Participatory Action Research

This book addresses a critical issue in the natural and social sciences: the difficulty researchers, experts and students face when trying to contribute to meaningful change in complex settings characterized by uncertainty. More than ever, researchers and actors need flexible means and grounded theory to combine people-based and evidence-based inquiry into situations that do not lend themselves to straightforward explanations and technical solutions alone.

The authors build on insights from many disciplines and lessons from the history of participatory action research (PAR), French psychosociology and related work in community development, education, public engagement, natural resource management and problem solving in the workplace. All formulations of PAR have in common the idea that research must be done 'with' people and not 'on' or 'for' people. Inquiry of this kind makes sense of the world through efforts to transform it, as opposed to simply studying human behaviour and views about reality.

The book contributes many new tools and conceptual foundations to this long-standing tradition, grounded in case studies and real-life examples of collective fact-finding, analysis and decision-making from around the world. It is a state-of-the-art modular textbook on PAR methods, theory and practice, suitable for a wide range of undergraduate and postgraduate courses, as well as working professionals.

Jacques M. Chevalier is Chancellor's Professor Emeritus in the Department of Sociology and Anthropology at Carleton University, Ottawa, Canada.

Daniel J. Buckles is Adjunct Research Professor in the Department of Sociology and Anthropology at Carleton University, Ottawa, Canada, and an independent consultant.

This book is a must for anyone seriously committed to research that ensures the authentic participation and empowerment of people from all walks of life, be they from oral or textual traditions, women or men, old or young, articulate or hesitant, outspoken or reserved.

Farida Akhter, Executive Director, UBINIG (Policy Research for Development Alternative), Dhaka, Bangladesh

This exciting and innovative book shows the patterns and processes that connect people and their social, practical and conceptual worlds in action. Its key themes of inter-dependence, relationship and the need for dialogue make it a book today for tomorrow's world. It should be on all reading lists as a key resource for developing socially-oriented pedagogies for a more peaceful, productive and interconnected world.

Jean McNiff, Professor of Educational Research at York St John University, York, UK and author of Action Research: Principles and Practice, *now in its third edition (Routledge, 2013)*

. . . a wonderful compendium, replete with practical tools and techniques that bring rigour and vigour to the international dialogue among action researchers . . . This is a serious volume worth the time of any action researcher who is curious about how western (including francophone) perspectives on PAR come alive. This volume makes a significant contribution to the collective craft of scholarly-practice among action researchers.

Hilary Bradbury-Huang, Professor in the Division of Management at Oregon Health & Science University, Portland, USA and Editor of the journal Action Research

Participatory Action Research

Theory and methods for engaged inquiry

Jacques M. Chevalier and Daniel J. Buckles

Routledge
Taylor & Francis Group
LONDON AND NEW YORK

This first edition published 2013
by Routledge
2 Park Square, Milton Park, Abingdon, Oxon, OX14 4RN

Simultaneously published in the USA and Canada
by Routledge
711 Third Avenue, New York, NY 10017

Routledge is an imprint of the Taylor & Francis Group, an informa business

British Library Cataloguing in Publication Data
A catalogue record for this book is available from the British Library

Library of Congress Cataloging-in-Publication Data
A catalog record has been requested for this book
Chevalier, Jacques M., 1949–
Participatory action research: theory and methods for engaged inquiry/Jacques M. Chevalier and Daniel J. Buckles.
p. cm.
Includes bibliographical references and index.
1. Action research. 2. Participant observation. 3. Social sciences – Research – Methodology. I. Buckles, Daniel, 1955– II. Title.
H62.C3757 2012
001.4 – dc23
2012024841

ISBN: 978-0-415-54031-5 (hbk)
ISBN: 978-0-415-54032-2 (pbk)
ISBN: 978-0-203-10738-6 (ebk)

Typeset in Stone Sans by
Florence Production Ltd, Stoodleigh, Devon, UK

MIX
Paper from responsible sources
FSC® C018575

Printed and bound in Great Britain by MPG Printgroup

Contents

Illustrations

FIGURES

PHOTOS

TABLES

Preface

This book has been ten years in the making, and marked by a world of adventures. Thanks to a series of grants from Canada's International Development Research Centre (IDRC), people on five continents contributed in various ways and at various times to developing a novel approach to participatory action research (PAR), using the project title SAS^2 (for Social Analysis $Systems^2$) as a temporary label. Community members, professionals in many fields, university students and faculty, working with the authors and on their own, engaged in hundreds of short- and longer-term inquiries into a wide range of topics meaningful to the people involved. These were combined with more than 100 capacity-building workshops involving some 2,080 people in twenty-two countries, facilitated by the authors and our many partners. At the heart of these research and training events was a process of constant dialogue and critical reasoning aimed at bringing about social change in community life, the workplace and civil society.

In Honduras, Juan Amilcar Colindres, Wilmer Reyes Sandoval and Ana Mireya Suazo led a core group of faculty and students at the Universidad Nacional de Agronomía (UNA) applying the proposed methods to research on the social dimensions of natural resource management. Dozens of thesis projects emerged from their training and research activities, leading as well to curriculum changes in two university degree programmes approved by the National Board of Higher Education. Laura Suazo and Raul Zelaya of IDRC played a key role in developing relationships with other national actors in Honduras, including the Regional University of the North (CURLA), a network of non-governmental organizations (NGOs) known as REMBLAH, an inter-institutional research project in the Rio San Juan area on the border with Nicaragua, the Universidad Agrícola Panamericana (Zamorano) and La Universidad Pedagógica, among others (see *ART* in Chapter 3, *Validation* in Chapter 8 and *Social Analysis CLIP* in Chapter 12). Laura Suazo, in a review of the Central American experience with PAR, argued that what had been missing, and now resonated with people working with this new approach, was the possibility of rigour combined with participation and a pragmatic focus to research. Earlier work by the authors with members of the Latin American Conflict and Collaboration Program (coordinated by Rolain Borel at the University for Peace in Costa Rica) had reached similar conclusions.

The Bolivian Centre for Interdisciplinary Studies (CEBEM), a prominent convener on development issues in the Andean Region led by José Blanes, stimulated small-and larger-scale inquiries in various countries through numerous collaborative training events, including a distance learning course. These were sponsored by regional universities, the Swiss Foundation for Technical Cooperation, the Ibero-American Model Forests Network, the Church-based Machaqa Amawt'a Foundation and Cuso International, among others (see *Activity Dynamics*, Chapter 17). Six case studies were later published by Edgar Pabón Balderas and many others appeared as unpublished theses and reports. The most comprehensive study was a doctoral dissertation by Jorge Téllez Carrasco on community forestry in Bolivia, work that eventually won a prestigious prize from Universidades de la Comunidad de Madrid (Spain) for excellence in research on international development in the field of engineering (see Chapter 13). David Mercado, based in Cochabamba, Bolivia was particularly prolific and creative in his use of a wide range of tools presented in this book, especially with indigenous peoples and municipal governments (see *Social Dynamics*, Chapter 17).

Our work in Bolivia contributed as well to the development of a methodology to engage municipal governments in planning local economic development initiatives. The initiative, launched by the Atlantic Community Economic Development Institute (ACEDI), the Federación de Asociaciones Municipales de Bolivia (FAM) and the Government of Bolivia, was a response to persistent gaps in the capacity of municipalities to design and implement local economic development policies and programmes, as required under the Bolivian Law of Participation. Under the direction of Juan Téllez (ACEDI), the research team leading this project developed and tested a quantitative economic evaluation methodology in a number of municipalities, using a process-oriented approach to engagement with municipal governments informed by the SAS^2 project approach.

In Chile, our work with Carlos Tapia brought the methods to numerous university settings and research projects including the Universidad de la Frontera, the Universidad de Chile and the Instituto de Fomento Pesquero (see *Option Domain*, Chapter 18). Jenny Menacho in Peru facilitated workshops for the Municipality of Lima (with Maria Fernández) and the Pontifical Catholic University of Peru. Most of these events were organized around multi-stakeholder groups with concrete projects in common. This grounded workshop practice contributed to new thinking about the problems at hand (on our approach to capacity building and higher education, see the *Conclusion*).

Most activities developed in Latin America involved formal research and higher education institutions. In Asia, grassroots organizations took the lead. In eastern India the authors worked closely with the Academy of Development Sciences (ADS) on a single, long-term study with the Katkari, a 'Particularly Vulnerable Tribal Group' fighting eviction from more than 200 hamlets near Mumbai, India. Eventually, the initiative helped the Katkari secure title to a large number of village sites (more than 60) and significantly enhanced the level of organization, leadership and self-confidence of the Katkari community. It also resulted in a major book by Daniel J. Buckles and Rajeev Khedkar, published in 2013 by Cambridge University Press India and used to illustrate various tools and themes in this book (see Chapters 4, 7, 9 and 12).

In addition to research with the Katkari, Rajeev Khedkar developed his own approach to training more than 40 grassroots organizations from eleven different states in India in the use of tools they found most useful for exploring problems and developing solutions with non-literate community groups. The German Catholic Church aid agency MISEROR and the Luxembourg-based organization Action Solidarité Tiers Monde (ASTM) funded much of this work. Khedkar also created a Marathi collection of tools to support the training, and worked closely with the Development Research Communication and Services Centre (DRCSC) located in Kolkata in eastern India. DRCSC made a similar collection of tools in Bengali and coordinated a series of training events with small, community-based organizations in Orissa and West Bengal (see *Disagreements and Misunderstandings* and *Levels of Support* in Chapter 14).

In Bangladesh, the authors worked with UBINIG (a Bengali acronym for Research for Policy Alternatives). This activist organization, led by Farhad Mahzar and Farida Akhter, works with a farmers' movement (the Nayakrishi Andolon) numbering more than 300,000 households. Many of the simple and advanced tools presented in this book provided a platform for engaging these farmers in detailed discussions of their livelihoods (see *Social Domain* in Chapter 18 and the detailed story of *Breaking the dependency on tobacco production*, Chapter 19). UBINIG later made use of this experience to design its own action-learning course for work with weavers, fishers, farmers and managers of small enterprises. They also developed a process for engaging professional journalists in a collaborative inquiry with farmers as a way to deepen journalistic assessments of key debates and issues in agriculture.

LIBIRD (Local Initiatives for Biodiversity Research and Development), based in Pokhara, Nepal was another key collaborator in Asia. LIBIRD is a well-established research NGO with a strong reputation and track record in the formal research system in Nepal. As in Latin America, the rigour and pragmatic focus of the concepts and tools presented in this book appealed to the organization's roots in plant breeding and other technical fields. Initially coordinated by Diwakar Poudel and later by Bimal Regmi and Bikash Paudyal, LIBIRD and its partners facilitated numerous training events. These led to dozens of case studies on gender-based crop preferences, the problems of livestock herders, disaster prevention in hillside environments and the challenges of wetland management. Neeraj Chapagain of the Livelihood Forestry Program in Nepal also took the concepts and tools to various parts of Nepal, and undertook research with a focus on relations of trust among groups involved in social forestry (see *Network Dynamics*, Chapter 17).

In Canada, innovative research and methodological training was grounded in other sectors and different institutional arrangements. The key partners were consulting firms, researchers in education and Canadian organizations working in international development. Canada World Youth (CWY), an NGO focussed on creating international educational opportunities for young people, was instrumental in bringing our approach to PAR to bear on evaluation questions as a distinct instance of action research. Together with Kate McLaren and Paul Turcot (at South House Exchange), the authors designed and implemented a five-country study of the impacts of youth exchange programmes on present and past participants and on host communities (see Chapter 7). Other evaluation designs and problem-solving applications inspired by this work followed in contexts as diverse as The United Way of Canada (an umbrella organization in the social service sector), Bhutan's Ministry of Education (Chapter 7) and YouthScape, a youth and environmental education programme funded by The McConnell Family Foundation and coordinated by the International Institute for Child Rights and Development (see Chapter 14).

Recently, we began working with ten Canadian international NGOs towards the development of new approaches to combining results-based management methodologies widely used by donor and government agencies with participatory approaches to planning, monitoring and evaluating projects and programme results (see *Rethinking evaluation methods in organizations*, Chapter 3). This initiative has also contributed to innovation in the field of evaluation by testing a new tool based on Anglo-Saxon legal reasoning and judgment entitled *Attribution and Contribution* (see Chapter 16). Work with other emerging communities of practice, coordinated by the Association québécoise des organismes de coopération internationale (AQOCI) and Crossroads International, focussed on problem assessment, priority setting and programme evaluation as applied to gender equity initiatives in the field of development.

Collaboration with partners in Canada led to applications of innovative PAR methods to the workplace and public engagement in problem solving, strategic planning and programme evaluation. Benoît Hurtel of the consulting firm Efficience International partnered with the authors to work with a number of major public sector agencies in Canada. Faculty and students at the Trent Centre for Community-Based Education, under the leadership of Todd Barr, and the University of Manitoba's Department of City Planning, also provided contexts for experimenting with workplace and public engagement processes. Other inquiries were carried out jointly with researchers and community groups such as the Cree Outfitters and Trappers Association (see *Idea Scenario* in Chapter 14), the Keewaytinook Okimakanak Research Institute (see *Competing principles of government consultation with natives in Canada*, Chapter 14), Carleton University (Chapter 10), the Bonnechere River Project (Chapter 9) and Canada's National Capital Commission (see Chapters 5 and 7 and Figure 16.1 in Chapter 16).

Francophone Canadian researchers in education emerged as a vital link to academics in Canada and source of new ideas and approaches to engaged inquiry. They also developed a robust community of practice in education, the Collectif des Savoirs Apprenants, a group working with teachers and school administrators in Quebec, Ontario and Belgium on a wide range of issues. This story is currently in the process of being turned into a book, under the leadership of Michelle Bourassa (Université du Québec en Outaouais).

Improvements to our teaching resources came from an unanticipated Canadian source – the Cree Outfitters and Tourism Association (COTA), an indigenous organization based in Northern Quebec. A workshop to build the capacities of COTA members was so successful the Association decided to commission a toolkit for First Nations community-based tourism development officers. After several rounds of testing, participants settled on tools they felt would be most useful in their work. These were then compiled with the help of Debra Huron and Zelie Larose into a set presented in a style based on principles of clear language and clear design. The learning from this process eventually resulted in a much larger collection of tools for use in workshops and training events, published by the authors in English, French and Spanish as *The Social Weaver: A Handbook for*

Participatory Action Research, Planning, and Evaluation (see www.participatoryaction research.net).

Designing flexible inquiries for a particular sector proved to be an effective way to combine innovative PAR with other methods used in specific disciplines and fields of study. This concept was further developed for the aboriginal tourism sector with Sylvie Blangy of the Université de Montpelier, France and UNEP's Secretariat of the Convention on Biological Diversity (see *Resource Mapping*, Chapter 9). Other designs for facilitating multi-stakeholder dialogue in specific sectors were created for work on accident prevention in the French construction industry, in close collaboration with Patrick Obertelli at the École Centrale de Paris (Chapter 10); on disaster relief efforts in the Philippines and Peru, in response to an invitation from the disaster relief network of the Ministers of the Infirm (Order of St. Camillus de Lellis) (Chapter 15); and on climate change adaptation in Nigeria, work undertaken with Ricardo Ramirez, Maria Fernández and John van Mossel (see Chapters 9 and 11). Designing an inquiry process to elicit community perspectives on key factors and concepts central to agriculture was also the focus for several other workshops held in Africa – in Senegal, with the Coalition pour la Protection du Patrimoine Génétique Africain (COPAGEN) and USC Canada (see *Ecological Domain*, Chapter 18) and also in Morocco, with the Institut National de la Recherche Agronomique (CIRAD) and the Centre de Recherche en Économie Appliquée pour le Développement.

A website (www.participatoryactionresearch.net) ensures ongoing public access to the results of this extensive collaborative initiative and the many tools and methods developed along the way.

To all of our partners, the people they work with and the many pioneers of PAR, we extend our heartfelt thanks.

Jacques M. Chevalier and
Daniel J. Buckles

Introduction

Engaging with participatory action research

THE RISK OF SCIENCE

Science is at a crossroads: either it continues to strengthen ivory towers and serve the interests of the few, or it embraces a firm orientation to society and the common good on a global scale. This book maps the second path and navigates through the many implications for theory and practice – by proposing concrete ways to reconnect knowledge making in the academic world with the diversity of perspectives on reality and ways to co-create meaning.

To achieve our purpose, we question the split between theory (*epistêmê*) and technique (*technê*) or the notion that inquiry essentially divides into substance and process. From this conventional viewpoint, substance stands as the subject matter of thought, that which is to be known, has real content and feeds into existing bodies of knowledge, theoretical or empirical. This is truth understood as cognitive output, the end-goal of the inquisitive mind – the research outcome that matters, is actively pursued and has value in the end. By contrast, process speaks to the journey, not the destination. It is the path to knowledge guided by 'small-m methods' and devices, the technical ways, step-wise procedures and technology used to gain a solid grasp over phenomena that are deemed to be real. When split from substance, tools to investigate reality cannot be ends in themselves. Rather, they are the instruments and means of advancing knowledge of the world.

Positive science is largely responsible for this division of means and ends in the field of knowledge. It is the main source of 'instrumental' views on methods to produce knowledge, using *technê* to discover things that are true in substance. The association between hard tooling and truth as the output of hard science is so close that many socially minded critics of positivism (and its many technocratic derivations) have opted to keep their distance from techniques and technology in general. In this book, we choose instead to reclaim the usage and development of tools, techniques, crafts, systems or methods of knowing to support the art of collaborative inquiry and thinking about the world and the experience of being.

The attention we choose to bring to the pathways of knowledge, treating them as objects of innovative thinking and practice, reflects a fundamental proposition: inquiries are part of the many ways in which humans interact with each other and shape the world 'about us'. The argument we make about science, amply confirmed by experience, is that the investigative *technê* is inseparable from everything we value in fact or in principle, including the well-being of others and the many objects of sensemaking and meaningful activity in everyday life.

Reinstating the interdependence and mutual conditioning of substance and process in social life is no small task. It means, among other things, that science must stop running away from self-reflection and its inevitable engagement with history. Until this happens, 'runaway science', unreflectively serving the interests of the few, will continue to create disastrous impacts on both local and global scales, to the point of undermining the lifespan of the current era. For better or for worse, the Anthropocene may end up being the shortest in geological history. Knowledge production poorly harnessed to life in society is a hazardous business leading to much collateral damage and 'accidents' of great proportion. This is so true that disaster has now become a 'normal thing' (Perrow, 1984), essentially because of the tight coupling of corporate risk-taking and science. Runaway technology, unregulated industry, erratic markets, greedy banks and polluted ecosystems all contribute to the many anxieties of current global history.

Science can no longer ignore the messiness of our Risk Society and Runaway World (Giddens, 1999). More than ever, researchers must inquire into long-term issues where facts are uncertain, not all factors are knowable and stakes are high. They are expected to cope with the fact that scientific explanations and theories compete for scholarly and political attention at the same time as stakeholder interests, values and sources of knowledge vary and clash. Given these requirements, multi-stakeholder involvement, public deliberation, workplace dialogue and community engagement become a necessity. Messy problems call for the active contribution of all those knowledgeable and/or affected by the issues at hand and willing to examine the available evidence, experience and views advanced by the parties concerned. Grassroots democracy, social movements and the wisdom of reasoned dialogue are key to getting unstuck from a world out of balance.

To some, meshing democracy and 'pure science' is pure fantasy. Keeping scientific and technical expertise in check is a safer move. Ravetz and Funtowicz (1999, p. 642) thus argue for the growth of 'post-normal' science, an approach that Kay, arriving at similar conclusions through research on thermodynamics and systems ecology, deems essential to make sense of problems and anomalies that existing paradigms are unable to solve (Kay *et al.*, 1999). Persistent anomalies bring into question the presumptions of conventional science, that anything scientific must be free of uncertainty, independent of values and the exclusive property of a technocratic elite. The claims of post-normal science echo worldwide civil society scepticism regarding the so-called breakthroughs of science.

Many academics and scientists voice similar concerns about the linkages between science, reflective modernization and democratic governance. Notions of 'sub-politics' advanced by Beck (1999) and 'multi-layered democratic participation' developed by Giddens (1999) are examples of this new way of thinking. Most of these discussions revolve around the disastrous consequences of scientific research (nuclear, industrial, pharmaceutical, biogenetic) harnessed to runaway technology and the interests of corporate industry. Gorz (2008), among others, argues for the self-limitation of science and a Habermasian revitalization of a truthful lifeworld and a thriving civil society. The ecological movement is an important contribution to this endeavour. It helps decolonize a lifeworld otherwise governed by armies of experts with the power to define the common good – a technocratic caste catering to the needs of neoliberal capitalism, with little concern for issues of environmental degradation let alone social justice and well-being in everyday life.

Positive scientists committed to strict measurements of replicability, reliability and validity view 'post-normal science' and eulogies about 'living knowledge' and 'democratic wisdom' as neo-Luddism, an anti-modern movement supporting inferior technology and methodologies in the service of political goals. Paradoxically, the two camps – hard scientists and critics of 'expertocracy' – share some common ground. For one thing, both deploy equal expertise when debating the issues at hand. More importantly, they both overlook an important fact: formal evidential reasoning now pervades many fields of investigation that are not 'exact sciences' as such.

Exact science is bound by rules of accurate quantitative expression, precise predictions and rigorous methods for testing hypotheses. While playing a critical role in modern history, there is no reason to equate this strict view of evidence-based thinking with the whole of science. Viewed more broadly, science is a bold foray into knowledge making of many kinds. From the start, science was a risky venture for the few who dared advance a radical shift in our understanding of humans and the universe, against the established views and vested interests of Church and theology. Over the centuries the scientific revolution inspired many shifts – in our understanding of Nature, to be sure, but also the role of observation, language and logic in the pursuit of knowledge and learning. In recent decades, the deep curiosity and open-mindedness of science gave rise to many new disciplines and an untiring effort to remove walls between them. The readiness of science to push the frontiers of knowledge has meant that no object can hide from scrutiny, not even science. The historical study of science is now an essential contribution to the science of social and natural history. This is science in one of its boldest moments, a methodical inquiry into its own remarkable journey.

The boldness of science reflecting upon itself, refusing to give itself immunity from self-examination and experimentation, has far-reaching implications. It means, among other things, that science can generate different hypotheses about its own logic and practice, each to be tested against experience and potentially proven to be false. This self-experimentation process in science is by no means new. Knowledge gained through evidential inquiry, theoretically informed, has acquired multiple meanings over the centuries, in fields ranging from medicine to law, psychology, ecology, economics and social sciences. There are now myriad 'sciences' where reasoning, facts and rigour matter. Some, however, do not have the luxury or pretence of controlling all key factors and variables associated with the phenomena they study. 'Exact science' itself has developed probabilistic models of reality that acknowledge indeterminacy, uncertainty and the unknown. This is a far cry from basic models of linear causality that evidence-based thinking is often associated with and tries to mimic. Linear positive science no longer has an exclusive monopole over evidential reasoning. In hindsight, it never did.

Science is a plural field. It is also part of a plural world. When viewed historically, science constitutes an array of theories and methods of knowing that mesh and interface with other knowledge systems and modes of learning. Webs of knowledge cannot be ignored, and many disciplines make it their business to investigate them. They include anthropology, cognitive science and neuropsychology, branches of learning that keep pointing to the complexity of a human mind capable of linear logic and causal reasoning but not limited to it. Intelligence takes many forms.

Science also interfaces with society. When science studies itself, it becomes a component part of larger systems, a field interacting with other fields evolving over time. Politics, science, industry and ecosystems are currently shaping each others' fate. It follows from this that science is bound to alter its own object of study and be altered in the process of changing its own environment, social and natural. Given these interrelationships, many objects of scientific study – science included – are moving targets that can never be systematically accounted for. Efforts to confine scientific inquiry to fixed concepts, methods and values run contrary to this larger view of science in society and history. Unreflective science, the unitary kind that merely mirrors itself, does not withstand logical and historical cross-examination.

THEORY AND *TECHNÊ*

Participatory action research (PAR), the central topic of this book, is an expression of science that assumes reflectivity and self-experimentation in history. Originating from the pioneering work of Kurt Lewin and the Tavistock Institute in the 1940s, PAR now represents a well-documented tradition of active-risk taking and experimentation in social reflectivity backed up by evidential reasoning and learning through experience and real action (Reason and Bradbury, 2008; Brock and Pettit, 2007; Kindon *et al.*, 2007). As we shall see (Chapter 1), PAR informs fields of study on issues ranging from organizations to group psychology, health, literacy, education, the workplace, community development, farming systems, intermediate technologies, environmental studies and public engagement. Much of this research goes a long way towards dissolving the apparent dichotomy of science and democracy – of methodical knowing and authentic dialogue, instrumental rationality and lifeworld communication.

PAR nonetheless has debates and challenges of its own. Given its middle-of-the-road stance between the received wisdom of science and the concerns and worldview of 'human relations', the approach has been struggling with a foundational tension verging on a double bind. On the one hand, PAR practice has had to tread softly on the path of scientific technique (*technê*) and theory (*epistêmê*). These are deployed on a human scale, typically through small group dynamics and context-specific theory. PAR practitioners typically stay clear of theories that are so lofty the ground disappears from sight or methods so complicated the results remain opaque to all but specialist eyes. On the other hand, engaged researchers have been careful not to overstate their humanist struggle against 'scientific management' to the point of renouncing the ideals of science.

Caught midway between two negative injunctions, PAR has not yet reached its full potential.

Three implications follow from the double bind and are taken up in this book. First, more work and creativity is needed to strengthen the theoretical foundations of PAR, and chart a path of methodological innovation and authenticity. Theory matters and makes a difference in the methods chosen and the way real-life research is conducted. In our view, this includes a sound theory of the PAR synthesis of evidence-based and people-based inquiry.

Second, PAR practitioners must pay more attention to the embeddedness of means in ends – building into the inquiry process the goals of a genuine encounter between self and other, those of truthfulness and responsibility but also the sheer pleasure of being-in-the-world. At stake here is a fundamental question in the research and teaching community: how to create a *careful action-learning* process based on abilities to think and act carefully, with rigour, combined with genuine *caring* for expressions of difference and otherness in social and natural history. To paraphrase E. B. White, if the PAR experience were merely intersubjective, that would be easy. If it were merely scientific, that would be no problem. But arising every morning torn between a desire to methodically save the world and a desire to savour it is something else. While daunting, this twofold challenge is at the centre of PAR practice.

Third, the advancement of PAR must take on the challenge of scaling up the inquiry process to address issues of complexity, especially those of 'another development' and alterglobalization. This requires that we develop and use more advanced techniques to shore up the PAR contribution to evidential reasoning and dialogue. Instead of scaling down the inquiry process to quick-and-easy conversations between the parties involved, PAR practitioners must make sure the questions asked and methods used do justice to the pressing issues at hand, the richness of participant knowledge and local views about the matters under investigation, and the broader lessons from research and field-specific knowledge. Our work over the last ten years, in organizations and communities struggling with issues of all kinds, confirms our view that participation and rigour in action and research can mutually reinforce each other, and contribute to social transformation and problem solving grounded in real settings.

Building on these themes from the history of PAR, Chapter 2 presents a theoretically informed alternative to positive science, one where the ends of human thinking and questioning are embedded in the 'skilful means' deployed. The existential grounding of the research process we propose harks back to a Stoic philosophy that celebrates the human mind engaging with social history and the 'art of living'. Other contributions to a theory of PAR are fleshed out in aphorisms and threads of theory dispersed throughout the book. These threads revolve around the three pillars of PAR and interconnections between them.

- Commentaries pertaining to **life in society** (participation) define research as an exercise in rational communication and knowledge making wedded to civil society and public life. Action-inquiry on a human scale is a local and global commitment to careful reasoning and caring that serves the needs of people and the values they hold. (See 'Threads of Theory' in Chapters 6, 11, 12 and 13.)

- Threads of theory on **engagement with experience** (action) propose several approximations of the pragmatic maxim, as applied to the process of collaborative inquiry. They emphasize the need for research activities and *technê* to actually 'work for people', the kind that has meaning in real settings. Pragmatic thinking requires that free subjects – humans condemned to be free, says Sartre – plan and develop the skilful means to understand the present, shape their own future and co-author the making of social and natural history. Given the messiness of human experience, however, god-like planning is never an option. Pragmatism of the existential sort, developed in the middleness of history, precludes all instrumental and mechanical views of *technê* viewed either with positivist optimism or deep humanistic fear. (See 'Threads of Theory' in Chapters 2, 3, 4, 5 and 9.)
- Commentaries on the framing of **soundness in thought** (research) draw inspiration from theories of 'ordinary language' – sensemaking shaped by rules on how to use words to communicate and get things done, as in Wittgenstein, but also struggles over reason and rules imposed by the few, as in Bourdieu. The commentaries also question mainstream views of research based on narrow views of causation, illusions of quantitative perfection and completeness, simple mirror-like representations of the world, and singular methods, models and theories to capture the whole of reality. If anything, engaged research is about the mediation of language and pluralism in means – ways to make sense of social history and efforts to transform it. (See 'Threads of Theory' in Chapters 8, 14, 16, 17 and 18.)

The review of the history of PAR in Chapter 1, the statement of our own theoretically informed practice in Chapter 2, and aphorisms and commentaries embedded throughout the text offer readers an opportunity to engage with other PAR practitioners in self-examination and theory building. The book also shows a wide range of ways to actually walk the talk of meaningful action-inquiry. These include detailed presentations of research designs and numerous flexible tools to support participatory action research, planning and evaluation. The tools and design principles are illustrated with stories from our own research, conducted in collaboration with partners around the world.

The methods and stories are organized into six modules that represent an integrated tapestry of ways to engage people and mobilize evidence in a wide range of situations, including complex multi-stakeholder settings. They are designed to assist people in the voluntary, academic, private and government sectors in carrying out key inquiry tasks, such as community-based action-research, project or programme planning and evaluation, organizational learning and problem solving. The methods proposed and their conceptual underpinnings build on lessons from different disciplines, scientific traditions and theoretical frameworks. Fully participatory and flexible, they are accessible to beginners and provide experienced researchers and facilitators with a new approach to educational, workplace, community and public engagement.

Module 1 is about the full tapestry, not the threads. It introduces central questions that are part of a methodology we call *Process Design*. The questions concern the relationship between action, research and training, between planning, inquiry and evaluation and between order and chaos in specific contexts. Answers to these and various practical concerns determine how a research process can effectively mix, sequence and integrate appropriate tools to support genuine dialogue and the exercise of reason in real settings, including complex situations marked by uncertainty and the unknown. The module also provides examples of simple combinations of tools designed for typical tasks (see *Combos*, Chapter 6). It outlines what the 'skilful means' of engaged research entail – by exploring the concrete implications of collaborative mediation, historical grounding, 'good enough' scaling, flexible technical navigation and the art of sensemaking.

Module 2 is a compendium of all-purpose tools for measuring, fact-finding and active listening. These are basic and critical to all other tools described in the book. Modules 3, 4 and 5 focus on three sets of questions applicable to any situation. What are the problems people face and must explore (Module 3)? Who are the actors or stakeholders affected by a situation or with the capacity to intervene, and how do they interact with each other (Module 4)? What future scenarios and options for action should be assessed against existing stakeholder interests and values (Module 5)? Deciding which of these questions to start with when designing an inquiry draws on the skilful means of Module 1.

Module 6 takes the participatory inquiry process to another level, by proposing tools for understanding systems in a complex world. The first chapter in the module includes *Attribution and Contribution*, a method to assess the contribution to meaningful change that can be attributed to a specific intervention (an action, project, programme). This is a perennial challenge in the field of impact evaluation. In two other chapters we present and illustrate several variations on *System Dynamics*, our collaborative take on classic input–output reasoning used in economics, and examples of *Domain Analysis*, our social adaptation of Kelly's Personal Construct Psychology. The tools acknowledge complexity from the start, using a soft systems approach to holistic thinking.

While this book offers many tools, it is not a toolbox. Nor is the proposed framework an exercise in lofty theory, with no effort to ground research in the messy journey of critical analysis for social change. The tools and the concepts we advance would be of questionable value had they not been extensively tested on the ground and significantly improved along the way in close collaboration with many colleagues and partners around the globe (see *Preface*). Throughout this book, we present a selection of experiences from our collaborative work and work by some of our partners (see Table of Contents and Index).

In our concluding chapter, we reflect on the challenge of getting university and college programmes to incorporate PAR theory and methods, as pioneering universities, colleges and institutes have in various parts of the world. This book outlines the 'skilful means' to respond to parts of that challenge, by showing how to bring rigorous inquiry and authentic dialogue to meaningful research and critical action for a better world.

REFERENCES

Beck, U. (1999) *World Risk Society*, Polity, Cambridge.

Brock, K. and Pettit, J. (2007) *Springs of Participation: Creating and Evolving Methods for Participatory Development*, Practical Action Publishing, Warwickshire.

Giddens, A. (1999) *Runaway World: How Globalization is Reshaping Our Lives*, Profile, London.

Gorz, A. (2008) 'L'écologie politique entre expertocratie et autolimitation', *Ecologica*, Galilée, Paris.

Kay, J. J., Regier, H., Boyle, M. and Francis, G. (eds) (1999) 'An ecosystem approach for sustainability: addressing the challenge of complexity', *Futures*, vol. 31, no. 7, pp. 721–742.

Kindon, S. L., Pain, R. and Kesby, M. (2007) *Participatory Action Research Approaches and Methods: Connecting People, Participation and Place*, Routledge, London.

Perrow, C. (1984) *Normal Accidents*, Basic Books, New York.

Ravetz, J. and Funtowicz, S. (1999) 'Post-normal science – an insight now maturing', *Futures*, vol. 31, pp. 641–646.

Reason, P. and Bradbury, H. (eds) (2008) *The SAGE Handbook of Action Research*, Sage, London.

CHAPTER 1

Action research history

PARTICIPATION, ACTION, RESEARCH

This chapter surveys the theoretical stances and methodological strategies applied to five areas where PAR has created a lasting legacy: work life approached experimentally (after Lewin), psychosociology (using the insights of psychoanalysis), Freirian education, community development in the international arena and the emerging technologies of public engagement. These contributions represent significant efforts to integrate the three fundamental components of participation, action and research. They also point to three key challenges within PAR.

First, on the **social plane** (see 'participation' in Figure 1.1) challenges revolve around twenty-first-century trends of accelerating globalization and the growth of social movements. Both lead to myriad forms of sociability and conflict that now criss-cross in complex ways. These topics and related issues are poorly addressed by models of collaborative action inquiry that still rely on using small group and site-specific dynamics to engage in 'fixed identity' politics inspired by the ideals of group autonomy and self-governance. More than ever PAR must reflect and act on the complex factors that currently shape the course of human interaction on a global scale.

On the **plane of experience** (action), a second challenge consists in overcoming PAR's mistrust of *technê*, a long-standing anxiety to keep tools of participatory inquiry 'humanistically and liberally soft' at all times. This must be done at the same time as links between society and psyche are duly explored. As noted earlier, caution exercised towards the 'hard tooling' of engaged research is largely a reaction to the dehumanizing effects associated with the modern industrial revolution and the technicism of positive science. PAR humanism argues against all forms of *technê* that treat people as objects of inquiry, scientific experimentation and production-oriented control. In the French tradition, psychosociologists also object to action-inquiry that serves primarily to pursue project goals and solve practical problems, with little attention paid to emotions and meaning (Michelot, 2008). Psychosociology attends to these issues using methods borrowed from clinical psychology and psychoanalysis. By contrast, Anglo-Saxon action-research is more 'instrumental and pragmatic' and less critical of the limitations of practical experimentation. Given this tension between the Anglo-Saxon and the French traditions, PAR tends to focus either on solving practical problems or strengthening the

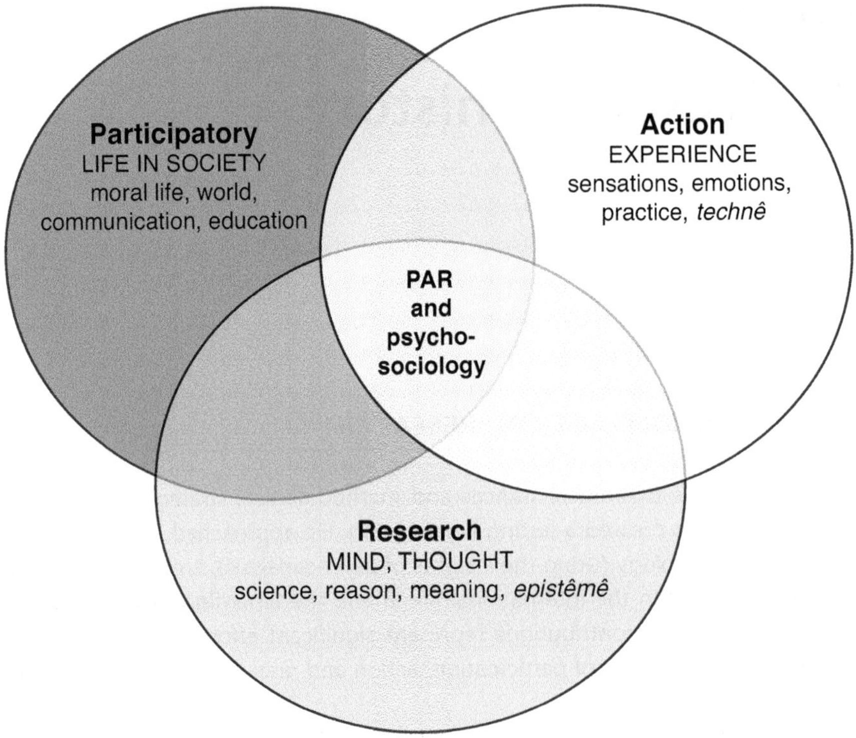

FIGURE 1.1 Participation, action, research.

interconnections of self-awareness, the unconscious and life in society. In our view, more effort is needed to develop a communicative *technê* that bridges the gap between pragmatic experimentation and the human psyche.

Finally, challenges on the **plane of mind** and thought (research) point to another deep anxiety built into PAR: the fear of *epistêmê*. By this we mean a tendency to keep the advancement of theory and philosophy in check because not inherently pluralistic and far removed from the grounding of research in social history. Interestingly, distrust towards both technology and groundbreaking theoretical investigation is a strategy to avoid a key question: how can engaged researchers hear others and be heard at the same time? The challenge is to work with a methodological and philosophical singularity in the art of doing research 'with people', in lieu of doing it 'on them' or 'for them', and not betray the spirit of dialogue that guides the construction and transformation of history. Can researchers engage with the infinite expressions of experience and society and at the same time develop a coherent art of thinking and learning that avoids the straight jacket of either technicism or theoreticism? Stoecker's question is central here: what is the role of scholarship in participatory research (Stoecker, 1999)? As we argue in various parts of the book, tentative answers to this question lie in a better understanding of 'the social construction of reality' and explorations into the phenomenology of knowledge, experience and society.

ORGANIZATIONAL LIFE

It is customary to trace the history of action-research to Kurt Lewin's groundbreaking work in organizational studies, a contribution heralding a pragmatic and democratic shift in the social sciences. His approach to group dynamics, experiential learning and research directed to solving social problems is key to understanding the beginnings of PAR. In his paper 'Action Research and Minority Problems', Lewin coined the expression 'action research', defining it as 'comparative research on the conditions and effects of various forms of social action and research leading to social action'. His perspective on the making of knowledge echoes Dewey's concept of learning from experience. It involves a flexible, scientific approach to planned change that proceeds through a spiral of steps, each of which is composed of 'a circle of planning, action, and fact-finding about the result of the action' (Lewin, 1946, 1948, pp. 202–203).

The first step in the action-research spiral is a problem awareness phase that seeks to 'unfreeze' a situation through fact-finding and diagnostic thinking. Shifts in understanding create the possibility of movement and support the formulation of an overall idea or plan of action to dismantle the existing mindset and overcome defence mechanisms and inertia. Decisions regarding immediate steps lead in turn to a phase of experimentation with transformative action. Progressive learning from these experiments feeds back into earlier plans and invites adjustments between objectives and actions. Iterative motions of research in action and action under research prepare the last phase, a closing of the spiral as new plans 'freeze' new forms of behaviour based on effective corrective action (Lewin, 1948, p. 206).

Lewin's action-research integrates theory building and practical grounding. It assumes that 'there is nothing so practical as a good theory' (Lewin, 1951, p. 169) and that the best way to understand something is by trying to change it. But the founder of social psychology was not committed to the goals of pragmatic inquiry alone. His work also sought to put science in the service of rational behaviour and the dynamics of democratic teamwork and organizational learning. From Lewin's perspective, socially relevant research and theory looks at behaviour understood as a gestalt, a whole psychological 'field' or 'lifespace' constructed in the mind. This situational field is the totality of coexisting facts observed in the here and now, mutually interdependent parts that cope with tensions between perceptions of the self and the environment (Lewin, 1951). Each lifespace is a 'force field' comprising both the forces that are driving movement towards a goal and those that counteract the same movement and call for adaptive behaviour. In keeping with gestalt theory, the field involves forms of social interaction that go beyond group membership based on similarities in beliefs, dispositions or behaviour. Group dynamics are ruled instead by relations of interdependence where the fate of each member depends on the fate of the group as a whole and the achievement of common tasks and goals. As in Dewey's work, organized social life does not thrive on patterns of aggression, hostility, scapegoating and discontent commonly observed in *laissez-faire* and autocratic climates. Rather it hinges on the 'interdependence of fate and tasks' and a 'climate' of democratic leadership and responsible participation that promotes originality, group-mindedness, objective praise and criticism and collaborative work (Lewin, 1948, p. 82).

Lewin's work revolves around questions of group productivity and communication, social perception, inter-group relations and group membership, democratic leadership and better group functioning through sensitivity training. Science helps answer these questions and enhance organizational performance and democratic management. But there is more. Lewin's research on organizational democracy is also committed to democracy in the area of research, with a view to transforming the practice of science itself. Principles of dialogue and engagement inform his work with basic skill training groups – T-groups where community leaders and group facilitators use feedback, problem solving, role-play and cognitive aids (lectures, handouts, film) to gain insights into themselves, others and groups with a view to 'unfreezing' and changing their mindsets, attitudes and behaviours. Group thinking and experimentation involves feedback mechanisms where learners use participant observation and information about the effects of actions in the here and now to bridge the gap between results that are aimed for and those that are achieved. The views and voices of participants matter when it comes to taking a step back and interpreting group dynamics. The change agent and the client group thus carry out all phases of the action research process jointly. The negotiated analysis and interpretation of data and observed behaviour is no longer the prerogative of the analyst or the expert alone. The client system fully engages in diagnostic thinking, active learning and problem solving.

The scientific logic of forming and testing hypotheses, gathering measurable data and interpreting the results plays a central role in Lewinian practice. Researchers contribute an important set of skills through their active involvement, including the ability to make sense of group dynamics and to identify the need for change, the problems involved, the steps required to bring about change and the appropriate methods to measure, monitor and evaluate results. Through T-groups, researchers also build client capacity in democratic leadership and the integration of action, research and education in a comprehensive process of rational learning. However, unlike conventional scientists and teachers, action researchers are fully involved in the learning process and must develop the skills needed to facilitate communication and feedback among participants (Kolb, 1984, p. 10). This is all the more important as the goal is no longer to generate and share scholarly theory and findings for their own sake. Rather scientific and analytic detachment from immediate experience and emotion is expected from both the researcher and the client system who must work together to identify specific problems and their root causes and develop plans for coping with them realistically and practically. Learning through collaborative experimentation in real settings produces behavioural change and self-analysis to support long-range, cyclical, self-correcting mechanisms that enhance the effectiveness of the client system.

Lewin adapted the logic of science and management to the task of collective self-inquiry and critical understanding undertaken by participants struggling with real-life issues. More than a method, action research is a commitment on the part of both researchers and actors to jointly observe, problematize and transform behaviour. Lewin's work is an inspiring meshing of scientific theory with real-life experimentation and the ideals of democracy.

While groundbreaking in many ways, Lewin's action-research also has limitations that have become recurrent themes in the history of PAR. His work is both inspired and constrained by the assumptions of liberal humanism, a micro-perspective on life in society and faith in rational behaviour (and labour) abiding by the rule of scientific experimentation and social engineering (see Dubost, 1987, pp. 49–53, 56–57). As we shall see, other formulations of PAR have attempted to address these limitations, with varying degrees of success.

Lewin's understanding of action-research coincides with key ideas and practices in organizational life developed at the influential Tavistock Clinic and Institute (created in 1947), save perhaps for the clinical orientation of Tavistock. Initially Tavistock broke new ground by combining general medicine and psychiatry with Freudian and Jungian psychology and the social sciences to help the British army face various human resource problems, such as low morale, officer selection and civil resettlement for repatriated prisoners of war (Dicks, 1970). Led by multidisciplinary, democratically functioning work groups, the Tavistock approach began with preliminary studies of critical problems, followed by the co-design of innovative solutions with military staff, handing over the developed model to the army and disseminating it to other units and branches of the organization. The same process – action-oriented inquiry, group-based and democratic – was extended later to civilian society, starting with a focus on the National Health Service and crisis management applications within the Clinic and the Tavistock Institute. Difficulties in obtaining untied research funds eventually forced the Institute to develop projects with private industry and diversify its action research portfolio while maintaining the goals of scholarly thinking, publishing and capacity building.

Sociotechnical analysis in the organizational context is an influential offshoot of Tavistock's contribution to action research. It emphasizes pragmatic inquiry into the social aspects of workplace behaviour and organization. The approach was first developed during the post-war period in response to an industrial sector facing scarce capital and low productivity problems, with a focus on self-regulating work groups in a coal mine (Trist and Bamforth, 1951). The methodology that emerged from these problem-solving experiments seeks to enhance performance in complex organizations. It assumes that improved technology alone is not sufficient to achieve greater productivity or efficiency. What is needed is the interaction and 'joint optimization' of the social and technical components of organizational activity. In a sociotechnical perspective, the best match between the social and technical factors of organized work lies in principles of 'responsible group autonomy', as opposed to deskilling and top-down bureaucracy inspired by Taylor's scientific management and linear chain of command. Sociotechnical theory advocates a shift of emphasis, towards internal supervision, leadership, cohesion and self-regulation at the level of small work teams, the primary unit of production. Semi-autonomous groups present many advantages, including greater trust and more efficient communication and risk management behaviour. Multi-skilled work groups are better suited for accomplishing 'whole tasks', provided of course they have a clear notion of the objectives to be achieved and some latitude in determining how to achieve them. Unlike hierarchical structures, semi-autonomous groups encourage creative problem solving and flexible adaptation to situations characterized by uncertainty and complexity (Ackoff, 1999; Liu, 1997).

Applications and further developments of sociotechnical theory have been undertaken in numerous contexts, including the Indian weaving industry (Rice, 1965) and the marketing of 'pleasure foods' such as ice cream, smoking and drinking (Emery *et al.*, 1968). The research process typically involves a project officer and two Institute staff members working closely together. This reduces the dangers of personal bias and related effects of transference and countertransference. Socio-ecological thinking transposes the same reasoning to larger organizations in a post-industrial era. In order to adapt to increasing levels of interdependence, complexity and uncertainty, organizations cannot simply compete and govern themselves through chains of hierarchical command between centre and periphery. Self-regulation and collaborative networking between organizations operating flexibly and democratically become the main drivers of post-industrial societies faced with endemic problems of individual stress and socio-economic turbulence (Trist *et al.*, 1997).

In France, **strategic organizational analysis** advocated by Crozier (2000) and Friedberg (1993) also focusses on the interaction between the technical and the social aspects of work and organizational life. The emphasis, however, is on relationships between different groups within an organization rather than small team interaction and dynamics. Also the action inquiry methodology used is somewhat conventional, to the point that the approach looks more like applied research driven by experts than 'action research' led by all the parties involved. The process usually starts with intensive interviews involving a sample of people representing the different segments of an organization. The interview material collected is subjected to content analysis and the formulation of interpretive hypotheses concerning key stakes, group strategies and related rules of the game and the power structure, bureaucratic and informal. The next phase involves an extensive survey to test the researcher's hypotheses, followed by data analysis and synthetic interpretation, to be shared and discussed with the interested parties. Researchers use their scientific and theoretical understanding of organizational sociology to frame the analysis and pursue scholarly goals in the process, cognizant that their findings are always context-specific. Action-research findings contribute to 'middle range' theory building and a functionalist understanding of rational actions, individual and collective, observed within existing organizations (Merton, 1968).

Lewin's action research and its adaptation to sociotechnical and strategic organizational analyses illustrate a firm commitment to innovating in the field of workplace intervention and scientific theory. The approach is based on the assumption that human behaviour and performance at work (B) is a function of person-centred psychology (P) and its environment (E), hence $B = f(P, E)$ (Lewin, 1936). The formula is a founding principle in social psychology. It is also a recurrent theme in the prolific body of literature and practice known as **Organizational Development (OD)**. OD is a response to calls for planned change and 'rational social management' involving a normative 'human relations' approach to capital-dominated economies (Dubost, 1987, pp. 84–88, 294–297). Its principal goal is to enhance an organization's performance and viability, with the assistance of a consultant, a change agent or catalyst that helps the sponsoring organization define and solve its own problems. Unlike Lewin's laboratory experiments involving 'stranger groups', OD is usually undertaken with 'family groups' located within real organizations. The process includes some form of inquiry or self-analysis combined with active learning or training sessions (typically focussed on effective communication skills, leadership, teamwork or conflict management). Diagnostic and capacity-building activities are informed, to varying degrees, by psychology, the behavioural sciences, organizational studies, or theories of leadership and social innovation. Rigorous data gathering or fact-finding methods may be used to support the inquiry process and group thinking and planning. On the whole, however, science is always a means, never an end. In the OD ethos, all activities are first and foremost problem-based, action-oriented and client-centred.

A recent development that offers novel ways of carrying out OD assessments is **Appreciative Inquiry** (AI), an offshoot of PAR based on positive psychology (Seligman, 2002). AI starts with the assumption that organizational change towards enhanced performance hinges on people's ability to change gears from a problem finding and solving mindset to reflection on group life that emphasizes stories of success, positive experiences and dreams, relations of trust, existing assets and opportunities for effective change. Instead of dwelling on what doesn't work and inquiries into related gaps, faults and deficiencies, AI concentrates on the basic goodness, core strengths and main assets of people, situations and organizations. The end result is a methodological path to excellence where participants envision, prioritize, plan and implement organizational processes that show promise and take inspiration from stories of past and present success. The inquiry process usually involves bringing very large, diverse groups to examine, discuss and build on assets and best practices in an organization or community (Srivastva and Cooperrider, 1999; Cooperrider *et al.*, 2004).

The Lewinian, sociotechnical, strategic organizational, OD and AI formulations of PAR emphasize the interpersonal and social aspects of well-being in the context of organizational adaptation to advanced industrial society. The focus is on group dynamics, which reflects a critical reaction against Taylorism and the dehumanizing effects of mass-scale industrial production, including the loss of community belonging and social solidarity. Action research undertaken in this spirit thus revolves around the humanistic and pragmatic struggle against raw capitalism. It does not, for all that, advocate fundamental changes in larger power structures based on revolutionary thinking and action. Organizational PAR practitioners are generally distrustful of macro-sociological perspectives on history (Dubost, 1987, pp. 104–109, 146, 162). A direct consequence of this is a tendency to isolate group life and organizational behaviour from the supralocal forces at play (with the notable exception of the Norwegian Industrial Democracy experiment; see Thorsrud and Emery, 1964; Emery and Thorsrud, 1969; 1977). At best, liberal concepts of individual freedom and self-determination are extended to group life through methods that enhance small-scale expressions of collective autonomy and self-management. The participation ethos is scaled down to action-oriented communications among team members or groups within an organization or defined community. The approach assumes groups and organizations have clear boundaries and common interests can prevail over the forces of competition and conflict, to the benefit of all the parties concerned. Where power differentials exist, efforts are made to 'level the playing field', if only in the time and space created by the action-research process itself.

Pragmatic applications of PAR in the workplace environment propose a win-win approach to personal and interpersonal well-being and organizational performance guided by the exercise of reason and problem solving on a local scale. They offer a creative blend of scientific rigour and interactive group dynamics (using role-play, for instance). The mix, however, is rife with tensions and ambiguities. The participation-action-research triad is so loosely understood it is often confused with any organizational capacity or awareness building process that involves group thinking and interactive learning. Science, in this context, is reduced to a means serving OD, not an end served by it. OD interventions into client systems are informed by theories of organizational performance, communication, leadership and teamwork, but they do not return the favour by helping with the advancement of knowledge. Basic concepts and theories are located upstream of the action-research process and do not evolve heuristically, through trial and error or a journey of collective discovery. The focus is on finding workable solutions to concrete problems framed by the requirements of liberal capitalism.

PSYCHE AND SOCIETY

Action research as initially conceived by the Tavistock Institute explored the meshing of psyche and society with a view to making sense of group dynamics and supporting both personal growth and institutional change in family life, the workplace and the educational system. Efforts by Tavistock to develop an engaged research paradigm at the intersection of psychology and the social sciences gave rise to a field of scholarly research and professional intervention loosely known as psychosociology, formally recognized in France as *la psychosociologie d'intervention*. The profession is represented by several schools of thought and 'social clinical' practice that have evolved at some distance from the experimental and expert mindset of social psychology (Dubost, 1987, pp. 287–291).

Most formulations of psychosociology share with organizational PAR a commitment to the aspirations of humanized work and democracy, best expressed through the relative autonomy and active participation of individuals and groups coping with problems of motivation and goal effectiveness within larger organizations and institutions. In addition to this humanistic and democratic agenda, psychosociology emphasizes the relationship between personality and culture or society, using concepts of psychoanalytic inspiration to address interpersonal relations and the interplay between self and group. The role of the unconscious in social behaviour and collective representations is acknowledged, including the inevitable expression of transference and counter-transference – language and behaviour that redirect unspoken feelings and anxieties to other people or physical objects taking part in the action inquiry.

Studies in group psychology and therapy have played a pivotal role in adapting psychoanalytic theory to group thinking and transformative action in organizational settings and the workplace. Apart from Lewin's T-groups, pioneering work includes Mayo's study of the impact of group dynamics on employee motivation and factory productivity (Mayo, 1933). Mention should also be made of the influential person-centred approach to therapy developed by Carl Rogers in the post-war period (Rogers, 1970) and his method of non-directive, active listening applied to 'encounter groups'. Of equal importance is Moreno's (1931) use of improvisational theatre (combined with interactive sociometrics and sociograms) as cathartic therapy for conflict resolution. Psychodrama is now a widely used method of group psychotherapy, creative learning and communication that uses role-play, symbolic language and theatrical props to express and analyse people's experience, memories, interactions, mindsets or feelings about particular themes or issues, towards new ways of thinking and fresh responses to real-life situations.

The contributions of Balint (1954), Jaques (1951) and Bion (1961) are turning points in the development of psychosociology. Their work introduced key concepts and techniques framed in a psychoanalytic perspective, including the use of free association, experiments in leaderless groups and the analysis of group defence mechanisms, the collective unconscious and signs of transference and countertransference. This is a tradition guided by the idea that interpretation unfolds not through inductive or deductive reasoning but rather through a progressive 'working through' of meaning in context, subject to the layering of multiple issues and signs of resistance. This is a concept known in psychoanalysis as 'perlaboration'.

The work of Anzieu and Martin (1966) is perhaps the most faithful to the psychoanalytic tradition. While limited in its sociological implications, their method of **group psychoanalysis** shows some innovative adaptations of Freudian theory and practice to fit the needs of collective thinking and social transformation on a small scale. It consists of intensive seminars that combine psychodrama and unstructured discussions with interpretive assessments proposed by the analyst. The psychodrama, a key moment in the process, establishes a topography of participants divided into concentric circles. Those in the smaller circle or nucleus, from one to six participants, are invited to address a precise theme by acting it out in ways that are creative and freely express individual concerns and anxieties. Those in the periphery are asked to act as observers. Another option is for participants in the periphery to form two circles. Seen through a psychoanalytic lens, spectators in the outer circle stand as the institutional, rule-setting superego to those in the nucleus. They remain silent. By contrast, those in the intermediary circle, from two to ten participants, can intervene and speak out. They create a 'transitional space' (Winnicott, 1965) between individuals and the institution and help bring out things otherwise left unsaid in the here and now. While socially 'neutral', the analyst can join the middle circle or move between the three circles so as to facilitate the expression of conflicts and contradictions. The process helps develop a 'group psychic apparatus', a sense of collective identity comprising group illusions, symbolic representations and defence mechanisms that speak to the issues at hand and related anxieties or suffering experienced by individuals and the group as a whole. The analyst offers interpretations of interpersonal and group behaviour formulated along psychoanalytic lines, with a focus on expressions of transfer, intertransfer and countertransfer between participants and between the group and the analyst. These interpretive comments play a critical role in the process. Anzieu and Martin frame these comments within their own theory of the 'skin-ego'. This *moi-peau* is a highly sensitive narcissistic envelope that regulates the experience of well-being by fulfilling two basic functions: protecting the individual or group ego from persecution and allowing it to 'reach out' and 'keep in touch' with others to avoid abandonment.

Dejours's brand of psychosociology, also informed by psychoanalysis, focusses on the **psychodynamics of work** and related issues of work-induced suffering and defence mechanisms (Dejours, 1988). The inquiry process starts with a particular request from workers followed by site visits and some preliminary training by the research team. Discussion groups and events are then organized on a voluntary basis, in the workplace environment, with a focus on gaps between norms and actual behaviour and the relationship between the organization of work and the subjective experience of suffering and distress. The research team eventually develops its own interpretation of the views expressed, highlighting the paradoxes and contradictions they detect throughout the discussions. Far from defining their analysis as a scientific explanation of observed behaviour and perceptions, researchers interpret what they hear and see in the psychoanalytic spirit of 'perlaboration' achieved through narrative conversations and comparisons between the workers' views and those expressed by researchers. The process is one of hermeneutic interpretation (Ricoeur, 1986), a dialogical invitation to 'work-through' and lift the symptoms of suffering and distress. The goal is to identify, understand and address existing mechanisms of collective defence, pathogenic responses and seemingly absurd behaviour. Findings and insights are eventually shared with other groups. The research team facilitates discussions between groups, prepares a report, modifies it in light of the feedback received from participants and disseminates the final version within the organization, in the hope that change will occur and that workers take responsibility for effective strategies to overcome suffering and distress. Researchers, however, do not provide direct assistance in facilitating organizational change.

Other commonly cited authors currently working in the French tradition of psychosociological intervention and clinical sociology are Amado (1993), Barus-Michel (1987; *et al.*, 2002), Dubost (1987), Enriquez (1992), Lévy (1997, 2001, 2010), Gaujelac (1997) and Giust-Desprairies (1989). By and large, these practitioners have in common the attention they pay to small group dynamics over long periods and the interaction of the psychological and social dimensions of human behaviour, which are not mutually reducible. They also emphasize the role that power relations, authority and conflict play in creating dysfunctions within society and the psyche. Another leitmotiv is the need to address expressions of transference and countertransference, anxiety and resistance, in real-life settings. The rule of neutrality that psychosociologists must follow when responding to demands or pressures from groups and the client system is generally accepted.

Psychosociological interventions may nonetheless diverge in some important respects. Key differences between interventions stem from the thematic or sectorial issues they address, their scope, the time dedicated to each intervention and the contractual arrangements they put in place. Other differences concern the use and combination of individual and group interviews and discussions, as well as verbal and non-verbal (theatre, music, etc.) modes of expression and analysis. More fundamentally, interventions differ in the status they assign to the analyst's external understanding of group behaviour and views; the relative weight they attribute to the social and psychological aspects of group behaviour; and the extent to which they are critical of broader institutional and social systems. The use of psychoanalytic concepts and the relative weight of effort dedicated to the research, training and action components of the intervention also vary.

Psychiatry is another area where some researchers and practitioners have challenged the ethics of positive science as applied to human subjects and used action research to explore the pathogenic effects of institutions. Tosquelles, for example, argues that asylums need as much attention and treatment as patients. This is the starting point of **institutional psychotherapy** (Tosquelles, 1984, 1992). The observation is a call for systemic thinking and creativity in the world of medicine, using psychodynamic and outpatient practices to help patients interact and communicate, express their experience of uniqueness and difference, develop a sense of autonomy and take responsibility for their own therapy. Institutional psychotherapy supports heterogeneity in 'the art of living', by creating group encounters, dialogues and sites of sharing. These are open spaces where people are encouraged to move freely, speak out, engage in creative work and develop bonds of affection (Oury, 1982, 1993; Schotte, 2006). The approach requires of caregivers and institutions that they reflect on their own emotional reactions and behaviour. They must reflect on the social and material conditions they set in place when caring for patients. These include the many 'objects' of transference and counter-transference that caregivers generate or institute, be they human or physical, individual or collective, positive or negative. Critical and creative thinking helps to address institutional conditions that reproduce or create feelings of alienation, 'chains of signification' so rigid and constraining that they deprive patients of the powers of language, symbolic imagination and desire. The chains are tied to powerful machines of institutional alienation such as patient incarceration, dependence on medical technocracy and the bureaucratic compartmentalization of caregiving services and disciplines. Other obstacles to humanism in psychiatry include claims to hard scientific objectivity and universal frames of diagnostic interpretation and metatheory. Institutional psychotherapy is diagnostic and institutional action that attempts to address these issues in a spirit of creativity and resistance to the powers that be. It affirms a pluralism of 'untamed differences', and a commitment to the anthropology and politics of mental suffering and medical care. These critical insights are closely associated with the anti-psychiatry movement of the 1960s (Cooper, 1967) and played a key role in the medical-philosophical inquiries of Guattari (1972) and the 'linguistricks' of Lacan (1978).

While also addressing issues in sociological theory and philosophy, the approach known as **socianalysis**, developed by Lapassade and Lourau, reflects some of the principles of institutional analysis or psychotherapy proposed by Tosquelles and Oury (Lourau, 1970; Lapassade and Lourau, 1971). Socianalytic interventions target institutions defined not as establishments or fixed systems but rather as processes that structure, dismantle and recompose norms and rules of social interaction over time. The goals and methods of socianalysis have changed over the years, towards a pragmatic, long-term approach to institutional analysis and intervention (Lourau, 1996). In its early version, socianalysis usually starts with a formal agreement or contract drawn between the client organization and the research team, following a careful examination of the initial request. The body responsible for overseeing and managing the inquiry process is the 'socianalytic assembly', which includes the analytic staff or research team. The inquiry usually extends over a few intensive days and revolves around the collective determination and open discussion of 'analyzers', with interpretive input from the research team, subject to validation. An 'analyzer' is anything pertaining to a group, an individual, a situation, an event or a scandal that will cause truth to come out into the open because freely expressed in the here and now, whether it be verbally or through expressive behaviour and acting out, as in Reichian therapy.

When addressing the analyzer, attention is paid to conflicts and contradictions buried and left unspoken within the institution. Researchers are careful not to act as external consultants transmitting expert advice and objective knowledge. They merely facilitate conversations and debates around analyzers viewed as 'hot moments of history', social events that drive the analysis and discovery process. The relationship between the analytic staff and the client group is an integral part of the analysis and is subject to the principles of social 'implication' and 'transversality' (Guattari, 1972) – i.e. the maximum communication of all views expressed at all levels, towards an understanding of the interests shared by the parties concerned.

Action research framed in a 'sociopsychoanalytic' perspective (Mendel, 1980; Mendel and Prades, 2002) is another influential contribution to French psychosociology. The main concern of **sociopsychoanalysis** is with how organizational life constrains the psyche and motivation at work, by imposing limits on the power that people exercise over their own productive activity and discouraging collaborative strategies to achieve individual and collective ends. The inquiry process invites small groups sharing the same occupation in a real setting to reflect on work-related problems, their level of satisfaction at work and the organizational factors that have a negative psychological impact on them. The methodology revolves around group discussions about existing problems and potential solutions. Written reports of these discussions are shared horizontally and vertically, between different groups within the organization and with the researchers who facilitate the process. When applied in the school context, similar procedures of 'Students' Collective Expression' allow teachers and students to engage in a constructive, problem-solving dialogue, in a spirit of solidarity and equality among students (rather than elitism, individualism and competition). Strategies to counter the pathogenic aspects of the organization are explored, typically by attenuating or neutralizing the technical, social and organizational forces that sustain patterns of patriarchal authority, conformity through identification, social fragmentation and powerlessness at work.

Sociopsychoanalysts expect expressions of retreat and resistance to change based on feelings of guilt and submission to authority. In addition to facilitating the inquiry process, they must be able to detect, understand and address these expressions of resistance, but without imposing any interpretation, not even of Freudian inspiration. The cannons of psychoanalysis recede in the background and give way to principles of human agency and the emancipation of self through social empowerment. Over time, sociopsychoanalysis aims at creating a 'movement of appropriation of the power act' such as to enhance pleasure, creativity, democratic participation and shared responsibility within the organization.

What *la psychosociologie d'intervention* brings to PAR is both challenging and inspiring. It is a reminder of the insights that psychological and social scientific theory and philosophy can contribute to meaningful knowledge. Engaged research can be pragmatic and democratic as in other PAR traditions but without abandoning its own 'transitional space', a place for creativity in language and symbolic interaction with others and their surroundings. This is a complex space where social interconnectedness means not only the exercise of reason but also the creation and communication of meaning and affect.

DEVELOPMENT

PAR has left an important imprint on the field of rural and community development, especially in the Global South. For the last four decades there have been countless experiments in technological innovation (Farming Systems Research, Appropriate Technology), alternative natural resource management (Participatory Rural Appraisal, Participatory Learning and Action) and the promotion of traditional, indigenous or local knowledge systems (TKS, IKS, LKS). On the whole, PAR applications in this field are committed to problem solving and adaptation to nature at the household or community level, using friendly methods of scientific thinking and experimentation adapted to support rural participation and sustainable livelihoods (Pound *et al.*, 2003; Gonsalves *et al.*, 2005).

Farming Systems Research and Extension (FSR-E), which started in the 1960s, is the first attempt at rethinking conventional science in the field of rural development. Historically, FSR-E was a counterpoint to mono-crop research on experimental stations isolated from the realities of capital-poor farmers who grow several food crops and have multiple sources of income and diverse biophysical resources at their disposal (Collinson, 2000). The farming systems perspective brings attention to the effects of complexity and the interaction of biological and socio-economic factors on the decision-making environment of farmers. It also introduces a strategic approach to livelihood planning by focussing on key variables rather than complete farming systems (Byerlee *et al.*, 1982). Methods used include exploratory surveys and participant observation to assess system dynamics, identify groups of farmers with roughly similar practices and circumstances ('recommendation domains') and select possible leverage points for biological research. On-farm research methods bring researchers, their ideas and their procedures into an environment where farmer conditions can test and weed out potential recommendations coming from scientists.

While client-oriented and needs based, early forms of FSR-E focussed largely on making better use of new technological components emerging from the Green Revolution, including hybrid seed, fertilizers, pesticides and farm machinery. Little attention was paid to improving traditional agronomic practices or existing farmer seed systems. The mounting costs of the Green Revolution for the environment and the vulnerability for farmers created by reliance on external inputs and corporate science and technology were initially ignored. Nevertheless, FSR-E opened the door to farmer involvement in setting research priorities, assessment of the performance of technological alternatives and eventual implementation or adoption. The survey methods of FSR-E later gave rise to Rapid Rural Appraisal (RRA) as scientists looked for faster and cheaper ways to understand system dynamics and engage farmers in identifying opportunities for new technology and livelihood strategies.

While still committed to a technical approach to development, the **Appropriate Technology (AT) Movement**, launched by the economist Schumacher (1973), is a more critical contribution to PAR that seeks to address the technological gap between rich and poor. Appropriate technologies are those that users can build, operate and maintain with little outside assistance, wherever they may come from originally. Inspired by Gandhian principles of self-reliance, AT calls for a reorientation of technology, with new methods of production and patterns of consumption respectful of the Earth and the dignity of work. The approach draws on ideas and technologies emerging from science at the same time as it emphasizes the use of local or readily available materials, including labour and local knowledge and skills.

Participatory Technology Development (PTD) has developed and carried forward the local and small-scale orientation of the original movement, and to some extent the underlying critique of the modern philosophy of work and nature responsible for the environmental crisis (Reijntjes *et al.*, 1992). In PTD, traditional technologies are adapted and retooled for today's conditions, and new ideas scouted among innovative farmers, trades people and operators of cottage industries (Gupta, 2006). The potential for local innovation, what Schumacher called 'room for human creativity', is enhanced by filling key gaps in local knowledge (for example, farmer knowledge of insect reproduction; Bentley and Andrews, 1996) and teaching simple experimental designs (Bunch, 1982). Direct farmer-to-farmer communication through exchange visits among innovators in different settings and support to farmer organizations supplement conventional approaches to technology transfer and rural extension (Holt-Gimenez, 2006).

Questions remain, however, regarding the extent to which farmers are actually responsible for managing on-farm agricultural experiments involving researchers. While farmer-based, many expressions of PTD are still not farmer-led. Moreover, it is not clear exactly what new technologies have emerged from this research strategy (Bentley, 1994). Most examples of technological change are minor adaptations of existing practices or very site-specific innovations. These do not have anything like the scope or potential impact of the Green Revolution technologies emerging from FSR-E and conventional agricultural research strategies. Many proponents of PTD also recognize the inherent limitations of a technical approach to system change and the need to foster social movements if self-reliance, environmental sustainability and dignified work are to be achieved (Holt-Gimenez, 2006).

Participatory Rural Appraisal (PRA) and its successor **Participatory Learning and Action** (PLA) are the most widely known of participatory methods in the international development field. They broaden the idea of rural development to include all aspects of livelihood and natural resource management, beyond the technical focus of FSR-E and AT. PRA and PLA draw inspiration from earlier efforts to engage poor and marginalized groups in self-directed analysis, problem-solving and emancipatory action. The study

PHOTO 1.1 Villagers in West Bengal, India assess community projects with DRSCC and UBINIG staff, using *Activity Domain*. (Source: D. J. Buckles)

clubs of the Canadian Antigonish movement (Coady, 1939), work with First Nations in the United States and Canada (Hall, 1992; Park *et al.*, 1993), community-development initiatives of the 1960s, Freire's adult education methods and other pioneering work showed that regular small meetings among poor people with low levels of education could generate meaningful understandings of the situations they face and agreement on actions needed to address them. The main contribution of PRA and PLA to this work is the creative, pluralistic and dynamic use of visual and tangible forms of expression and analysis addressing issues of livelihood and natural resource management. Maps, models, diagrams, pile sorting, ranking and rating, storytelling, ice breakers and role-play are the signature tools of the practice, giving rise to numerous and large collections of techniques adapted to various contexts with support from donor agencies across the world (cf. Pretty *et al.*, 1995).

Practical adaptations of PRA and PLA to planning, monitoring and evaluation (M&E) have mushroomed over the years. Many toolboxes are dedicated to specific sectors, such as health, agriculture, horticulture, forestry, fisheries and watersheds. Other sets of techniques are concerned with local development processes or issues of conflict and natural resource management (Means *et al.*, 2002). Underlying these many tools is a commitment to eliminate bias in community-oriented initiatives: that is, the spatial bias of urban perspectives over remote rural realities, the bias of the educated and the powerful over people with low literacy and low social standing, and the bias of scientists and professionals over 'non-professionals' who have expert knowledge of their own (Satheesh, 2009). While the tools help in this regard, turning researchers into facilitators and participants into leaders and learners of the action-research process ('role reversals') is a critical and difficult requirement of the practice (Chambers, 1993).

The strengths of PRA and PLA, including flexibility and the license to 'use your own best judgment at all times' (Chambers, 2008), also present significant risks. As with FSR-E, PRA and PLA can easily override existing legitimate decision-making processes, fall prey to powerful voices within a group and displace local and traditional ways of thinking and learning (Cooke and Kothari, 2001). The consensual focus can obscure diverging interests and the actual exercise of power during the action-inquiry process (Cornwall, 2004). Cooptation of PRA and PLA by development bureaucracies and insufficient attention to the power structures from which it is advocated and promoted have led to highly manipulated outcomes (Brown, 2004). A common lament is that the practice of PRA and PLA may simply legitimize agency-driven agendas, making too much of participation and too little of who decides and what actions are ultimately taken. A lack of rigour in the tools can also lead to quick and dirty assessments and complaints from scientists and policymakers that results are anecdotal and of questionable substance. These persistent gaps and insufficient attention to theorizing strategies for social transformation (Bebbington, 2004; Hickey and Mohan, 2004) explain, at least in part, why the practice of PRA and PLA has made few inroads into academic research and training.

Natural scientists and anthropologists committed to action research for development have played a key role in promoting an idea that is fundamental to PRA and PLA: the notion that the rural poor, if heard, can contribute to the creation of useful knowledge and better livelihoods. They have also contributed an important body of literature and research that acknowledges and promotes long-standing **indigenous, traditional or local knowledge systems** (IKS, TKS, LKS) that can be mobilized in support of endogenous development. While Western science has its merits, it has much to learn from knowledge that is built into the cumulative wisdom, practical knowledge and oral teachings of place-based communities. The wisdom is embedded in stories, legends, folklore, songs, rituals and norms of conduct and technical practices that are part of day-to-day livelihood activities and interactions with nature (Warren *et al.*, 1995; Berkes, 1999). Students of LKS thus delve into what local or indigenous populations know about plants and animals, watercourses, soils, landscapes and elements of nature such as wind, rain, weather and climate. The methods they use, primarily empirical, help describe local know-how, classifications and properties of soils, plants and animals and their interaction with elements of nature and human populations. Some studies in ethnogeography, ethnobiology, ethnobotany, ethnoforestry, ethnoagroecology and ethnomedicine include the conceptual, symbolic or spiritual underpinnings of traditional knowledge, using methods that vary from one study to another, whether ethnographic, ethnomethodological or structuralist. The primary intent of LKS studies is often purely academic, or a well-intended contribution to salvage ethnography – preserving 'age-old' non-Western wisdom against extinction. Some noticeable exceptions to this rule include mergers of LKS and GIS (Geographic Information System) or LKS and Participatory Video. Both of these mergers involve the collaborative gathering and processing of local knowledge for use in cultural transmission, land rights disputes, natural resource management, historical impact assessments and economic development planning (Fox *et al.*, 2005; Kindon *et al.*, 2007; Satheesh, 2012).

LKS has found its way in science and industry. However, endeavours to tap into bodies of traditional knowledge have been the object of debate at the international level, as reflected in discussions of the CBD (Convention on Biological Diversity), the WIPO (World Intellectual Property Organization) and WTO (World Trade Organization on Trade-Related Aspects of Intellectual Property Rights). Discussions revolve around two positions. Either traditional knowledge is part of the public domain, designed for local and universal benefit, especially as it relates to issues of biodiversity. Or it deserves the protection of existing intellectual property rights (patents, copyrights, trademarks, trade secrets) or new *sui generis* laws against two recurring threats: misappropriation of indigenous people's cultural heritage (including symbols, stories and songs) and the practice of pharmaceutical and agro-industrial bio-piracy, especially in regards to the patenting of plant life (Posey, 1996). Middle-of-the-road solutions advance the idea of rewards to generators and custodians of traditional knowledge, and equitable exchanges among the communities and institutions accessing biodiversity around the world (Gupta, 1994).

Other debates revolve around validity claims. How reliable is wisdom transmitted orally and acquired empirically, by trial and error, in specific contexts, without the benefit of objective documentation and scientific theory? To what extent is traditional knowledge generated under conditions that are becoming obsolete due to problems of environmental degradation, biodiversity loss and climate change? When faced with these questions, ethnoscience may attempt to salvage LKS by rehashing the principles of cultural relativity. Another option is to fall back on conventional methods of data gathering, analysis and scholarly dissemination to better understand worldviews and bodies of knowledge deemed to be authentically 'traditional' and interesting in their own right. Alternatively, ethnoscience may be carried out in a pragmatic spirit, to promote the creative and adaptive features of LKS (Sherwood and Bentley, 2009) and the dialogue of knowledge and learning systems needed to help people cope with social and environmental problems on a local and global scale (Brokensha *et al.*, 1980).

The inroads of PAR in the field of development in the Global South are significant. They point the way to a pragmatic, pluralistic and egalitarian approach to knowledge making that attempts to counter the devastating impact of modern industry and technology on rural forms of livelihood, community life and resource bases around the world. These contributions are nonetheless faced with limitations that impede their further development. As with organizational PAR and psychosociology, they generally underestimate the scale and depth of transformation needed to achieve democracy in the production of knowledge and well-being at all levels, local and global. They create a rift between a positive stance in the practice of science (as in FSR-E) and a populist plea for knowledge-generating tools that are quick-and-easy, i.e. scaled down on purpose in order to be universally accessible (as in PRA/PLA and AT). Last but not least, as in the Lewinian tradition, they tend to neglect forms of understanding and consciousness that are not directly related to rational means-ends considerations and concerns of material livelihoods.

EDUCATION

Freire's **critical pedagogy** (Freire, 1970) represents one of the most critical perspectives on the twin issue of knowledge and grassroots, community-based development. His work is a widely cited source of PAR inspiration in both education and development studies. It is firmly committed to the politics of emancipatory action, with a focus on dialogical reflection and action as means to overcome relations of domination and subordination between oppressors and the oppressed, colonizers and the colonized.

In the Freirean tradition, research is a critical inquiry adjusted to the task of promoting radical democracy and 'transformational liberation' (Lykes and Mallona, 2008) in all spheres of life, starting with education. Class struggle and self-liberation of the 'wretched of the earth' (Fanon, 1963) requires a revamping of traditional education, which tends to control and limit people's creative power and ability to transform their own lives. This means that the banking approach to schooling must be abandoned, and students no longer treated as empty pots that passively receive knowledge from authoritative teachers. After Rousseau and Dewey, Freire views the transmission of mere facts and existing bodies of knowledge to be futile as a learning strategy and as a way to promote well-being in a just and equal society. He challenges the teacher–student dichotomy itself, advocating a relationship of deep reciprocity that takes its inspiration from the dialectics of Socratic teaching. Education is both key to the struggle for democracy and a battlefield on its own, a site where teachers must fight alongside the people for the recovery of their stolen humanity.

PHOTO 1.2 Specialists in Canada reflect on the practice of Environmental Education. (Source: J. Wonnacott)

Critical pedagogy challenges the conventions of science, philosophy and theology. It subverts oppressive regimes of knowledge and power through the exercise of critical consciousness, inviting people on the margins of society to interrogate and question dominant thinking and systems of power, and take action against them. The end result is a dialectical movement that goes from *action* to *reflection* and from *reflection* upon *action* to new *action*. The approach is well illustrated in Freire's adult education method that brings oppressed people to both literacy and political consciousness by focussing on visual representations of everyday life situations and the 'generative words' that people use, with emotional content, to describe and confront the social, cultural and political reality in which they live. Freire's endorsement of Liberation Theology (Gutierrez, 1974) is another expression of his support for critical thinking and the interpretation of text and reality as a bottom-up movement led by lay practitioners rather than the Church hierarchy.

Critical pedagogy is more concerned with rethinking adult education than collective action or full-fledged research to support social change. It offers no means to bridge the gap between the development of critical consciousness and the exercise of scientific reason – methodical action-research based on pragmatic, evidence-based thinking. Fals-Borda's **critical PAR** attempts to close this gap, by extending the spirit of Freirean methodology to the field of action research (Fals-Borda and Rahman, 1991). His approach incorporates community-based needs, knowledge and action learning into the inquiry plans and theoretical concerns of traditional science. The task is carried out not with extractive and scholarly intent but rather to transform society and subvert existing systems of oppression. Fals-Borda's views on engaged inquiry and knowledge making are far-reaching and worth quoting at length:

> Do not monopolise your knowledge nor impose arrogantly your techniques, but respect and combine your skills with the knowledge of the researched or grassroots communities, taking them as full partners and co-researchers. Do not trust elitist versions of history and science that respond to dominant interests, but be receptive to counter-narratives and try to recapture them. Do not depend solely on your culture to interpret facts, but recover local values, traits, beliefs and arts for action by and with the research organisations. Do not impose your own ponderous scientific style for communicating results, but diffuse and share what you have learned together with the people, in a manner that is wholly understandable and even literary and pleasant, for science should not be necessarily a mystery nor a monopoly of experts and intellectuals.
>
> (Fals-Borda, 1995)

Like Freire, Fals-Borda has a profound distrust of conventional academia matched only by his confidence in popular knowledge, sentiments that have had a lasting impact on the history of PAR, particularly in the fields of development and counterhegemonic education (see Carr and Kemmis, 1986; Fine and Torre, 2008; Noffke and Somekh, 2009).

Feminist research, among other traditions (Maguire, 1987; Williams and Lykes, 2003; see Minkler and Wallerstein, 2008), has made important contributions to rethinking the role of scholarship in challenging existing regimes of power, using qualitative and interpretive methods that emphasize subjectivity rather than the quantitative approach of science working with human 'subjects' (Tolman and Brydon-Miller, 2000). While less critical in tone and purpose, more recent attempts to reconnect academic interests with education and community development needs, through **Community-Based Research and Learning** (CBR-L) programmes and networks (Westfall *et al.*, 2006), show greater confidence in the potential for conventional scientific methods to be carried out democratically and in meaningful contexts. The Global Alliance on Community-Engaged Research, recently created and led by several universities, networks and civil society organizations in Canada, is a promising effort to 'use knowledge and community–university partnership strategies for democratic social and environmental change and justice, particularly among the most vulnerable people and places of the world' (communityresearchcanada.ca). The Center for Community Based Research based in Ontario (www.communitybasedresearch.ca) is also committed to these principles. Its primary goal is to support and strengthen community-based research, towards the creation and sharing of knowledge that addresses pressing issues of justice and well-being and promotes positive social change and empowerment. The hallmark of community-university learning is an inquiry process that is action-oriented and community situated, i.e. grounded in practical community needs and learning, as opposed to serving scholarly interests alone (Brydon-Miller *et al.*, 2003, p. 24). It calls for the active involvement of community members and researchers in all phases of the action inquiry process, from defining relevant research questions and topics to designing and implementing the investigation, sharing the available resources, acknowledging community-based expertise and making the results accessible and understandable to community members and the broader public. Several guides show how students and faculty can engage in community-based participatory research and meet academic standards at the same time (Kemmis and McTaggart, 1988; Sherman and Torbert, 2000; Herr and Anderson, 2005; Burns, 2007; Coghlan and Brannick, 2007; Stringer, 2007; McNiff and Whitehead, 2009; Smith *et al.*, 2010; James *et al.*, 2012).

Service learning or education (e.g. Moely *et al.*, 2009; www.trentcentre.ca) is a closely related endeavour designed to encourage students to actively apply knowledge and skills to local situations, in response to local needs and with the active involvement of community members. University programmes inspired by these principles connect post-secondary students and faculty with local organizations to offer experiential education opportunities to students and grounded research services and support to community members. While innovative and beneficial to the student learning experience, research projects stemming from service learning programmes are often faced with the difficult task of adjusting course-based requirements and time frames to complex community situations and needs. Other problems include the limited involvement of faculty (whose research interests often lie elsewhere) and the fact that students have limited training or experience in the use of participatory methods and must fall back on conventional methods, such as literature reviews, content analysis, questionnaires, interviews and participant observation. The tendency to limit the notion of community to people residing in the same locality also imposes constraints on strategies to address issues on a broader scale.

Desgagné's take on **collaborative research in education** (CR-E) is community-based research where pre-university teachers are the community. Research is done on educational practices, with teachers and for their benefit. The approach provides some useful guidelines as to how researchers can support the educational community without losing sight of their own research goals. This calls for a process of interpretive mediation or dialogue between teachers and researchers – between 'knowledge in action' and formal scientific inquiry (Desgagné, 2001; Desgagné *et al.*, 2001; Desgagné and Bednarz, 2005). Mediation informs all the usual steps and tools of academic research, from theory building to research design, data collection and analysis and the dissemination of results. Collaboration between researchers and teachers is key to success for the creation of new interpretive meaning and knowledge. Conversations between the two knowledge systems, theoretical and practical, contribute to advances in science and the professional development of teachers. While providing an alternative to extractive, expert-based approaches to the advancement of knowledge in the human sciences, Desgagné's collaborative research agenda does not involve experimentation with new methods of teaching or research, let alone action learning and problem solving in real educational settings (Sebillotte, 2007). The primary goal is to produce new knowledge on relevant issues in education, building scientific knowledge on top of teachers' own interpretation of their experience and reality.

PUBLIC ENGAGEMENT

PAR strategies to democratize knowledge making and ground it in real community needs and learning represent genuine efforts to overcome the ineffectiveness and elitism of conventional schooling and science, and the negative effects of market forces and industry on the workplace, community life and sustainable livelihoods. The results have left visible imprints on the history of engaged research. They are nonetheless weakened by considerable timidity in addressing systems of power and societal challenges on a large scale (see Mead, 2008). The tendency is for action research to keep things small and close to natural communities and environments, even when conceived in a subversive or transformative mode. This micro-perspective on social action and analysis either ignores or remains naively optimistic in its opposition to the exclusionary and authoritarian character of positive science and an academic life largely deaf to pressing individual and community needs.

Novel approaches in the public sphere provide some useful strategies to scale up the action-inquiry process and the meshing of science and experience in the public sphere. Touraine's contribution to social movement theory and practice is a case in point. In the late 1970s, Touraine asked, what it is that sociologists actually do beyond what it is they think? To answer the question, Touraine (Touraine *et al.*, 1980), Dubet (1991, 2001) and others proposed a **sociology of intervention** involving the creation of artificial spaces for movement activists concerned with particular problems and for non-activists affected by them to meet voluntarily and debate views with other concerned parties (allies, adversaries, experts, policymakers, ecologists, unions representatives, business people). Intra- and inter-group discussions, organized iteratively or on an ongoing basis, allow key actors or agents to reflect on the meaning of their collective actions, by responding to provocative insights and 'plausible' reframing offered by the research team, usually an analyst interacting closely with the actors and a more distant interpreter responsible for taking notes. In principle, this dialogical inquiry is designed to generate group-driven conversions in systems of meaning, beyond the fixed categories of ideological discourse, towards the formulation of alternative courses of action. In practice, however, experiments in sociological intervention have served mostly to develop social movement, post-industrial thinking among researchers. Impacts on the real world have yet to materialize.

Citizen science is another recent move to broaden the concept of social engagement in scientific work, to include broader 'communities of interest' and citizens committed to enhancing knowledge in particular fields. In this approach to collaborative inquiry, research is actively assisted by volunteers who form an active public or network of contributing individuals. Participants may or may not have scientific expertise or share the same geographic, occupational, cultural or educational background. This emergent path to collaborative science is particularly effective in scaling up scientific programmes in the natural and environmental sciences (biology, astronomy, etc.), by employing volunteers to monitor natural phenomena, resources and species through observation and measurement (Cooper *et al.*, 2007).

The recent proliferation of citizen science activity owes a lot to the revolution in information and communication technology (ICT). **Web 2** applications play a critical role by supporting virtual community interactivity and facilitating the development of user-driven content and social media, without restricted access or controlled implementation. Social media that can fulfil these functions include networking, blogs, wikis, video sharing, crowdsourcing, hosted services, web applications, mashups (to aggregate and reuse data in new ways) and folksonomies (generated through the collaborative tagging and categorization of content). Web-based citizen science is still not widely used and is not necessarily committed to efforts in social transformation. The approach nonetheless shows great potential in refreshing and scaling up the social and technical components of PAR, otherwise limited to small-scale community endeavours and the conventional methods of collaborative inquiry and group dynamics.

The ICT revolution also plays a key role in formulating and promoting the principles of **open source governance** (Rushkoff, 2004). At stake here is a philosophical plea for applying the open source and open content movement to democratic institutions, allowing citizens to actively engage in wiki-based processes of virtual journalism, public debate and policy development. Experiments in open politics typically use ICT and the mechanics of e-democracy to facilitate communications on a large scale, towards achieving decisions that best serve the public interest. The methods used are highly flexible and can make provisions for anonymity, geographic rootedness, the standing law and institutions of a jurisdiction and the rule of accountability to persons affected by the decisions of open politics. They also take into account the difference between free speech and outright defamation.

PHOTO 1.3 Cuban youth discuss what civic engagement means in their national context. (Source: J. M. Chevalier)

In the same spirit, discursive or **deliberative democracy** is a call for public discussion, transparency and pluralism in political decision-making, lawmaking and institutional life (Cohen, 1989; Bessette, 1994). True to the Habermasian tradition of discourse ethics, it involves a theory of civics that recognizes multiple interests and grounds for dissent and offers ways to address them, through the exercise of communicative reason and the incorporation of scientific information and evidence-based reasoning in the deliberative process. Fact-finding and the outputs of science are made accessible to participants and may be subject to extensive media coverage, scientific peer review, deliberative opinion polling (Fishkin, 2009) and adversarial presentations of competing arguments and predictive claims. Although scientific arguments matter, experts must convince all those participating in the process. The methodology of 'citizens' jury' is pioneering in this respect. It is made up of people selected at random from a local or national population who are provided opportunities to question 'witnesses' and collectively form a 'judgment' (Wakeford *et al.*, 2007). In principle, deliberations based on the exercise of reason and authentic dialogue contribute meaningfully to decisions that are binding.

In practice, exercises in open source governance and deliberative democracy are few and far between. They are also poorly supported by existing national and international institutions so far have had little discernable impact on the functioning of liberal democracies and the global governance of pressing issues such as poverty, the loss of agricultural biodiversity and climate change. As for web-based inquiries, they may enhance the scale and efficiency of data gathering and analysis under the control of expert researchers. However, whether they are wedded to deep transformations in self and society, towards greater justice and well-being, is strictly a matter of choice and is not predetermined by the technology.

Still, ICT and open politics point to a fundamentally different perspective on social life, one which challenges the organismic view of 'Society' and replaces it with the sliding rule of 'Sociability'. The organismic model portrays social interaction as analogous to relations between the parts of a living organism. In this perspective, of functionalist inspiration, each society has well-defined boundaries and patterns of behaviour that constitute a distinct entity or cultural identity. Much like every living species in nature, each body social has its own institutions, biological-like organs created and interacting to serve the functional needs of the social whole, an entity greater than the sum of its parts. Interaction across social boundaries and trends towards globalization are the aggregations of decisions by individual collectivities defined politically or culturally, of varying sizes and life expectancies. Any action-inquiry conceived along these lines must commit to exploring and enhancing particular social identities and their immediate interactions.

By contrast, ICTs and open politics draw attention to simple and complex networks and movements that mesh and intersect in many ways and on many levels. Multitudes of nodes, flows and connecting lines give rise to rhizomatic growth rather than clearly delineated systems. No overarching structure, language or perspective can merge all pathways into a single road map, system or culture. Clear delineations of human identity, individual and collective, give way to myriad threads of inter-humanity and constructions of subjective reality, individual and collective. This is the complex world of interaction and sociability that the practice of action-research has yet to address, by establishing the right point of entry into each inquiry process and the corresponding path of social engagement.

ICTs and open politics also usher in new strategies to engage governments, scientists, civil society organizations and interested citizens in policy-related discussions of science and technology. They are becoming a permanent feature of 'metadeliberations' about how macro-level governance ought to be structured, nationally and internationally, towards greater inclusivity and accountability to the public space. These trends represent an invitation to explore novel paths of social inquiry and action. They also call for a revised understanding of *technê*, a shift from previous views of technology based on modern industry – the top-down division and control of repetitive labour harnessed to assembly lines of mass production. We know that ICT and advanced capitalism can lie in the same bed; large businesses derive massive benefits from using computer technology and a flexible specialization of labour to customize and manufacture products at mass-production prices. ICT companies are among the largest corporations in the world. All the same, the applications and effects of ICT are wide-ranging and profound to the point that the simple dualism between Technology and Humanism, a PAR leitmotiv for the last seventy years, is no longer justified. More than ever, engaged researchers must adapt to new ways of understanding and constructing social life, beyond small groups and organic communities. They must also show greater flexibility and creativity in their use of *technê* to support the kind of collaborative inquiry and social engagement that can be brought to bear on the pressing issues of our age.

REFERENCES

Ackoff, R. (1999) *Ackoff's Best: His Classic Writings on Management*, Wiley, New York.

Amado, G. (1993) 'La résonance psychosociale', Ph.D. Thesis, Université Paris-VII, Paris.

Anzieu, D. and Martin, J.-Y. (1966) *La dynamique des groupes restreints*, PUF, Paris.

Balint, M. (1954) 'Training general practitioners in psychotherapy', *British Medical Journal*, vol. I, pp. 115–120.

Barus-Michel, J. (1987) *Le sujet social: étude de psychologie sociale clinique*, Dunod, Paris.

Barus-Michel, J., Enriquez, E. and Lévy, A. (2002) *Vocabulaire de psychosociologie: Positions et références*, Erès, Paris.

Bebbington, A. (2004) 'Theorizing participation and institutional change: ethnography and political economy', in S. Hickey and G. Mohan (eds) *Participation – From Tyranny to Transformation? Exploring New Approaches to Participation in Development*, Zed, London, pp. 278–283.

Bentley, J. (1994) 'Facts, fantasies, and failures of farmer participatory research', *Agriculture and Human Values*, vol. 11, no. 2–3, pp. 140–150.

Bentley, J. W. and Andrews, K. L. (1996) *Through the Roadblocks: IPM and Central American Smallholders*, Sustainable Agriculture Programme, Gatekeeper Series, no. 56, International Institute for Environment and Development, London.

Berkes, F. (1999) *Sacred Ecology: Traditional Ecological Knowledge and Resource Management*, Taylor & Francis, Philadelphia and London.

Bessette, J. (1994) *The Mild Voice of Reason: Deliberative Democracy and American National Government*, University of Chicago Press, Chicago, IL.

Bion, W. R. (1961) *Experiences in Groups and Other Papers*, Tavistock, London.

Brokensha, D. W., Warren, D. M. and Werner, O. (eds) (1980) *Indigenous Knowledge Systems and Development*, University Press of America, Lanham, MD.

Brown, D. (2004) 'Participation in poverty reduction strategies: democracy strengthened or democracy undermined?' in S. Hickey and G. Mohan (eds) *Participation – From Tyranny to Transformation? Exploring New Approaches to Participation in Development*, Zed, London, pp. 278–283.

Brydon-Miller, M., Greenwood, D. and Maguire, P. (2003) 'Why action research?' *Action Research*, vol. 1, no. 1, pp. 9–28.

Bunch, R. (1982) *Two Ears of Corn: A Guide to People-Centered Agricultural Improvement*, World Neighbors, Oklahoma City, OK.

Burns, D. (2007) *Systemic Action Research: A Strategy for Whole System Change*, Policy Press, Bristol.

Byerlee, D., Harrington, L. and Winkelmann, D. (1982) 'Farming systems research: Issues in research strategy and technology design', *American Journal of Agricultural Economics*, vol. 65, no. 5, pp. 897–907.

Carr, W. and Kemmis, S. (1986) *Becoming Critical: Education, Knowledge and Action Research*, Routledge, London.

Chambers, R. (1993) *Challenging the Professions: Frontiers for Rural Development*, Intermediate Technology Development Group, London.

Chambers, R. (2008) 'PRA, PLA and pluralism: Practice and theory', in P. Reason and H. Bradbury (eds) *The SAGE Handbook of Action Research*, Sage, London, pp. 297–318.

Coady, M. (1939) *Masters of Their Own Destiny: The Story of the Antigonish Movement of Adult Education Through Economic Cooperation*, Harper, New York.

Coghlan, D. and Brannick, T. (2007) *Doing Action Research in Your Own Organization*, Sage, Thousand Oaks, CA.

Cohen, J. (1989) 'Deliberative democracy and democratic legitimacy', in A. Hamlin and P. Pettit (eds) *The Good Polity*, Blackwell, Oxford, pp. 17–34.

Collinson, M. (ed.) (2000) *A History of Farming Systems Research*, Food and Agricultural Organization of the United Nations, Rome.

Cooke, B. and Kothari, U. (eds) (2001) *Participation: The New Tyranny?* Zed, London.

Cooper, D. (1967) *Psychiatry and Anti-Psychiatry*, Paladin, London.

Cooper, C. B., Dickinson, J., Phillips, T. and Bonney, R. (2007) 'Citizen science as a tool for conservation in residential ecosystems', *Ecology and Society*, vol. 12, no. 2: 11.

Cooperrider, D., Diana, L. W. and Jacqueline, S. (2004) *Appreciative Inquiry Handbook: The First in a Series of AI Workbooks for Leaders of Change*, Berrett-Koehler, San Francisco, CA.

Cornwall, A. (2004) 'Spaces for transformation? Reflections on issues of power and difference in participation in development', in S. Hickey and G. Mohan (eds) *Participation – From Tyranny to Transformation? Exploring New Approaches to Participation in Development*, Zed, London.

Crozier, M. (2000) *À quoi sert la sociologie des organisations?* 2 vols, Seli Arslan, Paris.

Dejours, C. (1988) *Plaisir et souffrance dans le travail*, AOCIP, Paris.

Desgagné, S. (2001) 'La recherche collaborative: Nouvelle dynamique de recherche en éducation', in M. Anadon (ed.) *Des nouvelles dynamiques de recherche en éducation*, Presses de l'Université Laval, Québec, pp. 51–76.

Desgagné, S. and Bednarz, N. (eds) (2005) 'Médiation entre recherche et pratique en éducation', *Revue des sciences de l'éducation*, vol. 31, no. 2, pp. 245–258.

Desgagné, S., Bednarz, N., Couture, C., Poirier, L. and Lebuis, P. (2001) 'L'approche collaborative de recherche en éducation: un nouveau rapport à établir entre recherche et formation', *Revue des sciences de l'éducation*, vol. 27, no. 1, pp. 33–64.

Dicks, H. V. (1970) *Fifty Years of the Tavistock Clinic*, Routledge, London.

Dubet, F. (1991) *Les lycéens*, Seuil, Paris.

Dubet, F. (2001) 'Plaidoyer pour l'intervention sociologique', in D. Vranken and O. Kuty (eds) *La sociologie et l'intervention*, De Boeke, Bruxelles.

Dubost, J. (1987) *L'intervention psychosociologique*, PUF, Paris.

Emery, F., Hilgendorf, E. L. and Irving, B. L. (1968) *The Psychological Dynamics of Smoking*, Tobacco Research Council, London.

Emery, F. and Thorsrud, E. (1969) *Form and Content in Industrial Democracy*, Tavistock, London.

Emery, F. and Thorsrud, E. (1977) *Democracy at Work*, Martinus Nijhoff, Leiden.

Enriquez, E. (1992) *L'organisation en analyse*, PUF, Paris.

Fals-Borda, O. (1995) 'Research for social justice: Some North-South convergences', Plenary Address at the Southern Sociological Society Meeting, Atlanta, April 8.

Fals-Borda, O. and Rahman, M. A. (1991) *Action and Knowledge. Breaking the Monopoly with Participatory Action-Research*, Apex, New York.

Fanon, F. (1963) *The Wretched of the Earth*, trans. Richard Philcox, Grove, New York.

Fine, M. and Torre, M. E. (2008) 'Theorizing audience, products and provocation', in P. Reason and H. Bradbury (eds) *The SAGE Handbook of Action Research*, Sage, London, pp. 407–419.

Fishkin, J. S. (2009) *When the People Speak: Deliberative Democracy and Public Consultation*, Oxford University Press, Oxford.

Fox, J., Suryanata, K. and Herschock, P. (eds) (2005) *Mapping Communities: Ethics, Values, Practice*, East-West Center, Honolulu.

Freire, P. (1970) *Pedagogy of the Oppressed*, Continuum, New York.

Friedberg, E. (1993) *Le pouvoir et la règle*, Seuil, Paris.

Gaujelac (de), V. (1997) 'Introduction', in N. Aubert, V. de Gaujelac and K. Navridis (eds) *L'aventure psychosociologique*, Desclée de Brouwer, Paris.

Giust-Desprairies, F. (1989) *L'enfant rêvé*, Armand Colin, Paris.

Gonsalves, J., Becker, T., Braun, A., Campilan, D., Chavez, H. de, Fajber, E., Kapiriri, M., Rivaca-Caminade, J. and Vernooy, R. (2005) *Participatory Research and Development for Sustainable Agriculture and Natural Resource Management: A Sourcebook*, 3 vols, IDRC, Ottawa, ON.

Guattari, F. (1972) *Psychanalyse et transversalité, Essais d'analyse institutionnelle*, Maspero, Paris.

Gupta, A. (1994) 'Suggested ethical guidelines for accessing and exploring biodiversity', *Madras Agricultural Journal*, vol. 84, no. 10, pp. 569–573.

Gupta, A. (2006) 'From sink to source: The honey bee network documents indigenous knowledge and innovations in India', *Innovations: Technology, Governance, Globalization*, vol. 1, no. 3, pp. 49–66.

Gutierrez, G. (1974) *A Theology of Liberation*, SCM, London.

Hall, B. (1992) 'From margins to center? The development and purpose of participatory research', *The American Sociologist*, vol. 23, no. 4, pp. 15–28.

Herr, K. and Anderson, G. L. (2005) *The Action Research Dissertation: A Guide for Students and Faculty*, Sage, Thousand Oaks, CA.

Hickey, S. and Mohan, G. (eds) (2004) *Participation – From Tyranny to Transformation? Exploring New Approaches to Participation in Development*, Zed, London.

Holt-Gimenez, E. (2006) *Campesino a Campesino: Voices from Latin America's Farmer to Farmer Movement for Sustainable Agriculture*, Food First/Institute for Food and Development Policy, Oakland, CA.

James, E. A., Slater, T. and Bucknam, A. (2012) *Action Research for Business, Nonprofit, and Public Administration – A Tool for Complex Times*, Sage, Thousand Oaks, CA.

Jaques, E. (1951) *The Changing Culture of a Factory*, Tavistock, London.

Kemmis, S. and McTaggart, R. (1988) *The Action Research Planner*, Deakin University Press, Victoria, Australia.

Kindon, S. L., Pain, R. and Kesby, M. (eds) (2007) *Participatory Action Research Approaches and Methods: Connecting People, Participation and Place*, Routledge, London.

Kolb, D. A. (1984) *Experiential Learning: Experience as the Source of Learning and Development*, Prentice Hall, Englewood Cliffs, NJ.

Lacan, J. (1978) *The Four Fundamental Concepts of Psychoanalysis*, J. A. Miller (ed.), trans. Alan Sheridan, Norton, New York.

Lapassade, G. and Lourau, R. (1971) *Clés pour la sociologie*, Segher, Paris.

Lévy, A. (1997) *Sciences cliniques et organisations sociales*, PUF, Paris.

Lévy, A. (2001), with Amado, G. *La recherche-action*, Eska, Paris.

Lévy, A. (2010) *Penser l'événement, Pour une psychosociologie critique*, Parangon/Vs, Lyon.

Lewin, K. (1936) *Principles of Topological Psychology*, McGraw-Hill, New York.

Lewin, K. (1946) 'Action research and minority problems', *Journal of Social Issues*, vol. 2, no. 4, pp. 34–46.

Lewin, K. (1948) *Resolving Social Conflicts; Selected Papers on Group Dynamics*, G. W. Lewin (ed.), Harper & Row, New York.

Lewin, K. (1951) *Field Theory in Social Science; Selected Theoretical Papers*, D. Cartwright (ed.), Harper & Row, New York.

Liu, M. (1997) *Fondements et pratiques de la recherche-action*, Harmattan, Paris.

Lourau, R. (1970) *L'analyse institutionnelle*, Minuit, Paris.

Lourau, R. (1996) *Interventions socianalytiques*, Anthropos, Paris.

Lykes, M. B. and Mallona, A. (2008) 'Towards Transformational Liberation: Participatory and Action Research and Praxis', in P. Reason and H. Bradbury (eds) *The SAGE Handbook of Action Research*, Sage, London, pp. 106–120.

Maguire, P. (1987) *Doing Participatory Research: Feminist Approach*, University of Massachusetts, Amherst, MA.

Mayo, E. [1933] (2001) *The Human Problems of an Industrial Civilization: Early Sociology of Management and Organizations*, Routledge, London.

McNiff, J. and Whitehead, D. (2009) *Doing and Writing Action Research*, Sage, London.

Mead, G. (2008) 'Muddling through: Facing the challenges of managing a large-scale action research project', in P. Reason and H. Bradbury (eds) *The SAGE Handbook of Action Research*, Sage, London, pp. 629–642.

Means, K., and Josayma, C. with Nielsen, E. and Virayasakultorn, V. (2002) *Community-Based Forest Resource Conflict Management: A Training Package*, FAO, Rome.

Mendel, G. (1980) 'La sociopsychanalyse institutionnelle', in J. Ardoino, J. Dubost, A. Lévy, E. Guattari, G. Lapassade, R. Lourau and G. Mendel (eds), *L'intervention institutionnelle*, Payot, Paris, pp. 237–301.

Mendel, G. and Prades, J.-L. (2002) *Les méthodes de l'intervention psychosociologique*, La Découverte-Syros, Paris.

Merton, R. K. (1968) *Social Theory and Social Structure*, Free Press, New York.

Michelot, C. (2008) 'Le discours de la méthode de Guy Palmade', *Nouvelle revue de psychosociologie*, vol. 1, no. 5, pp. 97–104.

Minkler, M. and Wallerstein, N. (eds) (2008) *Community Based Participatory Research for Health: From Process to Outcomes*, 2nd edn., Wiley, San Francisco, CA.

Moely, B., Billig, S. and Holland, B. (2009) *Creating Our Identities in Service-Learning and Community Engagement*, Information Age, Charlotte, North Carolina.

Morenos, J. L. (1931) *Group Method and Group Psychotherapy*, Beacon, New York.

Noffke, S. and Somekh, B. (2009) *The SAGE Handbook of Educational Action Research*, Sage, London.

Oury, J. (1982) *L'aliénation*, Galilée, Paris.

Oury, J. (1993) 'Psychiatrie et psychothérapie institutionnelles', in P. Kaufmann (ed.) *L'apport freudien: éléments pour une encyclopédie de la psychanalyse*, Bordas, Paris.

Park, P., Brydon-Miller, M., Hall, B. and Jackson, T. (eds) (1993) *Voices of Change: Participatory Research in the United States and Canada*, Bergin and Garvey, Westport, Connecticut.

Posey, D. A. (1996) *Traditional Resource Rights: International Instruments for Protection and Compensation for Indigenous Peoples and Local Communities*, IUCN, Gland, Switzerland.

Pound, B., Snapp, S., McDougall, C. and Braun, A. (eds) (2003) *Managing Natural Resources for Sustainable Livelihoods: Uniting Science and Participation*, Earthscan/IDRC, Ottawa, ON.

Pretty, J., Guijt, I., Thompson, J. and Scones, I. (1995) *Participatory Learning and Action: A Trainer's Guide*, International Institute for Education and Environment, London.

Reijntjes, C., Haverkort, B. and Waters-Bayer, A. (1992) *Farming for the Future: An Introduction to Low-External-Input and Sustainable Agriculture*, ILEIA, Leusden.

Rice, A. K. (1965) *Learning for Leadership*, Tavistock, London.

Ricoeur, P. (1986) *Du texte à l'action. Essais d'herméneutique II*, Seuil, Paris.

Rogers, C. (1970) *On Encounter Groups*, Harrow, New York.

Rushkoff, D. (2004) *Open Source Democracy*, Text. eBook-No. 10753.

Satheesh, P. V. (2009) 'Why PRA?' Unpublished document, Deccan Development Society, Pastapur Village.

Satheesh, P. V. (2012) 'Participation and Beyond: Handing Over the Camera', www.ddsindia.com/papers&publications.htm, accessed 15 March, 2012.

Schotte, J. (2006) *Un Parcours: Rencontrer, Relier, Dialoguer, Partager*, Le Pli, Paris.

Schumacher, E. F. (1973) *Small is Beautiful*, Blond and Briggs, London.

Sebillotte, M. (2007) 'Quand la recherche participative interpelle le chercheur', in M. Anadó (ed.) *La recherche participative: Multiples regards*, Presses de l'Université du Québec, Québec.

Seligman, M. E. P. (2002) *Authentic Happiness: Using the New Positive Psychology to Realize Your Potential for Lasting Fulfillment*, Free Press, New York.

Sherman, F. T. and Torbert, W. (2000) *Transforming Social Inquiry, Transforming Social Action: New Paradigms for Crossing the Theory/Practice Divide in Universities and Communities*, Kluwer Academic Publishers, Boston, MA.

Sherwood, S. and Bentley, J. W. (2009) 'Katalysis: Helping Andean farmers adapt to climate change', *Participatory Learning and Action*, no. 60, pp. 65–75.

Smith, L., Ronsenzweig, L. and Schmidt, M. (2010) 'Best practices in the reporting of participatory action research: Embracing both the forest and the trees', *The Counseling Psychologist*, vol. 38, no. 8, pp. 1115–1138.

Srivastva, S. and Cooperrider, D. (1999) *Appreciative Management and Leadership: The Power of Positive Thought and Action in Organization*, Williams Custom, Euclid.

Stoecker, R. (1999) 'Are academics irrelevant? Roles for scholars in participatory research', *American Behavorial Scientist*, vol. 42, no. 5, pp. 840–854.

Stringer, E. T. (2007) *Action Research*, Sage, Thousand Oaks, CA.

Thorsrud, E. and Emery, F. (1964) *Industrielt Demokrati*, Oslo University Press, Oslo.

Tolman, D. L. and Brydon-Miller, M. (eds) (2000) *From Subjects to Subjectivities: A Handbook of Interpretive and Participatory Methods*, New York University Press, New York.

Tosquelles, F. (1984) *Éducation et psychothérapie institutionnelle*, Hiatus, Nantes, France.

Tosquelles, F. (1992) *L'enseignement de la folie*, Privat, Toulouse, France.

Touraine, A., Hegedus, Z., Dubet, F. and Wievorka, M. (1980) *La prophétie antinucléaire*, Seuil, Paris.

Trist, E. L. and Bamforth, K. W. (195l) 'Some social and psychological consequences of the longwall method of coal-getting', *Human Relations*, vol. 4, no. 1, pp. 3–38.

Trist, E. L., Emery, F. and Murray, H. (eds) (1997) *The Social Engagement of Social Science: The Socio-Ecological Perspective*, University of Pennsylvania Press, Philadelphia, PA.

Wakeford, T., Singh, J., Murtuja, B., Bryant, P. and Pimbert, M. (2007) 'The jury is out: How far can participatory projects go towards reclaiming democracy?', in P. Reason and H. Bradbury (eds) *The SAGE Handbook of Action Research*, Sage, London, pp. 333–349.

Warren, D. M., Slikkerveer, L. J. and Brokensha, D. (eds) (1995) *The Cultural Dimension of Development: Indigenous Knowledge Systems*, Intermediate Technology, London.

Westfall, J. M., VanVorst, R. F., Main, D. S. and Herbert, C. (2006) 'Community-based participatory research in practice-based research networks', *Annals of Family Medicine*, vol. 4, no. 1, pp. 8–14.

Williams, J. and Lykes, M. B. (2003) 'Bridging theory and practice: Using reflexive cycles in feminist participatory action research', *Feminism and Psychology*, vol. 13, no. 3, pp. 287–294.

Winnicott, D. W. (1965) *The Maturational Process and the Facilitating Environment*, Hogarth, London.

CHAPTER 2

Society, experience, knowledge

PLURAL CONVERSATIONS

Despite Lewin's call for sound theory, PAR practice does not often advance theoretical speculations of its own. These are thought to be of limited use in promoting social change. To grow and gain greater credibility, however, more theoretical thinking should go into understanding the conceptual underpinnings of engaged inquiry, with a focus on the dialogical foundations of knowledge and its grounding in history. To do this, knowledge must bring some attention to itself, in order to better act on its implications. That is, it must address the subject matter and concerns of epistemology.

One such concern, of direct relevance to engaged research, pertains to the creative tension that brings together two basic aims in PAR: acknowledging the multiple constructions of reality, and seeking a framework or theory to acknowledge and promote this multiplicity. Researchers bring forth this tension whenever they facilitate co-investigation grounded in real life at the same time as they offer their own expert framing of PAR in action. Paradoxically, they are experts at helping groups tap into their own individual and collective expertise.

Two positions have been developed to accommodate this paradox and avoid charges of inconsistency. The first position, commonly adopted in the field of development and organisational inquiry, consists in not dwelling on the paradox and simply getting on with facilitating the co-investigation, which is what matters in the end. While understandable, non-reflective pragmatism can never flesh out a full argument for the posture. The researcher's field of expertise (PAR) is denied, undervalued or exercised with excessive humility. At best, mastery in doing research is embedded in the researcher's practical wisdom and competent involvement with real-life issues and people. At worst, practice is at odds with concealed intents and concepts that have not been given much thought (Cooke and Kothari, 2001).

The second position, more typical of *la psychosociologie d'intervention*, is less modest. It recognizes the value added of theory, and treats research as a distinct profession and science, after Freud and Lewin (Dubost, 1987, pp. 90–101). Unlike PAR facilitators, those who adopt this stance commit to the advancement of knowledge. They work at producing insights and generalizations that hopefully transcend each specific instance and can be transposed to new situations. To sustain this twofold enterprise, practical and theoretical, psychosociologists assume a clear distinction between 'reflective action' and 'theoretical practice' and functional connections between the two. Reflective action harkens back to the classical notion of *technê*. It is what actors (e.g. accident prevention counsellors) do whenever they try to understand and act on reality, by going through the motions of diagnostic thinking, planning the immediate or long-term future, implementing decisions skilfully, evaluating the observed results and adjusting existing practice in light of the lessons learned. Unlike positive scientists, engaged researchers support the practical wisdom and reflective action of human subjects coping with real problems in meaningful context (e.g. frequent accidents at work). But they also pursue an activity of their own, which is the practice of theoretical reasoning – for instance, developing a general understanding of risk-taking behaviour based on existing evidence. This is *epistêmê*, which is what researchers seek when they attempt to rise above each particular situation, in search of more abstract propositions and models to inform interventions in other settings.

The distinction between *technê* and *epistêmê*, mentioned in the introduction and discussed in detail at the end of this chapter, has its problems. It reintroduces the logic of hierarchy – between doing and thinking, the concrete and the abstract, the specific and the general – in a PAR tradition otherwise critical of the top-down outlook of mainstream science. On the whole, psychosociology is careful to avoid extreme positions. While it recognizes the paradox of researchers striving to be 'experts at not being experts', it should be credited for staying the course with a long tradition of theoretical investigations, especially those of psychoanalysis. A difficult question, however, remains to be answered: how can researchers carry out the speculations of theory at some distance from their lifeworld, *but not above it*.

To stay on the ground, PAR theorists must refrain from turning their art into a science or metatheory of democratic action. Instead of developing propositions that transcend history, they must find ways to integrate theoretical guideposts into social history. This means acknowledging theory building for what it is: a social investment in language and discourse, carried out at some distance from day-to-day speech, equally rich and complex but less on the move. Like poetry, abstract propositions are strange because they come from distant places. They speak to other possible worlds and are committed to voyages of the mind.

Research that reflects on itself is an essential task that engaged researchers should tie in with their commitments to changing social history. But this is a fine line to walk. When tying the delicate knots between *technê* and *epistêmê*, falling back on conventional discourse that plainly contradicts the principles of engaged research is a common error. Some conditions must be met for research to engage with both reason and history. They converge on the idea that theory evolves dialogically.

At a basic level, dialogism is dialectics. It implies that the wisdom of reflective action (again, the example of accident prevention) feeds into theoretical practice. In return, developments in theory (e.g. explaining risk-taking behaviour) contribute to the growth of practical reason. Engaged theory informs practice and is informed by it. To create this feedback loop, however, the specificity of theory in relation to practice must be acknowledged. Theory and practice must be constructed as *ongoing activities and conversations* that remain distinct even as they interact and overlap. The goals, steps, time frame and audience involved in each conversation can never be exactly the same. This means that engaged researchers cannot tread along the reflective action path alone. They must take part in other conversations and communities as well, including those concerned with investigating theory. They are nodes and mediators, not guides and counsellors. They do not merely sit at and facilitate tables of thoughtful action. They also bring something from other tables (the insights of theoretical practice) and take something away, as input into other debates and cross-examinations of thoughts and actions in social history.

With PAR the path of theory is a crossroad of migratory views and ideas. Like any approach to research, PAR requires a set of propositions to account for key phenomena in particular settings. To assess the soundness of these propositions, some discussion of complementary and alternative lines of reasoning inspired by different perspectives and disciplines is in order. A theoretical stance follows from the discussion and sheds light on the phenomena at hand (risk-taking behaviour in the construction industry, for instance). For action to be taken in this field, however, a theory of intervention is also required. *Propositions to understand a field of intervention are never enough; intervention as a complex field must also be investigated theoretically.* This is where our review of PAR (Chapter 1) comes in, by offering a theory of social intervention negotiated and grounded in history (Dubost, 1987, pp. 55, 164–65, 233–34). Similarly, Chapter 10 investigates theoretically the foundations of accident prevention as a field of intervention. Essentially, the PAR standpoint emphasizes the ways in which multiple perspectives advanced by the concerned parties, PAR researchers *among others*, can contribute to researching and making sense of reality and ways to change it, each in their own manner and through conversations bound to overlap and interconnect.

A plea for conversations in the plural may seem so obvious as to be harmless. Yet it flies in the face of every PAR approach that defines participation as accountability to a single, well-delineated and self-directed community, those with whom all phases of the action research cycle is carried out, at least in principle. In reality, genuine participation is a journey along multiple paths. It consists in trying to do the right thing at the right time with the right people, knowing well that things, time frames and people criss-cross, get out of sync and keep fluctuating.

Dialogism goes beyond the simple notion that *epistêmê* is a field opposite to that of *technê* and that the two must connect. More importantly, it is a call to acknowledge diversity and multiplicity in both fields and ways in which they interface, in real settings. As with any practice, theoretical activity becomes sterile if it refuses to evolve, mutate, diversify and intermesh. The theory of engaged research is no exception to this rule. As it stands, PAR constitutes a richly diversified stance on the issue of knowledge and history. It does not constitute a full paradigm. Nor should it aspire to create an all-encompassing discipline or framework, rallying all practitioners around a contender to the throne of metatheory. In a globalized world, nodes, lines and flows of knowledge and communication overlap and criss-cross in so many places and directions that they defy any representation in a single map, a holistic theory or a comprehensive body of knowledge.

As Chambers (2008) suggests, PAR must eschew the temptation to totality, in theory building as well as in practice.

In keeping with Levinasian philosophy (Burggraeve, 2002), attention should be given to multiplying conversations about engaged research practice, including old and new directions in theory that can intermesh and shed light on human history. These conversations require a good dose of Derridean decentering and dissemination (Derrida, 1992), reflecting on immediate and deferred communications that go in different directions and criss-cross at the same time. A flexible weaving of multiple conversations, however, does not preclude efforts to develop tentative outlines of the founding principles of engaged research, including those advanced in this book. Distrust towards any theory that purports to explain everything is not an excuse to simply move on, get things done and avoid philosophy at all cost. No theory is not the alternative to only one theory. While invaluable, practical tools to support action-inquiry tend to go stale if not kept fresh with innovative views on key debates, including the role of methods and theory in meaningful research.

THREADS OF THEORY: SKILFUL MEANS

Methods and technology are skilful means to interact with others and the world we live in. Sound ones embed ends in means. Those that don't are meaningless, broken tools that should be fixed.

'Small-m methods' (such as interviews, questionnaires, archival research, statistics, etc.) are inquiry techniques that vary according to discipline. They require procedural know-how, technology and a practical mind. By contrast, 'big-M methods' involve key choices concerning the logic of inquiry – whether the inquiry should be qualitative or quantitative, value-free or value-laden, positivistic or phenomenological, and so on. Both kinds of methods are important to the inquiry process. They require the development and application of great skill. Both can also do harm, especially if they are handled without care, disconnecting us from others and the world we live in. This is what happens when technology and methods are used as lowly tools or means that are merely 'present-at-hand', handy things that are just lying there, without life and soundness of meaning, like cold machines or broken equipment, says Heidegger. They are no longer 'ready-at-hand', part of what we are – thoughtful beings that strive to reach out and communicate. For tools and techniques to come alive, ends must be embedded in skilful means. A skilful means is doing the right thing at the right moment and in the right way, planning or seizing the moment to bring out potentialities in learning and create a shift in understanding and action. It is an effort to embed the ends in the means-moment, which becomes part of the transformation we wish to see. Authentic inquiry seeks change in the world and starts with change in the world of inquiry. Ghandhi was right: 'means are after all everything'. Skills in means matter greatly.

Commentary

What is inquiry? This is not an easy question to investigate. For the investigation to reach its goal, we need to know how to go about inquiring into the matter. *That is, we need to possess the answer before we raise the question.* The endeavour seems like time wasted; it focusses on a story that ends before it starts.

One compelling solution to this riddle requires that we tread a risky path. It consists in letting the inquiry add something to what we already know about inquiry, creating the story at the same time as it unfolds. Although this may sound illogical, we cannot 'inquire about inquiry' without adding something new to what we're looking for. Sooner or later, something new must be said on the process whereby the question is investigated and answered in the first place. This means that probing into probing is an endless experience, a process of eternal return.

Accomplished artisans will appreciate the paradox. They are used to re-discovering their own skills and trade though trial and error, with endless apprenticeship and practice, cognizant that the mastery they achieve and possess is admirable only because it is always perfectible. The invitation to 'try their best' and improve on what they do is constant. The results they obtain will of course vary, depending on their learning skills and the art they practise.

Much of philosophy looks down on skilled artisans as those who have empirical knowledge only, with little to contribute to the subject of knowledge as such. Aristotle (1999) and his followers thus advise against reducing the inquiry process to the 'experience' (Gr. *empeiria*) and applied knowledge of a mere artisan (Gr. *cheirotechnês*). In their view, there is more to inquiry than familiarity with toolboxes and small-m methods, 'instrumental' techniques that barely get off the ground. For greater wisdom, we should look up to the craftsperson (Gr. *technitês*) who masters *technê*. Aristotle defines *technê* as the knowledgeable practice or practical thinking (Gr. *praktikê dianoia*) of a calculating soul attending to contingencies of everyday life. *Technê* is a craft or art guided by ends that vary and may be attained 'for the most part'. Results depend on how skilled the *technitês* is when striving to produce things according to expectations (health in the case of medical practice, for instance). They also depend on the means used and whether accidents happen or regularities hold true. All of this is true of an artisan's empirical work and know-how. Unlike the artisan, however, a capable *technitês* can communicate his or her reasoning to others, through clear accounting and teaching. Plato (1997) makes the same point: the master craftsperson can communicate the theoretical knowledge that guides his or her *technê*, by conveying the rational understanding (Gr. *gnôsis*) of what is fine, just and good in his or her own practice.

When applied to inquiry as an activity, craftsmanship involves explicit thinking about the inquiry process, a logic teachers now pass on through writings and lectures in 'big-M methods' and theory. The art of inquiry thus entails an ability to outline higher-ground reasons for carrying out the investigation in such and such a way (doing a controlled experiment or a survey, for instance). Such reasons should hold true 'for the most part' and be as accurate as possible. Since inquiry is an art, some exceptions and errors will occur. Absolute certainty and accuracy (Gr. *takribes*) cannot be expected and must be adjusted to what is aimed for and the means or methods used.

In short, inquiry viewed as *technê* is a reflective practice involving a rational approximation of what the investigator does or tries to do. This Aristotelian view is not without problems. It may be 'roughly true', but it is not 'good enough'. It ignores the fact that accounting and teaching are just other skills, namely, experience in choosing, shaping and combining words, numbers and sentences to communicate meaning. Like carpentry or medicine, wordsmithing is an art, to be mastered and continuously perfected. It can be deployed in ways that complement and strengthen other skills. For instance, the ability to communicate in words can support the ability to communicate in deeds. 'Walking the talk' is one skill enhancing another. This means that inquiry is always an art, even when it turns upon itself and 'makes sense' of itself, through discourse that tries to tailor word to deed. Whether the query concerns health or the art of inquiry, investigation is always a disposition (Gr. *hexis*) to produce methodical action and its expected results or findings. Theoretical and big-M investigation is no exception to the rule. What it adds to the practice of inquiry is 'surplus meaning' produced through wordsmithing, another art unto itself.

Asking questions about the art of questioning generates different responses and exercises in wordsmithing. A well-known response consists in splitting up the nexus of experience, know-how, language and reasoning, with the aim of imposing hierarchy, distance or detachment and the rule of order. Mastery turns into a chain of command. This is the Aristotelian ploy to detach the 'experience' of inquiry (day-to-day probing) from higher parts of the inquisitive soul, those of knowledgeable craftwork (Gr. *technê*) and, on a higher level, the lofty pursuit of science for its own sake (*epistêmê*). While *technê* evolves on a higher plane in comparison to *empeiria*, it moves closer to the earth and the ground when compared to theory and philosophy. The latter is pure *epistêmê*, the kind that does not aim for a down-to-earth *ergon*, i.e. an end product, function or goal that exists beyond the inquiry process. Instead of being driven by practical ends, theoretical and philosophical knowledge investigates things that exist of necessity and admit of no change. The endeavour represents the highest expression of the inquisitive soul, inspired by the spirit of sheer curiosity and wonder.

Aristotelian and Platonic wordsmithing speaks of science as fundamental knowledge and contemplation for its own sake. Its main product is the rational soul detached from worldly action and desire – from practical calculation or experimentation in regards to nature and the material world. Philosophical inquiry commands faith in pure theory and the mathematics of life informed by first principles, theorems of things that are invariable and cannot be otherwise. Great skill, eloquence and strong rule are needed to maintain faith in this chain of command.

In Western history, inquiries into the nature of true knowledge owe a lot to Platonic and Aristotelian thinking. The legacy includes Plato's vision of wise rulers that govern the city, by harmonizing the commanding knowledge and practice of legislators, judges and generals, under the reign of pure philosophy – an *epistêmê* designed to grasp the essence of what is truly fine, just and good. It also draws on Aristotle's view of virtue (justice, courage, moderation) as a disposition of character to do the right thing because it is the right thing to do, even if it goes against the impulses of animal life. Also, unlike *technê*, virtue chooses an action for itself (rather than as a means towards an end) and can only have virtuous effects.

A very different path consists in weaving all skills together, towards a full reinstatement of *empeiria* and *technê* in the process of knowing. On this course of knowing, all relevant practices, from number-crunching to storytelling, creative brainstorming and conceptual wordsmithing, are recognized for their contribution to the art of inquiry. To tread this path, the chain of command that subordinates experience to practical knowledge, and knowledgeable practice to pure *epistêmê*, must be questioned and overthrown. The apparent hierarchy of small-m and big-M methods, both value-free and under the rule of grand theory and epistemology, calls for the same treatment. Top-down reasoning must be toppled. It is not conducive to acknowledging and developing the many skilful means of practical wisdom and engaged inquiry.

While forward-looking, the path of 'many skills in means' brings us back to a long-standing challenge: abandoning all notions of god-like philosophy and value-free science, forcing us to question the way we conduct ourselves when conducting any inquiry. Xenophon's (1979) insights are important in this regard. This Greek admirer of Socrates, born *c.*334 BC, defines knowledge making as an art or craft that requires care and diligence, practice and experience. Pure theory achieved without virtuous conduct is neglected skill.

Zeno's contribution to Stoic thinking goes even further in the weaving of virtue (Gr. *aretê*) into experience, craftwork and knowledge (Arnim, 1903–1924). His account of virtue centres on training in the difficult art of reasoning (Gr. *dianoia*), a *technê* driven by the pursuit of what is naturally good and therefore morally right. However, as with medical practice that may fail to achieve its goal, virtue can go wrong and turn into vice and moral weakness, producing fickleness in the exercise of judgment and faulty knowledge in regards to good and evil and laws of the universe. Virtuous conduct is moral craftsmanship in recognizing and choosing truth and rightness at each juncture in life. The highest good, however, does not lie in obtaining the primary objects of nature, which we do not control (e.g. life, health). Rather, it is to be found in the constant effort to satisfy all impulses (Gr. *hormê*) that are true to nature and suited to the circumstances. This must be achieved through means that are socially sound and just. Why? Because human solidarity is not any different from health. It too is a primary object of human nature and therefore a virtue.

Experience, practice, tooling, reasoning, virtue and morality, all mesh in the art of life. The only thing desirable for itself is not virtue but rather the 'art of life', which consists in knowing how to go about choosing the appropriate means of living. This is morality understood as both the means and the end of life. Moral reasoning and conduct is enhanced by the number of natural ends that are aimed for, and the rational means used to pursue them. We strive for a life of plentiful satisfactions, knowing that the fullest satisfaction comes from the myriad ways we strive.

Our initial question regarding the nature of inquiry can now be answered 'for the most part', using Zeno's rich insights into the practice of wisdom. Investigation (of any object, including the art of knowing) is usually viewed as a means towards an end, which is knowledge. Inquiry is a question in search of an answer, theoretical or practical. Stoicism invites us to go beyond this conventional view and value the questions we ask as much as the answers we seek. Inquiring into truth is not an instrument of knowing but rather an integral part of life. Better said, it is the art of life (Sellars, 2009) – everything we experience and do when inquiring into what is true 'for the most part', probing into life and nature with care, diligence and concern for what is both good and right. To use the language of Mahayana Buddhism, practical wisdom is *upaya-kaushalya*, a Sanskrit expression denoting 'skills or cleverness in means'. In this tradition, practitioners may use any method or technique that fits the situation and potentialities in life, provided it is for the benefit of all sentient beings. As with all things that are good, skills in means must be welcomed for what they are, fleeting moments in a world that is forever perfectible.

REFERENCES

Aristotle (1999) *Nicomachean Ethics*, 2nd edn., trans. Terence Irwin, Hackett, Indianapolis.

Arnim, H. F. A. von (ed.) (1903–1924) *Stoicorum Veterum Fragmenta*, 4 vols, Tuber, Leipzig.

Burggraeve, R. (2002) *The Wisdom of Love in the Service of Love: Emmanuel Levinas on Justice, Peace, and Human Right*, trans. Jeffrey Bloechl, Marquette University Press, Milwaukee, WI.

Chambers, R. (2008) 'PRA, PLA and pluralism: Practice and theory', in P. Reason and H. Bradbury (eds) *The SAGE Handbook of Action Research*, Sage, London, pp. 297–318.

Cooke, B. and Kothari, U. (eds) (2001) *Participation: The New Tyranny?* Zed, London.

Derrida, J. (1992) *Given Time: I. Counterfeit Money*, trans. Peggy Kami, The University of Chicago Press, Chicago, IL.

Dubost, J. (1987) *Intervention psychosociologique*, PUF, Paris.

Plato (1997) *Complete Works*, J. M. Cooper (ed.), Hackett, Indianapolis, IN.

Sellars, J. (2009) *The Art of Living: The Stoics on the Nature and Function of Philosophy*, Bristol, London.

Xenophon (1979) *Memorabilia and Oeconomicus*, trans. Edgar Cardew Marchant, Loeb Classical Library, Harvard University Press, Cambridge.

MODULE 1

Grounding and uncertainty

MODULE 1: GROUNDING AND UNCERTAINTY

This module, on grounding and uncertainty, presents tools and processes that are foundational in our practice of PAR. The tools in Chapter 3 help practitioners reflect on what it means to create an action learning system, illustrated with stories from Honduras and Canada. *ART* is a tool to assess the current and desired integration of action, research and training activities in projects, programmes or individual profiles. As discussed earlier, the question of integration between these three components is a basic concept in PAR. *PIE* examines integration from an organizational perspective. It supports learning systems that balance and integrate planning, inquiry and evaluation.

Chapter 4 proceeds to another foundational tool called *Order and Chaos*, informed by chaos and complexity theory. The tool helps craft the planning process either as a blueprint for systematic action, suitable when key factors are easy to predict, or as a working hypothesis developed in complex settings, to be tested against experience and changing circumstances and needs. The experience of working with the Katkari of India, a non-literate and highly vulnerable tribal population living on the margins of Mumbai, illustrates how real-life planning changes in response to complexity.

These foundational tools serve in turn to introduce *Process Design* (Chapter 5), the point of entry and practical grounding for all the participatory inquiry methods proposed and illustrated in the book. *Process Design* is an integrative methodology that shows how to select, combine and adapt tools for collaborative inquiry and action. It encourages practitioners to make plans at the right time and at the appropriate level of detail and adjust them to real settings. *Process Design* is supported by *Process Mapping*, a visual planning tool that helps ground an inquiry, including monitoring and evaluation, in the context of broader, ongoing activities that inform and interact with the research process. The authors' experience facilitating discussions among managers and users of a federal park in Canada illustrate both the mapping of a process and the decisions that go into designing each step along the way.

Guidelines and tips for process design in different settings call on researchers to develop the 'skills in means' (Chapter 6) needed to facilitate dialogue and support the exercise of reason in real context. At the end of Chapter 6, we describe different ways to combine and sequence tools in events or processes that support collaborative thinking around common tasks (see *Combos*).

Each chapter in the module concludes with an aphorism and theoretical commentary on key assumptions underlying the processes of grounding and responses to uncertainty.

CHAPTER 3

Creating an action learning system

INTRODUCTION

Organizational, community and multi-stakeholder processes often fail to deal with recurrent problems because they ignore the many opportunities to feed inquiry into collective action and action into collective learning. In this chapter we present two foundational tools that allow participants to address these issues. The first technique is called *ART*, which speaks to learning processes that bring together *Action, Research and Training*. The tool captures the spirit of participatory action research as well as experiential learning and problem-solving inquiry in general. But this is not merely a concept. It is also a powerful tool, relatively simple and with far-reaching implications, to assess the current and ideal balance and integration of the three elements of 'A', 'R' and 'T' within an organization, programme or project. Group work with the tool helps stakeholders describe their particular *ART* profile and also decide what adjustments they need to make.

The second tool, titled *Planning, Inquiry, Evaluation (PIE)*, probes further into what makes for an effective learning system. It explores the extent to which existing practices integrate planning, evaluation and inquiry and ground them in meaningful action. *PIE* also asks whether a knowledge system effectively mobilizes stakeholder participation and makes use of a variety of tools at the proper time and scaled to the right level of detail.

Both tools serve a twofold purpose: introducing concepts that are central to the art of meaningful inquiry, and assessing existing knowledge systems against these concepts.

The chapter illustrates the use of *ART* in Honduras and *PIE* in Canada. The concluding section proposes a commentary on a critical theme that underlies both tools: the notion of 'meaningful inquiry'.

THE ART OF ENGAGED RESEARCH

Action, Research, Training (ART)

Purpose

To assess the current and desired balance and integration of three components within a learning system:

1 actions, including deciding, planning and doing things to achieve concrete goals;
2 research, consisting of data collection, inquiry and analysis;
3 training or teaching, involving capacity-building events and strategies.

Step 1

Define a key project, programme or institution and list major **actions, research and/or training activities** of the previous six months to a year.

Step 2

Assess and compare the overall and relative **weight** or importance given to action, research and training over the specified time. Draw a **Venn diagram** representing the three *ART* components (*Action, Research, Training*) and place one mark in the intersecting circles that best reflects the *ART* profile.

Step 3

If the profile includes more than one component, assess the extent to which each component **contributes** to the other(s). For instance, if the profile combines *R* and *T* mostly, are the results of the research used in the teaching activities, and is the teaching useful to the research? Use a code or symbol between each (one way, thin or thick arrows, for instance) to indicate the **level of interaction** among the components of the resulting *ART* profile.

Step 4

Review the *ART* profile and discuss how satisfactory it is. Decide where **more effort** is needed and why, and place a mark in the Venn diagram to show what the profile should be. Draw an arrow from the current profile to the ideal profile (see Figure 3.1). Explore what can be done to achieve this profile, and define the first steps in the desired direction.

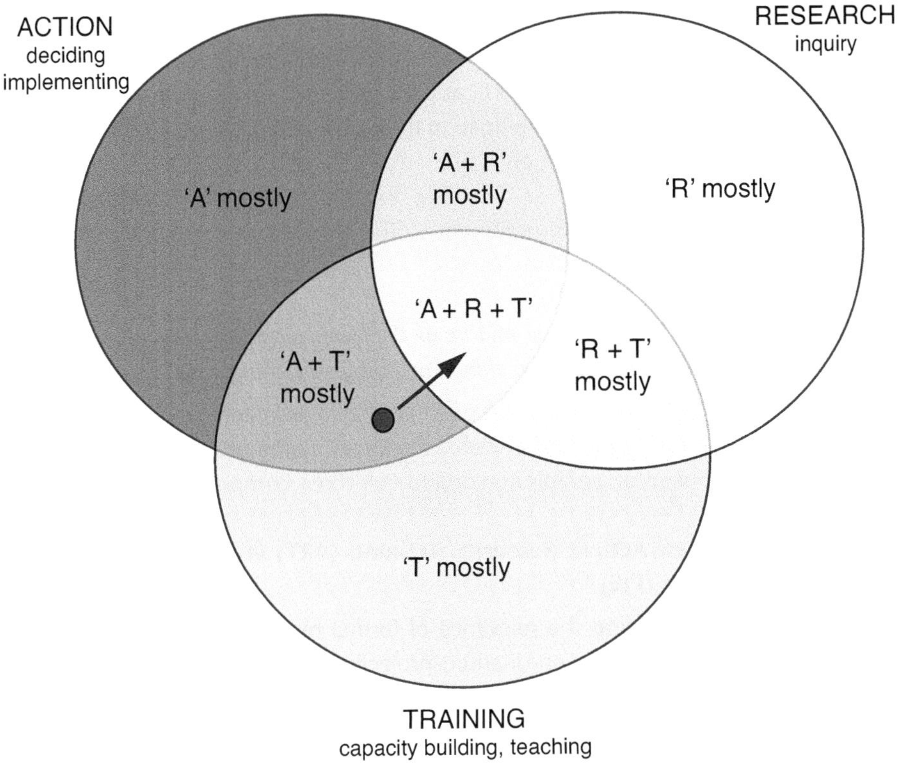

FIGURE 3.1 The *ART* Venn diagram.

FAQ

- ***Aren't research and training also activities?***

Yes, they are. But the word 'action' is used here in the conventional sense of 'doing things' (e.g. implementing a poverty reduction plan) as opposed to better 'understanding something' though research or teaching activities (e.g. inquiring into the causes of poverty).

- ***Is there a difference between research and day-to-day inquiry?***

Fact-finding and analysis is something that humans do on a day-to-day basis. Even simple things like crossing a busy street involve estimating when and how fast one must walk to avoid getting run down. All humans have inquisitive minds. Inquiry becomes research proper when the investigation proceeds consciously and systematically, with formal rules of data gathering, analysis and theoretical understanding aimed at creating new knowledge.

- ***What's the difference between* ART, *action research, applied research and experiential learning?***

Unlike the integrated approach to *ART*, applied research (investigation for practical applications) and action research (investigation through a reflective process of progressive problem solving) combine *A* and *R* only. They may be carried out with no educational or capacity-building activities *per se*. Similarly, experiential learning combines Action and Training only, without any commitment to the creation of new knowledge or the advancement of science.

- ***Is combining* A, R *and* T *(in the middle of the Venn diagram) always preferable to combining only two things or doing one thing only?***

Not necessarily. The best *ART* profile is the one that meets real needs and can be achieved through a realistic and timely use of available resources. Some projects, programmes or institutions may not need or be able to combine all three components all of the time.

- ***When should we use* Action, Research, Training (ART) *instead of* Planning, Inquiry, Evaluation (PIE)*?***

ART is helpful when discussing the relevance of formal research in relation to capacity building or problem solving, action-oriented projects. By contrast, *PIE* addresses issues of knowledge management in an organization or project, including questions of effective stakeholder participation and the proper tooling, timing and scaling of planning, inquiry and evaluation.

Variations

- Use the *ART* Venn diagram to survey and compare the views that different participants have of the same project, programme or institution, and what the profile should look like.

Combinations

- Use *Activity Dynamics* to measure the level of interaction among the components in the *ART* profile and strengthen their overall integration (see Chapter 17).

Applying *ART* in Honduras

The *ART* tool is well suited to the university environment where faculty and students often struggle to combine and integrate research, course-based learning and community service. Questions about the effectiveness of classroom teaching underlie numerous experiments with experiential approaches to university pedagogy such as field placements (coop, practicum, internships) and community-based education (service learning, student research for communities). Dissatisfaction with the broader impacts of research, particularly in complex social settings dealing with messy problems, also prompts faculty members to seek out real-life settings where student work and learning can contribute to a broader process of social change. The curricular implications of these shifts for universities as institutions are not well explored, however. They remain the largest single barrier to re-engaging universities, students and communities as partners in the creation of new knowledge that serves a larger purpose. As noted in the *Conclusion* to this book, the challenge lies in changing fundamentally the interface between university activity and community life.

In 2008 the National Autonomous University of Honduras (UNAH) undertook a group-based assessment of ways to link the university teaching environment to local communities and communities of shared interests. Laura Suazo (2008) facilitated the process, prompted by the decision of the university to establish a new regional branch that would serve both the interests of the surrounding rural economy and student learning.

Some twenty professors and the Director of the recently established regional branch of UNAH convened in 2008 to review ten established programmes in relation to three components in university life: (1) actions, such as community outreach and extension; (2) disciplinary research; and (3) teaching and other capacity-building strategies. Participants in this daylong workshop discussed each programme in terms of the relative

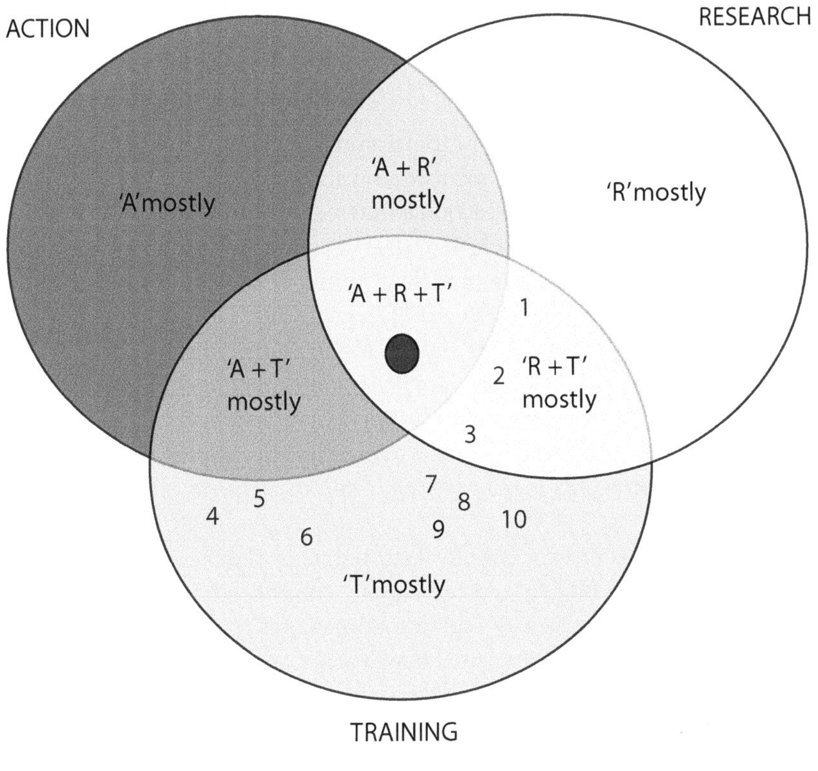

FIGURE 3.2 Current and ideal profiles of UNA programmes (Honduras).

PHOTO 3.1 Honduran faculty discuss ways to link the university teaching environment to local communities. (Source: L. Suazo)

weight or importance it gives to each *ART* component, and the level of interaction between components, from low to high. They based their assessments on course descriptions and mission statements for each programme and on actual practices established during the previous year of operation.

Figure 3.2 shows that most of the programmes (4 through 10) focus mainly on transmitting disciplinary knowledge and assessing students on their ability to show what they had learned. Minor elements of action and research in the mandate and operations of each programme are shown by their relative proximity to the boundary with other components. For example, programme 5 is mostly concerned with training, but occasionally applies the skills learned to real-life settings. By contrast, participants placed three programmes (1, 2 and 3) in the part of the Venn diagram representing balance in weight and integration between the research and teaching components. They noted that in all three cases research results are actively used in the teaching activities. Also students and teaching contribute directly to new research. The level of interaction between the two components is relatively high due to elements such as experimental trials and lab work.

None of the programmes currently incorporate a significant action agenda or practice. This observation highlighted the current imbalance between action and academic pursuits within the university and immediately led to a discussion of what was right for UNAH given its new regional mandate. Participants concluded that much more attention needed to be given to combining all three components in at least some programmes and building into them strong interactions between research, action and teaching activities. They decided to move the overall university profile firmly towards the middle part of the figure over the coming years.

The commitment reached at the end of the *ART* exercise in Honduras triggered an immediate question: what programmes and topics to focus on first? The facilitator suggested a strength-based approach to the question. To achieve this, participants used *Free List and Pile Sort* (Chapter 8) and *Option Domain* (Chapter 18) to list and analyse their research interests and relate these to problems faced by local communities. This helped ground the priority setting exercise in what the people involved had to offer and were committed to personally, while at the same time taking on board the collective commitment to community-oriented teaching and research.

SYSTEMS THAT LEARN

Planning, Inquiry, Evaluation (PIE)

Purpose

Planning (*P*) creates logical schemes for doing things to achieve goals with appropriate inputs. **Inquiry** (*I*) examines and explains facts and situations, using the appropriate tools. **Evaluation** (*E*) assesses results or outcomes against goals, using well-defined criteria and indicators of progress. A **learning system** combines all three processes. It also **grounds** them in meaningful action, mobilizes stakeholder **participation**, and applies a wide range of **tools** at the proper **time** and **scaled** to the right level of detail.

Step 1

Define a key project or programme and list major planning, evaluation and inquiry activities.

Step 2

Assess and compare the relative **weight** or importance given to planning, evaluation and inquiry over a specified time. Draw a triangle to represent *PIE* components in each corner, and add circles to indicate components that play a significant role in the project or programme. Adjust the **size** and **density** of the circle to reflect the relative weight or level of effort dedicated to each component.

Step 3

If more than one component plays a significant role, assess the extent to which each component **contributes** to the other(s). Does the planning (*P*) build on the collection and examination of relevant facts (*I*) and lessons learned about results or outcomes of the past (*E*)? Is the evaluation (*E*) well integrated into ongoing plans and reflect an adequate examination and explanation of facts and relevant experience (*I*)? Is the inquiry (*I*) well informed by existing plans and evaluation findings?

Draw **arrows** to indicate which component contributes to another. Adjust the thickness of the arrow to reflect the importance of the contribution.

Step 4

Rate each component on five criteria, starting with the extent to which each component is **grounded** in meaningful action. A rating of 3 would indicate that the component strongly informs action and is strongly informed by actions meaningful in the life of the organization. A rating of 0 would indicate that the component has little or no impact or significance. Also rate the extent to which each component **engages** stakeholders and mediates differences through dialogue, using a scale of 0 to 3 (where 3 represents the highest rating). Using the same scale, rate three other criteria: the extent to which each component uses a range of **tools**, at the right **time** and **scaled** to the right level of detail (see Figure 3.3).

Review the *PIE* profile and discuss how satisfactory it is. Decide where **more effort** is needed and why. A flexible learning system that continuously balances and integrates *PIE* may be particularly important in complex situations.

FAQ

- ***What do the terms grounding, participation, tooling, timing and scaling mean precisely?***

The section entitled *Skills in Means* (Chapter 6) unpacks them in greater detail.

- ***Isn't evaluation a form of inquiry?***

When used in its strict sense, evaluation assesses results or outcomes against goals using criteria and indicators. It answers the 'how well are we doing so far?' question (e.g. is the project contributing to improvements in livelihood conditions?). The primary task is to systematically determine the worth and significance of something, and adjust plans accordingly. The inquiry process is more concerned about **explaining** facts and situations and may in some cases contribute to the advancement of knowledge through formal research. It asks 'why is it so?' (e.g. why are livelihood conditions getting worse over the years?). An evaluation may also try to explain success or failure in achieving results. Likewise, an inquiry may pass judgment on the role of different actors in making things happen or not. The difference between inquiry and evaluation is thus a matter of emphasis.

- ***Do informal planning, inquiry or evaluation count?***

They certainly matter in real life. They are essential to carrying our day-to-day business of anticipating things we intend to do or that may happen and gathering relevant information in the process, including evidence about results and why things are the way they are. Planning, inquiry and evaluation of the formal kind is conscious and systematic,

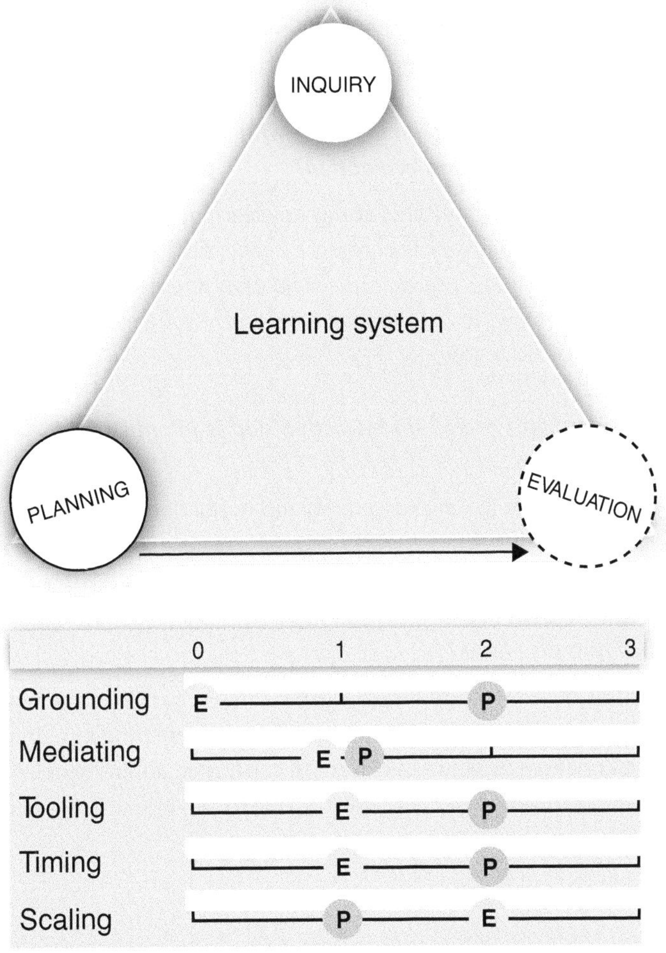

FIGURE 3.3 *Planning, Inquiry, Evaluation (PIE).*

Summary of this example: This organization pays attention to planning (in detail) and evaluating its work but not to inquiry (represented in Figure 3.3 by a blank circle). Scores for the rating criteria show that evaluation currently makes a poor contribution to the system as a whole. It is not well grounded in action and only weakly involves stakeholders with the right tools at the right time. Planning also fails to strongly involve stakeholders or scale its activities appropriately. Improvements in the learning system should focus on these aspects of planning and evaluation.

with explicit rules on how to gather and analyse information, plan effective ways of achieving goals and use evidence to determine the significance of project or programme outcomes.

- ***Can there be an effective learning system without a systematic integration of formal planning, inquiry and evaluation?***

The *PIE* technique raises key questions about any learning system. However, conclusions drawn from the analysis will vary according to each situation. For instance, the extent to which informal planning, inquiry and evaluation succeeds in meeting needs may determine the extent to which additional time and resources should be dedicated to systematic and formal *PIE* learning.

- ***An effective learning system informs action and is informed by it. Does* PIE *address this question?***

Yes. *PIE* explores the extent to which planning and evaluation are *grounded* in meaningful action (see Step 4).

- ***When should we use* Planning, Inquiry, Evaluation (PIE) *instead of* Action, Research, Training (ART)*?***

PIE addresses issues of **knowledge management** in an organization or project, including questions of effective stakeholder participation and the proper tooling, timing and scaling of planning, inquiry and evaluation. *ART* is more concerned about the relevance of **formal research** in relation to capacity building or problem solving, action-oriented projects.

Variations

- Use different colours or lines (continuous, dotted) on the same *PIE* chart to visualize and compare two learning system profiles, i.e. the current and the desired.

Combinations

- Use *Activity Dynamics* to measure the **level of interaction** among the components in the *PIE* profile and strengthen their overall integration (see Chapter 17).

Rethinking evaluation methods in organizations

Many civil society organizations (CSOs) working globally are looking for ways to bridge gaps and address problems in their learning systems. The search is prompted by a desire to learn about and improve the effectiveness of their international development programming, and satisfy the demands of widely used accountability frameworks such as results-based management. The government sponsored Paris Declaration on Aid Effectiveness, and CSO responses to the agreement, highlight the challenge, which consists in striking a meaningful balance between two legitimate expectations: honest learning from ongoing work and accounting for both resources and results to donors and the beneficiaries of development.

An informal Community of Practice (CoP) facilitated by the authors and involving eleven Canadian CSOs has been experimenting with ways to bridge this gap (also see Canada World Youth's use of *The Socratic Wheel* in Chapter 7 and Uniterra's use of *Attribution and Contribution* in Chapter 16). The tool *PIE* helped support discussions of what learning systems are all about and the extent to which organizations are satisfied with the learning systems they have in place. For some the diagnostic assessments focussed on learning systems at the organizational level while others chose to focus on specific programmes and projects.

The assessments, completed in 2011, converged around a common tendency to emphasize planning over inquiry and evaluation. For example, the organization Solidarité, Union, Coopération (SUCO) determined that the level of effort by the organization is highly skewed towards planning, followed by evaluation and inquiry as a distant third (Figure 3.4). This conclusion followed a systematic review and classification of the activities of the organization, including both formal and informal modes of planning, inquiry and evaluation (Lemieux, 2011). SUCO planning takes place during annual programme meetings and staff meetings in the field. Evaluation builds on project reports and meetings with donors. Inquiry is carried out through web searches on particular topics and the gathering of information and critical analysis at conferences.

SUCO staff also assessed the interaction of planning, inquiry and evaluation components in their organizational learning system. Group discussion led them to conclude that they were generally satisfied with the contribution of planning to their evaluation activities. Planning establishes the goals and the activities they pursue against which results are evaluated. SUCO described this as a strong contribution by planning to evaluation, represented in Figure 3.4 by a thick arrow in one direction. However, the reciprocal relationship – evaluation contributing to planning – is weaker. SUCO, like many other members of the CoP, typically evaluate at the end of projects, too late to affect the implementation process and with limited impact on subsequent planning. Informal observations and conversations regarding how well things are going inform day-to-day problem solving, but this evaluative thinking is not documented and systematically fed into formal changes in plans.

Contributions to and from SUCO's inquiry activities are also limited. Critically, inquiry is not planned well in advance and supported intentionally through the allocation of human and financial resources. As for the interaction of inquiry and evaluation, SUCO staff recognize that they give little attention to collecting information that can help **explain** the specific results documented in evaluations. Evaluations tend to be descriptive, without investigating and explaining why things turn out as they do. As a result, the causal links between planned interventions and observed changes remain sketchy. The arrows between the three components shown in Figure 3.4 reflect these uneven relationships. Assessments by other CSO members of the CoP also show considerable unevenness between different components in their learning system.

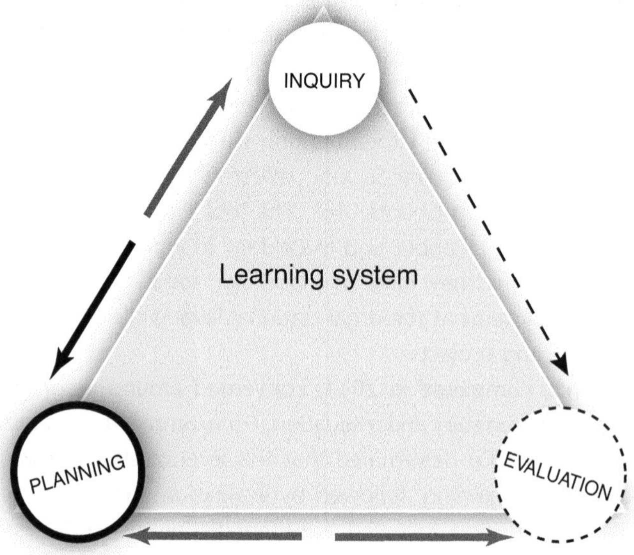

FIGURE 3.4 The balance and integration of *PIE* at SUCO.

Ratings for each component brought out common threads and concerns among the organizations involved. Overall, planning by members of the CoP tends to be well **grounded** in actions that are genuinely useful and meaningful, such as preparing proposals for funding, building team consensus and assigning roles and responsibilities. SUCO staff, for example, assigned a high rating of 3 (in a scale of 0 to 3) to show that their planning (*P*) is grounded in actions meaningful to the organization (Table 3.1). Ratings for effective **mediating** and **tooling** also received relatively high scores (2.5). That is, SUCO engages most of the right stakeholders in the planning process. Planning tools are relatively varied, including both formal and informal procedures in the office and in the field. Participants felt, however, that the **timing** of their planning processes is not optimal. Plans are usually made when specific funding opportunities arise, in response to deadlines and programming priorities set by external demands. Furthermore, plans are not **scaled** to the right level of detail. The requirements of RBM for detail from the beginning to the end of a project tend to overload plans with speculative statements and planning decisions that are premature. This is a common concern regarding current planning processes expressed by many of the CSOs in the CoP – they plan everything in some detail far out into the future, even when they are not ready to do so.

SUCO's approach to inquiry (*I*), while not weighty, scored well on most criteria. The participants felt that inquiry activities by the organization are well *grounded* in the themes of their mission statement and in key programmes. They are also satisfied with the range of inquiry *tools* used: internet searches, scouting for information at conferences, exchanges between partners and reviews of sector-based lessons. These seemed reasonably well suited to their needs and limited resources. The level of inquiry detail

TABLE 3.1 Ratings on the features of *P*, *I* and *E* at SUCO

Features	*0*	*1*	*2*	*3*
Grounding			*I*	*P E*
Mediating	*E*	*I*	*P*	
Tooling		*E I*	*P*	
Timing		*E I*	*P*	
Scaling		*P E*	*I*	

(*scaling*) is also sufficient. The participants recognized, however, that their inquiry activities are typically undertaken by individual staff and do not engage other stakeholders actively in generating information and diagnostic thinking. Little attention is given to *mediating* differences in perspectives among stakeholders (indicated by a low score on this criterion). This situation is partly a result of the tools used to inquire into the themes of interest (static websites and conferences attended mainly by other like-minded professionals). Furthermore, the *timing* of inquiry activities is haphazard. Since inquiry activities are not planned well in advance, results may not be available when they are needed.

Members of the CoP also examined evaluation activities, giving them low scores on most features. This reflected widespread dissatisfaction with various aspects of current evaluation practices. SUCO staff, for example, recognized that their evaluations do little to stimulate dialogue among stakeholders about how well programmes are doing. The range and flexibility of tools used to evaluate projects and programmes is limited and most evaluative effort is not timely. Evaluations also tend to lack the right level of detail. Some evaluations contain a lot of data but lack analysis of what really matters. Other evaluations are too sketchy to give clear guidance on what is working and what is not. On the positive side, SUCO staff felt that current evaluation practices do contribute directly to project completion reports and the renewal of programme activities. In this sense they are grounded in actions meaningful to the organization.

SUCO decisions following on the results of the assessment focussed mainly on making adjustments to the evaluation process. Priorities were to make evaluation activities more participatory and more frequent, and to try new evaluation tools. This, they argued, would help all staff feed evaluation results directly into ongoing planning and inquiry activities at various points in the project and programme cycle. They also noted later that the assessment, which took just a few hours, was instrumental in launching a new organizational approach to creating a learning system.

Other CSOs in the CoP also identified specific gaps in their approach to planning, inquiry and evaluation, and fine-tuned their learning systems. At Cuso International, for example, the *PIE* tool was used to assess the learning system of an internal capacity-building framework. The Human Resources manager responsible for the framework made changes to ensure that the right people evaluated specific things as needed. The earlier version of the framework called for scheduled meetings at regular intervals,

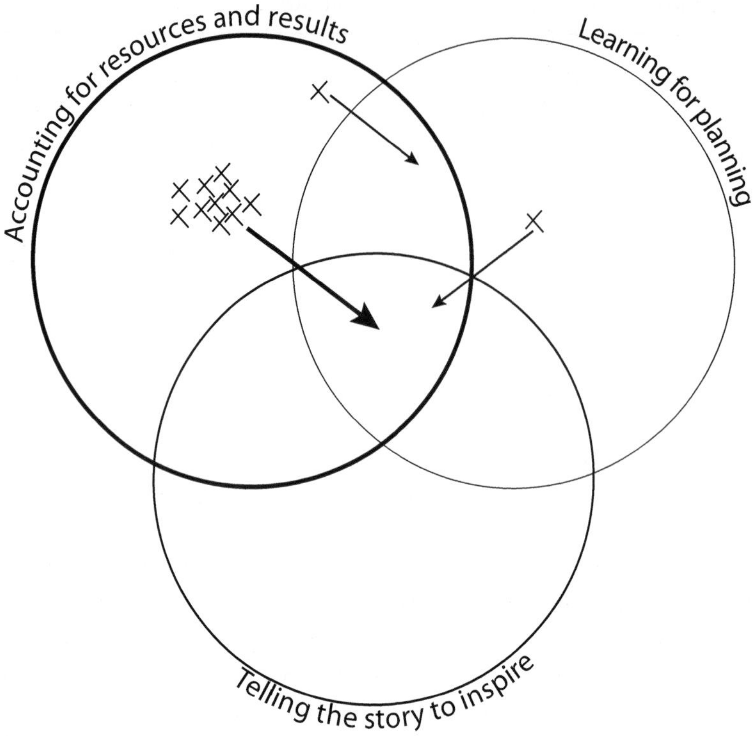

FIGURE 3.5 Current tendencies and desired directions for evaluation at CESO.

regardless of who needed to be involved and why. The revised framework also flagged the need to inquire into why and how people are learning rather than just assessing how well they are meeting their learning objectives. The manager adjusted the capacity-building framework accordingly.

Specific gaps highlighted in the *PIE* analysis by another organization (CESO) prompted senior managers there to launch a full review of the organization's monitoring and evaluation system. They found through the review that their current evaluation activities do not direct enough feedback to stakeholders or contribute as much as they would like to dialogue and the mediation of views on lessons and planning implications for future programmes. Evaluation activities are often out of sync with planning processes. Furthermore, data collection methods for evaluation are repetitive and generate uneven or incomplete information. These 'dead ends' fail to inform actions directly.

Dissatisfaction with the current system at CESO found an echo in a closely related exercise conducted some months later, facilitated by D. J. Buckles during an annual meeting of CESO staff from regional offices. Participants took time to reflect on the actual uses of their current evaluation system, and where they would like to see it go. Figure 3.5 shows the result. The vast majority (eleven people out of thirteen involved in the exercise) indicated that the evaluation findings are mainly used to account for resources (and to some extent results). They recognized that they had other needs as well not addressed by the current evaluation system, including learning for planning and telling their story to inspire others. Discussions that followed focused on ways to design each evaluation and select evaluation methods to fit the specific use or combination of uses important to stakeholders. They recognized that assessments with several uses in mind (accounting and story telling, for example) would need to use different methods (descriptive statistics and video, for example) to achieve both goals. This line of questioning is compatible with utilization-focused evaluation, an approach to monitoring and evaluation pioneered by Michael Quinn Patton (2012) and now widely used in the evaluation community. Attention to use sets in motion the whole evaluation process, including the development of the key evaluation questions and the selection of methods and data collection tools.

THREADS OF THEORY: MEANINGFUL RESEARCH

Greater synergy between university work, civil society and community life is needed urgently. While this call is widely heard, the obstacles are poorly understood. One important barrier to community-based research and pedagogy concerns the proverbial 'how' question – how to effectively 'walk the talk' of social engagement and mobilize the right set of skills and innovative methods that go beyond mere observation, interviews, focus groups and questionnaires. This is a central question for this book. It is also the key problem we raised and briefly illustrated in this chapter, through the use of *Action, Research, Training (ART)* and *Planning, Inquiry, Evaluation (PIE)*. The methods served their purpose: to facilitate dialogue and rigorous thinking about the balance and integration of the different components of effective learning systems and processes in real settings.

ART and *PIE* is a good place to start treading the multiple pathways of engaged research. It is also a good starting point for discussions about a key issue in PAR theory: the extent to which the creation of knowledge should mostly serve practical ends and grounding in real action, as it does in all applications of PAR. This is an old issue based on long-standing tensions between science, industry and humanism – tensions played out in the many transformations of university life since the end of the Middle Ages. Engaged research adopts a pragmatic and critical position in this debate: knowledge making cannot be complete until it contributes something to people's lives. In the aphorism and commentary that follow, we tackle this issue by taking inspiration from critical comments in the writings of Dewey, Peirce and James, the founders of pragmatism. The questions we ask are central to the advancement of PAR. How do we recognize what constitutes a worthy contribution to knowledge and social history? What about the humanities, pure mathematics and fundamental science in a PAR perspective? What 'cash value' do they have, as James's pragmatic expression goes? To what extent is the art of engaged research compatible with a true appreciation of the arts and the pleasure of knowledge for its own sake?

What follows is the second of a series of aphorisms and commentaries that engage with issues in abstract theory. Our incursions into theory unpack the conceptual underpinnings of the methods presented in this book and support critical thinking. Readers are warned: speculations of this kind will not appeal to those concerned with 'learning how' and 'getting things done'. But action-orientated practitioners should be wary. Interventions based on concepts and theories that simply 'go without saying' can cause great harm.

We don't devote enough research to finding a cure for useless research.

If we knew what we were doing, it wouldn't be called research, Einstein says. This is true. Nevertheless, questions about the relevance and the broader impact of academic learning and research must be raised and addressed. Part of the answer lies in the exercise of sheer curiosity and the pleasure of discovering the real world 'about us'; people's licence to study the world freely should never expire. But there's another side to what research should be doing, which is to raise questions and design a learning process that engages people in thinking that has meaning and serves a larger purpose. Let's be honest: university research creates too many non-events. More grounded theory and inquiry is needed. This is what we do when life counts and when the future has meaning. This is when thinking hits the road and things get real.

Commentary

Engaged research is pragmatism at work. It is meaningful because it serves a practical purpose and is grounded in real life. Pragmatism implies that not all topics are worth researching. For instance, some believe that the earth is flat, that Elvis Presley still lives and that Machu Picchu is the work of extraterrestrials. For reasons that are undoubtedly human, worthy of understanding, these beliefs work for them. To use William James's pragmatic metaphor, they have 'cash value', banking on a social currency accepted in the circle of believers. Is the truth value of these claims worth investigating by those convinced of their untruth, if only out of respect for the diversity of belief systems and pluralism in the pursuit of knowledge? Peirce (1902), the first to formulate one of many pragmatic maxims, answers the question in the negative. Why? Because further inquiry into such claims would be an exercise in futility. Less bluntly, an inquiry is only as good as its results or practical consequences.

In a Peircian perspective, usefulness that can be demonstrated is the arbiter of meaningful research. The true value of inquiry lies in its conceivable effects, realistic 'would-bes' that can be determined through sensory experience and scientific activity. An inquiry is meaningful if it makes a tangible difference to our lives, helping us to make up our minds, achieve clarity and act on what we say to be true. If we firmly believe that a diamond is hard, Peirce says, we can use a diamond ring accordingly (to symbolize everlasting love, among other things), confident that it will not be scratched by other solid objects (or by the hard knocks of strife and war).

Inquiry is the process of wedding our thoughts and statements to their practical consequences and the experience of our senses. For the marriage to be effective, it must take into account prior weddings between propositions and experience. In Peirce's version of pragmatism, this matching process is essentially social and collaborative. This is so for a reason: the effects of truth occur between people and communities. They can be publicly debated. For instance, the connection between roundness and the Earth has been widely publicized and celebrated, and firm arrangements made to navigate accordingly. Too many air travellers and past accounts of great overseas expeditions and world history count on it. Likewise, the legal heirs to Presley's wealth do not entertain doubts concerning the death of Elvis and have chosen to move on with their lives. Nor do the Peruvian people indulge in fantasies about the extraterrestrial origins of Machu Picchu. They continue to take great pride in their pre-colonial past and the awe-inspiring accomplishments of their ancestors. The cultural and legal consequences of knowing for sure that the Incas built Machu Picchu and that 'the king' is truly dead are as real as they can get. They leave little room for research into nonsense.

Not all founders of pragmatism share these views on the close relationship between science, truth and society. Unlike Peirce, the nineteenth-century contemporary William James (1978) advances his own version of pragmatism. On the one hand, James is more open to non-scientific reasoning. He reminds us in his writings that hard science faces serious limitations when it comes to making sense of the myriad ways in which humans go through life. On the other hand, as in much of traditional philosophy, especially since Descartes, James focusses on the thinking process and experience of the individual subject. His pragmatism gives little attention to the social construction of knowledge and conversations about reality – questions and answers raised and negotiated across differences between subjects and communities.

In our view, engaged research carried out in a pragmatic spirit is at odds with methodological individualism. Unlike James, it assumes that probing into the way each or all of us experience life is by necessity a social experience, with ripple effects that are inseparable from what Dewey and Bentley (1949) call the many 'transactions' of social and natural history. Inquiry is not just about what works for the inquisitive subject or the researcher. It is about what works or doesn't work for communities and webs of life.

Knowledge is not the product of an individual subject or mind hovering like a spirit over the real world, at great distance from the wanderings of social history. Any metaphysical notion that detaches the mind from life in society and nature is bound to be the least plausible hypothesis ever made. More to the point, knowing is brain activity glued to the social and natural 'world about us'. To use James's own reasoning, the mind-world connection is a fact among other facts. This is so true that the simple act of observing and 'making sense' of 'what is' inevitably contributes something to our lives and the world we live in. The same reasoning can be extended to Homo Sapiens and the Anthropocene, the current geological era. The human species is so involved with reality that it is now shaping the course of natural history – accelerating the rate of species extinction, climate change and ecosystem degradation. Humans must assume responsibility for this involvement. More than ever, we are called upon to sustain and intensify the many transactions of mind, community and world (Dewey, 1927) – local and global 'communities of inquiry' involving teachers, students, scientists, decision-makers, journalists, actors and concerned publics committed to addressing the social and environmental challenges of our age. Engaged research responds to the call by seeking to inquire and act on the world. To do so, it must also dwell on the world of inquiry and its involvement with being and history. It must take a stance on what it means to know.

Researchers are free to meet this responsibility in one of two ways: mostly with fear, or mostly with pleasure. Paradoxically, it is the first reaction that prompts the pursuit of absolute objectivity and god-like detachment built into dogmatic science and metaphysics. Feigned detachment is borne of fear – the fear of human error and uncertainty, to be sure, but also a reluctance to disclose what has 'cash value' for the powerful and the few. Fear and fight-or-flight responses (closely studied by James) can be found in many expressions of dogmatic truth. They include neoliberal appeals to freedom from coercion and harm inflicted by others. These are phobic calls for liberty that deny the free expression and hosting of otherness in self. With neoliberalism, the primitive flight from the threat of otherness – the physical fright caused by James's celebrated bear – makes us attack or retreat from other human beings and myriad forms of life. Dogmas, scare tactics and stories of life fleeing from life are costing us the earth. Clearly, they don't work.

The second response to what it means to know goes in the opposite direction. It takes its cue from the pleasure principle, a disposition that is equally primitive but 'works' differently. The pleasure of being and knowing is an invitation to acknowledge the engagement of mind, otherness and the world we live in, mutual commitments that science can never dissolve into component parts. Instead of dissecting the experience of life, minds engaging with the world 'about us' pay attention to the interlacing of senses and sense – observations that attract interest because meaningful in context. They support thinking grounded in the will to live, an exercise in curiosity (from Latin *curiosus*, care) that shows care and compassion for other people, forms of life and things that exist and populate the universe. The effects of knowledge pursued in this spirit are pragmatically oriented, but they also respond to human beings' 'epistemophilic' impulse. The latter drives us to discover the world jointly, by taking pleasure in learning experienced as a shared instinct.

Knowing is an impulse, a full engagement of both body and brain activity. Knowing this implies that researchers must acknowledge many kinds of knowledge other than their own, including things that the living body, inseparable from the body social, knows without the conscious mind knowing that 'it' knows. Like beggars sitting on mountains of gold, researchers inquiring into 'bodies of knowledge' can tap into the 'larger intelligence' that lies not above but rather below, in things felt and known through the interactions of heartbeat, blood flow, breath, neurons and dopamine. James's famous insight was right: the knowing body comes before the body of knowledge.

The various insights of Dewey, Peirce and James help guide the art of engaged research – sensemaking through conversations about lifeworld experiences and the 'sensational' hosting of world and otherness in self. If anything, this approach to pragmatism is a tribute to pluralism. It is at odds with all brands of humanism that bring diversity and dialogue into line with a single-minded conception of human nature and the exercise of abstract logic and reason by the self-centred subject.

This nuanced pragmatism also departs from the utilitarian concept of the greatest good for the greatest number of people actively pursuing their own interests using all available resources, material and social. Utilitarianism betrays the rule of 'consequentialism' by making otherness merely a measure or a means. In this perspective, otherness is never a finality or an end in itself, let alone an existential grounding beyond economic calculations of means and ends. Experience is seen instead as behaviour that pursues maximum benefit, reducing the web of life to quantity, a medium or milieu held hostage to the attainment of self-interest. Likewise, utilitarianism converts the work of inquiry into means-ends experimentation that 'pays off'. The end result is a short-sighted attitude that limits research to problem solving and productive activity supported by the applied contributions of science and education.

Engaged research must embrace the full spectrum of human learning, including the enjoyment of literature, art, music, philosophical and spiritual meditation, speculative mathematics and physics. All of these investments in living knowledge, expressed in different cultural forms and traditions, feed into the higher moments of learning (Dewey, 1934; Dewey and Bentley, 1949). They also support a host of aesthetic emotions. At stake here is sheer sensitivity to the world, the most primitive welcoming of otherness in self. This is the pleasure of living inquiry as an immediate experience, to be wedded to ongoing experimentation with future sources of happiness and better lives. When brought together, as they should, experimentation and experience point to E. B. White's often-quoted understanding of the pragmatic maxim – a healthy tension between a will to save the world and a desire to savour each and every moment of our lives.

REFERENCES

Dewey, J. (1927) *The Public and its Problems*, Henry Holt, New York.

Dewey, J. (1934) *Art as Experience*, Penguin, New York.

Dewey, J. and Bentley, A. (1949) *Knowing and the Known*, Beacon, Boston, MD.

James, W. (1978) *The Writings of William James: A Comprehensive Edition*, University of Chicago Press, Chicago, IL.

Lemieux, E. (2011) 'Compte rendu de la session de planification, évaluation, recherche (PER) pour évaluer le système apprenant de SUCO', unpublished report, Montreal.

Patton, M. Q. (2012) *Essentials of Utilization-Focused Evaluation*, Sage, Thousand Oaks, California, CA.

Peirce, C. S. (1902) 'Pragmatic and pragmatism', in J. M. Baldwin (ed.) *Dictionary of Philosophy and Psychology*, 3 vols, Macmillan, New York.

Suazo, L. (2008) 'Setting priorities for an applied research agenda in a new university', in D. J. Buckles (ed.) *Proceedings of Celebrating Dialogue: An international forum*, www.participatory actionresearch.net/Skillful-Means/proceedings-celebrating-dialogue-international-forum, accessed 20 January, 2009.

CHAPTER 4

Managing complexity

INTRODUCTION

The two techniques entitled *Action, Research, Training (ART)* and *Planning, Inquiry, Evaluation (PIE)* raise critical questions about learning and understanding grounded in meaningful action. Both tools raise another key challenge: how to ground the planning of an inquiry process and the actions that follow in a complex world? How can people investigate real-life situations and act on them collaboratively at the same time as they factor in uncertainty and the unknown?

In this chapter, we address the question of uncertainty through contrasts of order and chaos and propose a tool to support thinking and dialogue around ways to portray the future and make plans accordingly. A vivid example of how *Order and Chaos* was used to support the Katkari struggle against eviction from their homes near Mumbai, India is provided. The chapter ends with philosophical notes on the question of planning and the long-standing riddles of foreknowledge, determination and free will.

COPING WITH UNCERTAINTY

Order and Chaos

Purpose

To decide on the planning approach needed by answering two questions: what are the **chances** of achieving project or programme goals, and how **certain** or confident are people that the information and knowledge they have (about the conditions and factors affecting the project or programme) is complete and reliable?

Step 1

Define the project or programme and review its **goals** and plans to achieve them.

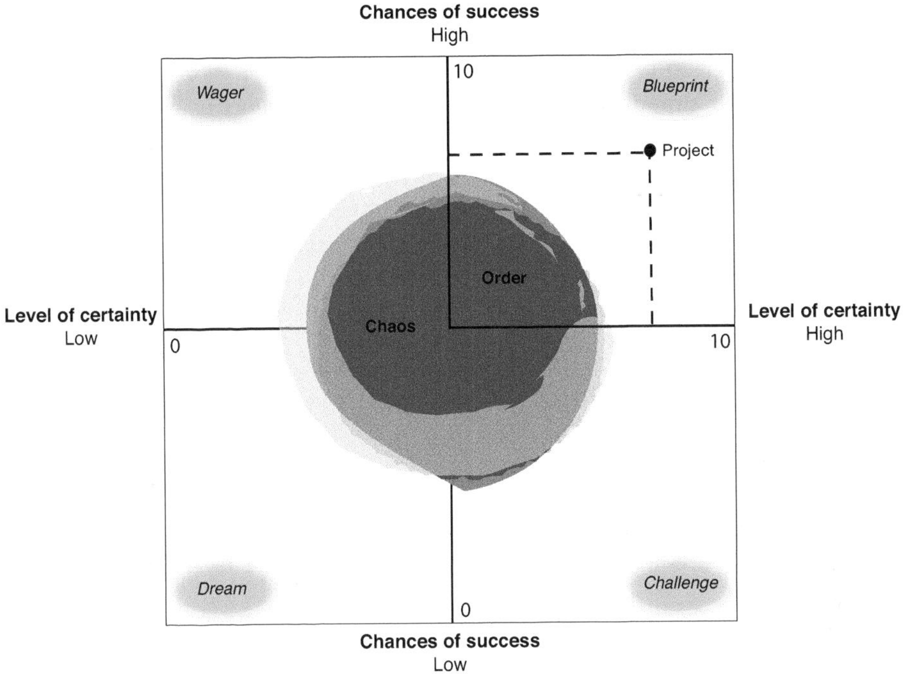

FIGURE 4.1 *Order and Chaos.*

Step 2

Prepare a graph (on the wall or the floor) by drawing a vertical line that crosses a horizontal line of equal length. Discuss and plot on the vertical line the chances of achieving the project or programme goals, using a scale of 0 to 10. A value of 10 would indicate that the current conditions are highly favourable and the chances of achieving the goals very high. A value of 0 would show the opposite (the **chances of success** are very low, see Figure 4.1).

Step 3

Discuss and plot on the horizontal line the level of confidence that people have in the information and knowledge they possess about the current conditions and factors affecting the project or programme. How **certain** are they that this information and knowledge is complete and reliable? A value of 10 would indicate that knowledge about the conditions and factors affecting the project or programme is detailed or informed by extensive experience. A value of 0 would show the opposite (knowledge about the current conditions and factors is sketchy and not informed by experience).

Step 4

Mark where the values from the two lines meet and label or place a drawing representing the project or programme at this intersection.

Step 5

Use the same graph to plot the chances of success and the level of certainty needed and that should be **aimed for** before going on with the project or programme. Mark the place where the two plotted values meet and draw an **arrow** from the mark showing the current situation to the mark showing the situation aimed for. Discuss ways to bridge the gap between the current situation and the situation that is aimed for. This may involve strategies to **increase knowledge** about the conditions and factors affecting the project or programme or strategies to modify the current conditions and **improve chances for achieving** goals.

FAQ

- ***What do the four quadrants mean?***

The four quadrants created by the graph reflect different types of projects or programmes:

1. A **dream** or vision (in the bottom left of the graph) points to an ideal that may seem unpractical and unclear.
2. A **challenge** (in the bottom right of the graph) is a project or programme pursued with awareness of the difficulties involved.
3. A **wager** (in the top left of the graph) is a project or programme that looks promising but is risky, because of limited knowledge of the key conditions and factors involved.
4. A **blueprint** (in the top right of the graph) is a project or programme likely to succeed for reasons that are well known.

- ***Is the upper right quadrant the best place to be?***

It all depends. Sometimes projects worth doing are still dreams that need to be thought through further before people can resume meaningful work. Also there are many urgent situations where projects and programmes must proceed despite obstacles to achieving success and limited knowledge of key factors (as in the medical profession, for instance). Planning projects or programmes located in these 'chaos' quadrants would benefit from the development of working hypotheses, further inquiry and iterative and continuous revision as ways to accommodate uncertainty and complexity. Orderly projects and programmes such as building a bridge call instead for rigorous planning methods and work executed according to the plans, with a view to delivering the expected results (as in the engineering profession, for instance). In short, each project or programme has a certain character and requires an appropriate approach to planning. Imposing the same planning approach in all situations is unwise.

- ***Shouldn't we use precise indicators to measure levels of certainty and chances of success?***

This is a question that can be asked of all techniques in this book. The short answer is that it all depends . . . on the amount of time that is available to develop good indicators and gather the relevant information, and how important these indicators are to the inquiry process. The 'good enough principle' is key to answering this question correctly. We return to it in Chapter 6.

Variations

- Identify **several objectives or activities** that are part of the project or programme, and then use the graph to plot the chances of success and the level of certainty for each objective or activity. Different planning approaches may be needed, depending on their location in the graph.
- Use the graph to **survey and compare** the views that different stakeholders (for example, donors and project staff) have of the same project or programme and the situation they would like to aim for. This 'reality check' may lead to negotiation of the planning process and investment in different kinds of activities needed to increase the chances of success or certainty regarding conditions and factors.

Combinations

- Use *Order and Chaos* before or after *Process Mapping* (see Chapter 5) to make sure that the planning process and its level of detail fit the situation.

The Katkari of India

The Katkari were at one time a forest people, with a special relationship to forest creatures such as the *Wagmare* (tiger), a common Katkari surname. Today they are a fragmented and very scattered tribal community, dependent on others for their livelihoods and for a place to live. Beginning in the 1950s, Katkari families migrated permanently from the high hills of the Western Ghats to the coastal plain near Mumbai. They settled on tiny parcels of marginal land on the outskirts of caste (Hindu) villages, often at the request of landholders and other employers in need of labourers that could be easily bonded. They are now at risk of enclosure and eviction from the hamlets they have lived on for several generations. Landholders who once valued their labour have started to sell lands in response to rapidly rising land prices. This has broken the patron-client relationship that once provided some security to the Katkari. Barbed wire fences now surround entire communities as landlords attempt to intimidate residents into moving to other locations. In some cases, houses have been levelled and families forced to move. For the Katkari, a people already living on the edge of survival, the situation is replete with pain and expense. It is also a significant cause of conflict and hardening of relationships with the caste communities they interact with.

A small team of people from two community-based organizations active in the area heard about the rising threat of eviction in March, 2005. Several Katkari women informed them that a Religious Trust had erected a barbed wire fence tightly around their hamlet, within a few feet of each house. A small gate was left for people to enter and leave. Representatives of the trust had purchased several properties to establish an ashram,

PHOTO 4.1 Katkari youth in Milkatkarwadi, India, discuss legal options with Bansi Ghedve, a member of the research team. (Source: R. Khedkar)

including the hamlet site. They told the Katkari to move elsewhere. Conflicted over what to do, the women sought the advice and assistance of a member of the team with whom they had a long-standing relationship. They said they felt like prisoners, but could not leave the place where their ancestors were buried.

The request led to a research project with the Katkari aimed at resolving the insecurity of this and other hamlets in the area (Buckles and Khedkar, 2013). Before committing to the process, however, the team used *Order and Chaos* to reflect on whether or not to get involved. Based on this exercise, we concluded that the situation was well defined and clear-cut, with a strong body of land reform legislation and special constitutional rights to protect Scheduled Tribes (ST) and Particularly Vulnerable Tribal Groups (PVTG) such as the Katkari. The state government seemed to have a process and source of funding for meeting housing needs in rural areas dating back several decades. A direct approach seemed possible, relying on the existing legislation, self-evident housing rights and established housing programmes financed by the state. The political climate for addressing the most extreme cases of human rights violations also seemed to be favourable given the economic boom in Maharashtra at that time and the state government's apparent interest in projecting an image of prosperity for all. The financial cost seemed low as well. Katkari hamlets are very small, often only a few acres, and typically located on extremely poor lands of no agricultural value. Given these considerations, we estimated that the

chances of achieving the goal of securing title for this and other Katkari hamlets were relatively high (about 75 per cent probability).

We also discussed our **level of certainty** regarding our knowledge of the conditions and factors affecting the goal. The community-based organizations had been working with the Katkari and with local government officials for many years and had good knowledge of who to speak to and how they might react. We had good information on the location of Katkari communities scattered throughout three districts, based on years of criss-crossing the area on motorbike and by vehicle. Relationships with the Katkari were personal and trusting in many hamlets. We also had on hand detailed information on the relevant land rights legislation and provisions regarding marginalized populations. Members of the research team had collected the information over the years when lobbying in support of tribal rights to forestland and other land resources. We understood what was involved in making land claims in the state of Maharashtra. The strength of these various sources of information gave us confidence that we had a fairly complete and reliable picture of the conditions and factors affecting the situation. We concluded that our information and knowledge base also merited a relatively high score (80 per cent certainty that it was complete, accurate and reliable).

The assessment conducted by the research team showed that not only were the **chances of success** good but also that we actually felt **confident** that we knew the situation well enough to justify our optimism. This conclusion, summarized by point A in Figure 4.2, suggested to us that we could plan an action-research process in detail and with considerable confidence, much like a **blueprint** for building a house. While it would involve a lot of work on everyone's part, and might take some time, one thing would lead to another until Katkari rights to the land under their houses were secured.

As readers might suspect, our experience was quite different from the plan, due to many problems that emerged along the way and new information challenging the knowledge we had when we developed the plan. Imponderables and unknowns that played havoc with our plans were many. To begin, record rainfall and widespread flooding jeopardized our immediate engagement with Katkari in their villages. These weather conditions cut many hamlets off from major roads and delayed a planned survey. When the survey was finally completed three months later, it showed that the **scope** of tenure insecurity among the Katkari was much greater than anticipated. We determined that 212 Katkari hamlets out of 313 in three districts, i.e. 68 per cent, did not have title to a village site. It became evident from this that the risk of eviction was widespread. As small organizations, we could not engage with more than a few of the affected hamlets. We also realized that the government would have to dedicate significant human and financial resources to address the problem in all communities.

It also became evident after the first few community meetings that working with the Katkari on this issue required a lot more time and skill on our part than we originally thought. Unlike cases of individual land rights addressed by team members in the past, mobilization around the right to a village site is a collective action. This means that high levels of community participation and agreement are needed. Given the extremely difficult living and livelihood conditions of the Katkari, full and immediate participation in a collective action by all or even a majority of residents in a hamlet was simply not possible.

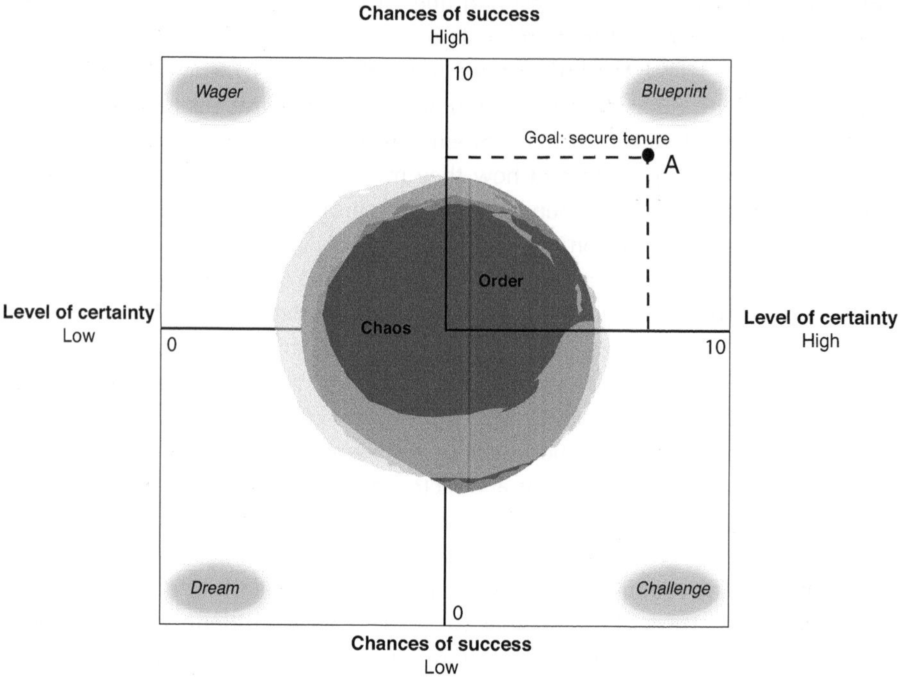

FIGURE 4.2 Assessment 'A', chances of success and level of certainty.

> **Summary of this example**: Point 'A' shows the interaction of two estimates. On the vertical axis, the chances of successfully securing village sites received a high rating. On the horizontal axis, the level of certainty regarding knowledge of conditions and factors affecting the proposed action also received a high rating. The point where the two ratings intersect places the action-research project in the upper right quadrant. This is the quadrant of relative 'order', where precise plans can be made and implemented with confidence, much like a blueprint describing what is to be done in great detail. The other quadrants refer to the world of relative 'chaos', where the chances of success are weaker and/or the level of certainty is lower due to limited understanding of the conditions and factors influencing success.

Almost from the beginning what seemed like a straightforward path led into a tangled briar patch. A year after launching the inquiry only one hamlet had acquired legal title to village land. The apparent reason for this modest result was the intense reaction of a single landholder in one village. His threat of using violence struck fear into the hearts of Katkari in many hamlets and undermined their resolve to make public demands. This happened despite careful analysis with the Katkari about the conditions needed for success, and many months of diligent and promising work to create these conditions (see further details in Chapter 9, and the full story in Buckles and Khedkar, 2013).

In hindsight, some of the obstacles we faced could not have been predicted. For instance, government plans to extend the limits of Mumbai announced a few months after the research began dramatically pushed land prices up. The effects were particularly strong near major highways. Landholders in these areas were enthused by the sudden increase in the value of land and went on high alert for any opportunities to gain from it, and to any threats to their ownership. By contrast, land prices in areas further from Mumbai did not experience these effects. The impact of these macro dynamics varied enormously at the micro-level, from place to place and depending on the idiosyncratic interests of particular landholders.

Twists and turns in the struggle for a secure hamlet were a fundamental challenge to the assumptions the research team had used to make sense of the situation and plan detailed and targeted actions with the Katkari. While successful in one hamlet, the attempt at holistic and strategic thinking developed with the Katkari quickly fell apart in others once the depth of opposition was revealed. Further analysis showed that the unequal relations of power between landholders and the Katkari, anticipated from the beginning, went far beyond direct confrontation with landholders. They were expressed as well in the relationship of the Katkari to government officials, the *Gram Panchayat* (village authorities) and all potential employers of unskilled labour. A long history of severe exploitation and social exclusion had fragmented the community and deeply eroded self-confidence. Many things would need to change on many fronts simultaneously in order to achieve the apparently straightforward goal of a secure village site. There would be no easy solution.

Given these many obstacles, the team decided to rethink its approach to working with the Katkari. We stopped going to the study villages, to ensure we were not putting any pressure on the Katkari to take further public action. The risks to the Katkari directly involved, their families and their neighbours were real, and the team wanted to avoid making their situation any worse. We learned through indirect queries and discussions with Katkari outside of their communities that many people were demoralized. They now felt they could not advance their cause and would eventually be evicted. Later, however, the various organized groups in the hamlets once again began to contact the team and ask for meetings. The threat of eviction was as tangible as ever. People said that they wanted to do something, but were not sure what. The research team was not sure either. We agreed, however, to investigate the reasons why people in some hamlets were not willing to take a public stand, and to use this understanding to plan future actions.

The invitation to return to the hamlets prompted us to redo our initial assessment of the research plan, and to revise downward our estimate of the chances of successfully securing village sites. When we reflected on what we had learned, we concluded that we now had more complete and reliable information and knowledge regarding the various conditions and factors affecting the project goals. By trying to solve the problem, we had increased our understanding of the main hurdles and the strongest barriers. All in all, we knew that the chances of success were low, and we knew what we were up against. The action-research endeavour, summarized by point 'B' in Figure 4.3, was now

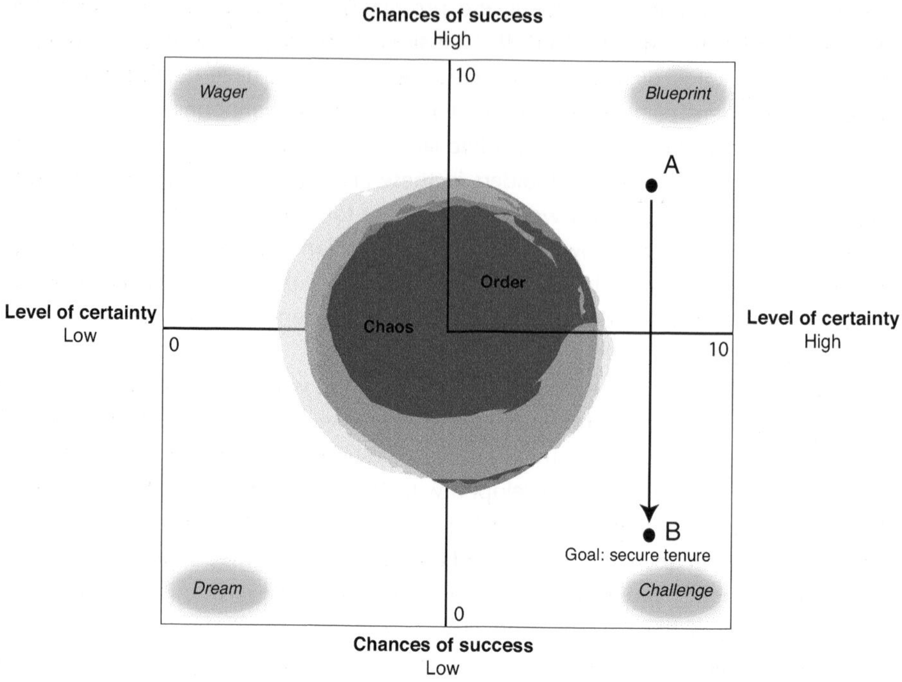

FIGURE 4.3 Assessment 'B', chances of success and level of certainty.

> **Summary of this example**: Point 'B' combines two estimates. On the vertical axis, the chances of successfully securing village sites received a low rating. On the horizontal axis, the level of certainty regarding knowledge of conditions and factors affecting the proposed action received a high rating. The point where the two ratings intersect places the action-research project in the lower right quadrant. This quadrant is part of the world of relative 'chaos', where plans are working hypotheses subject to multiple factors and streams of action and reaction by different parties.

more correctly seen as a significant **challenge**, rather than a blueprint that could be simply planned and implemented.

The shift in thinking about the nature of the inquiry and the kind of planning it required, consolidated in the new assessment, was unsettling and a test of the team's own expectations and resolve. Suddenly, the inquiry was a very uncertain endeavour with no clear end in sight. While this was cause for worry, it was also a useful conclusion as it pointed to a new kind of planning. We began to ground every step of the inquiry in **working hypotheses** regarding what needed to shift in the situation in order to increase the chances of success. Three working hypotheses emerged: addressing government neglect, breaking the bonds of migratory labour and filling gaps in both hamlet-level and collective organization. Together with the Katkari, the team tested these hypotheses over several years and adjusted plans along the way, 'in the middle' of multiple factors and streams of action and reaction by different parties.

Recognizing the complexity and uncertainty of the goal did not mean we abandoned all efforts to plan. We still needed to be efficient in the use of limited time and other resources to pursue the goal of securing village sites. We just didn't plan everything out well in advance and in great detail, under the assumption that we could anticipate the outcomes and results of each activity with great confidence and certainty. Plans became more flexible and iterative, while maintaining a sense of purpose. The Katkari and the research team began to work on various fronts simultaneously and with varying levels of intensity over time and in different spaces. Work unfolded unevenly over a number of years, in response to small successes, setbacks and stakeholder interventions that could not be predicted in advance. The design of new inquiries often depended on the prior assessment of the performance of key factors (e.g. the organizational capacities emerging in Katkari communities). Progress and decisions regarding what to do next had to wait for the results of prior activities and responses from particular stakeholders (e.g. securing caste certificates to support applications for government assistance, and then waiting for government replies to written applications for land).

Instead of a plan-and-implement framework, the team adopted a **continuous action–reaction** approach guided by the working hypotheses. We paid more attention to how the outputs of one activity fed into the next activity, and adjusted the design accordingly. This strategy of flexible and continuous planning required that the team and the Katkari constantly adjust the focus and time dedicated to activities aimed at the desired outcomes. It was like a voyage at sea: the energy and enthusiasm of some groups of Katkari buoyed spirits, obstacles arose during various interactions with government officials, and new information appeared to guide us in the use of legal countermeasures. As with any real-life voyage, the definitive set of waypoints or coordinates could only be placed on a chart once the ship was safely in port. Knowing that the route would be chaotic rather than orderly was nonetheless invaluable as it forced the inquiry to remain open to the lessons of failure, the reality of dead ends and the possibility of new directions unplanned and unanticipated.

THREADS OF THEORY: THE PLANNER

To navigate in perilous times, we must learn rules of navigation, plan our journey, prepare ourselves to cope with uncertainty and tame the unknown. Still, when in troubled waters, only fools let rules and plans navigate the ship.

Grounded inquiry is like conflict, commerce, work or marriage: in order to make the necessary arrangements, proper 'terms and rules of engagement' must be created. Failing to plan the process equals planning to fail in the process. Anticipating the future is all the more important when clear links between actions and their effects can be established and trusted; no one wants a bridge or a flight to London to be a working hypothesis, a best bet or lesser evil compared to swimming. In perilous times, however, the path of inquiry should never be so rigid that navigation becomes inflexible and robotic. Planning that maps out all aspects of the journey is irresponsible if it denies the unknowable, by assuming that all events can be counted on to unfold mechanically and inexorably.

Planning for the unexpected is not only perilous. It is also an oxymoron. Events that simply go according to plans, as expected and without surprise, are not events. Plans that deal with complex issues rarely survive contact with history. This means that the mainstream approach to project management and the inquiry process – plan before, execute after – offers a linear pathway not suited to complex endeavours, such as defusing a conflict, eradicating injustice or illness, or coping with climate change. When problems are messy and hard to define, the process of 'doing' cannot be a simple derivation of efficient thinking and planning. In difficult circumstances a good plan should not be a small picture outline of everything that needs to be done to achieve results. It should be more like a big picture riddled with working hypotheses and loose ends, subject to validation or falsification, second thoughts and new ideas on where things are heading and where to go next.

Real-life events call for logic and rigour, to be sure. But they also call for creativity and flexibility, the kind that allows people to move in and out of risky plans in response to new circumstances and information acquired step by step, along the way, through trial and error. Good planning in complex settings includes decisions not to decide and also plans to plan later, when the exercise is useful and possible, if at all. As with medicine, knowledge to address messy problems is a science of uncertainty and an art of probability. This is Aristotle's phronesis, Freire's praxis or Checkland's soft-system thinking. It is Lyotard's work of 'art emerging in the doing of it'.

Commentary

Planning the inquiry process (or anything else for that matter) is a juggling act that brings three things together and keeps them in motion: human **intelligence**, the exercise of **free will** and a **commanding voice**. Intelligence is the knowledge of things that were and that are, and the science of relations between them, all of which contribute to predictive reasoning and the determination of things that can be or will be. Free will is the ability of human agents to make choices free from absolute constraints. Humans make plans and project to do certain things because they so choose and know they could decide and do things otherwise. The commanding voice is the last ingredient essential to any plan. It directs certain ideas or decisions to be followed or obeyed by virtue of the will or reasoning that gives them compelling force.

To some, the juggling act of planning tosses things into the air that cannot be brought together. Incompatibilists prefer to doubt and not juggle at all, by arguing one of two things. The first argument consists in letting free will prevail against the tyranny of 'chains of causality'. This view is characteristic of libertarian metaphysics and Feyerabend's plea 'against method'. It also evokes Sartre's existentialism, a philosophical standpoint appealing to the radical freedom that characterizes the human condition. Humans are condemned to be absolutely free.

The second argument heads in the opposite direction: determinism obliterates free will, reducing human volition to a faint idea or a 'velleity', as Hume (1999) calls it. Variations on these views can be found in Lutheran and Calvinist theology and in the speculative thinking of Laplace (haunted by an all-powerful demon). The Stoic teachings of Chrysippus should also be mentioned here. According to Chrysippus, nothing exists or has come into being without a cause. The notion that there can be an uncaused cause is unthinkable and would be sufficient to destroy the entire universe, if it were it to come true.

Compatibilists are greater in number (McCann, 1995). They believe it is possible to reconcile the constraints of human existence with the ability of human agents to determine random alternative possibilities for action and act on their preferred option. The more optimistic see no problem in merging intelligence, free will and a commanding voice, all under the perfect control of a rational subject acting as a god-like Planner. They adopt what might be called a theistic standpoint (developed in a lay perspective) whereby the Planner is the creator of all things that truly matter. This implies three things. First, the Planner is **all-knowing**. For each statement that pertains to the past, the present or the future, the rational subject generally knows whether it is true or false. This knowledge does not change and is not liable to error. In the unfolding of his Plan, the Planner is infallible. Second, the Planner is **all-powerful**. All projects that occur in the planning universe take place under his or her sovereign guidance and control, and anything that is logically possible and feasible, he or she can do. Finally, the Planner is **all-benevolent**. In all circumstances he or she acts as a providential father, working all things for good and providing the best possible outcome for all those concerned by his or her creation. As in Leibniz's theodicy, the world he creates is the best of all possible worlds (Leibniz, 1985).

'Theistic planning' requires faith in the providence of scientific planning and the application of principles of 're-engineering' to human activity and social change. A curious riddle must be ignored in the process: perfect planning is trusting the systematic application of free will and reason to eliminating free will and reason in human activity. The more knowledgeable and powerful the Planner is, the less latitude there is for the human will to make different plans. The end result is man-made determinism, an unshakeable logic or superior plan created 'out of necessity'. A good illustration of this mindset is the notion, eminently modern, that 'in the past the man has been first; in the future the system must be first' (Taylor, 1911). The pronouncement evokes modern-day Taylorism and its glorification of dangerous and demeaning work guided by the scientific management of human activity and life in society. This is the Master Plan of Science and Industry founded on a dark paradox: the exercise of reason towards the denial of free will.

Solutions to the riddle, beyond the naive version of theistic planning, are many and date back to philosophical speculations of great antiquity. They include Boethius inviting the Planner to think beyond the dimension of time, Molina's proposal of a Middle Science, and Augustine's defence of the Planner's Plan to let others plan.

Boethius (2001), a Christian philosopher of the early sixth century, offers an elegant strategy to accommodate both foreknowledge and free will: let the Planner and his knowledge exist outside of time, in an eternal present that gives him access to the powers of planning. Through great detachment from history, the Planner gains, in a single act of awareness, full comprehension of the essence of planning, past and future, just as though it were now occurring. While the Planner is all knowing, what he knows to be true is external to time and cannot therefore be treated as foreknowledge. Epistemological debates about the compatibility between 'prescience' and free will are therefore pointless. After Boethius, theorists of positive philosophy and predictive methodology are prone to disconnect themselves from the uncertainty and messiness of everyday life. Their detachment from the vagaries of life on earth invites scepticism. The notion that what they know and are able to predict has no history and is not an integral part of history can be safely taken with a grain of salt.

Molinian efforts to promote 'theistic planning' without fatalism take us in a more interesting direction back to the sixteenth-century idea of 'subjunctives of freedoms' (Molina, 1988). In this scenario, the Planner possesses the *Scientia Media*, knowledge that stands in the 'middle' of two forms of knowing handed down by Aquinas: what the Planner knows about necessary truths embedded in logic and nature (the law of gravity, for instance), and his free knowledge of contingents truths – things that actually exist in one grammatical tense or another, including those that may or may not happen (global warming 'might have receded' had the Kyoto Protocol been enforced, for instance). Middle knowledge gives the Planner advance notice and understanding of what any human being would decide and do if placed in any possible circumstances. This enables the Planner to make all the arrangements that are needed for the right things to happen, outcomes that fit some true 'subjunctive of freedom'. The lay Planner does not have complete sovereignty over things that are true of necessity. But he can act on the free knowledge that he has of all things that are possible in his own creation, those that lend themselves to the intervention of human providence.

Many echoes of Middle Science reasoning can be found in modern-day thinking. A good example is scenario thinking and planning (Fahey and Randall, 1998), an adaptation and generalization of classic methods used by military intelligence. The approach uses systems thinking and simulation games for policymakers and planners based on known facts about the future, ranging from demographic to geographic, military, political, environmental and industrial information. The aim of the exercise is to generate alternative trends that are plausible. They include key driving forces from which precise plans of action can be derived.

Scenario-based science has its critics. As should be expected, concerns include the limits of existing knowledge; the infinite number of possible futures that can be imagined; the many judgment calls, methodological decisions and theoretical assumptions that inform each plan; and the intractable nature of uncertainty and complexity. Scenarios regarding discoveries that have yet to happen – the historical impact of what we will know later but don't know yet – constitute another quagmire of no small proportions. As Popper remarks, the conditional predictions of science only 'apply to systems which can be described as well-isolated, stationary and recurrent. These systems are very rare in nature and modern society is surely not one of them' (Popper, 2004, p. 457). The spectre of scientism and managerial technocracy – the imposition of top-down planning sanctioned by science – looms large in this lay version of Molina's Scientia Media.

For a more convincing strategy to reconcile knowledge of the future with the exercise of freedom, the insights of Augustine and Aquinas are well worth revisiting. According to the Church Fathers, an all-powerful Planner whose activity is the first cause of everything can enable his followers to choose and plan things freely, moving human agents to act in accordance with their voluntary nature. This means that the Prime Mover can be the first cause of all things willed and done by his agents without determining their actual decisions or actions. Everything that happens is under the Planner's full control and reflects his will. His will, however, includes a sovereign decision to let his followers make decisions along the way, wrong and wicked ones included, for which only the followers can be blamed. As in Sartrian philosophy, the gift of moral and responsible autonomy orders humans to act according to their own will, condemning them to be free. They are given the opportunity to freely accept the Planner's call to muster their own knowledge, power and benevolence in such ways as to please the Planner. But they have to work hard at emulating their enlightened Creator, knowing that they are bound to make errors and be responsible for their mistakes and wrongdoings. Erring is a necessary evil (Plantinga, 1974). Efforts to overcome ignorance, weakness and evil, with all the blessings and the colossal sufferings that follow, are part of the Master Plan. So is the human show of will and wisdom in making plans for defeating evil and achieving the good. In short, the planning of freedom explains the freedom to plan.

The idea that freedom is part of a larger scheme and contributes to the greater good is by no means evident. Well-intended plans multiply like locusts, yet hell insists on breaking loose and beautiful things continue to perish. A positive theodicy that explains the grand design of real choices made by human agents and the necessary role that ruin and wrongdoing play in real life seems so lofty and counterfactual as to be far-fetched. The opposite view, more plausible, defines freedom as the absence of any plan or scheme and the essential liberty that humans have in choosing 'what they do with what's been done to them', as Sartre aptly puts it. Once thrown into the world, humans are fully responsible for everything they do. Freedom either is or is not. If it exists at all, it must be inalienable and cannot be shackled to a master plan originating from the Creator or some earthly spirit created in his commanding image.

In reality, aspirations to radical freedom are as vain as great hopes of theistic planning. Human planning works but is still fallible. Likewise, human freedom takes command but has limited reign. These are the two sides of the same coin. Predictive knowledge as we know it implies free decisions to plan and the planning of decisions freely taken, all of which are subject to limitations, risks and erring. The planner, now spelled with a lower case 'p', has some but not unlimited power to foresee possible futures and act on them. He can do so by virtue of the ordinary randomness that is constitutive of the universe, some 'quantum indeterminacy' that supplies elbowroom for human intervention. Actually, his choices can be made not despite but rather because of known determinations of causes and effects. Were it not for probable and predictable relationships between things we observe and experience, all events would occur in perfectly random ways. Things would happen so 'freely' as to leave no room for humans to identify alternative courses of action to be followed in some orderly way, with good enough certainty in how things are likely to unfold. Radical indetermination is a curse – freedom without choices that have consequence and truly matter. In the end, theories that choose to crown freedom above all are profoundly unreliable. They have no way to justify their own freedom and power to choose.

While they have opposite characteristics, determinism and free will are both essential to human existence and forward thinking. The idea that we have absolute freedom of choice in the way we run our lives is as foolish as the notion that we have no choice at all. Middle-road thinking offers greater wisdom. It is the middle-path reasoning of *pratitya-samutpada*, a Sanskrit term to denote the Buddhist concept of 'interdependent arising', or the 'co-arising' of 'this and that'.

Thinking in the middleness of things points to Sartre's notion of an essential ambiguity built into the human condition, a form of being that brings together two regions fated to coexist but never merge (Sartre, 2003). One region harbours every solid, self-identical thing that simply is, was or will positively be. Sartre calls it the in-itself, an expression that captures the 'facticity' of every form of life, existence and event on earth. In this region lie all the givens of language, facts of the environment, the many prior choices and rules that shape people's history, and the inevitable prospect of everyone's death. The other region, the for-itself, is hollow, fluid and dynamic. It is packed with emptiness and becoming. Consciousness dwells there, always at some distance from its factitious self, torn between two forms of nothingness in time: being in the past that is no longer, and becoming in the future that is not yet – the future that opens up possibilities for the freedom of the for-itself. Non-being in time means that foresight and hindsight is by necessity a hit and miss affair, a projection that always ventures a new perspective and never brings planning to rest. All planning horizons are 'iffy' entanglements in time. They comprise the memory of possible futures that can no longer be, and the anticipation of past events that may be revisited and appraised in new light. Fixed frames of reference are suspect. In Eisenhower's words, 'plans are nothing; planning is everything.'

> 'Do not believe in anything simply because you have heard it. Do not believe in anything simply because it is spoken and rumored by many. Do not believe in anything simply because it is found written in your religious books. Do not believe in any-thing merely on the authority of your teachers and elders. Do not believe in traditions because they have been handed down for many generations. But after observation and analysis, when you find that anything agrees with reason and is conducive to the good and benefit of one and all, then accept it and live up to it.'
>
> (Hindu Prince Gautama Siddharta, the founder of Buddhism, 563–483 BC)

Every foresight into possible futures is an interlacing of facticity and transcendence, a mixture of fullness and emptiness that never bows to necessity and perfection in planning. The awareness of cracks in being and time detaches human existence from the rock-solid facts of life. It also creates a fundamental task for human beings, which consists in defining and projecting a possible lifeworld and assuming full responsibility for the choice made. This is the option of authenticity and the ethics of responsibility – projects that try to coordinate transcendence and facticity, mixing them in good faith, with all the attendant risks and a stubborn refusal to deny one region of being or the other. Planning in good faith advances claims to what has value in life and takes responsibility for such claims all at once.

REFERENCES

Boethius, A. M. S. (2001) *Consolation of Philosophy,* trans. Joel Relihan, Hackett, Indianapolis, IN.

Buckles, D. J. and Khedkar, R. with Ghevde, B. and Patil, D. (2013) *Fighting Eviction: Tribal Land Rights and Research-in-Action,* Cambridge University Press India, New Delhi.

Fahey, L. and Randall, R. M. (1998) *Learning from the Future: Competitive Foresight Scenarios,* Wiley, New York.

Hume, D. (1999) *An Enquiry Concerning Human Understanding,* T. L. Beauchamp (ed.), Oxford University Press, Oxford.

Leibniz, G. W. (1985) *Theodicy: Essays on the Goodness of God, the Freedom of Man, and the Origin of Evil,* trans. E. M. Huggard, Open Court, La Salle, IL.

McCann, H. (1995) 'Divine sovereignty and the freedom of the will', *Faith and Philosophy,* vol. 12, no. 4, pp. 582–598.

Molina, L. de (1988) *On Divine Foreknowledge: Part IV of the Concordia,* trans. Alfred J. Freddoso, Cornell University Press, Ithaca, NY.

Plantinga, A. (1974) *The Nature of Necessity,* Clarendon Press, Oxford.

Popper, K. (2004) *Conjectures and Refutations: The Growth of Scientific Knowledge,* Routledge, London.

Sartre, J.-P. (2003) *Being and Nothingness: An Essay on Phenomenological Ontology,* trans. Hazel E. Barnes, Routledge, London.

Taylor, F. W. (1911) *The Principles of Scientific Management,* Harper & Brothers, New York.

CHAPTER 5

Mapping the process

INTRODUCTION

We now turn to *Process Mapping* and *Process Design*, the critical threads that weave together all the tools and concepts presented and illustrated in this book. We present them here, near the beginning of the readers' journey, because practice cannot really begin without them. Using any tool without having reflected on how it fits into the stream of activities it seeks to understand and change is an invitation to failure and disappointment. Mapping a real-life process, even tentatively and over the short term, provides grounds for selecting and scaling appropriate tools for use.

This chapter presents a flexible planning methodology that helps ground the inquiry in orderly project cycles and in the middle of complex and messy situations as well. When key factors and conditions are easy to predict, *Process Mapping* and *Process Design* allow inquiry to be planned in some detail, well in advance. In more difficult situations, the same methodology allows questions and ways to answer them to evolve over time and adjust to ongoing learning and planning circumstances and needs. Goals and results are established through continuous testing and learning from failure – through an ongoing feedback, action–reaction loop, as in medical practice.

Step-by-step instructions on *Process Mapping* and *Process Design* presented in the chapter are illustrated using a story of tensions around the delivery of park services in Canada. This is followed by an exploration of the general implications of the approach for monitoring and evaluation (M&E), one of the most widely used forms of inquiry outside of the university environment. We conclude the chapter with a philosophical discussion of how planning 'in the middleness' of an evolving world relates to linear and non-linear conceptions of time.

CHARTING THE JOURNEY

Process Mapping

Purpose

To plan action and inquiry at the right time and at the appropriate level of detail, and to adjust the two in light of unforeseen events and new knowledge.

Step 1

Define the project and discuss overall **goals** and expected results. List all current and/or proposed project **activities** on cards using keywords (one activity per card). Use concrete action verbs to describe each activity or set of activities, instead of words for objectives or topics. For example, use 'raise funds' instead of 'resources', or 'lobby' instead of 'policy impact'. To clarify the distinction between activities and goals, use one side of each card to describe the activity and the other side to describe the corresponding goal.

Step 2

Organize the activity cards into **sets and subsets** based on principles of similarity among activities (see *Free List and Pile Sort*, Chapter 8). If need be, create a label or **title** for each set and for each subset.

Step 3

Create a process map, beginning with a title card, drawing or object representing the project placed in the centre or in the upper left corner of the map. Then add the sets and subsets of activity cards to the **map**, creating branches and sub-branches as in a tree or a shrub.

Step 4

Decide which activity or set of activities needs to be planned in some detail and whether this can be done immediately. Focus detailed planning on **immediate activities** (four months and sooner, for instance).

Some activities may not require formal planning or can be **planned at a later date**, when **more information** is available about the results of prior activities, the actions of stakeholders, or key conditions that need to be met. Discuss these information gaps and add new inquiry or **fact-finding** activities to the process map, as needed.

Step 5

Write the details on the back of those activity cards that require immediate planning, including the start and finish **dates, people** involved (and their roles), material **resources** needed (equipment, budget), the **information** required, **methods** to be used and the expected **results** or outcomes. Create and use a visual code to highlight in the map some of these details or any other aspect such as levels of **priority** or the **stage** of completion for each activity. Provide the optimal level of planning detail, and decide whether further planning is needed. Use tape to fasten the cards in place, thereby creating an overall picture of the process map.

Step 6

If needed, compile the planning details from sets and subsets of activity cards to produce **a table**. In Column 1, list project activities (some or all of all of them). Use other columns to record information for each activity on **who** does **what, why, when** and **how**. Alternatively, use 'mind-mapping' software to arrange and track the data.

Step 7

When new or more detailed plans are made, **modify the map**.

FAQ

- ***Shouldn't the process map highlight general and specific objectives instead of sets and subsets of activities?***

Process Mapping uses programme or project activities (**goal-oriented actions**) as the point of entry instead of the general and specific objectives (**action-oriented goals**) emphasized in conventional planning methods such as results-based management. Action-oriented goals (such as promoting democratic governance in the management

PARK DIALOGUE

In 2010 the Gatineau Park in Canada's Capital Region creates a multi-stakeholder platform known as Park Dialogue to address the increasing volume of user complaints about the park's management of winter trails and related services delivered by a private contractor. Facilitated by J. M. Chevalier, Park Dialogue held several meetings since then and contributed to a diagnostic assessment of user complaints and finding ways to address them.

Figure 5.1 illustrates the *Process Mapping* method used to construct meeting agendas, facilitate discussions at each meeting (by projecting and revising the map on screen), record minutes, flag issues to be discussed later, point each activity or event to relevant websites, and hyperlink all relevant documents uploaded on a shared site. (For a detailed account of this story, see example in *Process Design*, below.)

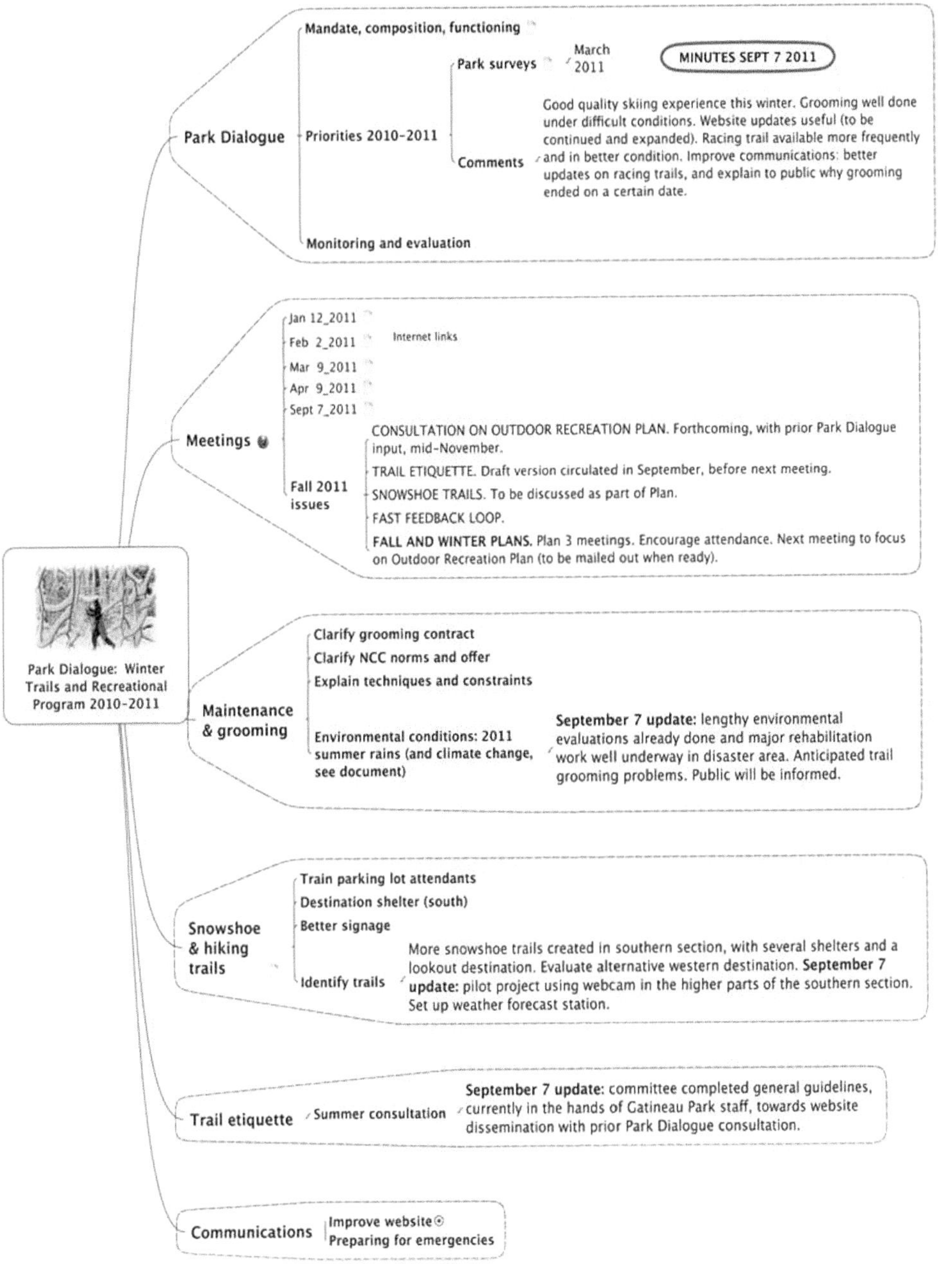
Park Dialogue: Winter Trails and Recreational Program 2010-2011
Park Dialogue
Mandate, composition, functioning
Priorities 2010-2011
Park surveys
March 2011
MINUTES SEPT 7 2011
Comments
Good quality skiing experience this winter. Grooming well done under difficult conditions. Website updates useful (to be continued and expanded). Racing trail available more frequently and in better condition. Improve communications: better updates on racing trails, and explain to public why grooming ended on a certain date.
Monitoring and evaluation
Meetings
Jan 12_2011
Feb 2_2011
Internet links
Mar 9_2011
Apr 9_2011
Sept 7_2011
Fall 2011 issues
CONSULTATION ON OUTDOOR RECREATION PLAN. Forthcoming, with prior Park Dialogue input, mid-November.
TRAIL ETIQUETTE. Draft version circulated in September, before next meeting.
SNOWSHOE TRAILS. To be discussed as part of Plan.
FAST FEEDBACK LOOP.
FALL AND WINTER PLANS. Plan 3 meetings. Encourage attendance. Next meeting to focus on Outdoor Recreation Plan (to be mailed out when ready).
Maintenance & grooming
Clarify grooming contract
Clarify NCC norms and offer
Explain techniques and constraints
Environmental conditions: 2011 summer rains (and climate change, see document)
September 7 update: lengthy environmental evaluations already done and major rehabilitation work well underway in disaster area. Anticipated trail grooming problems. Public will be informed.
Snowshoe & hiking trails
Train parking lot attendants
Destination shelter (south)
Better signage
Identify trails
More snowshoe trails created in southern section, with several shelters and a lookout destination. Evaluate alternative western destination. September 7 update: pilot project using webcam in the higher parts of the southern section. Set up weather forecast station.
Trail etiquette
Summer consultation
September 7 update: committee completed general guidelines, currently in the hands of Gatineau Park staff, towards website dissemination with prior Park Dialogue consultation.
Communications
Improve website
Preparing for emergencies

FIGURE 5.1 *Process Mapping,* documentation and Internet links.

of forest resources in a certain region) tend to be abstract and overly ambitious compared to goal-oriented actions (for example, setting up a multi-stakeholder platform to co-manage a region's forest resources more fairly). This makes the latter easier to discuss and to assess. Goal-oriented actions are more grounded, and closer to the day-to-day language that people use to make plans and evaluate their progress. As in other methods, the goals built into the actions can still be defined and negotiated collaboratively.

- ***What's the difference between* Process Mapping *and other planning methods such as results-based management* (RBM)*?***

Process Mapping is a **visual tool** that helps people discuss project plans and, while doing so, see the forest from the trees, features that are generally absent in planning methods that use mostly text, tables and spreadsheets. Also the focus is on concrete **activities** and their corresponding goals and desired results, as opposed to general objectives that translate into activities. This approach has the advantage of accommodating a **plurality of stakeholder interests** and potential outcomes around a common set of actions. Finally, *Process Mapping* is more **flexible**. It acknowledges the fact that some activities require formal, immediate and detailed planning while others don't.

Variations

- Use meaningful symbols or **images** to represent different activities within the map.
- Arrange the activities in the order or **sequence** of implementation. Place those activities that are ongoing throughout the project or not yet scheduled in a separate area of the process map.
- Include in the process map references to major **activities** carried out **before or following the planning period**. This encourages recognition that planning occurs 'in the middle' of complex situations involving other stakeholder contributions that have a prior history and no clear ending.
- When working on complex projects, you can divide participants into **groups**, ask each group to use *Process Mapping* to map out their own set of activities, and then adjust group plans through discussions and negotiations between all groups.
- Use **mind-mapping** software (such as Mindjet's MindManager or free software on the Internet) to create a process map and compile planning details for sharing. (See example in *Process Design*, below.)

Combinations

- *Process Mapping* combines with *Process Design* (below) to create an iterative or continuous planning methodology. Ongoing and future activities, including diagnostic assessments (using the appropriate methods) designed to inform the planning process, are woven together into a visual guide to navigation.

Process Design

Purpose

Process Design is a flexible systems approach to planning and managing an inquiry process grounded in action. It is the starting point leading to the selection of tools and methods deemed useful to the inquiry. The following guidelines help with the practical grounding of tools for collaborative inquiry in the context of an action-learning process (see Figure 5.2). They show how to plan an inquiry at the right time and at the appropriate level of detail, and inform action plans in light of unforeseen events and new information.

Step 1 Consider the general context

Define the general context where the inquiry needs to be planned in detail.

Step 2 Define the planning situation

To ground the inquiry in a real setting, it is useful to distinguish three scenarios based on varying levels of uncertainty and complexity (see *Order and Chaos*, Chapter 4).

Scenario 1: Continuous planning

The first scenario involves complex, multi-stakeholder situations rife with **uncertainty**. Planning in this scenario (the world of chaos) recognizes that general and specific objectives may **interact and evolve**, subject to negotiations, compromise and change over time. Planning needs to occur in the middle of an ongoing process where the results of prior activities, the performance of key factors and stakeholder interventions or responses cannot be fully predicted. Information and knowledge are incomplete, links between causes and effects are not linear and straightforward, and chains of actions, partners and results are complex.

For this kind of situation, characterized by some degree of chaos, use the tool *Process Mapping* to make project or programme plans with varying and optimal levels of detail and time frames. Create and mobilize knowledge and engage people along the way by formulating working hypotheses and integrating multiple, flexible inquiries or diagnostic assessments into the plans, as needed to inform actions and the planning process. Keep in mind that some activities do not require a formal inquiry either because there is no pressing need, the results are clear, or they can be monitored through **day-to-day tracking** (using informal exchanges, for instance).

Scenario 2: Plan first, implement after

Some situations are **predictable** enough to plan most activities in advance with considerable detail, followed by implementation. Planning in this relatively orderly scenario assumes that there is a coherent set of objectives shared by all stakeholders, and that these objectives are clearly achievable with a well defined set of inputs (time, resources, people). Under these conditions, use the tool *Process Mapping* and selected tools (from this book or from other sources) to do four things in sequence:

1 **assess** the initial situation;
2 make **detailed activity plans** based on assessments of the initial situation and the logical link between planned activities and expected results;
3 **monitor** the ongoing results of implementation against the initial set of observations or findings; and
4 **evaluate** the final results against initial objectives using relevant criteria, indicators or progress markers (see *Scoring tips* in Chapter 8). The initial situation can also be re-examined in hindsight, to produce effects of Socratic learning (such as 'Now we know we knew' or 'Now we know we didn't know'; see *The Socratic Wheel*, Chapter 7).

Results-based management may also be appropriate in this scenario. Planning in detail well in advance relies on high levels of information, consensus and confidence regarding the chances of achieving particular goals. As with more complex scenarios, do not plan more inquiries than are needed. Some activities do not require a formal inquiry either because there is no pressing need, the results are clear, or they can be monitored through **day-to-day tracking** (using informal exchanges, for instance).

Scenario 3: Single event

Some situations are so uncertain or pressing only immediate events can be planned. Comprehensive planning tools are not really needed or useful. Use *Process Design* and the appropriate inquiry tools (from this book or other sources) to facilitate a single or **one-off event**, and plan follow-up actions based on the results. If the focus is on a single event or activity, go immediately to **Step 3.**

Step 3 Identify prior decisions

To design the inquiry, identify decisions that can be made upfront regarding: (a) **who** is to be involved in the inquiry; (b) the participants' **profiles** and **roles**; (c) how much **time** will be dedicated to the inquiry; (d) the available **inputs** from previous events (knowledge, other decisions); and (e) the role(s) that the **facilitator**(s) should play.

When defining roles, decide whether the facilitator or facilitating team is expected to combine various roles, such as instructor, expert-consultant, researcher, note-taker, or stakeholder. Teamwork and a clear division of labour may be necessary when the facilitator(s) must combine several roles.

Use tools in this book to answer these questions, if needed.

Step 4 Define the inquiry purpose

Define the type of inquiry needed, its goal, its scope and the expected results (see definitions, below). Make sure that the purpose is compatible with the decisions made in Step 3.

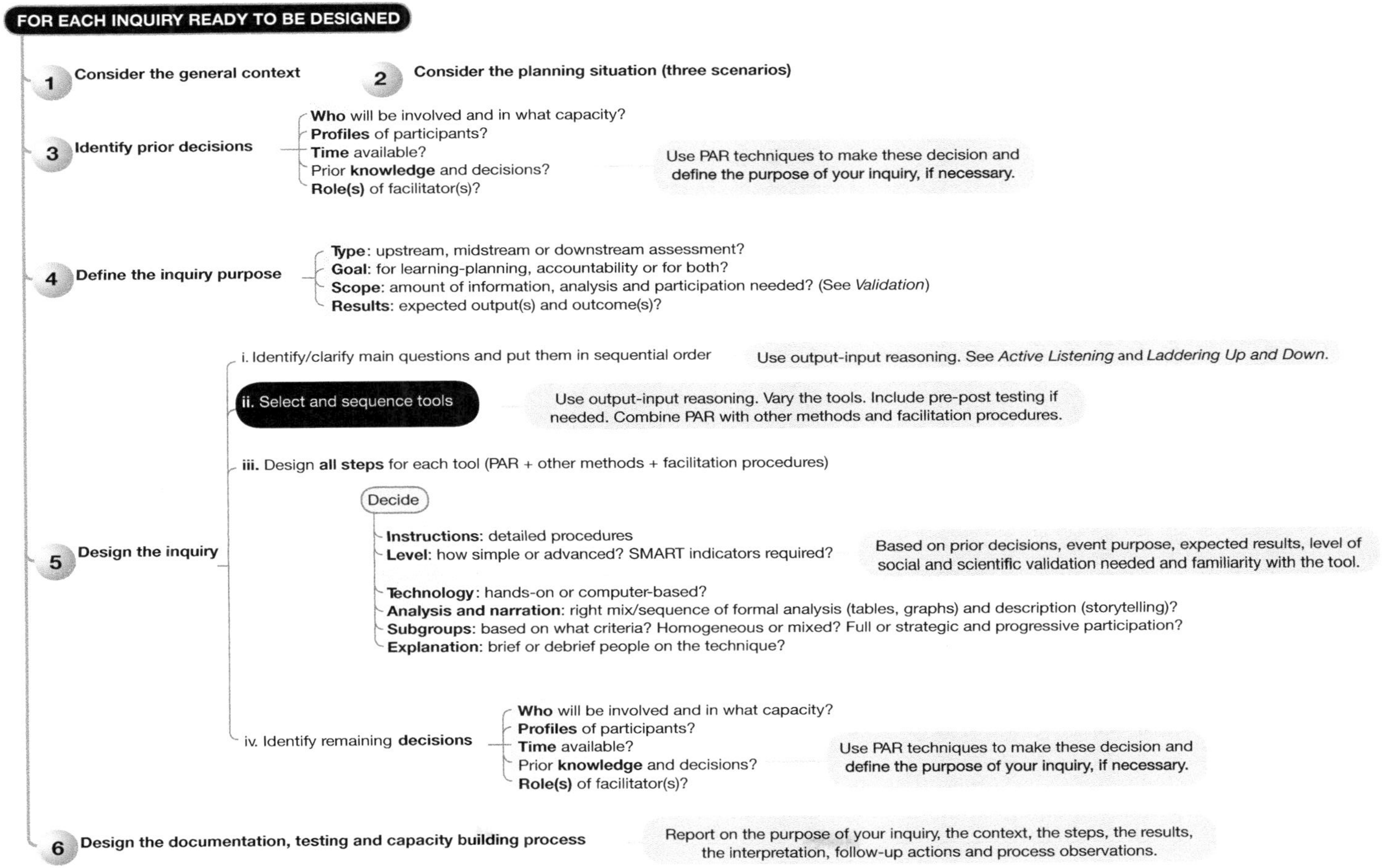

FOR EACH INQUIRY READY TO BE DESIGNED
1 Consider the general context
2 Consider the planning situation (three scenarios)
3 Identify prior decisions
Who will be involved and in what capacity?
Profiles of participants?
Time available?
Prior knowledge and decisions?
Role(s) of facilitator(s)?
Use PAR techniques to make these decision and define the purpose of your inquiry, if necessary.
4 Define the inquiry purpose
Type: upstream, midstream or downstream assessment?
Goal: for learning-planning, accountability or for both?
Scope: amount of information, analysis and participation needed? (See Validation)
Results: expected output(s) and outcome(s)?
5 Design the inquiry
i. Identify/clarify main questions and put them in sequential order
Use output-input reasoning. See Active Listening and Laddering Up and Down.
ii. Select and sequence tools
Use output-input reasoning. Vary the tools. Include pre-post testing if needed. Combine PAR with other methods and facilitation procedures.
iii. Design all steps for each tool (PAR + other methods + facilitation procedures)
Decide
Instructions: detailed procedures
Level: how simple or advanced? SMART indicators required?
Based on prior decisions, event purpose, expected results, level of social and scientific validation needed and familiarity with the tool.
Technology: hands-on or computer-based?
Analysis and narration: right mix/sequence of formal analysis (tables, graphs) and description (storytelling)?
Subgroups: based on what criteria? Homogeneous or mixed? Full or strategic and progressive participation?
Explanation: brief or debrief people on the technique?
iv. Identify remaining decisions
Who will be involved and in what capacity?
Profiles of participants?
Time available?
Prior knowledge and decisions?
Role(s) of facilitator(s)?
Use PAR techniques to make these decision and define the purpose of your inquiry, if necessary.
6 Design the documentation, testing and capacity building process
Report on the purpose of your inquiry, the context, the steps, the results, the interpretation, follow-up actions and process observations.

FIGURE 5.2 *Process Design.*

PARK EXAMPLE

Step 1 Context

The Gatineau Park in Canada's Capital Region receives 2.7 million visits per year. The Park has various means of identifying client needs such as open house sessions for park users, suggestion boxes and logbooks, the Infocentre, the Visitor Centre, e-mails, contacts with park staff, volunteers and tourist guides, and attendance at community meetings. With the emergence of new media (e-mail, blogs, etc.), an increasing number of users are voicing complaints about the park's management methods and services delivered by a private contractor. Responding to complaints draws considerable time and scarce resources away from other park management activities. With the assistance of J. M. Chevalier, the Park team wishes to review its response to service-related complaints and reduce their volume. It also wants to shift its approach from a client service focus to building solid partnerships with park stakeholders.

Step 2 Planning situation

The Park team hopes to address the increasing volume of user complaints by analysing the problem and designing solutions that reflect a good understanding of the situation. Given the many views and interests involved, the process should be **planned progressively**, in close collaboration with key stakeholders, starting with those concerned by recreational services (see Figure 5.3). Once the key problem and objectives are clearly defined, a workshop should be held with team members and the Park contractor to assess the situation, identify priorities and develop a plan of action. The plan should include the creation of a Park Dialogue platform, a process that will involve several steps, to be **planned in due time**. If successful, the same process should be extended to other Park services and stakeholder groups.

Definitions

- **Type**
  Is the assessment an upstream **inquiry** into an existing situation for planning purposes? Is it a midstream **monitoring** exercise to take stock of progress towards results? Is it a downstream **evaluation** of the results and outcomes of actions against goals or against initial observations?

- **Goal**
  Is the intent of the inquiry mainly to **account** for resources and results, to **learn** and adjust plans for ongoing or future actions, and/or to tell the project or programme story and **inspire** others with lessons learned? (See *Monitoring and evaluation*, p. 97.)

- **Scope**
  How much information, analysis and participation are needed to perform the inquiry? (See *Validation*, Chapter 8.)
- **Results**
  What are the expected or desired results (outputs and outcomes) of the inquiry, who is the audience and what are they expected to do with the information and conclusions?

Step 5 Design the inquiry

Identify and clarify the main question(s)

Focus on the question(s) that the inquiry is expected to answer, using terms that are meaningful to the participants. To do this, identify and unpack the different questions that may seem relevant, and clarify each of them. Then identify the questions that are the most important and that reflect the purpose and prior decisions, as defined in Steps 3 and 4. For tips on how to clarify the main question(s), see *Active Listening* (Chapter 8).

PARK EXAMPLE (*continued*)

Step 3 Prior decisions

The analysis of the problem at hand (increasing volume of park user complaints) is to be done with a group of about twelve people, including Park team members, four head office administrators and the Park contractor. The inquiry involves several tasks, including compiling and synthesizing all relevant documents, co-designing and holding a one-day workshop and writing up a final report. Completing these tasks requires about seven days of work, to be done within a five-week period, with the assistance of a university-based consultant (J. M. Chevalier) using a PAR approach to collaborative inquiry and stakeholder engagement.

Step 4 Inquiry purpose

The first workshop activity to be designed involves a short-term, midstream assessment of an existing problem, using available information and the existing knowledge and experience of key stakeholders to evaluate responses already in place and define priorities for planning purposes. Workshop discussions will also revolve around the creation of a multi-stakeholder platform and defining its mandate, composition and functioning (see Figure 5.3).

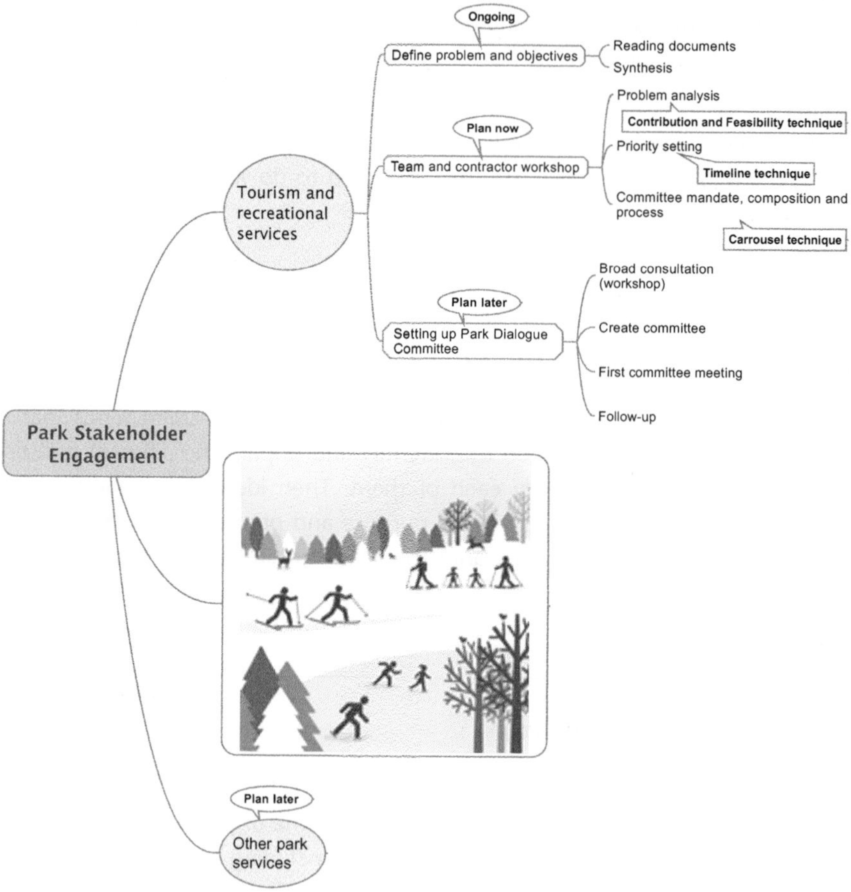

FIGURE 5.3 Park Dialogue process map.

JUST DO IT

Include in the inquiry plans familiar and well-established ways of doing things that reflect **local culture, procedures** and **customs**. Judge when the established ways to gather and analyse information, create priorities, resolve problems, take action and interact with others in the process are working well enough, and just do it! Introducing new tools or methods is never an end in and of itself, unless capacity-building for future assessments is a key goal of the inquiry. Overdoing the use of PAR methods, when local methods will do, is an insidious form of 'tyranny' in the name of participation (Cooke and Kothari, 2001).

Organize the main questions in sequence

Organize the main questions in sequence using output–input reasoning (where the answer to one question serves as the input to the question that follows).

Select and sequence tools

Select and sequence tools in this book and from other sources needed to answer the main questions of the inquiry. (Consult the list of tools in each module.)

Choose the **combination of tools and facilitation procedures** that suit the inquiry needs and the culture of the people involved.

Design all steps

Define and adjust all the **steps** and **procedures** to be used in each tool. Choose the right level of depth and the kind of technology needed in the situation and adjust the relative weight of quantitative data gathering, formal analysis, description, narration and storytelling. Decide how explicit and detailed the instructions should be and how participants can effectively engage in the process. This is a process of **scaling** to fit the purpose and time available (see *Skills in means* in Chapter 6).

Identify remaining decisions

Identify the remaining decisions using the planning questions listed in Step 3. Make sure that the decisions are compatible with the purpose of the inquiry and all other decisions taken when designing it.

Step 6 Plan the documentation, testing and capacity-building process

Decide how extensively to report on the group discussions, and determine the exact purpose or use to be made of the documentation. Define the activities needed to document the results during and after the inquiry and assign the related responsibilities.

Consider documenting the following elements:

- the **context** or situation in need of attention;
- the **purpose** of the inquiry;
- a **summary** of the process;
- a descriptive **analysis** of the results;
- an **interpretation** of the findings;
- **follow-up actions** identified by the participants;
- **observations** regarding what went well or difficulties met during the process.

Determine the need for prior testing and capacity-building activities to support the inquiry process, and make the corresponding plans. Far from being linear, the design process often requires going back and forth between steps in an iterative fashion, until a satisfactory understanding and plan is created.

PARK EXAMPLE (*continued*)

Step 5 Inquiry design

The initial inquiry will focus on three sets of questions. The first, to be addressed in the morning of a one-day workshop, concerns actions already in place to manage park users' complaints, what remains to be done to implement them fully, how feasible this is, the amount of time dedicated to each action and their projected effectiveness if fully implemented.

The technique used to address these questions is *Contribution and Feasibility* (Chapter 15). To save time, the list of actions in place will be prepared by the consultant and the team director and supplied at the beginning of the exercise; no particular technique is needed to complete this task. Workshop participants will be invited to divide themselves into small groups, evaluate two actions each using the tool, present their assessments in a plenary discussion and validate their views with other groups. The exercise will end with an invitation to prioritize some actions based on the compilation of results from the *Contribution and Feasibility* assessments.

In the afternoon, the group will be invited to organize its priority actions in sequential order, using the *Timeline* technique (in Chapter 9). This one-hour discussion may involve revising some of the decisions taken in the previous step regarding what actions should be prioritized.

The last exercise will focus on a new strategy that the Park management wishes to introduce as part of its approach to public relations: setting up a multi-stakeholder Park Dialogue roundtable. Two techniques, *The Carrousel* (in *Ideal Scenario*, Chapter 14) and *Free List and Pile Sort* (in Chapter 8), will be used to address three questions: the mandate, the composition and the functioning of the roundtable. Participants will form small groups, formulate a roundtable mandate, make a list of stakeholders (on cards) that should be part of it, and propose key rules on how the roundtable should function. To inform the discussion, the consultant will provide one or two examples of public advisory committees implemented in other parks. When ready, each group will present its suggestions to the whole group. Participants will be invited to identify similarities and differences between the views expressed (piling up similar stakeholder cards and identifying key words and ideas proposed by different groups), and progressively identify suggestions that meet their expectations and could be adopted as recommendations to the Park.

PARK EXAMPLE (*continued*)

Step 6 Documentation, testing and capacity-building

The *Contribution and Feasibility* technique (Chapter 15) should be tested first with the Park director, to make sure that the key questions are well grounded and meaningful. No capacity-building activity is needed before the event as the consultant will be facilitating. Notes prepared for the workshop and taken during the event will be used to write up a short report after the event. The consultant will ask workshop participants for permission to publish the results and share the experience with other audiences.

MONITORING AND EVALUATION

When research is combined with transformative action, monitoring and evaluation (M&E) matter. The results of action-research can and should be assessed against goals and inform ongoing learning and planning in context. Still, M&E is not research proper, at least not in the sense of an investigation towards the 'advancement of knowledge'. M&E information gathering and analysis focusses rather on answering questions such as 'What are the results of this programme or project thus far?', or 'What are the implications of the evaluation findings?' (For more on the difference between evaluation and research, see *Planning, Inquiry, Evaluation* in Chapter 3.)

Almost every major government and development agency has its own management system that staff and partners must use to plan and report. Results-based management (RBM) is one of the most widely known, with concepts and techniques to plan actions, assess progress along the way and at the end of a project cycle. The approach is prompted by two legitimate expectations: on the one hand, honest and useful learning and improvements in ongoing work, and, on the other hand, accounting for resources and results to both funders and intended beneficiaries (United Nations, 2010). While RBM has something to contribute in relatively simple and orderly situations (see *Order and Chaos*, in Chapter 3), in our view no all-purpose framework can address all possible situations where M&E is needed. The goals and activities people want to monitor and evaluate are as varied as the projects and programmes they are involved in. So too are the baseline conditions against which the activities are assessed. The implication of this diversity is that there can be no fixed M&E framework or methodology, **only M&E questions**. Consequently, any tool or technique, whether it's a soil test or stories about struggles to end poverty or prevent violence, can be used to effectively inquire into relationships between planned action and observed results, provided it is the right tool to answer the right question, at the right time, at the right level of detail and with the right people. Practically all of the inquiry tools described or cited in this book can serve to address M&E questions, through pre- and post-assessments (baselines and measures of results). For instance, parties to a conflict management process may monitor progress towards results by applying *Social Analysis CLIP* at one point in time, before new plans are made and implemented, and then later, to see what has changed and why (see the Katkari example in Chapter 12).

Every M&E process must be designed and tools selected to fit the purpose and situation under investigation (see *Canada World Youth*, in Chapter 7, and *Uniterra and HIV/AIDS prevention and treatment in Burkina Faso*, in Chapter 16). This may require that evaluators scale tools up or down to meet specific user needs and constraints (scarce time, financial and human resources). Methodological pluralism and creativity is also needed to go beyond current tendencies to emphasise upward accounting for resources and results, and to draw on a narrow range of methods (field observations, surveys, descriptive statistics, interviews, focus groups and storytelling). In some situations inquiries into results must be designed to create ongoing feedback and action-reaction loops (as in medical practice) to acknowledge learning from failure and support planning. In others they may need to accommodate the use of findings to inspire others with lessons learned (see *Rethinking evaluation methods in organizations*, in Chapter 3). There is scope for many more methods to be used in M&E, especially those that factor in the effects of uncertainty and **complexity**, as opposed to assuming linear chains of causation and overly schematic theories of change typical of RBM (Buckles and Chevalier, 2012).

The need to address complexity, longer-term results and system-wide effects is of increasing importance to governments and Civil Society Organizations (CSOs) working at national and international levels. The challenge, however, is to assess the extent to which changes in a situation can be attributed to a particular intervention, apart from other factors and actors (Cohen and Easterly, 2009).

M&E theorists and practitioners have different views on how they can infer or demonstrate cause-effect relationships to assess project or programme results in complex settings (Stern *et al.*, 2012). Thinking about this issue has resulted in what has been characterized by some as 'the causal wars' of impact evaluation, much of which revolves around the perennial debate between quantitative and qualitative approaches (Scriven 2008; White, 2006). The acrimony in the debate can be traced to the popularity in policy circles of the experimental approach to evaluating impacts in the field of international development. The approach is most fully developed by Banerjee and Duflo (2011). Duflo's work in this area won her the John Bates Clark Medal, the most prestigious award for economists after the Nobel in economic science. It also attracted the attention of The World Bank and many quantitatively oriented economists and policymakers, quickly becoming the 'gold standard' for mainstream impact evaluation. As a result the experimental approach starved funding and attention to other equally valid methodological approaches to programme evaluation and causation research. Critics (Scriven, 2008) argue that the level of attention and exclusionary tendencies of this approach to evaluation is not merited by the facts or its 'special features'.

Characteristically, the experimental approach uses some (but not all) of the rules for randomized control trials (RCT) common in the medical field to create a **counterfactual scenario** — a description of how things would have turned out differently to the way they actually did. The method requires that part of the target group (a 'control group') be isolated from the effects of the intervention or 'variable of interest' (Banerjee and Duflo, 2011; White, 2006). Randomization gives all individuals an equal chance of being in one group or the other. Surveys are then used to collect information on observed changes. This makes it possible, at least in theory, to see the difference between what happened with the programme, project or activity, and what would have happened without it, for the same target group.

Critics question both the practicality and ethics of control groups in real-world settings (Scriven, 2008; Stern *et al.*, 2012). In a complex world, effects are context specific, with no guarantee they will occur in the same way in another future setting or for a neighbouring community or population. This is so true that many fields of intervention (e.g. improving rural livelihoods) lack clear and internationally recognized indicators of project performance or other standards against which they can be assessed (Catley *et al.*, 2009). Moreover reliance on large-scale surveys and sophisticated statistical analysis creates important gaps between the experimental approach and the resources of many organizations. It is in part for these reasons that the vast majority of studies conducted using this approach are commissioned by large donor agencies and led by university-based academics. While CSOs often invest a lot of time and resources undertaking surveys of various kinds, they rarely have opportunities or reasons to work with control groups.

In addition to these flaws, the experimental framework ignores many debates in causal theory, including alternative approaches to counterfactual thinking, a form of evidence-based reasoning that can be found in other fields and professions, such as legal practice (see Chapter 16). In the process of formulating legal judgments regarding responsibility, judges and juries must reflect on the extent to which the harm observed is justly attributed to the actions of the accused. They go through this fact-finding and reasoning process rigorously, by bringing together evidence and logic to understand how events unfolded and how things would have turned out *had it not been for the human actions under examination.* Conclusions regarding causation 'beyond reasonable doubt' are reached without relying on random control trials. Similarly, stakeholders in a project or programme can assess the extent to which the observed changes would have occurred had the intervention not taken place, keeping in mind the details of the intervention and well-developed evidence regarding tangible outcomes.

The M&E principles we have just outlined, those of meaningful grounding in use, methodolological pluralism, flexible design and coping with complexity, provide direct inspiration to the many tools, the 'skilful means' and the overall approach to process mapping and design outlined and illustrated in some detail in this book. They also inform the tools we offer for M&E proper, including *Planning, Inquiry, Evaluation (PIE)*, Chapter 3; *The Socratic Wheel* and *Weighting*, Chapter 7; *Validation*, Chapter 8; *Contribution and Feasibility* and *What If*, Chapter 15; and *Attribution and Contribution*, Chapter 16. As already pointed out, however, all inquiry tools can help monitor and assess project or programme results, provided they apply to the situation at hand.

A final point about M&E that we stress in this book concerns the principle of **interactive** engagement and **mutual** learning that informs much of PAR thinking. This is a principle often ignored in self-evaluations (isolated from factual challenges by others) as well as in evaluations by proxy (assessing one's work by reporting on the results of one's partners) or carried out by third party experts (using survey, interview and narrative data). Applying this principle, however, poses many challenges. It requires, among other things, that we bring together and bridge the processes of fact-finding, analysis, interpretation and decision-making and invite parties to contribute relevant expertise and views on observed results. Most mainstream M&E, and many 'participatory' inquiries for that matter, keep these processes clearly separate, and reduce frontline staff, partners or actors to providers of raw data in the fact-finding phase of the evaluation. Another challenge lies in acknowledging and tapping into day-to-day tracking (e.g. informal exchanges) and non-literate forms of planning and learning that reflect differences in language and modes of communication. These are key to people engaging in the evaluation of ongoing activities and the longer-term and broader outcomes of efforts to bring about meaningful change in complex settings.

THREADS OF THEORY: IN THE MIDDLENESS

Unlike Hollywood characters, humans are thrown into an evolving world with no absolute beginning or ending. They must ground thinking, planning and acting in the middle of ongoing events and sensible things that are both the medium and the scene of living knowledge and meaning.

Engaged research is skilful thinking and acting always in the middle of ongoing events. It applies 'middle-m' methods (neither pure theory nor mere technique) to foster understanding and help shape our social milieu and natural surroundings in the context of an evolving story. The heuristic action that follows an inquiry has no absolute beginning or ending, no definitive source or final destination. Even when ends are met, they become means at best, to be kept in motion, with a sense of purpose, and a readiness to be found unready for hazardous findings and random events to come.

Grounded thinking calls for a perpetual involvement of means and ends. The more we meddle with this simple rule, by gearing every thought and action to first causes and final ends, the less mindful we are and the more muddled everything gets.

Commentary

The impact of science and industry in world history is undeniable. Its scope is such that many investigators do not hesitate to emulate the linear, neatly planned logic of science and engineering, even when dealing with messy problems such as poverty, armed conflict or economic crises on a global scale. When adopting this plan-and-implement model, the investigation usually starts with a solid framework that contains well-defined questions and methods to answer them, together with a survey of relevant documents and the broader literature that sheds light on the issues at hand. This is the design phase. The implementation phase involves the gathering of data, which may require field research and experimentation, followed by analysis and interpretation, towards possible recommendations for action, depending on the nature of the investigation.

At the end of the process, all findings and conclusions are written up, by applying existing standards of communication in writing. The dissemination phase comes last, using the appropriate medium to share findings and conclusions with a broader public, in the hope that good things will ensue. If recommendations are heard, action-oriented projects may follow, guided by the same linear logic. In short, key questions set the inquiry process in motion and clear answers bring it to an end. Actions that may follow are pinned down through proper planning and executed and delivered through efficient deeds.

The linear approach to knowledge making (and actions that follow, if any) is based on an idealized story of science and engineering developed over the last two centuries. The edges of truth obtained in this scientific mode are sharply defined, using straight lines rather than clouds and shades of light and dark. When reunited, the straight lines of knowledge point to three age-old spirits: *genea*, *telos* and *anagoge* (Chevalier, 1997). Each spirit speaks to a different aspect of linear thinking.

The first spirit invites a genealogical account of the path of inquiry where all steps have clear origins and beginnings. Each step of the process is part of a series of actions that can be traced back to root questions, original intents, formative concepts and initial circumstances. Inaugural ideas and plans are the prime movers. *Genea* provides the ancestry of the inquiry process understood as a linear narrative – a story that tells us where results come from 'in the first place' and the efficient steps and actions that followed suit.

Telos retains a linear plot but heads in the opposite direction, towards the future. It harnesses research and action to the forward movement of design and purpose, hence final ends or causes and related promises of things and findings to come. Prediction is the prime mover of *telos*, which takes many forms other than science, such as divination, astrology and prophecy. Science is a particular expression of *telos*, a disposition to predict that pays close attention to the efficient connections and step-wise procedures of *genea*. Things predicted must leave trails of prior hypotheses and step-by-step reasoning to support them.

The last spirit, *anagoge*, is the line itself – the notion that a single abstract dimension can bridge and fix the distance between first causes and final ends. This is the disposition to create a ruling order, by establishing inquiry on stable foundations and firm grounds. Anagogy is usually known as an allegorical interpretation of biblical symbolism that conveys meanings of eternal life in heaven. The Morning Star in John's *Book of Revelation* symbolizes God's light shining in the New Jerusalem (as opposed to the reign of the Antichrist contending for the same title), for instance. Allegorical thinking harks back to Platonic philosophy where pure ideas serve to elevate the true and the authentic above false claimants vying for an abstract essence, say the idea of Courage or Wisdom. Each Platonic essence or pure type is therefore understood 'idealistically'. In Aristotelian thinking, difference obtained by analogy divides a genus into opposing species through contrary predicates (as in 'man' versus 'animal'). Platonic difference reflects instead the distance between reality and ideality, to be measured against the rule of the golden mean, which is the desirable middle between extremes (e.g. while a deficiency in courage is cowardice, its excess amounts to recklessness) (Guattari, 1995, p. 72; Deleuze and

Guattari, 1987, pp. 27, 52; Deleuze, 1994, pp. 37, 59, 62, 67, 69, 265, 272). The result is a slanted construction of difference founded on morals and virtuous thinking.

Anagoge is not a Platonic invention. Signs of anagogical desirability can be found in everyday language, elevating expressions of higher order above ideas of lesser things. By way of example, the 'cycle of life' subsumes the opposition between life and death, placing the standard of life above the recurrence of death. The 'higher class' notion of 'man' denoting the unity of man and woman is another telling example of 'ideality' and 'pure type' mapped into the politics of language. Just as the wishful 'cycle of life' elevates itself above the opposition of life and death, so 'man' is summoned to rise above the divisions of gender in God's moral creation.

In the social sciences, investigation inspired by the politics of 'pure types' and 'classes in logic' is common practice. Concrete events and phenomena that are discrete and diffuse are explained as derivations, sequels or manifestations of ideal types – Capitalism, the Protestant Ethics, Fascism, Archetypes, the Unconscious or the Oedipus complex, to name just a few pillars of grand theory. These references to higher-order explanations are rife with moral intent. While Max Weber thinks 'ideal types' can be morally neutral, we beg to differ. The extent to which a real-life process resembles or manifests a 'standard model' is a question commonly asked with prescriptive intent, consciously or not.

The rule applies to positive science itself, an 'ideal type' guided by its own morality, a framing of knowledge designed to elevate the value of neutrality above all other competing values. It seeks lines of reasoning and explanation that transcend all differences in notions of rightness and goodness. Social sciences that follow the ideal-typical canons of positive science ignore the unique stories and lessons they have to tell. They move instead from alpha to omega, from opening questions to final answers, under the guidance of strict methods and predictive theory, in search of straightforward explanations that can be generalized across time and space. Positivism elevates sameness above difference, sedentary explanation above nomadic exploration. Actions 'engineered' to achieve precise outcomes abide by the same linear narrative. They bring about predictable results and social change according to plans, through clear roadmaps and efficient interventions.

Practical wisdom dictates that a sound inquiry should proceed rationally, with a sense of planning and orientation in time, using the measurements of *genea*, *telos* and *anagoge*. Still, linear pathways to questions asked and answered tell only one side of the story. The other side features an explorative journey that proceeds and evolves in the middle of complex events and messy situations. This is the narrative path of *mésos*, a term denoting anything that is 'in the midst' of everything else. The spirit of *mésos* evokes the middle way of Buddhist wisdom. It is also the medium and the middleness of time, as conceived by Augustine. What the Church Father says about the nature of time can also be said of knowing.

To begin with, common sense suggests that there are three moments in the inquiry process: steps that are part of the past, those happening in the present and those planned in the future tense. This is straightforward linearity and chronology, essential to planning and mapping the journey. Augustine is not fully convinced, however, by this timeline.

He proposes a deeper understanding of differences in time. In his words, 'there are three times; a present of things past, a present of things present, and a present of things future.' The Church Father adds that all three times of the present 'exist in the soul'. The 'present of things past' belongs to memory. The 'present of things present' pertains to sight. And the 'present of things future' is the object of expectation (Augustine, 1955, XX 26).

Inquiry that consciously engages with history is not a series of presences of the mind to its immediate surroundings. Rather it is a meshing of three dispositions. The first disposition is a sustained attention of the mind to the presence of things under consideration. The second consists of memories of past inquiry that are still alive. The third involves ongoing expectations of things to be considered and investigated in due time. This threefold ability to 'consider, remember and expect', and all at once, is at the heart of an inquisitive soul that is truly alive, in constant motion, 'distended' in time (Augustine, 1955, XXVIII 37–38). To paraphrase Ricoeur, authentic inquiry is the wisdom of *distentio*, or the Augustinian 'dialectic of expectation, memory, and attention, each considered no longer in isolation but in interaction with one another'. Engagements of the mind consist 'in the active "transit" of what was future in the direction of what becomes past.' It is this combined action of expectation, memory and attention that drives the inquiry process, stretching it in three different directions all at once (Ricoeur, 1984, pp. 3, 14–15, 30).

The *distentio* effect is reminiscent of Barthes's action code. This is the code involving the ordering of scenes, sequences and stages of actions and events situated in narrative time. To this 'action catalogue' Barthes adds the hermeneutic code governing the narrative enigma. Problems raised and solved by an investigative story revolve around the formulation of a question, the promise of a response, admissions of defeat and replies that may be ambiguous or partial, delayed or misleading. Real-life inquiry is the unfolding of a mystery, not the fulfilment of chronology (Barthes, 1970, pp. 26, 91–92, 215).

Given its narrative wanderings, inquiry points to 'what a conversation is – simply the outline of a becoming' (Deleuze and Parnet, 1987, p. 2). By this Deleuze (1994, p. 76) and Guattari (1995, p. 59) mean a world of differences ruled by chance and multiplicity, a 'chaosmos' governed by the eternal return of dissemblance and disparateness, the repetition of that which keeps differing. This is the middle ground of thinking, a groundless milieu constantly evolving, without metaphysical foundations (Derrida, 1973, pp. 51–52; 1981, pp. 17–18, 32).

The *distentio* principle ensures continuity and fluidity in the movement of inquiry. But it also has the opposite effect, which is to create dissonance in things that are considered, expected and remembered. The dissonance generates tension with findings that may be unforeseen, may fail to happen or that come to pass only to be ignored or forgotten (Ricoeur, 1984, pp. 20–21). As in real life, disputes (e.g. the causes of climate change) can arise midway in the investigative process, which really means at all times. Contentious issues are inevitable and point to the politics of active inconsideration, oblivion and short-sightedness in the making of knowledge. Inconsideration is expressed through the imposition of an inflexible framework that protects received or proposed wisdom against criticism and fickle thinking (giving in to the infinity of viewpoints on reality). Oblivion is selective memory, or the tendency to sift the facts and the evidence at hand according to what they can do for the proposed perspective or theory, the one that commands attention. Short-sightedness is a slanted look at obvious things that are worth keeping an eye on, hoping they are enough to speak to the ongoing investigation and the story that must be heard. All of these positions introduce tension in the narrative present — shifts of attention and speculative thinking in the inquiry process. In the end, every research has a story of arbitrary, risky and fearful thoughts to tell.

REFERENCES

Augustine, S. (Bishop of Hippo) (1955) *The Confessions of Augustine*, trans. Albert C. Outler, www.ccel.org/a/augustine/confessions/confessions_enchiridion.txt, accessed 12 January, 2012.

Barnejee, A. and Duflo, E. (2011) *Poor Economics: A Radical Thinking of the Way to Fight Global Poverty*, Public Affairs Book, Philadelphia.

Barthes, R. (1970) *S/Z*, Seuil, Paris.

Buckles, D. J. and Chevalier, J. M. (2012) 'Assessing the Impact of International Volunteer Co-operation: Guiding Questions and Canadian Experiences', IVCO 2012 http://cusointernational.org/IVCO2012/research, accessed December 15, 2012.

Catley, A., Burns, J., Abebe, D. and Suji, O. (2009) *Participatory Impact Assessment: A Guide for Practitioners*, Feinstein International Centre, Tufts University, Medford.

Chevalier, J. M. (1997) *A Postmodern Revelation: Signs of Astrology and the Apocalypse*, University of Toronto Press and Vervuert, Toronto and Frankfurt.

Cohen, J. (1989) 'Deliberative Democracy and Democratic Legitimacy', in A. P. Hamlin and P. N. Pettit (eds) *The Good Polity: Normative Analysis of the State*, Blackwell, Oxford, pp. 17–34.

Cooke, B. and Kothari, U. (eds) (2001) *Participation: The New Tyranny?* Zed, London.

Deleuze, G. (1994) *Difference and Repetition*, trans. Paul Patton, Columbia University Press, New York.

Deleuze, G. and Guattari, F. (1987) *Mille Plateaux*, trans. and Foreword by Brian Massumi, University of Minnesota Press, Minneapolis, MN.

Deleuze, G. and Parnet, C. (1987) *Dialogues*, trans. Hugh Tomlinson and Barbara Habberjam, Columbia University Press, New York.

Derrida, J. (1973) *Speech and Phenomenon, and Other Essays on Husserl's Theory of Signs*, trans. David B. Allison, Preface by Newton Garver, Northwestern University Press, Evanston, IL.

Derrida, J. (1981) *Positions*, trans. and annotated by Alan Bass, University of Chicago Press, Chicago, IL.

Guattari, F. (1995) *Chaosmosis: An Ethico-aesthetic Paradigm*, trans. Paul Bains and Julian Pefanis, Indiana University Press, Bloomington and Indianapolis.

Ricoeur, P. (1984) *Time and Narrative*, vol. 1, trans. Kathleen McLaughlin and David Pellauer, University of Chicago Press, Chicago and London.

Scriven, M. (2008) 'A Summative Evaluation of RCT Methodology: An Alternative Approach to Causal Research', *Journal of MultiDisciplinary Evaluation*, vol. 5, no. 9, pp. 11–24.

Stern, E., Stame, N., Mayne, J., Forss, K., Davies, R. and Befani, B. (2012) 'Broadening the range of designs and methods for impact evaluations', Working paper no. 38, Department of International Development (DIFID).

United Nations (2010) *Results-Based Management Handbook: Strengthening RBM Harmonization for Improved Development Results*, United Development Group, New York.

Watson, C. (2008) *Literature Review of Impact Measurement in the Humanitarian Sector*, Feinstein International Center, Medford.

White, H. (2006) 'Impact evaluation: the experience of the Independent Evaluation Group of The World Bank', Independent Evaluation Group, Washington, DC.

CHAPTER 6

Walking the talk

INTRODUCTION

When inquiry involves human subjects, higher learning institutions expect their students to develop standardized skills. Dedicated courses help students learn the rudiments of conventional inquiry, which consists of gathering and analysing data based on observation (participant or not), experimentation, surveys, interviews and focus groups. Other courses address bodies of literature in various fields, with an emphasis on key concepts and abstract theory. Programmes proceed from introductory courses to advanced studies, a logical pathway that seems as normal as breathing. In most cases, effective student learning is measured through essay writing, open-question exams and multiple-choice testing. If per chance students move on to graduate studies or jobs that require them to undertake 'real' research, they are most likely to use the mainstream methods already outlined in their undergraduate textbooks.

The concepts and tools presented in this book propose a different perspective on the 'logic of inquiry'. They emphasize research grounded in action and dialogue with the parties involved, towards the integration of action, research and training as well as planning, inquiry and evaluation (see *ART* and *PIE*, Chapter 3). The skill sets required to achieve this extend well beyond the routinized teachings of mainstream post-secondary education. They include the ability to deal with situations that are complex and chaotic (see *Order and Chaos*, Chapter 4). Equally critical is knowing how to design processes that are rigorous but also flexible and collaborative (see *Process Mapping* and *Process Design*, Chapter 5). Engaged research is bringing people together to skilfully inquire into messy situations and act on them, as opposed to treating people and society as problems to be investigated and re-engineered from above.

Skills to investigate and act on complex situations cannot be acquired in a linear manner, from introductory to advanced studies, from the learning of simpler things to studying things that are progressively more complicated. Rather complexity must be embraced from the start, with a progressive application of the many skills needed to inquire and intervene in situations otherwise unexplained and intractable.

This chapter explores core skills that enable learners to develop the art of engaged inquiry. It offers guidelines on ways to put these skills into effective practice, towards inquiry processes that are designed to fit the situation. The chapter ends with a theoretical commentary on the twofold disposition of skilful inquiry – carefulness and caring as the roots of reason and concern for the common good.

SKILLS IN MEANS

Following is an outline of the five skills that come together when designing and facilitating a collaborative inquiry (see Figure 6.1).

1 **Mediating**
Engage people and mobilize knowledge from different perspectives by facilitating dialogue across social boundaries, cultural settings and modes of learning.
2 **Grounding**
Build inquiry and learning on felt needs and ongoing processes, towards meaningful actions and decisions appropriate to people's goals and available resources.
3 **Navigating**
Select and combine the forms of inquiry, planning and participation that help people deal with complexity (the uncertain, the unknown) in a timely fashion.
4 **Scaling**
Adjust inquiry methods and actions to fit the depth of evidence, planning and participation needed to achieve meaningful results.
5 **Sensemaking**
Co-create meaning in complex situations by integrating information, analysis (quantitative, qualitative) and theoretical insights into stories and explanations that inspire and persuade.

> Use *The Socratic Wheel* (Chapter 7) to assess individual or group abilities to mediate, ground, navigate, scale and co-create meaning through collaborative inquiry and to set learning objectives.

Combining and applying these core skills to the engaged inquiry process requires much practice and the constant exercise of judgment. It involves learning to make many decisions on how to facilitate group thinking and dialogue – small and major decisions that will make a difference for the people involved and success or failure in achieving goals. Since the devil is in the details, we offer guidelines on key choices that must be made when exercising these skills in real settings.

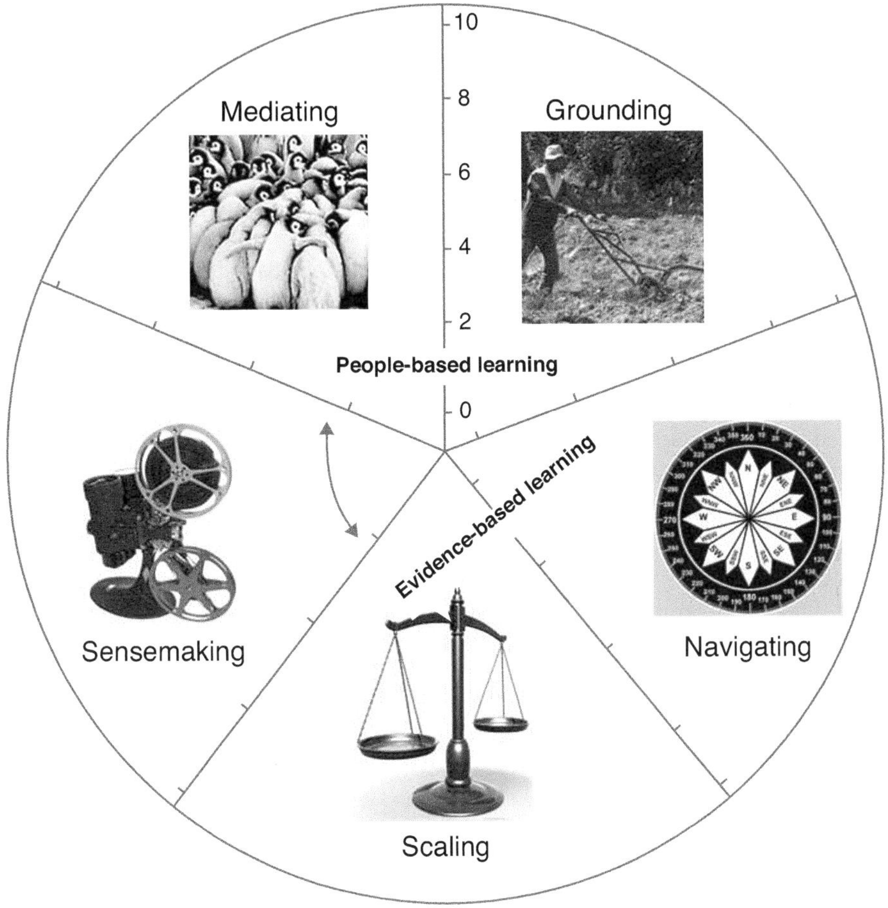

FIGURE 6.1 Skills in means.

When mediating

Consider local language and forms of inquiry, learning, planning and interaction (see Just do it, in Chapter 5)

- Explore ways to accommodate differences in language, meaning and symbolism. Build on local forms of inquiry, learning, planning and interaction that are well established and work well in either literate or non-literate contexts.

Build on group and individual differences

- Determine whether participants should first address key questions individually, in groups or both (e.g. start with an individual rating exercise and then form subgroups that share similar views and prepare recommendations for plenary discussion).

- Decide whether subgroups should include a mix of people with different characteristics (heterogeneous groups) or participants that share a particular set of characteristics (homogeneous groups). Mixed groups are preferable if the exercise is intended to draw out views representative of the entire group. Each subgroup can be assigned the same or a different task, depending on whether all participants need to be involved in all parts of the inquiry.
- When forming groups pay special attention to differences in views and knowledge that may affect how people assess the same issues. Subgroups based on age, gender, marital status, ethnic origin, religion, education, their place of residence, the amount of time they have lived in a certain place, their occupation, or their role in an organization or project may be important in some contexts.
- If participants disagree about some issues, clarify the differences and discuss how important they are to the purpose of the inquiry.
- When differences arise regarding numbers and measurements, facilitate discussion of the reasons for particular ratings and go with the majority view rather than an average. One way to facilitate and mediate differences in ratings is to make them visual: place numbers on the floor for each point on the scale and invite participants to stand next to the number they think is correct for a particular criterion. Agreement and differences on ratings will be easy to see. The group can then focus on major differences only, the reasoning of participants, and adjustments needed to obtain a single rating (using a majority view rather than an average).

Facilitate multi-site and interactive engagement

- If the chain of actions and partners has multiple sites and organizational layers (local, national and international, for instance), determine key inquiry questions that are specific to each site or layer, those that concern the broader interaction of sites and layers, and those that apply to all sites and layers and can be rolled up at the programme level.
- Establish how mutual accounting and learning between partners can help answer key inquiry questions and address the concerns and contributions of each partner and what is attributable to their collaborative work (see *Attribution and Contribution*, Chapter 16).
- Define the responsibilities of each partner in the inquiry process. Design the inquiry to include measures of interactive engagement, conversations that may be combined with self-evaluation and third party assistance, when appropriate. Interactive engagement presupposes the use of tools other than self-reflective stories or data extracted through surveys, interviews or focus groups conceived and led by outside experts.

Define the role of facilitators and third parties

- Normally, facilitators help create safe space for people to express their views and reach collective decisions. They can state their own opinions on the issues being

raised if they have permission from the group to do so or if they are stakeholders or members of the group doing the exercise.
- A third party may be needed in a context where there is considerable tension or mistrust, parties take rigid positions, participants do not express themselves freely, or clear rules of order are needed.

When grounding

Create a safe and inviting environment

- Safety is key to learning. It is based on trust in the convening body, the relevance of the inquiry topic, the questions guiding the inquiry and the skills of the facilitating team. It also requires a physical environment that is both comfortable and enabling. Whenever possible, use an open space large enough to accommodate about three times the number of participants, with moveable chairs and tables for small group work. Natural light will improve people's comfort as will periodic breaks and an absence of clutter.

Encourage creative expression

- Use humour, games, physical movement, floor democracy and other forms of creative expression (drawing, mime, sculpting, stories) to build awareness, energize the group and connect to emotions. This will help facilitate teamwork, release tension and ground learning in real-life settings.

When navigating

Identify the point of entry

- What is the ideal point of entry into a collaborative inquiry process – analysing the problem(s), knowing who the stakeholders are and how they interact, or assessing the options for immediate action? The question is rhetorical because the answer is a judgment call regarding what is the right thing to do at a particular time in a specific context. Choose an entry point in light of the main question(s) to be answered as well as the context, the purpose and the decisions made prior to the inquiry. Focus on what is more pressing or relevant and leave the other issues in the background until people are ready to explore them in detail. In complex and dynamic situations, going back and forth between a focus on problems (Module 3), actors (Module 4) and options (Module 5) is inevitable.

Describe characteristics or assess interactions

- The distinction between 'domain characterization' and 'dynamic interaction' is useful when selecting a tool for a particular inquiry. The *Domain Analysis* tools presented in Chapter 18 are social adaptations of Personal Construct Psychology designed to describe or characterize how people see a particular domain or topic. They help assess the levels of similarity among elements of a domain, leading to an understanding of clusters and broader categories of elements in the domain. By contrast, *System Dynamics* tools (in Chapter 17) build on the logic of input–output analysis used in economics. They focus on the interaction between elements in a system, leading to an understanding of system boundaries and levels of integration.

Be flexible

- Plans often change along the way. A tool may need to be adjusted or replaced with a different one on the fly. A clear understanding of where the group wants to go with an inquiry will help manage the transition.
- To avoid fatigue, vary the tools and the kinds of tables or diagrams designed to support collaborative thinking.

Choose the right technology and facilitation techniques

- Determine what facilitation techniques and technology should be used and how to gather and analyse information with the support of user-friendly and visual, kinaesthetic tools (people moving in space) that help see and discuss patterns emerging from the findings.
- Make a list of the supplies and equipment needed for each inquiry, such as cards, post-its, masking tape, scissors, low-odour markers of different colours, sculpting wax, drawing paper, flip charts and stands for all groups, a laptop computer and video projector, etc.
- Decide whether to use software, flip chart, note-taking or 'floor democracy' to facilitate data collection and analysis. *Social Analysis CLIP* and *Domain Analysis* are currently supported by specialized software (see www.participatoryactionresearch.net). Data from many other tools can be displayed graphically using commonly available software such as Excel.

When scaling

Manage time

- Plan enough time to go through all the steps of an inquiry tool (about two to four hours per tool, on average), with breaks during the process as needed. The group may decide at any time to stop the exercise, find more information about the questions being raised and complete the exercise later.
- To save time, divide the group into smaller groups, and then ask each one to complete one part of the assessment (e.g. each group can assess a different option or use a different criterion to rate the same set of options).

Adjust the level of participation

- Plan realistic ways to help people participate in an inquiry process. This includes determining whether all the key actors should be present or not. In some cases it may be better to work only with stakeholders that are keen to cooperate. In other cases stakeholders may prefer to adopt a 'shuttle' approach: that is, a third party facilitates a multi-stakeholder inquiry by engaging with individuals or small groups separately and then presenting the results at a general meeting where all the parties are together.

Aim for the right level of application

The steps involved in each inquiry and the number of tools used can be reduced or expanded. Decide how simple or advanced the application of a tool or process needs to be, considering the following factors:

- How much time and resources are available to dedicate to a particular inquiry.
- How complex the issues are. Summary indicators that are SMART – specific, measurable, applicable, realistic and timely – may provide sufficient understanding

PHOTO 6.1 Clockwise: a pot used in India as a symbol of worms in a child's belly; dividing into smaller groups at Cuso International; visioning by environmental educators in Canada; Katkari in India assessing their livelihoods. (Source: D. J. Buckles)

of an issue, and allow for fewer steps in an inquiry. Dividing a key variable into its component parts – looking at the various expressions of the power variable in *Social Analysis CLIP*, for instance – may also be needed to expand the analysis.
- How reliable do the results need to be. If important decisions are expected to follow immediately from the inquiry, or they are irreversible if proven wrong, high levels of evidence and consensus may be needed (see *Validation*, Chapter 8). Tentative decisions and actions to be verified later or monitored closely can be made on less detailed information and a narrower base of stakeholder agreement.
- How familiar the facilitators are with the tools. It is usually safer to learn with simpler applications of a tool and progress to more advanced applications and combinations of tools as experience is acquired. Facilitators should become familiar with a tool by testing their knowledge and design in a safe context.

There are two extremes to avoid when applying tools. The first consists in using tools to generate exhaustive data, analysis and text-heavy reports that make authentic stakeholder participation difficult and push actions out into a distant future, once all factors are fully analysed. The other involves using tools hurriedly and superficially, without providing the details, nuances and analyses needed to make the inquiry meaningful, useful and reliable. The middle way is to aim for a level of detail and engagement that reflects existing constraints and goals, and is 'good enough' in the context. (See *Validation*, Chapter 8.)

When making sense

Combine formal analysis and narration

- Formal analysis supported by diagrams and tables helps to organize information and findings in ways that are clear, logical and succinct. Narration (whether oral or written) gives the context, the sequence of events, a sense of purpose and details that add richness and texture to understanding of the situation. Mesh the two kinds of thinking and adjust the relative weight of each to suit the context. When relevant, convert the findings of one kind of thinking into the starting point for another kind of thinking (for example, use storytelling based on the *Most Significant Change* method to determine the criteria to be used in *The Socratic Wheel*).
- Consult instructions provided in the tools to ensure that the collection of data is fully integrated with analysis and interpretation of the results through group discussion. Avoid separating the people and the timing of data collection, analysis and interpretation.

Elicit concepts or start with predefined terms

- Tools such as *Gaps and Conflicts, Social Analysis CLIP* and *Legitimacy* start with concepts adapted from the social sciences such as power, legitimacy, interests and values. While these are informed by social scientific theory, they may not be meaningful in some contexts. Tools that use *Domain Analysis* and *System Dynamics* as their base intentionally allow participants to elicit their own terms and concepts. Other tools such as *The Socratic Wheel* also lend themselves to elicitation techniques. Decide which approach is needed at what point in the inquiry.

Use numbers and measurements wisely

- When using a tool that includes ratings or ranking, keep in mind that numbers are not ends in themselves. Measurements are means to provide information, clarify people's views or knowledge about a topic, define priorities, focus the attention during a group discussion, structure the conversation and find patterns. Numbers and measurement may also reduce tensions by providing an external point of reference or bring out differences among stakeholders that were unspoken. How much attention is given to numbers and measurements depends in part on the weight given to different knowledge systems, such as science and local experience and know-how, and the importance of dialogue between knowledge systems.

Explain tool instructions or not

- Explaining all the steps of a tool before using it can confuse and detract participants from the substance of a discussion. Instead, outline and seek agreement on the inquiry's expected results, and then proceed step-by-step.
- When moving from one tool to another, clearly state the main question that the tool will address and invite participants to reformulate the question if necessary.
- In some cases, explaining the technique in advance can help a group focus on a task and reduce tension. In other cases, participants may want to get right into the substance, trusting in the expert judgment of the facilitator regarding what technique to use. In the later case, the facilitator may use a technique discreetly to guide a group facilitation process and to organize the findings in the facilitator's mind, notebook or in a table (during or after the event). Participants can decide whether they want to learn more about the technique and begin to use it themselves independently.

COMBOS

There are different ways to skilfully combine and sequence tools in events or processes that support collaborative thinking. The following are examples of methodological designs that can be implemented in a one-day workshop (setting aside time for introductions) or in several short meetings. Other chapters in this book also describe and illustrate processes that involve a number of inquiry tools used in a sequence. These action-inquiry processes can extend over a few hours, weeks, months or even years (as in the Katkari and the Bangladesh stories illustrated in various chapters).

Many other designs for the same task are possible. The planning process varies as well. Tools brought together in a PAR process can be planned in advance or may be developed along the way, according to circumstances. The amount of time, the level of planning and the number of meetings needed depend on how important and complex the issues are, the amount of information required and the number of people that need to engage in the process (see *Validation*, Chapter 8).

Defining project goals and mission

1. *Ideal Scenario (True or False)*: share stories of great things already accomplished or dreamed about and that contribute to a successful project.
2. *Ideal Scenario (The Carrousel)*: develop and share statements towards a common vision of a successful project.
3. *Order and Chaos*: discuss ways to improve the likelihood of a project succeeding and the knowledge needed to make plans.

Developing a resource management proposal

1. *Resource Mapping*: draw a map of all the sites and key resources that can contribute to a project.
2. *Timeline* and *Stakeholder Identification*: identify current activities (placed in a sequence) that make use of different sites and resources. Indicate the key stakeholders involved in each resource management activity.
3. *Contribution and Feasibility*: identify actions that would make the greatest contributions to the goals of the different stakeholders involved, and are feasible.
4. *Levels of Support*: determine if there is enough support from stakeholders to go with a proposal or course of action (based on the conclusions reached in previous steps).

Setting priorities

1. *Free List and Pile Sort*: identify the main options to resolve a problem or achieve project goals.
2. *Weighting*: assess the options against weighted criteria developed by the group.
3. *Values, Interests, Positions (VIP)*: discuss the extent to which the preferred options coincide with people's values and interests.

Monitoring and evaluating a project

1. *The Socratic Wheel*: define the indicators and information needed to measure current, ongoing and expected progress in achieving project results.
2. *What If:* develop a plan to monitor risk factors and adjust activities accordingly.
3. *Process Mapping*: plan the activities needed to achieve and monitor progress towards project goals.

PHOTO 6.2 Stakeholders in a Bonnechere River conservation organization. (Source: J. Wonnacott)

Solving a problem

1 *Stakeholder Rainbow* or *Social Analysis CLIP*: identify the key stakeholders who can influence or may be affected by a key problem or issue to be discussed.
2 *Force Field*: identify ways to act on the key factors that contribute to the problem and those that stop it from getting worse.
3 *Validation*: discuss the additional evidence and stakeholder involvement needed to better understand the problem and make plans.

Managing a conflict

1 *Timeline*: reconstruct the chronology of events that created or maintained the conflict.
2 *Values, Interests, Positions (VIP)*: discuss the extent to which the positions adopted by the parties coincide with their values and interests.
3 *Lessons and Values*: discuss the values held by the parties and apply the lessons learned from successful actions that are consistent with those values.
4 *Ideal Scenario*: imagine a scenario that describes what would happen if the conflict were resolved.

Creating a community of practice

1 *Action, Research, Planning (ART)*: assess the balance between action, research and training goals in current profiles.
2 *Social Domain*: describe and compare the skills and learning goals of members of the community of practice.
3 *Process Mapping*: plan the activities needed to achieve and monitor individual and collective progress towards learning goals.

Manage change

1 *Sabotage*: identify and resolve to overcome behaviours that are barriers to success.
2 *Activity Dynamics*: examine how to strengthen the integration and synergy of ongoing activities.
3 *Ideal Scenario (The Carrousel)*: develop and share plans to implement change successfully.

Working together

1 *Force Field*: identify ways to act on the factors that contribute to a key problem and those that stop it from getting worse.
2 *Negotiation Fair*: discuss and plan concrete actions that stakeholders can take to meet their mutual expectations and resolve a key problem.

THREADS OF THEORY: CARING AND CAREFULNESS

Carefulness and caring are the roots of reason and concern for the common good. This twofold disposition is embedded in our being, one that invites us to think carefully, with rigour, while authentically caring for others and the world we live in. The invitation calls for sound reasoning and genuine dialogue applied to problem solving and sensemaking in context. Acknowledging the invitation gives wisdom. Knowing how to respond procures invaluable skills.

Thoughtful inquiry combines evidence-based and people-based learning. It acknowledges the careful precision and intelligence that people must apply to understanding and shaping reality. It also supports the sense of caring that people show in their mindful engagement with other people and myriad forms of life to achieve the common good.

But this is easier said than done. Many skills are needed to walk the talk. To begin with, people-based inquiry hinges on our ability to **ground** learning in real settings and ongoing processes that provide a sense of meaning and social purpose. It also requires that we develop the art of **mediating** different views and knowledge systems, by engaging people and knowledge from different perspectives and facilitating truthful dialogue across social boundaries, cultural settings and modes of learning. To succeed, a well-crafted inquiry must also integrate evidence-based thinking, the kind that is achieved through skilful **navigation and scaling.** Navigation is knowing how to select and combine the forms of inquiry, planning and participation that help people deal with complexity (the uncertain, the unknown) in a timely fashion. It means doing the right thing with the right people, at the right time and in the right way, to create a shift in understanding and action. **Scaling** is going for the right level of detail and complexity – the art of adjusting inquiry methods and action to fit the depth of evidence, planning and engagement needed to obtain meaningful results.

Of all skills that must be mastered, **sensemaking** is often the most critical. In it lies the ability to construct meaning in complex situations by integrating information, analysis and insights into stories and explanations that inspire and persuade. All of this may be common sense, but making sense is not all that common.

Commentary

Western culture displays an enduring disposition to set subject apart from object, spirit from body, mind from matter and people from things. It also detaches humans from everything else that exists on earth, and elsewhere for that matter. This Manichean thinking creates two factitious moods: the objective and the subjective. The objective mood sees objects as things that are simply present at hand and 'have been there all along', existing independently from humans. It does as if humans had never existed or could simply live 'along with' objects for some time, and then pass away quietly, anonymously, without consequence. The subjective mood prefers to apply the disappearing act to objects presenting themselves in the mind only. Their existence hinges on human perception, consciousness, or signs in language.

The subject/object distinction is a denial of being in the world. The two moods it sustains betray a fugitive and forgetful attitude towards what it is to be human, which is to be immersed in the middleness of everything. The bipolar attitude shows little concern for death, treating the disappearance of either things or humans as a trivial fact of mental or material life. When subjects are pitted against objects, the involvement of world and humans trying to live together meaningfully breaks down. Mind and matter stand each in their own full presence or absence, either alive or dead, forever hiding from each other, unready to engage. The gravity of being 'thrown out of the world' and 'no longer being there' is ignored. The angst that comes with humans 'no longer belonging' is forgotten (Dreyfus, 1991; Heidegger, 1962).

Whatever mood they adopt, humans are inextricably involved with myriad things, life forms and other humans. Thrown into the world, they experience a multitude of moods and ways of being that dispose them to encounter people and things that are here or there, lying or hiding before them, to be understood and discovered through what they are and the many questions and concerns they raise. Concerns about the manifold expressions of life can give rise to inauthentic considerations, as when theorists or polluters get absorbed by idle talk about subjects living independently from objects. Futile thinking can also convert death into a vague rumour, forgetting that it is forever present in our lives and plays a vital role in our measurement and understanding of time.

Authentic care works differently. It is all encompassing. Far from being a purely subjective or intersubjective mood, caring for a world that makes sense calls for careful interventions in the world 'about us', using all means and measures of phenomenal involvement – i.e. *technê*, everyday skill, and *phronesis*, practical wisdom. Dispositions to act carefully, with precision and patience, enable humans to act and deal with tangible situations and unique circumstances. They allow people of practical wisdom (*phronemos*) to show resolve, decisive action and skilful coping, to be sustained by risk-taking experience, the exercise of judgment and the appropriate use of equipment – tools of experimentation and measurements in space and time.

Caring and carefulness is at the root sensemaking, the greatest skill. This is the ability to generate insights that lead to the transformation of self and world. The art of 'making sense of it all' can be nurtured on condition that humans face the anxiety of radical change, including death, and be ready to mourn all that is taken for granted in their everyday lives. Thrown into the world for a while only, humans are fated to experience angst and take interest in other beings and the world about them, until such time as they change or pass away. Caring for what is and can be is in the nature of humans who, from the moment they are born, are old enough to evolve and die.

REFERENCES

Dreyfus, H. (1991) *Being-in-the-World: A Commentary on Heidegger's Being and Time, Division I*, MIT Press, Cambridge.

Heidegger, M. (1962) *Being and Time*, trans. John Macquarrie and Edward Robinson, Harper & Row, New York.

MODULE 2

Fact-finding and listening

MODULE 2: FACT-FINDING AND LISTENING

Module 2 includes two chapters on multipurpose tools for fact-finding and listening, richly illustrated through examples from Bhutan, India, Burkina Faso, Honduras, Nepal, Bangladesh and Canada. The chapters reflect basic processes and principles built into every tool in the book, and speak to the facilitation skills and procedures practitioners need to develop when walking the talk of engaged research.

Chapter 7 starts with variations on *The Socratic Wheel*, a flexible tool to support evidence and people-based inquiry and evaluation. Deceptively simple and powerfully visual, *The Socratic Wheel* lends itself to a wide range of applications including setting priorities in light of baseline conditions, monitoring and evaluation as well as assessing and comparing individual and group profiles. Many examples are provided to illustrate the multiple ways this tool can be reinvented in the service of Socratic learning – knowing now what you did or did not know before.

Chapter 8 proceeds to a wide range of tools for seeking evidence and consensus, starting with *Validation*, a technique to provoke thinking about whether more evidence and/or consensus is needed before action can be confidently taken. The chapter also presents the tools most familiar to PAR practitioners and facilitators, from *Free List and Pile Sort* to *Rating, Ranking, Participation* and *Active Listening.* To these basic fact-finding and listening tools and illustrations from various settings, we add theoretical commentaries on the meaning of measurements and the perennial debate between quantitative and qualitative methods in the social sciences.

CHAPTER 7

Reinventions of the wheel

INTRODUCTION

This chapter is about a participatory rating tool, *The Socratic Wheel*, and its varied applications in real-life settings. The stories presented below provide vivid examples of how *Process Design* (described in Chapter 5) works on the ground. They show how the core skills outlined in Chapter 6 come together in an apparently simple technique to facilitate group thinking.

The chapter starts with a story of how the tool made its way into the management of school education for gross national happiness (GNH) in Bhutan. We then provide step-by-step instructions for the tool and describe a nautilus-shaped version of a similar group rating exercise called *Weighting*. As the title suggests, *Weighting* allows participants to visualize the weight of rating criteria according to their relative importance to the matter at hand.

The rest of the chapter narrates applications of *The Socratic Wheel* in various settings, with a focus on one of two distinct questions: how to assess results against expectations and related actions (the heart of monitoring and evaluation), and how to describe and compare different profiles in a domain (projects in a programme portfolio, people with different skills or interests, etc.).

In a concluding theoretical commentary, we once again take up the issue of monitoring and evaluation and make a case for tools that ground measurements in everyday life and meaningful action.

EDUCATING FOR 'GROSS NATIONAL HAPPINESS' IN BHUTAN

The Fourth Druk Gyalpo or King of Bhutan challenged the world and Bhutan with his statement twenty-five years ago that 'Gross National Happiness is more important than Gross National Product'. The concept of gross national happiness or GNH quickly became the focus for a number of efforts in various countries to develop indicators and a composite index that measures quality of life or social progress in more holistic and psychological terms than gross domestic product. It also set out a vision for building an economy and society in Bhutan based on Buddhist spiritual values. Embedding GNH in the structure of the country's institutions and the consciousness of its people became an official goal, carried on by the current king and constitutional government.

Recently, attention by the Royal Government of Bhutan began to focus on major school reforms that would bring the spirit and practice of GNH into the educational system. Several conferences were organized to describe what this might mean, including an international conference held in December 2009 and a follow-up event involving all 541 principals from across the country. In these two events education specialists and principals jointly defined the areas of change needed, including aspects of the school curriculum, the broader learning environment and linkages to community life. The goal of these changes was to bring holistic, ecological and human principles and values, including daily meditation and critical thinking skills, into everyday school activity and the education of students. Far-reaching reforms of this nature had never been attempted on a national scale, and plans were needed to guide, monitor and evaluate these changes.

PHOTO 7.1 While archery is Bhutan's national sport, field dart throwing is popular among urban and rural youth. The target is the same shape in both sports. *The Socratic Wheel* exercise made use of the dart and archery metaphor to convey the notion of precision when setting targets. (Source: D. J. Buckles)

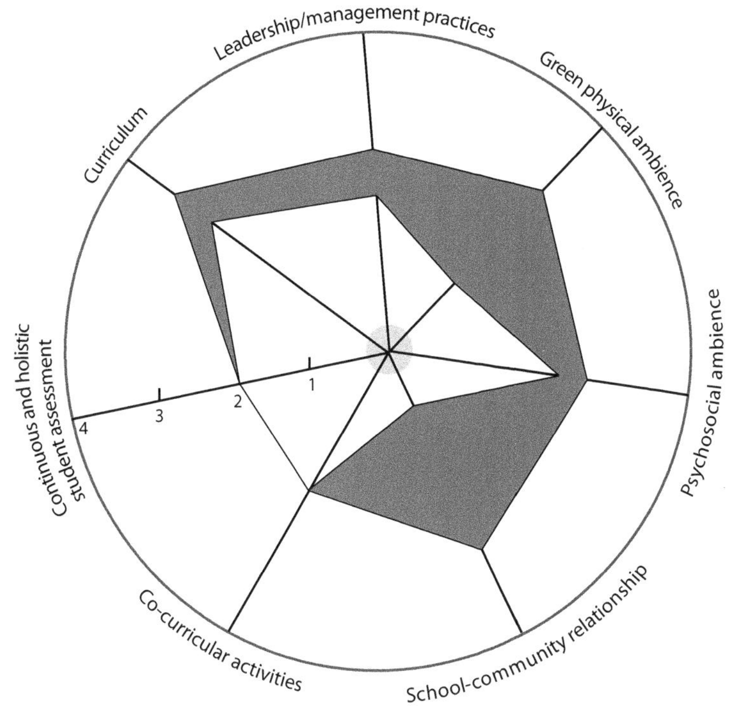

FIGURE 7.1 The GNH school improvement plan, Bhutan.

Summary of this example: For one rural school discussed during the workshop, participants indicated two significant improvement targets for the coming year: school-community relationship and green physical ambience. Plans to improve the school-community relationship included organizing several cultural events on occasions important to local communities. Participants said this would in turn make it more feasible for the school to engage parents in collective work parties to green the physical ambience. A school representative in the workshop described the parent network as a cluster of dandelions, a flower with many seeds and yellow petals. The imagery expressed genuine efforts to spread the value of caring to every nook and cranny of the school community. Modest targets were also defined for curriculum improvements, inspired by ideas presented during the international conference and teaching guides from other countries. Improvement targets for the psychosocial ambience were also modest, to be met by inviting local monks to lead morning meditations at the school. They added that some work should be done to share leadership and management responsibilities fairly among the various teachers at the school. Participants explained through other ratings in the wheel that they were relatively satisfied with the school's application of GNH principles and values to co-curricular activities and the student assessment process. Consequently, no targets for the coming school year were set for these two areas.

Against this background, the Evaluation, Monitoring and Support Services Department (EMSSD) of the Ministry of Education held a workshop in Thimphu, the capital of Bhutan, before the first day of the 2010 school year. At this workshop, facilitated by D. J. Buckles, some thirty staff, teachers, principals and students came together to co-design a continuous planning and strategic evaluation tool for use by schools.

The tool needed to pose three questions:

- Where is the school now, in relation to the principles and values of GNH applied to distinct areas of school life?
- What improvement targets can be set for the current year?
- How are schools planning to achieve these targets?

The tool had to be simple enough for use by all schools across the country without any training. *The Socratic Wheel* offered this potential and lent itself, with some adaptation, to a self-assessment process later integrated into formal monitoring and evaluation plans.

Workshop participants were first tasked with reviewing GNH values and principles discussed during the previous events and applying these to an assessment of distinct areas of school life (see spoke titles in Figure 7.1). They decided they would use a simple rating process and scale of 1 to 4 (low to high) to engage the various stakeholders in each school (principals, teachers, older students, active parents) in discussions of the extent to which the school was applying the principles and values of GNH in different areas of school life. When rating, they were to provide concrete examples on how the school demonstrated the principles and values of GNH. For example, a principal in the workshop said the school promoted the concept of continuous and holistic student assessment (level of achievement on multiple tests, attendance, level of improvement, contribution to class activities, etc.) rather than over reliance on a single final exam. The school principal said he reminded his teaching staff of this approach using the metaphor of a colour wheel. When spun, the colour wheel appears white, the colour of an overall assessment.

The self-assessments generated during the workshop produced a snapshot of where specific schools were in relation to the principles and values of GNH as applied to distinct areas of school life. They also helped school stakeholders make specific plans for improvements, by setting targets for the coming school year, beyond the levels already achieved and recorded on the wheel. People determined the level of improvement the school should be aiming for and developed detailed plans for what they intended to do to move from the current to the target level. When compiled in *The GNH school improvement plan* (Figure 7.1), the results expressed concretely and visually the current level of achievement on each spoke, the target levels and the actions needed to bridge the gaps.

After further testing and adjustment, the EMSSD integrated the tool and detailed instructions into a system-wide guide for School Self-Assessment and Improvement Planning. This guide is now fully implemented nationally across the Bhutanese school system. It provides, for the first time in a Bhutanese school setting, a flexible and group-based tool for planning, monitoring and evaluation. Combined with other evaluation tools developed by the EMSSD, *The GNH school improvement plan* creates opportunities for self-directed learning in relation to the principles and values of GNH and for planning of concrete actions for school improvements. It stands, when decorated and posted in an appropriate location at the school, as a friendly reminder of school aspirations and planned commitments, and a reference for ongoing monitoring of progress. In an update on use of the tool, the EMSSD noted that the wheel supported 'a culture of inquiry and reflection focussed on continuous improvement' inspired and guided by the principles and values of GNH (EMSSD, 2011, p. 1).

DESIGNING THE WHEEL

The planning, monitoring and evaluation tool developed in Bhutan is a particular version of *The Socratic Wheel* applied to a visionary goal: measuring the pursuit of GNH in educational institutions. The process designed to achieve this represents one possible spin of the wheel, unique in many ways. Before we say more about other applications, some simpler and some more advanced, we advise readers to familiarize themselves with the generic version of the tool. Detailed instructions are given below, followed by a summary list of optional features to consider when adjusting the tool to a real setting. We also describe *Weighting* – a wheel with spokes that vary in length to represent rating criteria that vary in levels of importance.

The Socratic Wheel

Purpose

To evaluate and rate one or several elements or alternatives (project goals, options to choose from, individual skills, leadership styles, products, activities, etc.) on multiple criteria.

Step 1

Define the situation and identify **criteria** useful to evaluating it. **Elicit** the criteria from the group (by putting the question directly to the group or with the help of *Free List and Pile Sort*, storytelling, photography, etc.), **supply** predefined criteria based on established or agreed upon goals or characteristics or **negotiate** some or all the criteria, depending on the purpose of the inquiry and time available. The criteria should be concrete, distinct and clearly defined.

Example criteria if rating alternative actions: cost and time efficiency, net impact, feasibility, gender equity, environmental sustainability, fit with local culture, local skills available, expected buy-in, etc.

Step 2

Decide on a **rating scale** (0 to 3, 0 to 5, or 0 to 10), and give the highest value for each criterion a **positive meaning**. For more precision, use **indicators** or progress markers to define the meaning of each number on the scale. For instance, a score of 4 out of 5 on the criterion 'community support' could mean there is strong majority support for the proposed action.

Step 3

Create a wheel on paper, a flip chart or on the floor and assign a criterion to each spoke in the wheel. Mark the scale on each spoke, from the centre (0) to the outer edge of the wheel (the highest value). **Label** each spoke with a title card, or use a drawing, an object or a person to represent the criterion. A relevant metaphor (see the dream catcher example below) can be identified to represent the purpose of the exercise.

Step 4

Rate the element on each criterion, using the scale from Step 2. Discuss ratings and the reasoning behind the ratings until all participants agree. If agreement is not possible, use the majority rating. Record each rating on the corresponding spoke and draw **straight lines** between the marks to create a shape that defines the overall profile for the situation defined in Step 1 (see example in Figure 7.2).

Review in detail the *Scoring tips* (Chapter 8). They are critical to proper application of *The Socratic Wheel.*

Step 5

Plan and evaluate

Use *The Socratic Wheel* to plan ways to achieve goals. Start by defining a time frame and rating both **current and desired levels** on each criterion. Then identify and plan the actions needed to move from one level to the other. Incorporate these specific actions into work plans. (See *Process Mapping* and *Process Design*, Chapter 5.)

Monitor or evaluate **progress over time** using three ratings for each criterion: (a) the **initial rating or baseline**, (b) the **rating aimed** for within a defined time frame, and (c) the **final rating** obtained once the time is reached (see Table 7.1). The ratings for (a) and (b) can be recorded at the beginning of a process, followed in due time by the rating for (c). Use different colours to indicate the profile shape at each stage in the process.

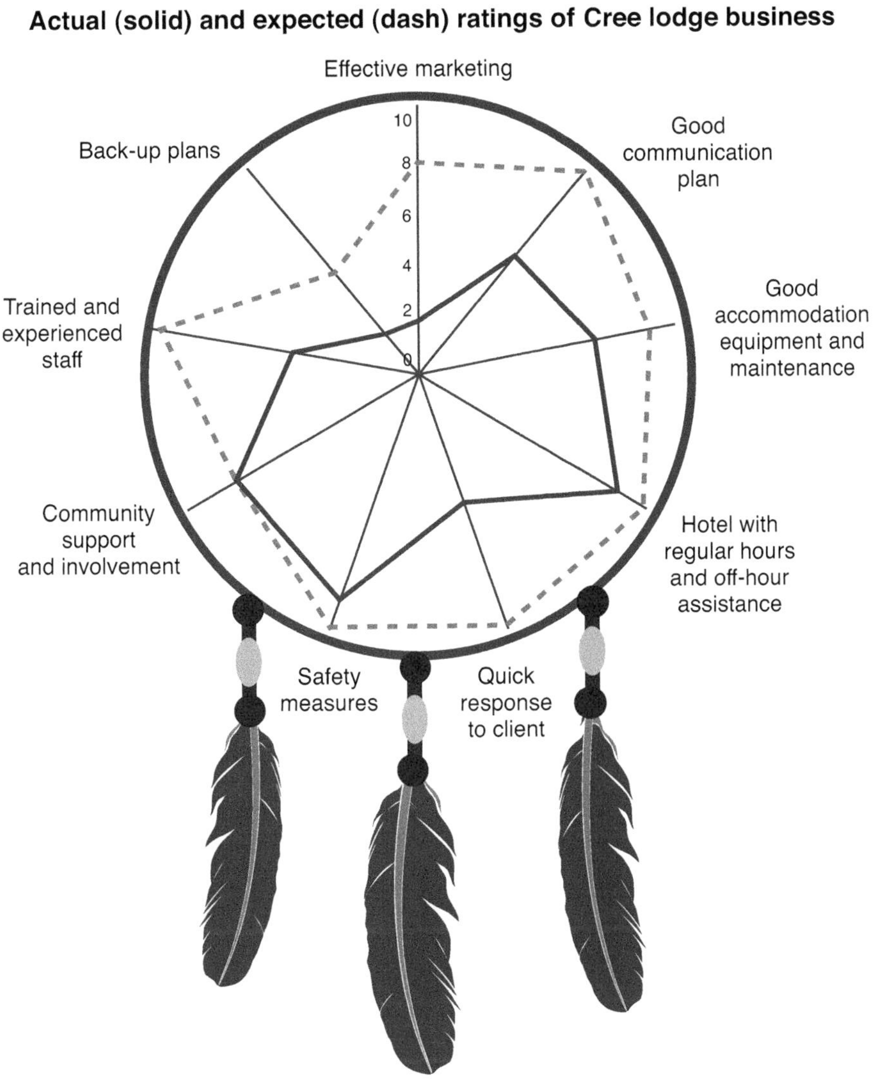

FIGURE 7.2 Assessment of a Cree lodge business in Northern Quebec.

Summary of this example: A Cree lodge business owner evaluates his business using nine criteria identified with the assistance of local tourism officers. Solid lines drawn in Figure 7.2 indicate how well the lodge is doing against the corresponding criteria. The dotted lines indicate the level of improvement the owner is aiming for within a year or so. The most important challenges include developing an effective marketing strategy and communication plan, recruiting trained and experienced staff and making sure that clients receive quick responses to their queries and needs.

Socratic learning

To capture Socratic learning, add a fourth set of ratings to the monitoring and evaluation wheel: the **initial ratings revised.** The starting point on each criterion is assessed again, after a final rating is obtained at the end of a process. People may discover that what they knew or had already achieved at the beginning was either greater or lesser than what they had thought. To evaluate the **real progress** over time, compare the 'final rating' with the 'initial rating revised' (see column D–C in Table 7.1). The Socratic learning may inspire learners to seek the knowledge they lack, or appreciate more the knowledge they already have (see *Assessing profiles*, this chapter).

Table 7.1 Socratic learning

Rating criteria	*Initial rating* *A*	*Expected rating* *B*	*Expected progress* *B–A*	*Initial rating revised* *C*	*Final rating* *D*	*Real progress* *D–C*
Effective marketing	2	8	6	1	6	5
Trained, experienced staff	5	10	5	6	8	2

Compare

Participants can compare the profiles reflected in wheels made by different individuals or groups. To do so, **cluster** individual wheels with similar overall profiles and assess their distance from other clusters by comparing the shapes on each wheel (created after rating on the various criteria). To do this clustering dynamically, ask participants to move around with their wheel figures looking for other wheels that resemble their own, forming twins, triplets and then **families of wheels** with a similar overall profile. Each family (including small families or orphan participants) can then prepare and present to the whole group a brief description of what their wheels have in common. When a family of wheels presents their similarities, other groups can move away if they feel their family wheel profile is very different in several ways, or come closer if the similarities are more important than the differences. At the end of the exercise, participants can plan strategies that draw on different but complementary family wheel profiles (to create well balanced work teams that draw on different leadership styles, for instance). Another method for comparing wheels is to rank the scores using the tool *Disagreements and Misunderstandings* (Chapter 14).

FAQ

- ***What are the common errors made when using this tool?***

Common errors include failing to define concrete and discrete criteria or cluttering the wheel with too many criteria or indicators (more than six spokes). The tool can also be overused and applied inappropriately (e.g. in cultural contexts where inserting a zero value in the centre of a wheel makes little sense).

- ***What is the advantage of mapping numerical values on a wheel figure instead of simply organizing the data into a table?***

The Socratic Wheel is essentially an exercise in rating, a bar chart adapted to a circular frame. As with other graphs in this book, its appeal does not rest in its technical features but rather in the intent that sets the technique in motion: in this case, reflective dialogue and action in a meaningful context. This is the intent of any whole brain exercise, analytic and visual, cognitive and evocative, the kind that allows views and data to be discussed and organized synthetically, to support collective thinking and action in complex settings. Unlike a table, a wheel figure drawn by a circle of people can launch a discussion of what should be measured (the spokes) and what has been achieved (the ratings) (see the Katkari example, this chapter).

Variations

- Rate several elements or options (represented by spokes in the wheel) using one or two criteria (overall feasibility and net contribution, for instance) on the same spoke.
- If some criteria should be given more weight than others, use *Weighting* instead of *The Socratic Wheel.*

Design options: questions to consider

Purpose

- Should the tool serve to assess profiles (e.g. leadership skills), set priorities, monitor progress, or evaluate final results?
- Should the assessment involve several wheels to represent and compare projects, activities or individual profiles? Or should it focus on a single project wheel generated by the entire group? If a single wheel, should the spokes stand for criteria or for the activities to be assessed (against one or two criteria)?
- Should the wheel(s) express individual, subgroup or collective assessments of the topic at hand?

Criteria

- Should some or all of the criteria be generated, negotiated or supplied?
- Should participants start with storytelling or *Free List and Pile Sort* to generate meaningful criteria?

- How many criteria should appear in the wheel? Are sub-wheels needed to represent more precise criteria for each spoke?
- Would the exercise gain from using objects, drawings, pictures or people to represent each spoke on the wheel?

Ratings

- Should the ratings involve indicators or progress markers (see *Scoring tips* in Chapter 8)?
- What rating scale (short or long) should be used?
- Should the scale vary according to the importance of each criterion (see *Weighting*, Figure 7.3)?
- Should the ratings be negotiated, averaged or determined by the majority?
- Should ratings be done in subgroups (mixed or homogeneous), divided by spoke or wheel, to save time?
- When should the ratings be done: before, during or after goals are implemented? Should initial ratings be revised at a later point in time?
- Should prior fact-finding inform the exercise?

Reporting

- Should the wheel be drawn with flip charts, masking tape on the floor or software (Excel or RepGrid)?
- How should the exercise be documented?

Combinations

The Socratic Wheel is a rating tool than can be combined with a wide range of techniques to answer multiple questions, depending on the purpose of the inquiry. Here are some examples of possible combinations:

- When using *The Socratic Wheel* to determine priority actions, use *The Carrousel* (see *Ideal Scenario*, Chapter 14) to first compare and discuss the views of different groups.
- Combine *The Socratic Wheel* with *Force Field* (Chapter 10) to monitor and evaluate ongoing activities and to assess factors that help or limit the achievement of each goal represented in the wheel.
- Use *The Socratic Wheel* to assess differences between stakeholders (individuals, groups) and then *Negotiation Fair* (Chapter 14) to discuss what stakeholders can expect of each other.
- Use *Social Domain* and the RepGrid software (Chapter 18) to analyse the ratings of individual or group profiles obtained from *The Socratic Wheel.*

Weighting

Purpose

To rate and compare elements in a list using multiple criteria and scores weighted according to the importance that people assign to each criterion.

Step 1

Define the **situation** and create a list of **relevant elements** to be rated, such as options for action (see *Free List and Pile Sort*, Chapter 8).

Step 2

Define the **criteria** on which to rate the elements using **positive terms. Elicit** the criteria from the group (by putting the question directly to the group or with the help of *Free List and Pile Sort*, storytelling, photography, etc.), **supply** predefined criteria based on established or agreed upon goals or **negotiate** some or all the criteria, depending on the purpose of the inquiry and time available. The criteria should be concrete, distinct and clearly defined (see examples in Step 2 of *The Socratic Wheel*).

Step 3

Decide on a **rating scale** or maximum score for each criterion according to the importance that the criterion has for the group. For more precision, use **indicators** or progress markers to define the meaning of each number on the scale.

Step 4

Create a graph on paper or a flip chart using spokes (or ribbons on the floor) to represent the different rating criteria established in Step 2. Adjust the **length** of each spoke to reflect its maximum score, and organize the spokes in **ascending order**. Mark the scale on each spoke, from the starting point (0) to the other end of each spoke (representing the highest value). **Label** each spoke with a title card, a drawing or an object representing the criterion. A relevant metaphor can be identified to represent the purpose of the exercise.

Step 5

Individually or as a group, **rate** each element in the list on each criterion (several elements may receive the same rating). Record the ratings on the corresponding spokes on the graph. Keep track of the **reason(s)** given for each score on cards or a flip chart. If rating is done as a group, discuss each rating until participants agree based on consensus or a majority vote. Alternatively, calculate the average ratings for each element.

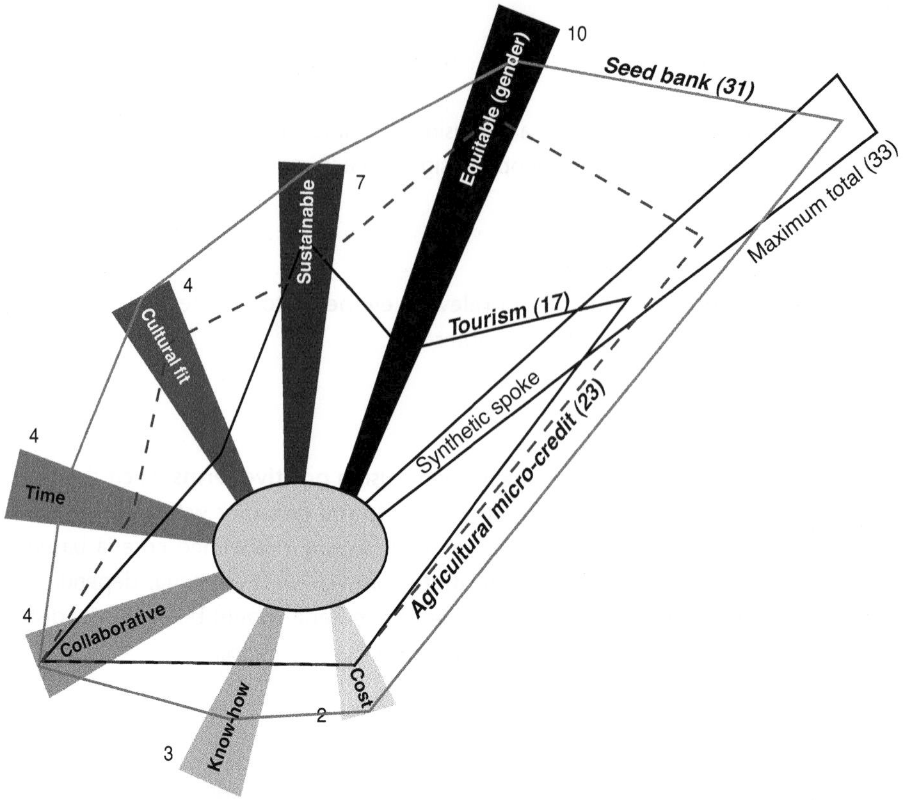

FIGURE 7.3 Setting priorities for local development.

Summary of this example: A community in Burkina Faso must choose between three possible local development strategies, using six criteria of different weights. The two most important criteria are the degree to which each option is equitable, especially when based on gender, and how sustainable it is. Considering the ratings discussed and assigned by the group, the seed bank is by far the best strategy, and tourism, the least attractive.

Review in detail the *Scoring tips* in Chapter 8. They are critical to proper application of *Weighting*.

Step 6

Add another longer spoke to the graph. Record the Maximum Total rating at the end of this **synthetic spoke**. Calculate the **Total** rating for each element. Record it on the graph, with a mark on the synthetic spoke.

Step 7

For each element, draw **straight lines** between all the corresponding marks to create a shape that defines the element's overall profile.

Step 8

Review the results and reasoning that went into the rating process and discuss the **priorities** based on the scores. Also discuss ways to modify the elements to make them more feasible, achieve greater impact, etc.

FAQ

See FAQ under *The Socratic Wheel.*

Variations

- See Variations under *The Socratic Wheel.*
- Create a table. Insert the elements in the first row. Record the rating criteria and their maximum scores in the left column, in descending order. Calculate the Maximum Total rating for any element, and record it at the bottom of the left column. Insert the ratings in the corresponding rows and columns.

Combinations

- See combinations under *The Socratic Wheel.*
- To compare the weighted ratings of two individuals or groups, see *Disagreements and Misunderstandings* (Chapter 14).

VARIATIONS ON THE WHEEL

Baseline and priority setting

We now turn to other applications of *The Socratic Wheel*, starting with an exercise in baseline assessment and priority setting by an association of the Katkari, an adivasi people in India. The Association used a version of the wheel to assess the current situation in different areas of their lives and make plans for collective action. In this application of the tool, participants defined the areas they wanted to explore, made use of powerful symbols to represent each area of interest to them, and provided vivid descriptions and sound reasoning to make sense of current and target ratings on each spoke. The result was an exercise in strategic planning, based on an understanding of the baseline situation and new priorities.

Strategic planning by an adivasi association

The Katkari have been marginalized from the wider society by a long history of exploitation, land alienation and social exclusion (Buckles and Khedkar, 2013). They are not passive victims of their situation, however, and have organized themselves into a regional association representing many hamlets and villages scattered throughout Raigad Distinct in Maharashtra near Mumbai, India. The Association was initially a forum for resolving conflicts both within Katkari communities and between communities and outside groups. To remain relevant, however, the Association needed to refocus its priorities and broaden its activities. A meeting in February 2010 of the Association leadership brought together twenty-two men from different hamlets to discuss the challenges and opportunities facing their communities, and plan what the Association should do on a priority basis. Together with D. J. Buckles, three activists with whom they had a long-standing relationship facilitated the strategic planning process.

After lighting incense and breaking a coconut to launch the meeting, the group settled down in a large circle for several hours of discussion. The mood of the group was very positive because they had recently completed construction of a modest meeting hall in the commercial town of Pali. This hall provided the Katkari with a rare and highly appreciated common space for a variety of needs. It offered a place for people to rest or sleep while waiting for medical appointments or government paperwork, a storage space for wood, dried fish or other products not sold in the Pali market, and a space for Association meetings and broader celebrations. In recognition of the confidence created by this significant accomplishment, and informed by prior discussion with the Association executive, the facilitators launched the discussion with an appreciative question – what things were going well in their communities and where could improvements over the previous ten years be clearly seen? After discussing the question, participants agreed that it was time to build on these strengths when setting the priorities of the Association for the future. They also decided that a time frame of two years was needed as a planning period, because the challenges were many and the resources of the Association very limited.

Areas of improvement in the lives of the Katkari were elicited directly from the group and discussed one by one. As each area emerged in the discussion sticks were placed on the floor progressively, in the middle of the circle of people like the spokes of a wheel. Participants identified objects to represent each topic and placed them at the outer end of each stick as visual labels.

One person in the group said that various Katkari had established **small enterprises** in recent years and that this was an emerging livelihood option. He and others in the group provided various examples, including very small brick operations, a tree nursery, vegetable cultivation, provision shops and charcoal contracting. He noted that entrepreneurial Katkari with knowledge of the brick industry and easy access to skilled workers had responded to the emerging demand for bricks near urban areas and the doubling of brick prices. They had set up their own very small units close to Katkari communities and the many small towns and villages experiencing a housing boom. Others said that even in more remote locations Katkari had been able to access government livelihood

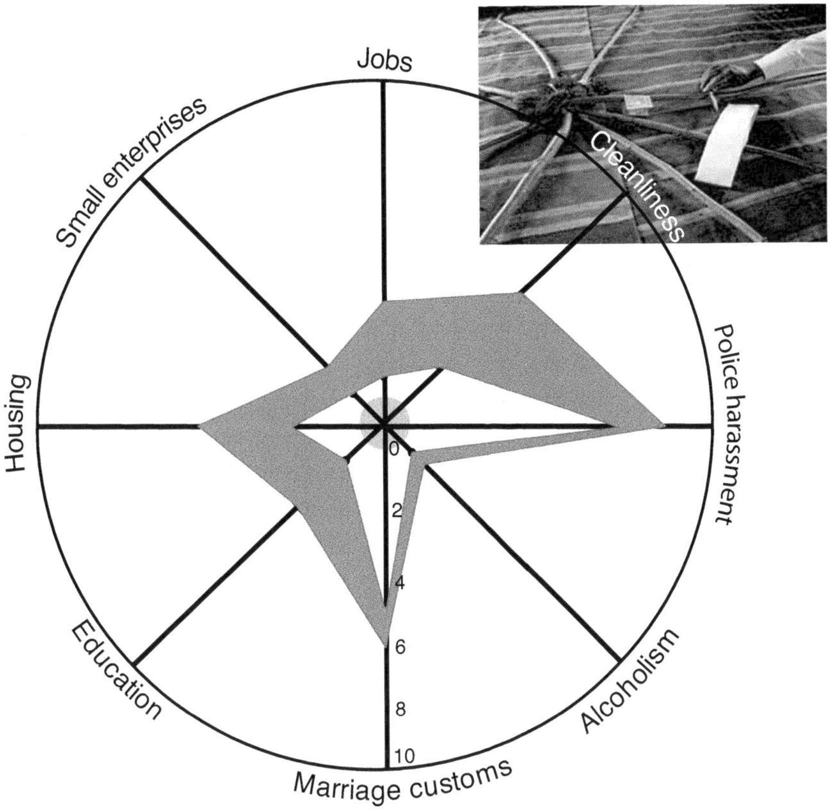

FIGURE 7.4 Setting priorities among the Katkari in India.

Summary of this example: The wheel represents eight areas of interest to the Katkari Association and the broader community, showing the current level (inner shape) and target level of improvement (outer shape). The biggest gaps between current and target levels represent areas where the Association intends to give priority attention (housing, education, jobs and cleanliness). The area with the lowest current level of achievement (controlling alcoholism) will also receive attention not only because it is low but also tending to get worse. Expected gains in controlling alcoholism are nevertheless very modest due to the complexity of the problem and limited scope of the Association to make a difference. Members agreed to treat these five areas as their collective priorities, and to develop plans accordingly.

schemes to purchase a pair of ploughing bullocks, establish a small herd of goats, or set up a small shop. A brick was selected by the group to represent the idea of new businesses. Everyone recognized, however, that only a handful of individuals had actually made this livelihood shift successfully. Most Katkari were still dependent on casual agricultural wage work and bonded employment on large brick operations in various parts of the state. They decided to give a score of 1 out of 10 to show that the current situation was nevertheless a slight improvement on the past.

When it came to setting a goal for the topic many remarked that there were many limitations, especially with respect to the management capabilities of the Katkari. Money and assets such as bullocks from government schemes is often poorly spent, used for other purposes, or sold off. Also the Association has little need to play a role in this process and could not be responsible for managing schemes and putting energy into enterprise development. Besides, they noted, successful enterprises are usually individual, not group endeavours. Based on this discussion they set an improvement target of only 2 out of 10 over the next two years. While the Association would continue to inform people about government schemes and help young people interested in brick or nursery enterprises to get management training, it would not treat this topic as a high priority for the organization.

Government employment was another area where participants felt there had been some improvement in recent years. A paper bill was selected as a symbol for this change, and the current level rated at a 1. People said that they have always had access to government jobs, due to quotas for adivasi and other marginalized groups, but that many didn't stay in these government jobs. One of the participants provided an example from his experience as a government watchman. He and his cousin had been offered jobs as part of a reservation quota. The cousin lasted four days only. He didn't show up at the work site at all, for fear of being separated from his family. For a year he received notices from the government about the job. Looking ahead, however, participants recognized the potential value of these jobs to the youth, and that competition was now fierce. Even with reservations, bribes are often needed to get government jobs such as entry into the police or as a watchman. Other types of private sector employment were also increasing and of great interest to young men who want to be tractor drivers or work in company security. The Association set a goal of reaching 3 out of 10 for livelihood improvement over two years. To achieve this they said they would encourage and assist applications for government jobs and organize career guidance for educated youth. Some even suggested that senior members would accompany candidates to interviews to ensure that they received proper attention.

Harassment by police, symbolized by a stick used to beat people, was an area where participants felt significant improvements had occurred over the previous years, already reaching a point of 7 on the scale. This improvement, they said, was mainly due to the work of the Association to reduce conflict and sort out problems within the village. Now, police don't pick up Katkari randomly for any crime, unless there is evidence the person was involved in some way. The group decided that the Association needed to remain vigilant for police harassment and to continue its work on legal aid and conflict resolution, with a view to achieving a level of 8 over the coming two years.

The group agreed that **cleanliness**, an expression of pride and a minimum standard of living, was another area where improvement from the past could be seen. Using a traditional white cap to symbolize the topic, the group gave a current rating of 2 out of 10. They said that earlier people did not take baths for a month or more, houses were very dirty, utensils were not cleaned properly, and areas surrounding houses and the hamlet were littered. One participant told of how he set an example by having a clean house, ensuring his children go to school, taking a bath daily, wearing washed clothes, reducing litter around the house and providing clean food in the house. He also felt that illnesses had declined as a result. The group agreed, however, that there was still a strong need for improvement in cleanliness by the community as a whole. They set a goal of reaching a level of 5 over the coming two years, through a campaign the Association would lead to dispose of plastic bags in a proper manner. These, they felt, symbolized the litter in their community because they never rot away and are highly visible. By eliminating litter from plastic bags the general message of cleanliness would be conveyed.

Great dissatisfaction and concern was expressed by participants regarding the lack of progress with **alcoholism** in their communities, symbolized by a discarded plastic water bottle often used to contain alcohol. They rated the current level at less than 1. Participants recognized that this was a difficult problem to resolve. When husbands drink, women also drink, even when pregnant. Then there are fights, leading to the abuse of women. Various participants expressed concern about the future impact of this practice on the youth in the community, influenced as well by increasing levels of alcohol consumption among non-tribal youth in the area. They also noted that past efforts to control the problem by banning the making of alcohol, including requests for help from the Police in enforcement of the ban, had come to naught or simply shifted production from Katkari communities to other adivasi communities. Katkari families had lost livelihoods as a result of the ban but not stopped drinking. Reduced availability also simply drove people to the town of Pali to drink, where the addiction was even more expensive. While local spiritual leaders had inspired some Katkari to stop drinking, they had little influence in the broader region. For all these reasons, reflecting what participants consider to be a very persistent and difficult problem, they felt that as an Association and a community they could only aspire to very modest improvements, perhaps reaching a 1 over the following two years. Actions by the Association would focus on discouraging families from taking advances on wages to spend on drinking during festivals.

The Association had overseen significant improvements in the practice of customs related to **marriage** and other religious ceremonies (*pujas* of various kinds), symbolized by a flower necklace brought for the inauguration of the meeting. It received from the group a 5 out of 10 for the current level of improvement. The main focus of this work had been to keep under control the pressures from the wider Indian society to host elaborate and very costly marriages. Unlike Hindu families, the Katkari traditionally followed a bride price system rather than the dowry, and organized their own marriages. Feelings of inferiority arising from this difference created continuous pressure to scale up the marriage ceremony, by issuing invitations to large numbers of people, asking Brahmins to officiate and organizing a *puja* (Hindu ritual). In response, the Association had established norms for expenditures to be incurred during marriages and specified the amount of bride price paid to different parties. These norms were written down and widely used in the hamlets. During the assessment, the members of the Association resolved to continue to promote these norms and to monitor their implementation. The group also reaffirmed earlier decisions to authorize representatives to impose fines on families that did not respect the norms. As a group, they agreed that over the following two years the Association should pursue a modest overall improvement to a rating of 6 out of 10.

Education was another area where the participants felt there had been some improvements in recent years. The school drop-out rate seemed to be going down. Children aged from six to fourteen tended to be in school and there were more schools being built in Katkari hamlets. More Katkari children, while still few in number, were studying beyond the tenth standard. Using a pen to symbolize the topic, participants set the current level at 2. Still, they noted that many Katkari parents do not take education seriously because they themselves are not literate. Moreover, even educated children cannot get jobs without paying bribes. Parents wonder about the relevance of education for the Katkari. They decided as an Association, however, to continue to create awareness about the value of education by meeting with groups of parents. They also resolved to lobby the government to build schools in Katkari communities, and set a goal of reaching a target level of 4 over the next two years through these actions.

Finally, improvements in **housing** and household facilities such as televisions, fridges and bathrooms, symbolized with a flat stone for a foundation and a piece of brick for a wall, were also noted, and rated at the 3 level. While most Katkari families had in the past lived in wattle and daub houses, more were making houses with a stone foundation and brick walls and acquiring various household amenities. The Association now expected rapid progress since many families had started collecting materials on their own rather than waiting for a government scheme. One person reported that in Kumbhargharwadi hamlet 25 or so people acted on their own and collectively built new houses. The Association felt that they could support this trend by sharing stories of how people were building their own homes. They would also continue to lobby for greater security of land tenure in their villages, thereby reducing the threat of eviction from their homes by landholders. They set a target level of 5 within a two-year time frame.

The picture of the current situation and target levels for further improvement emerging from the exercise showed meaningful, albeit modest, accomplishments in several areas and priorities for the future. These became the basis for strategic planning by the Association (Figure 7.4). The participants reviewed each current and target level, and decided which ones to focus on over the following two years. They singled out four areas (where the gap between current and target levels was greatest) for special attention from the Association: government jobs, education, cleanliness and housing. People agreed that these were important to all communities making up the Association, and consistent with the mandate and capabilities of the Association. The various actions identified during the process were summarized and agreed to by the group as a whole.

Participants also revisited the alcoholism question in light of the overall analysis of priorities. While they felt they could not be ambitious in this area, they expressed concern that improvements made in the past were actually slipping backwards. Non-tribals were drinking more, and this was influencing the younger people, creating a serious threat to the community. The Association needed to pay attention to this problem, even though the target level was modest. It was consequently added to the strategic plan. Participants recognized that successes in controlling norms for marriages were a strength they could use to impose sanctions and fines against behaviour related to alcohol consumption. They consequently made commitments to tighten the rules around the purchase of alcohol for marriages and festivals. They also decided to organize against the taking of advances for bonded labour on brick kilns and other migratory work sites as these were often spent largely on drinking.

The President of the executive committee concluded the strategic planning exercise by calling on members of the Association to always keep the priorities in mind in the work they were doing in their hamlets, and to dedicate their time accordingly. He also expressed surprise at how the process had stimulated so much discussion, both in appreciation for their collective accomplishments and in recognition of challenges yet to be met.

Monitoring and evaluation

In Bhutan, *The Socratic Wheel* contributed to the design and testing of a tool for ongoing monitoring and planning in the field of education on a national scale. The conveners supplied rating criteria and detailed indicators, those of GNH, and invited stakeholders in the schools to discuss and decide on school improvements that would bring them closer to achieving their aspirations. Although equally meaningful, the Katkari version of *The Socratic Wheel* is more narrowly focussed on deciding what to do, without delving into how their priorities will be pursued or establishing criteria against which progress might be assessed. The Katkari application involves a quick upstream assessment and planning exercise in the field of tribal community development, using concrete stories and descriptive actions (instead of measurable indicators) to evaluate current situations and set realistic targets for improvements in people's lives.

The next series of examples described below take place in Canada. They all address issues of monitoring and evaluation, but with significant variations in the design of each tool in light of the needs of the parties involved. The Park Dialogue story, introduced earlier (Chapter 5), is an example of a quick-and-easy exercise in designing and using a tool to monitor progress. This version of the wheel works for this purpose without any obligation to use indicators of measurable progress let alone gather reliable information about observed results. The Canada World Youth example is very different. It provides a downstream illustration of *The Socratic Wheel* used to assess impact in combination with a range of other tools to gather information and views on the key results of youth exchange programmes. It is a large-scale assessment involving reflections by different stakeholder groups (youth, community hosts, programme staff) involved in the programme over a ten-year period, with an effort to roll up analyses from several countries and continents.

While different in many respects, all these stories take inspiration from a constant principle: making sure that monitoring and evaluation supports learning and practical planning as well as meaningful dialogue between the people involved.

Park Dialogue

Public spaces are often hotly contested. In Canada's Capital Region, just fifteen minutes' drive from Parliament Hill, the Gatineau Park is a heavily used public space in both summer and winter. With hundreds of kilometres of trails through forested hills, abundant wildlife and numerous crystal-clear lakes typical of the Canadian Shield, the Park receives approximately 2.7 million visitors per year, mainly from the Capital Region.

Satisfying the needs of different individuals and groups and managing competing demands is a challenge for the National Capital Commission (NCC) responsible for the Park. With the emergence of new media (e-mail, blogs, etc.) an increasing number of users are voicing an opinion on the needs, resources and management methods of the NCC and the private contractor providing the majority of winter recreational and visitor services. The volume of comments, suggestions and complaints is particularly high during the winter season, reflecting the divergent interests and competing uses of trails by cross-country skiers, downhill skiers, snowshoers and people seeking walking trails. Handling these communications responsibly and resolving differences and competing interests overwhelmed the processes in place, prompting a decision by the NCC to shift from a client-service approach to a strategy of effective interactive engagement with winter trail user groups.

The first step in this transition was to create a forum for discussion between Park managers and winter trail users, facilitated by J. M. Chevalier. After collectively establishing the mandate, functioning and composition of what came to be known as Park Dialogue (see Chapter 5), discussions turned in subsequent meetings to issues revolving around the offer and standards of service of Gatineau Park's winter recreational programme and new proposals and requests expressed by Park users and managers. Various matters were discussed and resolved, including decisions to create a destination shelter in the south section of the Park for snowshoers and hikers, investments in better signage and training for attendants, preparation of information posters about trail etiquette, and clarifications by staff of specific services offered to park users.

Two months into the Park Dialogue process, conceived as a sixteen-month pilot, informal feedback suggested that the forum process was achieving its goal. Members seemed satisfied, but expectations were high as well. While they believed the forum to be generally on track, members agreed to develop a self-monitoring tool to establish parameters for evaluation and follow-up, using a simple version of *The Socratic Wheel*. One by one, the group identified the criteria to monitor progress and posted them directly to a wheel-shaped figure on a flip chart (using *Free List and Pile Sort*). As each new criterion emerged, the group checked to be sure it was clear and distinct from other criteria already posted. One person in the group argued that discussions must lead to real change, a feature labelled as 'tangible results'. Others proposed attendance by members at regular meetings and a spirit of mutual respect reflected through listening

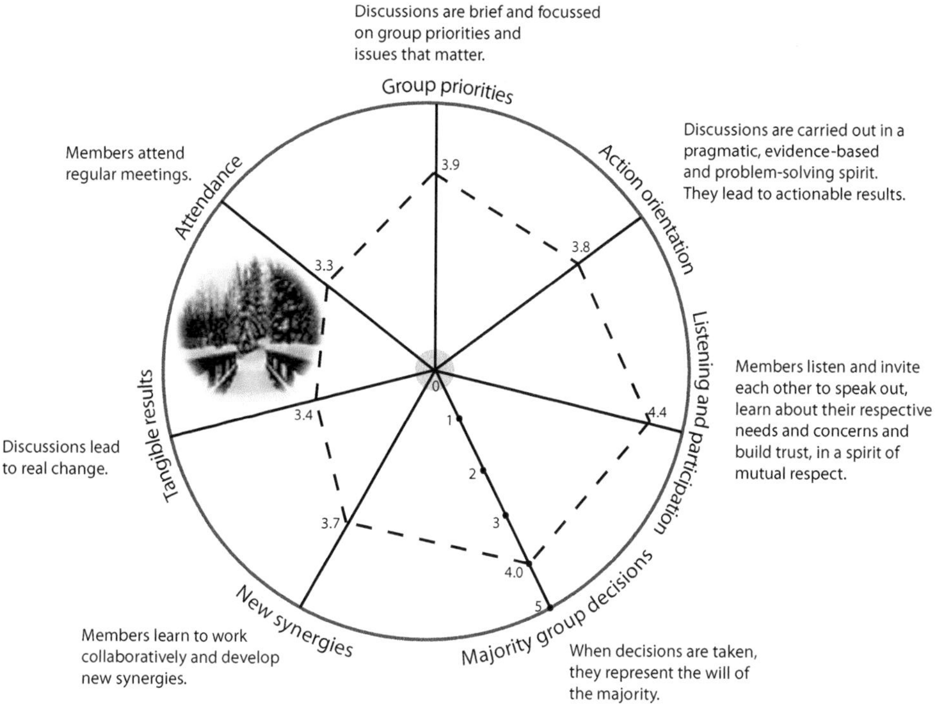
Discussions are brief and focussed on group priorities and issues that matter.
Group priorities
Discussions are carried out in a pragmatic, evidence-based and problem-solving spirit. They lead to actionable results.
Action orientation
Members attend regular meetings.
Attendance
Listening and participation
Members listen and invite each other to speak out, learn about their respective needs and concerns and build trust, in a spirit of mutual respect.
Tangible results
Discussions lead to real change.
New synergies
Members learn to work collaboratively and develop new synergies.
Majority group decisions
When decisions are taken, they represent the will of the majority.
3.9
3.8
3.3
4.4
3.4
3.7
4.0
0
1
2
3
5

FIGURE 7.5 Monitoring Park Dialogue progress.

Summary of this example: Ratings on the wheel drawn in Figure 7.5 (on a scale of 0 to 5) show that participants are generally satisfied so far with the Park Dialogue process. The sense of being heard and engaged is very high (4.4/5) and decisions made represent the will of the majority. The work of the forum has focussed primarily on group priorities and taken an action orientation. Attendance at regular meetings is an area of some concern (the lowest score) and tangible results not yet fully evident. Signs of observable results are hopeful but judgment is reserved. The NCC, as convener of the forum, is encouraged by the group feedback on the process and guided in its support to what participants want to see continue or improve.

and participation as equally important criteria. Three other criteria emerged quickly through the discussion: a focus on group priorities, action orientation, and decisions that represent the will of the majority (Figure 7.5). The group went on to discuss and rate their level of satisfaction with the forum process on each criterion, using a scale of 0 to 5. Discussion of the reasons behind each rating continued until there was full or majority agreement.

The picture emerging from the exercise, generated from start to finish within less than an hour, confirmed for the group and for the NCC that Park Dialogue was on track. People were surprised by the ease with which the criteria emerged, and their confidence buoyed by the result. The criteria, ratings and thinking behind them also highlighted what aspects of the process needed to continue or improve. The exercise provided the basis for ongoing self-monitoring of Park Dialogue and support to possible extension of the Park Dialogue concept to summer user groups.

Canada World Youth

Canada World Youth (CWY) is a Canadian NGO focussed on youth programming in Canada and abroad. Previous assessments of CWY programmes suggested that knowledge and skills is an important impact area from the point of view of past participants and future programme design. In 2006 the organization undertook a new assessment of the impact the Youth Exchange Program had on participants and communities in five countries, including Canada, Cuba, Ukraine, Benin and Thailand. One-day workshops for past participants in the Youth Exchange Program were organized in each country, covering six impact areas identified in previous CWY assessments (Figure 7.6). CWY also convened half-day workshops with representatives of participating communities and conducted an online survey with a sample of Canadian past participants and representatives of communities.

The evaluation team included CWY staff in each country and was lead by J. M. Chevalier and two experienced consultants from South House Exchange (Kate McLaren and Paul Turcot). The team selected, tested, adapted and sequenced various evaluation tools for the purpose of assessing how and to what extent the Youth Exchange Program contributed to the mission of CWY (McLaren *et al.*, 2006).

The evaluation team convened one-day workshops in seventeen different locations involving a total of 289 past participants in the Youth Exchange Program between 1995 and 2002. They explained each impact area and made sure that skills were understood to mean a concrete ability to do something, rather than something like being open-minded, which is an attitude. Each participant was then asked to **score the impact** of the Youth Exchange Program on five knowledge and skills areas, using a scale of 0 to 5. Individuals charted their **scores on a wheel** and noted details explaining their scores (knowing that the results would be used in reports on the programme). Participants then looked for others with similar scores marked on their wheels and formed **groups with similar impact profiles**. The members of each group discussed what they had in common and chose an image or symbol that represented the set of knowledge or skills the group had most developed or strengthened through the CWY experience. Similarities and differences between groups were discussed, along with the reasons why the programme had more impact in some areas and less impact in others. The participants strongly endorsed the conclusions reached through this exercise. Many noted that the visual display of the scores and group presentations that followed made it easy to appreciate the overall impact of the programme on skills.

Participants rated five specific impact areas identified by CWY:

- knowledge;
- organizational skills;
- communication skills;
- learning skills; and
- technical skills.

Examples provided of **knowledge impacts** included the increase among participants in their knowledge of history, culture, geography, politics, development issues, aid, or any other related knowledge area. **Organizational skill impacts** referred to improvements in teamwork, leadership, facilitation, mediation, planning, or any other related ability. **Communication skill impacts** referred to abilities in language, cross-cultural communications, non-verbal communications, listening, interviewing and speaking in public or any other related ability. Examples of **learning skill impacts** were improvements in analytical logic, data collection, capacity to adapt, creative thinking and other related abilities. **Technical skill impacts** referred to farming, computer use, teaching or any other ability requiring technical know-how.

The rating scale used by the participants was from 0 to 5, where

0 = No impact
1 = Very small impact
2 = Small impact
3 = Moderate impact
4 = Important impact
5 = Very important impact

Facilitators encouraged participants to flag the skills they were already very strong in before the programme started so that the team could interpret the ratings correctly.

Findings

Data compiled from all countries indicate that the top two skill areas were **communication skills** and **organization skills**. These two received the highest impact rating in every country (except in Thailand where communication skills were rated lower than organization and learning skills). By contrast, **technical skills** received the lowest impact rating in every country (except Benin).

The impact areas with the highest variability between the countries were **knowledge and learning skills**, scoring higher on average in some countries and lower in others. For example, participants in Benin rated knowledge at 3.1, their lowest rating among all of the impact areas in this exercise. Participants in Cuba rated this impact area at 4.3. Impact on learning skills received ratings from as low as 3.5 in Canada to a high of 4.2 in Cuba. It is interesting to note that while the Cuban rating was the highest for this impact area, learning skills received a relatively low score compared to other impact

TABLE 7.2 Averages of individual scores for knowledge and skills, by country

Country	*Number of participants*	*Average of individual scores*[a]					
		Communication skills	*Organizational skills*	*Learning skills*	*Knowledge*	*Technical skills*	*Average score*
Cuba	61	4.5	4.5	4.2	4.3	4.0	4.3
Ukraine	28	4.5	4.3	3.9	4.0	3.3	4.0
Canada	64	4.3	3.9	3.5	4.0	2.4	3.6
Benin	74	4.0	4.0	3.7	3.1	3.4	3.6
Thailand	62	3.8	4.1	4.1	3.8	3.6	3.9
Weighted average for all 289		4.2	4.1	3.9	3.8	3.3	3.9

a The maximum possible score is 5.

areas. This may be explained by the fact that the Cuban participants are all teachers by profession and view themselves as expert learners.

While these variations may be significant, aggregated data show an average score of 3.9 out of 5 on all impact areas (Table 7.2). This indicates an important impact of the Youth Exchange Program from the point of view of past participants. The average of individual, small group and workshop scores for each country also shows a consistent pattern of high impacts on the knowledge and skills of past participants (Table 7.2). Subtle variations in average impact ratings were nonetheless observed. For example, the skills that consistently benefited the most from the Youth Exchange Program are **communication and organizational skills**. This confirms the centrality of impacts on interpersonal relationships flagged in other parts of the impact assessment. These skills are targeted in various programme activities and strengthened through educational activity days, group activities and in the interaction between counterparts and their host families and work placements.

The evaluation team combined the results of the exercise with results from other parts of the impact assessment, towards an overall assessment of the impact the Youth Exchange Program had on participants and communities. The overall design, summarized in Figure 7.6, addressed questions related to impacts not only on knowledge and skills (using *The Socratic Wheel*) but also the influence of the programme on the values and attitudes of participants, perceived personal and professional gains, and influence on involvement in civic and community engagement activities later in life. Importantly, hosts also provided feedback and perspectives regarding the impacts of the programme on their families and communities. The final assessment recommended that CWY *ground its emphasis on individual learning objectives in specific community projects*. This subtle strategic shift implied adjustments to the work placement component of the exchange programme, to put both *work and community experience* at the centre of the learning

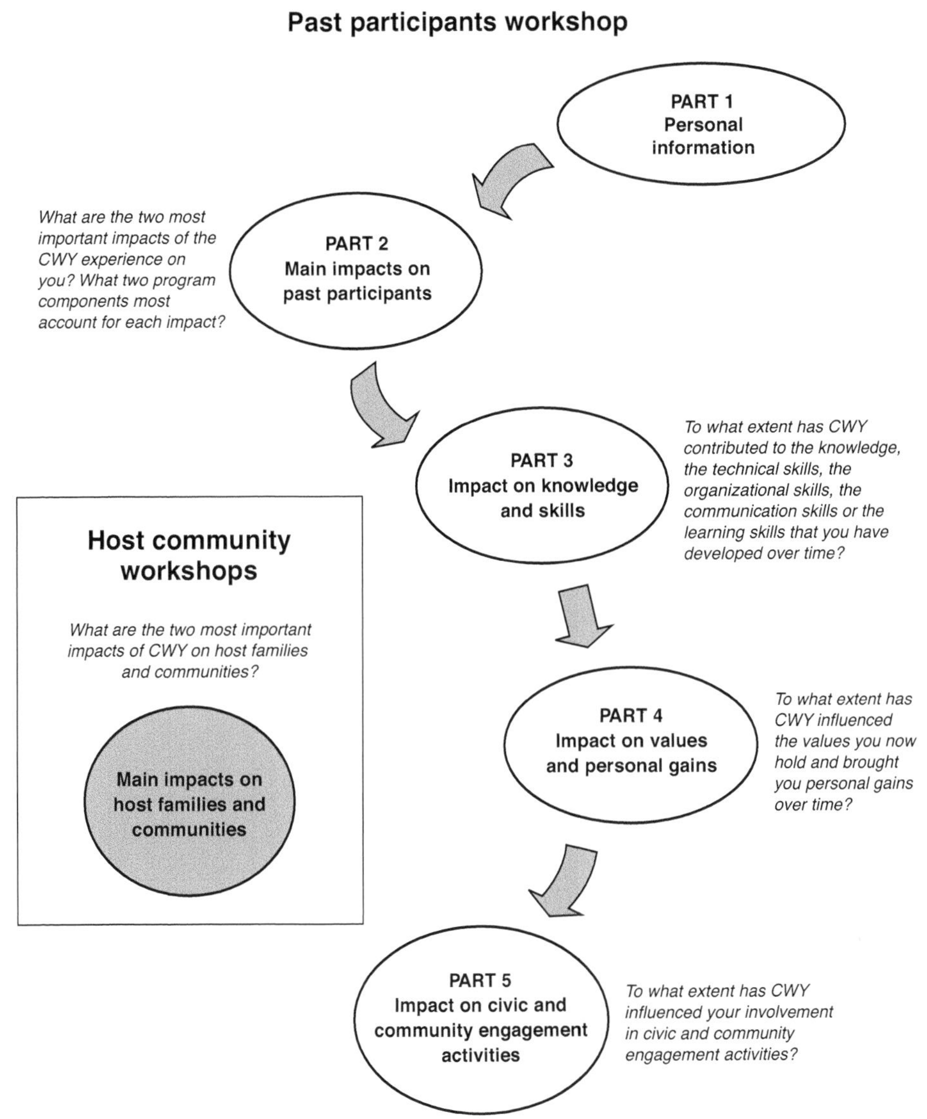

FIGURE 7.6 CWY impact questions and process design.

agenda. The anticipated effect would be to have a longer-term impact on host communities while at the same time building relevant individual technical or professional skills, in addition to communication, learning and organizational skills.

Assessing profiles

The Socratic Wheel is flexible enough to support step-by-step monitoring and evaluation on a small or large scale, by itself or in combination with other M&E tools (storytelling, surveys, etc.), with or without the use of indicators. Readers with a particular interest in monitoring and evaluation should review our general comments on the topic in Chapter 5, and an advanced M&E tool (*Attribution and Contribution*) presented in Chapter 16. The tool can do other things as well. As we could see in the Katkari story, above, it can support strategic planning starting with a baseline assessment of the situation (supplemented, as needed, with information from other sources) and priority setting. It can also be used to examine the similarities and differences that exist between people or between actions. The brief stories below are examples of *The Socratic Wheel* used in this manner, with a focus on the learning profiles and aspirations of health care and community development workers in Canada and Nepal.

Setting learning goals, and planning steps to achieve these goals, is a common function of educational learning as well as human resource development in organizations. The authors have had many opportunities over the years to facilitate discussions around skills and learning goal in schools, community organizations and the workplace. One example involved a group of twenty five or so healthcare workers in Saskatchewan who generated a list of five broad categories of skills important in their work:

1 ability to apply knowledge;
2 time management;
3 emotional intelligence;
4 planning a step-wise process; and
5 reflecting and adjusting.

Each of these categories of skills emerged from a *Free List and Pile Sort* exercise where people shared thoughts and stories on important skills and sorted these into categories. The purpose of the exercise was to assess where each individual stood with respect to each skill category, set individual learning goals and develop a plan to address them collectively and individually. The planning brought individuals with similar strength profiles into groups, a process that helped people identify peers and potential allies with different strengths in areas relevant to their own learning goals. This laid the ground for designing collaborative strategies between people that wanted to develop complementary skills by working with one or more potential allies already strong in a desired area. Participants could thus make specific training offers to others and request training and technical support in areas of priority learning (see *Negotiation Fair*, Chapter 14).

Another example is from work by D. J. Buckles in 2009 with fifteen community development workers in Pokhara, Nepal. They created a list of skills that reflected the unpredictability and complexity of working in very isolated and remote places in the hills of Nepal. The needed skills in this environment are:

- creative at problem solving;
- willing to face challenges;

- ability to focus clearly on goals;
- good at time management; and
- knowledge of a relevant technical subject.

The community development workers rated themselves in response to the question 'How good am I at . . . (each skill)', using a score of 1 to indicate that much improvement was needed to 5 indicating that they could teach others the skill. The rating process allowed everyone to create an individual profile using *The Socratic Wheel* and set learning goals to be achieved over the following twelve months. The exercise grounded learning goals in a prior discussion of what was feasible in the time frame and considering the training resources and opportunities available to them.

Back in Canada, a group of ten consultants and staff from organizations working in the social services sector in Calgary with D. J. Buckles also identified five strategic skills in their work: group leadership, active listening, generating enthusiasm, being flexible in response to different situations and suspending judgment. These reflected their roles primarily as facilitators of diverse and sometimes contentious initiatives involving highly marginalized populations. They rated themselves individually on each skill using a scale of 1 to 5 to express how strong they felt they were in each skill area. They also set personal improvement goals for the coming six months, knowing that training in these skills was available to them through workshops and individual coaching sessions. As with the health workers, the gap between the starting point and the target level for each skill formed the basis for group formation. By comparing individual wheels people gradually identified twins, triplets and then families with the same gaps between where they felt they were now and where they wanted to be. These reflected common, primary learning goals regardless of the absolute level of the starting point.

For example, one 'family' of two people wished to make significant improvements in two skill areas: being flexible and suspending judgment. Discussion helped them flesh out why this was so and what they could do to act on their goals. They learned that both worked with many different kinds of groups, a challenge that demanded a broad range of tools and techniques to respond to the context or focus at hand. They needed greater flexibility in their approaches. They recognized in each other as well a tendency to quickly form and express opinions on topics they had strong feelings about. This had landed them in hot water on many occasions. Cultivating the ability to suspend judgment and broadening their repertoire of active listening questions and approaches to accommodate different situations emerged for both as strategic learning areas. A drawing by the group helped explain their learning goals to others, using the scales of justice surrounded by an irregular fence as a reminder to be careful about forming judgments too quickly, and to recognize that every case is unique. They also flagged facilitation as an area where they felt they were already very strong, and in a position to teach others.

Each profile was re-examined after three days of intensive facilitation and PAR training. Socratic learning effects emerged when individuals revisited their initial rating for each skill, and considered whether or not they had over or underestimated what they were good at (see Table 7.1). For example, one of the two people targeting flexibility and the suspension of judgment as strategic learning areas realized that she had overestimated her skill level with respect to group leadership. She felt that the training had opened her eyes to many new leadership skills she had never thought about previously, and provided her with a new perspective on what leadership is all about and how she could use that understanding to help her adjust to situations, listen actively and suspend judgment.

REFERENCES

Buckles, D. J. and Khedkar, R. with Ghevde, B. and Patil, D. (2013) *Fighting Eviction: Tribal Land Rights and Research-in-Action*, Cambridge University Press India, New Delhi.

Evaluation, Monitoring and Support Services Department (EMSSD) (2011) 'Towards Educating for GNH – A guide to school self assessment tool and school improvement plan', unpublished document, Ministry of Education, Thimphu.

McLaren, K., Turcot, P., Chevalier, J. M. with Patterson, H. (2006) 'Canada World Youth Impact Assessment Synthesis Report', Canada World Youth, Montreal, QC.

CHAPTER 8

Seeking evidence and consensus

INTRODUCTION

Selecting the right tool and using it in the right way, with a good blend of rigour and flexibility, is key to success in practising the art of engaged research. The preceding chapter showed the many ways in which a basic tool such as *The Socratic Wheel* may be adapted and scaled up or down to support effective group thinking in a wide range of settings.

In this chapter, we offer other basic concepts and methods for participatory action research, starting with a theoretical commentary on the importance of developing, using and mastering a wide range of inquiry methods to support PAR. This preamble is followed by a tool to validate the results of an inquiry in light of two fundamental criteria: those of evidence and consensus. The tool, entitled *Validation*, points to both the social and factual aspects of knowledge considered to be valid. It can be used before or after people take action based on the results of an inquiry, to make sure they are ready to proceed and that no further research or prior stakeholder involvement is required.

The chapter also includes a variety of basic tools to facilitate brainstorming (*Free List and Pile Sort*), generate measurements through *Rating* and *Ranking*, or gather, analyse and share information (*Information GAS*) that feeds into collaborative research. It also puts forward general concepts and technical guidelines for *Active Listening*, a fundamental skill for any researcher working *with* people. Finally, in *Participation* we raise the tricky question of what 'participation' actually means and build on this concept to investigate the rules of ethical conduct for participatory action research, drawing on innovative thinking from Canada's main research funding agencies.

THREADS OF THEORY: COOKWARE AND HEAT IN THE KITCHEN

With all its aspirations to scholarly diversity and haute intellectual cuisine, social scientific inquiry as currently practised keeps employing the same, relatively simple containers to capture social phenomena – observation, survey questionnaires, interviews, content analysis and focus groups. It lacks novelty when it comes to the tools in the kitchen. Also, ironically, the means and measures of the social

sciences are in many ways the least social of all, often serving to merely gobble up data. Good inquiry methods should be crucibles designed to process competing ideas and take social heat.

To act in our complex world, we need to learn the art of browsing and navigating in many fields of learning, communication and knowledge. Applying the same recipes routinely to all questions of interest will not help or satisfy. Today's researchers and planners must be ready to explore different paths. They must be able to gather the information they need and select, mix and adjust tools to achieve a social purpose. They must know how to sharpen and sequence tools in ways that can adapt to changing circumstances and take the heat of social history. They must learn to sift through many sites and sources of knowledge, technology and methods of inquiry. Measures to log in and out of different sets of collaborative engagement strategies for learning and action in complex settings are needed more than ever.

Commentary

Multi-methodology is a growing trend that challenges the debate between the qualitative and quantitative stances in the social and human sciences. Fixed methods are giving way to mixed methods. This 'third movement', as Tashakkori and Teddlie (2003) call it, is long overdue. It introduces a breath of fresh air into a world of polarized theory, upholding a pluralistic and flexible attitude in the advancement of knowledge. Multi-methodology calls for the development of the many skills needed to mesh qualitative and quantitative methods, with a view to extending the breadth and range of inquiry to address increasingly complex, interdisciplinary problems (Creswell and Garrett, 2008; Creswell and Plano Clark, 2007).

The benefits are many. Triangulation corroborates results obtained from the use of different methods. Complementarity occurs when each method sheds additional light on the subject at hand. Development of findings is when the results of one method help develop another inquiry involving another method – the findings of a focus group help design survey questions, for instance (Spratt *et al.*, 2004). Last but not least, multi-methodology serves to initiate new thinking, by discovering the paradoxes, contradictions and multiple perspectives that emerge from the different strategies used (Greene *et al.*, 1989).

Multi-methodology is an important contribution to framing the inquiry process. The trend, however, represents an incomplete settlement of the qualitative/quantitative dispute. For one thing mixed methods do not challenge the basic dichotomy that created the controversy in the first place. The story of a divorce in the world of methods, now ending in reconciliation, was contrived from the start. It assumes that quantitative methods exist that are not also qualitative in some way. The contrast oversimplifies how measurements really work.

It is difficult to imagine how survey questions can be put into words using tools that are strictly quantitative, for instance. Some qualitative thinking is required to determine the right questions and terms to be used, not to mention the concepts needed to interpret the results. The same can be said of observations of measurable behaviour – violence or poverty in different social surroundings, for instance. Observations must rest on some prior notion of what 'violence' or 'poverty' means to researchers and their audience, to be deliberated prior to gathering information on the subject at hand.

The other assumption – qualitative methods cannot be quantitative – is equally problematic. Language stripped of any form of measurement is hard to imagine. Actually, researchers play games on laypeople when they use obscure mathematics and statistics to conceal a simple fact of history: numbers originate from everyday lives and stories that count. Measurements speak volumes in our lives, as when we write songs or poetry, cook meals, keep time, inquire about speed and distance, ponder about weight and weather, or number the blessings of youth and old age. Day-to-day calculations also include the constant estimation of risks of accident, illness and death. People use numbers to add value to conversations about life.

The rift between quantitative and qualitative methods perpetuates an odd assumption: the notion that measurements are strictly technical and instrumental (positively viewed by some and disdained by others). The debate ignores the fact that it is never quality or quantity that really 'counts', but rather the measures of life and meaning. In response to this criticism, one might argue that multi-methodology is simply an invitation to mix methods that 'tend to' be of opposite kinds, with a formal emphasis on either qualitative or quantitative thinking. When compared with qualitative studies, quantitative inquiries use measurements of a different order, more advanced. While more subtle, this argument raises another problem: it ignores methods that belong to neither camp because inherently mixed. A researcher can use a mixed method without having to mix methods.

Construct analysis is a good example (see *Domain Analysis*, Chapter 18). In the works of Kelly (1963), personal constructs identified through a qualitative technique known as triadic elicitation are the ways in which individuals perceive the world. If applied to a topic such as violence, construct analysis starts with participants listing concrete expressions of violence in their own surroundings, to which they can add real stories. Participants then choose three expressions of violence at random and ask themselves how two expressions are different from the third. The bipolar constructs elicited in this manner (e.g. physical as opposed to psychological violence) are then used to assign a numerical value to each expression of violence on a continuum from one pole to the other, using a simple scale of 1 to 3 or a more elaborate scale, such as 1 to 9. Participants provide descriptive arguments and narrative evidence to support each rating.

The end result of construct analysis is a single unified method that blends qualitative and quantitative reasoning. *Domain Analysis*, our social version of Kelly's Personal Construct method, is all the more powerful as it integrates analytical reasoning and narration in a participatory mode. That is, participants contribute both storytelling and logical attributions, measurements and classification to the exercise. In many ways, this meshing of analytic logic and storytelling, not to mention rigour and dialogue, is more advanced than efforts to combine qualitative and quantitative methods.

Domain Analysis goes to show that mixture differs from plurality. If multi-methodology is to be a third movement, it must offer robust ways of uniting qualitative and quantitative thinking, mixing both forms of reasoning into a new blend of inquiry. A weak strategy in this regard consists in juxtaposing and linking methods that are distinctively quantitative and qualitative. A stronger strategy consists in choosing and developing methods that are inherently 'mixed', as in the works of Kelly.

Multi-methodology raises another critical question: how does a method mix its component parts and work as a component part in a larger mix? To answer this question, we need to come back to some basic part-whole notions that tend to be glossed over. The inquiry process brings together several levels of thinking. Every inquiry consists of technique interfacing with method, methodology, epistemology and ontology. A **method** normally denotes an integrated set of **techniques** or procedures. For instance, the method of construct analysis proceeds from the free listing of elements in a particular domain (e.g. concrete expressions of violence) to a triadic elicitation of bipolar constructs (e.g. physical vs. psychological violence), followed by the rating of all domain elements against the constructs, and then cluster or principal component analysis to identify statistically significant groupings of expressions of violence.

But the inquiry process doesn't stop here. A good inquiry is never merely technical. To explain why and how a method is used, with or without other methods, one needs a **methodology**, i.e. a discourse on method(s). This is the set of principles and rules of organization that govern one or several methods that are part of the inquiry in a particular discipline. If using construct analysis, *The Easy Guide to Repertory Grids*, by Jankowicz (2004), offers a methodological exposé on construct analysis, for instance. As we shall see, Chapters 18 and 19 recast personal constructs into a different methodology centred on social constructs.

Methodology – i.e. methods, and arguments about them – requires in turn some thinking about **epistemology**. This is the theory of knowledge, claims that lie behind the techniques and methods used. In Kelly's work, psychological constructivism informs his understanding of knowledge making, a theory that assumes, among other things, that anticipation and prediction are the main drivers of constructions in personal grids or mindsets. Tools to investigate constructs presented later head in a different direction, towards the social anticipation and predictions of language and knowledge.

Ontology is the last ingredient in an inquiry framework. It is an explicit theory of reality, a formal specification of what we think is true of the component parts of our subject matter, and relationships among them. The notion that individuals essentially behave according to how they 'construe' the world around themselves represents Kelly's view on the subject matter of human behaviour, for instance. Materialists would beg to differ on this one.

These distinctions are helpful in understanding what mixed methods in the human and social sciences look like and other levels of thinking they must 'mix with'. Multi-methodology is mostly concerned with the first issue: techniques and methods to be mixed in different ways. On the quantitative side of the divide, available methods include survey questionnaires, structured interviews, observations and experiments designed to generate data that lend themselves to some frequency and distribution analysis. On the qualitative side, methods range from archival and content analysis to individual or group interviews that may be open-ended or structured, with a focus on life histories, key themes or critical incidents. Other qualitative methods, often used in the social sciences, include participant or non-participant observation performed without measurements, using formal procedures or not.

Qualitative and quantitative methods can be used alone or in combinations. However, researchers cannot apply them in isolation from theories of knowledge and social reality. This raises a question that goes well beyond the merits of methods that are either 'mixed' or 'fixed' along qualitative or quantitative lines. The question is, what motivates the choice of inquiry techniques in the first place? When doing participatory action research, for example, being able to move between methods and blend them is essential. This pluralistic stance, however, is not a statement about the inherent superiority of multi-methods. Rather it is a statement about what drives the inquiry process, which is the **fit** between chosen methods and the actual contribution that the inquiry seeks to make to transformations of knowledge and social reality. Whether this contribution can be achieved through a single or many methods is a question that cannot be resolved a priori. In the end, fit determines the choice between mix and fix. The rule is simple: work with tools that work.

To apply the rule, one must probe into the purpose of social science. Pragmatic philosophy (and eclecticism) seems to offer a natural fit between purpose and mixed methods studies, with its general emphasis on selecting and pulling together all tools and concepts that may help collect, analyse and interpret relevant data in a given context (Brewer and Hunter, 1989; Creswell, 2003; Creswell and Plano Clark, 2007; Greene, 2007; Morgan, 2007; Spratt *et al.*, 2004; Tashakkori and Teddlie, 2003). Pragmatic researchers insist on having access to a plurality of means and methods of inquiry that can be put to work and lead to a better understanding of reality.

A true pragmatist, however, should not assume that mixed methods are always better. Using a single method is also a legitimate option, provided it works. As Greene and Caracelli (1997) point out, 'using multiple and diverse methods is a good idea, but is not automatically good science'. Medical practice, the most pragmatic of all, illustrates the point. When inquiring into a possible brain tumour, medical practitioners do not automatically combine a tissue sample (biopsy), a white blood cell count, an MRI test (magnetic resonance imaging) and a CT scan (computerized tomography), on the simple assumption that more tools are better than fewer. If the inquiry can succeed in achieving its purpose with a single tool, say the blood cell count, why bombard the patient with the full artillery of tests? The fit between tool(s), purpose and circumstances (such as available time, burden experienced by the patient and resources) is what matters above all.

For a stronger foundation in multi-methods, variations on constructivism (Williamson, 2006), post-modern thinking (Hesse-Biber, 2010) and critical social theory (Mertens, 2003) may be more promising. They suggest that multi-method designs are more effective in bringing out multiple voices and theoretical perspectives to shed light on social reality, including the views of under-represented groups. Again, this reasoning is problematical in several regards. First of all, there is no reason to assume that multi-methodology and multi-theory necessarily go hand in hand. Just as one method can effectively bring out different views on the same subject, so multiple methods can converge on the same understanding of reality. Second, constructivism and post-modernism suggest that no conceptual discourse or philosophical framework exists in a pure state, without multiple influences that meet and intertwine in the process of theory building. Conversations across modes of thinking are pervasive and unavoidable, irrespective of the methods chosen to make sense of reality. Lastly, social purpose matters more than mixity in methods, or plurality for its own sake. While an inquiry can be designed to capture a plurality of perspectives that shed light on the phenomenon of violence, it can also aim for a shared understanding of violence, with a view to eliminating it, using the appropriate method(s), mixed or not. In some cases, acknowledging lines of sight that do not converge is the aim. At other times, working to construct new lines of sight across existing horizons is a priority. Purpose guides the choice.

It is commonplace to say that we now live in a complex world. From this observation, it is tempting to conclude that mixed methods are inherently better (Spratt *et al.*, 2004). In reality, complexity lies elsewhere: in choosing and creating the stand-alone or composite tools and designs that suit the purpose of meaningful research.

ENGAGING STAKEHOLDERS AND MOBILIZING EVIDENCE

Validation, described below, is central to answering the question of methodological fit. It reaffirms the importance of both fact-finding and consensus building in PAR. It is also a critical reminder that a dynamic, process-oriented approach to action-inquiry requires time. Whenever time permits, people engaging in the process must make sure to gather enough information and build sufficient consensus before acting on the conclusions of the inquiry, if they are to achieve results. Short-changing this essential requirement of reflective action is not without consequence. We illustrate this point by telling a short story of how people assessed and made plans to improve their account of the history of cooperative milk production in the Department of El Paraíso, Honduras (using *Timeline*). The stakes were too high to leave parts of this history incomplete and unknown.

Validation

Purpose

To validate the results of an inquiry and decide whether more evidence and/or consensus is needed before action can be taken based on the results.

Step 1

Review the overall results of an inquiry, including proposed actions.

Step 2

Prepare a **graph** (on the floor or a flip chart) by drawing a vertical line that crosses a horizontal line of equal length. Write 0 and 10 at the opposite ends of each line. Discuss and **plot** on the horizontal line the extent to which the inquiry is based on evidence (sound and sufficient information and analysis). A value of 10 would indicate that the inquiry is based on **strong evidence**. A value of 0 would show the opposite (the evidence is sketchy and unreliable).

Step 3

Discuss and plot on the vertical line the extent to which the inquiry is based on stakeholder consensus (participation and agreement on the conclusions). A value of 10 would indicate a **strong consensus** achieved through active stakeholder involvement in the inquiry and complete agreement with the conclusions. A value of 0 would show the opposite (no stakeholder involvement and/or strong disagreement with the conclusions). Consider and include in the rating past consultations used to inform the inquiry.

Step 4

Mark where the values from the two lines meet and label or place a drawing representing the results of the inquiry at this intersection.

Step 5

Use the same graph to plot the level of **evidence and consensus needed** to reach a firm decision and begin to act on the conclusions. Mark the place where the two desired values meet, and draw an arrow from the first mark to the second.

Step 6

Use the results of this exercise to identify what people are ready to decide and act on now. Then, identify what can be done to **complete the inquiry** to their satisfaction through (1) further information gathering and analysis and/or (2) further stakeholder involvement and stronger agreement. Keep in mind that not every context requires the same level of evidence and consensus before action can be taken.

Before deciding how much evidence and consensus is needed to reach a firm decision, discuss the **factors** that should influence the decision, such as how well the stakeholders understand the issue being analysed, how much time and information is available, the urgency to act, the impact the inquiry conclusions have on stakeholder activities, how much stakeholder approval and involvement is required, etc.

FAQ

- ***Does first-hand experience count as evidence?***

Knowledge and understanding acquired through experience certainly counts, especially if it extends over time.

- ***Is consensus limited to those actually participating in the* Validation *exercise?***

To answer this question, participants should discuss and identify all stakeholders that should be involved in the inquiry under review and contribute to consensus building.

- ***Isn't evidence-based thinking sufficient to validate the results of an inquiry?***

Well-informed or knowledgeable stakeholders, including scientific experts, may have different views on how to generate, analyse and interpret evidence that is relevant to the topic at hand. Cross-examination of these views may strengthen confidence in an inquiry process and its findings and makes it easier to discuss possible courses of action. By tapping into real diversity of views more information gets weighed, typically leading to better decisions.

Variations

- To be more precise, identify **indicators** that define the meaning of each number on the scale used to assess the level evidence and the level of consensus associated with an inquiry.

Combinations

- *Validation* can be used to assess the results of any inquiry, including any diagnostic assessment using tools or methods from this book.

Timeline validation in Honduras

The Jamastrán Valley and Highlands of Danlí are farming and ranching areas in the Department of El Paraíso near the border Honduras shares with Nicaragua. Most ranchers there raise cattle for two reasons. They sell some male animals for meat while the milk from cows is sold to cheese-makers. Over the years, the owners of livestock have tried to organize themselves to negotiate milk prices, develop regional and export markets for their meat products and address technical problems that arise. These attempts to organize have had uneven results. Many of the producers' organizations failed a few years after they got started.

The Board of Directors of the United Producers Agricultural Cooperative (COAPUL), the largest cooperative in the region, decided to examine the history of the organization and the older organizations from which it had emerged. The purpose of the assessment was to identify the events and actions that had helped or hindered the development of regional cooperatives. They planned to use this information to write a proposal for new funding. At the request of COAPUL, a university-based consultant (Laura Suazo) used the *Timeline* technique to facilitate the assessment. The group also validated the result, as reported here (Suazo and Buckles, 2008). They felt that it was important to do so before final decisions on the focus and rationale for the project proposal. The following summary describes the validation process, not the *Timeline* assessment per se.

The *Timeline* exercise was conducted during a half-day meeting with ten people that knew about the origins and evolution of COAPUL. It concluded, among other things, that having a large and committed membership improves the organization's capacity to negotiate milk prices and attract the investment needed to improve production methods. In the past, producers would sell part of their production on their own and part of it through the cooperative. This made it difficult for organizations to present a united front to buyers. Membership would inevitably decline after a few years when it became clear that the cooperative could not offer members better prices for milk than the open market. Participants recognized as well that COAPUL's investments in improving the sanitation and storage of milk made it possible to offer a better quality product to cheese-makers in the region. An effective membership drive in 2001 and commitment by members to sell their milk collectively also enhanced COAPUL's negotiating power. These developments happened thanks to technical and financial help provided by a research group and some members' administrative skills, acquired in previous organizations.

Participants went on to validate the *Timeline* result by asking two questions:

1 To what extent was the assessment based on solid evidence (sound and sufficient information and analysis)?
2 To what extent was there agreement on the views expressed through collaborative thinking?

In response to the first question, the group rated its *Timeline* analysis at level 6 for evidence, using a scale of 0 to 10. This reflected uncertainty regarding some of the local and national events that contributed to successful development of the cooperative (see Figure 8.1). The second question obtained a similar rating. The group rated its *Timeline* analysis at level 5 for consensus, also using a scale of 0 to 10. Participants understood that a 0 would show that there was disagreement within the group or that many key actors had not been consulted regarding the results of their previous analysis. A level of 10 would show complete agreement among key stakeholders. The level 5 rating for consensus reflected the group's view that some people who had been leaders or activists in relevant producer organizations had not been consulted. Also the group did not fully agree on the main reasons why some of the prior organizations had failed to achieve their goals, especially with respect to competitiveness in the open market.

Participants concluded that their *Timeline* analysis was not good enough for their purpose. The assessment had helped the group understand links among the many different organizations that had existed and the different legal structures and names they had used. However, some confusion remained. They also felt that greater consensus regarding the reasons for past failures would ensure that most members would support the conclusions and implications of the assessment for new activities of the cooperative. The group felt that a level of 7 on both evidence and consensus would be good enough to support plans for use of *Timeline* and its conclusions in the funding proposal. This would strengthen claims in the proposal about the long-standing legitimacy of COAPUL. More analysis of the factors that affected their evolution would also bolster a key argument about the importance of member solidarity, namely, that selling milk as individuals rather than collectively had a strong negative impact on the survival of past organizations. Greater consensus around these results would enhance confidence in new

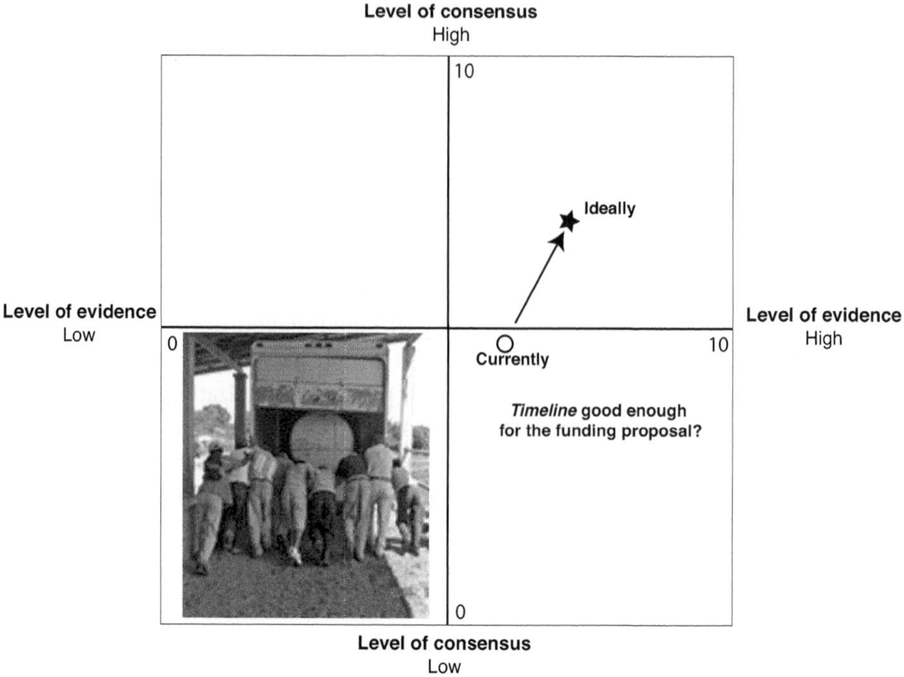

FIGURE 8.1 Validation of a *Timeline* assessment in Honduras.

directions and bolster the sense of solidarity among all members, by helping the younger and newer members of the organization to appreciate the struggles of older members.

Participants made plans to interview a few older members of producer organizations and collect more information on name changes and dates of registration of related organizations. More information on trends in membership would also be obtained from secondary sources (the archives of the Honduran Institute for Cooperatives). Once the information was compiled and integrated into a revised document on the history of the organization, it would be shared with the General Assembly and revised further, as needed, before being used in the project proposal.

BRAINSTORMING AND ORDERING

We now turn to basic participatory fact-finding and measurement tools, starting with *Free List and Pile Sort*. Free listing is an adaptation of brainstorming, a basic tool for group thinking. Brainstorming often provides the first step to a more advanced assessment, by allowing participants to generate a list of elements in the domain under analysis (events, activities, problems, factors, actors, skills, resources, options, etc.). To be manageable, however, list making should be combined with pile sorting. This helps to organize a list into fewer categories that become the focus for group discussion.

Free List and Pile Sort

Purpose

To create and compare lists and categories of elements relevant to a particular topic.

Step 1

Define a **topic** and ask each participant or small group to identify two or more examples of the topic. Give several cards to each participant or small group and ask them to write one example or meaningful **element on each card**. They should use key words, and add details on the reverse side of the card. The elements should be concrete, distinct in some way and relevant to the topic. If they are vague, use the *Laddering Down* method in *Active Listening* (below) to make them more specific and meaningful.

Step 2

Ask a participant to present one element and then group other cards that mean the same thing into a pile. Participants can place the cards under each other when they are the same, and below each other when they represent variations or shades of meaning. Continue sharing examples, one card at a time, until all cards are **sorted into piles**. Give a label or create a drawing to identify each pile or column of cards.

Step 3

Identify what may be important but **missing** from the list of elements organized into piles. If need be, **reduce** the number of piles and columns by combining them into broader categories, or by recognizing some as less urgent or less important and deciding not to include them in subsequent steps of the exercise.

Review in detail the *Scoring tips* (below). They are **critical** to proper application of *Free List and Pile Sort.*

FAQ

- ***Is* Free List and Pile Sort *the first step for any exercise in group thinking and analysis?***

Not necessarily. There are situations where the elements in a domain have already been determined through prior studies and discussions (core skills for instance), or they are clearly known to everyone and need not be free listed and pile sorted (e.g. existing project activities).

Variations

- Ask participants to pile sort the elements between themselves, **without facilitation**.
- Use **brainstorming** to make a list on a flip chart, without pile sorting. Start by defining a topic and a time frame not exceeding twenty minutes. Invite people to offer elements for the list using short phrases without lengthy explanations. Ask people to agree to suspend judgment or criticism of their own ideas and the ideas of others during the brainstorming session. Mirror what people say, write down all ideas and encourage people to take turns. End the session by reviewing the list of elements and deciding which ones to carry forward for further discussion. For information on the theory and technique of suspended judgment, see Kaner (1996).

Ranking and advanced comparisons

Concentric circles

- **Rank** each pile based on the number of cards (piles with elements that people mention most often may be the most important). Visualize the ranking by placing piles in three **concentric circles**. In the inner circle, place the core piles that have the most cards; in the middle circle, the average-size piles; in the outer circle, the piles that have the fewest cards. Discuss why some piles have more cards than others.

PHOTO 8.1 Managers of a community seed wealth centre in Tangail, Bangladesh discuss priorities for conservation. (Source: Abdul Zabbar)

- Determine how **familiar** a participant or group is with a topic by counting the number of core elements appearing in their list and the number of core elements appearing in a list created by all participants. Also count the number of peripheral elements in each list.
- Evaluate the level of **compatibility** between two individual or group lists by counting the number of times the same elements are mentioned in both lists and divide this number by the total number of elements.
- Evaluate the level of **agreement** between two individual or group lists that contain the same elements by counting the number of times the elements are placed in the same circles and divide this number by the total number of elements.

Comparison table

- Compare two different lists and negotiate **a common list**. Start by creating a table where the rows represent one party's elements or piles of elements, and the columns represent the other party's elements or piles (see Table 8.1). Identify the row and the column elements or piles that have the **same meaning**. Rearrange the rows and the columns so that the elements or piles that have the same meaning appear at the beginning of each party's list and in the same order. Mark an 'X' in the cells with the same meaning and insert the cards representing these elements or piles in the corresponding cell.
- Calculate the level of **agreement** between the two lists by counting the number of elements or piles that are placed in the marked cells, and divide the result by the total number of elements or piles in the table. Discuss the elements or piles that appear only in one list until parties reach a **common understanding** of most elements or piles. Redefine the elements, create new ones or change the way elements are grouped into piles, as needed. Verify the revised list by asking each party to organize the elements into piles again, and compare the results using the same table.

TABLE 8.1 Comparing and negotiating *Free Lists and Pile Sorts*

Party 1				*Party 2*		
	Equity	*Conservation*	*Peace*	*Development*	*Identity*	*Spirituality*
Fairness	x					
Sustainability		x				
Peace			x			
Progress				x		
Education						

Tree mapping

- Create a **map of elements and categories** using a tree trunk and branch metaphor. **Sort** all elements into two piles of any size, according to what participants think is the **most important difference** between all the elements provided. Give a label to each branch leading out from the tree trunk. Sort each pile again into two smaller piles reflecting the most important difference between the remaining elements in the pile, and label each branch. Repeat the process until each element is placed at the end of a branch.
- **Compare** individual or group tree maps involving the **same elements** by exchanging trees showing the branch labels only. Each individual or group can then locate the elements on the map according to the differences already labelled on the tree. Calculate the **level of agreement** between the resulting tree maps by counting the number of similar element cards placed at the same branch level, and then divide the number by the total number of element cards.
- **Compare different interpretations** of tree maps by exchanging the branch labels written on cards and trees showing the elements only. Participants can then assign the labels to the differences they see between piles of elements placed on the branches. Calculate levels of agreement in the interpretation of tree maps by counting the number of labels assigned to the same branches and divide the number by the total number of labels.

Combinations

- Use **drawing, pictures, objects, description and storytelling** to explore the topic (for example, by describing cases of success and failure), and then use this information to identify the elements relevant to a particular topic.
- Participants may put the piles or elements of each pile in a *Timeline* **sequence** that makes sense to them, especially when planning or doing a step-by-step presentation of the elements and piles.

MEASURING

Ranking and *Rating* are widely known techniques to facilitate group thinking about things that need to be weighted and measured, with varying degrees of precision. They should be used when quantity matters.

> Einstein reminds us that not everything that counts is measurable, and that not everything that is measurable actually counts. Still, there are countless instances in research as well as in everyday life where things can be measured and do actually count.

Ranking

Purpose

To develop order within a hierarchy, from first to last, using one or several criteria.

Ranking using one criterion

Step 1

Define the **topic** and create a list of relevant **elements** to be ranked from first to last (see *Free List and Pile Sort* and *Information GAS*, in this chapter). The elements should be **concrete**, distinct and clearly defined. If they are **vague**, use the *Laddering Down* method in *Active Listening* (below) to make them more specific and meaningful. Write key words or draw each element on its own card, with details on the reverse side.

Step 2

Identify a **criterion** on which to rank the elements (e.g. feasibility). Define the criterion using **positive terms**.

PHOTO 8.2 Women in Purba Medinipur district of West Bengal, India discuss project priorities separately from men, prior to weighting them on different criteria. (Source: D. J. Buckles)

Step 3

Individually or as a group, **rank** each element in the list from first to last based on the criterion. Keep track of the **reason(s)** given for each score. If ranking is done as a group, discuss the rank until participants agree based on consensus or a majority vote. Alternatively, calculate the **average ranking** for each element by adding all scores (or each score multiplied by the number of times it is given to an element) and divide the result by the number of scores received by that element. If using one criterion only, go to Step 8.

Ranking using two or more criteria

Step 4

If necessary, define **other criteria** relevant to the topic. Write the criteria on cards using positive terms, or create a drawing to represent each criterion.

Step 5

Create a large **table** (on the floor using masking tape, for instance) with the cards for the list of elements in the top row and the cards for ranking criteria in the first column. Add a **final row** to record the average ranking for each column element (see Table 8.2). Ensure that the elements and the ranking criteria are clear to everyone.

Step 6

Under each criterion, **rank** the elements from first to last. If the ranking is done as a group, discuss each rank until participants agree based on consensus or a majority vote. Alternatively, use the method of average calculations, pile sorting or paired comparisons described below.

Record the scores on separate cards and place them in the corresponding cells. Keep track of the **reason(s)** given for each score on the back of the corresponding card.

TABLE 8.2 Ranking using multiple criteria

Criteria	*Clinic*	*Sewage*	*Road*	*Electricity*
Cost effectiveness	4	2	1	3
Sustainability	3	2	4	1
Buy-in	4	2	3	1
Gender equity	3	2	4	1
Average ranking	3.5	2	3	1.5

Step 7

Record the **average ranking** for each column element in the final row, by adding all column scores (or each score multiplied by the number of times it is given to an element) and dividing the result by the number of scores received by that element.

Step 8

Review the results and reasoning that went into the ranking process. Discuss the implications of the ranking for people's understanding of the topic and decisions to be made. Participants can **compare** the tables and final ranking by different individuals or groups using the same ranking criteria, or compare final rankings based on different criteria.

Review in detail the *Scoring tips* (below). They are critical to proper application of *Ranking*.

Variations

Paired comparisons is another ranking procedure. Start by making a ranking choice (first and second) between two elements chosen at random. Then, choose one other element at a time and find the most similar among those already ranked. Where there are many elements to compare, use a table with all the elements in both the top row and repeated in the first column. Then, make **one-to-one ranking choices** (first and second) and enter the results in the cells along the top diagonal of the chart (see example in Table 8.3). The bottom diagonal consists of cells that represent false pairs (A by A) or pairs that appear for a second time (B by A is the same as A by B). Use the last two columns to record the number of times each row element (A, B, C, etc.) is preferred *in all cells* and the **final rank** for each element based on these numbers. If there is a tie between two elements, decide which of the two should be ranked above the other.

TABLE 8.3 Paired comparison table

Options	*Fisheries*	*Grain bank*	*Road*	*Children's nursery*	*Total*	*Rank*
Fisheries	x	Grain bank	Road	Fisheries	1	3
Grain bank	x	x	Road	Grain bank	2	2
Road	x	x	x	Road	3	1
Children's nursery	x	x	x	x	0	4

Combinations

- To calculate levels of disagreement and misunderstanding between the ranking tables of two individuals or groups, see *Disagreements and Misunderstandings* (Chapter 14).

Rating

Rating is an all-purpose technique widely used in the field of participatory inquiry, planning and evaluation. Together with *Free List and Pile Sort*, it is a key component of many techniques presented in this book.

Purpose

To grade elements using one or several criteria. Rating differs from ranking in that it creates scores that may be the same for several elements in a list.

Rating using one criterion

Step 1

Define the **topic** and create a list of **relevant elements** to be rated (see *Free List and Pile Sort*, above). The elements should be concrete, distinct and clearly defined. If they are vague, use the *Laddering Down* method in *Active Listening* (below) to make them more specific and meaningful. Write key words or draw each element on its own card, with details on the reverse side.

Step 2

Identify a **criterion** on which to rate the **elements** (see sample criteria in Table 8.4). Define the criterion using **positive terms**.

Step 3

Establish a **rating scale** and assign a value of 1 to one end of the scale and a value of between 5 and 10 to the other end of the scale. To be more precise, identify **indicators** or progress markers that define the meaning of each number on the scale. For instance, a score of 2 out of 10 on the criterion 'community support' could mean that about 20 per cent of the community is likely to support a particular action.

Step 4

Individually or as a group, **rate** each element in the list on the criterion. In a rating exercise, several elements may receive the same score or value. Keep track of the **reason(s)** given for each score on a flip chart. If rating is done as a group, discuss each rating until participants agree based on consensus or a majority vote. Alternatively, calculate the **sum of ratings** for each element. If using one rating criterion only, go to Step 9.

TABLE 8.4 Rating using multiple criteria

Criteria	*Arts and crafts*	*Fishing*	*Hunting*	*Historical route*
High impact				
Cost efficient				
Skills available				
Benefits the community				
Environmentally friendly				
Total rating				

Rating using two or more criteria

Step 5

If necessary, define **other criteria** relevant to the topic. Write the criteria on cards using positive terms, or create a drawing to represent each criterion.

Step 6

Create a large **table** (on the floor using masking tape, for instance) with the cards for the list of elements in the top row and the cards for rating criteria in Column 1 (Table 8.4). Add a **bottom row** to record the total score for each column element. Ensure that the elements, the rating criteria and the rating scale are clear to everyone.

To weight scores according to the importance the group assigns to each criterion, add a column for the **maximum score** allowed for each criterion. (See *Weighting*, Chapter 7.)

Step 7

Rate each element on the criteria. When rating, the same score can be assigned to two or several elements. Discuss each score until participants agree based on consensus or a majority vote. Alternatively, calculate the total score for each element. Record the scores on separate cards and place them in the corresponding cells. Keep track of the **reason(s)** given for each score on the back of the corresponding card.

Step 8

Calculate and record the **total rating** for each column element in the final row.

Step 9

Review the results and reasoning that went into the rating process and **discuss** the priorities based on the bottom row totals. Also discuss ways to modify the elements to make them more feasible, achieve greater impact, etc. Participants can compare the tables and final ratings by different individuals or groups using the same rating criteria or compare final ratings based on different criteria.

Review in detail the *Scoring tips* (below). They are critical to proper application of *Rating*.

Variations

- Many tools presented and illustrated in this book (*The Socratic Wheel, Domain Analysis, System Dynamics, Force Field,* etc.) include a rating exercise where scores are organized into figures, diagrams or charts to facilitate their analysis and provide visual support for group discussion.

Combinations

- Use *The Socratic Wheel (*one for each element) to create a visual representation of the rating results.
- To calculate levels of disagreement and misunderstanding between the rating tables of two individuals or groups, see *Disagreements and Misunderstandings* (Chapter 14).

Scoring tips

Identifying elements and criteria

- Elements and criteria to evaluate them should be concrete, distinct and clearly defined. If they are **vague or overlap**, use the *Laddering Down* method in *Active Listening* (below) to make them more specific and meaningful.
- If using measurements, decide whether they should be based on **observation** (e.g. of behaviour) or reported views and **perceptions** (e.g. levels of agreement with a statement).
- Determine whether you should use **progress markers** (what people 'expect to see', 'would like to see' and 'would love to see') as proposed in Outcome Mapping (Earl *et al.*, 2001) or SMART indicators (specific, measurable, applicable, realistic and timely).
- Determine if the facilitator should **supply** or **negotiate** some or all the elements and the criteria, invite participants to **generate them**, or identify them through a combination of methods (supplying general categories and generating specific criteria, for instance).
- A simple procedure to identify several criteria is the **catchall question**: 'Can you think of some relevant criteria to assess the elements?' Another option is the **full context**

procedure: review all elements and find two that have a positive characteristic in common, and then the element that is the most different from these, and why. Use the discussion to identify one or more criteria.

- Use **description and storytelling** to explore the topic (for example, by describing examples of success and failure, observed or imagined), and then use this information to identify the elements or criteria relevant to a particular topic.

Rating scales

- Decide if the **rating scale** should be the same for all criteria (e.g. 0 to 5) or vary according to the importance of each criterion (as in *Weighting*).
- Make sure that the highest value for each element has a **positive meaning**. This usually makes more sense intuitively and is key to interpreting the sum of ratings in rating tables.
- **Middle scores** in a rating scale may have ambiguous meanings. Results may be easier to interpret if middle scores are avoided, using a rating scale with an even number of points (such as 1 to 4 or 1 to 6).
- To be more precise, identify **indicators** or **progress markers** that define the meaning of numbers on each scale.
- If numbers are a barrier, use simple **phrases** first and then convert the phrases into measurable objects (from 1 to 5 stones, for example). Another option is to score each element with the help of a grey scale: white (value 1), light grey (value 2), medium grey (value 3), dark grey (value 4) and black (value 5). A grey scale makes it easier to see patterns in a table.

Rating process

- Determine if the rating should be done **individually**, by **subgroups** or by the **group** as a whole.
- **Pile sorting** is a simple ranking or rating procedure. Start by dividing all the elements into three piles: those with high scores, those with middle scores and those with low scores. Repeat the process with each pile until a distinct ranking or rating is identified for each element.
- Another option is to place cards showing the **two polar values** (0 and 5, for instance) at a distance from each other. Then ask participants to locate each element somewhere along the **continuum**.
- **Multiple flip charts** are an alternative to creating a table. On separate flip charts, post all the information for each element: the description, the ranking or rating criteria, the actual scores and the reasons for each score.
- When differences arise regarding scores, facilitate discussion of the reasons for particular ratings or rankings and go with the **majority view** rather than an average.

Saving time when rating

- To do ratings in **less time**, divide all participants into **subgroups** that are representative of the larger group. Then, divide the criteria among the subgroups and ask each to rate all elements using the criteria assigned to each subgroup. Use this technique only if the participants don't need to be involved in making all the ratings.
- Place **numbers on the floor** for each point on the scale and ask participants to stand next to the number they think is correct for a particular criterion. Agreement and differences on ratings will be easy to see. The group can then focus on major differences only, discuss them and adjust positions until a single rating is obtained.

Working with large groups

- Novel methods to scale up action research from small groups to broader publics and multi-stakeholder groups are much needed (see Chapter 1). When working with large groups using rating or ranking, write each element and its description on its own flip chart (e.g. each contributing factor in *Causal Dynamics* or each rating criterion in *Weighting* or in *Domain Analysis*). Place each flip chart in a separate part of the assembly room or in a separate room. Create a small jury responsible for each flip chart element. Select jury members and adjust the timing of selection according to purpose (e.g. a mix of people that are representative of the larger group may be selected in advance and contribute to designing the inquiry process). Make sure that each jury and all participants understand the scoring process and the corresponding instructions. Invite all participants to visit any jury to express their views as to how they assess the corresponding element and their reasons. Set a time frame during which visitors can circulate. To help visitors take other views into account, jury members may progressively synthesize prior results and reasons expressed by visitors and invite further contributions. Another option is for each jury to start with one or two rounds of small group discussions leading to a formal assessment of their element, with documented reasons. Follow this with an open round of visits from participants wishing to review, validate or challenge prior group ratings or rankings as summarized by the jury.

  Once the discussions and visits are completed, each jury deliberates on the final score(s) and the arguments that justify them. The deliberation takes into account the views and evidence expressed by participants, and jury members' informed understanding of the topic under examination. The jury then prepares a summary of their deliberations, including any relevant information about arguments or conclusions that diverge from the majority view.

  When planning the process, decide what evidence or prior inputs are needed to inform the deliberations, whether external experts or observers should be involved, and how each jury can contribute to the other jurys' deliberations, if time permits. When working with a wider public, consider using a web-based platform to support these deliberations.

INVOLVING PEOPLE

The validity of PAR findings hinges on the quality and quantity of information gathered or generated with the appropriate methods, including group techniques such as *Free List and Pile Sort*, *Ranking* and *Rating*. However, while participatory action research is a commitment to sound research, it is also a constant effort to pay more than lip service to participation in research. *Validation* is thus a social process that seeks agreement through reasoning and persuasion. For this to happen, the parties involved must develop the art of effective communication that brings reason to bear on problems to be understood and solved. The art includes the ability to speak. It also requires a disposition to listen. Successful and truthful communication hinges on the listening skills of those engaging in collaborative research to make sense of the world and make it better as well.

This section focusses on the implications of engagement, starting with a brief discussion on PAR ethics as they relate to mainstream rules of consent and confidentiality. This is followed by a tool that raises critical questions about the levels and conditions of authentic participation, with complementary guidelines on *Active Listening*.

Participatory action research ethics

Research involving humans is subject to considerations of ethical conduct, norms that guide the relationship between researchers and participants, with a view to protect the latter from suffering harm, disrespect or unfair treatment. A clear and detailed expression of such norms can be found in Canada's *Tri-Council Policy Statement: Ethical Conduct for Research Involving Humans*. The statement, published in 2010, represents the joint policy of Canada's three federal research agencies: the Canadian Institutes of Health Research (CIHR), the Natural Sciences and Engineering Research Council of Canada (NSERC) and the Social Sciences and Humanities Research Council of Canada (SSHRC). Informed by leading international ethics norms, the policy recognizes that the search for knowledge aimed at understanding and improving our world is a fundamental human endeavour. This implies that research has its own requirements, those of academic freedom, to be balanced against three competing sets of ethical considerations: respect for persons, concern for welfare and justice. The way the Tri-Council interprets these principles, particularly in reference to research practices that are critical, action oriented and community based, is most helpful.

The first principle recognizes the inherent worth and dignity of all human beings. Researchers are under the obligation to **respect** the autonomy and freedom of individuals and groups to deliberate about a decision and act on it. Respect for people implies that researchers must seek the **free, informed and ongoing consent** of all those participating in research, with authorized third party involvement in the case of persons lacking the capacity to decide. This is particularly important in situations of power imbalance and potential coercion or undue influence affecting the relationship between researchers and participants. Consent must be informed, which means that measures must be taken to make sure that participants have a reasonably complete understanding of the purpose of the research, what it entails and all risks and potential benefits that may result from participation, at least those that can be foreseen. Normally, evidence of this voluntary and informed consent is obtained through a **signed consent form**.

The second principle involves the obligation to protect the **welfare** of living individuals or groups, by not exposing them to any unfavourable balance of benefits and risks associated with participation in the research, especially those that are serious and probable. Since privacy is a factor that contributes to people's welfare, **confidentiality** tends to be the norm. Respect for privacy regulates the control of personal information about participants and those who are important to them – information that is identifiable and not in the public domain. Confidentiality is usually obtained through the collection and use of data that are **anonymous** (e.g. survey data) or anonymized (irrevocably stripped of direct identifiers).

The last principle, **justice**, requires that all people be treated with equal respect and concern for fairness and equity. Criteria of **appropriate inclusion** are needed to ensure that no particular people or groups (defined by age, gender, language, religion, ethnicity or disability) bear an unfair share of the direct burdens of participating in research. Nor should any population or group be overprotected or discriminated such as to be excluded from research without appropriate justification, arbitrarily depriving them of the potential benefits of participation (e.g. information sharing, capacity building, community action-learning and problem solving). Concern for justice also calls for mechanisms to identify the dual or multiple roles of researchers and those assisting them, with a view to disclosing, minimizing or eliminating related **conflicts of interest**, whether real, potential or perceived.

At first sight, Canada's Tri-Council policy seems to limit the application of norms of ethical conduct for research to activities that are within the scope of Research Ethics Boards and related review processes. **Research** is restricted to its mainstream definition – *a disciplined inquiry or systematic investigation aimed at* the *advancement of knowledge for the benefit of future generations and society as a whole, usually with little or no direct benefit to participants*. While the definition is restrictive, topics that may be researched are limitless. They include 'attempts to understand the broad sweep of history, the workings of the human body and the body politic, the nature of human interactions and the impact of nature on humans' (Tri-Council, 2010, p. 7). Excluded from this list, however, are non-research inquiries that may employ methods and techniques similar to those employed by researchers. Non-research comprises practical fact-finding activities such as programme evaluation, quality-improvement studies, performance reviews, educational testing and works of artistic interpretation. While fulfilling an important role in society, these inquiries lie outside the scope of the Tri-Council policy and may be subject to legal, professional or institutional norms of their own.

This brief outline of rules of ethical conduct for research involving humans will be familiar to most researchers. The reasoning and related measures provide important guidance against attacks on the dignity and welfare of fellow humans, examples of which can be found in a long history of scientific endeavours that reduce people to observed subjects and mere objects of research. When generalized and rigidly codified, mainstream ethics are nonetheless problematical. They interpret the principles of deliberative autonomy, welfare and justice in ways that leave little room for alternative perspectives on what research is, who owns it and what 'participation' means in the first place.

Well aware of the limitations of conventional thinking in these matters, the Tri-Council offers extensive guidelines to support ethical conduct in what is an accepted yet less conventional research paradigm: i.e. engaged research. The following summary is largely inspired by Tri-Council thinking on research endeavours that are critical, qualitative or promote the engagement of aboriginal populations, organizations or communities of interest. These guidelines, well worth reading (see the Policy Statement, Chapters 9 and 10), should not be read as waivers of the normal rules of signed consent and anonymity and the policies of appropriate inclusion and non-conflicting interests. They are not exemptions that can be justified in exceptional cases only. More to the point, they reflect a different understanding of what consent, welfare and justice entail when researchers take inspiration from the ethics of collaborative engagement.

To begin with, PAR entails a broader perspective on research, to include approaches other than the 'disinterested advancement of knowledge'. Alternative approaches to the pursuit of knowledge involve research codes and practices grounded in action, experience and dialogue. Research thus defined may flourish outside the walls of academic or corporate science. It is wedded to social context and will reflect or transform existing worldviews. Engaged research serves immediate or long-term benefits to the parties involved, contributing to the pursuit of collective goals in particular historical settings.

Given this alternative stance on the advancement of knowledge, the notion of '**participation in research**' acquires a fundamentally different meaning and has several ethical implications.

- When carrying out a PAR project, participation calls for research that is conducted by, for and with particular communities (i.e. collectivities defined territorially, organizationally or as a communities of interests). The people involved are not 'subjects' or 'participants' but rather **partners** engaged in all phases of the process, from conceiving and designing the project to gathering and analysing relevant information, interpreting the results, deciding on actions to follow and disseminating the results. Accordingly, the terms and conditions of the collaborative process must be set out in a **research agreement** based on mutual understanding of the project goals and objectives between the parties, subject to preliminary discussions, negotiations and adjustments over time.
- Agreements are guided by ethics that acknowledge collective rights, interests and obligations and view **community welfare** as a complement to individual well-being.
- Expressions of agreement can take many forms, depending on the context. They include **informal agreements** that are binding and appropriate manifestations of mutual trust and respect. In some contexts, verbal consent or a simple handshake is less threatening and a better indication of agreement than signing a consent form. Some collaborative research projects may lead to deep relationships where questions of ethics are interwoven with personal commitments extending over a lifetime.

- Agreements sensitive to indigenous knowledge and value systems may require the extension of ethical obligations to respectful relations and partnership with the deceased, future generations and **life forms** other than human.

Ethical considerations regarding the potential harm and benefits associated with engagement in collaborative research also take a different path.

- In a PAR perspective, **risks** to all parties are best addressed in the language of respect for self, others and the diversity of views and interests at stake, rather than the protection of 'others' who 'participate' but exercise little control over the research. To mitigate the risks associated with a collaborative project, mutual expectations and obligations should be set out in the research agreement, subject to review as the project unfolds.
- **Recognition** and 'being heard' may matter more than privacy and confidentiality. Respect for individuals and groups who wish to be heard and identified for their contribution to research must be shown through proper quoting, acknowledgements, co-authorship, or the granting of intellectual property rights.
- Given its commitment to social justice and transformative action, PAR may be **critical** of existing social structures and the policies and practices of governments, institutions, interest groups and corporations accountable for their actions. As a result, research may legitimately entail negative consequences for some individuals or groups (other than those engaged in PAR).

Research is a step into the unknown. As a result, it may **evolve** and create new risks over time. This inherent feature of research is particularly salient in the case of PAR methods, which tend to be consciously dynamic and flexible, inductive and reflective.

- Given its emergent quality and responsiveness to social context and needs, PAR cannot limit the question of ethics to the design and proposal phase. The ongoing assessment of expectations that are met or not met is key to success and must take place at the appropriate time, as the project unfolds.

It should be emphasized that levels of engagement vary considerably from one PAR project to another, depending on the nature of the research, the contribution of the parties or community involved and the corresponding assignment of multiple roles. This means that the choice of appropriate rules of ethical conduct is rarely an either/or question. For instance, collaborative work between academics, formal leaders and customary authorities within an indigenous community does not preclude seeking consent from individual 'participants' and the involvement of groups otherwise excluded and disempowered, such as women and the poor. This is to say that judgment must be exercised when selecting and balancing the ethics of engagement with measures of informed consent and privacy (to protect the dignity and welfare of individuals). Rules of ethical conduct depend largely on what 'participation' really means in each context.

Participation

Purpose

To determine the level of participation in an ongoing or proposed project and assess the extent to which existing conditions limit or enable it.

Step 1

Discuss and use the guidelines below to describe the existing **level of participation** in the project. Draw a **diagonal line** on a flip chart and mark the observed level of participation on one side of the line, using a scale of 0 to 7.

Step 2

Discuss the **conditions** needed to achieve effective participation in project activities (see *Conditions of participation* in Figure 8.2). Mark on the other side of the line the level at which these conditions are actually met, using a scale of 0 to 7.

Step 3

Discuss **gaps** between levels of participation and conditions needed to achieve them. Explore **ways to address** those gaps.

Levels of participation

1. **Inform and educate**: gather and share the information needed to identify problems, make plans, promote awareness on a topic or change stakeholder attitudes and behaviour.
2. **Consult**: present information, plans and results and invite stakeholders to communicate their views on an existing situation and what should be planned. Assess the impact of project activities, after implementation.
3. **Support participation**: offer resources or incentives to engage stakeholders in the implementation of project or programme plans.
4. **Facilitate independent action**: encourage stakeholders to independently implement activities consistent with project goals.
5. **Seek group consent**: agree to go on with a plan of action only if there is informed consent from other key parties.
6. **Delegate authority**: transfer responsibilities to plan and carry out some activities to one or more parties, within a broader joint work plan or governance structure.
7. **Decide and act jointly**: engage with all stakeholders in assessing a situation, deciding what actions to take, and sharing or dividing responsibility for implementing tasks and accounting for the results achieved and the resources used.

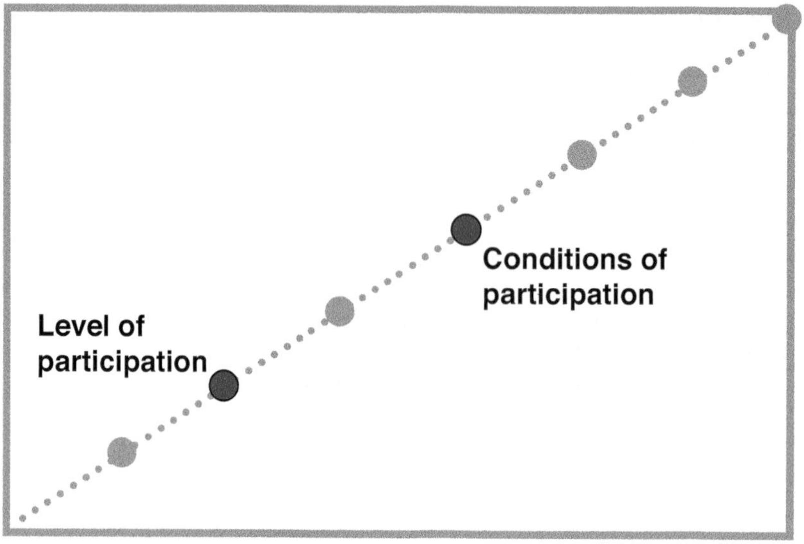

FIGURE 8.2 Levels and conditions of participation.

Conditions of participation

- Local *culture* and customs
- The *time available* for the activity and the *urgency* of the issues to be addressed
- The *resources* that are available
- The *inequalities* that exist among participants (the 'uneven playing field')
- The *workload* implications for all parties concerned
- The *expectations* likely to be created and whether those expectations can be satisfied
- The desired level of *formality* (or informality)
- The need for *trust*
- The current level of *conflict or sensitivity* connected to the issues at hand
- The need for better communication or *consensus building*
- The importance of *discussing differences*
- The need for a *formal outcome* or binding decisions
- The need for *new ideas* and creative output
- The number of *options* (few, many) to be explored when addressing key issues
- The level of *clarity* and *complexity* connected to the issues at hand
- The level of *leadership and commitment* that can be applied to any plan
- The extent to which the expected *gains* will be greater than the expected losses
- The need for adequate levels of *stakeholder representation* and accountability
- The amount of reliable *information* (neither too little nor too much) that participants need to access or produce

FAQ

- ***Does this technique suggest that full participation is not always realistic?***

Correct. To put it succinctly, participation is doing the right thing at the right time with the right people, with success in mind. This is different from the jamboree approach to participation – doing all things with all people at all times, irrespective of the risks and benefits involved.

Variations

- **Revise** the list of conditions and levels of participation.
- To be more precise, identify **indicators** that define the meaning of each level of participation.

Combinations

- Several methods can be used to further discuss conditions and levels of participation, including *Storytelling* (see *Information GAS*, below), *Timeline* (Chapter 9), *Force Field* (Chapter 10), *Social Analysis CLIP* (Chapter 12), *Ideal Scenario* (Chapter 14), *Sabotage* (Chapter 14), *Negotiation Fair* (Chapter 15) and *Network Dynamics* (Chapter 17).

> As with democracy, participation is both an end and a means to achieve it, among other ends.

Active listening

Purpose

To engage people and help all participants listen and be heard. (See *Sabotage*, Chapter 14.)

Step 1

Review the purpose of the inquiry and become familiar with the diversity of people involved (see *Stakeholder Identification* and *Stakeholder Rainbow*, Chapter 11).

Step 2

Use various forms of *Active Listening* (below) to engage all stakeholders, considering the culture and customs of the people involved.

The verbal

Open questions

Pose open questions that do not lend themselves to 'yes' or 'no' answers, such as *Tell me about your experience . . .* or *What do you think would happen if . . .* Make sure the person or group understands the question. If not, restate it using other words.

Paraphrases

Restate what someone has said, using the speaker's key words and starting the sentence with phrases such as *What I'm hearing is that . . . I see that . . . If I understand you well . . .* or *In other words what you're saying is that . . .*

Summaries

Periodically summarize the main ideas expressed during a discussion, as needed. Use key words and begin the sentence with *To sum up this point . . .*

Note-taking

When facilitating a group discussion, gather ideas on flip charts by printing clearly and alternating colours for each idea. Decide whether to take notes on one, two or three flip charts. The first could be used to capture all the points that are made, the second to summarize and organize the main points, and the third to list issues that may have to wait until later to be discussed in detail. If possible, have one facilitator write on the flip charts while the other listens carefully to the participants and summarizes what should be written.

Synthesis and validation

End the discussion with a synthesis and validate the synthesis (*Can we conclude that . . ., Is it fair to say that . . .*).

The non-verbal

The implicit, body language, emotions

Reflect on and draw out the implicit meanings, feelings and non-verbal messages that people are expressing (without necessarily being aware of it). These may add meaning to what is being said (*If I hear you well, it seems that . . ., Perhaps we should talk about . . .*).

Rhythm, humour and silences

Welcome good humour, laughter and enjoyment of the process. Accept and welcome silence as well, either when people call for it, or when it arrives on its own. Avoid rapid

PHOTO 8.3 Varied views on environmental priorities on the Bonnechere River (Source: J. Wonnacott)

speech and frequent interruptions; don't try to fill silence. Allow time for people to pause and reflect on the topic (possibly in writing) before the dialogue begins. Listen while others are speaking and let go of planning what you will say when it is your turn.

Self-awareness

Take time to reflect on your state of mind before beginning a discussion. While listening to what others have to say, be aware and let go of immediate concerns, bias, feelings or immediate reactions that may affect your ability to listen actively. Observe non-verbal language, and adjust behaviour if necessary. Acknowledge information held by others and invite them to share it. Recognize gaps in your own knowledge.

Empathy

Show empathy and appreciation while listening (*I understand . . ., I see/hear what you're saying . . ., I appreciate the fact that . . .*). Do not describe similar experiences you or another person had in the past. Encourage active listening and empathy toward third parties that are being talked about (*How would you state, in one sentence, what they are trying to tell you?*). Be aware of moments that are intense. Do not try to rush through them.

Suspended judgment

Avoid making positive or negative judgments (*Lucky you . . ., I envy you . . ., Poor you . . ., How awful . . .*). Don't start a sentence with *Yes but . . ., I believe that . . ., In my opinion . . .*. At the start of a new discussion, begin with a brainstorming or free listing exercise where all ideas can be expressed freely, without being judged or interrupted by others.

Orientation

Clarifying the goals

Discuss and clarify what people expect from a process (*What do you expect from this meeting? If I understand you well, you'd like to . . .*). Take into account how much time is needed and available to achieve these goals. Use various forms of active listening to make sure people's expectations are clearly understood.

Framing

Unpacking

Keep track of and note different lines of thinking (*I'm hearing three topics being raised. They seem to be . . .*). When several issues are raised in a discussion, unpack them so that people can address each of them separately and establish priorities.

Sequencing

Identify the issue that should be addressed first (and those to follow). Choose the right moment to end one topic and move on to the next *(Perhaps we could move on to the next topic concerning . . .).*

Parking

Identify topics that may need to be discussed later.

Prior information

Plan in advance so the documents, facts or evidence needed to have a well-informed discussion are on hand.

Reframing

Positive reframing

If needed, restate negative statements as positive statements (*If I understand you well, you'd like meetings to be short and to the point . . .*).

Congruency

When statements seem to contradict each other, try to clarify them, without expressing judgment (*On the one hand . . ., On the other . . .*). When needed, note areas of both disagreement and likely agreement (*Some people seem to be saying that . . ., Others think that . . .*).

Scaling

Laddering up or down

When statements seem too general or vague, use laddering down questions to make them more specific or concrete. (*For instance? Can you give an example? What makes you say that? What do you mean by this? Can you tell us about a situation that describes what you're saying?*). When statements seem too specific or concrete, use laddering up questions to make the meaning clearer. (*Why is it so? What have you learned from this? Why does this matter? What do these things have in common?)*

The good enough principle

Make sure that the information and analysis that are part of a discussion are 'good enough' to satisfy needs and expectations, without being either superficial or exhaustive and exhausting (see *Validation*, Chapter 8).

Process observations

Welcome questions or comments about the process being used in a discussion. State what needs to change in a positive way, and adjust when possible. When unsure on how to proceed, share doubts and ask for help (*Are there suggestions on how we should proceed?*).

MOBILIZING KNOWLEDGE

Research methods to gather, analyse and share information are many. All methods may serve a useful purpose, provided they fit the circumstances and are skilfully applied to the situation at hand. While some are simple and others are technically more advanced, selecting, combining and adapting tools to support meaningful research is truly an art, an exercise in complex thinking and reasoning. Below we provide a brief outline of well-known methods of inquiry, interpretation and communication ranging from participant observation to surveys, secondary data analysis, qualitative interviews, storytelling, improvisation theatre, popular performance, graphics, audio-visual productions and the Internet. The list and description of strengths and weaknesses for each method is by no means exhaustive. It should be read as an incentive to learn more about the many paths of knowing and sensemaking (in lieu of always falling back on surveys or interviews, for instance) and show an open mind and creativity when designing and carrying out an insightful action-research project.

Information GAS (Gathering, Analysis, Sharing)

Purpose

To select methods for gathering, analysing or sharing information best suited to the needs and culture of the people involved.

Step 1

Discuss how information is likely to be used in a project or programme, for what purpose and by whom.

Step 2

Select and combine methods for information gathering, analysis and sharing appropriate to the context. Consider the culture and customs of the people involved and how formal and methodical the inquiry needs to be and the importance of storytelling as part of the process of gathering, analysing and sharing information.

Information GAS *methods*

- **Qualitative interviews** use a semi-structured or informal framework to gather information from individuals or focus groups. They usually start with general questions on a particular topic and then probe for details. A focussed, two-way conversation can emerge that covers both predefined topics and emerging issues as interviewees expand their answers and share experiences and feelings about a situation or topic.
  - *Strengths*: Supports the collection of detailed information about people, behaviours and perspectives on issues. Comments from interviewees and new lines of questioning can be incorporated into the framework. The privacy and flexibility of an individual interview may make it easier to discuss sensitive topics and to deeply probe for underlying issues and detailed explanations.
  - *Weaknesses*: The views of the people who are interviewed may not represent the views held by a majority of community members or vulnerable groups. Unless the interview is done in a focus group, the information cannot be easily compared or verified by others.

- **Narrative interview, life history, storytelling and diaries** generate stories about real or hypothetical events and situations. The methods can gather broad personal or community knowledge, either in writing or orally.
  - *Strengths*: Supports the reconstruction of a series of events or situations from particular points of view. Allows researchers to probe deeply into the importance and interests of stakeholders, the relationships among them, their beliefs, the management of time, possible ways to manage problems and the roots and scope of a problem (relating to ethnicity, religion, kinship, politics, laws, etc.).
  - *Weaknesses*: These methods can be emotionally challenging for all parties. The information may be difficult to organize and analyse.

- **Improvisational theatre, role-play and simulation** connect theatre to research. Short, structured games may be used to create an experience that enhances creativity, teamwork, leadership and learning. Participants may be asked to put themselves in a story or a pretend situation or to respond to guided imagery by acting out a scene from their point of view or the point of view of a particular stakeholder. Debriefing questions help share observations, feelings and learning from the activity.
  - *Strengths*: These methods help people step out of a given reality and empathize with the position of others (using role reversals), making it possible to express

views and ideas in ways that are not limited by present circumstances or personal interests. This may be important when the group's ability to analyse a situation is limited or empathy is lacking. New understanding and ideas are experienced through the body and emotions as well as the intellect, potentially deepening the personal impact. The methods may use humour and other forms of creative expression, thereby building energy and releasing tension.

  - *Weaknesses*: Simulation and role-play may differ too much from reality to be compelling. If not grounded in a topic or task, the methods can seem trivial or superfluous. Skilful debriefing is needed to ground the activity.

- **Audio-visual presentations** share information, tell stories and stimulate multi-stakeholder discussions in an organized way. Text, images, video and audio can be combined in various formats including presentation software such as PowerPoint, DVDs or websites.
  - *Strengths*: A readily accessible way to reach large numbers of people with particular messages, information and statements on outcomes. Can stimulate response and discussion among multiple stakeholders and across language barriers.
  - *Weaknesses*: Effective audio-visual presentations require the careful selection of high quality visual inputs, and can be both costly and time consuming.

- **Still visuals** such as photography, drawings, cartoons, murals, posters and flannel boards offer ways to engage community members and professional artists in the co-creation of visual information. It may include calendars, maps and other visual material to raise awareness, provoke discussion, gain feedback for analysis and monitor issues.
  - *Strengths*: Still visuals cross cultural boundaries as well as language and literacy barriers. They are inexpensive to produce and provide creative ways to engage various kinds of stakeholders, including youth and children.
  - *Weaknesses*: Still visuals present information selectively and can oversimplify issues. Effectiveness as conveyors of information depends a lot on the selection and quality of the images and may require professional assistance.

- **Graphics** include tables, graphs, charts, maps and various kinds of pictograms that present and summarize large quantities of information in a visual form.
  - *Strengths*: Graphics provide a sharp focus for discussion of the underlying data supporting main findings and conclusions.
  - *Weaknesses*: Interpreting graphics may require specialized technical knowledge. Graphics can be misleading.

- **Popular performance** includes mime, dance, song, jokes, verse and theatre. They provide creative and emotionally engaging ways to create awareness and communicate key messages directly and simply.

- *Strengths*: Large numbers of people who speak different languages or have different literacy levels can be reached. Popular performance can draw on local culture and customs. It can be both educational and engaging, and combines well with other *Information GAS* methods.
- *Weaknesses:* Popular performance can oversimplify complex information.

- **The Internet** provides a wide range of options for gathering, analysing and sharing information including chat rooms, electronic mailing lists, forums and networking sites. These allow participants from different places to discuss issues instantly during virtual meetings. Participants can also exchange and post information before, during, or after the virtual meeting.
  - *Strengths*: The Internet and its various spaces for chat rooms and forums make collaborative work possible when physical meetings cannot be arranged or are too costly. These spaces involve an anonymous or controlled sharing of information. They allow large quantities of information to be stored and easily retrieved through search engines.
  - *Weaknesses*: Effective use of the Internet requires some technical knowledge and good Internet connections among all participants. To avoid frivolous or inappropriate messages, clear protocols are needed regarding who can be involved, the purpose of the discussion and boundaries regarding how information is to be shared. Organizers may not be able to confirm the identity of participants and therefore the validity of their information.

- **Surveys** involve the use of standardized questions designed to gather information about people and their opinions and behaviours. Many surveys are designed for in-depth statistical analysis of the responses by ensuring an appropriate and randomized sample size and by using scales or indexes to measure the same idea in different ways (for example, several questions may be combined to help measure the idea of 'occupational stress'). A number of procedures can be used to collect the information in a questionnaire including face-to-face interviews, telephone interviews, the post, etc.
  - *Strengths*: Surveys allow researchers to see how a wide range of people living in different circumstances answer the same questions on a particular topic. Objective information about individuals and households such as income, age, profession, etc. can be combined with subjective information on opinions and behaviours. It allows researchers to track changes by asking the same questions at different times, and comparing responses.
  - *Weaknesses*: Interviewing an appropriate sample of a population can be a challenge as updated lists of names from which to draw a sample may be hard to come by. Questionnaires typically require a considerable amount of time from both respondents and interviewers. Because survey questions are often simple and responses may be given out of context and without discussion, results

can be superficial, difficult to explain or undermined by low response rates. All the key decisions about survey design must be made before the survey begins and cannot be changed once the survey has started. Use of appropriate statistical techniques for analysis requires specialized knowledge.

- **Participant observation** involves becoming a member of the community being researched, with a distinct and accepted role as an observer. Information is gathered over an extended time using a variety of methods.
  - *Strengths*: An insider's view of an organization, group or community can be created. Makes use of well-developed rules for observing, taking field notes and analysing observations.
  - *Weaknesses*: Gatekeepers can block access to certain individuals and topics. Training is needed to protect sources and maintain researcher neutrality. Information is collected, analysed and interpreted by the participant observer who controls the inquiry process.

- **Analysis of secondary data** involves the use of information that has already been gathered by another researcher, perhaps for another purpose. Sources include published books, databases and public documents collected by governments, libraries and museums.
  - *Strengths*: A wide range of information on a topic can be collected and contrasted. This may be particularly useful at the beginning of a research process when little is known about a topic. Secondary sources may contain detailed interpretations of information and links to theory.
  - *Weaknesses*: Secondary sources can be biased, out-dated or unreliable, and should be selected critically.

REFERENCES

Brewer, J. and Hunter, A. (1989) *Multimethod Research: A Synthesis of Styles*, Sage, Newbury Park, CA.

Creswell, J. W. (2003) *Research Design: Qualitative, Quantitative, and Mixed Methods Approaches*, Sage, Thousand Oaks, CA.

Creswell, J. W. and Garrett, A. L. (2008) 'The "movement" of mixed methods research and the role of educators', *South African Journal of Education*, vol. 28, pp. 321–323.

Creswell, J. W. and Plano Clark, V. L. (2007) *Designing and Conducting Mixed Methods Research*, Sage, Thousand Oaks, CA.

Earl, S. Carden, F. and Smutylo, T. (2001) *Outcome Mapping: Building Learning and Reflection into Development Programs*, International Development Research Centre, Ottawa, ON.

Greene, J. C. (2007) *Mixed Methods in Social Inquiry*, Jossey-Bass, San Francisco, CA.

Greene, J. C. and Caracelli, V. (1997) 'Advances in mixed-method evaluation: the challenges and benefits of integrating diverse paradigms', *New Directions for Evaluation*, no. 74, Jossey-Foss, San Francisco, CA.

Greene, J. C., Caracelli, V. J. and Graham, W. F. (1989) 'Toward a conceptual framework for mixed-method evaluation design', *Educational Evaluation and Policy Analysis*, vol. 11, no. 3, pp. 255–274.

Hesse-Biber, S. N. (2010) *Mixed Methods Research: Merging Theory with Practice*, Guilford, New York.

Jankowicz, D. (2004) *The Easy Guide to Repertory Grids*, Wiley, London.

Kaner, S. (1996) *Facilitator's Guide to Participatory Decision-Making*, New Society Publisher, Gabriola Island, Canada.

Kelly, G. (1963) *A Theory of Personality. The Psychology of Personal Constructs*, Norton, New York.

Mertens, D. M. (2003) 'Mixed methods and the politics of human research: The transformative-emancipatory perspective', in A. Tashakkori and C. Teddlie (eds) *Handbook of Mixed Methods in Social and Behavioral Research*, Sage, Thousand Oaks, CA, pp. 135–164.

Morgan, D. L. (2007) 'Paradigms lost and pragmatism regained: Methodological implications of combining qualitative and quantitative methods', *Journal of Mixed Methods Research*, vol. 1, no. 1, pp. 48–76.

Spratt, C., Walker, R. and Robinson, B. (2004) *Practitioner Research and Evaluation Skills Training in Open and Distance Learning: User Guide, Module A5: Mixed Research Methods*, Commonwealth of Learning, Vancouver, BC.

Suazo, L. and Buckles, D. J. (2008) 'Validation of a timeline assessment by a milkproducers' cooperative in Honduras', in J. M. Chevalier and D. J. Buckles, *SAS^2: A Guide to Collaborative Inquiry and Social Engagement*, Sage/IDRC, New Delhi, Ottawa, pp. 161–164.

Tashakkori, A. and Teddlie, C. (eds) (2003) *Handbook of Mixed Methods in Social and Behavioural Research*, Sage, Thousand Oaks, CA.

Tri-Council – Canadian Institutes of Health Research (CIHR), Natural Sciences and Engineering Research Council of Canada (NSERC), Social Sciences and Humanities Research Council of Canada (SSHRC) (2010) *Tri-Council Policy Statement: Ethical Conduct for Research Involving Humans*, Ottawa, ON.

Williamson, K. (2006) 'Research in constructivist frameworks using ethnographic techniques', *Library Trends*, vol. 55, no. 1, pp. 83–101.

MODULE 3

Exploring problems

MODULE 3: EXPLORING PROBLEMS

The next three modules reflect basic questions that apply to any situation: what are the **problems** people face and must explore, who are the stakeholders or **actors** affected by a situation or with the capacity to intervene, and what **options** or alternatives for action do people need to consider and assess? This module illustrates concepts and tools for exploring problems. We do not, however, argue that this is the best point of entry for a collaborative action-inquiry process. In fact, the sequencing of the three modules is arbitrary. What question needs immediate attention varies according to the circumstances of a group process or project. Judgment must be exercised, based on the setting, the inquiry purpose and decisions made prior to the inquiry (see *Process Design*). This is grounding as a skilful means. Action-research that is well grounded focusses on short- or long-term questions that are pressing and leaves the other issues in the background until people are ready to explore them in detail. In complex and dynamic situations, going back and forth between a focus on problems, actors and options is usually recommended.

The module contains two chapters on exploring problems. Chapter 9 shows how to analyse the causes and the effects of a problem (*Problem Tree*); visualize and acknowledge the resources of communities (*Resource Mapping*); tell a story of changes over time, or identify stages in a theory of change or steps in current or planned activity (*Timeline, Critical Path*); assess the ways that key stakeholders have managed a core problem in the past (*Previous Responses*); and examine whether a core problem is mostly about gaps or conflicts in power, interests, moral values, or information and communication (*Gaps and Conflicts*). Stories of tribal land struggles in India and adaptation to climate change in India and Nigeria illustrate these techniques for getting to the root of a problem.

Chapter 10 presents and applies two other tools to assess problems. The first tool, *Force Field*, is of Lewinian inspiration. It looks at the factors that contribute to a problem and those that counteract it. The second, *Paradox*, is our adaptation of paradoxical psychology. It explores how efforts and practices to handle an existing problem can be undermined by unspoken benefits, values and attitudes that are veiled and may be difficult to comprehend. Both tools, combined with *Timeline* (Chapter 9) and *Hazards* (Chapter 15), are brought to bear in an accident prevention study of the construction industry in France. The study, co-authored by J. M. Chevalier and Patrick Obertelli, illustrates how PAR methods creatively developed and applied with rigour can go beyond site-specific inquiries and contribute to debates on broader questions such as risk analysis and the causes and prevention of hazards in modern society (also see *Disaster relief and risk reduction in the Philippines*, Chapter 15).

ENTRY POINTS

While they play an important role in framing the inquiry process, assumptions about the ideal point of entry for action-research are rarely discussed. This raises a question that may be worth putting to partners in a PAR initiative or learning process: what is the ideal point of entry into a collaborative inquiry process? Analysing the problem(s), as in Module 3? Knowing who the stakeholders are and how they interact, as in Module 4? Or assessing the goals and options for immediate action, as in Module 5? Those participating in this exercise can form groups around their preferred entry points and then try to recruit others by convincing them of the validity of their reasoning. The discussion can then proceed to a quick survey of methods that represent different stances on this issue. For instance, the Japanese *Project Cycle Management* method and the *ZOPP* or *GOPP* (Goal Oriented Project Planning) approach promoted by the German International Cooperation (GIZ) begin with a stakeholder analysis and then proceed to a problem analysis using the *Problem Tree.* Realistic options for action and expected outcomes are considered last. By contrast, *Appreciative Inquiry* and *Future Search* are critical of the focus on existing problems and unmet needs because of its deficit-minded assumptions. They prefer instead to launch group thinking and planning with a positive vision of the future based on existing assets and strengths.

In our view, taking a general stance on this question, without reference to time and place, creates what is essentially a chicken and egg riddle. How can we identify key actors if we ignore the problems or goals that bring them together in the first place? Likewise, how can we determine problems or options if we don't know whose interests they speak to? How can we say that something is a problem if we don't define the goals that have not yet been met? Conversely, how can we develop goals for the future if we have no sense of current failures and problems in achieving these goals? In the end, problems, actors and options are inseparable. The question to ask is, 'What would be useful to investigate and learn more about at this point in time?'

CHAPTER 9

Getting to the root

INTRODUCTION

Most PAR practitioners are familiar with *Resource Mapping* and other basic techniques such as *Timeline* and the *Problem Tree*. The tools are designed to engage people in discussions of what resources are important to them, and the root causes and history of situations in need of collective attention and action.

What follows are instructions on how to facilitate each tool. We also offer two detailed stories of their use. A *Problem Tree* assessment of the roots and consequences of insecure land tenure among the Katkari in India proved to be a pivotal moment in strengthening their resolve to resist eviction. A comparative story of climate change initiatives in Nigeria and India shows how all three tools were combined to support rich community-based discussions.

The chapter includes two new techniques that are equally helpful in defining the problem(s) at hand. *Previous Responses* draws from theories of leadership style and Alternative Dispute Resolution. *Gaps and Conflicts* takes its inspiration from the conflict management literature.

Techniques to inquire into the nature, the roots and the history of a problem can help find solutions. That is their ultimate goal. The solutions may be technical, or not. In the conclusion to this chapter, we explore the issue of *technê* in more detail, and challenge two common attitudes that are diametrically opposed: the technical fix approach to research and its subject matter, on the one hand, and the fear of any advanced technical or technological device for understanding and acting on life in society, on the other. In our perspective, technophilia and technophobia have more in common than might be expected.

ROOT CAUSES

Problem Tree is a common tool in Participatory Rural Appraisal (PRA) and an integral part of Goal Oriented Project Planning (known by the German acronym ZOPP) championed by Japan's JICA and the German international development agency GIZ. It is typically used to broaden thinking about a problem and see how it is linked to other issues in a linear cause-effect manner. The focus on root causes and effects seeks to move thinking about a problem beyond the immediately obvious symptoms, with a view to identifying deeper corrective actions. To provide a bridge from understanding of the problem to the corrective actions, a *Problem Tree* exercise is often followed by an *Objectives Tree* or *Tree of Means and Ends*. This involves restating the core problem as though it had already been resolved, converting it into a positive scenario (see Chapter 14). The effects are rephrased into **ends** that are realized when the positive scenario is in place. Similarly, the root causes are turned into the **means** to resolve the problem at hand. Means-ends thinking thus provides a basis for project and programme definition and strategic planning (see the example below).

Problem Tree

Purpose

To understand the causes and the effects of a problem.

Step 1

Define the **core problem** and place a card with key words, a drawing or an object representing the core problem in the middle of the workspace. This corresponds to the trunk of the problem tree.

Step 2

Ask 'Why has this problem occurred?' Identify four or five causes directly responsible for the core problem. Focus on causes that can be observed directly. These are the **first-level causes** (or thickest roots) of the core problem. Describe each first-level cause on its own card using a drawing or a few key words, and add details as needed to the back of the card or on a flip chart. Place all the cards that show first-level causes in a row below the trunk showing the core problem.

Step 3

For each first-level cause, ask 'Why has this occurred?' The reasons are the **second-level causes** directly responsible for each first-level cause. Write (or draw) each second-level cause on its own card using a few key words, and add details as needed to the back of the card or on a flip chart. Place the new cards in a row below the corresponding first-level causes.

Step 4 (optional)

Use the same method (Step 3) to determine the causes directly responsible for each second-level cause. Place these **third-level causes** in a row below the corresponding second-level causes. Connect the first, second and third level causes with lines representing the thickest surface roots and the finer deeper roots of the core problem.

Step 5

Go through the same steps (Steps 2 to 4) to determine the **first-level, second-level and third-level effects** or implications (branches and fruit) of the core problem. Ask participants 'What is the result or consequence of this problem (or this effect)?' Keep in mind that effects of a core problem may include **actions** people are already taking in response to the situation, whether successful or not. Write each effect on its own card, and place the new cards in layered rows above the core problem. When noting an effect, avoid using words that emphasize the **lack** of a particular solution to the problem; describe instead the **consequences** of what is lacking.

Step 6

Review the result and look for causes and/or effects that fit into both the roots and the branches of the problem tree. These may point to **loops** or 'vicious circles' that reinforce each other through direct or indirect connections to the various levels of causes and effects.

Step 7

Identify the most important, the most pressing or the least difficult causes to handle. These may be **priorities** for action. Identify the effects that are most troubling to the people involved in the exercise, or that point to new opportunities. These may help to motivate and focus attention on the core problem and its causes.

FAQ

- ***What are the common errors made when using this tool?***

When identifying the causes and effects, participants sometimes write the cause and its effect(s) together on the same card or create cards that describe the same cause using different words or sentences. Failing to drill down into deeper causes of causes is another common problem.

Variations

- Other metaphors such as parents and ancestors (for the roots) and children and grandchildren (for the branches and fruit) may help identify the various levels of the *Problem Tree*.

Combinations

- To convert a *Problem Tree* into a *Tree of Means and Ends*, see *Ideal Scenario* (Chapter 14). This involves restating the core problem as though it had already been resolved. The problem is converted into a positive scenario, the causes into **means** to achieve it, and the effects into **ends** that are realized when the positive scenario is in place. (See example below.)

Insecure tribal land in India

The Katkari, a traditionally nomadic adivasi people in India, feel the bite of insecurity when landholders enclose their hamlets with barbed wire. Communities in this situation are forced to act against eviction and to seek help from any quarter that will offer it.

Our engagement with the Katkari began in March 2005 when several Katkari women from a village in Karjat taluka near Mumbai told a member of the research team that a barbed wire fence had been erected around their hamlet. A religious trust had recently purchased several properties to establish an ashram. The sale included title to land settled some eighty years earlier by about twenty Katkari families. This incident launched an action-research process designed and facilitated by Daniel Buckles and Rajeev Khedkar that eventually led to greater security and much enhanced confidence and resolve among Katkari living in more than 200 affected villages (Buckles and Khedkar, 2013). However, when the research team talked with people in hamlets not facing immediate eviction, many were puzzled by our focus on land tenure and sense of urgency. They recognized that they did not have title but did not think this was a key problem in their community. For them the problem of ownership seemed remote, compared to more pressing matters such as hunger, water scarcity, sickness and the constant struggle to find employment. The research team was uncertain how to respond to this apparent indifference. Our research in 313 Katkari hamlets had shown that 212 of them did not have legal title to a village site. Given that land prices were skyrocketing everywhere, it was only a matter of time before they too were threatened with eviction. The dilemma we faced was how to raise this issue in villages not threatened by immediate eviction, without imposing the topic or ignoring other matters of immediate concern.

The *Problem Tree* offered an opportunity to raise the question: should the Katkari pay attention to the legal status of their hamlets? Figure 9.1 illustrates the reasoning that emerged in a hamlet called Siddeshwarwadi. The participants, a group of eight men and four women, developed the chain of causes leading to the core problem – no land title. They stated the main reasons why they did not have title and then identified the reasons underlying each of these. They worked down from first to second to third level reasons to create a rich network of logically connected causes.

While the roots of the problem contained no surprises for the group, the shift to the fruit or branches of the problem brought a lot of energy into the discussion. A few years earlier government officials had offered to build a school in the hamlet but the landholder had objected. This was very telling for participants. Because of the objection, the new school was built in a much smaller, non-tribal village some distance away. Katkari

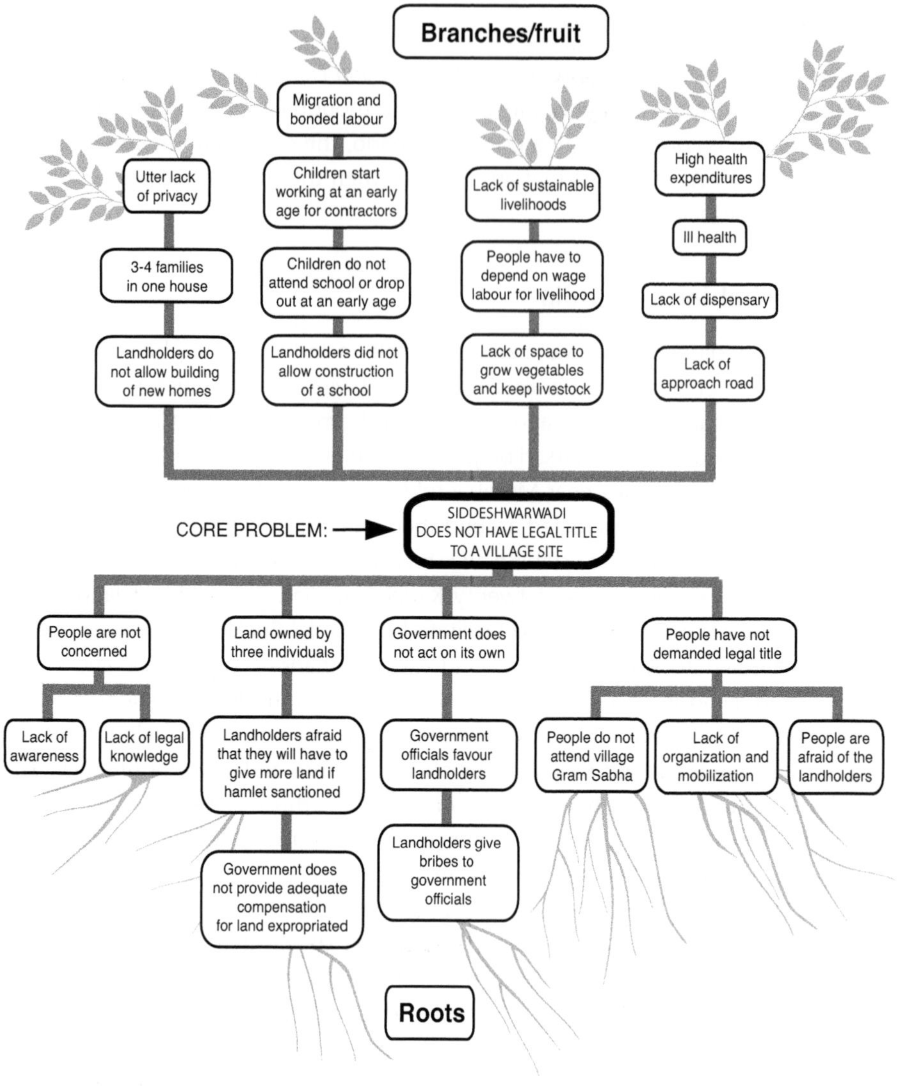

FIGURE 9.1 Roots and consequences of not having legal title to a village site in Siddeshwarwadi.

children did not attend regularly, or they dropped out at an early age. Children not in school are usually taken to work on the brick kilns where they can be cared for on a daily basis. Participants lamented this situation, which they felt ultimately brought their children into bonded labour at an early age.

As they recounted this story each link was drawn in chalk on the floor to show the chain of effects (summarized in Figure 9.1). Other consequences of not having title to land for the hamlet were also identified until participants felt that the story was complete.

In the meetings with the Katkari, participants decided to replace the metaphor of a tree trunk, roots and branches with the notion of 'parents' and 'children' of the situation, a language they felt better reflected their relationship to the hamlet.

The *Problem Tree* assessments in various Katkari hamlets made the specific problem of legal title visible to the Katkari, and to us, in a way it had not been before. It brought related ideas into a single conversation and larger picture linking insecure tenure to other matters of direct and immediate concern to the Katkari. In villages where enclosure and eviction were hard realities, the chance to tell their stories broadened people's understanding of the problem's scope and the root causes they would need to address if they were to take control of the situation. In villages that had not previously thought seriously about legal title to the village site, reasons to do so were identified. For many this produced a shift in their thinking, an effect similar to what Freire called a process of 'problem posing'.

In all cases, the collaborative analysis showed that the problem was a very difficult one to resolve. It had several root causes well beyond the control of the Katkari. Some participants concluded that they simply could not dream or hope of any improvement in their situation. Others, while desperate to avoid eviction, were overwhelmed by the challenge of organizing the entire community around the issue.

To provide a bridge from understanding of the problem to the corrective actions, the research team later engaged the same groups in converting the *Problem Tree* into a *Tree of Means and Ends* (Figure 9.2). People in Siddeshwarwadi reviewed and then reworded the original problem and its causes and effects as though they had been resolved positively. This built a gradual pathway to a future where, for instance, children would have an opportunity to complete school, and various potential improvements to the village site and individual households would be realized. The end that generated the most excitement in the group, however, was an idea not mirrored in the original *Problem Tree*. One of the participants, inspired by the positive image of the village emerging from the discussion, said that with a secure village site they could build a community stage for cultural events. The Katkari are very fond of celebrations of all kinds and have a unique style of music and dance they enjoy greatly. Other participants enthusiastically agreed that having a stage on which to perform their music would bring immense benefits to community life and foster the unity among residents needed to pursue any number of other collective actions. This vision galvanized the discussion and launched people into thinking about means to achieve their dreams. They concluded that a legal title for their hamlet was worth pursuing and that they could do things to begin to make it happen. This kind of energy, and the many smaller conversations it generated afterwards, also helped to overcome the indifference people felt in hamlets not threatened with immediate eviction.

In the days and weeks following the various assessments, participants began to speak with greater confidence about the importance of legal title to the future of their hamlet, and the need to make it happen through their own efforts. As a symbol of their resolve,

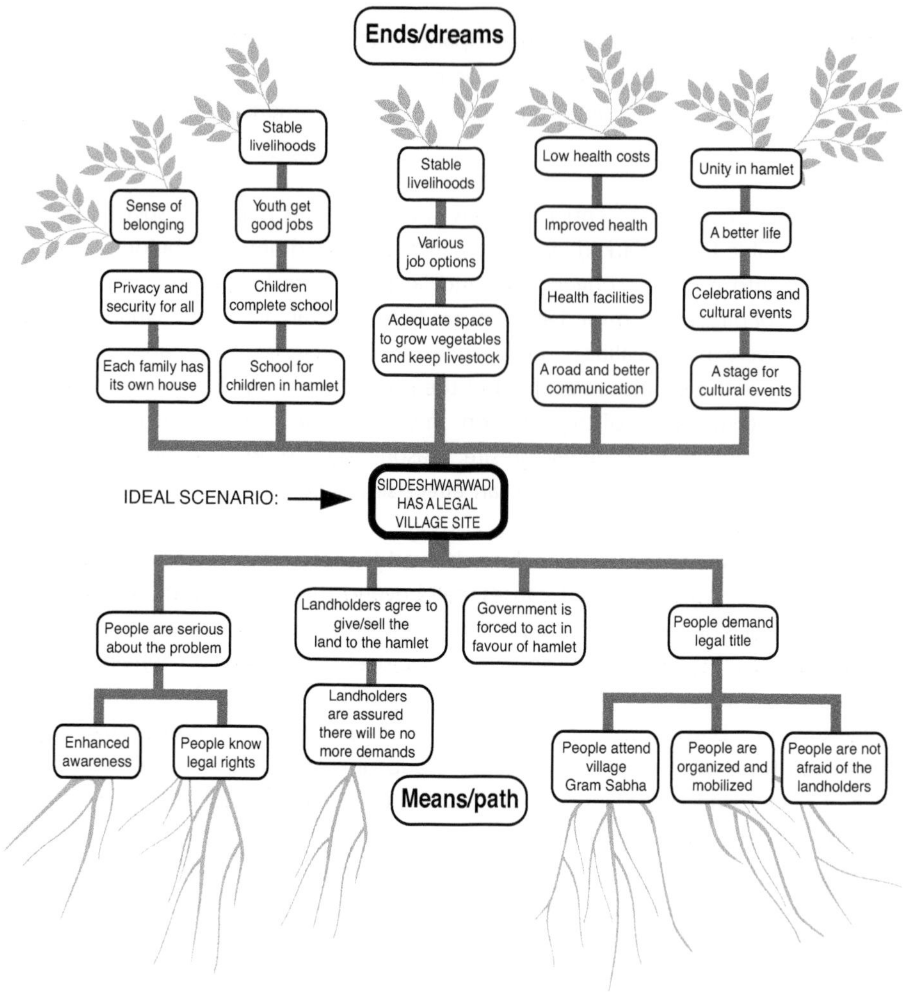

FIGURE 9.2 Dreams and a path to a legal title for Siddeshwarwadi.

the community elders and other residents of Siddeshwarwadi later raised and ceremoniously anointed a stone pillar (*ves*) marking the entrance to their hamlet. Rituals of this kind had been used in the past to mark the boundaries of Katkari communities. They were hopeful that the gesture would not raise alarm among the landholders but rather would be seen positively as a symbol of the boundary of their village site and their resolve to stay.

ACKNOWLEDGING RESOURCES

Participatory Resource Mapping (PRM) is perhaps the most widespread participatory technique used in the field of development over the last twenty years or so. It is designed to help local and indigenous communities map their territories and associated resources, assets and conflicts together with references to cultural history and mythology. PRM is typically carried out in close partnership with researchers and NGOs engaged in land-based development and community planning. The method supports inter-generational dialogue as well. It builds on local knowledge held by resource users and elders at the same time as it helps develop new village-level capacities in resource management, customary land rights issues and 'counter-mapping' politics. These are critical contributions to understanding 'the inherently spatial dimensions of participatory approaches' (Kesby, 2007, p. 2827).

PRM is a good example of a tool that can be kept simple or scaled up into a full methodology, depending on purpose and available time and resources. If delivered in a short time frame, the exercise may involve hands-on map-making (using paper, objects, chalk, masking tape, etc.) with a view to ground the group planning process in local or regional space and associated issues. This is the version presented below. If scaling up is needed, participants may produce maps of the past, the present and the future, projected or desired. They may opt for a 3-D modelling method (using sheets of cardboard, pushpins, coloured string and paint) combined with more detailed information obtained from transect walks, videos, aerial and satellite images and printed maps (covered with clear plastic sheets to capture local knowledge). More advanced applications combine PRM with GPS (Global Positioning Systems), GIS (Geographic Information Systems) and other digital computer or Internet-based technologies (see Wood, 2010).

Resource Mapping

Purpose

To visualize and acknowledge the land-related resources of communities.

Step 1

Define the topic and the boundaries of the community involved. Invite participants to draw an outline of the area on the ground using chalk, on the floor using masking tape or on large sheets of kraft paper. Alternatively, use existing maps of the area covered with transparent plastic people can write or draw on. Add landmarks and objects that can act as reference points.

Step 2

Locate and mark places of activity, interest or concern relevant to the topic. Encourage the use of colour and objects to represent resources and their spatial relationships.

Step 3

Review the result by asking people to describe what they have included in the map and why. Add new information to the map that emerges from the discussion, and photograph the result. Conclude by inviting observations about the scope and importance of resources held by different community members and the community as a whole, and opportunities they offer to address problems.

FAQ

- ***What are the limitations of participatory resource mapping?***

Resource mapping is often used as a stand-alone methodology, without other tools to inquire into local power relations and broader structures that determine local land rights and use.

Like any application of PAR, participatory mapping initiatives may not achieve community ownership and control over the action-research process. If not adequately grounded in felt needs, it can serve agendas that are primarily external.

Local mapping may be carried out with little or no administrative commitment to scale up the results from the local level to higher-level research and decision-making processes.

While advanced applications of PRM using GIS and computer or Internet-based technology are easier to sell at higher levels, they entail significant costs in labour, time and equipment. They also require local training, outside expertise, external funding and long-term support.

PMR may raise questions of intellectual property rights. It can also bring out sensitive issues that create tension or conflict (within the community or between community members and outsiders) while leaving them unresolved.

Combinations

- *Resource Mapping* with *Storytelling*
  The mapping exercise can include individual **stories** about sites that bring back vivid memories of personal experiences.

- *Resource Mapping* with *Timeline*
  When reviewing the resource map, ask people to comment on major changes in the resources compared to the past and create a timeline of these changes. Alternatively, use a Venn diagram to map resources of the present, resources of the past and resources the group wants to develop in the future.

PHOTO 9.1 Places on the Bonnechere River with meaning and value to stakeholders. (Source: J. Wonnacott)

Summary of this example: The Bonnechere River is a relatively healthy tributary of the Ottawa River in Ontario, Canada supporting dozens of small communities. Representatives from throughout the watershed gathered to discuss ways to become better environmental stewards of the watershed, and what information they needed to play this role. The assessment, facilitated by D. J. Buckles, began with a large map on the floor showing the outline of the Bonnechere River, from its headwaters to its mouth. Participants gathered along the river at places especially meaningful or important to them. They then told short stories about why it was a meaningful place and identified things they needed to know or see monitored to ensure their continued enjoyment of the place. Informed by this discussion, recorded by participants with key words and images on cards placed on the map, participants then defined the kinds of issues around which information on the watershed could be organized: recreation, education, environmental protection, culture/history and livelihood development. Groups were formed using *The Socratic Wheel* based on similarities and differences between individuals in terms of the issues they were most concerned about. The day concluded with the assessment of options for dissemination and public engagement using *The Carrousel* (Chapter 14). The results of the exercise provided the convenors (an environmental NGO) with a rationale for structuring their communication efforts and many details on what information was needed by residents and for what purpose.

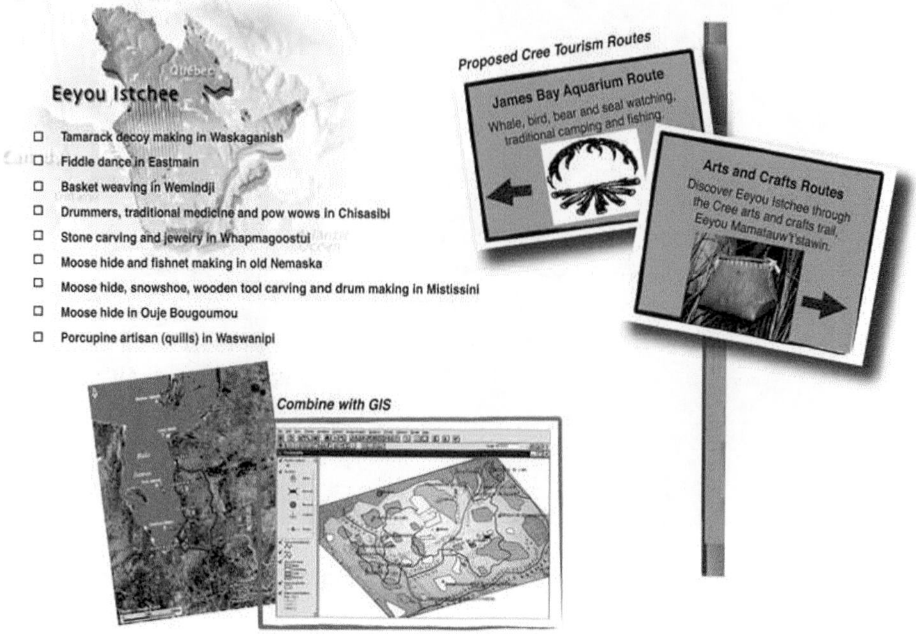

FIGURE 9.3 Cree resource mapping and community tourism planning.

Summary of this example: In her work, Sylvie Blangy (2010) narrates rich applications of various tools described in this book. They are combined with simple and advanced participatory resource mapping methods focussed on the issue of aboriginal tourism. Her doctoral thesis reports on twenty workshops (several of which were co-designed and co-facilitated with J. M. Chevalier) with thirteen communities from Northern Canada (Cree and Inuit) and Northern Scandinavia (Saami). It also describes a collaborative process spanning several years that lead to the creation of an Aboriginal Destinations Guidebook and a website (www.aboriginal-ecotourism.org) on 200 aboriginal tourism initiatives from around the world.

TELLING THE STORY

Timeline, past or forward-looking, is another powerful and well-known technique used in participatory action research. Generic steps for this technique are provided below, followed by examples of how it was applied to issues of climate change in India and Nigeria, in combination with *Resource Mapping* and the *Problem Tree*.

Timeline

Purpose

To tell a story of changes over time, significant events of the past or the chronology of steps in a current or planned activity.

Step 1

Define the **topic** and **time frame** for the analysis, and create a timeline on the floor or on a flip chart with the 'starting point' at one end and the most distant reference for the time frame at the other end. Invite participants to add one or two milestones in-between that can stand as additional reference points on the timeline, if needed.

Step 2

Invite each participant to think of a **key moment** relevant to the topic (a change, historical event or a step in a current or planned activity). Write (or draw) it on its own card. Add closely related **facts** to the back of the card or on a flip chart, such as the date, the positive and negative aspects associated with the key moment, the key parties involved, what they did, etc.

STEPS IN A TYPICAL CREE TOUR: NEMASKA, THE LAND OF PLENTIFUL FISH

1. Visits the COTA and community websites
2. Calls the tourism officer by phone
3. Drives to Nemaska, refills at the gas station
4. Sees posters (welcome, fishing) along the road
5. Enters the community and goes to the restaurant
6. Checks in at the Nemaska lodge
7. Looks for information, goes to Band Office
8. Meets and plans expedition with local outfitter and tourism officer
9. Visits old Nemaska, goes shopping
10. Goes fishing, sees wildlife with local guide
11. Shops for local crafts and souvenirs
12. Visits the Hydro-Quebec dams
13. Drives back home

Summary of this example: In a workshop facilitated by J. M. Chevalier among the Cree of Northern Quebec, participants used *Timeline* to describe the typical journey of a tourist visiting the village and land of *Nemaska*. The tool was expanded to include a description of the key actors and problems involved in each step of the journey. (See Blangy, 2010.)

Step 3

Discuss each key moment card and place it in the appropriate place on the timeline. Continue until the group has **reviewed** all the key changes, historical events or steps relevant to the topic and arranged them in chronological order on the timeline. To simplify the story, place minor moments under the cards for the major moments occurring in the same time period. If the exercise concerns significant changes or events of the past, you can move the cards for **positive changes** or events to one side of the timeline and the **negative** ones to the other side.

Step 4

Review the result by looking for **trends** or patterns in the story. Identify actions relevant to the situation today based on **lessons** of the past.

FAQ

- ***Is* Timeline *reliable, given that people's recollections of the past are not always accurate?***

As with all other inquiry techniques, participants can decide to plan further fact-finding studies to make sure that their understanding of history is well-informed (see *Validation*, Chapter 8, for a story about Honduran members of a cooperative deciding to improve their initial timeline on the history of the cooperative with interviews of more past members).

Variations

- **Past and future**
  Events along the timeline can be divided into two parts: to the left, those that occurred in the past and, to the right, those that will result if events follow their current course or if things happen according to new plans.
- **Ups and downs**
  Events along the timeline can go up or down depending on their positive or negative contribution to a situation evolving over time, as perceived by participants.
- **Before and after**
  Instead of a timeline, create a 'Before-and-after' table with five columns that describe the domains of change (Column 1), what used to be (Column 2) and the present situation (Column 3) for each change area, how important these changes are (Column 4), and then the causes or reasons (Column 5) behind each change. In the last row, describe the overall difference between the past situation and the present (see Table 9.1).

TABLE 9.1 Before and after

Domain of change	*Before (20 years ago)*	*Now*	*Importance (from 1 to 3)*	*Causes*
Jobs				
Environment				
Family				
Religion				
Overall				

Combinations

- *Timeline* with *Stakeholder Identification* (Chapter 11)
  Draw or write on separate cards the key people or groups involved in each change, historical event or step. On the back of each card, record information about each stakeholder involved, such as how they contributed to the event, change or step, how they are affected by it, and the gains or losses incurred in each case.
- *Timeline* with *Force Field* (Chapter 10)
  Another option is to create columns on the upper side of the timeline for each major **factor** that **contributed** to a particular change or event. Create columns on the lower side for major factors that **counteracted** or limited the impact of a particular change or event. Show the weight or intensity of each factor by varying the height of the column.

CLIMATE CHANGE IN INDIA AND NIGERIA

The following material is a comparative story of project initiatives that combine *Problem Tree*, *Resource Mapping* and *Timeline* with several tools from other chapters – *The Socratic Wheel* (Chapter 7), *Rating* and *Validation* (Chapter 8), *Force Field* (Chapter 10) and *Stakeholder Rainbow* (Chapter 11) – to support rich community-based discussions about climate change and adaptation in India and Nigeria. The India story draws from the People's Coalition on Climate Change (2009) while the Nigeria story uses results reported by NEST and Woodley (2011) and Woodley (2011) based on a methodology designed by D. J. Buckles, R. Ramirez, M. Fernandez and J. van Mossel.

Farmers, fishers, pastoralists and forest people feel the local impacts of climate change acutely because they depend directly on biological resources for their livelihoods. Within these communities, women and children often suffer the most. And yet these are also the communities with the least influence on broader debates regarding who is responsible for causing the climate crisis, and what must be done, locally and globally. This 'democratic deficit' has prompted civil society organizations and ordinary people to ask 'whose climate, whose change?'

Separate initiatives in India and Nigeria explored this question with rural communities using a similar process, albeit for different purposes. In India, the inquiry was launched by the People's Coalition on Climate Change, comprised of ten grassroots civil society organizations. Each of them had a long history of doing community development work in rural areas of India, and a shared interest in bringing community perspectives to policymakers and a general public largely unaware of the local issues. The process produced a Community Charter on the Climate Crisis, drawing on the results of weeklong deliberations in twenty communities in five different ecosystems of India (People's Coalition on Climate Change, 2009). Climate change mitigation – action to reduce the release of greenhouse gases into the atmosphere – is embedded in the Charter's call to stop the spread of industrial agriculture and further erosion of local food systems.

In Nigeria, community engagement guided actions by Nigerian organizations and investments by Canada's International Development Agency (CIDA) aimed at helping communities adapt to the worst effects of climate change. The seven implementing groups included university-based teams and NGOs selected by the Canadian NGO Cuso International and ICF Marbek, an international consulting firm, through a competitive process. Over a period of eighteen months, teams in each Nigerian organization worked with fifteen communities from the Sahel in the Northeast to the coastal and rainforest environments of the Southeast (NEST and Woodley, 2011). They generated and tested a large number of locally relevant strategies to reduce the vulnerability of rural people and enhance their capacity to adapt to climate change.

Both initiatives used participatory methods across multiple sites. D. J. Buckles designed the selection and sequencing of tools, later adapted by instructors (R. Ramirez, M. Fernandez and J. van Mossel) and adapted again by each Nigerian organization. The Nigerian organizations gathered before launching their work to learn and test a combination of tools selected to support the planning stage of community-based pilot projects on climate change. They then used the results of the planning process to guide the design of project investments and monitor outcomes. The Indian organizations also met to review and agree on a common set of participatory tools to meet their needs, drawing on the long history of community-led facilitation anchored in the work of the Deccan Development Society. Each organization used the tools to elicit climate-related stories with people and generate a specific Community Charter on the climate crisis. Both initiatives used many of the same tools and combined them with other methods.

In India, the process began with wide-ranging discussions of significant concerns facing villagers, and selection of one for analysis using the *Problem Tree*. Fishers on the Gulf of Mannar in Tamil Nadu, for example, selected the diminishing fish catch as the most critical problem, represented by a tree trunk drawn on the ground in chalk. They then identified and drew pictures of various causes arranged in levels as roots and sub-roots of the tree. Rising sea surface temperatures, they argued, drive fish into deeper and cooler waters beyond their reach and redirect seawater currents in unpredictable ways. A chalk drawing of a burning sun represented the underlying cause of the

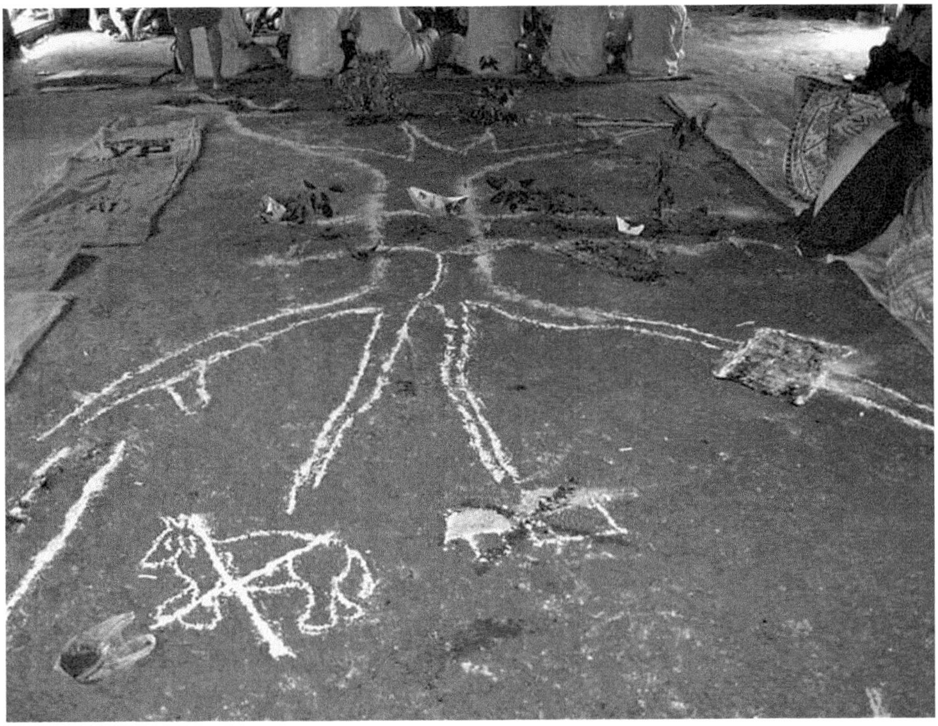

PHOTO 9.2 Fisherfolk and farmers in the coastal area of Sunderbans, West Bengal discuss the causes and effects of river bund erosion.
(Source: Deccan Development Society)

diminishing fish catch. A decline in rainfall, represented by fishers with a chalk outline of blue clouds and yellow raindrops, affects the growth of cultivated fish in ponds and consequently the fish catch. To these climate-related causes of the diminished fish catch participants added several others related directly to human activities: the industrial use of 'killer nets' that sweep the sea of all fish (including the fish-fingerlings and species that rely on estuaries), pollution from coastal industries, the dumping of plastic and other waste into the sea and the use of dynamite by small-scale fishers. They used various colours and images to represent these causes as roots of the tree. In another setting, a coastal community of West Bengal, people selected flooding due to erosion of the bund containing the river for the core problem. Discussion generated a chain of causes: the scarcity of fuel prompted cutting of the mangroves, which in turn made the mangrove barrier protecting the river vulnerable to the effects of severe storms. Participants also argued, based on information from popular media, that melting polar ice caps was the cause of the rising estuary they observed directly.

Discussion of effects flowing from the core problems discussed in various villages brought out a myriad of considerations. Erosion of the river bund, for example, allows saline water to enter and stagnate on agricultural fields. The salt settles and turns green fields a brownish black. Fresh water fish in the ponds die. These livelihood impacts in turn force households to migrate in search of alternative work. The core problem discussed in Kulathoor Thankammalpuram village in Tamil Nadu – the ground water has become salty – imposes constraints on vegetable cultivation, makes fish ponds impossible, undermines fodder production and provokes diarrhoea in goat livestock and urinary infections in people. 'Now the situation here', said one participant, 'is that all women in the village go around with pots in search of water' (People's Coalition on Climate Change, 2009, p. 55). This has a chain effect on social relationships. Due to the lack of fresh water, relatives are not invited during festivals and other villagers are reluctant to give their girls in marriage to their village boys. A village elder summed up the feeling of despair: 'We should not live in a village that has no pond' (People's Coalition on Climate Change, 2009, p. 56).

Sorting through the root causes and effects of problems experienced by the various Indian communities supported a discussion of how these relate to weather events and broader climate change issues. The *Problem Tree* analysis embedded the climate change theme in a felt experience, and launched the discussions that followed. In Nigeria, knowing the actors was the entry point for community engagement rather than problem assessment. The process thus started by getting communities and organizations involved in the development of a common rationale for targeting the use of resources for climate change adaptation. A *Stakeholder Rainbow*, illustrated in Chapter 11, helped identify key actors considered to be the most vulnerable to climate change and those with influence on the success of potential projects. Local women, children and youth typically emerged as the most vulnerable, and village heads and organized groups as the most influential.

The results of the *Problem Tree* in India and *Stakeholder Rainbow* analysis in Nigeria were immediately applied to a *Resource Mapping* exercise. In Nigeria, men (including youth and elders) drew community maps pointing out resources, vulnerable areas and infrastructure relevant to particular groups identified in the stakeholder analysis. In some cases this involved transect walks to help staff in the organizations become familiar with resources people felt were important. Their maps were compared to and combined with community maps generated by women. For example, in Daudu, a village in the Guinea and Sudan savannah zone, the women identified spring wells and an abandoned borehole that the men had left out. This highlighted expectations of the women and motivated the Nigerian Greenwatch Initiative responsible for the project to focus later discussions on the importance of rehabilitating drinking water sources. Resource mapping by the men alone would have placed attention in this village on farmlands and forest areas.

Resource Mapping in Sahelian communities of the north highlighted resources that had been lost. Six of thirteen oases previously available to two communities had silted up as had large areas of agricultural land now covered over by mobile sand dunes. Important tenure issues also emerged through the mapping process. As the oases belonged formally to the Village Head in trust for the community as a whole, the loss of one oasis required that remaining oases accommodate all villagers. The cultural practice of sharing losses equally, a traditional strength documented and discussed explicitly through the resource mapping process, later made it possible to mobilize the entire community in a large-scale effort to revitalize specific oases previously used by some families only.

PHOTO 9.3 Farmers mapping the resources of rainfed, dryland agriculture in Zaheerabad, Andhra Pradesh. (Source: Deccan Development Society)

Resource Mapping in India highlighted the resources people could use to address problems identified in the *Problem Tree*. In Zaheerabad, Andhra Pradesh, for example, people used coloured powders, chalk and small objects to create a detailed map of the houses belonging to various social groups, forest areas, water sources, transportation routes and farmlands differentiated by soil type and related crops. The process of co-constructing the map inspired elders to share proverbs and stories depicting the interaction between rainfall patterns, cloud formation, wind direction and crops suited to the various climatic conditions. In some settings resource mapping was followed by a finer description of the crop resources available in the communities using a rating table with multiple criteria (see *Rating*, Chapter 8).

The detailed baseline of current strengths and assets subsequently grounded an historical analysis of trends. Using *Timeline*, people traced the history of how they had managed climate-related crises in the past. In Zaheerabad, elderly people established reference points on the timeline by noting events in their lives they thought were significant to everyone in the village: namely, the Hyderabad Police Action of 1948 which annexed the state into the Indian union, a major drought in 1972 and the end of Indira Gandhi's government in 1984. People then discussed changes in farming practices and other livelihood activities before and after each of these reference points. Participants flagged periods when traditional seeds of several crops were lost, new crops were introduced, labour practices changed and new industries were established. The sequencing of events over time helped draw out lessons from the past. For example, a sugar cane factory that put new pressure on fodder resources later made it increasingly difficult to raise livestock and manure fields.

In some settings people also used *Timeline* to create a seasonal map showing the chronology of agricultural activities, complementary livelihoods and health problems commonly encountered in each season. These results prepared the ground for the final step in the collaborative diagnostic process: a discussion of what climate change might look like when 'it visits our lives' (climate risks) and responses they could plan now based on the resources they had. People consolidated in a single table all previous observations regarding climate risks and resources they could use to manage these risk, including agricultural biodiversity, specific water management knowledge, drought-tolerant tree species and hardy livestock breeds.

The Nigerian organizations also reconstructed the local history of severe climatic events. The exercise combined *Timeline* with *Force Field* analysis of the impacts of the climatic events and peoples' responses. After establishing a few historical points of common reference, participants developed a detailed sequence specific to their communities: a year of decreased rainfall, heavy winds, flooding, severe sandstorms, intense heat waves, etc. They placed labels for these on a flip chart or on the ground, and at the same time described the actual impacts each severe climatic event had on their community and how different people responded. Progressively, a timeline emerged with impacts on one side of each event and responses on the other. For example, in Tosha, a village in the Sahel, a severe drought in 1972 produced a major crop failure and the loss of livestock. To cope with these impacts, people drew on stored food and fodder from the previous harvest and moved some livestock into neighbouring areas. A severe sandstorm in 1984 also provoked soil erosion and created a new threat: the movement of massive sand dunes towards the village. These blocked access routes and threatened to overrun the settlement. People responded by initiating a tree planting campaign and drilling a borehole well to care for the trees. Some moved out of the most affected sites. Heavy rainfall in 2007 and 2008 flooded an oasis and crops planted nearby. Homes were also destroyed. People responded by making more intensive use of upland farms.

The timelines in Nigeria provided a basis for linking the assets identified in the resource maps (e.g. stored grain and fodder, upland farmlands) to past and potential future responses. In Tosha, people discussed strategies for stabilizing sand dunes, improving fodder production and storage and diversifying food sources from the various kinds of lands available to them. These were then modified and ranked in light of priorities and concerns expressed separately by men and women. For instance, women said that the quality of drinking water, not the quantity, was of primary concern. The initial plan of the University of Maiduguri, the Nigerian implementing organization, to construct a reservoir (surface dam) was consequently dropped in favour of a coordinated effort to rehabilitate several dry oases using bore wells and trees to stabilize sand dunes. New ideas introduced by the university were also reviewed and approved or rejected by communities in light of the analysis of impacts on the most vulnerable groups, feasibility, reliance on community capacities and contribution to local abilities to adapt to climate change. A rating table using these and other criteria supported separate discussions by men, women and male youth. The findings, once compiled, pointed to project interventions acceptable to the various community groups. For example, priorities in Daudu converged around interventions all groups agreed were feasible and would make an acceptable contribution to the ability of vulnerable groups (especially women, children and youth) to adapt. Priorities involved the deepening of the existing earth dam, tree planting along dry stream banks, bee-keeping and the introduction of early maturing varieties of various crops. Fish farming and sewing machine projects initially identified by the Greenwatch Initiative were rejected as they would only benefit men and did little to build capacity in the community. The tool *Validation* (Chapter 8) further reinforced the Greenwatch Initiative and community confidence in the proposed actions, showing that there was a high level of consensus among the different groups and a high level of evidence used to support the conclusions. The Greenwatch Initiative and other Nigerian organizations also developed a monitoring and evaluation tool using *The Socratic Wheel* (Chapter 7). The tool revolved around the criteria generated by communities to assess the interventions in the first place. This established the goals for each project and helped all parties monitor progress.

The organizations involved in the Nigeria initiative observed some meaningful changes after only eighteen months, including very high levels of local engagement and contribution to project implementation and some livelihood improvements as well (Woodley, 2011). Importantly, many observed that women's voices were heard during the consultations and that women were very committed to project activities. They considered this a major accomplishment in a culture where women are often isolated from others and from each other. There are also early signs that local organization is stronger, and that both local men and the Nigerian organizations involved understand and support investments in local climate change adaptation projects that intentionally benefit the most vulnerable. The results of the India initiative were less tangible but meaningful to both the communities and the organizations involved. The work formed the basis for drafting in each village a Community Charter on the Climate Crisis. In the charter, local voices confidently affirmed the value and importance of local resources they could use to combat the climate crisis ('Our strengths'). They also articulated specific demands that governments respect and support the community assets that farmers, fishers, pastoralists and forest people use to protect the ecological integrity of the planet.

THE SHORTEST ROUTE

Critical Path

Purpose

To plan the shortest route to completion of a project, by distinguishing the tasks that must be completed in a sequence from those that can be done in parallel to other tasks.

Step 1

Define a **plan of action** and list the **activities** that are part of the plan. The activities should be concrete and distinct from each other. Write a few key words for each activity on its own card and describe the activity briefly on the back of the card.

Step 2

For each activity, determine the **earliest date** by which it could start and estimate the **time** it will take. Record the information on the activity card.

Step 3

Identify the activities that must be completed **sequentially**, before other tasks can begin. Distinguish these from tasks that can be done at any time, as **parallel** tasks. Organize all the activity cards in the order that would take the shortest time, taking into account both parallel and sequential activities.

Step 4

Create a **critical path diagram** based on the organized cards using a code for the key information (see Figure 9.4). For example, use numbered **circles** to show the start and finish of each activity. Draw **arrows** (from left to right) between circles to show the activity that needs to be completed before another can start. Write the **time** required to complete the activity above each arrow. Above each circle track the cumulative **time** it will take to complete the project.

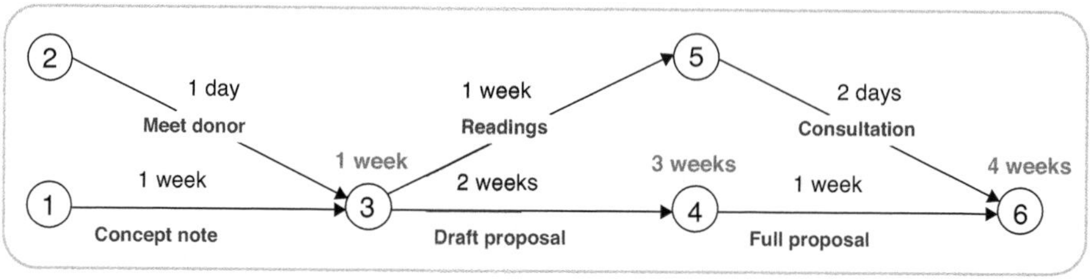

FIGURE 9.4 *Critical Path.*

Step 5

Review the result and **adjust the amount of time** dedicated to different stages of the plan of action. Plans can be completed in shorter periods of time by investing more resources (human or financial) in some stages or reducing the scope of some activities. Postponing activities that are not part of the critical path is another option for managing time-sensitive plans.

KNOWING THE HISTORY

Previous Responses brings together two key questions that may be asked when assessing past responses to a given problem or situation. The first revolves around the well-known distinction between task-orientation and people-orientation, dating back to the pioneering work of Lewin and the Ohio State Leadership Studies carried out in the 1940s. The second points to basic distinctions in the conflict management field – between force, concession, accommodation, negotiation and consensus and also between customary, legal-administrative and Alternative Dispute Resolution (ADR) responses to conflict.

Previous Responses

Purpose

To assess the ways that key stakeholders have managed core problems in the past.

Step 1

Define the **core problem** and create a drawing or identify an object to represent it. Then identify the key **stakeholders** involved (see *Stakeholder Identification*, Chapter 11).

Step 2

Identify the typical response of each stakeholder to the core problem during a defined period. Write the **stakeholder response** on its own card, using a short sentence or key words that are concrete and clear to everyone. If the stakeholder responded to the core problem in different ways at different times, select one period and the most typical response during that period.

Step 3

Create a **table** (see example). In Column 1, insert the typical response of each key stakeholder.

Step 4

Assess whether each stakeholder response involved **local customs**, **legal-administrative measures**, or other strategies such as **Alternative Dispute Resolution** (involving negotiation, mediation or arbitration). Record your assessment in Column A.

Step 5

Rate the extent to which each stakeholder has generally emphasized the importance of getting the **task done** ('Task oriented responses'). Use a scale of low, medium or high.

Step 6

Rate the extent to which each stakeholder has generally emphasized the importance of **meeting the expectations** of other stakeholders ('People-oriented responses'). Use a scale of low, medium or high.

Step 7

Locate each stakeholder in the **diagram** that combines the two kinds of responses (task-oriented on the horizontal axis, people-oriented on the vertical axis) established in Steps 5 and 6. The diagram (Figure 9.5) helps determine whether the main stakeholder strategies have been characterized by **force, concession, accommodation, negotiation,** or **consensus.** Record the results in Column B.

Step 8

Discuss strategies with positive effects on the core problem (and how to **reinforce** them) as well as strategies that produced negative effects (and how to **break** from them).

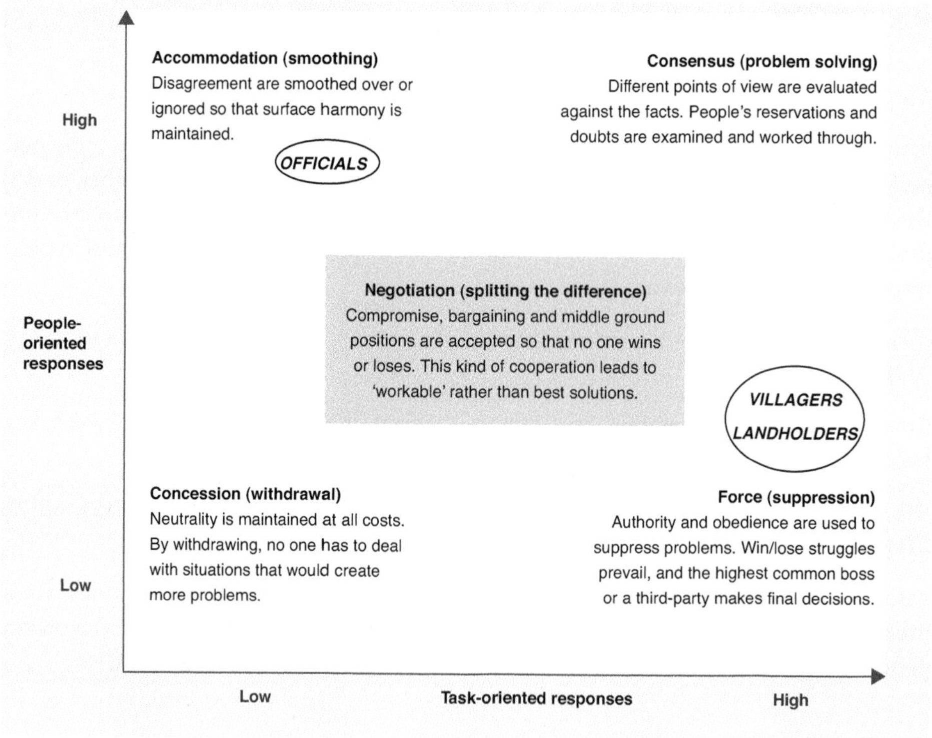

FIGURE 9.5 Force, concession, accommodation, negotiation and consensus.

Source: adapted from Warner, 2001, p. 12. See also Worchel and Austin, 1986, p. 76.

TABLE 9.2 Tribal land claims in India

Response by stakeholder	A **Type of response** *Customary, legal-administrative or alternative*	B **Overall strategy** *Force, concession, accommodation, negotiation or consensus*
Villagers petition local leaders for a village site and then make written demands on elected representatives	Customary followed by legal-administrative	Force
Landholders openly oppose the land petition and pressure officials informally	Customary	Force
Government officials calculate and survey the land, but do not transfer ownership for fifteen years	Legal-administrative	Accommodation

Summary of this example: Bapu Hilam, a social worker, convinced the ten Katkari families in Narsurwadi hamlet to petition local leaders for a legal village site. The hamlet had been established on private lands many decades earlier with permission from several landholders who needed their labour. The villagers' petition was opposed by the landholders, who continued to benefit from the cheap labour of villagers and wanted to retain the option of eventually selling the land on the open market. Government officials responded to these forceful pressures by surveying the land but not following up with a land transfer. This amounted to a partial accommodation of the opposing parties (landholders and villagers) in an effort to smooth things over without resolving the underlying problem. Villagers then took their case to elected officials. Through legal and administrative pressure, villagers hoped to force the transfer of land. Persistent appeals by villagers eventually resulted (some fifteen years later) in a transfer of house plots to individual families, but not recognition of a village site. This outcome meant that villagers could not access government infrastructure programmes available only to villages, or create common-use areas. Meanwhile, the landholders received minimal compensation for their land (well below market value) and retaliated by trying to block villagers from access to employment. In hindsight, participants in the assessment felt that the villagers should have claimed a smaller area in exchange for agreement from the landholders to support a village site. Also, in the future, more effort should be given to direct engagement and negotiation and using a mediator to explore possible trade-offs early on in a conflict (Buckles and Khedkar, 2013).

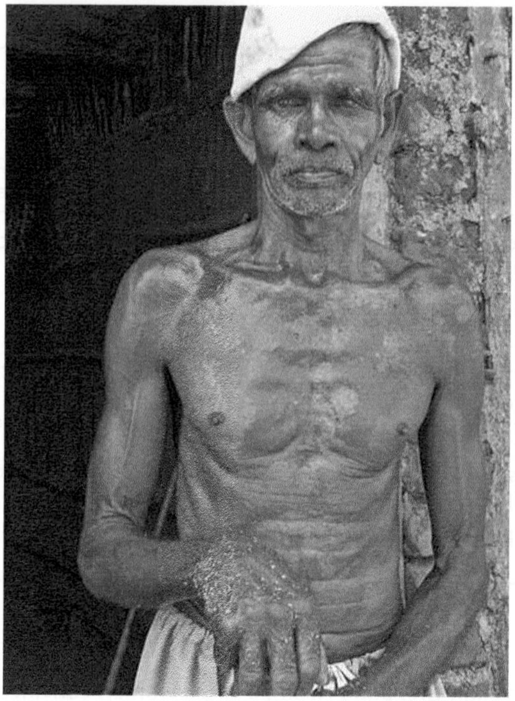

PHOTO 9.4 Shripat Waghmare (meaning tiger, a common Katkari surname) rests after threshing rice for a landholder. (Source: D. J. Buckles)

Combinations

- Use *Timeline* to focus the assessment on critical periods in the history of the problem.
- To know whether or not the conditions exist for negotiation, and to identify potential allies, used *Social Analysis CLIP*.

TYPES OF PROBLEMS

Gaps and Conflicts helps investigate the nature of a key problem and strategies to improve the situation. In some cases, parties must deal with competing interests or conflicts in power. Other situations call for incentives to do things differently, more effective communications, or discussions about underlying values.

Gaps and Conflicts

Purpose

To identify the issues underlying the core problem and find out if these issues are mostly about gaps or conflicts in power, interests (gains and losses), moral values, or information and communication.

Step 1

Define the **core problem** and create a drawing or identify an object to represent it. Then identify the **main causes** of the core problem. *Free List and Pile Sort* or *Timeline* may help identify these causes. Write each cause on its own card, using a short sentence or key words that are concrete and clear to everyone.

Step 2

On each card that describes a different cause, write the **kind of issue** it represents. Is the issue one of **power**, **interests** (gains and losses), moral **values**, or **information** and ways of communicating (see definitions, below)? Discuss and clarify the kinds of issues, using local examples and terms. Create a label or identify an object to represent each issue. If the cause raises more than one issue (such as power *and* interests), write the same cause on two or more cards and record a different kind of issue on each card.

Step 3

Create a *Gaps and Conflicts* **table**. Place labels for the four kinds of issues in the first column. Place Gaps, Conflicts and Ranking labels in the top row.

Step 4

Take each cause of the core problem and decide whether it involves a **gap** that needs to be filled or a **conflict** that needs to be resolved (see definitions, below). Record and explain each assessment on the back of the corresponding card or on a flip chart. Place the cards in the corresponding cells of the table.

Step 5

Use the last column to **rank** the combined weight of row issues according to the number and importance of the cards that appear in each row. Use a ranking scale of 1 for the greatest combined weight to 4 for the least combined weight.

Step 6

Review the result of the analysis. Consider whether the issues with the greatest combined weight are mostly about gaps that need to be filled or conflicts that need to be resolved. Discuss **priorities** for action. Keep in mind that the act of filling a *gap* (such as getting information on land ownership) can sometimes lead to a *conflict* between parties.

TABLE 9.3 Gaps and conflicts in national park management practices, Canada

Issues	*Gaps*	*Conflicts*	*Rank*
Power	Hiring new park staff is impossible due to financial constraints	There is little public consultation when park management plans and decisions are made	2
Interests (gains and losses)	Park managers are overworked and morale is low		4
Moral values	Park users are seen and see themselves as clients rather than stakeholders and potential partners		3
Information and communication	Communications between park staff and park users are slow and time-consuming	Some unsatisfied park users can be aggressive	1

Summary of this example: National Park administrators experience several problems regarding its winter trail services to the public. The most pressing and stressful issue is communication – the amount of time that park staff must dedicate to managing tensions and conflicts with a vocal group of park skiers (row 4). Issues that rank second in importance include the lack of financial resources to hire additional staff and the fact that park management plans and decisions are made with little public involvement (row 1) (see Table 9.3).

Definitions

- **Power** is your ability to achieve what you want by influencing others and using resources you control. These resources include economic wealth, political authority (an office, position or role recognized by an institution or by local customs), the ability to use force or the threat of force and control over information (including knowledge and skills) and the means to communicate.
- **Interests** are the gains and losses that you will experience based on the results of ongoing or proposed actions. Gains and losses affect the resources you control such as economic wealth, political authority, prestige, the ability to use force, information, means to communicate, legitimacy or social ties.
- **Values** are beliefs, judgments, norms or principles about what is important, or the degree to which something is viewed as morally right or wrong.
- **Information** is what you know 'for a fact' and believe to be true.

- **Communication** is how you exchange information and make your views known to others.
- A **gap** involves a lack of power or control over resources; the absence of incentive or interest (gains or losses); a failure to appreciate the moral worth or value of something; a shortage of information and effective means of communication.
- A **conflict** is a struggle over how decisions are made and who makes them; how gains and losses are distributed; the values that people believe in; the information that is given out and the ways that people communicate.

THREADS OF THEORY: TECHNOPHILIA OR TECHNOPHOBIA

An inquiry looking for a technical fix is perfection of means and confusion of aims. It includes precise applications of high explosives to social problems. So, let's be wary of analyses that offer magic bullets: they can be lethal.

When a computer breaks down, we look for ways to fix it. A technical inquiry into the problem makes sense, assuming we know why we need to use computers in general and the one that is broken in particular. After all, it's the purpose that creates the machine, not the other way around. Einstein's advice regarding the relationship between technique and purpose is relevant here: 'Concern for man and his fate must always form the chief interest of all technical endeavors. Never forget this in the midst of your diagrams and equations.'

Imagine now a more complex problem: peace talks break down and conflict breaks out. The temptation here is to examine the problem as a social machine that needs fixing, by entering the 'human factor' into the equation, ensuring that it is properly computed, and then delivering hard and fast solutions according to plans. While science and technology matter, they represent only one part of the solution when examining complex issues. In some cases, they are part of the problem. Any well-engineered research plan or blueprint for action that fails to acknowledge uncertainty, and the social issues involved, is misguided. It may also be suspected of wrongdoing, as when an election is 'fixed' or when nuclear science and explosives are applied to international disputes. There's no magic bullet or easy fix for an intractable problem. Even when paved with good intentions, blue-sky pathways that experts contrive to explain and eradicate injustice, poverty or violence are like Shakespeare's remedies 'ascribed to heaven': they are poor substitutes for down-to-earth solutions that 'oft in ourselves do lie'.

Commentary

Inquiring into the *Question Concerning Technology* (Heidegger, 1977) is not a simple task. Among other things, it requires that we concern ourselves with the inquiry process and its own *technê*. To be more precise, we must investigate inquiry as just another *technê* – a human activity set up to work as a means to an end, a 'framing' instrument to carry out a particular task or, in this case, the *making of knowledge*. In an Aristotelian perspective, inquiry viewed as an activity involves material means (Gr. *hyle*), giving them a particular shape (Gr. *eilos*) that suits the context, all in pursuit of definable ends (Gr. *telos*). To Heidegger, all of these framing decisions are 'responsible' for the inquiry process 'coming into being' in real-life situations – for instance, making good use of aluminium conductors in Electronic Maximum-Minimum Temperature Sensors (MMTS) to measure surface air temperatures in the Arctic in the context of global climate warming. The proper framing of the inquiry owes a 'debt' to the careful consideration and craftsmanship of those who design and carry out the investigation and related methods. The activity owes its means, shape and purpose to the thoughtfulness (Gr. *logos*) that is freely given to bringing about or 'bringing forth' (Gr. *poiesis*) potential knowledge.

Inquiry is skilful know-how in granting the unknown an opportunity to come about and become 'present' (Gr. *aitia*) to our senses and the workings or our minds. Great expertise and know-how goes into manufacturing the nuts and bolts of meaningful inquiry. The latter do not for all that exhaust the subject matter of knowing. In reality, the essence (Gr. *eidos*) of an investigative *technê* is to reveal what exists outside the devices of knowledge making. Whatever critical role we may give them, thermometers will not be held responsible for global warming.

As with thermometers that are well designed and properly used, the skills and means of inquiry must be adequately framed if the job of knowing is to get done. Researchers are thus responsible for advancing their preferred means of inquiry, including those that may not be appropriate to the task, at their own risk. In a Heideggerian perspective, inauthentic means are those that keep the veil on the essence of knowing. They are accessory to one of two (mis-)orientations to the world. The first orientation, eminently modern, is technophilia, a strong enthusiasm for scientific measures that have no limit and can get everything explained and all works of knowledge done. This devotion to *technê* is commonly satisfied by extracting a 'standing reserve' of raw facts obtained from physical objects or human subjects, to be exploited mechanically and 'enframed' at will. Things known in this manner are boxed into bits of precise information that are worth our attention because they are 'good for something', i.e. instrumental in achieving one practical end or another.

Visions of techno-utopian intelligence to satisfy a 'needy humanity' are not lacking. They abound in science fiction. They also attract attention in debates concerning algeny and transhumanism, a movement that advocates the use of NBIC sciences (nanotechnology, biotechnology, information technology, cognitive science) to fundamentally alter the human condition ('H') and gain full control over its evolution. Futuristic 'H+' enhancements to eliminate existing cognitive barriers and achieve posthuman intelligence and enlightenment include 'strong artificial intelligence' research into neurobiological uplifts, brain engineering, mind uploading (whole brain emulation), reprogenetics, nanorobotics and human cyborgization.

The second way to orient ourselves to (un-)knowing goes in the opposite direction, i.e. technophobia, the fear or intense dislike of complex rules and devices for understanding. Those who fall prey to this fear curse the granting of power to technology and know-how. They distrust the precise framing of knowledge. They are suspicious of narrow minds and their mundane infatuation with 'small-m methods', instruments that are insignificant in comparison with the general 'logic of inquiry' and grand insights into knowledge, nature and society. What technophobes fail to see is the freedom and responsibility that goes with setting up the material means, the concrete shape, the specific ends and the overall orientation and purpose of human inquiry. They also forget the impulse that drives the 'art of inquiry' – the desire to learn and know with great care, a compelling force that connects us to everything and keeps us meaningfully and literally alive.

Visions of techno-dystopia in the field of knowledge are staple foods in science fiction, producing countless sequels of *Frankenstein* and *Metropolis*. These visions have a broader history. They harken back to metaphysics and metatheory, flights from the manifold expressions of practical knowledge and wisdom that form part of the rich experience of everyday life and constant experimentation in the world. The fear of *technê's* rule over *epistêmê* also finds its way into many corners of philosophy, including the anarchism of Feyerabendian arguments 'against method' and related declarations of 'anything goes' (Feyerabend, 1975). Methodological scepticism makes for many strange bedfellows. Uninvited guests include corporations that fund junk science to cast pseudo-rational doubt on climate change, the influence of the military-industrial complex, the causes of the diabetes pandemic or the negative impacts of tobacco farming on the health of farmers and the environment.

Technophilia and technophobia in the field of research have a lot in common. Both assume a narrow stance on method understood as mere 'instrument' – cognitive and technological tooling that holds infinite promise or inspires deep resentment and fear of alienation. Both represent misanthropic efforts to play God and gain full control over the inquisitive mind, either by pushing forward its mechanical *technê* or by pushing out the sensible fields and grounds of reason and wisdom. The worldly involvement of human understanding is denied, and with it, the freedom and responsibility that rests in the framing and making of knowledge.

An alternative orientation consists in welcoming the activity of knowing for what it is, by acknowledging the kernel of indetermination that lies at the heart of human questioning. After all, indetermination is what gives us the freedom to 'frame' the way we go about knowing. Our free relationship to the *technê* of knowing produces an openness to letting humanity exist, as an enduring question mark. Refusing the invitation to explore knowing and its involvement with being makes us vulnerable. However blind we may be to this freedom, the world will continue to reveal itself on its own terms, as indeterminate and existentially risky. It will send us on a self-destructive course that matches our own destructive path, pushing humans out of land and home. As beings with the license to act responsibly, humans can and must envisage the possibility of no longer existing, either for no reason at all (the license to be may expire due to some cataclysm) or because of humanity's collective failure to host its own freedom and carefully let it be.

REFERENCES

Blangy, S. (2010) 'Co-construire le tourisme autochtone par la recherche action participative et les Technologies de l'Information et de la Communication: Une nouvelle approche de la gestion des ressources et des territoires', Ph.D. thesis, Université Paul Valéry – Montpellier III.

Buckles, D. J. and Khedkar, R. with Ghevde, B. and Patil, D. (2013) *Fighting Eviction: Tribal Land Rights and Research-in-Action*, Cambridge University Press India, New Delhi.

Feyerabend, P. (1975) *Against Method: Outline of an Anarchistic Theory of Knowledge*, Verso, London.

Heidegger, M. (1977) *The Question Concerning Technology and Other Essays*, trans. William Lovitt, Harper and Row, New York.

Kesby, M. (2007) 'Spatialising participatory approaches: The contribution of geography to a mature debate', *Environmental Planning*, vol. 39, pp. 2813–2831.

Nigerian Environmental Study/Action Team (NEST) and Woodley, E. (eds) (2011) 'Reports of Pilot Projects in Community-based Adaptation – Climate Change in Nigeria. Building Nigeria's Response to Climate Change (BNRCC)', Ibadan, Nigeria.

People's Coalition on Climate Change (2009) *Community Charter on Climate Crisis: Outcome of an India-Wide Participatory Initiative*, Deccan Development Society, Andhra Pradesh, India.

Warner, M. (ed.) (2001) *Tools and Training, Module 5, Consensus Building*, Natural Resources Cluster Secretariat, Business Partners for Development, Canada.

Wood, D. (2010) *Rethinking the Power of Maps*, The Guilford Press, New York.

Woodley, E. (2011) 'Building Nigeria's response to climate change: Pilot projects for community-based adaptation in Nigeria', in Walter Leal Filho (ed.) *Experiences of Climate Change Adaptation in Africa*, Springer, Berlin, pp. 297–315.

Worchel, S. and Austin, W. G. (eds) (1986) *Psychology of Intergroup Relations*, Nelson-Hall, Chicago, IL.

CHAPTER 10

Factors and reasons

INTRODUCTION

Problem solving hinges on an adequate grasp of the situation that requires attention and of the forces and factors at play. In this chapter, we introduce *Force Field*, a tool inspired by Lewin's understanding of the situational field. For him this is a 'lifespace' that brings together forces that drive movement towards a goal and those that block the same movement and call for adaptive behaviour (Lewin, 1951). We also offer an original tool developed and applied in collaboration with Patrick Obertelli (École Centrale de Paris), entitled *Paradox*. It is inspired by the insights of paradoxical interventions in psychology. The tool looks at efforts and practices to handle an existing problem and explores at the same time individual and collective interests, values and attitudes that maintain or veil the problem and are difficult to comprehend.

Both tools are brought together in a single case study on accidents at construction sites in France. To achieve its purpose, the study incorporated two other tools: *Timeline* (Chapter 9) and *Hazards* (Chapter 15). The chapter tells this story in the broader context of theories of accident causation and prevention. We describe the research at some length with a view to showing how rigorous and careful research in a participatory mode can contribute to academic debates about broader questions, such as risk analysis and hazard prevention in the construction sector, and advance knowledge in regards to critical issues in society. This is a reminder that PAR can go beyond site-specific inquiries and engage as well in multiple conversations evolving in different directions and at different levels – in this case among and between researchers, workers and agencies involved in understanding and preventing hazards at work.

DRIVING AND COUNTERACTING FORCES

Force Field

Purpose

To understand the factors that contribute to a problem, a situation or a project and those that counteract it.

Step 1

Define the **topic** and place a card with key words, a drawing or an object representing the topic inside a long horizontal **bar** created on the floor, the wall or on a large sheet of paper.

Step 2

Identify the **factors that contribute** to or drive the problem, situation or project. *Free List and Pile Sort* may help identify these factors. Create **labels** to represent each factor and place them above the horizontal bar. Write descriptions of the factors on the back of the labels or on a flip chart.

Step 3

Identify the **factors that counteract** the problem or play against the situation or project. Create labels to represent the factors and place them below the horizontal bar. Write descriptions of these counteracting factors on the back of the labels or on a flip chart.

Step 4

Rate each factor using scores from 1 (weak) to 5 (strong). To be more precise, identify indicators that define the meaning of each number on the scale. **Record** the reasons participants provide for each score. Create **columns** for each factor and show the score by varying the height of the columns.

Step 5

Use **green dots** to identify the factors that people have some control over. Increase the size of the dot when people have greater control over the factor. Use **red dots** for those over which people have little or no control. Use **numbers** from 1 (short term) to 3 (long term) to indicate how long it would take to act on a factor.

Step 6

Discuss ways to achieve key objectives by **strengthening** or **reducing** the factors at play. Consider starting with the factors that people have some control over or can be addressed in the short term.

FAQ

- ***What is the difference between* Force Field *and* Problem Tree*?***

The *Problem Tree* (Chapter 9) focusses on the causes and the effects of a problem. By contrast, *Force Field* explores, in addition to the factors that contribute to a problem, those that counteract it. Also it leaves out the discussion about effects.

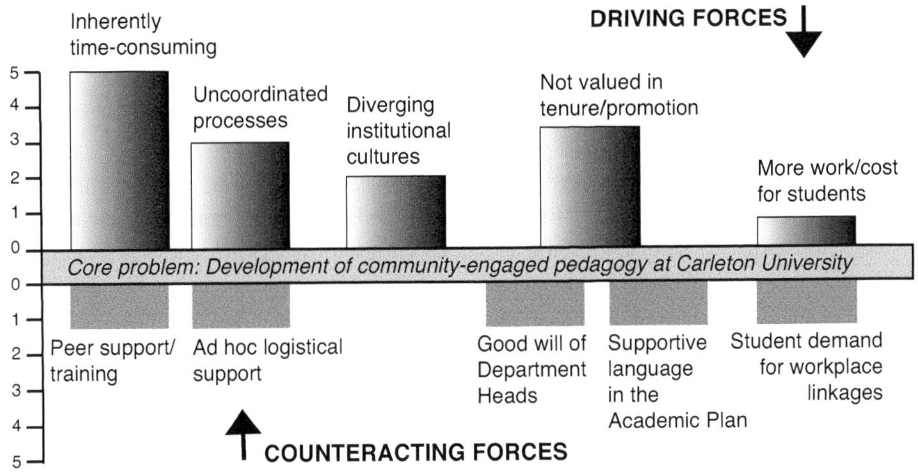

FIGURE 10.1 Factors creating and counteracting barriers to community-based pedagogy.

Summary of this example: In 2011, the Office of the Provost at Carleton University (Ottawa, Canada) and an informal network of professors in various faculties across the university came together around a common interest in improving the experiential basis for student learning through community engaged pedagogy. This agenda reflected a recent commitment at the highest levels in the university to promote active student learning through community engagement and to enhance excellence in teaching and learning. The assessment, involving nineteen faculty at two different meetings facilitated by D. J. Buckles, examined the barriers to community-engaged pedagogy (CEP) at Carleton and the institutional supports that currently counteract these forces. The barriers refer to the specific features of CEP, how the practice is perceived and managed within the university, and forces affecting the relationship between the university and communities (Figure 10.1). The discussion of current institutional supports and ways to strengthen them and reduce the weight of the barriers pointed in two strategic directions: (i) increasing the efficiency and effectiveness of engagement with community groups through a university-wide system of coordination; (ii) high-level dialogue to align the CEP mandate with appropriate student credit and faculty compensation for increased workload. Immediate actions were to enhance an existing web interface linking faculty and community groups, develop a CEP practitioner's toolkit to promote best practices, and ask the Office of the Provost to launch discussions around the wider applicability of extra teaching credits currently given to faculty involved in a special first year program of community engagement.

Combinations

- *Force Field* with *Paradox*
  See *Risk taking* and *risk thinking,* below.
- *Force Field* with *SWOT Analysis*
  Identify the factors in the *Force Field* that are existing strengths (*S*) and those that are external opportunities (*O*). Identify as well the factors that are existing weaknesses (*W*) and external threats (*T*). Use a colour code to distinguish these four kinds of factors.
- *Force Field* with *Timeline* (Chapter 9)
  Convert the horizontal bar into a chronology of key changes or events in the history of the problem, situation or project. Then, rate each as either a driving or a counteracting change or event using a scale of 1 to 5. Create columns for each change or event and show the score by varying the height of the columns (see climate change story in Chapter 9).

BEYOND LOGIC

Paradox

Purpose

To acknowledge efforts and practices to handle an existing problem and at the same time explore individual and collective behaviour that maintains the problem, is difficult to comprehend and draws little attention.

People often know what they must do to address a key problem and recognize at the same time that they are not taking action for reasons that remain obscure and little discussed. These tacit reasons may be of three types:

1 the **benefits** incurred from maintaining the problem;
2 the principles or **values** that, in some situations, may justify behaviour that maintains the problem; and
3 **attitudes** towards aspects of the problem that seem unpredictable or inevitable.

Step 1

Define the **core problem** briefly (e.g. construction worksite accidents). Create a **diagram** with a column to the left, a top row to the right and three columns below the row. Write the problem identified in Step 1 above the diagram.

Step 2

Examine what each group member and the group as a whole actually do to address or reduce the problem at hand (e.g. 'wearing personal protection equipment'). Draw

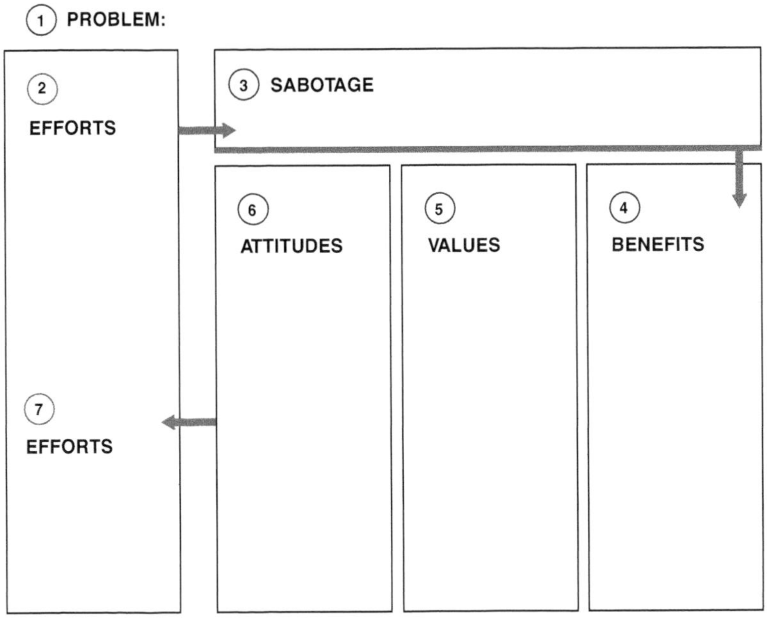

FIGURE 10.2 *Paradox* – construction worksite accidents.

or write the key words representing each **individual and group effort** to address the problem on its own card. Place the cards in the column to the left entitled *Efforts* (see Figure 10.2). Discuss how real the problem is despite individual and collective efforts to address it and what group members feel when the problem is evoked.

Step 3

Identify what each participant and the group as a whole can **possibly do** to make sure that the problem is **maintained or reinforced** (e.g. 'climbing without safety straps'). Draw or write the key words representing each response on its own card. Place the cards in the top row entitled *Sabotage* (see Chapter 14).

Step 4

Discuss what you would stand to gain individually or collectively from doing everything to maintain or reinforce the problem at hand (e.g. 'saving time'). Draw or write the key words representing each **benefit** on its own card. Place the cards in the column to the right entitled *Benefits.*

Advanced version: to assess the relative importance of each benefit, identify the benefits you would be willing to **sacrifice** in order to secure those that matter the most to you individually or collectively. For a more in-depth discussion, explore why these benefits matter in the first place and the **basic need(s)** they express.

Step 5

Identify some principles or **values** that you hold individually or collectively and that, in some situations, may justify the benefits sought through unsafe behaviour (e.g. 'taking pride in work well done completed on time'). Draw or write the key words representing each value or principle on its own card. Place the cards in the middle column entitled *Values*.

You can identify these values indirectly, by asking why each benefit from maintaining the problem matters in the first place (e.g. 'saving time allows us to meet the employer's expectations') or by exploring why these benefits do not matter to some people (e.g. 'they don't take pride in their work').

Advanced version: to assess the relative importance of each value, identify the values that you would be willing to **sacrifice** in order to secure those that matter the most to you individually or collectively. For a more in-depth discussion, explore why these values matter and the **fundamental value(s)** they express. Discuss the limits of each value and tensions between them (e.g. 'it is important to complete the work on time but the job has to be well done').

> Unlike rules and norms that leave little room for interpretation, values reflect the exercise of judgment in context and a balancing of ends and means to achieve them. (See *Lessons and Values* and also *Values, Interests, Positions*, Chapter 13).

Step 6

Discuss the extent to which there would still be a problem even if all measures were taken to address it (e.g. 'accidents are inevitable'). Identify concrete examples of **hazards** that are **unpredictable** or **inevitable** (e.g. 'working at height is always dangerous'), and discuss the individual or group **reaction** to them (e.g. 'we don't think about it. . .'). Write the key words expressing each unavoidable hazard and the reaction to them on its own card. Place the cards in the column entitled *Attitudes*.

Step 7

Discuss individual or group **measures** that could be introduced or reinforced in order to better handle the problem at hand (e.g. 'looking after each other's safety'). Discuss how these measures **negate** or **reinforce** the benefits, the values and the attitudes discussed in previous steps (e.g. 'mutual help is essential to doing good work and completing it on time'). Draw or write the key words expressing each measure on its own card. Add the cards to those already placed in the column entitled *Efforts*.

Step 8

Discuss the overall analysis, the method used and the findings.

FAQ

- ***Who should engage in this assessment?***

It all depends on what collective problem and behaviour is being examined and who the problems belong to – a small team, an organization or a stakeholder community, for instance.

- ***Does the technique assume that participants are essentially responsible for the problem at hand?***

Paradox assumes that participants are at least partly responsible for the problem they wish to investigate and can therefore act on it (through means that may not be strictly technical).

Combinations

- To explore values and attitudes, see *Active Listening* (Chapter 8) and *Lessons and Values* (Chapter 13).
- To further explore measures to better handle the problem (Step 7), use *Values, Interests, Positions* (Chapter 13), *Negotiation Fair* or *The Carrousel* (*Ideal Scenario*, Chapter 14).
- To combine *Paradox* with *Timeline, Force Field* and *Hazards*, see *Risk taking and risk thinking*, below.

RISK TAKING AND RISK THINKING

***Authors*: J. M. Chevalier and P. Obertelli**

While *Paradox* can be applied to a wide range of settings, the tool was designed to address health and safety issues in the European construction industry. It was tested with three small and medium size enterprises (SMEs) located on the outskirts of Paris (with twenty, seventy and 200 employees, respectively). The research and facilitation team (Jacques M. Chevalier and Patrick Obertelli, École Centrale de Paris) met with five small teams of workers and their immediate supervisors, on two separate occasions, in January 2011 and late in March of the same year. The study was part of a broader action-research project, under the coordination of P. Obertelli and jointly administered by the École Centrale de Paris, the OPPBTP and the Groupement National Multi-disciplinaire de Santé au travail dans le Bâtiment et les Travaux Publics (GNMST-BTP). Results of this study were presented to the pilot committee in April 2011, in a report entitled 'L'accompagnement des conduites individuelles et collectives face aux risques dans le bâtiment'.

The methodology developed for this study consists of *Paradox* preceded by an integrated *Timeline* (Chapter 9), *Force Field* and *Hazards* assessment of worksite hazards faced by workers of SMEs in the construction industry. (In Chapter 15, we present another story related to hazards of a different kind – typhoons, earthquakes, tsunamis and other natural disasters – using some of these tools and concepts.) A sample of our findings involving a small enterprise are presented below. But first we introduce key concepts and debates in theories of accident causation and prevention, starting with a general aphorism on the hazards of things we apprehend in life, some imposed on us and some of our own making.

> The literature review, to which we now turn, serves a critical purpose in this book. It illustrates the importance of reconciling two sets of considerations that are key to developing the full potential of PAR: on the one hand, the grounding of research in site-specific problem assessment and action and, on the one hand, engagement in conversations about broader issues – in this case paradigms of workplace safety and health in the modern construction industry. Inquiry and debates in this field also allow us to touch base again with a concept that is pivotal to this book: social engagement in support of meaningful science.

Accident causation and prevention theory

Science that fails to reflect upon itself produces conflicting messages and is inclined to cover them up at the same time. On one hand, science commands that strict rules of sound knowledge and learning be applied to all observable phenomena. On the other, positive science is reluctant to extend its scope to itself and accept the full implications of rigorous 'self-observation'. Given the difficulty in reconciling these two imperatives, many choose to impose observation-based reasoning as rock bottom knowledge, never to be questioned. As a result, science becomes what it is so successful at critiquing – an article of faith. A double bind takes command over rational means to understand the world and interact with it. To discover order in reality, the narrow scientific mind must treat science as a unique phenomenon, one that lacks root causality – an observable fact and process not determined or shaped by other facts of human history.

When narrowly defined, science also limits our understanding of the world, by promoting principles of control, scientific and managerial, to all observable phenomena, including those that are inherently complex and hazardous – i.e. marked by risk and the unknown. The science of hazard causation and prevention illustrates the point. Much of it assumes that the world we live in can be understood and ruled through positive science and the logic of command-and-control. While deviations from rational thinking and behaviour are bound to occur, they are mere 'accidents', to be accounted for through observable cause-effect relationships. This leaves all unobservable factors out of the equation. They do not count in our understanding or prevention of accidents that bring harm to men and women in real settings. As a result, accidents take on the appearances of 'pathology' – deviations from healthy systems that function normally and efficiently.

A chronic pathology well documented throughout the industrial world concerns accidents in the construction sector. Despite a wide range of effective measures adopted to prevent or mitigate risks on construction sites, the number of accidents, injuries, illnesses and deaths remains disproportionately high compared to other workplaces. In Europe, for instance, around 1,300 construction workers are killed in each year. Most of them are employed in SMEs representing more than 99 per cent of construction firms in Europe. The death rate, thirteen employees out of every 100,000, is more than twice the average of other sectors. The costs of accidents and ill health to individuals, employers and governments are immense.

A widespread and long-standing idea regarding construction accidents is that they are essentially a labour problem – the result of careless behaviour, errors and unsafe acts on the part of workers. Behaviour-based safety thinking goes back to Heinrich's pioneering work on accident causation and prevention based on his study of 75,000 workplace accidents, published in 1931. Heinrich (1959) visualized workplace injuries as the result of a chain of sequential events, like a line of dominoes falling over each other, one by one. The first domino is the social environment or inherited behaviour that contributes to creating the second domino – some fault in the worker's personality, such as recklessness or ignorance. The fault can in turn topple a third domino that plays a critical role in the chain: a failure to behave safely (e.g. standing under suspended loads, removing safeguards, starting machinery without warning) or to create safe work conditions, mechanical or physical (e.g. unguarded gears, insufficient light). The fourth domino is the accident and the fifth is the injury itself, which occurs in one of every eleven accidents, on average (leading to the 'iceberg theory' of accident causation). Heinrich claimed that 88 per cent of accidents are due to unsafe acts, 10 per cent result from unsafe mechanical or physical conditions and 2 per cent are 'acts of God'. Given this 88-10-2 ratio, behaviour-based safety focussed on the 'human factor' is the most effective way to interrupt the sequence of events leading to accidents and injuries.

Although still influential, Heinrich's mechanistic **domino theory** is a weak contribution to theories of industrial health and safety, compared to the many competing theories that have developed since the 1960s (Duclos, 2003; Manuele, 2002; Hovden *et al.*, 2008, Ch.56). Heinrich should nonetheless be credited for recognizing the relationship between human and environmental factors and the classical distinction between unsafe acts and unsafe conditions. Also the criticism usually levelled against his domino theory does not do justice to his insights on the issue of injury prevention. Heinrich was in fact the first to lay the foundations, if only prescriptively, for most work-related safety practices and legislation that have developed in modern industrial history. These foundations are briefly outlined in his ten *Axioms of industrial Safety* and the *Three E's* of his proposed *Corrective Action Sequence*.

The first 'E' stands for **Education**. It calls for action to train workers regarding all facets of safety and to persuade employers to prevent accidents for both humanitarian and financial reasons (axioms 6 and 10). Educational measures are all the more critical as most accidents are caused by unsafe acts and are preventable (axioms 1, 2 and 4). **Engineering**, the second 'E', is also needed for hazards to be effectively controlled. This requires making adjustments to product, mechanical, physical and process designs, applying the same methods as used to control the quality, the cost and the quantity of production (axioms 1, 3, 6 and 7). **Enforcement**, the last 'E', insures that workers and management alike follow internal and external rules, regulations and standard operating procedures. This implies the exercise of managerial responsibility, adjustments to personnel, the enforcement of discipline and close supervision of worker performance (axioms 6, 8 and 9) (Heinrich, 1959).

Mishaps that may cause injuries can be prevented but they will continue to happen as long as workers, managers and governments do not understand how and why they happen, do not design safe work and technology and are not constrained by safety regulations and procedures. Unlike his linear causal-sequence model, Heinrich's *Three E* principles and related axioms suggest that accidents result from failures in education, engineering and enforcement. This implicit theory of accident and injury causation and prevention is systemic in its own way. It is all the more holistic as it includes another 'E' worth naming: methodical **Enquiry**, the fourth pillar of hazard prevention. This is Heinrich's call for action-research in five methodical steps, those of accident and near-accident investigation, analysis, selection of remedy, implementation and evaluation of effects.

Education, engineering, enforcement and enquiry represent the four cornerstones of current wisdom in the industrial world on the matter of occupational hazards. When brought together they support a complex edifice that takes on different sizes and shapes from one occupational sector and country to another. Each cornerstone builds on important contributions from different disciplines and conceptual frameworks. The complex meshing of these *Four Es*, however, tends to be poorly reflected in most theories of accident causation and prevention. Most models and theories concentrate on some parts of the edifice rather than grasping the system as a whole. Trees receive far more attention than the forest. In Heinrich's work, unsafe behaviour is viewed as the main cause of accidents at the same time as it is subject to other forces both acknowledged and left unexplained. From a scientific perspective, the *raison d'être* of management, government and science in regards to unsafe behaviour at work remains a secret.

The domino theory of accident causation is science flirting with vagueness and confusion. Combined with the *Four E's*, the model creates a riddle: it refuses to target the system as a whole, choosing instead to concentrate on a principal cause that is left poorly investigated and has no root cause of its own. While clearly identified, means to act on this principal cause (controlling behaviour through adequate education, engineering, enforcement and enquiry) are never given a causal status. With Heinrich, non-workers are responsible for putting in place extensive measures that hold workers strictly responsible for accidents and measures to prevent them.

Given the confusion, many accident theorists have chosen to redirect the locus of responsibility and effective control to non-workers, through the development of the science of safety engineering and management. The current wisdom resulting from this shift, dating back to the 1960s, is that corporate industry and management is essentially responsible for health and safety issues at work. Although legislation varies from country to country, employers are now typically obliged to design and organize construction work safely, identify hazards, determine corrective actions, implement and monitor them, keep record of injuries and incidents, report them to the authorities, consult employees, provide training and inform workers of hazards and safe work practices. Section 5 of the

Occupational Health and Safety (OSH) Act passed by the US Congress in 1970 thus requires each employer to 'furnish to each of his employees employment and a place of employment which are free from recognized hazards that are causing or are likely to cause death or serious physical harm to his employees.' The European Council Directive 92/57/EEC, transposed into law in all member states, reflects the same philosophy.

Most safety and health theories and frameworks developed since the 1960s emphasize the importance of designing work for no risk or minimum risk, a task essentially under management control. The basic philosophy is summarized in the prosaic statement by the editor of *Hazards*: 'It's the hazards, stupid' (O'Neill, 2002; Frederick and Lessin, 2000). Less polemically, the argument is that health and safety depends on work process and managerial decisions about what and how to produce, not on well-instructed and well-behaved frontline workers. To prevent illness and injury at work, root causes must be addressed. Measures must be taken to remedy or eliminate the hazards altogether (e.g. dangerous chemicals, heavy weights, possible falls), by investing in plants and working environments that are safe, mechanically and physically, and introducing appropriate engineering controls and process design. Building safety requirements in the design specifications of work, product, equipment and environment already has a long history in many complex safety-critical systems such as rail and mass transportation systems, commercial airliners, air traffic control, spacecraft, nuclear power and complex weapon systems. The ergonomic design of equipment, physical environment and work tasks to eliminate or reduce operating hazards, such as work-related musculoskeletal disorder (WMSD), is another important contribution to creating failsafe, 'non-energy transferring' situations.

This brings us to **Energy Release Theory** and the critical role it played in making the shift. Borrowing concepts from Gordon (1949) and Gibson (1964), Haddon (1972, 1980), the father of modern injury epidemiology, argues that bodily injuries and property damage never happen simply 'by accident'. They must be addressed scientifically, by looking at the different factors and phases involved. Key **factors** include humans suffering the injury (the host), the vehicles (e.g. chemicals) and equipment (e.g. power saws) causing it, the physical environment (e.g. buildings) where the event takes place and also the social environment (i.e. regulations, laws, cultural norms or mores). These factors come together in situations where thermal, radiant, chemical, electrical or mechanical energy is out of control and transferred in excess of body injury thresholds, thus causing harm.

Energy transfers go through different **phases**, and countermeasures to keep them in check must adjust accordingly. The first phase, the pre-event, raises questions about the source of harmful energy and safety measures to eliminate it (e.g. substitute non-toxic for toxic chemicals). Other first-phase prevention strategies consist in limiting the amount of harmful energy or modifying its characteristics, preventing it from building up or being released (e.g. design power saws with a start button that prevents accidental starts), or modifying its rate and distribution if released. The second phase, the harmful event, calls for means to separate energy and humans in time or space (e.g. use remote control machines) or by means of physical barriers (e.g. use power saws with safeguards). The third phase, the post-event, involves the final release of energy and efforts to reduce the immediate and long-term consequences of an injury once the harm is done (e.g. apply first aid and minimize the time delay between injury and hospital care). Haddon's synthetic matrix, refined over time, brings together column **factors** and row **phases** in a single table. The matrix invites users to identify strategies for risk management and prevention in each problematical cell.

Haddon's etiological model substitutes a multiple-phase and root-cause framework for Heinrich's linear causal-sequence model, an approach now adopted in most accident causation theories (Kjellén, 2000). The model has been key to creating safety standards for motor vehicle design and driving in the United States and elsewhere. It encourages safety theorists and practitioners to avoid being locked into one phase of the matrix and to consider the different factors that underlie or determine the injury or harm caused by uncontrolled energy. As Runyan (2003) remarks, this is a flexible and pragmatic framework to examine risks and problems systematically and choose from a wide array of strategies the most effective in preventing injuries, including workplace behaviour, management decisions, technological innovation and policymaking.

Injury prevention cannot be limited to its behavioural aspects and must include planning for all conditions and phases that may cause injuries, including unsafe equipment and physical environments. On this point, Haddon notes that large amounts of harmful energy transfer require interventions in the pre-event phase, with a view to nipping the problem in the bud. He also remarks that passive countermeasures are more reliable in the long term because they act automatically and require no action or co-operation on the part of workers (e.g. interlocks that automatically stop machines when tripped). By contrast, active barriers requiring human action may be sufficient to handle immediate day-to-day problems (e.g. pressing an emergency stop button, using guards or escape and evacuation to maintain safe distance between workers and the danger zone).

Designing barriers to eliminate or effectively control hazards is now a basic principle of **safety engineering** and the 'hierarchy of hazard controls' framework, long employed in the aerospace industry. The framework ranks hazard control methods according to effectiveness. The top-ranking measures are *elimination* (e.g. performing a task at ground level rather than at heights) followed by *substitution* as the next best method (e.g. substituting water-jet cutting for mechanical sawing). *Engineering* comes third (e.g. safeguarding technology such as interlocks, two-hand control systems, safety edges, noise-dampening technology, mechanical lifting devices). All three measures are 'engineering controls' under management responsibility, to be promoted by workers, unions and governments. They directly affect the work process and ensure that jobs are designed to be safe or redesigned to be safer when hazards are detected. Less effective measures are of the cognitive and behavioural kind. They lay much of the responsibility on the workers and frontline staff. They include *administrative* controls (e.g. training, standard operating and safe working procedures, authorization, supervision) and distributing *information for use* (e.g. manuals, instruction sheets, labels, signs, signals). *Personal protective equipment* (PPE) such as safety glasses and helmets comes last since it requires compliance and supervision and adds a new physical burden on the worker, creating discomfort and even hazards. Also it is not fool proof. As with other methods, PPE is to be used only if higher-ranking controls are unavailable.

Similar causal-hierarchy frameworks inform other models of accident causation such as TRIPOD (Reason, 1991), the ILCI method (International Loss Control Institute, see Bird and Germain, 1985), MORT (Management Oversight and Risk Tree, see Cornelison, 1989) and SMORT (Safety Management and Organisation Review Technique, see Kjellén, 2000). A consistent theme in these models and related causal-factor checklists used for investigation is the lack or loss of top-management control over potentially harmful energy as the root cause of unsafe acts and injuries at work (Kjellén, 2000, pp. 37–39, 55). The basic idea is 'that there exists an ideal SHE (safety, health and environment) management system as specified in industry standards or handbooks. In this sense, they are prescriptive. By comparing the actual conditions with the ideal model, the analyst is able to identify gaps that represent the so-called root causes of accidents' (Kjellén, 2000, p. 45). Underlying causes include dormant deficiencies in the design and management of the industrial system, latent failures that can be triggered and overcome a system's defences if left unabated (Reason, 1991).

In a safety engineering perspective, accident investigation focusses on causes that are preventable and within the boundaries of company control. Guided by quality assurance management principles, the investigation goes beyond considerations of unsafe acts by workers alone. The inquiry (and planning) process avoids at the same time going too far in the opposite direction, back to Adam and Eve, by expanding the causal chain to include psychological, social, economic or political conditions and factors at play. As Kjellén (2000, p. 72) puts it, safety engineering is essentially about immediate causation and prevention, not about explanation and prediction.

Engineering for safety is far more effective than safe-behaviour education. Although attractive, the argument is by no means universally accepted. The notion that managerial and engineering controls at the company level can nip health hazards in the bud fails to make sense of many intervening actors and factors, including the necessary role of state agencies in matters of health and safety. If employers and employees have so much to gain from reducing costs in health, lives and property, why is there still a need for regulatory agencies and frameworks? Another puzzle consists in applying the principles of managerial science and control to small and medium size enterprises (SMEs). More often than not, safety-engineering theory is out of sync with SMEs that generally lack control over the design of the machinery or standard materials they use (forklifts, for instance). Nor do they control existing health services and technology that play a vital role in reducing the immediate and long-term consequences of injuries at work.

The notion that improved technology can resolve all SHE problems is no less convincing. Technological innovation is known to introduce new risks, a concept clearly understood in fields such as medicine, transportation and the nuclear industry. In the construction sector, safeguard technology and automation can create a sense of false security (Goguelin and Cuny, 1988, p. 102), produce boredom and reduce worker attention, for instance. More advanced technology may call for the development of specialized skills that may be acquired and applied unevenly, with the possibility of error. Regular maintenance requirements can also create hazards that cannot be countered through the engineering of 'passive barriers' alone. However reliable it may be from an engineering perspective, safety-designed hardware and equipment may fail to protect workers if it is not regularly tested and routinely maintained (e.g. gauge reading, leaky valves, metal fatigue). Another risk factor involves competing concerns, those of productivity and efficiency, considerations that may impede full managerial and worker compliance with extensive SHE instructions and regulations.

Hazards also emerge from temporary or mobile construction projects where workers and management are routinely faced with situations and problems that require deviations from the original plans (for reasons involving variations in construction projects, materials and external conditions, or pressures to complete the work on time and within budget). More generally, it is the nature of industry to undergo frequent transformations that give rise to new worksite hazards. Fast pace changes in industrial technology, information and communication technology (ICT) and global markets for products and labour profoundly affect everyday work life systems and processes. These changes may solve some problems but they also create new social, technical and communicational challenges – those of migrant labour, automation and ICT, for instance. Related stressors, such as workplace violence, cannot be fully anticipated or solved through company-based, 'engineering controls' (Hovden *et al.*, 2008).

In fairness to system safety theory, the argument that some risk is inevitable is not news to management science. As Stephenson observes, system safety represents 'a sub-discipline of systems engineering that applies scientific, engineering and management principles to ensure adequate safety, the timely identification of hazard risk, and initiation of actions to prevent or control those hazards throughout the life cycle *and within the constraints of operational effectiveness, time, and cost*' (quoted in Vincoli, 2006, p. 6, authors' emphasis). Its primary goal is not to eliminate risk altogether but rather to create the highest possible level of freedom from risk in a given environment, or reducing the hazard of risk to its **lowest acceptable levels**. Not all risk can be eliminated under all conditions and in all possible circumstances. If so, no forklift or drill press could be operated, automobile driven or aircraft authorized to fly (Kjellén, 2000; Reason, 1997). Nor would industry be able to maximize profits. Most governments act on this twofold concern for workers and the interests of capital when they pass SHE laws and regulations. In reality, enforcement measures are designed to create minimum health and safety standards at best and rely mostly on industry to implement them.

Historically, system safety is part of systems engineering, a broader discipline that is as much if not more about maximizing profits (or minimizing financial risk) as it is about safety and health. Its goal is to reduce hazard risk to its lowest acceptable level, usually well above zero. This raises a fundamental question: what level of risk will corporate industry, managers and engineers find acceptable given other considerations such as operational effectiveness, time and cost? As should be expected, the answer varies according to the perceived benefits and disadvantages associated with context. The acceptable risk level in the construction industry is not the same compared to other sectors such as road transportation or nuclear power.

Workers are also faced with the problem of defining tolerable safety risks in light of the various concerns they have, and adjusting their behaviour accordingly. As Hale and Glendon (1987) point out, the degree to which people expose themselves to safety and health hazards depends on the level of risk they are willing to accept or tolerate. Unless they change their target level towards greater safety, people may use innovations in system safety to pursue other goals, such as improved performance. Behavioural responses and adaptations of this kind are well documented, especially in the field of road traffic and accidents (e.g. people drive faster on roads that have wider lanes, paved shoulders, reflector posts or clearly painted edge markings, measures otherwise designed to reduce the frequency of accidents).

This is Risk Homeostasis Theory – people will be less cautious if perceived hazards are reduced. Using the insights of Surry (1969), Hale and Glendon (1987) add that people's hazard tolerance depends on the phase at which the hazard is detected. Workers react differently to early warning during danger build-up compared to an immediate threat caused by danger release. The way workers determine tolerable risk also reflects differences in work situations and levels of learning (Rasmussen *et al.*, 1987). The caution they exercise is lower in hazardous situations involving automatic skill-based behaviour informed by training and experience. By contrast, workers are more risk-conscious in situations where they must apply existing rules or when they use acquired knowledge to interpret, assess and cope with new hazards.

Engineering for safety at the company level, with proper measures to **educate** workers and **enforce** safety procedures and regulations, in compliance with existing laws, has many loopholes. The overall approach could always be treated as a working hypothesis, to be tested and refined through the fourth 'E' – a systematic **enquiry** into accident causation and, what is equally important, the effectiveness of current policies and practices in managing health and safety hazards. By and large, research on accidents focusses on the former issue and falls short in addressing the latter. The literature is dominated by methods and related checklists to collect data and analyse accidents, as described at great length in Kjellén (2000), Vincoli (2006) and DOE (1999). The most often used tools are the Ishikawa (fishbone) diagram, Fault Tree analysis, Event Tree analysis and Causal Root analysis. They focus attention on the causal or contributing factors associated with a sequence of logically and chronologically related events that deviate from plans and result in injury to personnel or damage to the environment or material assets. *Causal factors* are events or conditions in the accident sequence that are necessary and sufficient to produce or contribute to the unwanted result. More advanced models distinguish between direct causes (immediate events or conditions), contributing causes (collectively increasing the likelihood of an accident) and root causes (systemic, under managerial control, to be corrected in order to prevent recurrence of the accident). Unlike causal factors, *contributing factors* are more lasting and relate to issues of design, organizational processes and social systems. In some frameworks, factors are subdivided into categories, such as Material, Milieu (environment), Methods, Materiel (equipment) and Manpower. Investigative frameworks based on Energy Release Theory revolve around deficient barriers – controls that fail to impede harmful energy flows (e.g. equipment, administrative procedures and processes, supervision/management, warning devices, knowledge and skills).

Investigations into the causal and contributing events and conditions that produce accidents are essential to planning for no risk or minimum risk on construction sites. The visual, step-by-step nature of most methods encourages group discussions (at the company level) that help account for reported accidents. They are nonetheless insufficient to correct problems of recurrent illness and deaths in the construction industry, as current statistics sadly indicate.

The basic limitations of formal investigative methods into accident causation revolve around two stop-rules, both of which point to issues of 'control'. The first stop-rule, as described by Rasmussen *et al.* (1987) and Reason (1997), suggests that the investigation should stop when the causes identified are no longer controllable through means/ends analysis and formal planning. Since most models emphasize the role of company and management in preventing accidents at work, this stop-rule means that tracing causes back to failures at higher levels – looking at the roles of national regulatory and supervisory authorities, for instance – is unrealistic because too complex and out of reach. The second stop-rule, also inspired by the fear of going 'back to Adam and Eve', concerns the distinction between 'accounting' and 'understanding'. Techniques to investigate accidents are essentially designed to gather evidence, describe events and conditions and analyse logical relationships between them. The enquiry process thus accounts for unplanned events and helps gain greater control over hazards. Given their practical nature, the methods used preclude efforts to discuss, understand and dig deeper into cultural or psychological factors that are complex and do no lend themselves to measurable observations and plans to control them. Since they neglect the less tangible aspects of health and safety at work, most methods invite a technical, largely top-down investigative approach – a sequence of fact-finding steps and procedures to follow at all times, mostly for administrative and legal purposes.

In summary, accident causation and prevention theory is hampered by several double-bind attitudes concerning risk-taking in real-life situations. First, system safety thinking acknowledges the key role that the *Four E's* and related actors play in causing or preventing accidents. Narrow views of science and prevention nonetheless impose a command to refrain from further thinking and discussion about whatever lies outside the scope of a single-cause and key-actor approach to the subject at hand. Second, mainstream theory acknowledges the complexity and hazards of technological change and SME construction activity. All the same, all things that do not yield to a command-and-control logic are left out of the final equation. Third, hazards are clearly understood to be manageable up to a certain point only. Yet considerations that determine acceptable risk thresholds (for workers and industry) are ignored – all the more so if they involve non-observables such as safety culture in organizational settings and everyday life. As Obertelli (1995) points out, group norms in regards to these thresholds vary considerably and account for important differences in risk-taking behaviour.

In reality, accidents are intricate events, with multiple layers that should not be ignored as soon as they become complex – i.e. less easily observed, described, measured and controlled (see Faverge, 1967, p. 9). Relying on strict causal reasoning to figure out why accidents happen and how to prevent them is not as rational as it may seem. The approach imposes narrow views of 'methodical thinking and planning', with limitations on the potential for social reflectivity and collective action. The main limitation in this regard lies in the top-down technical approach to health and safety Education, Engineering, Enforcement and Enquiry, much of which ignores the value of stakeholder engagement. Stop-rules regarding the effective involvement, reflective and practical, of all contributing actors and factors, other than managerial, remain a key obstacle to a thriving safety culture at work.

Calls to develop a stronger safety culture through greater dialogue and reflectivity are many. Hale and Hovden (1998) describe 'safety culture' as a breakthrough in accident prevention thinking, an approach backed up by a long tradition of psychosociological and sociotechnical contributions to group dynamics dating back to the pioneering work of the Tavistock Institute. Reason (1990) makes the same argument when he emphasizes the need for top-management commitment to a safety culture permeating all levels of the organization (see also Kjellén, 2000, p. 14). Likewise, proponents of Risk Homeostasis Theory point out that people's health and safety depend essentially upon their desire to be safe and related tolerance toward risk (Wilde, 1982).

Petersen (2001) is another strong advocate of safety culture (defined as 'the way it is around here'). He holds that accidents are essentially caused by people, not by unsafe acts, conditions or things. The real question is why people engage in unsafe acts in the first place? To be more precise, why does an organization allow hazards at work and opportunities to behave unsafely? If safety committees, programmes and audits are set up, what is the real motivation behind them? According to Petersen, they are of little help if they represent administrative procedures and paperwork aimed mostly at regulatory compliance, as is often the case. They become effective only if they reflect a genuine culture of organizational commitment and employee involvement in accident prevention thinking and planning. What matters in the end is the value placed by all (industry, workers, governments) on safety and concrete actions that follow.

Given its many limitations, the models and muddles of 'managerial control' should be understood for what they are – neo-liberal euphemisms for the lack of close coordination between the many actors and factors of hazard prevention. Top-down command-and-control measures are no substitute for multi-stakeholder **Engagement** and dialogue to support reflectivity in the field of health and safety at work. This proposed fifth 'E', explored below, is a critical link missing in both theory and practice and weakening all expert-based pillars of workplace hazard prevention.

Health and safety among construction workers in France

Concepts of safety culture and social reflectivity expand the scope of thinking and action in regards to work-related illnesses and injuries, beyond technical and managerial approaches to the issues at hand. They invite organizations, workers and other key actors to address two vital questions that tend to be ignored or glossed over. Why do organizations and workers take or accept exposure to risks, real or perceived, despite the many calls and measures to prevent them? Also, why is there so much restraint in researching the hidden reasons of risk behaviour, individual and organizational?

The case study presented below attempts to answer these questions through a blend of dialogue and evidence-based analysis. Tested in France, on the outskirts of Paris, the methodology combines a novel tool called *Paradox*, inspired by the works of Bateson (1972) and Erickson *et al.* (1976), with three tools that address the more conventional aspects of accident assessment: the sequencing of events (*Timeline*, Chapter 9), contributing factors (*Force Field)* and the perceived risks of observed hazards (*Hazards*, Chapter 15). The methodology spans two sessions and proceeds through sequenced questions to guide conversations between workers and the facilitating researchers and between workers themselves. The first session concerns workers' perceptions of hazards as they relate to an ongoing construction project, factors that aggravate or attenuate these hazards, and the level of control that workers exercise over them. The second session delves into less observable phenomena: the effects of unspoken benefits, values and attitudes that lead workers to accept risks in particular organizational settings. Both sessions show the way out of the double binds of managerial command, by opting out of simple notions of control. By lifting the ban on 'risk taking and risk talking', the proposed methodology substitutes positive paradoxical reasoning for unexpressed dilemmas, using 'skilful means' to strengthen checks on hazards at work.

Session 1: Timeline, Force Field *and* Hazards

The first session grounds group thinking in a real worksite setting, using three integrated diagrams: *Timeline* combined with *Force Field* and *Hazards* (Chapter 15). *Timeline* (Chapter 9) allows each team to map on a horizontal line (drawn on a flip chart) the sequence of steps or phases in an ongoing construction project and the specific hazards associated with each phase. Using *Force Field* analysis, participants add, above the horizontal line, columns to indicate contributing factors, those believed to give rise or exacerbate existing hazards; and, below the line, columns to indicate counteracting factors, those believed to keep existing health and safety problems from getting worse (see Figure 10.3). Participants discuss and estimate the relative weight of each contributing and attenuating factor and adjust the length of each column accordingly. They also draw on each column-factor a dot to indicate the level of control they feel they can exercise over the factor, from low (solid dot) to moderate (half-tone dot) and high (open dot). A separate Cartesian graph allows participants to assess and discuss the relative gravity and probability (or past frequency) of each hazard (see Figure 10.4). The session ends with a discussion of things that the team can do to further prevent worksite accidents and injuries. They can do this in one of two ways: by targeting factors that show higher levels of gravity and/or probability, or by altering the weight of contributing and counteracting factors (those over which they have some control).

Widely used accident investigation methods (e.g. causal tree analysis) also gather information about the sequence of worksite events and phases, associated hazards and their relative gravity and probability. Less familiar questions built into our first session concern (a) counteracting factors that keep risk factors in check; (b) levels of control over counteracting and contributing factors; and (c) different perceptions that team members have in regards to the relative gravity and probability of health and safety hazards. While less conventional, these questions are key to moving away from frameworks that ignore grassroots lessons to be learned from factors that help counter-act existing hazards; from workers' assessment of their capacity to change things; from

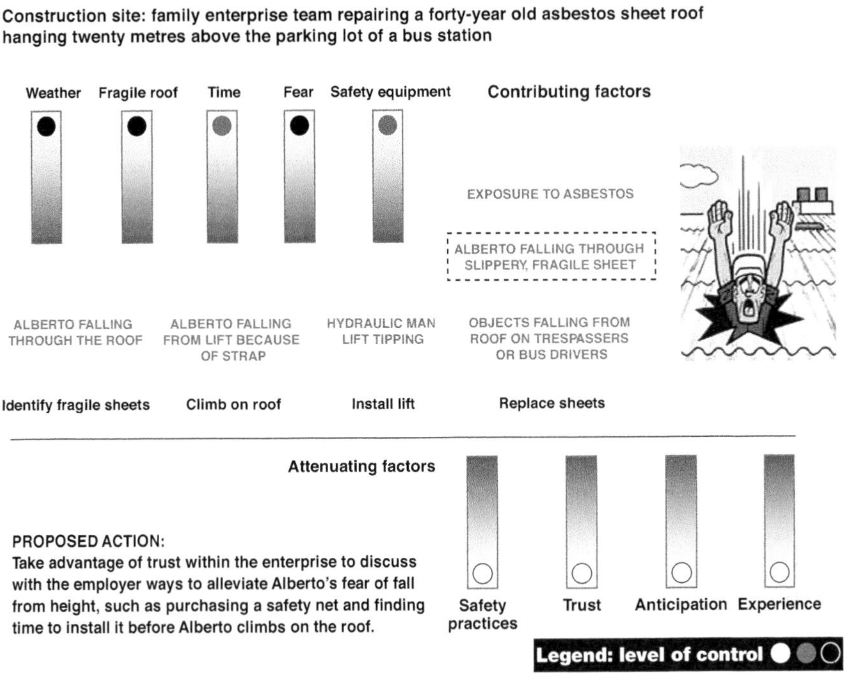

FIGURE 10.3 Factors counteracting and contributing to construction worksite hazards.

Source of pictures: Copyright ISSA Construction Section.

differences in level of exposure and vulnerability to risk. These considerations need to be factored into priorities for preventive action.

We now turn to a detailed illustration of this first session assessment of worksite hazards. All participating teams used the proposed methodology to reflect on a worksite already under way. One enterprise and work team we met had been called upon to repair a 40-year-old asbestos sheet roof hanging 20 metres above the parking lot of a bus station (measuring about 2,000 square metres). The team drew a *Timeline* sequence of steps to repair the roof together with the main risks associated with each work phase. Principal hazards included prolonged exposure to asbestos; the hydraulic man lift tipping due to strong winds or improper installation; objects falling from the roof on trespassers and bus drivers walking below. Much of the discussion, however, revolved around another danger: Alberto, a team member, risking a fall whenever he climbs to the roof, unstraps himself from the man lift, and walks on the roof to identify and replace fragile asbestos sheets. Team members said they use safety traps at all times to prevent such falls. But they know that straps are fallible. They wear out over time and may be poorly fastened to the worker, the man lift or the roof.

Force Field analysis, the next step, helps identify factors that contribute or aggravate worksite risks, some more so than others (usually shown as taller factor columns). Also some factors are more easily controlled or corrected than others (shown by open or half-tone dots drawn on each column). Again, most comments revolved around the team's fear of Alberto falling from the man lift or the roof. Factors that aggravate this risk include **environmental conditions** and the roofing **material** under repair, both of which are difficult to control. Exposure to wind, rain and freezing makes Alberto's work even more hazardous. The only thing the team can do under such circumstances is to stop working until the weather improves. The roofing material is also a danger. Some sheets are worn out, break easily and become slippery when covered with moss. Again, not much can be done to remedy this problem. Nor is it possible to anticipate sheets that are likely to collapse under new weight. Alberto needs to inspect them and runs the risk of falling through the roof in the process.

Equipment is another risk factor, partly controllable this time, through management intervention. The hydraulic man lift and safety straps are rented and may at times break or require maintenance. Workers can signal the problem to the employer who is responsible for contacting the rental business and see to it that the problem is corrected.

The other two factors, known as Manpower and Methods in the Ishikawa diagram (widely used in France), weigh considerably more in the team's assessment of worksite hazards. **Manpower** is the so-called 'human factor' – how individual workers and teams do their job. A factor that considerably aggravates Alberto's situation is his fear of heights and the vertigo he experiences when standing or moving on elevated platforms, especially those that are narrow or unstable. This fear dates back to a traumatic accident he had about fifteen years ago when he slipped and fell on waste gravel from the top of a three-story building, plummeting through a fifty-centimetre interstice between the scaffold and a brick wall. The event reminds Alberto of two fall-from-height accidents that his sixty-five-year-old father suffered at a younger age. The father is now unable to climb ladders and work at height.

Alberto considers his fear of heights to be uncontrollable and irreversible. His fear of falling is real and creates a feeling of insecurity that takes its daily toll. The team believes that the problem could be remedied by placing a safety net below the roof. However, this raises another issue that further complicates things, a work **method** issue (the fifth 'M' in the Ishikawa diagram) that workers and companies are constantly confronted with: the all-too-familiar race against time. This is a constant source of stress and tension within the team and the enterprise. Installing a safety net takes time and is expensive. As it is, creating a safe worksite absorbs more time than repairing the roof. The employer is not about to authorize another safety procedure, especially one that is costly in time and money.

Researchers invited the team to take a pause from the safety net discussion to rate worksite hazards using two criteria: the relative severity and probability (based on past frequency) of each hazard, mapped on a Cartesian graph drawn on a separate flip chart (see Figure 10.4). The exercise quickly confirmed the fact that falling from the roof was the greatest hazard, even if less probable and not a threat to everyone. It highlighted the greater vulnerability of Alberto, traumatized by a previous accident and now suffering from vertigo. The assessment reflected a tacit and common sense understanding of factors of 'vulnerability' and 'preparedness' to handle danger, two notions that are key to accident prevention and priority setting from an organizational perspective.

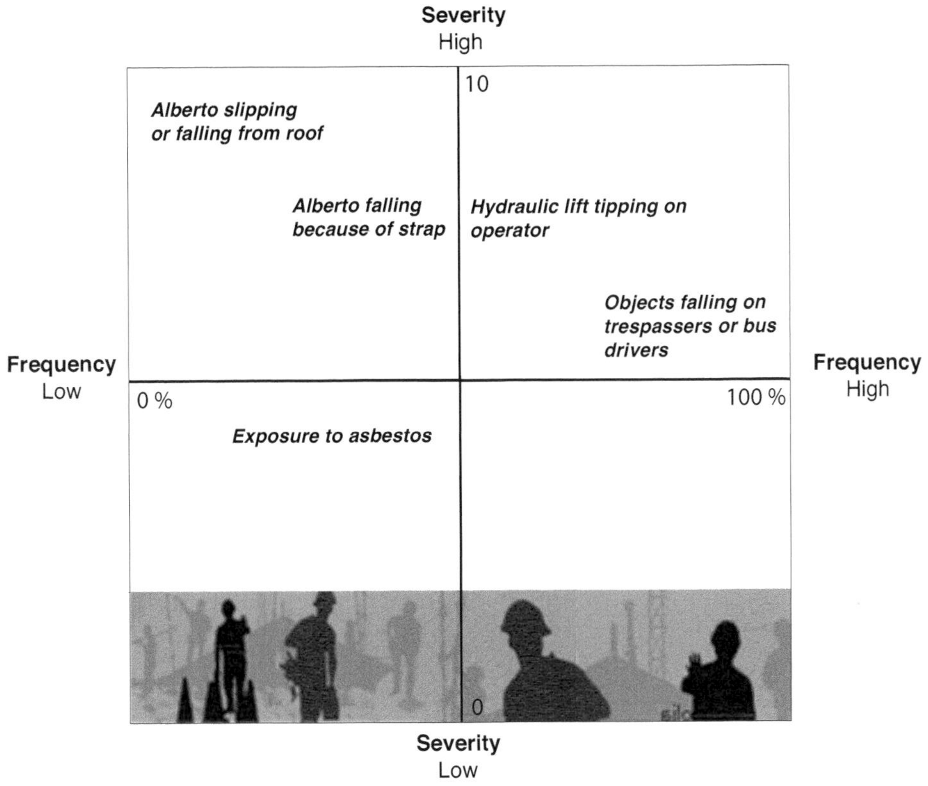

FIGURE 10.4 Construction worksite hazards.

Coming back to the *Force Field* exercise, team members identified factors that attenuate existing hazards (drawn below the *Timeline*), those they can build on to further prevent risks. The discussion converged on the spirit of trust prevailing within the team and the enterprise as the most important factor. Other factors that keep hazards in check include safety-critical practices such as wearing PPE, using and maintaining reliable equipment, and creating a safe and well-organized workspace. These are things they already do and are under their control. Experience is another factor that helps. Unlike younger workers, the team feels it does not need training on scaffolding and work at height, for instance. Team spirit and the ability to handle tensions and resolve problems, however, are far more critical to accident prevention. Workers who trust each other and enjoy working together (as they do) are more likely to help each other and show concern for everyone's safety and health in general (by ruling out alcohol consumption or cell phone interruptions, for instance). The team feels that trust is missing on many worksites. This is particularly true of larger team and multi-team construction projects where workers don't know each other well and regularly step on each other's toes. Conflicts over minor irritants (smoking in the worksite cabin, for instance) can turn into real fights.

Thus far, the discussion and diagram to capture it provide a clear picture of existing hazards associated with an ongoing construction project and the factors, more or less controllable, that aggravate or counteract them. Findings give the team a better handle on possible actions to remedy the key hazard of falling from height, a priority for the team. When invited to identify those actions, the team focussed their attention on two critical factors moving in opposite directions (drawn above and below the timeline diagram): on the positive side, the fact that trust and good will exists within the family enterprise; on the negative side, the cost in time and money associated with the safety net solution. Since the decision to purchase new equipment belongs to the employer, the team proposed to involve the employer in the discussion and explore what the enterprise could do about Alberto's fear and risk of falling from the roof.

The session ended with comments on the extent to which hazards are actually discussed within the team and the enterprise. Participants also evaluated the *Timeline, Force Field* and *Hazards* assessment process they had just experienced. In response to the first question, the team noticed the tendency they have of raising safety issues at the start of a project. They frequently warn each other and trespassers of potential dangers during the job, as needed. Words of caution are also important to guide every step in getting Alberto on the roof and helping him identify and replace decrepit asbestos sheets. Participants mentioned again that on-the-spot communications regarding safety matters are more likely to happen in smaller teams, among workers who know and trust each other as they do.

General remarks about Session 1 shifted the attention from risk taking to the question of risk talking. For one thing, the team felt that the process 'authorized' a safe space to address delicate issues of health safety at work. It gave workers an opportunity to pause and discuss past events and possible accidents, something they rarely do because always pressed for time. Also workers find it hard to talk about past traumas and life-threatening incidents. (The discussion concerning Alberto's fear of falling from height was emotionally charged to the point that Alberto spoke only briefly and in a low voice throughout the session. Many of the comments about falls from height actually came from Alberto's older brother). Participants agreed that speaking about these issues, including among family members, is key to promoting safety at work. They also felt it useful to compare different views and perceptions of worksite hazards and levels of danger. In their view, this kind of discussion could help integrate young co-workers and check up on everyone's appraisal of potential hazards at the start of a project. The exercise could also help manage tensions at work, with the assistance of an accident prevention officer, if needed.

The team recommended that employers be part of the discussion and contribute to the assessment. They recognized that discussions about corrective measures such as the safety net will not be easy. In this regard, having someone from outside to facilitate the discussion can make a difference.

On a concluding note, participants likened Session 1 to a family enterprise tradition that once existed – a friendly gathering at Christmas time when employees freely exchanged with the employer on work-related incidents of the year, including issues of health and safety prevention. In those days, taking time to talk things through and enjoying the process was the normal thing to do.

Session 2: unspoken benefits, values and attitudes

Session 1 focussed on workers' perceptions of worksite hazards, their relative importance and factors aggravating or attenuating them. It raised questions about what workers can do about these factors and the hazard that worries them the most: Alberto's potential fall from the bus station roof. Session 2, held two months later, started with a debriefing of things that had occurred since the first session. In response to this query, one team member said that Session 1 had prompted him to wear his safety helmet at all times. As for the safety net, participants reported on the discussion they had with older employees and the enterprise owner who showed genuine interest (and is usually accommodating when requests for equipment are made). But the issue of time and the imperative of 'speed, speed' came up again. The idea was abandoned because not realistic.

Team members thus had little to report on the technical side of prevention. However, they informed researchers that discussions continued well after Session 1, within and outside the team, especially in regards to the question of trust. The issue was particularly important and timely as two young workers had joined their team – workers they know little, have difficulty working with and whose behaviour they find impossible to anticipate (when working at heights, for instance). Session 2 picked up on a related risk situation mentioned only in passing in Session 1: the stress and lack of trust associated with larger-team projects. In keeping with this topic, the team revisited a concrete action proposed at the end of Session 1, namely, engaging in dialogue with new and young team members on matters of health and safety at work.

On the whole, Session 1 made the team more conscious of the many risks involved in the work they do, things 'you don't think about'. But there is still the problem of having to work with other teams and 'people you don't know on other worksites – having to work with all those people around us, those wild teams that get carried away. It's all about speed. They take no precaution. Sometimes just to save five minutes. . . When teams are mixed, everyone tries to go first. There is no respect between workers.'

Enlarging the work team with to young recruits produces similar hazards. The team did try to raise health and safety issues with the new co-workers, but with poor results. Even when warned, younger workers don't wear safety helmets or masks (because not 'stylish') and continue to wear running shoes instead of the heavier construction boots. The only way to get youth to comply with safety rules is by 'telling the boss'. Team members admit they once behaved the same way, when they were young and 'controls didn't exist'. Over the years, however, they saw other workers get sick or die. 'So-and-so would still be with us had he strapped himself to the roof.' When you get older you realize your hands will bleed if you don't wear gloves. Also you know better than to rush all the time and risk hurting yourself or falling from height.

Insights into tensions between younger and older co-workers set the scene for Session 2's main question, and a fundamental riddle in the field of accident prevention theory and practice: why is it that workers expose themselves to hazards in the first place? The question was explored in seven steps designed to facilitate further thinking around issues of health and safety, the integration of young co-workers and the critical factors of stress and trust at work.

On a theoretical note, it stands to reason that the root causes or reasons for risk-taking behaviour within a team, a profession, an organization, an industry or a society are key to understanding why people do what they do and how things can change. But the statement is not as harmless as it may seem. Oddly enough, the question of root causality, which is central to scientific thinking, attracts little attention in much of accident causation and prevention theory and practice. Accidents tend to be viewed not as the predictable effects of causes worthy of scientific inquiry, but rather as the consequence of plans not being made or followed – a lack or loss of managerial control and worker compliance. As in legal practice, inquiries into 'faults' and related evidence thus revolve mostly around questions of responsibility, i.e. final ends (intent) and means (actions) not taken to prevent harm. As a result, accidents remain unexplained. This non-scientific mindset is reminiscent of scholastic philosophy where the 'accidents' of human existence matter little in comparison with the master plan of God, as expressed through his moral Creation. In the writings of Thomas Aquinas (inspired by Aristotle), an 'accident' thus denotes an attribute, known to exist through the senses, which may or may not belong to a subject, without affecting its essence – the whiteness of the teeth of a human being, for instance (a man remains a man even if his teeth turn green). Unlike essences, accidents are fortuitous, transient and changeable. Ultimately, they are of little interest to philosophy, as they have no logically necessary connection with their essences. 'Accidents' in the modern world generally suffer a similar fate. However much sadness and concern they may cause, they are mere incidents on the margins of the master plan of management and industry. Essentially, an accident is a plan in need of further perfection.

Accidents in the construction industry have root causes that beg to be investigated. Some of them happen to be less observable than others. They matter no less in our understanding of worksite health and safety problems and ways to resolve them. The most delicate causes, and the most systematically ignored, have to do with 'reasons' for taking risks or not preventing accidents, i.e. motives for management and workers to accept or tolerate hazards at work. Below we describe a step-by-step process and conversation to unpack three sources of hazard tolerance, all of which converge on what might be called the 'hidden rationality' of unsafe behaviour. They consist of the unspoken *benefits*, the underlying *values* and the deep-seated *attitudes* associated with risk exposure at work.

Safety (Step 2)

The proposed method starts with an exercise in positive psychology, i.e., an appreciative conversation about good health and safety habits already in place – all the things that team members do on a regular basis to prevent work-related accidents and illnesses. More specifically, participants describe what they each do to promote everyone's safety at work. The question is rarely asked (given the emphasis on safety education) and was well received. In response, participants mentioned their habits of installing protective barriers around holes; making sure that the worksite is safe; wearing PPE and reminding young workers to do the same; watching over younger co-workers ('they fool around with cement mixers and don't realize how dangerous they can be'); refusing to do

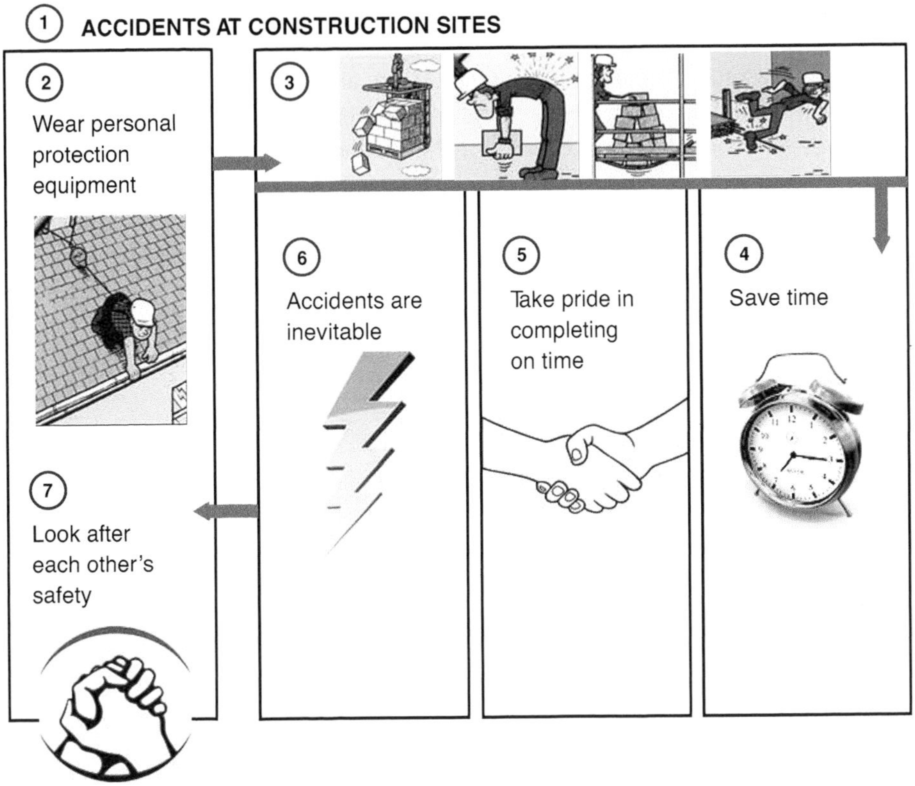

FIGURE 10.5 *Paradox* – construction worksite accidents in France.

Source of pictures: Copyright ISSA Construction Section.

something if it doesn't feel safe; strapping oneself when working at height; and, last but not least, looking after the safety of others at all times (by warning them of hazards, such as lifting heavy loads without bending the knees), insisting to the point of nagging, getting stressed and forgetting about one's own safety in the process. Alberto's older brother admits that while he is good at assessing worksite problems and hazards, he also tends to worry a lot. He exercises authority when things go wrong and does so even if it irritates younger guys and creates tension within the team.

The research team used a flip chart diagram to capture the main points of the discussion and facilitate their immediate analysis and interpretation by the group (Figure 10.5). The diagram consisted of a column to the left (for Steps 2 and 7), a top row to the right (for Step 3) and three columns below the row (for Steps 4, 5 and 6). Existing health and safety practices identified by the group were recorded in the upper half of the left hand column, under Step 2.

Unsafe behaviour (Step 3)

From an exercise in positive group psychology, the attention turned to paradoxical thinking framed around an unusual question, equally unexpected: what is it that each team member and the group as a whole can possibly do to make sure that unsafe behaviour prevails at work? Facilitators encouraged participants to respond without concern about whether these unsafe acts reflect actual behaviour and who should be blamed for it if and when it occurs.

Responses (recorded in the top row of the diagram) covered the usual suspects driven by time constraints. The list included refusing to wear PPE, climbing without safety straps, showing no caution when using machinery, ignoring the equipment maintenance schedule (every six months), burning waste material in the middle of the site and, lastly, working at height or mechanically lifting heavy loads with people below. Another good way to cause accidents consists in not placing safety barriers around danger areas, or letting strangers trespass into the site at their own risk (a wartime unexploded shell killed two children playing on a worksite a few years previously).

Benefits (Step 4)

The next three steps invite workers to reflect on the benefits (Step 4), the values (Step 5) and the attitudes (Step 6) associated with unsafe behaviour, individual or organizational (identified in Step 2, with humour). The group conversation around these issues, recorded in the three columns below the top row, helps participants wrestle with a double-bind situation. Either they assume the motives behind their behaviour and enact them intentionally or voluntarily, at some risk to their health. Or they give up some risk-taking behaviour and the motives behind it. In either case, the problem is no longer experienced as a lack or a loss of control. The real issue shifts: how to exercise control?

A simple query launches the discussion: what does the team and the organization stand to gain from maintaining unsafe behaviour at work, as illustrated in Step 3? The immediate answer offered by Alberto's team concerned the perennial issue of time. Saving time is by far the greatest benefit to be gotten from poor safety performance. Installing barriers, checking and maintaining the equipment, bagging and transporting waste material instead of burning it, waiting for the man lift to back up instead of walking behind it, all of these safety measures take time away from getting the job done. Two other minor considerations emerged from this discussion. Safety straps and PPE hinder physical movement. Also, team members believe that younger workers ignore PPE instructions for reasons of personal appearance and style.

Values (Step 5)

Previous steps set the scene for group thinking about the less visible aspects of unsafe behaviour. Step 5 takes the reflective process to a deeper level, by exploring the unspoken values that justify apparently odd behaviour. The issue of saving time is particularly interesting in this regard. While defined as an immediate gain, time saved through risk-taking behaviour begs the question: why is time so important? The first response offered by Alberto's team is predictable. Time equals money. That is, taking time adds to the employer's costs. If prevention procedures were dropped, construction work could be done in no time and cost less. When probing further into the issue, however, the group turned to issues of professional satisfaction – seeing tangible results of good work done at the end of each day. At times this means cutting down on safety measures that cause delays. Also there are situations when doing a good job requires taking risks, such as unstrapping oneself and going out of the way to add another screw in a difficult place. Due consideration for the family enterprise owner is another good reason for taking chances with safety. The team values their ability to meet the employer's expectations, by estimating the number of days or weeks needed to complete each task and doing it on time. Pride plays a role too, especially when competing with other teams to get the work done faster. This is less true of small projects where good work matters more than rushing to meet deadlines. It is also less true of younger workers who go faster and take risks for other reasons. They rush not because they take pride in their work and the speed at which they do a job. Rather they don't enjoy the work and want to accomplish each task as quickly as possible. 'In the construction industry, you have to like your job and value good work.' Youth appear to value other things, not work.

Step 4 highlighted the familiar tension of safety vs. time and money. Step 5 revealed a different tension: the difficulty in reconciling safety goals with the workers' sense of responsibility towards the employer (meeting deadlines), the pride that workers take in quality work (going 'out of the way' to do it right) and their ability to perform and compete (especially on larger projects).

Attitudes (Step 6)

Exploring the implicit benefits and unspoken values associated with unsafe acts is key to understanding and correcting unacceptable risk-taking behaviour. But this raises a burning question: how to define risks that are acceptable, if any? Step 6 triggers group dialogue around risk tolerance through a simple line of questioning. 'Would hazards still exist and accidents still happen even if all measures were taken to prevent them? If so, why, and how do you cope with these inevitable hazards?'

Alberto's team acknowledges that hazards will always exist, whatever people do to prevent them. Hazards are inherent to construction work. Handling cement blocks will 'break your back' over time. There are days when incidents and accidents are fated to happen. Machines may break. There are hazards you can't anticipate or things you can't see – an electrical wire in a wall that you're nailing, or the wind that starts blowing when you're on the roof. Whatever you do, working at height is hazardous. As for coping with these hazards, it is important to keep them out of your mind, to the extent possible. When there is danger, you adjust the work plan, take necessary precautions, get on with the job and remain vigilant. But there is a point where you have to stop worrying. Thinking about safety all the time creates anxiety, which makes things worse.

Reflective prevention (Step 7)

Health and safety at work is a juggling act. While workers want to prevent hazards, as everyone does, they feel responsible for meeting deadlines and take pride in the work they do and their ability to compete and perform. They also believe that risks are inevitable. Constant vigilance is needed. Obsessing about them, however, serves no purpose and may become a hazard. The overall reasoning is complex. Accident causation and prevention theory would do well to reflect on juggling acts such as this, instead of harping on technical solutions to observable faults and losses of control.

The conversation continues. Step 7 (in the left-hand side column, below Step 1) attempts to integrate all previous concerns and observations into new thinking and safety plans. The final discussion wraps up insights into how the team juggles the requirements of safety, competitive pride, quality work and professional responsibility in situations where some risk is inevitable. With this goal in mind, researchers invite participants to revisit the question initially posed in Step 1, using positive psychology now in a projective mode: what can be done to further prevent worksite accidents? On a deeper level, an informed choice is proposed between consciously enacting the goals, values and attitudes of risk-taking behaviour, or altering them through concrete actions such as to improve health and safety at work.

Much of the conversation summarized below reflects a subtle rethinking and integration of risk-related benefits, values and attitudes previously explored, towards a reinforcement of safety prevention. The shift underscores an overarching principle announced from the beginning of Session 2: genuine respect, trust and solidarity between co-workers. Team members opened the discussion by evoking concrete things they can do to prevent accidents, including placing safety posters on the worksite (requiring workers to wear safety helmets, for instance); showing films of accident injuries and the tragic consequences of poor safety performance; or confiscating cell phones from those answering calls in the middle of work (and not wearing helmets to be able to take incoming calls). Not surprisingly, all measures proposed by the team are addressed to younger, less experienced workers. The discussion reverts to a concern expressed in Session 1 and in the debriefing of Session 2, i.e. unsafe acts by younger, less trustworthy workers. The issue is all the more relevant as two new recruits have now joined the team. However, differences noted between 'us' and 'them' give way to a call for mutual respect and 'concern for them'.

As the conversation evolves, the team finds faults again with young co-workers who show less interest in their work and in meeting the employer's expectations or protecting his reputation. Participants explain these faults by the fact that younger workers do not project themselves into the future or think about long-term goals such as learning a trade, helping the enterprise prosper, securing a steady job and raising a family. Moreover, their schooling prepares them poorly for construction work (except for a few things they learn and can teach others, such as metal framework techniques). On the whole, younger workers feel less attached to the enterprise. They also lack respect for older, more experienced workers. This can be seen by the familiar tone and the slang they use when speaking to older co-workers. Also some drink at work or smoke pot the night before. They refuse to carry out the tasks they are told to do. Instead of following orders, they get angry or violent.

All the same, the team feels that younger workers should not be put down and treated like slaves. They are 'la relève', our future, those who will succeed us. They deserve respect. This a key value to the team and also the enterprise, one that has the potential to resolve many problems. If there is respect, the team remarks, there is room for healthy competition between workers and teams. There is less stress and people work calmly, as opposed to obsessing about speed (or safety for that matter). Co-workers get along, laugh together and help each other (when lifting heavy loads, for instance). As a result, there are fewer accidents.

Conclusion

Comments about the importance of respect echoes the discussion of trust, mutual help and team spirit in Session 1, ingredients that are lacking in some mixed teams and multi-team projects. They are essential to preventing stress, tensions, conflict and the incidents or accidents that may result. These concluding insights lay the ground for further safety-related discussions with younger workers, to be carried out in a spirit of mutual trust and with the interest of workers, the employer and his clients in mind.

When reflecting back on Session 2, participants felt that the discussion gave them the opportunity to slow down, reflect and consider alternative accident prevention strategies and gain more confidence in their ability to think and act. They also suggested that visiting other enterprises and multi-team worksites might give them a broader view on how to approach health and safety at work (knowing at the same time that larger enterprises can count on more staff to supervise safety at work). Again the team felt that sessions like this one could foster dialogue between the employer and staff and between co-workers. Real conversations are less irritating and more effective in preventing accidents compared to formal memoranda addressed to staff. Participants also believe that their enterprise offers fertile ground for dialogue. They look forward to sharing their diagram and thinking with their colleagues who have shown interest and 'constantly ask questions [about this research project]'.

To conclude, mainstream research on harmful accidents identifies where things go wrong and their immediate circumstances. It establishes whether the worker was wearing his helmet when he fell from a slippery roof on a windy day, in a rush to get the job done before letting another team occupy the worksite, for instance. Based on its findings, the investigation identifies measures that could or should have been taken to avoid the accident (management must instruct workers to postpone work at height on bad weather days, for instance).

Supported by factual evidence, 'counterfactual reasoning' pointing to the inadequacies of existing safety systems and practices is essential to explaining accidents. Still, there is more to causal reasoning than combining observable facts with thinking about how events could have unfolded differently. To serve its purpose, the enquiry process must go beyond surface-level description and prescription and probe into the deeper causes of worksite hazards, including the reasons that people and systems have for taking chances with peoples' health and lives. Why do some workers expose themselves to danger as they rush to get the job done or choose not to wear PPE? Why does management allow workers to take such risks? Until such questions are answered, measures to prevent accidents lack grounding in causal thinking. Meanwhile construction workers (in France and elsewhere) continue to face the prospect of tragedy at work. To address this problem, safety and health research must help lift the ban on risk taking and risk thinking. It must engage all parties concerned, from workers to managers, employers and legislators, in frank discussions about health and safety at work.

REFERENCES

Bateson, G. (1972) *Steps to an Ecology of Mind: Collected Essays in Anthropology, Psychiatry, Evolution, and Epistemology*, University of Chicago Press, Chicago, IL.

Bird, F. E. and Germain, G. L. (1985) *Practical Loss Control Leadership*, Institute Publishing, Division of International Loss Control Institute, Loganville, Georgia, GA.

Cornelison, J. D. (1989) 'MORT based root cause analysis', Systems Safety Development Center, EG&G Idaho, Working paper no. 27, Idaho Falls, ID.

DOE, US Department of Energy (1999) *DOE Workbook, Conducting Accident Investigations*, Washington DC.

Duclos, D. (2003), 'Attention, Risquologues! Analyse critique du champ socio-politique des risques techniques et sociaux,' www.geo-anthropology.com/recherche-bibliographique-et-thematique-sur-le-risque_a21.html, accessed 12 March, 2012.

Erickson, M. H., Rossi, E. L. and Rossi, S. I. (1976) *Hypnotic Realities: The Induction of Clinical Hypnosis and Forms of Indirect Suggestion*, Irvington, New York.

Faverge, J.-M. (1967) *Psychosociologie des accidents du travail*, PUF, Paris.

Frederick, J. and Lessin, N. (2000) 'Blame the worker: The rise of behavioral-based safety programs', vol. 21, no. 11, multinationalmonitor.org/mm2000/, accessed 12 June, 2012.

Gibson, J. J. (1964) 'The contribution of experimental psychology to the formulation of the problem of safety – a brief for basic research', in W. Haddon, E. A. Suchman and D. Klein (eds) *Accident Research: Methods and Approaches*, Harper and Row, New York.

Goguelin, P. and Cuny, X. (1988) *La prise de risque dans le travail*, Octares/Entreprises, Marseille.

Gordon, J. E. (1949) 'The epidemiology of accidents', *American Journal of Public Health*, vol. 39, pp. 504–515.

Haddon, W. (1972) 'A logical framework for categorizing highway safety phenomena and activity', *Journal of Trauma*, vol. 12, pp. 193–207.

Haddon, W. (1980) 'Advances in the epidemiology of injuries as a basis for public policy', *Public Health Reports*, vol. 95, no. 5, pp. 411–421.

Hale, A. R. and Glendon, A. I. (1987) *Individual Behaviour in the Control of Danger*, Elsevier, Amsterdam.

Hale, A. R. and Hovden, J. (1998) 'Management and culture: the third age of safety. A review of approaches to organizational aspects of safety, health and environment', in A. M. Feyer and A. Williamson (eds) *Occupational Injury. Risk, Prevention and Intervention*, Taylor and Francis, London.

Heinrich, H. W. (1959) *Industrial Accident Prevention – A Scientific Approach*, 4th edn., McGraw-Hill, New York.

Hovden, J., Albrechtsen, E. and Herrera, I. A. (2008) 'A need for new theories, models and approaches to occupational accident', Working on Safety Conference, Hellas, Crete.

Kjellén, U. (2000) *Prevention of Accidents Through Experience Feedback*, Taylor and Francis, London and New York.

Lewin, K. (1951) *Field Theory in Social Science; Selected Theoretical Papers*, D. Cartwright (ed.), Harper & Row, New York.

Manuele, F. A. (2002) *Heinrich Revisited: Truisms or Myths*, National Safety Council, Itasca, IL.

Obertelli, P. (1995) 'Le groupe de travail face aux risques en milieux industriels', in Groupe d'Études Interuniversitaires en Sciences du Travail (GEIST), *L'évaluation des risques professionnels – actes du colloque de Strasbourg*, Presses Universitaires de Strasbourg, Strasbourg.

O'Neill, R. (2002) 'It's the hazards, stupid', *Hazards Magazine*, no. 79, pp. 1–5, www.hazards.org/bs, accessed 12 March, 2012.

Petersen, D. (2001) *Safety Management*, 3rd edn., American Society of Safety Engineers, Des Plaines, IL.

Rasmussen, J., Duncan, K. and Leplat, J. (eds) (1987) *New Technology and Human Error*, Wiley, Chichester.

Reason, J. (1990) *Human Error*, Cambridge University Press, New York.

Reason, J. (1991) 'Too little and too late: A commentary on accident and incident reporting systems', in T. W. Van der Schaaf, D. A. Lucas and A. R. Hale (eds) *Near-Miss Reporting as a Safety Tool*, Butterworth-Heinemann, Oxford.

Reason, J. (1997) *Managing the Risks of Organizational Accidents*, Ashgate, Hampshire.

Runyan, C. W. (2003) 'Back to the Future – Revisiting Haddon's Conceptualization of Injury Epidemiology and Prevention', *Epidemiological Reviews*, vol. 25, no. 1, pp. 60–64.

Surry, J. (1969) *Industrial Accident Research: A Human Engineering Appraisal*, University of Toronto, Toronto, ON.

Vincoli, J. W. (2006) *Basic Guide to System Safety*, Wiley, Hoboken, NJ.

Wilde, G. J. S. (1982) 'The theory of risk homeostasis: Implications for safety and health', *Risk Analysis*, vol. 2, pp. 209–225.

MODULE 4

Knowing the actors

MODULE 4: KNOWING THE ACTORS

Module 4 is about actors reflecting on actors. It advances concepts and tools to identify stakeholders involved in a situation or proposed action and to assess relations between them. Chapter 11 presents the rudiments of stakeholder analysis, including different methods to identify stakeholders (*Stakeholder Identification*). *Stakeholder Rainbow* goes from identification to two critical questions: the degree to which each stakeholder can influence a situation or course of action, and the degree to which each stakeholder may be affected by it. The chapter begins and ends on a broader note – threads of theory on the need for democratic engagement in the making of knowledge and reflections on the web of human relations on a global scale.

Chapter 12 reflects further on ideals of participation, democracy and civil society. It also proposes more advanced tools to examine the characteristics and relationships of key stakeholders and explore ways to resolve social problems and mobilize people strategically. These more robust tools include *Social Analysis CLIP* (for Collaboration/ Conflict, Legitimacy, Interests and Power) as well as *Power, Interests* and *Legitimacy.* They are helpful in understanding and evaluating the sources and levels of power, legitimacy and interests that stakeholders hold in a given situation. To illustrate these tools, we continue the story of land eviction affecting the Katkari adivasi of India.

Chapter 13 moves on to *Positions and Interests* and *Values, Interests, Positions (VIP),* techniques to compare the positions that stakeholders take on a situation or action with their actual interests and the moral values they hold. A brief story of conflict over the control of timber in Bolivia shows how *VIP* works in real settings. A closely related technique is *Lessons and Values,* a diagnostic approach to manage a problem by becoming aware of what moral values are held and applying the lessons learned from successful actions that are consistent with those values. These methods are discussed against the background of the Harvard model of interest-based negotiation and an alternative approach centred on the values that people hold and that give them ample reason for 'Getting to NO: negotiating agreement without giving in'.

CHAPTER 11

Stakeholder identification

INTRODUCTION

Social analysis based on concepts of stakeholders and 'communities of interest' helps identify the people, groups and institutions involved in a situation or proposed action. It explores the resources, influence, authority or power that individuals, groups and organizations can apply to a situation and how existing or proposed actions may affect their interests. Stakeholder analysis thus urges social thinking and inquiry that reflects particular contexts and is grounded in real settings. The focus is on specific social actors and what they can do to solve particular problems and achieve their goals using the power and resources they already have or seek to obtain. In its own pragmatic way, the analysis of 'key actors' questions much of the standard wisdom of stratification theory and political economy based on handy class definitions that can be applied to all situations. It is also a social actor alternative to positivist methodologies that pay little attention to how actors 'act' on their own real-life conditions.

The idea of a social actor or stakeholder is relatively straightforward. Still, its application is not always simple. For one thing, the concept raises several tricky questions about **group boundaries**, i.e.:

- when to separate a group into various stakeholders;
- when to lump certain actors into one stakeholder group;
- when to recognize the community of all stakeholders as a group with its own profile; and
- when to factor in the fact that some people may belong to more than one stakeholder group (e.g. leaders and public officials have their own stakeholder profile at the same time as they speak and act for broader groups).

There is also the problem of who should answer these questions and determine who the stakeholders are. In principle, all those known to be directly affected by the action research should help answer the question or validate prior decisions on relevant stakeholder involvement, if interested and in a position to do so.

While pragmatic in spirit, stakeholder thinking is tricky. It is also limited in several regards. More often than not, tools for stakeholder analysis are descriptive and schematic.

They do not build on local ideas and terms to describe social status and relations. They assume that problems, interests and groups have clear boundaries and are stable over time. When applied to PAR, stakeholder analysis often ignores the question of who should conduct the inquiry and for what purpose – who is affected by the inquiry itself and who should be involved in that process. The analysis may be done in a top-down fashion, with a neo-corporatist view that seeks to promote 'dialogue' without challenging relations of domination operating at many levels. In an effort to avoid questions of appropriate representation, all stakeholders (the entire community, for instance) may be invited to participate in the analysis, irrespective of whether there is enough good will or practical means to do so. Given the complexity of real-life settings, stakeholder engagement often requires a strategic and progressive approach, with a focus on parties that can and should contribute to the inquiry and measures to empower marginal or voiceless groups that may otherwise be excluded from collective thinking and action.

While a strength, the site-specific character of stakeholder analysis and involvement also limits engagement with notions of democracy and citizenship on a global scale. The following aphorism speaks to this issue, revisited at the end of the chapter.

THREADS OF THEORY: CAPTAINS OF OUR SOULS

The global age is in urgent need of democratic engagement in the making and sharing of living knowledge and the exercise of reason, for the common good. Failing this, our future will soon be a thing of the past.

Theology reigned in the Middle Ages. Reason prevailed throughout the Enlightenment. Science triumphed in the Modern Age. Each era brought formidable insights into our understanding of the world and ability to act on it. But these forms of knowing and being in the world have also hindered humans from showing a sense of enduring care and carefulness in their interaction with each other and other forms of life. The institutions of religion, philosophy and science have too often supported hierarchies that served authority, upholding powerful interests that prevailed over the natural world and the common good. The global epoch we are now entering must tread a different path and embrace many forms of reasoning and truthful dialogue, or it will not be. It must build on previous accomplishments but also rise to the challenge of creating better and more effective forms of school, workplace, community and public engagement to solve problems on both local and global scales. These are times to create synergies among the living knowledge of people from all parts of the world, including the almost one billion poor or marginalized people, 'have-nots' wrongly branded as 'know-nothings' with little to contribute to human history. In collective wisdom and radical democracy lies our chance of becoming true captains of our souls.

Commentary

Truth can no longer be found in the lofty heavens or the lonely ponderings of the thinking subject. It dwells rather in humanity's potential for collective reason and dialogue, the kind envisaged in Freirean dialogics rooted in principles of freedom, justice and equality (Freire, 2004). Authentic democracy goes beyond the surface deliberations of liberal democracy and the manufacturing of consent, advertised and sold in the interest of the few. Rather, it is a lifeworld of difference and enabling dissent (Laclau and Mouffe, 1985). A truly humane and egalitarian world depends on the growth of critical consciousness and communicative reason, to achieve mutual understanding and joint action across social boundaries. The language points to Habermas's call for a full transformation of the public sphere (*Öffentlichkeit*), a lifeworld based on the constraint-free, consensus-generating force of the 'better argument'. Critical sociology turns Piaget's principle of 'social cooperation' into an evolutionary challenge on a social scale.

The Habermasian vision is not without risks. A vibrant public sphere implies the constant possibility that common understandings may not be reached. Collective decisions and conventions may go astray; claims cannot be evidenced and validated by social currency alone. Everyday life and webs of communication may be routinized and lose meaning. They may be co-opted by mass consumerism, the rule of state and the vested interests of capital. Given these perils, consensus may have to be contested and altered if is to be sustained (Habermas, 1983–1987, pp. 10–17).

Another peril consists in failing to ground public reason in history and anthropology – ignoring the diversity of cultural assumptions about the world, sound judgment and interpersonal communications. As Habermas points out (1983–7, pp. 32–40), reason, democracy and engagement in the public sphere can thrive outside the juridical, medical, managerial, scientific and aesthetic boundaries of Western history. For this to happen, however, lateral thinking must be extended to Habermasian and Piagetian concepts of rational thinking and communication. To make sense, reason and dialogue must be translated, revisited and transformed into myriad forms of deliberation and sensemaking.

Communicative reason exists only in the plural and thrives on the development and the meshing of singular lifeworlds. Anthropology cautions against Western notions of 'Reason' always creeping into critical thinking.

NAMING THE ACTORS

Stakeholder Identification

Purpose

To identify the stakeholders involved in a situation or proposed action.

Step 1

From the list below choose the method(s) needed to identify stakeholders. Modify or combine the methods as needed.

Flag in the list of stakeholders those who are doing the analysis. Consider when to **combine** groups into a single stakeholder category and when to **separate** broad categories into smaller groups (broad categories of stakeholders such as a geographic community or large organization may mask significant differences within the group). Decide whether to include the **community of all stakeholders** as a group with its own profile. Also the **representatives** of a group may be defined as a stakeholder distinct from those they represent. When identifying stakeholders, remember that some people may accept ancestors, future generations, spirits and non-human species as legitimate parties to the situation.

- **By experts**
  Use staff, key agencies (such as NGOs), local people or academics that know the situation well enough to identify stakeholders.
- **By self-selection**
  Use announcements at meetings, in newspapers, on local radio or other media to invite stakeholders to come forward. This will attract those who believe they will gain from communicating their views and wish to contribute to the process.
- **By other stakeholders**
  Identify one or two key stakeholders. Ask them to suggest other key stakeholders who share their views and interests, as well as those who may have a different way of looking at the issues.
- **Using written records and population data**
  Census and population data may provide useful information about the numbers of people by age, gender, religion, residence, etc. Obtain stakeholder information from directories, organizational charts, surveys, reports or written records issued by local authorities, donor agencies, government bodies, experts, academics, NGOs, business and industry, etc.
- **Using oral or written accounts of major events**
  Identify key stakeholders through oral or written descriptions of major events in the history of a problem and the people who were involved (see *Timeline*, Chapter 9).

Step 2

Review the result of the exercise after some time so that stakeholders initially left out or not involved at earlier stages can be identified.

Combinations

Use appropriate sampling procedures to develop a sample of stakeholders that need to be consulted or surveyed because they are part of larger stakeholder populations and may have no other way to represent themselves as a distinct group.

THE PLAYING FIELD

Stakeholder Rainbow

Purpose

To visualize the differences between stakeholders involved in a situation or proposed action.

Step 1

Define the situation or proposed action and make a list of the **stakeholders** (individuals, roles or groups) who can influence or may be affected by it. Write the name of each stakeholder on its own **card**.

Flag the cards of stakeholders who are doing the analysis. Consider when to **combine** groups into a single stakeholder category and when to **separate** broad categories into smaller groups (broad categories of stakeholders such as a geographic community or large organization may mask significant differences within the group). Decide whether to include the **community of all stakeholders** as a group with its own profile. The **representatives** of a group may be defined as a stakeholder distinct from those they represent. Also, when identifying stakeholders, remember that some people may accept ancestors, future generations, spirits and non-human species as legitimate parties to the situation.

Step 2

On each card, use one, two or three plus (+) or minus (–) signs to indicate whether the stakeholder is highly, moderately or little **affected** by the situation or proposed action. Plus signs indicate **net gains** resulting from the situation or proposed action. Minus signs indicate **net losses**.

Step 3

On each card use one, two or three 'I' signs to indicate whether the stakeholder has high (III), moderate (II) or little (I) **influence** on the situation or proposed action.

Step 4

Create a **rainbow diagram** with three bands on a flip chart or with masking tape on the floor. In the smaller band, **insert the cards** of stakeholders little affected (+ or –). Insert the cards of stakeholders moderately affected (++ or – –) in the middle band, and those of stakeholders highly affected (+++ or – – –), in the larger band.

Step 5

Divide the rainbow bands into three equal parts: one part to the left, one in the middle and one to the right (see example). **Move the cards** of stakeholders with high influence (III) to the right side of the diagram. Move those of stakeholders with low influence (I) to the left side. Leave the cards of stakeholders with moderate influence (II) the middle part of the bands.

Step 6

Discuss the resulting picture and effective ways to get important **stakeholders involved** in follow-up actions. Also discuss ways to adjust the **gains or losses** experienced by each stakeholder and the **level of influence** that some stakeholders have on the situation or proposed action.

FAQ

- ***Shouldn't stakeholder identification and analysis be done at the start of any project?***

Not necessarily. For instance, there are situations where stakeholders already know each other quite well and where differences in levels of influence are minimal or not an issue that requires immediate attention.

Variations

- Instead of using a rainbow diagram, locate each stakeholder in a Cartesian graph where the vertical line represents different levels of influence (from 0 to 10), and the horizontal line, the extent to which stakeholders are affected (from –10 to 10).

Primary Health Facilitators in Saskatchewan working with city officials needed to consider the perspectives of new Canadians and small-town farmers in planning an initiative focussed on healthy lifestyle choices. They used an improvisational theatre method (facilitated by D. J. Buckles) to undo some of the stereotypes and bring out variations in knowledge, cultural perspectives and life circumstances within the stakeholder groups. Beginning with a name, participants took turns offering a characteristic of the stakeholder group such as gender, age, ethnicity, occupation, income and residence relevant to the context. The description included information about the ways in which each stakeholder could **influence** or **be affected** by the city initiative. This continued, in several rounds, until the characters felt complete. The exercise prepared the ground for *Social Analysis CLIP* by creating a better understanding of the diversity of real-life situations of stakeholder groups.

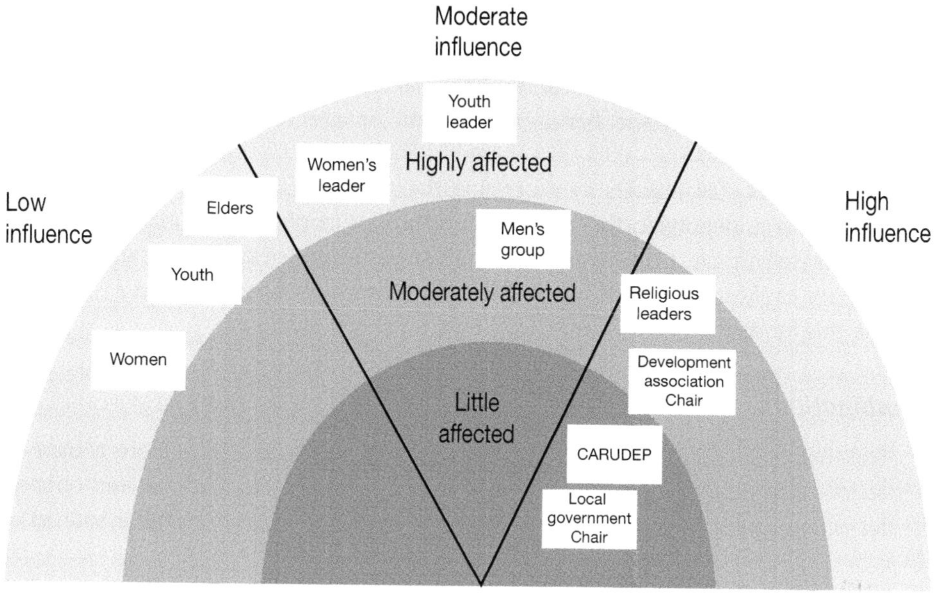

FIGURE 11.1 *Stakeholder Rainbow* and climate change in Nigeria.

Summary of this example: Figure 11.1 shows the configuration of stakeholders in Kwaikong village, Nigeria, including the Catholic Archdiocesan Rural and Urban Development Programme (CARUDEP), the organization that convened and facilitated the analysis with community members. The exercise helped build a common rationale for targeting the use of resources for climate change adaptation, by identifying stakeholders most affected by climate change and those with influence on the success of potential adaptation strategies. Project planning subsequently sought to enhance the influence of highly affected groups (women, youth, elders, etc.) by engaging them intentionally in action-research activities. Separate groups were organized to map existing resources that are important to them (*Resource Mapping*) and reconstruct the history of impacts and previous responses to major climatic events (*Timeline*) (see Chapter 9). Participants then discussed possible project actions and rated these using criteria meaningful to the stakeholder groups. CARUDEP also took steps to inform and seek feedback and assistance from influential stakeholders residing outside of the village. Decisions were then made regarding pilot project investments and validated with the various stakeholder groups (*Validation*, Chapter 8). Source: adapted from NEST and Woodley (2011).

- Adapt the rainbow diagram by using other characteristics that describe the main differences between stakeholders. For instance, use the three bands to identify stakeholders working at the local, the regional and the national levels. Use a single vertical line dividing the bands to separate private sector from public sector stakeholders.
- Make a list of stakeholders by describing the major events of the past or planned activities and identifying the key people or groups involved (see *Timeline,* Chapter 9). Storytelling can help identify and gain a better understanding of stakeholders that are easily stereotyped or have no way to represent themselves in a situation. Use this list as the first step in a *Stakeholder Rainbow* diagram.

Combinations

- Stakeholder analysis is often the first step in a PAR process to explore a plan of action or to understand a problem, its root causes, the factors at play and options for action (using the appropriate methods from this book or from other sources).

THREADS OF THEORY: THE WORLD ABOUT US

The world *about* us is never just about *us.* It is also the milieu all *around* us, the myriad sites ('mille lieux') existing in our nearness, in the middle of self and otherness.

More than never, knowledge making must be taken to a bold new level, with a vigorous orientation to life in society and being in the world. Humanity's global turn can no longer trust otherworldly calls for unity cast in the sectarian spirit of Church and religion. The 'world about us' must also evolve beyond narcissistic appeals to the individual psyche and the thinking subject. It must rise above pleas for critical self-awareness and realization, authentic 'I-you' communications and local 'we-group' dynamics. It must transcend the struggles of identity politics and self-governance and the ad hoc arrangements of multi-stakeholder mediation. Identity politics, the self-help enterprise and the effective communication industry have in common efforts to 'get the whole system in one room', so to speak. They conspire to get life on a larger scale squarely out of everyone's system.

Commentary

The history of coping with the world is a journey on two roads, the high and the low. The high road is world religion, the building of golden bridges between eternal gods dwelling in eternity and mortals living in the here and now. This is the pathway of Durkheim's moral order and solidarity developed across boundaries, first launched by 'international gods' drawn and synthesized from different tribes mingling since the origins of time (Durkheim, 2001; Inglis and Robertson, 2008). Throughout Antiquity, the road map to global history follows this otherworldly route, the heavenly, with inspiration from the golden sun-god ruling over the temporal order in all corners of the universe.

Religion has contributed to globalization for reasons that are not strictly angelic. Far from elevating solidarity to the highest plane of world morality, flights from our lifeworld have shored up the formation of ancient empires and vast markets of silver and gold money, currencies that date back to Lydian, Akkadian and Egyptian history. Precious metals gave systems of wealth and power the aura of the sacred – the flesh of gods, the golden calves and the gilded temples and thrones of Antiquity. On one side of ancient gold coins is engraved the business of faith in the Beyond and the commerce of vows and offerings to the gods. On the other side, there is material commerce, the golden opportunities of supply and demand and the financing of military campaigns ruled by all the powers that be (Chevalier and Larose-Chevalier, 2008).

The gods continue to shape world history throughout holy wars of the Middle Ages, well into the Enlightenment. The Renaissance brings about the rule of nation-states and absolute monarchs ordained by divine right and made wealthy by the discovery and pillage of the gold-rich New World. It also heralds the downfall of 'our world made in heaven', launching humanity on the pathway of Nature centred on the rational, self-serving 'subject'. The forward march of Modernity opens the low road to creating history, using a secular approach to globalization where all that is of value, including the tokens of Inca civilization, can be melted into ingots, bars and standards of gold. Measurements of wealth and history gradually take their distance from the sacred and engrave their value in the permanence of Nature, stable commerce and secure markets rising across colonial time and space. But aspirations to order and the stable growth of knowledge and wealth shine like fool's gold. They are undermined by the effects of greed without measure – periodic economic crises, wide-scale depressions and the many atrocities of conquest and war.

On the low road to global history, the modern subject becomes king. Freed from the religious and kingly forms of tyranny, the subject is crowned Man at the centre of the universe. When coming together, subjects constitute the sovereign 'people' empowered to think and act rationally and govern themselves via representatives who protect their interests, starting with the ownership of private property, forever exchangeable for gold. Individual interests can and must be reconciled with the 'common good', which matters more than ever. Benefits of the collective will, however, hinge on the individuation of groups of 'people' and their particular interests: usually the enfranchised citizens of a nation-state, to the exclusion of slaves, the propertyless, people from other nations and life forms other than human. Like species in nature, each 'people' exists on to itself, formed by those who constitute a community, a tribe, a nation, a society, or any other group by virtue of a common culture, lifestyle, history, religion, occupation (such as 'salespeople') or the like, to the exclusion of all others that people the land and the world as a whole.

Representations of individual and collective identities are now as many as the competing gods and demiurges of Greek mythology. Advances in democracy, science and social philosophy have given rise to numerous concerns and struggles for self-realization, civil rights, the empowerment of women, gay liberation, cultural survival, the protection of animals and environments, consumer voice, stakeholder engagement, and so on. The proliferation of legitimate 'subjects of political, economic and moral interest', however, has the paradoxical effect of dissolving rigid boundaries of Self and Other. It does so by bringing attention to a host of 'multi', 'inter' and 'trans' phenomena that affect the interfacing of disciplines, subjects, cultures, nations, genders, sexes, gene pools and life forms, interactions and webs of communication on a scale never seen before. This heralds the opening of history's middle road – an oecumenical pathway to globalization that can be ruled neither by God nor any particular 'people', let alone the sum of all gods and people merely living and coexisting.

Global history forged in the middleness of everything points the way to an ecology of being. Subjects are grounded in the web of humanity and life, a universe where the 'world about us' can never be 'us' versus 'the world around us'. Humanity is now called upon to fashion its own history and become, in the words of Jean-Jacques Rousseau, 'the wise power that governs the world' (Rousseau, 1999). This is not a power that can be cast and take refuge in the absurdity of fetishes of gold. It cannot give assurances of the absolute or guarantees of a sacred or permanent natural order that transcends history. Neither is it a power that can be handed over to a trust nor a single authority that captures and monopolizes the power of trade and arms. For this power to become truly wise, the fiduciary principle – from the Latin *fiducia*, 'trust' that is the basis of all human exchange – must take flight and flow to all of humanity, which alone is able to create its own values and give meaning to history. This anthropological and forever evolving project will come to pass when the world takes full responsibility for its own freedom, without the numerous crimes committed in its name.

REFERENCES

Chevalier, J. M. and Larose-Chevalier, Z. (2008) 'Gold and a Brief History of Eternity', in H. Dionne (ed.) *Gold in the Americas*, Septentrion, Sillery and Musée de la Civilisation de Québec, Québec, pp. 181–187.

Durkheim, É. (2001) [1912] *Elementary Forms of the Religious Life*, trans. Carol Cosman, Oxford World's Classics, Oxford University Press, Oxford.

Freire, P. (2004) *Pedagogy of Hope: Reliving Pedagogy of the Oppressed*, Continuum, New York.

Habermas, J. (1983–1987) *The Theory of Communicative Action. Volume 1: Reason and the Rationalization of Society*, trans. Thomas McCarthy, Beacon, Boston, MD.

Inglis, D. and Robertson, R. (2008) 'The elementary forms of globality: Durkheim and the emergence and nature of global life', *Journal of Classical Sociology*, vol. 8, no. 1, pp. 5–25.

Laclau, E. and Mouffe, C. (1985) *Hegemony and Socialist Strategy: Toward a Radical Democratic Politics*, Verso, London.

Nigerian Environmental Study/Action Team (NEST) and Woodley, E. (eds) (2011) 'Reports of Pilot Projects in Community-Based Adaptation – Climate Change in Nigeria. Building Nigeria's Response to Climate Change (BNRCC)', Ibadan, Nigeria.

Rousseau, J.-J. (1999) [1754] *Discourse on the Origin of Inequality Among Men*, trans. Franlin Philip, edited with an Introduction and Notes by Patrick Coleman, Oxford University Press, Oxford.

CHAPTER 12

Stakeholder analysis

INTRODUCTION

Chapter 11 introduced basic tools for stakeholder identification and analysis. In this chapter, we present a more robust method for delving into stakeholder profiles and relationships involved in a core problem or proposed action. *Social Analysis CLIP* explores existing ties and the record of conflict and collaboration (C) among parties. It also brings these relationships together with three key factors of social life, those of legitimacy (L), interests (I) and power (P). Given the complexity of each factor, three other tools are available to go deeper, as needed, by assessing the sources and levels of *Legitimacy, Interests* and *Power* that stakeholders hold in a given context. PAR practitioners may apply these tools to scale up the investigation of each dimension to a finer level. In Chapter 13, we also consider two other factors that determine the stakeholder configuration in a given situation: the actual positions and the values that stakeholders express in real situations (see *Positions and Interests* and *Values, Interests, Positions*). These may or may not coincide with their individual or group interests. All of these considerations are incorporated into CLIP, an original web application available at www.participatory actionresearch.net.

Issues of power, interests, legitimacy, values and relations of conflict and collaboration are critical to action-research initiatives that go beyond technical thinking and interventions. The way these factors play out affects the existing stakeholder structure and related scenarios for problem solving and social transformation. By exploring these scenarios and the problems they raise, strategies can be found to manage them. This may involve taking steps to transform social relations, including measures of cooperation and compromise to reduce conflict, efforts to empower weaker and vulnerable groups, or appeals to values and the ideals of justice and democracy. We explore these possible measures at the end of *Social Analysis CLIP.*

The chapter provides a detailed example of how *Social Analysis CLIP* was used to fight eviction and overcome unequal power relationships among stakeholders in rural India. It ends with a theoretical note on the twofold requirements of democracy: hardware institutions, laws and procedures that support effective representation, public deliberation and rational thinking, on the one hand, and flexible software processes to facilitate authentic dialogue and well-informed reasoning, on the other.

SOCIAL ANALYSIS

Social Analysis CLIP (Conflict/Collaboration, Legitimacy, Interests, Power)

Purpose

To describe the characteristics and relationships of key stakeholders and to explore ways to resolve social problems and engage people strategically.

Step 1

Define the **situation or proposed action** clearly and precisely. Make a list of the stakeholders (individuals, roles or groups) who can influence or may be affected by it, including those that are doing the analysis (see *Stakeholder Identification* and *Stakeholder Rainbow*, Chapter 11). Draw or write the name of each stakeholder on its own stakeholder profile **card** (see Figure 12.2).

Flag the cards of stakeholders who are doing the analysis. Consider when to **combine** groups into a single stakeholder category and when to **separate** broad categories into smaller groups (broad categories of stakeholders such as a geographic community or large organization may mask significant differences within the group). Decide whether to include the **community of all stakeholders** as a group with its own profile. The

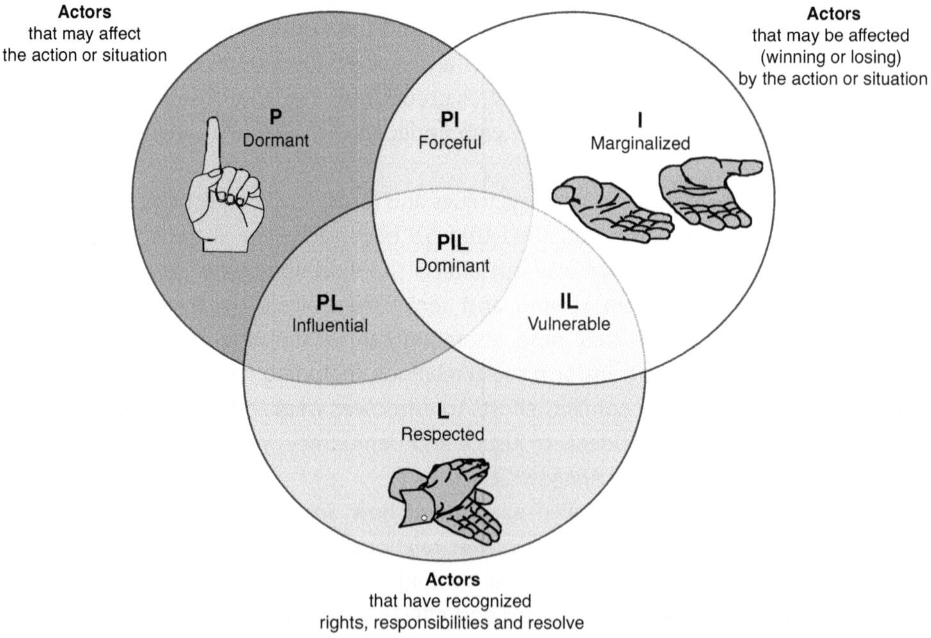

FIGURE 12.1 Power, interest and legitimacy profile.

Situation or proposed action: ....

Stakeholder (individual or group): ....

(P)OWER	High	☐	Middle	☐	Low/none	☐
Description:						
(I)NTERESTS	High +	☐	Middle +	☐	Low/none	☐
	High –	☐	Middle –	☐		
Description:						
(L)EGITIMACY	High	☐	Middle	☐	Low/none	☐
Description:						

FIGURE 12.2 Stakeholder profile card.

representatives of a group may be also defined as a stakeholder distinct from those they represent.

Step 2

Ask participants for **examples** of power, interests and legitimacy that are relevant to the situation or proposed action, and discuss the definitions below. Clarify the ideas and modify them using the participants' own definitions and terms, if they prefer. Use symbols or drawings to represent each idea, such as raising a fist or finger for power, holding out the hands for interests, or clapping hands for legitimacy (see Figure 12.1).

Step 3

Discuss and describe the **power or resources** that each stakeholder can use to oppose or promote the situation or proposed action defined in Step 1. Exclude forms of power (e.g. force) that stakeholders would not realistically apply to the situation or proposed action being discussed. Rate the level of power on each stakeholder card using one of three values: **high, middle or low/no power**. On the same card, record a description of the power or resources discussed.

Step 4

Discuss and describe the **interests** of each stakeholder – the gains that each makes from the situation or proposed action and the estimated losses. Pay special attention to stakeholders' estimation of their own gains and losses. Rate the **net interests** (gains minus the losses) on each stakeholder card using one of five values: high net gains (++), middle net gains (+), low/no interests (0), middle net losses (–), or high net losses (– –). On the same card, record the description of the interests discussed.

Step 5

Discuss and describe the **perceived legitimacy** of each stakeholder – that is, the recognition by law or by local customs of rights and responsibilities relevant to the situation and exercised with resolve. Rate the level of legitimacy on each stakeholder card using one of three values: **high, middle or low/no legitimacy**. If a stakeholder's legitimacy is highly disputed, assign the 'middle' value and note the dispute along with the description of legitimacy on the card.

Definitions

- **Power** is the ability to influence others and use resources controlled to achieve goals. Resources may include economic wealth, political authority (an office, position or role recognized by an institution or by local customs), the ability to use force or threats of force, access to information (knowledge and skills) and the means to communicate (see *Power*, below).
- **Interests** are the gains and losses experienced as a result of an existing situation or proposed action. These gains and losses affect the various forms of power and uses of resources. Make sure that participants do not confuse this idea of interests with 'taking an interest in' or 'being interested in something' (see *Interests*, below).
- **Legitimacy** is when the rights and responsibilities of a stakeholder are recognized by other parties through law or local customs, and are exercised by the stakeholder involved with resolve (see *Legitimacy*, below).
- **Social relations** involve existing ties of collaboration and conflict (including group memberships) that affect stakeholders in a certain situation and that they can use to influence the situation or a course of action.

Step 6

Create a **table** listing categories of gains and losses in the top row and stakeholder categories in the first column (grouped into upper, middle and lower blocks; see example). **Place** each stakeholder card in the column that corresponds to its **interests** (high, middle or low/no net gains or losses) and in the row that corresponds to its **PIL profile**; apply each letter to a stakeholder only when the corresponding score is 'high' or 'middle'.

Don't place cards in the cells that combine contradictory attributes (such as 'dominant' stakeholders with 'low/no' interests). These cells are marked with the letter 'x' in the example. Use bold letters (or any other code) to identify the stakeholders who are participating directly in the analysis.

Step 7

Discuss the history of **collaboration or conflict** among particular stakeholders and use **a visual code** (such as lines in Figure 12.3) to identify these social relations and their relative strength. Include all relevant ties, even if they are unrelated to the situation or proposed action identified in Step 1. Note that stakeholders may collaborate in some areas and be in conflict in other areas.

Step 8

Discuss the resulting **stakeholder structure** showing the distribution of power, interests, legitimacy and social relations involved in the situation or proposed action. Pay particular attention to conflicts of interests, differences in power and perceptions of low legitimacy. Assess how existing ties of **collaboration or conflict** make the situation easier or more difficult to manage.

Step 9

Identify the **actions** and the steps that stakeholders can take to achieve their goals while dealing with existing stakeholder tensions. Consider ways to modify existing social relations of power, interests and legitimacy such as to produce greater fairness and more effective responses to the situation or proposed action identified in Step 1. Develop **strategies** to manage conflict, make use of neutral parties or draw on existing or potential alliances among stakeholders. If the exercise concerns a proposed action, decide whether the proposal should be modified to better reflect existing or possible stakeholder scenarios.

- If **power differences** are an issue, find ways to increase the resources available to vulnerable or marginalized stakeholders (or measures to empower them); involve these stakeholders in decisions regarding proposed actions; strengthen organizations and alliances between powerful and weaker organizations; or create opportunities for shared leadership and broader participation.
- If **conflicting interests** are an issue, find ways to modify the situation or proposed action to reduce losses; develop a common vision of shared goals and explore underlying interests; share a detailed analysis of the costs and benefits of the situation or proposed action; create new incentives or mechanisms for the redistribution of gains.
- If low **legitimacy** is an issue, find ways to use the legal system to demonstrate rights and responsibilities; uphold the importance of local norms; inform people about their rights and responsibilities; increase public awareness; organize demonstrations of stakeholder resolve.
- All stakeholders may benefit from a situation or proposed action (thereby appearing on the right side of the table) but have a **history of poor or limited collaboration** or open conflict. If this is the case, discuss actions and steps to develop or strengthen

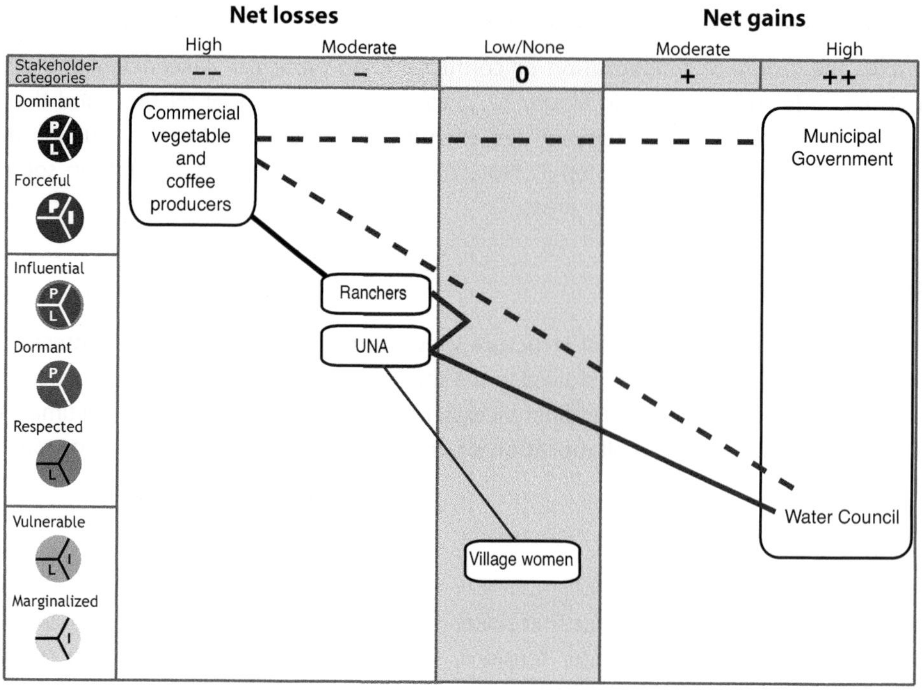

Figure 12.3 Water contamination in Honduras.

Summary of this example: The Water Council is tasked by the Municipal Government with monitoring and ensuring the supply and quality of water to a variety of groups along the Taluga River in Honduras. More than 2000 people depend on this source for domestic use and to support various economic activities. A *Timeline* assessment by the Council of trends affecting the river determined that water contamination is a growing and worrisome trend. Water analysis confirmed the presence of chemicals and heavy burdens of organic matter, especially from coffee plantations and commercial vegetable farms. With the backing of the Municipal Government, the Council proposed to control dumping of coffee husks and prohibit the use of pesticides in close proximity to the river.

Before proceeding with the action, Council members examined the stakeholder structure using *Social Analysis CLIP*. The exercise determined that a large and unified block of stakeholders would oppose the initiative. Vegetable farmers and coffee producers, the two groups responsible for much of the contamination, would lose a lot if prohibitions on the use of pesticides and dumping of coffee husks were enforced. Ranchers would also lose, although to a much lesser extent. On balance the benefits of cleaner drinking water for their animals and themselves would offset, in part, the cost of washing their cattle further from the river. Similarly, the university (UNA) would need to find alternatives to current practices on experimental plots it owns near the river bank. Women participating in the analysis recognized that river contamination created problems for them, but they didn't want to oppose the other stakeholders on whom they and their husbands rely for employment. One said that 'I'm not in agreement with what the boss does [heavy use of pesticides and washing sprayers in the river] but my husband needs the work!' Women thus take a neutral position.

The thinking by the Council and other participants that went into describing the stakeholder structure included discussions of the history of conflict and collaboration between the various parties (solid and dotted lines, respectively). Their interpretation of the stakeholder structure (including the limited power the Council has to enforce the proposed action, indicated by the lower position in the figure) dissuaded them from imposing new regulations. They decided instead to make use of their past relationship with UNA to engage with the ranchers and to raise awareness with them about the costs to all of water contamination. The goal was to eventually influence other stakeholders with whom the ranchers have a history of collaboration. The Council also decided to work with UNA to develop and test new practices on their own lands, which others could also put in place to reduce pesticide use and recycle coffee waste. Other actions included the introduction of a prorated system of water user fees to finance community washing stations that would address women's concerns. While tentative, they felt that the strategy had the potential to frame efforts to reduce contamination in a more favourable light for all. Source: adapted from Reyes Sandoval, 2006.

coalitions or reduce conflict by seeking third party mediation or building trust. For a more detailed analysis of trust, use *Network Dynamics* (Chapter 17).

- Some of the stakeholders identified in Step 1 will not appear in the table if they have no/low interests at stake and little power or legitimacy in relation to the situation or proposed action. In these cases, leave these non-stakeholder groups or actors out of the analysis or find ways to engage them.

FAQ

- ***When is* Social Analysis CLIP *most useful?***

For this in-depth analysis of stakeholder relations to be useful, understanding issues of unequal power or conflicting interests must be key to addressing the problem at hand. If these issues do not play a critical role, use simpler tools such as *Stakeholder Identification* or *Stakeholder Rainbow* (Chapter 11).

Variations

- Use Steps 1 to 5 to describe each stakeholder profile, locate each stakeholder card in Figure 12.1, and then go directly to Step 9.

Combinations

- In Chapter 13, we show how *Social Analysis CLIP* and the software CLIP (www.participatoryactionresearch.net) can incorporate two other factors: the actual positions and the values that stakeholders express in real situations and that may or may not coincide with their individual or group interests (see *Positions and Interests* and *Values, Interests, Positions*).

LAND EVICTION IN INDIA

Rising land prices on the rural periphery of Mumbai, India are prompting landholders to sell to real estate developers and expanding industries. This has led to attempts to evict people from village sites they do not own but have lived on for generations. The Katkari, formerly called a 'Criminal Tribe' because of their nomadic livelihood, are particularly vulnerable. In 2005 D. J. Buckles and a grassroots organization working with the Katkari community (Academy of Development Studies, ADS) launched an action-research process to address the threat of eviction, an initiative that has continued to this day (Buckles and Khedkar, 2013). They proposed to take the fight to the *Gram Panchayat*, the local governing body at the village and small town level. The research team believed that without support from these authorities, higher-level officials would ignore the claim. While this strategy was clear enough, developing and presenting a petition for approval by the *Gram Panchayat* was a significant challenge for the Katkari. Most Katkari had never attended a General Assembly of the village *Gram Panchayat*, and few had ever been elected to formal positions. People would need to stand up collectively and as individuals in a local situation fraught with sharp power imbalances and unknown risks. Given this uncertainty, discussed at length in small groups and informal meetings, the Katkari decided that before they could take any action they needed to know more about what to expect from the *Gram Panchayat* and other stakeholders, such as the landholders and various government officials.

The research team selected the tool *Social Analysis CLIP* to engage the Katkari in a discussion of who the petition would affect and who had influence over its success. Figure 12.4 shows the assessment of local stakeholders done in Ambewadi, a hamlet that had recently been enclosed by a landholder. Katkari in this hamlet had decided to stay and fight eviction. Over the course of an evening, twelve Katkari (seven men and five women) gathered to discuss the situation and the prospect of presenting a petition in the General Assembly. This group had formed a committee to mobilize support from others and formalize a collective petition.

The picture that emerged from their analysis was a stark reminder for them and for the research team of how isolated and vulnerable the Katkari were on this issue, and what would need to change to improve their chances of success. Of the six stakeholders identified, four would likely reject the application, including the landholder, the *Gram Panchayat*, the Secretary (*Gram Sevak*) paid by the Revenue Department and the officer with the Integrated Tribal Development Project (ITDP) (upper left side of the figure).

PHOTO 12.1 Real estate agents lure Mumbai elites with advertisements like this one along Highway 17 near Nagothane. Evictions are becoming common. (Source: D. J. Buckles)

The thinking that went into describing the stakeholder structure and what Katkari could expect from the proposed petition was richly detailed. Participants identified examples of the use of power in other situations familiar to them and rated the extent to which each stakeholder they identified could use their power to oppose or promote the petition. In the case of the landholder, they talked about his power to purchase support for his position (economic power) and to hire goons to harass the Katkari (coercive power). Consequently, they rated his power to oppose the petition as high, an assessment that placed the landholder in the upper half of the figure. Participants also recognized that the landholder would lose a lot if he were forced to sell his land at government rates rather than to external land agents. This placed him on the far left side of the figure, showing high net losses ('– –'). Furthermore, the landholder had a legal land deed, a fact that gave him legitimacy in the eyes of other stakeholders. He had already shown his resolve to evict the Katkari by enclosing the hamlet with a fence and would likely make use of his past relations of collaboration with the other stakeholders (represented by arrows) to reinforce his opposition.

Participants recognized the political authority of the Revenue Department, the *Gram Panchayat* and the ITDP as other forms of power that could be applied to the situation. Participants gave high ratings on power to both the Revenue Department and the *Gram Panchayat* in view of their formal authority in the General Assembly. According to the

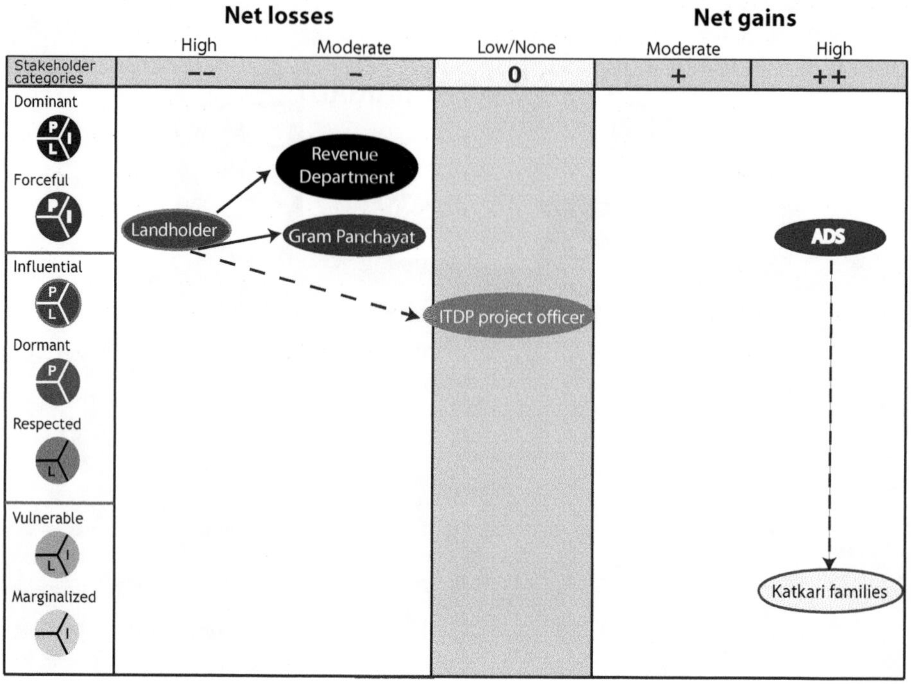

FIGURE 12.4 Stakeholder positions on a proposed Katkari village site, Ambewadi, period 1.

Summary of this example: Positions in the table reflect the presence or absence of power (P), interests (I) and legitimacy (L) held by each stakeholder. Of the six stakeholders identified (body of the table), three would likely reject the petition because their losses would be from medium to high (left side of the table, showing medium to high losses represented by '–' and '– –' headings, respectively). They include the landholder, the *Gram Panchayat*, and the Secretary representing the Revenue Department. These same actors are relatively powerful in the situation (upper half of the table, in rows that include P for power, reflecting stakeholder categories with medium to high levels of power). The landholder would likely make use of his past relations of collaboration with the other stakeholders (represented by solid or weaker dotted arrows) to reinforce his opposition to the petition. In this scenario, the Katkari are isolated and vulnerable; while they have a lot to gain ('+ +' rating), they have little power (lower stakeholder category). They also have only one ally (ADS) linked weakly (dotted arrow) to the community through a recent history of collaboration on some land issues.

Katkari, both stakeholders would likely see more losses than gains from the proposed petition. Recognition of Katkari rights to a village site would require the Revenue Department to order a survey of the hamlet and compensate the landholder financially. They would see the petition as nothing but trouble given the many other demands on their time and resources. The *Gram Panchayat* would see losses as well due to opposition from the landholder and new demands on village services if the hamlet were eventually incorporated into the village site. Participants concluded that, on balance, the *Gram Panchayat* had little to gain from supporting the petition and had a legitimate right to object. The ITDP officer was also recognized as a legitimate stakeholder but with less power and less to lose from the petition. While he is responsible for addressing adivasi concerns, their hamlet is outside his jurisdiction and consequently less important to him. The Katkari also knew he collaborated occasionally with local contractors when providing

PHOTO 12.2 Katkari woman carrying some 38 kilograms of red clay brick while working at a brick kiln in Maharashtra, India. (Source: C. Cousin)

services to adivasi communities, a relationship that participants felt might lead him to support the landholder's position.

According to participants, only ADS and the Katkari would gain from the proposed petition. They felt that the Katkari community had a lot to gain because it would help them resist eviction from the hamlet. The current location gave the community a base for seasonal migration to brick kilns and future access to job opportunities in the area. Moving to a new location would be difficult and costly and would probably result in the hamlet breaking up, with the loss of relationships among the various families formed during the forty-five years since it was established. Their dependence on the current landholder had declined in recent years, so opposing him would come with fewer costs. While the Katkari would stand to gain from approval of the petition, participants rated the resources, influence, authority and other forms of power they could use to achieve their goal as low. They had no money, lacked knowledge regarding their rights and were isolated from local and broader government bodies and external organizations. This isolation meant that others would not see the rights of the Katkari hamlet as legitimate. In the eyes of the landholder, the *Gram Panchayat* and maybe even government officials, the Katkari were vagabonds moving about in search of employment and without a history of prior participation in the institutions of village life. Participants also lacked confidence that their community had the resolve to develop and present the application collectively and forcefully. Overall, they saw themselves as having neither the rights nor the resolve of a credible stakeholder.

The participants considered ADS to be a relatively powerful stakeholder in the situation because of its prior work with officials in the Revenue Department and its detailed knowledge of legal issues affecting tribal populations. They gave a medium rating to ADS on this factor. They also recognized that ADS had something to gain from the petition because it would enhance the organization's ability to lobby on behalf of other Katkari communities and demonstrate the value of its work. Participants nevertheless wondered how long ADS would support them if things did not go well. ADS staff at the meeting expressed their commitment but had to recognize that the bonds of trust and collaboration were still relatively weak. In Ambewadi, ADS had mostly worked on the land rights of individual families and was not known by all households in the hamlet. The relatively weak relationship between the Katkari and ADS (represented by a dotted arrow) was especially critical to the Katkari participants considering the many collaborative ties they noted among other dominant and opposing stakeholders. The overall situation left the Katkari with few real or potential allies and in conflict with the landholder, their former benefactor.

The unequal and opposing relationships among various stakeholders involved in the situation suggested that gaining support for their petition would be an uphill battle. While this conclusion surprised no one, discussing the details grounded and stimulated thinking about ways to manage and transform the relationships. Discussion by the group turned to efforts to empower themselves through information, possible measures of cooperation and compromise with the landholder to reduce conflict, and appeals before the *Gram Panchayat* and government officials to public values of justice and the common good. Concrete steps emerged from the discussion. For example, participants decided to compile proofs of residence such as house taxes, electricity bills and voter registrations to document and demonstrate to the government and to local officials that they were not simply homeless vagabonds without ties to the community. They decided to talk to members of the *Gram Panchayat* about their difficulties, and assure them that their intention was to press the Revenue Department for fair compensation for the landholder. This was important, participants felt, to avoid placing blame and responsibility on the landholder alone. They would also do what they could to learn more about their rights and responsibilities as members of a village, and begin to participate in the institutions of village life. These actions might demonstrate their resolve to stay in the village and begin to build a positive relationship with local officials.

In the weeks and months that followed, the Katkari committee began the tedious work of collecting proofs of residence door to door. They made copies of house tax receipts, residence certificates from the *Gram Panchayat*, Caste Certificates, Ration Cards, voter identification cards, electrical bill payment receipts, school certificates and proof of age documents. It was difficult work. Most houses are in such disrepair that people lose their documents to the weather or neglect. Often the documents are not understood or valued. Many households simply never had basic identity papers in the first place. Nevertheless, documents were collected and copied for as many households as possible, focussing on those documents that could stand as proofs of residence. The committee, guided by elders in the community, also drew maps showing the boundaries of the hamlet and created a *Timeline* of when the community was first established and major events in the life of the hamlet. While travelling to work places or socializing in the evenings, members of the committee shared what they learned with others, raising the general level of knowledge and understanding in the hamlet.

The research team contributed to this process by compiling all of the documentation into a portfolio on the hamlet, and making copies to go back to individual households. It also collected the land deed from the regional headquarters of the Revenue Department. This document showed the legal ownership and boundaries of land where the Katkari now lived. With the support of the Katkari committee, ADS offered information sessions on land rights, the operations of the Gram Panchayat, and technical procedures for acquiring papers and services from the government. These sessions built on ADS's long history of practical activism, and addressed matters that were often of immediate and practical interest to people seeking supports that could bring some immediate relief to their poverty. Many attended, often in the evening, including some non-tribal members of the *Gram Panchayat* who were not familiar with the topics.

The research team facilitated similar assessments and follow-up activities in nine other Katkari hamlets where committees had resolved to develop and submit petitions in their respective *Gram Panchayat*. Visits by the research team opened relationships with some heads of the *Gram Panchayat* and with all of the Secretaries. Informal, personal interactions with these officials focussed on the legal and ethical issues at stake, including the long-standing contributions of Katkari labour to agriculture and industry in the area, their many years of residence in the villages and the existence of government provisions for extending a *Gaothan* and compensating landholders. The practical and potential social costs of evicting large numbers of families from their homes were also mentioned.

The goal of these discussions was not only to inform the stakeholders about the scope and impact of the problem but also to take stock of their position and possible response to Katkari petitions for support. Only a few attempts were made to discuss the matter directly with landholders as these often led to defensive reactions and an opposition to Katkari gestures of compromise and openness to negotiation. The involvement of ADS as an outside group was particularly troubling to the landholders and a source of additional tension that ADS tried to avoid by being discrete in its movements in the villages and avoiding direct contact with landholders.

The Katkari monitored the effects of these strategies and adjusted their actions periodically in light of new information and developments, including unanticipated outcomes. For example, after four months of work, the Katkari committee in Ambewadi decided to repeat their assessment of the stakeholder structure (Figure 12.5). It showed some important improvements. The regional head of the Revenue Department had asked his officials in a memo to provide all the help they could to securing a village site on behalf of Katkari families. Various elected representatives of the *Gram Panchayat*, including the Chairperson, said they now understood the situation better and recognized the legitimacy of the Katkari claim. They assured the Katkari they would help to the extent possible, and would call on the government to provide compensation to the landholder. Even the Project Officer for the ITDP, while rarely in the hamlet, did not want to be seen to be supporting the landholder against a tribal clientele. The landholder in Ambewadi, while still harassing the Katkari and threatening to evict them, was now alone, without assured support from other stakeholders.

The committee in Ambewadi was encouraged by the responses of key stakeholders. They were also happy with their own efforts to become better informed, their success at compiling relevant documents and the level of participation and agreement among Katkari in the hamlet. The new story they began to tell reflected greater confidence in themselves, expressions of support received from other stakeholders and a stronger and broader set of relationships to stakeholders. While initially they thought that they would lose because alone in their struggle with the landholder, the second assessment led them to conclude that the conditions were now much more favourable. As a result, the committee decided they were ready to present a petition and encouraged all Katkari families to attend the next General Assembly.

New assessments in other hamlets also showed positive shifts in stakeholder structure, attributed by participants to the actions they and others had taken to organize and persuade others regarding their claim. However, the timing of these shifts, and impacts on subsequent actions, varied. In one hamlet a second assessment after four months of concerted effort by the committee identified a change in the position of only one stakeholder, the regional head of the Revenue Department. Several visits to his office by members of the committee and the research team seemed to make him more receptive to the issue. On the last visit he told his officials, including the Secretary responsible for their hamlet, to cooperate if the petition was presented according to proper procedures. While the committee could not be sure of his commitment to follow through, his outward position was more favourable. Still, participants deemed this as insufficient to change their minds about presenting at the General Assembly. They

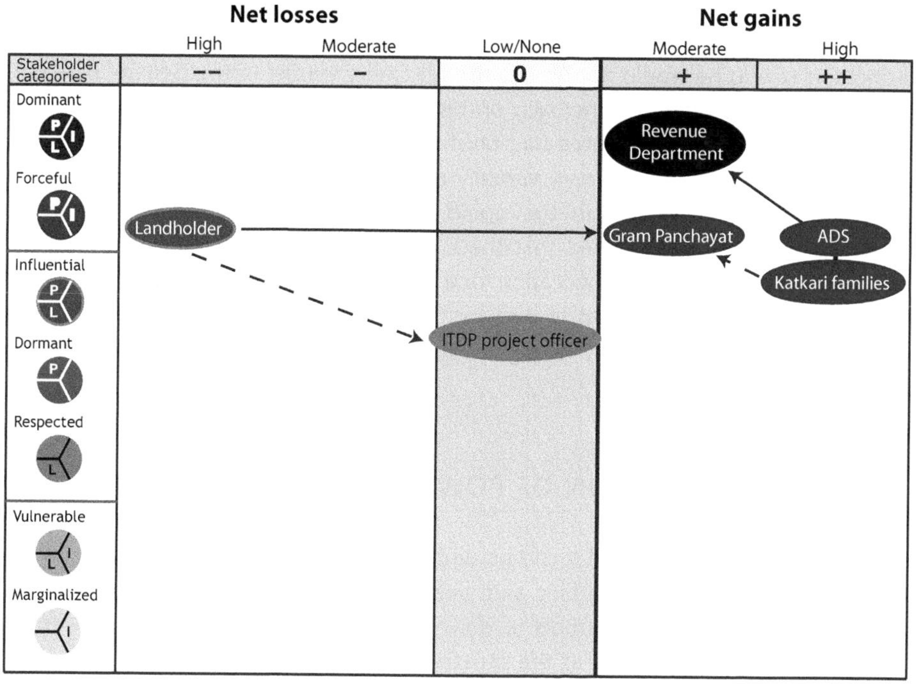

FIGURE 12.5 Stakeholder positions on a proposed Katkari village site, Ambewadi, period 2.

Summary of this example: Figure 12.5 shows that while the landholder remained opposed because of the losses he would suffer from a resolution in support of the Katkari (left side of the figure, showing high net losses represented by a '– –' heading), other stakeholders now recognized neutral or net gains from the resolution (middle or right side of the figure). Importantly, both the Revenue Department and the Gram Panchayat now recognized the legitimacy of the Katkari claim and the merits of incorporating the hamlet into a village site, factors leading to a shift in their position. The Katkari had gained in power through their own efforts to be better informed and organized at the hamlet level, and strengthened their relationship to ADS. Shifting alliances seemed to have isolated the landholder to some extent.

decided to wait and continue their work. Important shifts in the positions of other stakeholders in the hamlet only began to emerge some six months after the initial strategy was launched. Some members of the *Gram Panchayat*, including the Chair, began to openly support the idea of integrating the hamlet into the village site. The Chair argued that it would bring new resources into the community and be good for village development. The three landholders affected by the petition, while still opposed, seemed to be more isolated. Furthermore, a division between them emerged, with one of the landholders saying he would not go against a majority verdict in the General Assembly, provided the Katkari did not encroach on his neighbouring lands. Importantly, by the end of six months the committee had finished collecting proofs of residence from all households in the village. By now, virtually all families in the hamlet understood that legal title to the hamlet was a right they could demand, and many were highly motivated to present their claim. It seemed that the conditions were better than they had ever been and that approval of an application for a village site would be passed at the General Assembly. All that remained was to wait for the appointed day.

For the rest of this story, including the ups and downs of the petition, see Buckles and Khedkar (2013).

THE DISTRIBUTION OF POWER

Power is not a simple notion that can be understood through direct observation alone. The notion lends itself to variations and views on what matters in each context. The following is a participatory method to delve into the different sources of power and identify those that are relevant to the situation at hand.

Power

Purpose

To understand and evaluate the sources and levels of power that stakeholders hold in a certain situation.

Step 1

Define the situation and discuss the **sources of power** that people can use in the situation. Ask for examples of power relevant to the situation, and discuss the definitions of sources of power, below. Clarify the ideas and modify them using the stakeholders' social categories and terms, if necessary.

Step 2

Create a table (see Table 12.1). In the top row, insert the sources of power. In the first column, list all the stakeholders involved in the situation identified in Step 1. Indicate in the list those who are doing the analysis. Consider when to **combine** groups into a single stakeholder category and when to **separate** broad categories into smaller groups (broad categories of stakeholders such as a geographic community or large organization may mask significant differences within the group). Decide whether to include the **community of all stakeholders** as a group with its own profile. The **representatives** of a group may be also defined as a stakeholder distinct from those they represent.

SOURCES OF POWER

- **Economic wealth** includes access to or use of natural resources, the possession of material goods, property in kind, equipment, income and savings, financial capital, etc.
- **Political authority** is an office, position or role that is recognized by an institution or by local customs and that gives someone or a group the ability to reach decisions and pass or implement rules and regulations.
- The ability to use **force or threats** of force is the power to exercise physical strength or threaten to inflict bodily harm on others.
- Access to **information** and the **means to communicate** involves access to and control over facts, documents, knowledge, skills (technical expertise, experience) and the media (such as radio, television, the Internet, newspapers, publications, public demonstrations, etc.) to make one's knowledge or views known to others.
- **Social ties** (group memberships, alliances, histories of collaboration) and **legitimacy** (recognized rights and obligations and the resolve to exercise them) are other sources of power. Use *Social Analysis CLIP* or *Legitimacy* to assess these, if necessary.

Step 3

Rate the **level of power** that each stakeholder has for each source of power using a scale of 0 to 5. Record the scores in the corresponding cells. Add an **explanation** for each score to the table or on a flip chart.

Step 4

Total the scores for each stakeholder in a summary column. Use the total scores to identify the stakeholders that have relatively high levels of power, those that have middle levels of power and those have little or no power. Record this summary conclusion in the final column.

Step 5

Review the result and discuss how the **distribution of power** may affect the stakeholders' ability to influence the situation identified in Step 1. If tables are done separately by different individuals or stakeholder groups, compare the results and negotiate a common understanding of the actual and the ideal distribution of power in the situation.

TABLE 12.1 Stakeholder power profiles

Key stakeholders	*Wealth*	*Authority*	*Force*	*Information and communication*	*Sum*	*Level*
Landowner	8	2	8	4	22/40	high
Revenue Department	7	9	5	9	30/40	very high
Katkari	1	1	4	2	8/40	low

Summary of this example: In Table 12.1, based on work with the Katkari of India (Buckles and Khedkar, 2013), three stakeholders hold different kinds and levels of power in the situation. The landowner, who is trying to evict the Katkari from land they have occupied for several generations, has considerable economic wealth and has used it in the past to hire goons to harass people in several villages. He has also made use of his connections to local government officials to protect his ownership of the land and the rights of private property owners. The Revenue Department is the primary authority with respect to land issues in India and the registrar for land deeds and all legislative procedures associated with land. The Department can and has in the past made use of this authority and knowledge of the law to call on the police to enforce their decisions. It also levies taxes on land and can use existing legislation to purchase land from established sources of funding. By contrast, the Katkari only have their numbers to draw on as sources of power in the situation. They have been part of demonstrations and marches in the past (information and communication, and currently occupy the land directly (force). This makes it more difficult to displace them.

Variations

- To obtain stakeholder profiles that reflect the relative weight of each source of power, create a table and insert the sources of power in Column 1 (see Table 12.2). Then set a maximum possible score allowed for each source of power. This maximum possible score provides a weight to the different sources of power in the situation (see *Weighting,* Chapter 7). For more precision, discuss what each level of power means for each source and write (or draw) these descriptions in the corresponding cells. Post the table as a reference for the discussion to follow. Then create a new table (see Table 12.3) and insert the sources of power and the highest possible score for each source (between 3 and 9 in the example table) in the top row. Rate the level of power that each stakeholder has for each source of power and total the scores for each stakeholder in the summary column. Use these total scores to determine the overall level of power held by each stakeholder.

TABLE 12.2 Weighted sources of power

Sources of power	*Low*	*Levels of power*			*High*
	1	*3*	*5*	*7*	*9*
Wealth	description	description	description	description	description
Authority	description	description	description	←maximum	
Force	description	description	←maximum		
Information and communication	description	description	description	description	←maximum

TABLE 12.3 Weighted stakeholder power profiles

Key stakeholders	*Wealth (max. 9)*	*Authority (max. 5)*	*Force (max. 3)*	*Information and communication (max. 7)*	*Sum (%) (max. 24)*	*Level*
Overall						

GAINS AND LOSSES

Interests

Purpose

To evaluate the net gains and losses that may result for different stakeholders or a single stakeholder involved in a situation or proposed action.

Step 1

Define the situation or proposed action and identify the key **stakeholders** involved. The exercise can be done separately by all stakeholders or with a focus on one of the stakeholder groups. Consider whether to include the representatives of a group as a stakeholder apart from the group they represent, or the community of all stakeholders as a group with its own profile (see *Stakeholder Identification* and *Stakeholder Rainbow*, Chapter 11).

Step 2

Make a list of the major **categories of gains and losses** that may result from the situation or proposed action for any of the stakeholders. Include in the list gains or losses of any valued source of power or resource relevant to the situation or proposed action such as economic wealth, political authority, the ability to use force, information, the means to communicate, legitimacy and social ties (see definitions in *Social Analysis CLIP* and *Power*, above). Divide these resources into smaller categories, as needed. For instance, divide economic wealth into monetary returns, food security, levels of consumption, possessions (such as land, equipment), etc. Add other things of value, such as a clean environment or physical security, if they are directly relevant to the situation or proposed action.

Step 3

Create a **table** with the categories of gains and losses in Column 1 (see Table 12.4). In Column 2, write indicators of each category and the **information** needed to evaluate or measure the gain or loss.

Step 4

Set and record in Column 3 the **highest and lowest possible values** allowed for each gain and loss. The highest and lowest values should fall somewhere between +10 for gains and –10 for losses. The range in values shows the relative importance and weight of each category of gain or loss in the situation or proposed action identified in Step 1 (see *Weighting*, Chapter 7). Gains or losses in social ties may be a lot more important than gains or losses in time, for instance. Different stakeholders may want to establish a different scale from their perspective.

Step 5

Total the **maximum possible gains** allowed when evaluating the situation or proposed action. Then, total the **maximum possible losses**. Indicate the overall scale of maximum gains and losses at the bottom of Column 3.

Step 6

Complete the table for each stakeholder (using separate columns) or for a single stakeholder. Estimate the **gain or loss for each category** that may result from the situation or proposed action, using the range of values set in Step 4. Then, total the net possible losses or gains for each stakeholder. Record the total in the last row.

Step 7

Review the results and discuss the kind and level of gains and losses estimated by the stakeholders involved and the overall impact of the situation or proposed action on their

TABLE 12.4 Categories of gains and losses

Categories of gains and losses	*Graduated indicators*	*Scale*	*Net gain or loss*		
			Tobacco farmer	*Jute farmer*	*Mixed crop farmer*
Yield	– Yield much less than expectation (–10) – Yield not up to expectation – Expected yield achieved (0) – Yield more than expectation – Yield much higher than expectation (+10)	–10 to +10	+5	+2	–5
Monetary returns	– An additional loan to meet needs (–6) – Need of loan for the next crop – Loan has been repaid somehow (0) – Some money remaining in hand after the repayment of loan – Money available for purchase of cow (+6)	–6 to +6	–6	+6	0
Happiness	– Disagreement between wife and husband (–4) – Lack of peace in family life – No worry and anxiety (0) – Happy – Very happy (+4)	–4 to +4	–4	0	+4
Product quality	– Product half-ripe, unfilled, rotten (–6) – Low quality – Average quality (0) – Good quality – Very good quality (+6)	–6 to +6	+3	+3	+3
Food independence	– Lack of minimum food for three months (–8) – Lack of minimum food for one month – Minimum food independence ensured (0) – Enough food round the year – Surplus food for sharing among relations after meeting family needs (+8)	–8 to +8	–4	0	+6
Overall		**–34 to +34**	**–6**	**+11**	**+8**

Summary of this example: Farmers in Bangladesh assessed net gains and losses from ongoing tobacco production and alternative farming systems. This was part of a broader initiative to help farmers shift out of tobacco altogether, described in detail in Chapter 19. To launch the discussion, the research team elicited categories of gains and losses from farmers by asking them to contrast stories of a good farming season with a bad season. Several participants were invited to think of a neighbour or their own situation and act out a meeting in the regional market. One shared their good news of a stellar season while the other told the story of a poor season. During the storytelling, a member of the research team jotted down key words from the role-play, conducted in several rounds involving a range of participants.

The list of key words formed the basis for a pile sorting exercise by farmers, to generate categories of gains and losses. The group selected those that stood out for them, and added indicators showing graduated levels of performance within each category, drawing on the story details. The research team arranged the categories in a table with a graduated scale from 1 to 5. Farmers then took turns scoring their actual growing season and outlined the reasons for their scores. Overall assessments were made at the end. The values appearing in Table 12.4, estimated by the authors, reflect these discussions. The authors added the varying scales to show how the exercise can take into account the importance of each category of gains and losses, through weighting (see Chapter 7). The table, typical of the situation, highlights the appeal of consistent yields of tobacco leaf of average quality compared to more variable production outcomes in other farming systems. It also reflects the recurring indebtedness faced by tobacco farmers, and conflicts in the home due to uncertain food supplies and debt.

Farmers said that the exercise helped them think through the various considerations that implicitly go into an overall assessment of a farming season. 'I can now justify myself', said one farmer in reference to how he was now thinking about the strengths and weaknesses of his season and where he needed to pay more attention in future. For the research team the exercise helped to unpack the notion of profitability into something closer to a full cost accounting of economic performance from a farmer perspective. It also launched follow-up discussions regarding the relative weight of different categories of gains and losses, and new insights into the reasoning of farmers continuing to grow tobacco. Table 12.5 draws on the same exercise to illustrate how risk can also be introduced into assessments of gains and losses.

interests. If different individuals or groups calculate their own gains and losses, **compare** the results. Discuss how the distribution of interests may affect the stakeholder's ability to respond to the situation or proposed action identified in Step 1.

Variations

To obtain a **risk-adjusted value for gains and losses** for a single stakeholder, estimate **how likely** it is that expectations about gains and losses in each category will be met. This is a measure of risk. Choose a percentage likelihood and record it in Column B (see Table 12.5). Multiply the net gain or loss (recorded in Column A) by the probability (recorded in Column B) across each row. Record the results in the final Column (A x B). To calculate the **net gain or loss** that may result from the situation or proposed action, total the adjusted values in the final column.

TABLE 12.5 Risk-adjusted estimates of gains and losses

Categories of gains and losses	*Graduated indicators*	*Scale*	*Net gain or loss (tobacco farmer)*	*Probability (%)*	*Overall value*
			A	*B*	*A × B*
Yield		–10 to +10	+5	60	+3.0
Monetary returns		–6 to +6	–6	60	–3.6
Happiness		–4 to +4	–4	40	–1.6
Product quality		–6 to +6	+3	50	+1.5
Food independence		–8 to +8	–4	40	–1.6
Overall		–34 to +34	–6		–2.3

RIGHTS, RESPONSIBILITIES AND RESOLVE

Like power and interests, legitimacy can mean different things in different situations. The definition used in *Social Analysis CLIP* is one possible way to approach the concept. It revolves around the recognition of stakeholder rights and obligations and the expressed will or resolve to act on them. The following technique explores these attributes in greater detail.

Legitimacy

Purpose

To gain a better understanding of stakeholder legitimacy using the three 'R' factors, i.e. rights, responsibilities and resolve. Use this technique to investigate how the 'R' factors are distributed, and how this affects the ability of key stakeholders to handle a situation or proposed action.

Step 1

Define the situation or proposed action and list all the **stakeholders** involved (see *Stakeholder Identification* and *Stakeholder Rainbow*, Chapter 11). Indicate those who are doing the analysis in the list. Consider whether to include representatives of a group as a stakeholder different from those they represent and the community of all stakeholders as a group with its own profile.

Step 2

Discuss **examples** of the rights and the responsibilities of stakeholders in relation to the situation or proposed action identified in Step 1, and how important these are. Also discuss examples showing their resolve in exercising these rights and responsibilities. Use other terms to discuss these ideas, if necessary. If the three 'R' factors are not equally important, set a **range of values** for each factor showing their relative weight (such as 1 to 9 for rights, 1 to 6 for responsibilities, and 1 to 4 for resolve; see *Weighting*, Chapter 7).

Step 3

Draw a **Venn diagram** where the circles represent the three 'Rs' (see Figure 12.6). Identify the stakeholders who have high levels of rights, responsibilities and resolve. Locate these stakeholders in the middle of the diagram. Locate the other stakeholders in the diagram according to their levels of rights, responsibilities and resolve.

Step 4

Review the results of the Venn diagram. Discuss how the **distribution** of rights, responsibilities and resolve may affect stakeholder's ability to handle the situation or proposed action identified in Step 1. If different individuals or stakeholder groups do their own legitimacy analysis, **compare** the results.

Variation (advanced version)

Create a table with the list of stakeholders in Column 1 (see Table 12.6). Decide on one or several scales to be used to rate stakeholder rights, responsibilities and resolve. Record each stakeholder's **rights** related to the situation or proposed action in Column 2 using key words. Rate the importance of each right using the appropriate scale. Calculate the average importance of the rights of each stakeholder. This is **Score A**. If a stakeholder's rights are in dispute, assign a middle range value and note the dispute. Evaluate and rate the stakeholder's **resolve to exercise their rights** using the appropriate scale, and

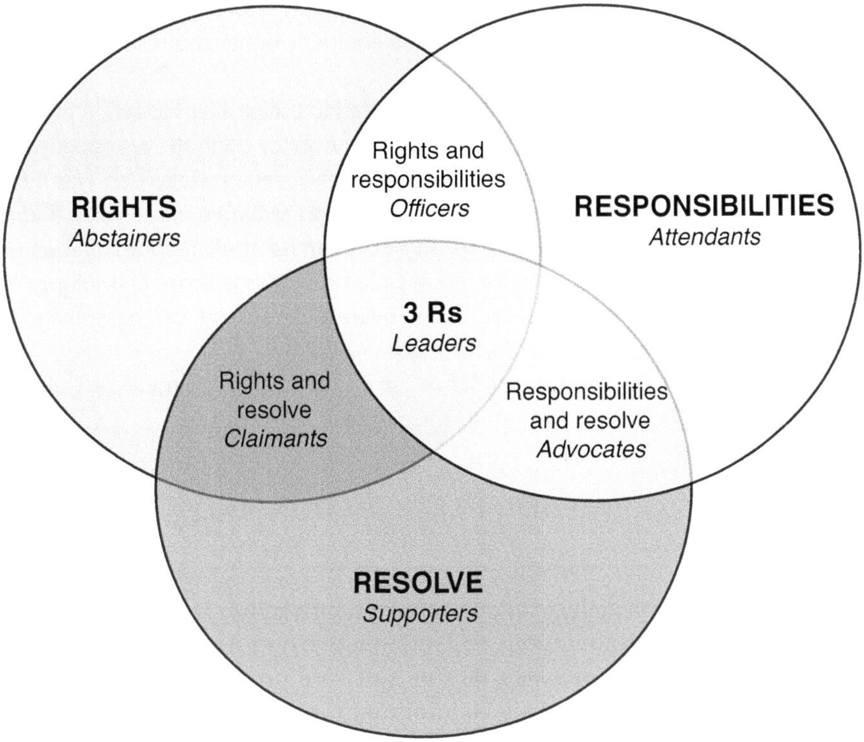

FIGURE 12.6 The three 'Rs'.

TABLE 12.6 Weighted estimates of rights, responsibilities and resolve

Stakeholders	*Rights*			*Responsibilities*			*Total legitimacy score*
	Details (Score A)	*Resolve* (Score B)	(A × B)	*Details* (Score C)	*Resolve* (Score D)	(C × D)	

record the rating in Column 3. This is **Score B**. Multiply Score A by Score B for each row to arrive at an overall assessment of the stakeholder's rights and resolve, and record the results in Column 4.

Record each stakeholder's **responsibilities** related to the problem or action in Column 5 using key words. Rate the importance of each responsibility using the appropriate scale. Calculate the average importance of the responsibilities of each stakeholder. This is **Score C**. If a stakeholder's responsibilities are in dispute, assign a middle range value and note the dispute. Evaluate the stakeholder's **resolve to exercise their responsibilities** using the appropriate scale, and record the rating in Column 6. This is **Score D**. Multiply Score C by Score D for each row to arrive at an overall assessment of the stakeholder's responsibilities and resolve, and record the results in Column 7.

To obtain the Overall **Legitimacy Score** for each stakeholder, multiply Columns 4 (A x B) and 7 (C x D). Record the result in Column 8.

THREADS OF THEORY: PARTICIPATION AND DEMOCRACY

Full democracy depends on institutions, laws and procedures that support effective representation, public deliberations and rational thinking. This is critical hardware. To work, however, it also requires flexible software processes – skilful means to facilitate authentic dialogue and well-informed reasoning at work, at school, in community life and in the public domain. Unfortunately, democracy is often sold piecemeal, without attention to the integration of hardware institutions and software processes. Governance by the people is chunked and hacked to artificial bits and bytes. The end result is a subtle programming of fraud and tyranny.

Democracy is both hardware and software. The hardware part consists of institutions, laws and procedures to implement collective decisions and sustain mechanisms of effective representation, communication and participation. Without them, we get only quick-and-easy voting, survey thinking, polling, lobbying, chatting, blogging and twittering, all of which represent the best argument against democracy, and an abuse of statistics. Democracy works if people know when to stop talking and start acting to create or strengthen the stable foundations of government by the people.

The software part is also essential. It involves flexible mechanisms and steps to support authentic dialogue and well-informed reasoning to achieve the common good. At stake here is a lifeworld that promotes transparent communication and rational engagement in social life and civil society, including the workplace, institutions of learning, the public sphere and community life, real and virtual. In the absence of the daily investments of people's minds and souls, democracy turns into governance by an elected aristocracy prone to accommodate those with the 'longest purse'.

The hardware and software of democracy must be brought together and regularly refreshed and upgraded if they are to do what they are supposed to do. Until this is done, Plato's suspicion that tyranny is bound to arise out of democracy will continue to haunt us.

Commentary

The notion that the authentic functioning of democracy lies squarely outside the hardware institutions of the State, in the software lifeworld and language of *communitas* and civil society, is naive. It ignores competing views on Cicero's *societas civilis*. In its current usage, the concept is closely associated with the rise and proliferation of NGOs, new social movements and technologies of e-communication and collaboration on a global scale. It evokes myriad forms of networks, associations, organizations and collaborative forms of communication and knowledge sharing that are independent of government systems and politically derived institutions, at least in principle. Activists suspicious of institutional power count on the uncoerced action of civil society to resist globalization and support struggles for participatory democracy and alternative visions of social and world order.

Great optimism lies in promises of lifeworld democracy and alterglobalization driven by civil society. Sceptics, however, are quick to remind us that civil society rhetoric may act as a neoliberal device to overthrow or precipitate the fall of regimes not in line with dominant financial and geopolitical interests. Keeping civil society busy also works to promote decentralisation and the international aid system, helping to reducing the power of state against market forces and putting pressure on governments to cut down on service provision and social care, especially in debt-laden states of the Global South.

Historically, civil society was and continues to be a pillar of market-ruled nation-states and a world economy ruled by capital, i.e. private property in the hands of the corporate few. Jean-Jacques Rousseau's thinking on this subject, as expressed in his *Discourse on Inequality*, written in 1754, has not lost its relevance: 'The first man who, having fenced in a piece of land, said "This is mine," and found people naive enough to believe him, that man was the true founder of civil society. From how many crimes, wars, and murders, from how many horrors and misfortunes might not any one have saved mankind, by pulling up the stakes, or filling up the ditch, and crying to his fellows: Beware of listening to this impostor; you are undone if you once forget that the fruits of the earth belong to us all, and the earth itself to nobody.' Marx's views on the evils of private property built into civil law and bourgeois politics are no less cynical, with reason.

Competing views of civil society have a long history (Edwards, 2004; Seligman, 1992). To philosophers such as Socrates, Plato and Aristotle, civility, social life and state politics meant basically the same thing. A good and virtuous society is composed of citizens who behave with civility and use rational arguments and dialectics to uncover truth and resolve disputes. This assumes the practice of virtue in everyday life, such as justice, moderation and courage, all of which ensure peace and order among rational citizens.

Humanism, the Scientific Revolution and the Enlightenment challenged the classical view on civil society. They radically transformed the old concept, by distinguishing the State (formed under the tyranny of Church and Monarchy) from expressions of 'the will of the people'. Social contracts and the rule of self-determination by the people became the precondition for the State to exercise legitimate power and maintain peace and order. Thomas Hobbes believed in the necessity of a strong Leviathan state and positive law to maintain civility and curb natural self-interested behaviour and anarchy. John Locke proposed instead a powerful society and a weak state, a two-treaty arrangement to protect peace and basic human rights. Despite important differences in strategies to uphold democracy, social contract philosophers shared the view that state institutions had to be wired to the laws of Nature, including the preservation of life, the practice of Reason, the exercise of free will and, never to be forgotten, the sanctity of private property.

Private economic interests were further enshrined in the writings of Hegel. The Romantic philosopher redefined civil society as a modern liberal market society governed by the satisfaction of individual interests and private property, to be distinguished from the State whose mission it is to correct the faults of civil society and sustain moral order. Alexis de Tocqueville had more confidence in the system of civilian and political associations and their capacity to keep liberal individualism and state centralisation in check. Marx rejected the positive role of both State and civil society, which he viewed as arms of the bourgeoisie. Antonio Gramsci and post-modernists restored faith in the potential of civil society, in its capacity to challenge the hegemony of capital and state bureaucracies overburdened by systems of power.

Long-standing concerns and debates about the limitations and three-way collusion of Civil Society, the State and Business are not about to be dispelled. In the global era, the dialectics of social and public life – engagement in the exercise of reason for the common good, as prescribed by Socrates – still remains a formidable challenge.

REFERENCES

Buckles, D. J. and Khedkar, R. with Ghevde, B. and Patil, D. (2013) *Fighting Eviction: Tribal Land Rights and Research-in-Action*, Cambridge University Press India, New Delhi.

Edwards, M. (2004) *Civil Society*, Polity Press, Cambridge.

Reyes Sandoval, W. (2006) 'Dinámica causal y el "CLIP" aplicados al manejo de cuencas hidrográficas', Universidad Nacional de Agricultura, Departamento de Manejo de Recursos Naturales y Ambiente, Catacamas, Olancho.

Seligman, A. (1992) *The Idea of Civil Society*, Free Press, New York.

CHAPTER 13

Positions and values

INTRODUCTION

Social Analysis CLIP looks at how factors of power, interests, legitimacy and histories of conflict and collaboration affect a given situation or the possible outcomes of a planned action. The software CLIP (www.participatoryactionresearch.net) adds two other variables to the equation: the **positions** and the **values** that stakeholder express in relation to a situation or action and that may or may not coincide with their interests as they perceive them. The notion that overt positions (in favour or against an observed or proposed action) may not reflect underlying interests is part of mainstream conflict management theory and practice. It is a reminder that stakeholders can make rigid demands or major concessions that leave no room for compromise and lead to win-lose solutions that produce poor results and may not last. Interest-based analysis and discussions are more effective because they encourage the parties to think of the concerns, fears and expectations that are important to each side in a conflict. The approach promotes thinking about trade-offs that can be made across multiple issues and measures that can be taken to share the pie fairly or enlarge it to everyone's benefit.

While useful in many settings, interest-based bargaining, also known as principle-based negotiations, is not a panacea for all conflicts. First of all, no distinction is made between negotiable interests and fundamental needs that should not be up for trade. Frameworks that gloss over this critical distinction are like theories that apply the concept of 'capital' to any asset that has some worth in a given situation. All 'parties' are conveniently lumped into a catchall category – actors using the 'capital' at their disposal to satisfy their individual or group 'interests', whether or not they have control over means of production. The language is general to the point that powerlessness and impoverishment disappear into thin air.

Second, no distinction is made between interests and values. Both aspects of human behaviour are lumped into a general notion of 'interests and principles', those that matter when seeking win-win solutions to real-life disputes. The language avoids thinking about moral conduct that may be disinterested. It also ignores the fact that many wrongs are committed by those who seek their interests without concern for others. What is euphemistically called 'principle-based negotiation' is in reality an interested plea for 'ethical egoism' – the claim that moral agents can pursue what is in their own self-interest at all times without qualms.

Third, interest-based bargaining theory deals with principles and values rather superficially. There is no appreciation for the difference that lies between explicit norms of conduct and deeply felt values that may be hard to express and yet influence the positions that stakeholders adopt in real settings. Deep-seated values are all the more important as other parties may actually share them. They can guide actions toward positive results.

Positions, values and interests are not absolutes in theory or clear-cut categories in day-to-day language. The notions overlap and invite grey-zone thinking where boundaries can be blurred. Is 'private property' a fundamental need and principle or is it a self-serving concept reflecting the interests of the few? Do competing positions on what is meant by freedom or justice point to differences in deeply felt values or conflicts in political and economic interests? Answers to these questions vary considerably and cannot be resolved once and for all, through rigid positions couched as general theory. This chapter suggests that, instead, the questions be grounded in real issues and put directly to the parties involved.

Below we present three action-research methods that help actors reflect on their positions as they relate to both the interests and the values they hold in concrete situations, knowing that both forms of reasoning may help them better understand existing problems and act on them. The approach we recommend is pluralistic and flexible: the usefulness of an interest-based or a value-based approach to negotiations depends on each situation and must be judged accordingly. Efforts to resolve a conflict affecting stakeholders in a community-forestry initiative in Bolivia illustrates how this can be done.

TAKING A STAND

Positions and Interests

Purpose

To compare the positions that stakeholders take on a situation or proposed action with their underlying interests.

Step 1

Define the context and describe the **situation** or **proposed action** where stakeholder views and interests may differ significantly. Decide which stakeholders will be included and who will engage in the exercise and the steps that follow (see *Stakeholder Rainbow*, Chapter 11 and *Social Analysis CLIP*, Chapter 12).

Step 2

Discuss and rate how strongly stakeholders feel about the situation or proposed action described in Step 1. Use values ranging from –10 (strongly opposed) to +10 (strongly in favour). This is **Score P** (for position). It is an estimate of each stakeholder's **support** for the situation or proposed action. For more precision, use **indicators** to define the meaning of each number on the scale.

Step 3

For each stakeholder ask what would the stakeholder gain if its position were adopted. Make a list of the **gains**, discuss how important the gains are and which ones are the most important.

Step 4

For each stakeholder ask what would the stakeholder lose if its position were adopted. Make a list of these **losses**. Discuss how important the losses are and which ones are the most important.

Step 5

Calculate the **net gains** (or net losses if the position is defeatist or disinterested) the stakeholder would realize if its position were adopted. Use values from –10 (high loss) to +10 (high gain). This is **Score I** (for interests). For more precision, use **indicators** to define the meaning of each number on the scale.

Make sure not to confuse the idea of 'acting in one's *interest*' with 'taking an *interest* in something'. Also, clarify the difference between **interests** and basic **needs**.

Step 6

Create the **table** shown in the example and insert the names of the stakeholders in Column 1 (see Table 13.1). In each row, insert the letters P and I in the cells that reflect the stakeholder's scores for position and interests. If relevant, use the results of *Social Analysis CLIP* to order the stakeholders in Column 1 by rank based on the factors of power, interests and legitimacy. Alternatively, insert the results of *Positions and Interests* in the *Social Analysis CLIP* table (see Figure 13.1).

TABLE 13.1 Comparing positions and interests

Stakeholders	*–10* *I: high net loss* *P: strong opposition*		*0* *Neutral*	*+10* *I: high net gain* *P: strong support*
Ranchers			I	P
Small farmers	P	I		
Women's association	P	I		

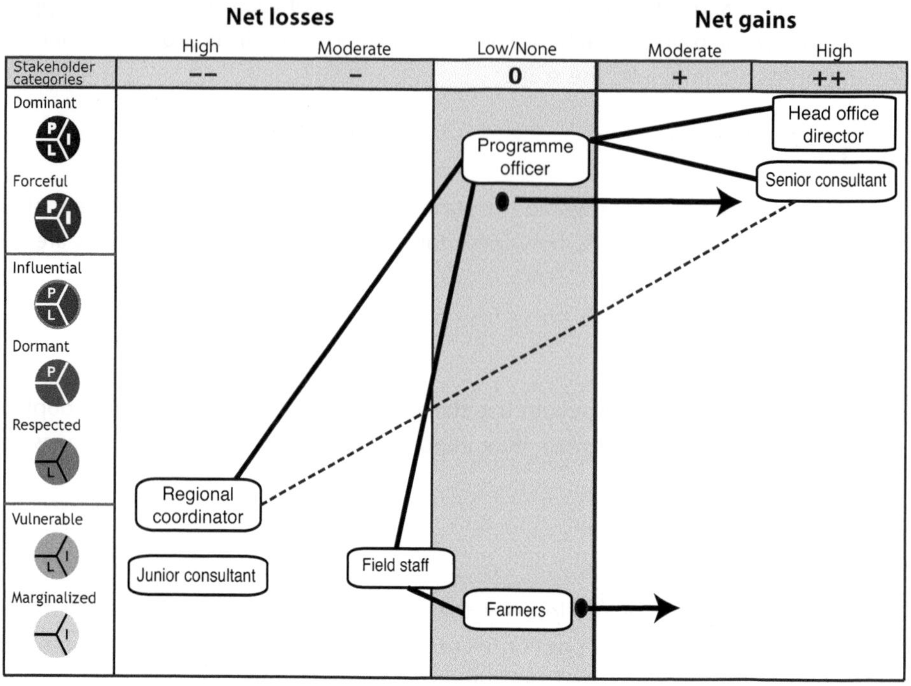

FIGURE 13.1 Adding positions to *Social Analysis CLIP*.

Summary of this example: The regional coordinator working in Western Africa does not see eye to eye (dotted line) with the Canadian head office director who decided to follow the advice of a senior consultant and *transfer funds and management responsibilities* from the regional coordinator to field staff and the programme officer. African farmers know little about the decision and take a neutral position. But they stand to gain from the transfer of funds to local offices and could therefore be convinced to support the move (the arrow represents the farmers' potential shift from a neutral position to active support for the head office decision). By contrast, the programme officer is taking a neutral stand but could oppose the move because he is sensitive to the key role the regional coordinator plays. Given a long history of close collaboration (solid lines) between most parties, all indications are that the problem can be resolved through mediation. (See *Social Analysis CLIP* and the software CLIP, Chapter 12.)

Step 7

Compare stakeholder net gains or losses (Score I) with the stakeholder's level of support for the current situation or proposed action (Score P). Assess the **degree** and the **direction of change** that could occur for each stakeholder if discussions and negotiations were based on interests rather than positions.

Step 8

Explore modifications to the situation or proposed action that could satisfy the interests of all parties concerned.

> Facilitators should not express positive or negative comments or **judgments** when discussing stakeholder positions and interests. Also, when using a 'why' question to identify stakeholder interests (such as 'Why do we take this position?'), keep in mind that stakeholders may adopt positions that do not reflect their own interests as they define them. People may give answers that focus on their values and **principles** or on **external factors**, not on their interests. If the answer is based on statements of rights or principles (such as 'We live here and this is our forest'), ask what are the **interests** at stake when rights or principles are being expressed. Continue asking this type of question until the underlying interests are made clear (such as 'We need firewood for cooking'). Ask in different ways, such as 'What are the benefits for us?', 'What would we gain if we did it our way?' or 'How would we be affected if it did not go our way?'

Combinations

- Use *Timeline* or *Previous Responses* (Chapter 9) to inquire into the history of positions adopted by stakeholders; *Interests* (Chapter 12), to examine interests in greater detail; *Values, Interests, Positions (VIP)* or *Lessons and Values* (below), to explore the values that people hold and that may reflect the positions they adopt; *Negotiation Fair* (Chapter 14), to assess and negotiate what stakeholders can expect of each other.

BETWEEN PRINCIPLES AND INTERESTS

Values, Interests, Positions (VIP)

Purpose

To compare the positions that stakeholders take on a **situation** or **action** (existing or proposed) with their **actual interests** and the **moral values** they hold.

Step 1

Define the situation or action where stakeholder positions must be discussed. This may be an action that stakeholders are taking and do not feel entirely satisfied with (for reasons yet to be identified). Determine whether participants should express their positions individually or as subgroups, and whether it should be done **openly** or **anonymously**.

Step 2

Create a diagram by drawing a vertical line that crosses a horizontal line of equal length. Write 0 where the lines intersect, and +10 and –10 at opposite ends of each line.

Step 3

Ask each individual or subgroup to **plot** on the vertical line the extent to which the situation or action **corresponds on the whole to the values** they hold. Use +10 to represent a situation or action that matches their values perfectly, and –10 to represent one that fundamentally contradicts their values.

Step 4

Ask each individual or subgroup to **plot** on the horizontal line the extent to which the situation or action supports their interests (e.g. financial, professional, political). These are the **net gains or losses**, expected or observed, that result from the situation or action. Use +10 to represent an action or project that brings high net gains, and –10 to represent high net losses.

Step 5

Mark where the values from the two lines meet. This represents the **position** of each individual or subgroup (see Figure 13.2).

Step 6

Discuss the results and explore how to **improve** or **modify** the situation or action so that it better matches stakeholder values or interests.

FAQ

- ***Isn't the distinction between values and interests rather subjective?***

It is. While making money serves material interests, it can also be viewed as an expression of hard work and merit in life. Still, there are countless situations in life where people see possible gaps between interests and the moral values they hold – between real conduct and their ideals of moral behaviour. These are worth exploring.

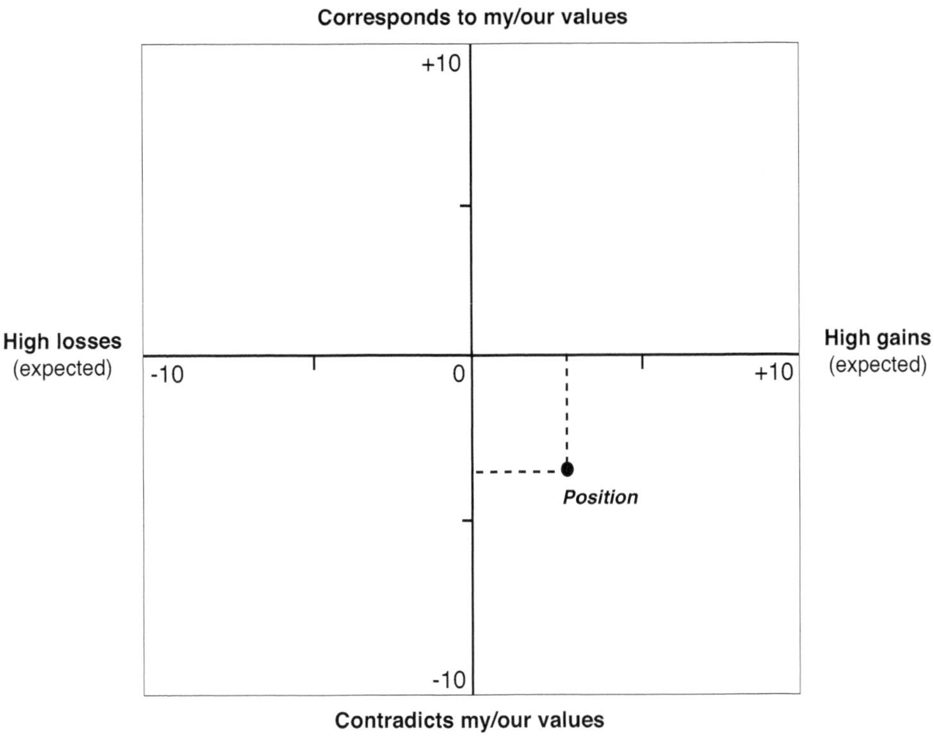

FIGURE 13.2 *Values, Interests, Positions (VIP).*

Variations

- Assess different proposed actions using *Values, Interests, Positions (VIP)*. (See *Conflict over the control of timber in Bolivia,* overleaf.)
- Label the four corners of the diagram with the name of a well-known profession, historical figure or life form (animal, plant, spirit) that best represents the position obtained by the combination of extreme scores in each corner.
- *Anonymous floor mapping option.* Create a large-scale version of the diagram on the floor using masking tape. Ask each participant to create the same diagram on a card and mark their position using their individual ratings on the two factors (values and interests). Then ask them to exchange their diagram with other participants several times so that it can't be traced. End by inviting all participants to stand in the floor diagram at the location marked on the diagram now in their hands. Discussion of the distribution of positions can maintain anonymity, making it easier to discuss sensitive issues openly.

Combinations

- Use *Timeline* or *Previous Responses* (Chapter 9) to inquire into the history of positions adopted by stakeholders; *Interests* (Chapter 12), to examine interests in greater detail;

PHOTO 13.1 Field staff and other members of an NGO assess the extent to which a shift in the programme is consistent with their individual values and interests. (Source: D. J. Buckles)

Lessons and Values (below), to explore the values that people hold and how they relate to the positions they adopt; *Negotiation Fair* (Chapter 14), to assess and negotiate what stakeholders can expect of each other.

Conflict over the control of timber in Bolivia

Timber in the Chiquitania region of Bolivia includes many precious woods of great value. Currently, timber buyers acquire timber from people and communities at a very low price. They do so by advancing money for basic needs in exchange for commitments to deliver timber at a fixed price. Since many local people have very low incomes, much of the better wood is captured in this way.

With help from the Spanish Government, a municipal government in the region set up a lumber mill and carpentry shop to purchase and partly process timber locally so that communities could realize more of the potential value of the forests. They also employed a Forestry Officer to help communities develop forest management plans and authorize and monitor all agreements between buyers and sellers. National laws support these and other efforts by municipalities to ensure that timber is cut legally and, to the extent possible, processed locally. While a priority for the municipality, making sure that the mill has enough high value timber is made difficult by the fact that other timber buyers use the existing loan and debt system to divert timber promised to the municipal mill. To address this problem, the municipal government convened a meeting of various stakeholders, facilitated by Jorge Téllez Carrasco, a Ph.D. student undertaking research in the region (Téllez Carrasco, 2009).

The meeting began using the tool *Social Analysis CLIP*. The assessment was interrupted, however, when a participant accused the Forestry Officer, who was married to a timber buyer also present during the meeting, of being in a conflict of interest. The participant accused her of ignoring efforts by her husband to capture timber committed to the municipal mill. He also called on the municipal government to fire her immediately. The mill manager hesitated to fire the Forestry Officer because he relied on her to deliver on many other timber agreements also important to the mill. The discussion began to falter. The facilitator then invited the participants to shift the focus to a discussion of ways to resolve the conflict. People representing four forest communities, the municipal government and the municipal mill agreed and began to explore the interests and moral values at stake using the tool *VIP*. The Forestry Officer and the timber buyer remained to defend themselves, but did not participate in the rating exercises.

Over a period of several hours, participants identified four possible actions in response to the conflict and assessed the moral acceptability and the collective gains and losses (interests) associated with each, using a scale of –10 to +10. They began by assessing the current situation where the timber buyer pays forest communities very low prices for high-value timber and diverts some timber away from the municipal mill, with the unspoken approval of the Forestry Officer. People argued that allowing the Forestry Officer to ignore the illegal actions of her husband was morally unacceptable to them. They gave a value of –5 to the moral acceptability of the current situation and a value of +1 to gains they now have from the sale of timber. This resulted in Position 1 in Figure 13.3.

A number of participants repeatedly argued that the Forestry Officer should be fired immediately. The group thought this was the right thing to do because government officials should not be allowed to favour their own family members when they hold public office. This action received a value of +5 in terms of its moral acceptability. They were aware, however, that doing so would undermine many agreements with the mill set up by the Forestry Officer and thus throw the municipal mill and several forest communities into an even deeper crisis. These outcomes would affect more than just the communities where the Forestry Officer's husband was active. They also noted that firing a local official would have a political cost for the municipal government who would suffer some embarrassment and have to admit a failure to deliver a successful mill project. On balance, the action would result in significant losses, rated by the group as –8. This assessment resulted in Position 2 in Figure 13.3.

During the discussion, the Forestry Officer threatened to organize a community petition to support her if the municipal government fired her. She argued that many

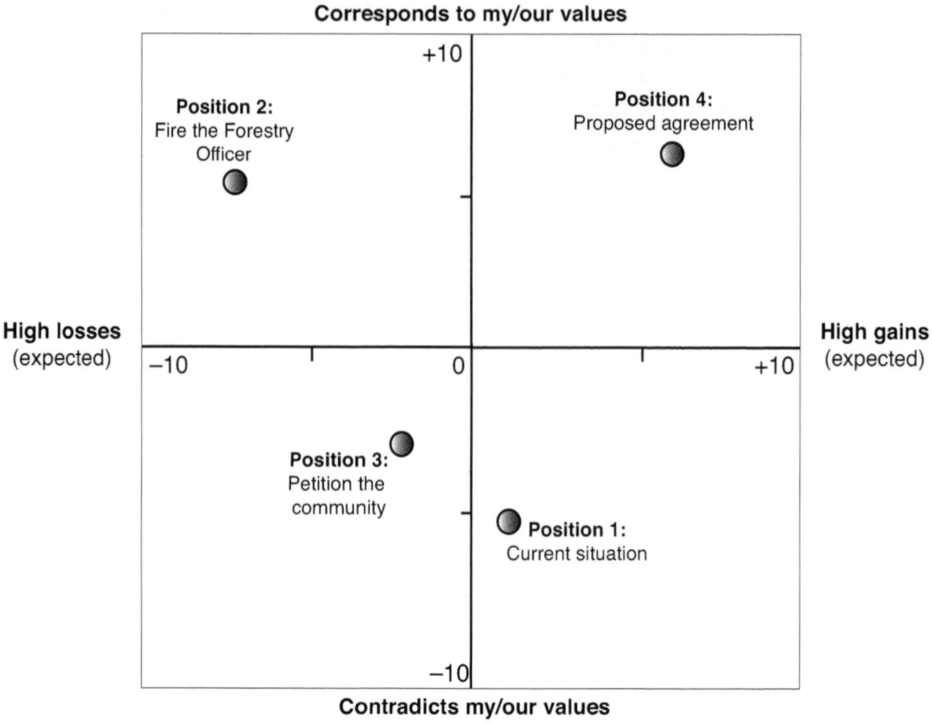

FIGURE 13.3 Forestry conflict management in Bolivia. (Source: Téllez Carrasco, 2009)

forest communities are satisfied with the harvest agreements they have with timber buyers. She also denied giving any favours to her husband. Participants assessed this proposed action by the Forestry Officer and decided that even if most of the forest communities supported her petition, it would still not satisfy their concerns about the moral acceptability of the situation (–3 on the scale of moral acceptability). While many of the current agreements in communities might go ahead, the municipal mill would still not be able to meet its needs because some wood would be diverted anyway and the municipal government would be still embarrassed by the situation (–2 on the scale of gains and losses). The group decided that this action would result in fewer losses than firing the Forestry Officer but that it remained morally unacceptable to them (Position 3, Figure 13.3).

After a lively discussion of these alternatives, the facilitator asked whether participants could imagine a compromise that would satisfy their interests and the moral values they hold. The group was aware that it needed to shift its position if the mill's season was to be saved. Any further delays or complications resulting from firing the Forestry Officer would reduce the short-term success of the municipal mill. This would in turn affect the way forest communities saw the long-term potential of the mill and their level of commitment to it. The group also recognized that the work of the Forestry Officer had brought some concrete benefits to forest communities.

Based on ideas emerging from the discussion, the group developed a series of conditions it would be willing to accept. First, the Forestry Officer would need to commit to active monitoring of all harvest agreements made by timber buyers, including her husband, to ensure that committed timber was not diverted away from the mill. Second, the Forestry Officer would need to cooperate with a representative of the municipal government who would monitor her work and make sure favouritism was not being tolerated. Third, the timber buyer married to the Forestry Officer would have to resell to the mill a certain amount of timber he collected, thereby ensuring the supply needed for the current season. Fourth, the municipal government, acting through the Forestry Officer, would promptly approve pending harvest agreements made by the timber buyer in question, assuming the forest communities agreed and had no other options. The group assessed the proposed agreement and concluded that it would satisfy their current interests (+6 on the scale of gains and losses) and would be morally acceptable to them (+6 on the scale of moral acceptability). Their position, shown by the number 4 in Figure 13.3, reflected the group's view that while the other actions failed to satisfy their interests and their moral values, the proposed compromise could satisfy both to some degree. Eventually, the Forestry Officer and the timber buyer agreed.

The exercise was very tense and difficult for everyone. Sometimes the municipal mayor had to use his authority to keep the discussion going. Occasionally the Forestry Officer and the timber buyer left the meeting, only to return after tempers had calmed. Overall, however, the process worked. The initial discussion using the *Social Analysis CLIP* tool, while aborted, had raised issues and provided the group with concepts needed to discuss the interests and values of stakeholders. Using a flip chart to graph the current situation and proposed actions helped to depersonalize the discussion while staying focussed on common understandings of the interests and values at stake. This helped the parties continue the discussion and shift from personal blame and criticism to exploring the values and interests the group was willing to negotiate. Tension was reduced over time and the discussion continued until a resolution was reached. Participants said that the result was satisfactory and more productive than they had initially thought was possible given the controversy.

The agreement held until the end of the harvest season. Although the municipal mill did not get all of the wood it needed, it got enough to show the potential to the forestry communities. The Forestry Officer was eventually fired and a new person was hired under much clearer working arrangements.

LESSONS LEARNED

Lessons and Values

Like interests, different values may intersect in a single situation. Some may be more important than others. Unlike interests, however, values tend to be more abstract and may be more difficult to put into words. They are also more difficult to ground in concrete action and behaviour. The technique presented below helps address these issues and solve problems in the process.

Purpose

To better manage a problem by becoming aware of what moral values people hold and applying the lessons learned from successful actions that are consistent with those values.

Step 1

Identify the **problem** that participants find difficult to resolve. Describe the **response** or position that participants have adopted to handle the situation and that they are **not entirely satisfied** with. Record the problem and the response to it on a card using a few key words or a short sentence. Add key details on the back of the card.

Step 2

Identify **why** participants are not satisfied with the response or position identified in Step 1, and record the answer on another card. If the reason is a negative statement, find positive terms to describe the principle or **value behind the reason**. Place this value card immediately above the first card (see Figure 13.4).

Step 3

Discuss why the value identified in Step 2 is important. Ask in a different way, such as 'Why does this matter?' or 'What will happen if we all apply this value?'. Record the **new principle or value** on its own card and place it above the other cards.

Step 4

Repeat this process until a **core value** is reached, and place it at the top. If there are two core values that are relevant to the problem, place both of them at the top.

Step 5

Identify at least one **situation where the core value was applied with confidence and positive results**. Describe what was done in that situation. If the description is vague, use the *Laddering Down* technique to make it more meaningful and detailed. Ask 'Can we give an example of this?', or 'How can we tell this response was respectful?', for instance.

Step 6

Go back to the situation identified in Step 1 and **imagine** a response or position using lessons learned about how core values can guide actions towards positive results.

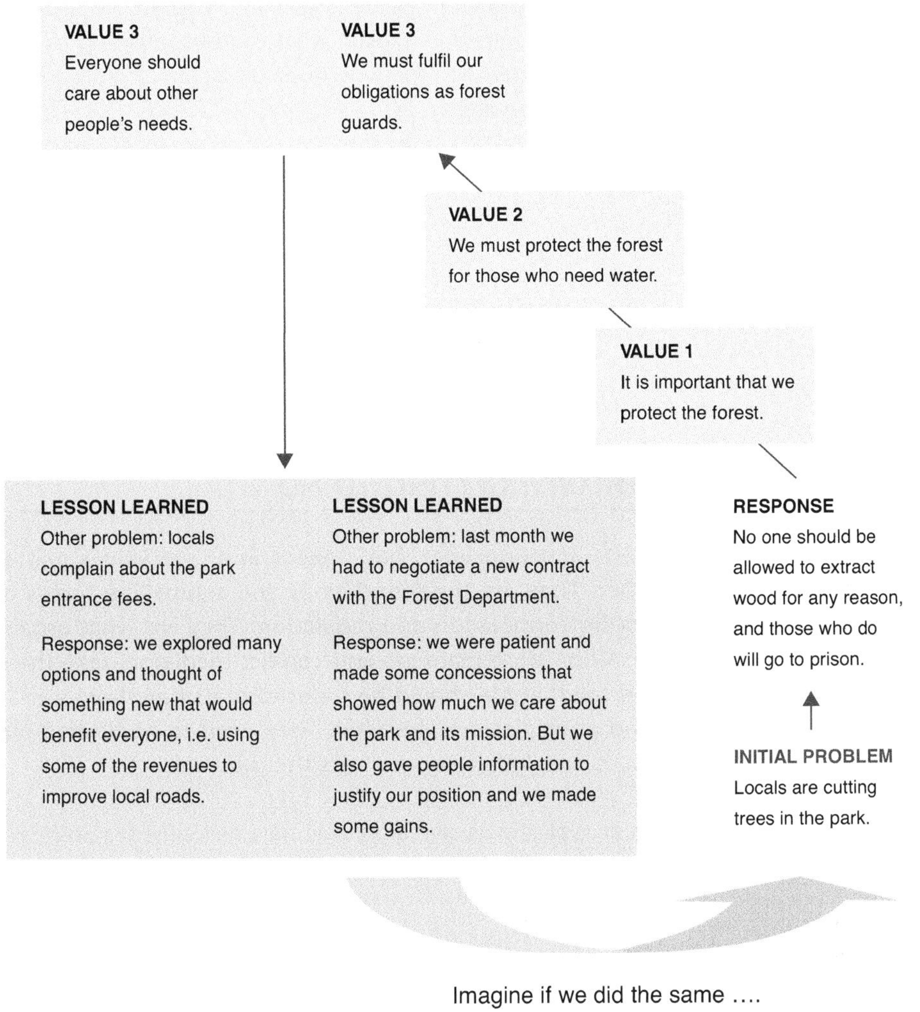

FIGURE 13.4 Forestry conflict management in Costa Rica.

Tips

- If a value sounds too concrete or like a **cliché**, use the *Laddering Up* technique to make it more meaningful (see *Active Listening*, Chapter 8). Ask 'Why do we think this (name the value) is so important?', 'Why is this (name the value) essential in life?' or 'What happens when people have this (name the value)?' These questions may help identify a higher value that expresses the participants' fundamental beliefs. Participants will recognize values that are higher up the ladder when they express things that are deeply felt and are central to the image they have of themselves. Participants often view these values as self-evident, essential in life and applicable to everyone.

- When using a '**why**' question to identify values (such as 'Why do we take this position?'), people may give answers that explain what causes something to exist or what their interests are. Respond with the why question again, formulated in a different way, until values are identified.
- Facilitators that are not also stakeholders in the situation should not make comments or express **judgments** about stakeholder values.

Combinations

- Use *Timeline* or *Previous Responses* (Chapter 9) to inquire into the history of positions adopted by stakeholders, or *Values, Interests, Positions (VIP)* to explore the interests underlying the positions they adopt.

THREADS OF THEORY: GETTING TO NO

When compared to interests and principles, basic needs and core values matter more deeply and last longer. They are the foundations and compelling forces of social life, not their day-to-day formulation and regulation. They are what organs and bones are to skin and flesh. Wise planners and conflict mediators take them into account. This is not to say that life should be reduced to its bare bones at all times. Surface interests and principles are also vital. They need to be fleshed out and kept in line with what is deeply felt and matters the most.

Conflicts that seem intractable typically revolve around entrenched either-or positions, emotional and principled claims regarding who is right and wrong, the imposition of rule and the exercise of power. An alternative to rights or power contests is interest-based negotiation. The focus is on discussing underlying goals, assessing key gains and losses to each party, and negotiating a win-win solution to the dispute. This kind of rational bargaining is effective in some situations, i.e. when the right conditions exist. It works when interests can be effectively reconciled, by 'enlarging the pie', for instance, and also when basic needs or core values do not have to be traded or deeply compromised. Addressing individual or group interests without first attending to the non-negotiables of life – without clearly saying 'no' when 'no' is clearly called for – is a solution looking for trouble. It is also profoundly objectionable. Food to the needy comes before money to the greedy.

Commentary

The Harvard model of negotiation is principled in that it is truthful and non-adversarial (Fisher and Ury, 1981). It calls for the exercise of reason and dialogue and an enlightened and creative understanding of self-interest. Interest-based bargaining is a friendly and honest approach to problem solving and the pursuit of win-win arrangements in real-life settings. The model makes an invaluable contribution to conflict management.

'Getting to YES' has nonetheless a darker side, a pragmatic orientation that can accept practically anything, including unprincipled behaviour. When closely examined, the primary purpose of interest-framed dialogue is to bargain for peace and order, not to eradicate injustice. The approach is not meant to challenge existing power imbalances. This orientation is reflected in tactical BATNA reasoning (Best Alternative To a Negotiated Agreement). The reasoning consists in doing or imposing whatever is in one's power, as long as one can get away with it, irrespective of the common good and concerns for what is right or wrong. Under this scheme, parties negotiate only to derive better outcomes than would otherwise occur. In the end, getting the parties to say yes to what they want and can reasonably get *under existing circumstances* is a mighty euphemism for saying no to what the powerless struggle for and ought to get.

When 'Yes' is simply not the 'right' thing to say, truthful dialogue must enable people to voice an intractable 'No'. This is the approach expressed in the resolve of Martin Luther King and Nelson Mandela. It also underlies Gandhi's philosophy and practice of active but non-violent resistance in the face of injustice. Through civil disobedience, non-cooperation and the positive statement of demands, the force of reason and moral conscience uphold a position of unarguable truth. This is not weakness or pacifism but rather *satyagraha*, 'truth force' as an alternative form of persuasion and politics in the pursuit of a just cause.

For Gandhi (1926), debate and respectful discussion with opponents are a crucial part of non-violent resistance. Adversaries are always worthy of regard, patience and even compassion. Dialogue and reason prevail over the use of force. There are no losers, only winners. The *satyagraha* path, however, is never complacent towards existing regimes of power and wrongdoing. Apathy and cowardice as a response to oppression and the pillage of Nature is not an option. Also, in this approach to conflict management, answers to problems are never simply utilitarian and pragmatic, placing reasoning or immediate interests above all else (Gupta, 2009, p. 30). Rather, core values always come first and are best expressed through non-violence, i.e. *ahimsa*, a resolve that is as demanding of the oppressed as it is of the oppressor. By steadfastly refusing to retaliate against violent acts, Gandhi drove opponents to defeat through the pressure of moral bankruptcy. By holding to this deeply felt value, he also reminded the world that people can engage in a principled struggle without submitting passively. In these teachings lies an instance of *Getting to NO: negotiating agreement without giving in*.

REFERENCES

Fisher, R. and Ury, W. L. (1981) *Getting to YES: Negotiating Agreement Without Giving In*, Penguin, New York.

Gandhi, M. K. (1926) *Satyagraha in South Africa*, trans. Valji Govindji Desai, Ahmedabad, Navajivan, India.

Gupta, D. (2009) 'Gandhi before Habermas: The democratic consequences of Ahimsa', *Economic and Political Weekly*, vol. 44, no. 10, pp. 27–33.

Téllez Carrasco, J. A. (2009) 'Aproximación a los proyectos de desarrollo forestal desde el diálogo entre los sistemas de conocimiento y los intereses involucrados. Los pequeños productores forestales en la Chiquitania (Bolivia)', Ph.D. Thesis, CID-CRUMA, Madrid.

MODULE 5

Assessing options

MODULE 5: ASSESSING OPTIONS

PAR attempts to understand the world by trying to make it better. As such, the approach must help people imagine possible futures, examine priorities and assess what they can expect by acting on key problems. Predicting what is likely to happen if nothing further is done (beyond current attempts to improve things) is also key to creating 'another future'. In this module, we look at different ways to imagine the change we wish to see (Chapter 14) and anticipate the consequences of things that are or might be (Chapter 15). We illustrate these tools with stories about youth engagement in Canada, competing priorities of men and women in West Bengal (India), and the different understandings government officials and natives have about consultation processes in Canada. We also propose a methodology for engaging people in disaster relief and risk reduction planning using several tools from this module and from previous chapters. The methodology is illustrated with information and analysis from the Philippines. All of these PAR tools speak to situations where options or alternatives for action need to be carefully considered and assessed, towards a positive vision of the future.

CHAPTER 14

Blue-sky thinking

INTRODUCTION

This chapter proposes techniques to assess existing options and engage in thinking about a better world (blue-sky thinking). It starts with various group processes to imagine an *Ideal Scenario* that recognizes and takes inspiration from past accomplishments and current strengths. They include *The Ideal Scenario Tapestry* and *The Carrousel*, a variation on the *World Cafe*, two effective techniques to develop a vision of the future or common action plan. *The Carrousel* is most helpful in situations where small groups or large assemblies need to develop consensus gradually. The process allows for sharing and several rounds of improvements to ideas. It is a good substitute for the conventional general assembly or plenary session more conducive to formal discussions and deliberations. Practitioners may also use *Sabotage*, a humorous exercise to identify and overcome habits, doubts, fears and other barriers to achieving goals (the tool is already built into *Paradox* and is illustrated in our story of *Health and safety among construction workers in France*, Chapter 10). As a complement to visioning PAR facilitators can use *Disagreements and Misunderstandings* to rank stakeholders' goals in order of importance, and review disagreements or misunderstandings people may have about these goals. The West Bengali and Canadian Cree examples of this tool are particularly telling of the importance of understanding difference as the basis for building agreement. *Levels of Support* (adapted from Kaner, 1996), illustrated with another story from West Bengal, is equally handy. This is a method that uses local language to determine whether there is enough support from stakeholders to go on with a proposal or course of action, before any final decision or vote is taken.

The last tool in the chapter is *Negotiation Fair*, a powerful technique to investigate and negotiate what stakeholders can expect of each other in the pursuit of multiple goals. We give an example of how we used this tool to address tensions between teams involved in a programme to engage youth in building resilient communities in Canada. It also builds on local concepts, language and symbols to inquire into future expectations. Since local and contextual expressions of meaning is a recurring theme in this chapter, we end with a theoretical commentary on the issue, with a focus on Wittgenstein's investigations into ordinary language.

VISIONING

Ideal Scenario

Purpose

To imagine an ideal scenario that recognizes and takes inspiration from past accomplishments and current strengths, using one or more of the following tools.

The Ideal Scenario Tapestry

Define a focus for a vision and invite participants to list the elements of an ideal scenario (see *Free List and Pile Sort*, Chapter 8). Collectively, create a tapestry made up of drawings of these elements on individual sheets of paper or a single drawing on a large sheet of kraft paper. If possible, use good quality art paper and pastels, intense colour pencils or colour ink so people can enjoy the drawing process. Participants may use real or imaginary life forms or scenes (such as animals, plants, landscapes, activities) to reflect their vision. Ask participants to explain their drawings to others and combine them into an ideal scenario tapestry.

True or False

Define a general topic and invite participants to think of a true story about a great thing they have accomplished, and a false story about something they would like to accomplish in relation to the topic and that builds on their existing strengths. Share the stories in pairs or small groups. The false story must be told convincingly while others try to guess which they think is the true story, and which is the false one.

The Carrousel

Define a focus for this exercise and divide participants into groups of five to eight people for rounds of small-group discussion (Figure 14.1). Decide whether each group will work on the same vision or mission statement or proposed action plan, or focus on a different aspect. Ask each group to prepare an outline of key aspects of their statement or plan, and elect a spokesperson for the group and a skilled note taker. Provide a common time frame for development of the outline. When ready, everyone from the group except the spokesperson and the note taker from each group visits another group to hear a presentation, provide comments and borrow ideas to advance their own thinking. Spokespeople and note takers stay at their original table to receive visiting groups, and to both present and take note of comments. Other rounds of visits to some or all other groups can follow, time permitting. Another option is for presenters and note takers to visit each group. Once the visits are completed, invite each group to reconvene and improve its initial outline based on the recorded comments and ideas received from other groups. The exercise ends with a plenary session where all groups present their revised vision, mission statements or action plan, with an emphasis on the new elements accepted from other groups (see Figure 14.1).

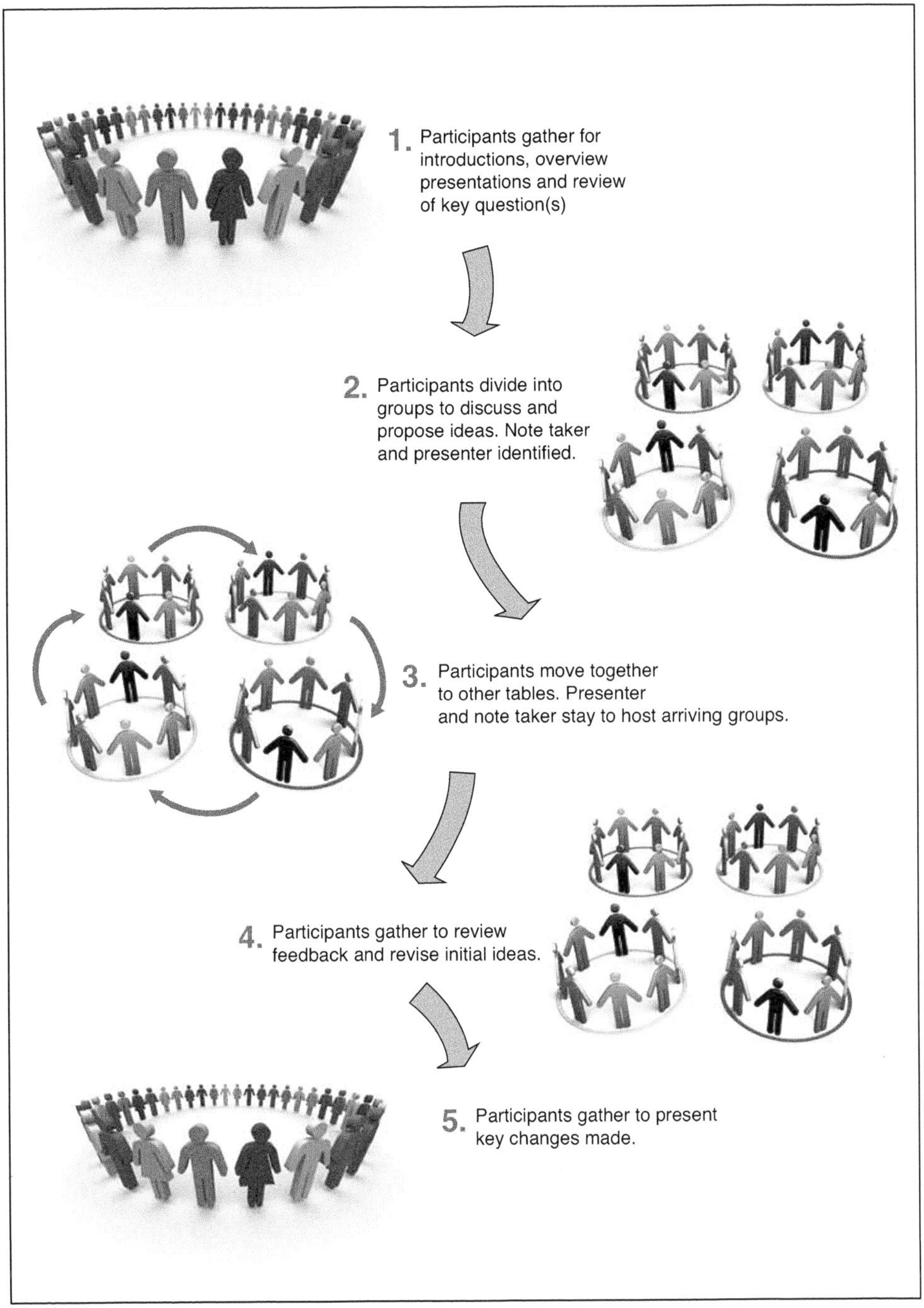
1. Participants gather for introductions, overview presentations and review of key question(s)
2. Participants divide into groups to discuss and propose ideas. Note taker and presenter identified.
3. Participants move together to other tables. Presenter and note taker stay to host arriving groups.
4. Participants gather to review feedback and revise initial ideas.
5. Participants gather to present key changes made.

FIGURE 14.1 Circulation of groups in *The Carrousel.*

Summary of this example: Quebec's ACCORD programme (Concerted Cooperative Action for Regional Development) fosters economic development in the province by supporting Niches of Excellence that are competitive in the North American context and globally as well. In October of 2010, the Ministère du Tourisme and the Ministère du Développement économique, de l'Innovation et de l'Exportation convened the first meeting of the committee responsible for consulting and engaging key players, businesses and leaders in developing a common vision of their niche and its brand image in the northern Quebec region of James Bay and Eeyou Istchee (Cree for 'The People's Land'). Sixteen Cree and non-native representatives from the region attended the meeting, which took place in the Cree community of Ouje-Bougoumou. In response to a request from the Ministry, J. M. Chevalier designed the meeting, in direct consultation with committee members, and facilitated the event.

The first day began with a brief presentation of the ACCORD programme and a brainstorming session on criteria to assess plans to develop a thriving tourism industry in the North. In the afternoon, participants prioritized criteria to be applied to the assessment of a formal statement and branding of their Niche of Excellence. On the whole, the committee felt that the Niche should be unique to the region, reach an international market and build on existing natural assets, infrastructure and human resources. It should be viable and sustainable, bring tangible benefits to the partners and communities involved, and remain under their effective control. Also, the overall approach used to develop the Niche should be participatory and be guided by principles of mutual trust, respect and effective teamwork.

The second day posed a greater challenge: agreeing on the precise wording of a shared vision of tourism in the North, a formal statement that would satisfy the above criteria and receive full committee endorsement and substantial financial backing from the government of Quebec. Several attempts at creating a regional committee around a vision that both natives and non-natives would endorse had previously failed. The facilitator proposed a twofold method to unblock the situation: *The Carrousel* (Figure 14.1) coupled with *The Socratic Wheel* (presented, with permissions, in the shape of a Dreamcatcher, an aboriginal symbol of unity). Participants formed three mixed groups (natives and non-natives) and used *The Carrousel* process to iron out differences in language and views regarding tourism in their region, towards a vision statement that everyone would be willing to endorse. In each round of discussion, participants were also asked to evaluate their own proposal and those of others against the criteria established on the previous day, now drawn as spokes in a Dreamcatcher diagram. At the end of the process, a brief plenary session allowed the committee to convert three negotiated statements into a final wording. This was done by underlining the key words and phrases that met with general approval, and using them to produce two complementary formulations: a message addressed to the general public, and a vision statement for ACCORD. The message invited the broader public to 'Discover the great open spaces of James Bay and Eeyou Istchee by travelling heritage routes through time. Learn and experience our living history and the Cree traditional land use and way of life.' The wording for ACCORD was slightly different and evoked an agreement to 'Position James Bay and Eeyou Istchee as a vast northern territory of rare natural beauty, rich in biodiversity, with a vibrant Cree culture to be discovered.' While they may seem noncontroversial, the two statements highlight the importance of Cree culture in a region inhabited by natives and non-natives, an issue that was debated and created some tension during the session. Both statements nonetheless received full support from all committee members, much to government officials' surprise. The rest of the day was dedicated to discussions about innovative products and services as well as strategies to further develop the proposed plan of action.

The Vision Circle

Define a specific focus for the vision, and invite participants to sit in a circle. Begin by asking participants to quietly think about an ideal situation relevant to the focus, including the gains that might result, the individual and group strengths and accomplishments that would be part of it, and the factors that would make it work. Then invite participants to close their eyes and offer one or two details of their vision, starting with the words 'I have a dream'. Others can join in whenever they are ready, without stopping to object or evaluate their own ideas or those of others. People can include the statements already heard and add new elements to the vision until the activity slows down naturally. The facilitator may ask questions about what the ideal situation looks like and ask if anyone has anything else they would like to add before the activity ends. Conclude with a brief discussion of what is exciting about the vision of the future, what feels possible and what was surprising in the visions shared.

The Tree of Means and Ends

Define a situation and draw a tree trunk that stands for a core goal shared by the group. Begin by asking participants 'What might happen if we achieve this goal?' and inviting them to write each response on a card using key words or a short positive sentence. Use *Free List and Pile Sort* to consolidate the cards into piles, and place them above the tree trunk as though they were branches and fruit. If the piles are directly related to each other, show this by placing them above or below each other, arranging them as main and secondary ramifications. Use the same process to identify the means or ways to achieve the goal, starting with the question 'What do we need to do or obtain to achieve our main goal?' Include all necessary means but leave out any that people think will have undesirable effects. Place these below the tree trunk and arrange them as main and secondary roots to show their interrelationship.

The Tree of Means and Ends is a mirror image of the *Problem Tree*, which centres on a core problem (the trunk) and its first-level and second-level causes (roots) and effects (branches). If the group has already done a problem tree, they can reframe the core problem into a positive statement as though it had already been achieved, and convert the causes and effects into means and ends. (See example in Chapter 9.)

MAKING IT WORSE

Sabotage

Purpose

To identify and overcome habits, established patterns, doubts, fears and other barriers to success, with a touch of humour.

Step 1

Define a plan, activity or project and ask participants to think of one or two things they or others could do to make sure it will fail completely. Record each **sabotage idea** on a separate card. Encourage creative responses and remind everyone that they are not committed to any of the sabotage ideas stated!

Step 2

Share the sabotage ideas. Use *Free List and Pile Sort* to organize them into categories (see Figure 14.2).

Step 3

Review the results and transform the sabotage ideas into positive statements, strategies or factors of success.

Variations

- Distinguish sabotage ideas that are certain to block or destroy all possibility of success, from those that are simply irritants or disruptions that are likely to undermine enthusiasm, efficiency or enjoyment of the plan, activity or project.

Combinations

- The Improvisational Theatre game *But versus And* can be a follow-up to *Sabotage* if one of the behaviours consists in being too critical or to censor oneself or others prematurely. To start, identify a proposed task or action related to the issues under discussion. Ask participants to comment negatively on the proposed plan or task, starting each sentence with 'Yes, but . . .' After a few minutes of critical feedback, ask the group(s) to comment on the same task or action starting each sentence with 'Yes, and . . .' Review and contrast the two rounds of discussion and how people feel about the plans emerging from each round. The exercise can incorporate other *Active Listening* tips (Chapter 8) as well.

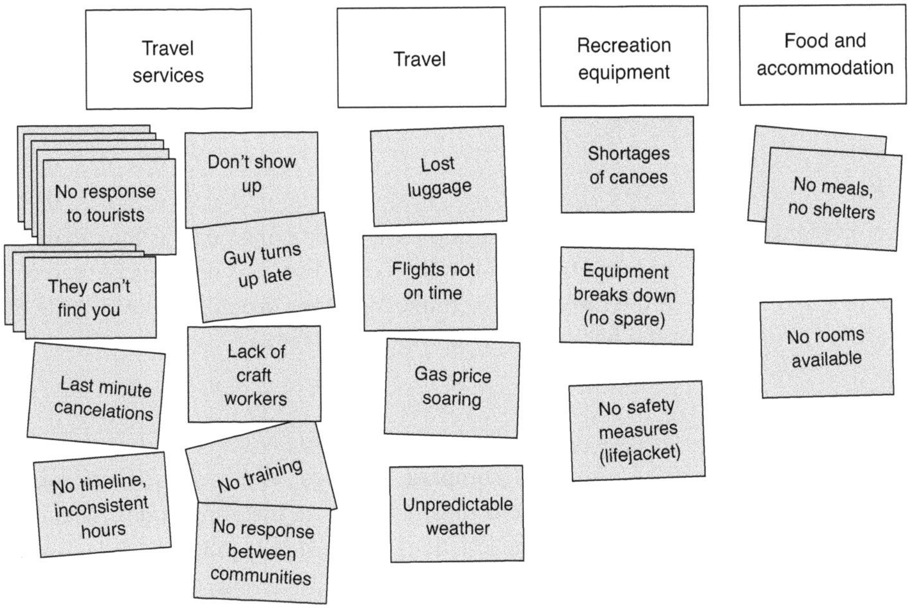

FIGURE 14.2 How to sabotage hunting and fishing tourism in Mistissini, Northern Quebec.

SOURCES OF DISPUTE

Disagreements and Misunderstandings

Purpose

To rank stakeholders' goals in order of importance, and review disagreements or misunderstandings people may have about these goals.

Step 1

Define the **situation** and ask participants to list the key **goals** and competing priorities they have using positive terms. Goals may be objectives, activities or the moral values that people hold. Define these goals clearly, using key words or a picture to describe each goal.

Step 2

Divide the participants into **two groups** based on some significant difference relevant to the situation (such as men and women, management and workers, community members and government officials, rich and poor, etc.). Ask each group to gather separately (perhaps in another room), write each goal on its own card, and then **rank** the goals in order of importance from first to last (see *Ranking*, Chapter 8). The most important goal should be numbered 1, with each score recorded below the goal written on the corresponding card.

Step 3

Once the ranking is complete, ask each group to rank the same goals as they think the other group would have ranked them. This will produce two rankings, one of their own priorities, and another of the **ranking they think the other group will have.** Write the second set of scores on the back of each corresponding card.

Step 4

Come together as a single group to **compare** rankings of the cards. First look for similarities and differences in **actual priorities**, and discuss the implications. Then look at each group's **understanding** of the priorities of the other group, and discuss the implications. Members of each group may wish to discuss these issues among themselves before sharing their views with the other group, especially if there is a lot at stake.

To show the order of priorities physically, ask members of each group to distribute cards among themselves and to form **two lines** facing each other, with cards in their hands, in the order of the groups' priorities. Discuss the differences, and then ask one line to reorganize itself as they thought the other group would have ranked the goals. Discuss the misunderstandings of this group, and then reorganize again to discuss the misunderstandings of the other group.

Step 5

Levels of disagreement combined with levels of misunderstanding produce **six possible scenarios** (see Table 14.1). Identify the scenario that best reflects the findings of the exercise.

TABLE 14.1 *Disagreeements and Misunderstandings* – six scenarios

Scenario	*Understanding*		*Misunderstanding*
Agreement	**Scenario 1** The parties agree and both know it	**Scenario 2** The parties agree but one doesn't know it	**Scenario 3** The parties agree but don't know it
Disagreement	**Scenario 4** The parties disagree and both know it	**Scenario 5** The parties disagree but one doesn't know it	**Scenario 6** The parties disagree but don't know it

TABLE 14.2 Competing project priorities of men and women in Mehi, West Bengal, India

Priorities	*Men*	*Women*	*Disagreement*	*Ranking by women for men*	*Women's misunderstanding*	*Ranking by men for women*	*Men's misunderstanding*
Mixed cropping	2	3	1	3	1	5	2
Fisheries	1	4	3	2	1	2	2
Grain bank	4	2	2	4	0	3	1
Road construction	6	6	0	1	5	6	0
Children's nursery	3	1	2	5	2	4	3
Kitchen garden	5	5	0	6	1	1	4
All activities			**8/18**		**10/18**		**12/18**

Summary of this example: Mehi is a small village some 336 kilometres from Kolkata in the district of Purulia, West Bengal. In May 2006 the non-governmental organization Development, Research, Communication and Services Centre (DRCSC) convened villagers as part of a strategic planning process. DRCSC wanted to know the priorities of male and female villagers before deciding on the renewal of six different development projects that had been in place for several years. At their request, D. J. Buckles designed and facilitated discussion among twenty or so villagers, most of whom were married couples. In separate men's and women's groups, the participants reviewed and ranked the projects from the most to the least beneficial. Differences within each group were resolved through discussion until a consensus was reached. Once both groups had finished ranking, they imagined the ranking the other group might have made (see Table 14.2). Participants then compared rankings by forming two lines of people (men and women) holding the pictures they had made of each project in the priority they had indicated. After a discussion of major differences between the two groups, the order was shuffled to show how each group guessed the priorities of the other group. This led to a discussion of misunderstandings between the two groups. People were able to see the conclusions right in front of them, without having to create and discuss a summary table.

Differences in priorities, and the negotiation of future plans, centred around three activities: maintaining fish ponds, the children's nursery and the grain bank. The exercise showed there was little disagreement on the relative priority of the other projects. The level of misunderstanding, however, was high for both groups. Women nevertheless showed a slightly better understanding of men's priorities than the other way around. Men overestimated the benefits women see in the kitchen garden project. They also underestimated the benefits women see in the children's nursery project. According to participants, the high level of misunderstanding when it comes to the priorities of the other gender pointed to a communication gap between men and women, even within households. Several of the men remarked on this communication gap and said they planned to discuss priorities with their wives more often. DRCSC used the results as a strategic input into future project planning.

Step 6 (optional)

To measure **levels of disagreement** and **levels of misunderstanding** between the rankings and priorities of the two groups, create a table (see Table 14.2). To assess levels of disagreement, total the differences between same-goal rankings of the two groups. Then, divide this number by the maximum difference that could have been generated by the two ranked lists. If ranks range from 1 to 6, then the maximum difference is 6 – 1, 5 – 2, 4 – 3, 3 – 4, 5 – 2, and 6 – 1, for a total difference of 18. Multiply the result by 100; this gives you the percentage level of disagreement. To assess **levels of misunderstanding**, use the same calculations by comparing the actual rankings of each group with the rankings attributed to them by the other group.

FAQ

- ***Can the use of different ranking methods by each group affect the result?***

Ranking, while a simple concept, is subject to misdirection and manipulation in a group context. Explore in advance any local methods for ranking, and consult the tool *Ranking* (Chapter 8) for ideas on how to minimize bias and the pressures of group cohesion. Consider asking the group if they are willing to use a common method suggested by the facilitator.

Variations

- To compare the rankings of **more than two groups**, identify the **two goals** where people seem to **disagree** the most. Create a diagram by drawing a vertical line that

PHOTO 14.1 Men's ranking of their development priorities in Edmonton, Alberta. (Source: D. J. Buckles)

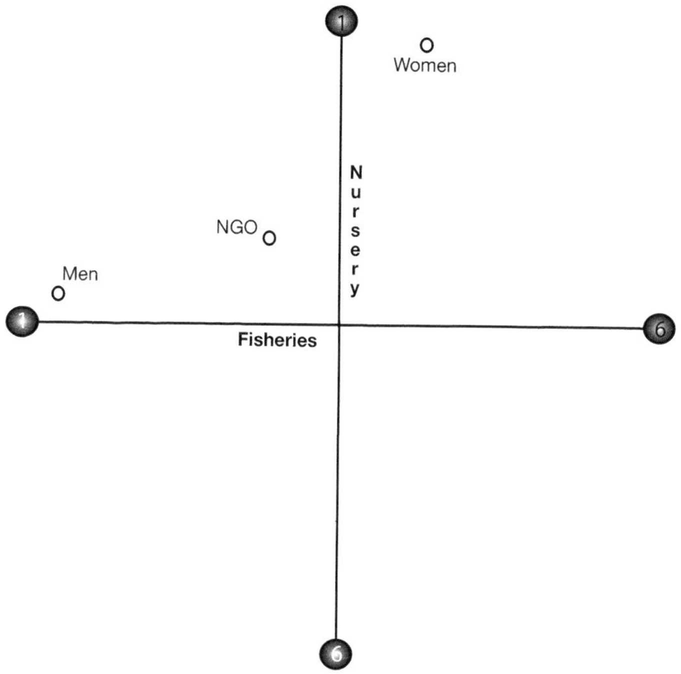

FIGURE 14.3 Comparing the ranking of two options by three different groups.

crosses a horizontal line of equal length. Use the vertical line to represent one goal, and the horizontal line to represent the other. Write the lowest and the highest ranking numbers at the opposite ends of each line. Place each group's name into the diagram where the group's rankings on the two goals intersect (see Figure 14.3).

Combinations

- To explore the reasons that may account for differences in group rankings, use *Interests* (Chapter 12) or *Values, Interests, Positions (VIP)* (Chapter 13).

Competing principles of government consultation with natives in Canada

In February of 2010, *Disagreements and Misunderstandings* helped Canadian government officials and native community land use planners in the Northern Ontario Oji-Cree community of Keewaywin compare their respective views on what effective consultation means and the competing principles behind them. The meeting was designed and facilitated by J. M. Chevalier.

The two groups created a common list of effective consultation criteria without difficulty (see Table 14.3). Comparisons between the rankings of these criteria by each group and their predictions of the other group's rankings showed disagreement regarding

TABLE 14.3 Competing principles of government consultation with natives in Canada

Priorities	*Government rankings*	*Community rankings*	*Disagreement*	*Government prediction of ranking by community*	*Government's misunderstanding*	*Community prediction of ranking by government*	*Community's misunderstanding*
Participation	2	1	1	3	2	4	2
Trust (authenticity)	3	4	1	2	2	5	2
Treaty rights	1	2	1	1	1	6	5
Rainbow dialogue	5	3	2	5	2	2	3
Timeline (results)	4	6	2	6	0	1	3
Conflict resolution	6	5	1	4	1	3	3
All activities			**8/18**		**8/18**		**18/18**

the importance of meeting deadlines (*Timeline results* more important to the government) and promoting dialogue between all the parties concerned (*Rainbow dialogue* more important to community participants). *Participation* and *Treaty rights*, however, were top priorities for both groups, a finding that surprised community participants who had considerable difficulty predicting the rankings of government officials. On the whole they underestimated the importance that government officials grant to *Treaty rights*, *Participation* and *Trust*. They also overestimated the importance that government officials grant to *Timeline (results)*, *Rainbow dialogue* and *Conflict resolution*.

When asked to explain this high level of misunderstanding of government priorities on the part of community members, two reasons emerged. First, the government had recently made a shift in its approach to native community consultation. Second, community participants felt that what the government says is not necessarily what the government does. For instance, while government officials consider that recognition of *Treaty rights* is a given, community participants believe that respect for *Treaty rights* has always been a problem and is likely to remain a source of mistrust and conflict.

READINESS TO PROCEED

Levels of Support

Purpose

To determine whether there is enough support from stakeholders to go on with a proposal or course of action, before any final decision or vote is taken (Adapted from Kaner, 1996).

Step 1

Identify or describe a proposal or **course of action** under consideration. Create a descriptive title or drawing, or identify an object that represents the proposal or course of action.

Step 2

Create an **agreement scale** to assess the level of support. The scale should consist of up to **nine statements** and no less than four statements ranging from the most negative to the most positive response to the proposal or course of action. Use phrases and local expressions that are meaningful to the people involved (see Table 14.4).

Step 3

Discuss whether participants should express their level of support as individuals, as subgroups or as a whole group. Also discuss whether they should express their level of support **openly** or **anonymously**.

Step 4

Ask each participant, subgroup or the whole group to choose the **support level** that best represents their response to the proposal or course of action, and to indicate their response on the agreement scale.

Step 5

Review the distribution of marks on the agreement scale. Discuss whether there is enough support from stakeholders to go on with the proposal or course of action, and concerns reflected in the responses. If the level of support is not as high as the group wants or needs it to be or if key stakeholders reject the proposal, participants may wish to **modify** the proposal or course of action so that it can address concerns and has enough support to succeed.

When discussing the distribution of marks on the agreement scale, invite participants to **express their concerns** directly, or use **role-play** to anonymously raise concerns people may have. Give special attention to low levels of support that may come from key stakeholders.

TABLE 14.4 Levels of support

X		X X X		X X X	X	X X X X X X X X X X X X X X X	X X	X X X X X X
I will fight this	I'm against it	I don't like it but I won't oppose it	I'm not sure	I agree, reluctantly	As long as others do the work	It's worth the risk	It's a good idea	This is great

FAQ

- ***Should the scale include an odd or even number of choices?***

An even number will force a choice, either slightly in favour or slightly against. An odd number will allow people to remain neutral or abstain if that is how they feel about the proposal. Context and purpose will point to one scale or the other.

Combinations

- Once a plan or key decision is reached using any inquiry or planning tool from this book (or from other sources), stakeholders may use *Levels of Support* to see if stakeholders are ready to proceed. If there is not enough support, *Social Analysis CLIP* (Chapter 12), *Contribution and Feasibility* (Chapter 15) or *Values, Interests, Positions* (Chapter 13) may help determine the reasons for the lack of support.

Levels of support for community woodlots in Kajla, West Bengal, India

Kajla is a village in the Purba Medinipur District of West Bengal, India. About 10 per cent of the people who live here are landless. The men from the village migrate seasonally for work in other areas, leaving their families without support for long periods of time. The Development, Research, Communication and Services Centre (DRCSC), an NGO based in Kolkata, has international funding to support the development of community woodlots in Kajla for use by landless households. For the last fifteen years, DRCSC has worked jointly with Kajla Jana Kalyan Samity (KJKS), a community-based organization. Support from KJKS staff, landless families and local authorities (known as the Panchayat) is vital for the project to succeed. Support from the irrigation department of the state government is also needed, since it controls some of the land in the village that might be used for woodlots.

To assess existing support for the initiative, S. Panda of DRCSC facilitated a consultation with stakeholders at the Kajla primary school (Panda, 2008). Some thirty-eight people attended, including sixteen landless villagers, six KJKS staff, several members of the irrigation department and other people from the village and the *Gram Panchayat*. The meeting began with the presentation of a proposal to establish community woodlots, including plans to plant trees on the roadside, canal banks and fallow areas. KJKS described the potential benefits of the plan, including the landless households' improved access to fuel, food and fodder. Participants stated their views and concerns about the proposal, which were noted on cards. They piled similar opinions together and chose the simplest phrase from among them to represent each pile. The facilitating team lined up the nine phrases, accompanied by pictures, on the ground, from the most positive at one end to the most negative at the other. Each participant then placed a piece of brick beside the opinion he or she most strongly agreed with. The exercise ended with a discussion of the overall level of support, the level needed for the proposal to succeed and possible revisions to make it better.

TABLE 14.5 Levels of support for community woodlots in Kajla, West Bengal, India

xx	*x*	*x*		*xxxx*	*xxxx*	*xx*	*xxx* *xxxx* *xxxx* *xxxx*	*xxxx*
Tree planting not possible	Trees can't be protected	Land needs to be prepared	Not all people will contribute	Tree planting is a good idea	Tree planting is important	Though risk of loss, will be done	We will plant on roadside	We will fully support woodlots

The level of support for community woodlots is presented in Table 14.5. Four participants gave their support to *all* aspects of the proposal. Almost half the group (15/33) gave full support for community woodlots on the roadside and indicated they were willing to invest time and effort in this project. A few recognized the risk of wasting their time on this but said they would help to get it done. When discussing the final results, participants remarked that most of those who were supporting the proposal were landless families who tend to welcome outside help and resources and stand to gain from converting unused roadside state property into community woodlots.

Some agreed that while the community woodlot was important they would not be willing to assist directly. Four individuals expressed very low levels of support or opposition to the proposal. They voiced concerns about the amount of effort needed to prepare the land properly and whether or not the trees could be protected. A community woodlot might also hamper cattle grazing. These comments came mostly from villagers with land of their own and little to gain directly from the initiative. Most of them were not directly involved in the proposed activity. Nor were they in a position to block uses of public lands by landless groups.

The participants, including the various organizations involved in the proposal, agreed to create community woodlots on only part of the roadside and canal bank, covering an area 2.5 kilometres in length. They would consider woodlots on other lands once there was evidence to show that the project benefitted all community members and did not hamper cattle grazing. KJKS would take on the task of making sure that group members share the workload needed to prepare the land properly and protect the trees.

The majority felt confident that there was sufficient support in the village to proceed with the revised proposal focussing on the roadside and canal bank. Several participants said that they appreciated how the exercise had led to modification of the proposal rather than a simple approval or rejection that might have resulted from a standard voting procedure.

STAKEHOLDER EXPECTATIONS

Negotiation Fair

Purpose

To assess and negotiate what stakeholders can expect of each other.

Step 1

List all the **key stakeholders (individuals or groups)** that wish to work together to achieve common goals. Consider whether to include representatives of a group as a stakeholder different from those they represent and the community of all stakeholders as a group with its own profile. Create a flip chart or 'post box' for each stakeholder able to participate in the exercise.

Step 2

Establish a **rating scale** for levels of interaction among stakeholders, from 0 to 3 or 0 to 5. Alternatively, use simple phrases or measurable objects (high, medium, low or colourful stickers, for instance) instead of numbers to set a scale.

Step 3

Ask each stakeholder to create one **card** for each other stakeholder. Each card should indicate who it is from and to whom it is addressed.

Step 4

On each card, rate the **current level of interaction** with the other stakeholder (and the community of all stakeholders) and a desired or **expected level of interaction**. Members within a stakeholder group can also rate the current and expected levels of interaction among themselves. Record the ratings on the corresponding card (see Figure 14.4). Determine the **time** needed to achieve the expected level of interaction.

Step 5

Write on the back of the card the **reasons** given for the two scores. Also describe what can be done to achieve the expected level of interaction. This should include **offering** to do something for the other stakeholder as well as saying what they would like to **receive**.

Step 6

Make a **copy** of each completed card for later discussions. **Post** all original cards on the flip chart or in the 'post box' of the stakeholder the card is addressed to.

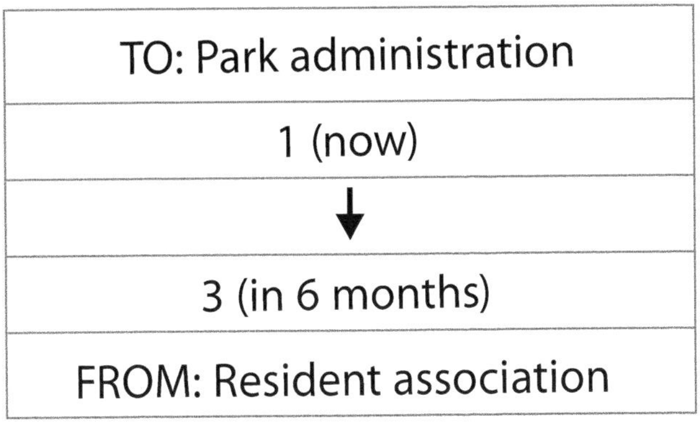

FIGURE 14.4 Levels of interaction, perceived and expected.

Step 7

Invite each stakeholder to **read the cards** they receive from others and decide which other stakeholder they would like to meet immediately to explore mutual expectations and reach agreements.

Step 8

Set a time for a **negotiation fair** during which any stakeholder can meet any other stakeholder to discuss mutual expectations and specific ways to meet them. When two stakeholders reach an agreement, they can put their agreement in writing and sign it, noting things that need more discussion or approvals from others that are still needed.

Step 9

All stakeholders can present their agreements in a **plenary session**, if they so wish. Consider ending the exercise by inviting all stakeholders to stand in a large circle to present their **expectations of the community of all stakeholders**, starting with the phrase 'Imagine if . . .' (and taking one step closer to the centre of the circle after each statement). Discuss these expectations and ways to meet them.

FAQ

- ***Isn't there a risk that some stakeholders will not receive cards from others?***

If people do not know what they can expect from each other, prior work may be needed to create the conditions for working together. If many stakeholders in a particular context do not need to interact with each other, focus on the level of interaction that exists between one or two key stakeholders and all other stakeholders.

Variations

- To facilitate the active negotiation of agreements, without detailed assessment of current and expected levels of agreement, focus only on the offerings and requests made by each party. These can be treated as 'letters' sent and received that express concrete ways of strengthening collaboration around specific activities.
- Introduce a touch of humour by asking each stakeholder to describe on the back of one card an offer or a request that is greatly exaggerated or completely unexpected, which other groups will try to detect. Each group can also choose a symbol (plant, animal) to represent themselves.
- Encourage parties to announce agreements or successful conclusions to a discussion by clapping, congratulating each other, launching a balloon or making some other celebratory gesture.

Combinations

- Use *The Socratic Wheel* or a Cartesian graph (see example below) to show the current and expected levels of interaction among stakeholders.

YouthScape engagement and project team expectations, Canada

YouthScape is a national initiative to build resilient communities by engaging excluded or marginalized youth in the planning and implementing of community development initiatives in five cities in Canada. The International Institute for Child Rights and Development (IICRD) facilitated and supports the initiative through ongoing research and by providing assistance in community-youth capacity building, developmental evaluation and broader web-based networking through TakingItGlobal (TIG).

In early November of 2006, IICRD held a symposium in Montreal and invited J. M. Chevalier to facilitate a half-day evaluation and strategic planning of YouthScape. The session was designed to assess existing levels of interaction and strategies to improve collaborative ties between YouthScape teams, using *Negotiation Fair*. The exercise began with the creation of six natural teams and animal totems to represent them: the advisory team (owls), youth and TIG (eagles), IICRD (thunderbirds), the administrators (marmots), the coordinators (beavers) and the developmental evaluators (butterflies). The second step consisted in each team rating its current and ideal levels of interaction within the team (self), with each other team and with YouthScape as a whole (all teams).

Discussions that followed allowed teams to explore each other's expectations and means to improve existing relations (Chevalier, 2008). Briefly, several tentative agreements emerged from bilateral discussions between YouthScape teams.

- Thunderbirds (IICRD) agreed to relay more clearly to eagles (youth and TIG) what role IICRD plays in the YouthScape initiative. They also agreed to work with TIG at improving transparency and involving more youth in gatherings and the planning of meetings.

- Butterflies (developmental evaluators) will give beavers (coordinators) more 'breathing room' and begin to focus more on community activity.
- Marmots (administrators) will draw more on the strengths of the owl team, by bringing advisors in as resource persons more often, at least when dealing with issues that go beyond daily tasks.

The time available (2.5 hours) to complete the *Negotiation Fair* was somewhat limited, at some cost to the breadth and depth of YouthScape's thinking and planning process. On the whole, however, the objectives of the session were largely met. The facilitator later undertook the task of preparing a more detailed report to support further YouthScape thinking and planning. Data presented in the report indicated that of all teams, the eagles (youth and TIG) had higher expectations in regards to increasing their level of interaction with all other teams. Also teams expected to increase their level of interaction mostly with thunderbirds (IICRD), eagles (youth and TIG) and beavers (coordinators).

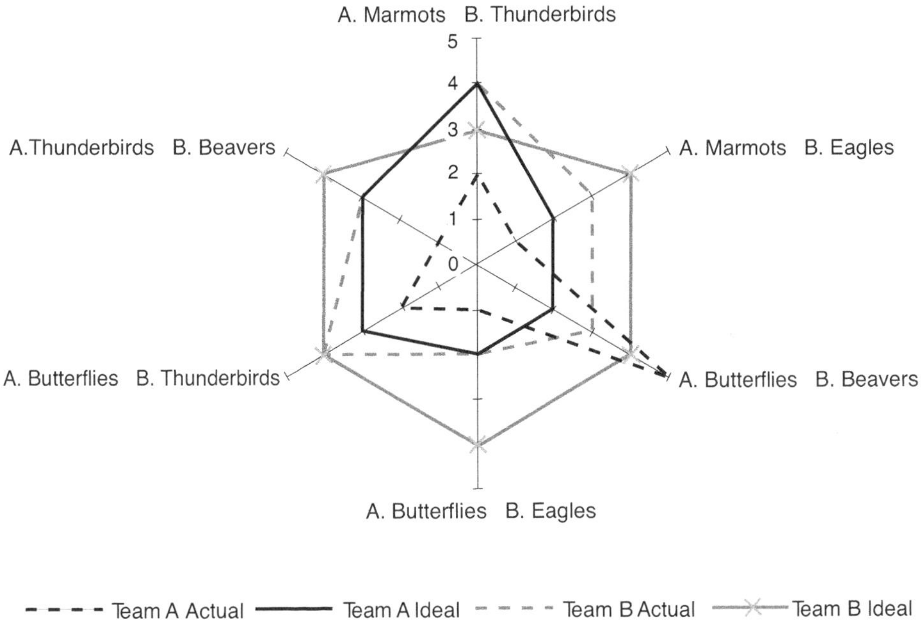

FIGURE 14.5 Comparing levels of interaction, perceived and expected.

The four lines appearing in this figure mark different levels of interaction for each pair of teams: i.e. how Team A rates its actual (dotted, black line) and ideal levels (black line, continuous) of interaction with Team B, on the one hand, as distinct from how Team B rates its actual (dotted, grey line) and ideal levels (grey line, marked by an X) of interaction with Team B, on the other.

Of the 30 ratings describing YouthScape team interactions and expectations, about two thirds reflected shared views of current and ideal levels of interaction. The remaining one third, described in Figure 14.5, pointed to significant differences between perceived interactions and expectations. For instance, the marmot team (administrators) wished to interact more (from 2 to 4) with thunderbirds (IICRD) who in turn would have preferred to interact less (going from 4 to 3). Similarly, marmots (administrators) and eagles (youth and TIG) wanted to interact more, but marmots planned on going from level 1 to level 2 while eagles wished to go as high as level 4.

The report presented a synthetic view of perceived and expected levels of interaction using network analysis software called InFlow. The upper diagram in Figure 14.6 shows existing ties, while the lower diagram represents the ideal scenario. One-way arrows indicate strong ties (rated 3, 4 or 5) in one direction only. Two-way arrows indicate strong ties in both directions. The close distance and thicker lines between teams or between each team and 'self' indicates stronger relationships.

The figure and related statistics generated with InFlow pointed to several important observations. One is that of the forty-nine potential ties that all teams could develop,

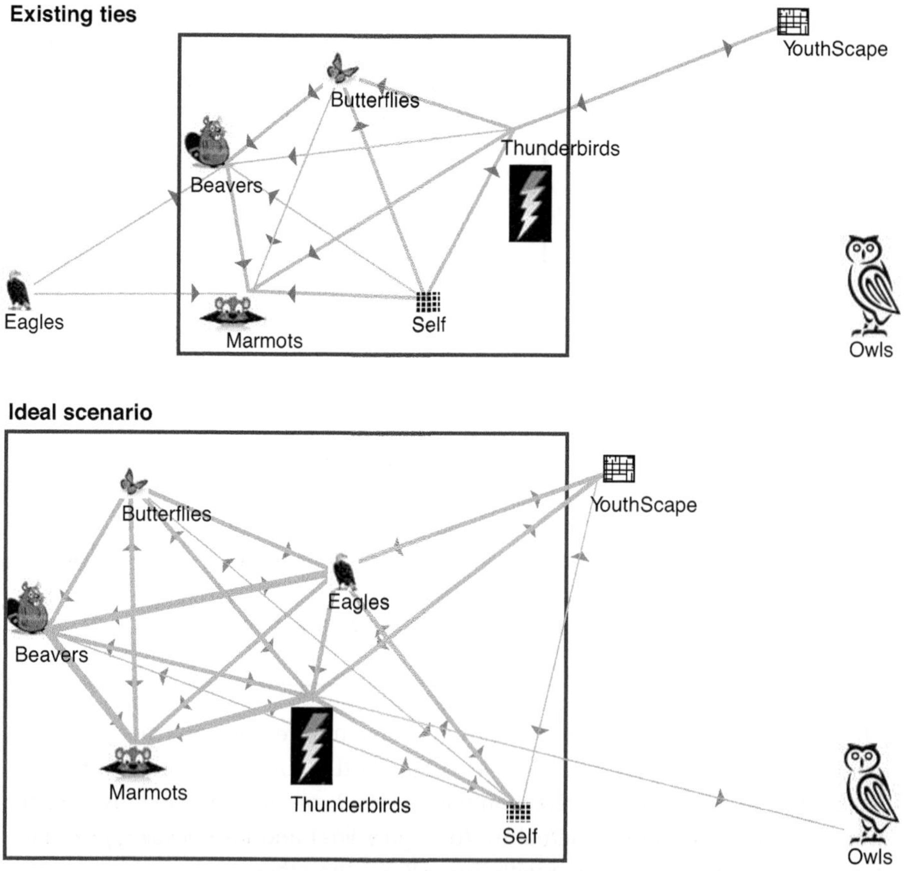

FIGURE 14.6 Existing YouthScape ties and ideal levels of interaction.

sixteen strong ties (rated 3 to 5) currently exist, for a network density of 33 per cent. In the ideal scenario reflecting team expectations, network density would practically double and go up to 61 per cent, with thirty-four strong ties (rated 3 to 5) developed out of fifty-six potential ties. Closeness or access to other team members, to other teams and to YouthScape as a whole would also double, from 37 per cent to 74 per cent.

THREADS OF THEORY: GLOBAL VENTRILOQUISM

Social scientists speaking a language that transcends culture and history are ventriloquists. They utter sounds that appear to come from elsewhere, usually from above. These are lofty voices that speak for everyone and that very few speak. 'Transcendental ventriloquism' turns actors into puppets and dummies. Language grounded in history and pluralism of the mind is silenced.

Thinking grounded in history is sensitive to nuance and variation in language and meaning. Research exhibiting the trappings of authoritative science and philosophy lacks this sensitivity. A case in point is the ruling wisdom of stratification theory or political economy based on sweeping definitions of class and the exercise of power, universal concepts spread around the world and across history. Definitive theories of conflict, violence, poverty, justice or well-being are equally problematical. Let's face it, when it comes to generating stories from Universals, every grand theorist is a director working in a competing studio.

Social scientists should let go of their commanding voices and universal stories, especially those that are full of voiceless puppets and have no audience other than themselves. Instead, they should write the kind of history that makes room at the table of knowledge and sensemaking and where all actors are invited to author compelling dialogues and scripts. While contributing to the grand narrative of science, social scientists should be stakeholders in the business of promoting pluralism of voice, language and meaning. They can draw their inspiration from a flexible use of language and a detachment from all definitive idioms and investments in hegemonic theory. If anything, the role of social inquiry and theory is to remind us that the invariants of life remain artificial essences, like oils extracted from the real world. In the language of Sartre, essences are crucial, but their strategic existence in language and history precedes and rules them. From this perspective, nothing should become a dogma, not even the idea that human universals are absolutely meaningless. Rebellious minds about to be shot at dawn will appreciate the paradox.

Commentary

To question the language of inquiry, one must inquire into the question of language. Answers to this query often revolve around the quintessential requirements of clarity and logic. In the first half of the twentieth century, analytic philosophers such as Russell, Frege, Carnap, Quine and the young Wittgenstein (1981) were of the view that ordinary language is too ambiguous and confusing to solve major issues in philosophy. Nor can it spearhead the forward march of science. Sweeping philosophical systems that use obscure language are also hopeless. As in the natural sciences, formal logic and clear reasoning, uninfluenced by culture, language and historical context, are needed to better deal with science and also with philosophy that speaks to the nature of knowledge and language. This idea is in many ways a return to the notion that mathematics is a universal language.

From the 1940s onwards, analytic philosophers such as Austin, Ryle and the older Wittgenstein took a radical turn towards ordinary language and language analysis, showing how a better understanding of native speech can help resolve some of the most abstract problems in philosophy. Ordinary language thinkers now pay attention to the multiple and malleable ways in which words function in different contexts. They no longer trust abstract words to capture universal ideas. This implies that no direct relationship can be posited between abstract words such as 'cause', 'evidence' or 'knowing' and clearly identifiable things that exist 'out there', like 'tables' and 'chairs'. The word 'cause' employed in the English language must be explored instead for its contribution to doing things and communicating on a day-to-day basis.

In his *Philosophical Investigations*, Wittgenstein (1999) thus abandons the search for a perfect language that brings together 'simples', ultimate logical facts or atoms that cannot be broken down any further. He warns us against the illusory problems that philosophy is prone to create through 'bewitchments by language', ignoring the fact that language is fundamentally part of how people conduct their lives and interact with others. Metaphysics err in forcing language out of its proper home and depriving it of the contextual clues needed to make it work. In real life, clarity of meaning doesn't come from strict dictionary-like rules of reference or the classificatory logic of 'essential' features, those shared by all items covered by a term. Intelligibility comes rather from the flexible and intuitive use of words grounded in social settings and 'forms of life'. What a word or sentence means thus depends on the language-game in which it is used and the particular rules that apply to that game, which are neither universal nor purely personal or private. The same word played out in different games will mean different things. Given its flexible application in context, a word like 'cause' or 'game' must connect things within a 'family of resemblance' characterized by overlapping similarities – common features that are spun roughly, like fibre on fibre, without a single thread that runs throughout the entire family. The strength of such words does not reside 'in the fact that some one fibre runs through its whole length, but in the overlapping of many fibres . . . For how is the concept of a game bounded? What still counts as a game and what no longer does? Can you give the boundary? No.' (Wittgenstein, 1999, pp. 67–68)

The same reasoning applies to words such as 'rule' and 'meaning'. Tying ourselves into philosophical knots over these terms is time wasted. The words have no essential meaning. They are deeply woven into our lives and stand for complex social phenomena that cannot be accurately defined. All acts of speech weave their way into actions that blend into each other through 'family resemblances', playing themselves out through multiple games that vary according to context and purpose. Paradoxically, this no-rule principle is a general rule, to which there is no exception. It applies to all word games, even those that revolve around the word 'game'. Wittgenstein's strategic handling of the word confirms the point. Wittgenstein uses the word in a particular context, to the exclusion of other possible connections within the broader family of activities called 'games'. When handling this word, the philosopher makes a move in language, taking sides in a family dispute that warrants further investigation.

What is Wittgenstein's stance on the 'language-game'? In his later writings, the expression denotes primitive forms of language that can be invented to help children learn language or philosophers clarify the workings of language. The expression also points to the infinite plurality of language practices and situations (including whole languages) that people can engage in and fashion according to purpose. This framing of 'language-games' creates a 'family of resemblance' that brings together four attributes: simplicity, usefulness, regulation and playfulness understood as elusive change and freedom of action and movement. If this framing is accepted, all other possible readings of 'language-game' into *Philosophical Investigations* must be ruled out. For instance, the expression cannot evoke people playing word tricks on each other, competing for alternative ways to manipulate a particular 'family of resemblance', gambling on some usages instead of others. Nor can it conjure up an imagery of deceitful moves, in the direction of power, a playing field where mastery for the few means a yoke for the rest. In Wittgensteinian philosophy, a language-game is not designed to ridicule or 'make game' of the weak and the defenceless, taking profit from those who are 'fair game' for exploitation reinforced by ideology and slanted discourse.

Political interpretations of Wittgenstein's language-game expression are mistaken, one might say. Declaring these proposed readings as misrepresentations of Wittgenstein, however, is self-defeating. After all, Wittgensteinian statements cannot be simply false or true; rather they are moves in language that make sense in context. Given this ruling, political 'misreadings' of Wittgenstein should be understood for what they are, namely, 'alternative moves', manoeuvres to see through ordinary language thinking, with the intent of giving the game away. If so, where is this secret game going? Could it be in the direction of scheming and plotting, as in 'hide and seek' – hide the playing field of power in language, by not letting anyone see through it?

Naming this counter-playing field gives us Lyotard's concept of the *differend*, partly inspired by Wittgenstein. A *differend* is a conflict between discourses that are incommensurable, with no rules that apply across the discourses, not even rules of appeal for the wrong suffered by those whose language is silenced (Lyotard, 1984, 1988). Wittgenstein's scheme against politics in language also conjures up Bourdieu's concept of agency and positioning in the field of language. As with any social field, language is a structured space governed by its own prereflexive rules and schemes of domination, practical dispositions that define the extent to which someone has the right to be listened to, ask questions and provide answers. Moves, positions and dispositions in language fall under the rule of an unconscious *doxa* that defines what is taken for granted and goes without saying in a particular setting, including the rulings of class distinction and domination (Bourdieu, 1977).

Language is more than a simple and useful game, a field of playful and flexible logic that achieves clarity and usefulness in context. It is also a dangerous game to play, with serious stakes, obscure motives and interests, not to mention attacks of the few on the freedom of speech and action by the many. Language is a battleground for words and interpretations competing for attention, contending for the status of authoritative meanings, universal buzzwords or categorical imperatives of the mind. In this perspective, the essentialism denounced by Wittgenstein is not an error. More to the point, it is a move in hegemonic theory. As Spivak (1987) observes, the move is wrong in the sense of being objectionable, worth opposing through counterhegemonic actions and subaltern voices that speak to and struggle for an alternative world. Paradoxically, the voices of otherness may welcome the opportunity to dress up their common cause in the language of essentialism, knowing that new 'universals' will last for a reason and for a while, confident that they have justice and history on their side.

If we were to look for the essence of language, if only strategically, where should we go? Perhaps in moves to resolve a fundamental family dispute centred on two competing games: one that features the rule of plurality and freedom, as in Wittgenstein, and another that disputes the exercise of power, as in Lyotard and Bourdieu. Language is playful enough that it can let these two games intersect. All parties stand to gain. They can take pleasure in voicing their views and 'coming together' to enjoy the game as a 'game' (from O.E. *gamen* 'joy, fun, amusement', and also Goth. *gaman* 'participation, communion', or 'people together'). At the same time they can contest competing pronouncements of language and rulings on discourse, without fear.

REFERENCES

Bourdieu, P. (1977) *Outline of a Theory of Practice*, Cambridge University Press, Cambridge and New York.

Chevalier, J. M. (2008) 'YouthScape network evaluation and planning', SAS^2 Community of Practice: IDRC Digital Repository, Ottawa, ON.

Kaner, S. with Lind, L., Toldi, C., Fisk, S. and Berger, D. (1996) *Facilitator's Guide to Participatory Decision-Making*, New Society Publishers, Gabriola Island.

Lyotard, J.-F. (1984) *The Postmodern Condition: A Report on Knowledge*, trans. Geoff Bennington and Brian Massumi, University of Minnesota Press, Minneapolis, MN.

Lyotard, J.-F. (1988) *The Differend: Phrases in Dispute*, trans. Georges Van Den Abbeele, University of Minnesota Press, Minneapolis, MN.

Panda, S. (2008) 'Levels of support for community woodlots in Kajla, West Bengal, India', in J. M. Chevalier and D. J. Buckles (eds) *SAS^2: A Guide to Collaborative Inquiry and Social Engagement*, Sage and IDRC, Delhi and Ottawa.

Spivak, G. (1987) *In Other Worlds: Essays in Cultural Politics*, Taylor and Francis, London.

Wittgenstein, L. (1981) *Tractatus Logico-Philosophicus*, D. F. Pears (ed.), Routledge, London.

Wittgenstein, L. (1999) *Philosophical Investigations*, trans. Gertrude Elizabeth Margaret Anscombe, Prentice Hall, Englewood Cliffs, NJ.

CHAPTER 15

Into the future

INTRODUCTION

Chapter 14 was mostly about visions and priorities for the future. In this chapter, we propose various methods to assess the consequences or risks associated with:

- things that are likely to happen if nothing is done to prevent them (*Hazards, Projections, What If*);
- possible courses of action (*Contribution and Feasibility, Results and Risks*).

Our foray into forward-looking diagnostic tools begins with a methodology to assess and plan community-based disaster relief and risk reduction, using illustrative material from the Philippines. The proposed methodology combines two tools from this chapter, *Hazards* and *Contribution and Feasibility*, with methods presented and illustrated in previous chapters, i.e. *Process Mapping* (Chapter 5), *Timeline* (Chapter 9), *Stakeholder Rainbow* (Chapter 11), *Values, Interests, Positions* (Chapter 13), *Levels of Support* (Chapter 14) and *The Carrousel* (Chapter 14).

DISASTER RELIEF AND RISK REDUCTION IN THE PHILIPPINES

The Philippines lies on the Pacific Ring of Fire. Volcanic eruptions and earthquakes are frequent because of the collision of tectonic plates along the Pacific rim and the presence of many volcanoes. The Philippines is also on the path of regular tropical cyclones (typhoons) with powerful winds, torrential rain, high waves and damaging storm surges. These hazards are not, however, what makes the country prone to disasters. Other places on the Pacific Ring of Fire, including San Francisco, Vancouver and Auckland, face similar dangers but not the same level of risk or number of casualties when disaster strikes. The difference lies in how the natural hazards interact with human sources of vulnerability to create risk. Inadequate prevention, lack of preparedness, haphazard responses to disasters and recovery activities that do not address underlying threats all conspire to leave populations exposed to the risk of harm when a hazardous situation comes to pass.

To explore these issues, and plan responses to disaster risks in the Philippines, members of a Roman Catholic religious order gathered for five days in February, 2011 at the Camillian Order Seminary in Quezon City next to Manila. Founded by Saint Camillus de Lellis in the sixteenth century to minister to the sick, the Camillian Order now runs hospitals and clinics in Europe, Africa, South America and Asia. It also provides immediate emergency medical response to disasters, and administers to the associated trauma and mental health impacts. This experience prompted the Order to develop a multi-stakeholder, participatory process to identify the risks associated with natural hazards, and plan responses that manage or reduce these risks. The process needed to achieve two complementary goals: to develop collaborative action plans people and organizations can use to support disaster relief and risk reduction (DR-RR), and to strengthen the capacity of people to protect themselves from harm. They asked D. J. Buckles to facilitate a process to these ends, co-designed with J. M. Chevalier.

The first goal reflects the centrality of planning to DR-RR. Well-developed plans worked out beforehand describe the actions and inputs needed to achieve the goals of reducing the loss of life, property and livelihoods. Given the complexity of the task, good planning and effective implementation depend on a high degree of cooperation and coordination among multiple stakeholders – individuals or groups affected by disasters or with the capacity to influence the emergency response or actions aimed at reducing risk.

While widely recognized as important, being proactive, strategic and inclusive in planning for DR-RR is a departure from the norm among relief agencies. Chandrasekhar notes that disaster plans and policies are often created quickly, after the fact, and may depend on power structures and lines of communication that 'can further reinforce inequities rather than redress them' (Chandrasekhar, 2010, p. 131). Periods of relative peace and stability are obviously much more appropriate moments to plan than during the chaos and turmoil of a disaster and its immediate aftermath. Experience also shows that the long recovery phase after immediate emergency aid has been provided is a vital window of opportunity for change, including potentially unpopular or difficult actions to affect structural change (Lettieri *et al.*, 2009).

The second goal goes to the heart of the human experience of disaster – the sense of helplessness in the face of an uncontrollable force. While it is well known that peoples' participation in planning at the local level is indispensable, how that participation is facilitated and for what purpose matters a great deal (Chandrasekhar, 2010). Top down strategies disempower and undermine peoples' capacities to independently manage the individual and collective tasks that must be carried out urgently when disaster strikes (IIRR and LWR, 2011). Moreover, they fail to tap people's ingenuity. On this point, Barrs remarks that while 'we may support some local responses, there are many more – particularly the discreet and unorthodox ones – that we fail to assist. Indeed there is a whole understory of local preparations against harm that we tend not to even recognize' (Barrs, 2010, p. 1).

Engaging a range of stakeholders and mobilizing knowledge from various sources when planning DR-RR is consequently both a practical and ethical imperative. It has enormous potential to broaden the range of planned responses and to support efforts aimed at self-preservation by people directly affected by a disaster. It is also a concrete mechanism through which people can develop the capacity to become the subjects of their own security, rather than objects of the plans and actions of others.

These twin goals – building capacities for self-preservation and co-creating action plans – provided direct inspiration for work with members of the Order. The workshop design, summarized in Figure 15.1, has two parts. Part A, the preparatory stage, leads to an overall plan to engage stakeholders. This is critical to ensure that planning is both participatory and multi-stakeholder from the beginning. Part B is the actual engagement process, involving the right stakeholders at the right time.

Part A, the preparatory stage, begins with the formation of a core planning group. For example, laypeople and members of the Order in The Philippines have a history of working with a vulnerable population living on urban wastelands in Manila. This relationship provided good conditions for engaging representatives in the initial planning process.

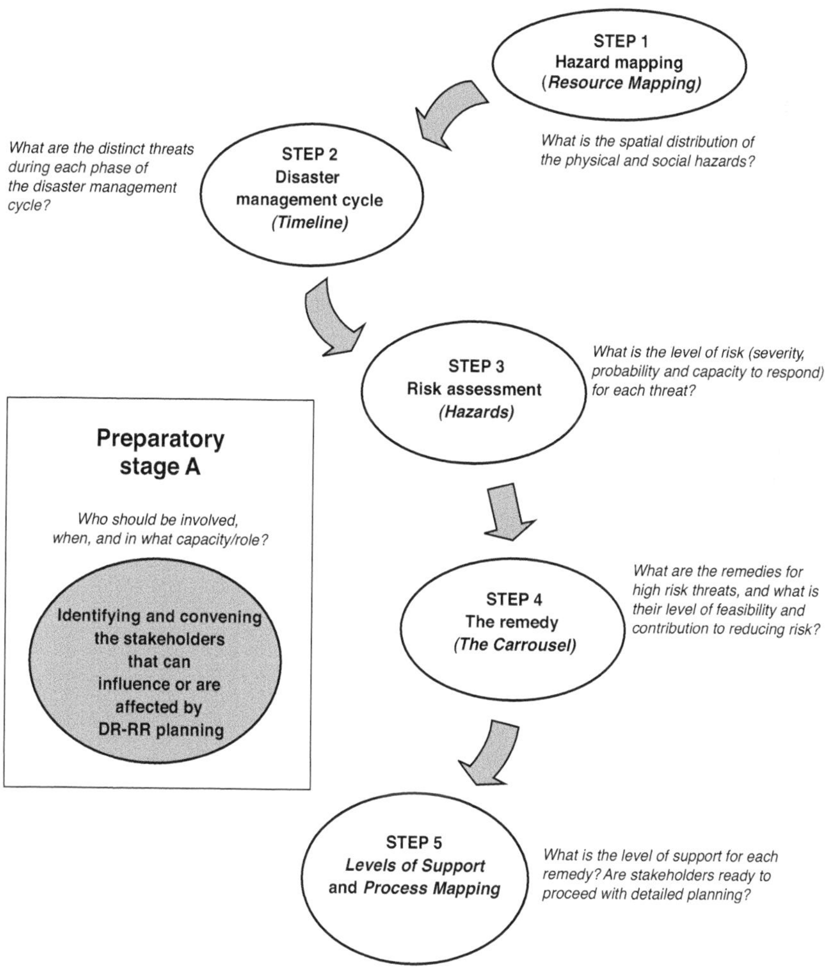

FIGURE 15.1 Planning disaster relief and risk reduction.

The work of the core planning group begins with a visioning exercise building on the concrete experiences and aspirations of the group. This may involve sharing of personal experiences during natural hazards and reasons why planning is needed, or a more structured discussion using tools such as *True or False* or *The Vision Circle* (Chapter 14). The purpose is to acknowledge the need for planning, recognize past accomplishments relevant to the goals of the planning process, and to define the general vision for the proposed planning process.

Based on this vision, and other preparatory work undertaken by the convening parties (for example, research on who-is-who in the DR-RR field in the country), the core planning group can then undertake a comprehensive stakeholder analysis (*Stakeholder Rainbow*, Chapter 12). The purpose of the exercise is to decide who else to engage in development of a detailed action plan, based on an assessment by the group of who is affected by disasters in a defined situation or context and who has influence over the success of any plans the core group might develop with them. The decisions of this group might recognize that power differences and the cultural norms of the various stakeholders work against convening a single process or meeting for all stakeholders at the same time. Separate or parallel meetings among stakeholders with a similar profile might be needed before bringing all stakeholders and their analyses together. For example, the workshop group working on planning for an urban slum of Manila noted that women and elders in this community are key stakeholders to engage in the planning process. They are both affected by disasters and have considerable influence over the actual implementation and success of any action plans that might develop for the urban slum. They also recognized that higher ranks of the security force and certain government agencies are probably critical to the development of effective action plans. They decided, however, that these actors could only be engaged later in the process, when the time was right and the local groups had developed their own capacities and independent analysis.

The third step in the initial planning process is to plan what needs to be done and when to engage the right people, based on the stakeholder analysis. This includes addressing logistical and operational questions and discussing the overall outline of the proposed process for engagement (Part B). Convenors can thus solicit feedback on plans for the next meeting and seek support for their role as facilitators. Workshop participants experimented with this step using *Process Mapping* (Chapter 5) as the planning tool, although any local method or planning procedure will also do.

Part B of the proposed methodology engages the right stakeholders at the right time and in the right number and order, according to the analysis of the initial planning group (Part A). The actual engagement process involves a sequence of assessments, starting in Step 1 (Figure 15.1) with an adaptation of *Resource Mapping* (Chapter 9) to the DR-RR context. Using maps of the planning context (group of villages, urban area, region) or creating maps of their own, stakeholders share their knowledge of the spatial dimensions of the hazards experienced in the past. For example, the Camillian team from Northern Mindanao in the Philippines created a hazard map for the city of Iligan profoundly affected by typhoon Sendong in December 2011. The typhoon had flattened homes, broken bridges and upended vehicles in various parts of the city, including areas where schools were located and one of the cities' hospitals. In the surrounding hillsides, torrents of water had stripped deforested mountainsides bare and flooded villages with mud. The map they created showed not only the affected areas but also the places in the city not directly disturbed. Unharmed places included schools that make up the primary system of evacuation centres established under the National Framework on Disaster Response. The group discussed the difficulties people encountered trying to get to these centres, and mapped the location of other key resources available to people such as communication nodes, hospitals and areas of stable high ground. Along the side of the map, created on a large chart paper, they noted details regarding the socio-economic profile of specific neighbourhoods devastated by the typhoon and neighbourhoods that escaped relatively unharmed. Once completed, the map showed that the impacts of the typhoon in Iligan were concentrated not on the coastal side but rather at the upper side of the city where many poorly constructed homes were located and landslides were very intense. The city's main transportation corridor along the entire length of the valley floor was also heavily affected by flash flooding.

Mapping the path of the hazard and discussions on the spatial and social distribution of the impacts helped participants identify factors and behaviours that contribute to the impacts and harm experienced by the population. These are the threats of harm having an element of human intent, negligence or error, or involving a failure in a social system. In Step 2, an adaptation of *Timeline* (Chapter 9), the threats were written by participants on separate cards, drawing on the previous mapping process and adding other threats as needed along the way. These were then situated in relation to four phases in the disaster management cycle: mitigation or prevention, preparedness (with a focus on individual and institutional behaviours during a disaster), emergency response and recovery. Four chairs in a row representing each phase provided the space for groups to take turns sharing their cards until they had created a richly annotated timeline. A fifth chair, in the middle, represented the moment the natural hazard struck. For example, people discussing disaster risks from typhoons in the **mitigation or prevention** phase noted failures to regulate the construction of houses near riverbanks and mistakes made when managing the seasonal flow of water from dams. They placed the cards for these threats on the chair representing the prevention phase because they felt that was when the threats should be dealt with.

Preparedness is a phase in the management cycle focussing on changing human behaviours that make a difference to survival in the moments the disaster strikes — knowing where to go, what to do and how to help. Participants in the workshop noted many threats of this nature such as blocked or unclear evacuation routes, the inability among the general population to provide first aid, the presence (or absence) of early warning signs, and stocking of emergency rations of food and water, among others. Participants also noted that some segments of the population were aware of what to do and where to go during a particular kind of hazard (an earthquake, for example) while others were not. Ensuring that all had the same knowledge and information, including children, was recognized as a key element in preparedness.

Given the experience of the Camillian Order with disaster relief, discussion of the third phase of disasters, the **emergency response**, was richly detailed. Their home base in hospitals and relationships with medical professionals and parish volunteers allows the Order to mobilize emergency services and responders when a disaster strikes. This includes working with databases and other lists of people with the right skills, coordinating the logistics and solving practical problems such as road blockages by mobilizing local knowledge of alternative routes. Participants discussed difficulties during the response phase associated with communications and coordination but also health threats due to overcrowding in evacuation shelters and the inability of traumatized people to clean their homes following a flood or mudslide. Dangers faced by field staff, and looting by desperate victims and opportunists, were also mentioned as common occurrences during the response phase. They also noted the tendency for men to delay fleeing to a safer place during a disaster in an attempt to protect their belongings, and failures to anticipate this behaviour.

The literature on DR-RR focusses a great deal of attention on the importance of the **recovery** phase in the disaster management cycle. It also highlights the difficulties relief agencies face making the transition from emergency response to disaster to dealing with the complex problems of shattered livelihoods and long-term trauma (Lettieri *et al.*, 2009). Once emergency relief is complete, and many professionals have gone home, the disaster victims are left on their own or with minimal support. It is precisely in this final recovery phase, however, that efforts must go into making sense of the disaster experience, and evaluating the underlying causes and potential strategies to prevent major problems from reoccurring. Participants gave examples of how pastoral care helped victims deal with trauma, and cases where professional treatment of trauma and related long-term mental health problems was lacking. They also pointed to the recovery phase as the appropriate moment to start engaging stakeholders in a new cycle of discussions about mitigation – about the construction of houses, reforestation, urban planning, etc., and the related issues of entrenched power and interests that exacerbated the disaster risks in the first place. Participants placed cards representing these threats on the chair associated with the recovery phase, and noted how they reinforced factors and behaviours they had associated earlier to the prevention phase.

Piling and sorting cards on the timeline of phases of the management cycle allowed participants to create a phase-specific list of potential threats. For example, participants from Samar Island in the Philippines noted five threats associated with the emergency response phase:

1 the lack of local logistical knowledge;
2 not having enough volunteers with the right skills;
3 road blockages;
4 poor coordination between agencies; and
5 the scarcity of expertise in trauma treatment.

They then sat together to assess the level of risk for each of these threats, using the tool *Hazards*. The tool, Step 3 in the workshop design, builds on the calculation of two components of risk (R): the magnitude or severity of the potential harm (S), and the probability (P) that the harm will occur. This approach reflects the equation used in quantitative risk assessment in various sectors including finance, environment and public health.

Participants rated each threat using a scale for severity or magnitude of the potential harm from 0 to 10. They also rated the probability that the harm will occur using a scale from 0 per cent to 100 per cent probability. Each threat was then placed on a Cartesian graph where the ratings on these two variables intersected. At the same time, they rated the current capacity (C) of stakeholders to manage the threat, using a scale of low, medium and high capacity. This rating was added to the graph by colouring the plotted threat green, yellow or red to show the 'C' value associated with the threat. The equation can be summarized as $R = (S \times P)/C$. This is a relatively simple and locally grounded model compared to the pressure and release model often used in the emergency management literature (i.e. Risk = Hazard x Vulnerability). Our alternative is easier to quantify and focusses attention on assessing local conditions, thereby addressing problems in the pressure and release model (Birkmann, 2006, p. 31).

The goal of the *Hazards* assessments completed during the workshop was to identify priority threats around which phase-specific action plans could be developed. For example, based on the assessment of threats during the typhoon response phase, the Sambar Island group decided that poor coordination between agencies and the scarcity of expertise in trauma treatment were too risky to ignore (Figure 15.2). They are severe and likely threats for which they and other stakeholders are little or only moderately prepared at present (as shown by solid and half-tone dots). By contrast, the threat of not having enough skilled volunteers available and the threat of not having the right local logistical knowledge, while potentially severe, are much less likely to occur. Moreover these are threats that they have prepared for in the past through careful development of databases of volunteers with different kinds of skills, and strong linkages to local organized groups that speak local languages and know the lay of the land (open dot showing high current capacity). Road blockages, while a severe threat and likely to happen in the wake of a typhoon, is a highly unpredictable threat for which they cannot really prepare (solid dot). Threats during the other phases in the typhoon disaster cycle were also assessed on these three criteria (severity, probability, capacity), and priorities selected for detailed planning of ways to manage or reduce the risks.

Hazards is an assessment that can be been done separately with different populations, local men and women for example, to see who might be more or less exposed to specific risks. This brings us to the concept of vulnerability, widely used in the emergency management literature but with different meanings (Birkmann, 2006). Essentially, risk is the way we measure and share 'true fear'– i.e. irrational feelings mixing with rational doubt based on experiences and personal circumstances such as age, gender, sexual orientation, income and other characteristics inherent in social interactions and institutions. Given this blend of subjective and objective considerations, people are likely to experience fear differently and assess the probability and severity of perceived risks accordingly. The DR-RR methodology, and Step 3 in particular, can address these issues in two complementary ways: by marshalling all the available information to support evidence-based analyses of perceived risks, on the one hand, and by supporting authentic dialogue between different views of existing threats. As noted above, the stakeholder analysis by

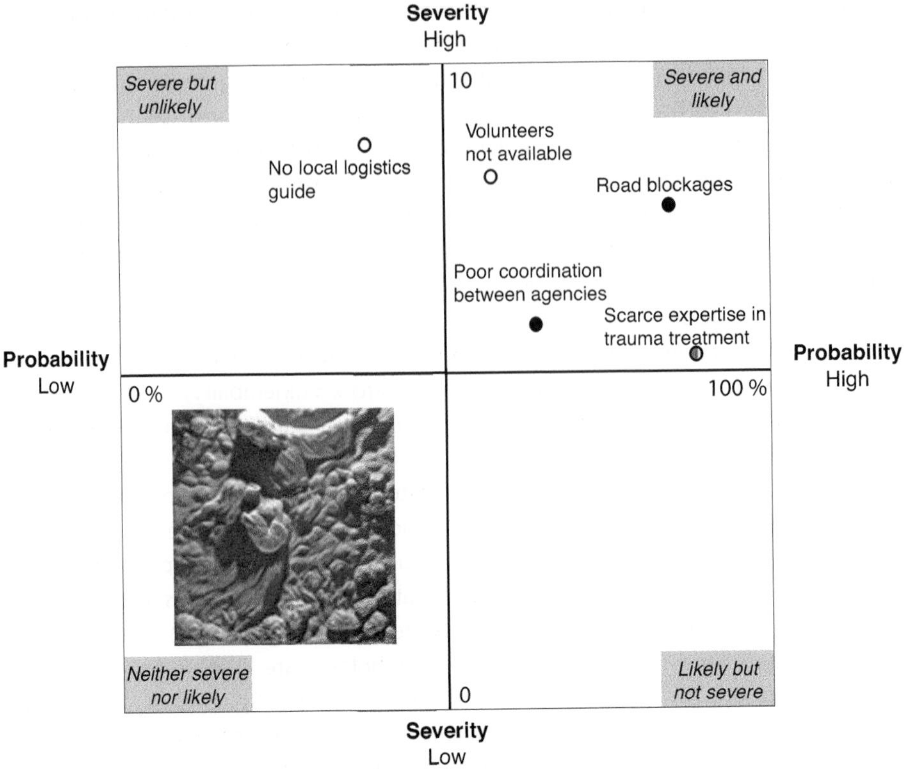

FIGURE 15.2 Threats during the response to typhoons.

the initial planning group (the preparatory stage, Figure 15.1) provides an opportunity to consider whether or not to plan separate assessments, such as between men and women, or the poor and the rich. Decisions to do so could apply to any of the subsequent steps, from *Resource Mapping* onwards. These are judgments to be made in light of the local context by the core planning group responsible for the process, and the extent to which different groups are or feel more vulnerable to risks than others.

Another key judgment concerns the depth of evidence, planning and participation needed to achieve meaningful results. Adjusting the number of steps and the level of detail to the right **scale** for the purpose and context is a skilful means (Chapter 6) critical to effective engagement. For example, the workshop participants in the Philippines used the *Problem Tree* to deepen their analysis of the root causes of the hazards under discussion before moving on to the development of remedies or solutions to priority threats. This optional step can be added to the methodology, if useful and if time permits. Similarly, prior and later steps can be scaled down or up to fit the context, so long as the spirit of a multi-stakeholder engagement process is maintained and the results are 'good enough' to guide development of a meaningful DR-RR action plan.

Priority threats identified through the risk assessment become, in Step 4 (Figure 15.1), the focus for developing remedies or solutions using a combination of *The Carrousel* (under *Ideal Scenario*, Chapter 14) and the *Contribution and Feasibility* tool (this chapter). During the workshop, participants organized themselves into four groups, one for each phase in the disaster cycle. Each group discussed the priority threats during the specific phase and formulated potential remedies or solutions. They then assessed the extent to which each remedy would **contribute** to solving or resolving the threat, and rated it on a scale of low contribution to high contribution. They also rated the **feasibility** of carrying the remedy through to a successful conclusion, in light of financial and human resource constraints. Review of the contribution and feasibility of specific remedies added a third variable: the extent to which the remedy enhanced **fairness or equity for vulnerable populations**. Steps taken to reduce vulnerabilities (for example, men not reaching safe ground because they stay with their possessions) could be important considerations when assessing remedies. This variable was represented by solid (high), half-filled and open circles (low) on the graph indicating three different levels of fairness impacts of the remedy.

Figure 15.3 shows the results of a rating exercise adapted from ideas discussed by the response phase group. They noted that having a logistics coordinator would go a long way towards resolving the severe and likely threat of poor coordination between agencies. After further discussion, however, the remedy was split into two different remedies and rated separately. Coordination between the Church Parish and government agencies at all levels would make a high contribution to reducing the threat. Building tight linkages between the Church Parish and government agencies would nonetheless take time (moderate feasibility) and could reinforce inequities affecting vulnerable populations rather than redress them (represented by a half-filled circle). By contrast, coordinating with NGOs would be relatively easy to do (high feasibility) and make a slightly lesser contribution to resolving the threat. A logistics coordinator at this level could enhance sensitivity to all sub-populations of victims, thereby achieving the goal fairly and equitably.

A second set of remedies emerged in response to the threat posed by the scarcity of expertise in trauma treatment. Expanding the number of professionals in the trauma team could contribute highly to solving the problem. Volunteer training, however, is a less expensive proposition (and therefore more feasible) and would be more likely to engage sub-populations such as local women and youth unrepresented in an entirely professional medical team. This became the preferred course of action.

The Carrousel method of facilitation (Chapter 14) provided each group with an opportunity to improve on their remedies based on feedback from other groups and learning about how other groups were proposing to handle the threats and remedies they had identified. A presenter remained at each table to explain the group's ideas and assessment, and gather feedback on the remedies. The others in the group collectively visited another table to provide feedback and collect good ideas for their own table. After several rounds of presentation and feedback, everyone (except the presenters) had an opportunity to hear and comment on the specific remedies emerging from each group, and their ratings on contribution, feasibility and fairness. Participants made many suggestions about how the remedies could be implemented so as to increase the contribution of the remedy to resolving the threat, make it more feasible and/or improve

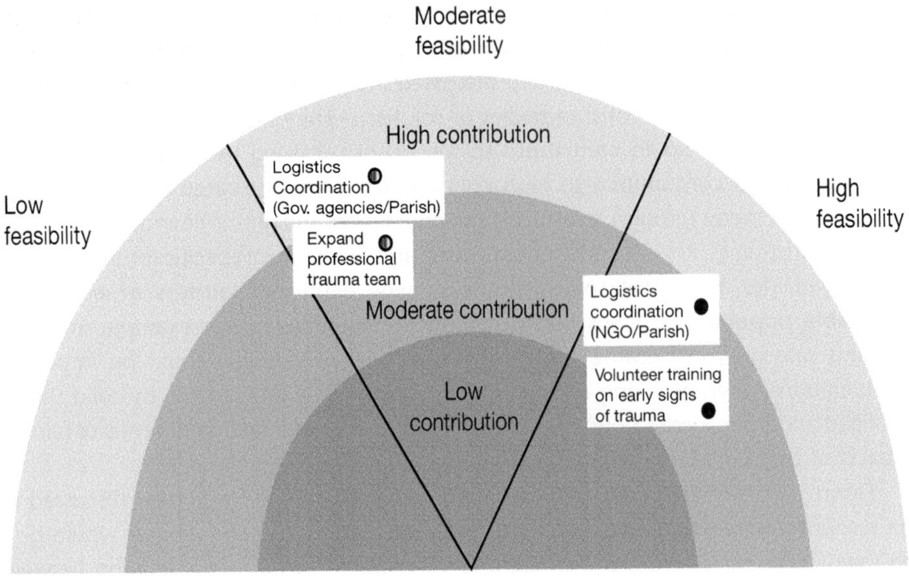

FIGURE 15.3 Remedies to priority threats when responding to typhoon disasters.

on its fairness. These suggestions led to various adjustments to the original formulation of the remedies once the original group reconvened to review the results of *The Carrousel* session. The feedback also helped to identify additional remedies not considered initially. For example, the group discussing priority threats during the response phase decided in light of the feedback received to modify their plan for volunteer training. It should focus, they decided, on the early signs of trauma as a complement to professional assessment. They also noted that while direct linkages with government responders would help enormously during the response phase, it seemed far from feasible given the very unequal power relationships between these stakeholders. To increase the feasibility of this remedy the group argued that they should first build relationships between local NGOs and the Church parish communities in the area so that this united front could then engage with the appropriate state-level agencies. This sequencing, they felt, would enhance the overall contribution the remedies would make to resolving the problem of poor coordination during the emergency response phase.

The proposed DR-RR planning methodology, when applied to risk assessments by the right stakeholder groups (see Part A, above), concludes with a final step (Figure 15.1). Step 5 contributes to consensus building around the action plans emerging from *The Carrousel* using either *Levels of Support* (Chapter 14) or *Values, Interests, Positions (VIP)* (Chapter 13). Both tools provide people with an opportunity to assess whether or not there is enough support to proceed with specific action plans emerging from *The Carrousel*. They also support discussion of further adjustments that could be made to address any remaining concerns. Detailed plans, using *Process Mapping* or some other local planning method, could follow.

In the Camillians' workshop, where risk assessment, remedies and plans were provisional and subject to validation through a future multi-stakeholder engagement process, *VIP* was applied to a more general question. Based on the experience with the methodology, each participant assessed the extent to which the approach corresponded to his or her values and sense of what was morally the right thing to do, and the extent to which the approach served their personal and professional interests as well (for detailed instructions, see *Values, Interests, Positions,* Chapter 13). Results were made anonymous by exchanging individual assessments several times and compiling all results on a single graph placed on the floor of the room. What was evident for all to see was that all but a few (anonymous) individuals were firmly in the same quadrant. The group position was that a multi-stakeholder and participatory planning process for DR-RR is highly compatible with the moral values they hold at the same time as it is consistent with their personal or professional interests in improving their ability to respond to disasters.

AT RISK

Hazards

Purpose

To assess and address existing or perceived hazards using three criteria: their severity, their probability and people's current capacity to respond to them.

Step 1

Define the **situation** and make a list of **the hazards** that are part of the situation (using *Free List and Pile Sort,* Chapter 8). Write each hazard on its own card. Organize these hazards into phases, if useful. For instance, in a disaster cycle, the phases are prevention, preparedness, emergency response and recovery (see our story of *Disaster relief and risk reduction in the Philippines,* above).

Step 2

Assess each hazard using three criteria: its **severity**, its **probability** and people's **capacity** to respond to it. Use a scale of 0 to 10 to represent the severity or magnitude of the harm potentially caused by the hazard. Represent the probability that the harm will occur on a scale from 0 to 10. Rate peoples' current capacity to respond to the hazard on a scale of low (L), moderate (M) and high (H).

Step 3

Create a **diagram** by drawing a vertical line that crosses a horizontal line of equal length (see Figure 15.2). Use the vertical line to represent the severity or magnitude and the horizontal line to represent probability. In each corner of the diagram, describe the **scenario** obtained when the two considerations (severity and probability) are combined.

Step 4

Locate each hazard in the diagram; use a dot to mark where the values from the two lines meet. Adjust the colour of each dot to indicate people's current **capacity** to respond to the hazard (for example, red for low, yellow for moderate and green for high current capacity to respond).

Step 5

Discuss how hazards are distributed. Pay special attention to hazards that are more severe and more likely to occur and those where the current capacity to respond can be improved.

Variations

Some people may be more **vulnerable** to some or all hazards compared to others. Views and responses to hazards will vary accordingly. If this is the case, invite each group (men and women, for instance) to do their own *Hazards* assessment separately and then discuss the results together. (For an illustration of different perceptions of vulnerability, see our application of *Hazards* to accident prevention in the construction industry in Chapter 10.)

Combinations

- Use *Timeline* (Chapter 9), *Force Field, Paradox* (Chapter 10) or *Projections* to gain a better understanding of existing hazards and responses to them.
- See *Health and safety among construction workers in France*, Chapter 10, and *Disaster relief and risk reduction in the Philippines*, above.

FORECASTING THE FUTURE

Projections

Purpose

To visualize what can be expected if current trends continue and stakeholders' actions do not change them.

Step 1

Define the **situation** and make a list of **the positive** and the **negative factors** that are part of the situation. Focus on the most important factors.

Step 2

Create a **table** and insert the list of positive and negative factors in Column 1 (see Table 15.1).

Step 3

In Column 2 indicate the importance or **weight** of each factor, using a scale of 1 (low) to 5 (high). Use plus (+) and minus (–) signs to distinguish the positive and the negative factors.

Step 4

Discuss the main cause(s) responsible for each factor and current trends underlying the cause(s). Record key words to describe the **main cause(s)** in Column 3.

Step 5

In Column 4 indicate whether each cause is likely to have **a stronger** or a **weaker impact** over time, assuming no one tries to change the current trends. Use a range of 0 per cent to 100 per cent and above, where 100 per cent indicates an impact that will remain the same over time, a value below 100 per cent a lesser impact and above 100 per cent a greater impact. Determine the **time** needed for these expected changes. Plan to get more information to estimate future impacts, if needed.

TABLE 15.1 *Projection* table

Current situation factors	*A* *Weight* –5 to +5	*Main cause(s)*	*B* *Future impact* <100% (lesser) =100% (stable) >100% (greater)	*A × B* *Projection score*
Positive factors				
1.				
2.				
Negative factors				
1.				
2.				

Step 6

Calculate the **projection score** for each row by multiplying scores A (Column 2) and B (Column 4). Record the results in Column 5. The more positive the overall projection score is, the more reason there is to be optimistic. The more negative the score is, the more reason there is to be pessimistic. When there are several causes for a factor, calculate the average projection score by totalling all the projection scores for the factor and dividing the total by the number of causes.

Step 7

Create a **diagram** by drawing a vertical line that crosses a horizontal line of equal length (see Figure 15.4). Use the vertical line to represent the maximum positive and negative weights that could be obtained for the factors that are part of the situation (+5 and –5). Use the horizontal line to indicate impact, from the weakest score (0 per cent) to the highest impact over time (>100 per cent). In each corner of the diagram, describe the **scenario** obtained when the two considerations (factors and impacts over time) are combined: positive factors that will get stronger (top right); positive factors that will get weaker (top left); negative factors that will get stronger (bottom right); negative factors that will get weaker (bottom left). To facilitate the analysis, find an idea or a symbol to represent each quadrant of the diagram.

Step 8

Using the results from Column A and Column B in the table, **locate** each factor in the diagram; use a dot to mark where the values from the two lines meet and write the factor. **Discuss** how the positive and negative factors are distributed. **Summarize** the situation that will result from the negative and the positive factors and the likely future impacts of their causes. Pay special attention to factors that are likely to **change a lot** over time (extreme scores for future impacts).

Tips

- Different stakeholders may weigh the various factors and the future impacts differently, and give them different symbolic meanings. When contrasting views are likely, do the *Projections* separately and then discuss together.

Combinations

- Use *Timeline, Problem Tree* (Chapter 9) or *Force Field* (Chapter 10) to explore the causes responsible for each situation factor and current trends.

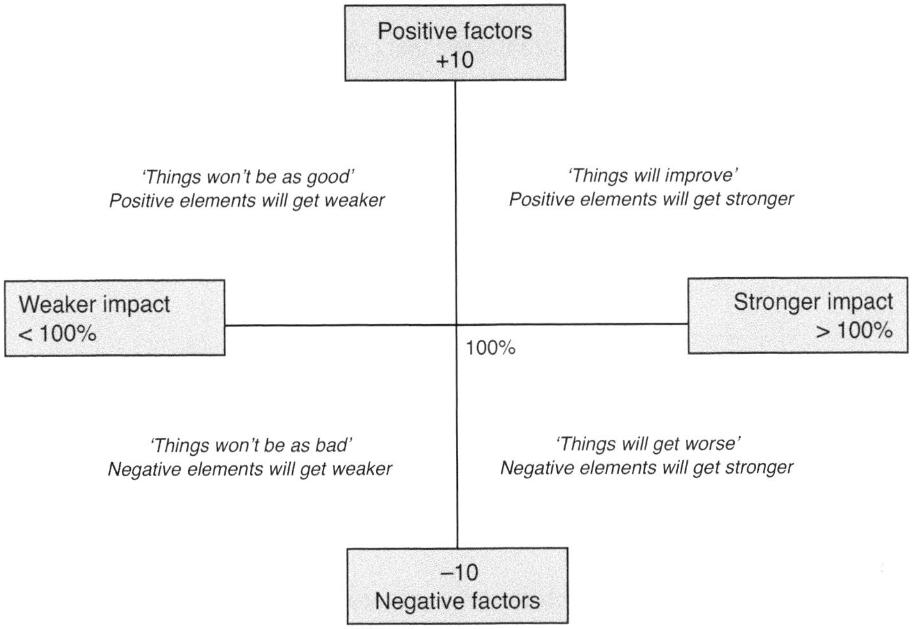

FIGURE 15.4 *Projections* scenarios.

MONITORING THE UNEXPECTED

What If

Purpose

To develop a plan to monitor risk factors and adjust activities accordingly.

Step 1

Define a plan, project or programme and make a list of key **factors** that may have a **high impact** and are **difficult to predict**.

Step 2

Review the list and select the **two factors** that may have the highest impact **and** are the most difficult to predict. Use *Ranking* (Chapter 8) if need be.

Step 3

Create a diagram by drawing a horizontal line that crosses a vertical line of equal length. On the horizontal line label **two opposite outcomes** for one of the factors (such as 'No more funds' versus 'More funds', see Figure 15.5).

Step 4

On the vertical line, label **two opposite outcomes** for the other factor (such as 'A new government' versus 'The same government').

Step 5

In each corner of the diagram, write (or draw) the **scenario** obtained when the possible outcomes are combined (Figure 15.5).

Step 6

Discuss the potential impact of each scenario and record this using key words or a visual symbol in each corner of the diagram.

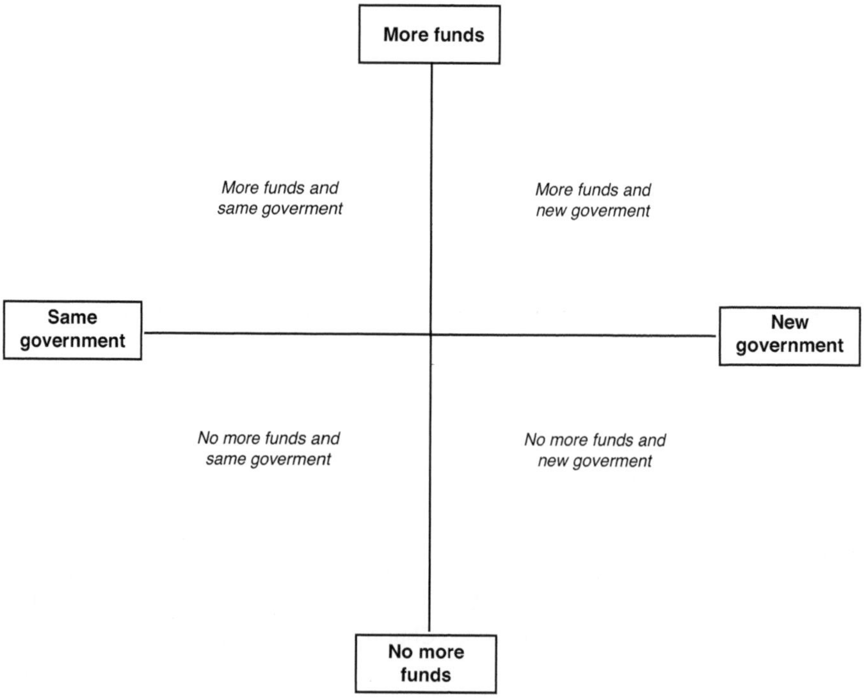

FIGURE 15.5 *What If* scenarios.

Step 7

Review the result and identify what kind of **information** is needed to track the two factors. Decide *when* and *how* the information can be obtained, and *who* will be responsible for doing this. Over time, adjust broader plans in light of the information collected.

FAQ

- ***What is the point of a monitoring plan based on things that are difficult to predict?***

Early warning can make a difference between failure and a disaster averted.

Combinations

- Use *Force Field* (Chapter 10) to determine the likely implications of each scenario.

MAKING A DIFFERENCE

Contribution and Feasibility

Purpose

To choose between several courses of action using two criteria: the contribution that each action would make to achieving goals, and how feasible each action is in light of favourable conditions (strengths, opportunities) and unfavourable conditions (weaknesses, limitations).

Step 1

Define the **situation** (project, problem) and create a list of current or proposed **actions** to be compared for planning purposes. Each action should be concrete, distinct and clearly described. Draw or write each action on its own card, with some details about the action on the back of the card or on a flip chart.

Step 2

Assess and indicate on each card whether the action will make a high (C-H), moderate (C-M) or low (C-L) **contribution** to resolving the problem or achieving goals. For more precision, use **indicators** to define the meaning of levels on the contribution scale. Record the **reason(s)** given for each potential contribution on the corresponding action card or on a flip chart. If rating is done as a group, discuss each rating until participants agree based on consensus or a majority vote. Alternatively, calculate the average rating for each action. (Review the *Scoring tips* in Chapter 8. They are critical to proper application of the *Contribution and Feasibility* tool.)

Step 3

Assess and indicate on each card whether the action is highly (F-H), moderately (F-M) or barely (F-L) **feasible**. When discussing feasibility, take into account the favourable conditions (strengths, opportunities) as well as the unfavourable conditions (weaknesses, limitations) associated with the action (see *Force Field*, Chapter 10). For rating procedures, see Step 2.

Step 4

Create a **rainbow diagram** with three bands on a flip chart or with masking tape on the floor. In the smaller band, insert the cards of low contribution options (C-L). Insert the cards showing actions of moderate contribution (C-M) in the middle band, and those of high contribution (C-H) in the larger band (see Figure 15.3).

Step 5

Divide the rainbow bands into **three equal parts**: one part to the left, one in the middle and one to the right. Move the cards of highly feasible options (F-H) to the right side of the diagram. Move those that are barely feasible (F-L) to the left side. Leave the moderately feasible actions (F-M) in the middle.

Step 6

Discuss the picture that emerges and overall course of action based on the level of contribution and feasibility of each action. Also discuss ways to **improve or combine** the actions so they make a greater contribution to resolving the problem or achieving goals, or become more feasible.

FAQ

- ***Are contribution and feasibility the only criteria that really matter when choosing a course of action?***

The strength of these two criteria is that they bring together two tightly connected questions – will it make a difference and can we do it? However, other considerations (gender equity, for example) may be important and could be included in a rating table using multiple criteria. Also questions of contribution and feasibility are complex and may be unpacked into specific measurements or indicators.

Variations

- Instead of using a rainbow diagram, locate each option in a Cartesian graph where the vertical line represents different levels of contribution (from 0 to 10), and the horizontal line, different levels of feasibility (from 0 to 10).

- Use **visual codes** (colours, numbers, icons, etc.) to add other information on each action, such as the order in which each preferred action should be carried out and dependency relationships between actions. Other information that may be useful is the level of completion for the corresponding course of action (indicated by a small pie chart or clock symbol, for instance).
- Use a nautilus diagram to represent the assessment of each option against its potential contribution, its feasibility and how complete it is. Steps to this nautilus-shaped assessment of possible options or courses of action are slightly different from those described above. The adjustments are as follows:

  1. Instead of assessing the potential contribution of each option (as in Step 2), from low to high, determine how far each option would go in **resolving the problem** or **achieving project goals**, using a percentage figure (from 0 per cent to 100 per cent). Use a table (see Table 15.2) to record these potential contributions. Place them in Column A, in descending order.
  2. Create a **graph** on paper or a flip chart using spokes (or ribbons on the floor) to represent the different options or actions under discussion. Adjust the **length** of each spoke to reflect its potential contribution, and organize the spokes in a clockwise ascending order. **Label** each spoke with a title card, a drawing or an object representing the option or action. A relevant metaphor can also be identified to represent the purpose of the exercise (see the snail in Figure 15.6).
  3. Estimate the actual **level of completion** for each option as part (a percentage) of the total effort needed to realize its full potential. Record each percentage

TABLE 15.2 Assessing park complaint management options

Strategies to manage park user complaints	*A Potential contribution (%)*	*B Level of completion (%)*	*A × B Potential contribution of completed actions (%)*	*Feasibility*
Public information campaign	50	20	10.0	Moderate
Follow due process	25	30	7.5	Low
Improve service quality	20	30	6.0	High
Staff capacity building	20	10	2.0	High
Stakeholder engagement	20	0	0	Moderate
Complaint CRM management system	15	40	6.0	Low
Clarify norms	10	20	2.0	High
Revise park maintenance contract	5	70	3.5	High
Total problem solving contribution	165		37.0	

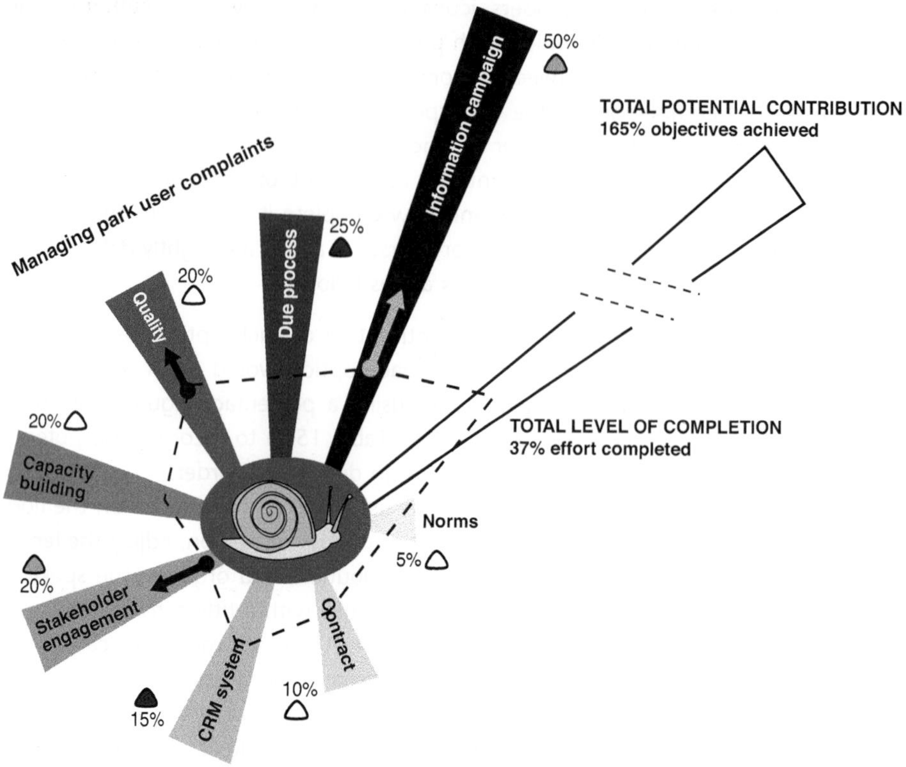

FIGURE 15.6 Assessing park complaint management options.

Summary of this example: National Park staff decide to reassess the various strategies they use or could use to handle suggestions and complaints from park users more effectively. Three strategies stand out as priorities (see arrows in Figure 15.6). The team estimates that *engaging stakeholders* in problem solving and establishing *quality standards* to be applied when delivering park services would contribute significantly to reducing complaints. They would resolve the problem by 40 per cent. While the stakeholder engagement process has yet to be designed, the work involved in defining quality standards has already started (by 30 per cent) and is easier to achieve (high feasibility, indicated by a white triangle). A public *information campaign* about what the Park has to offer (and services not available) could also make a significant contribution, reducing the problem by another 50 per cent. However, much of this work remains to be done and may be somewhat challenging (moderate feasibility, indicated by a grey triangle).

rating in the table, in Column B. **Mark** each rating on the corresponding spoke, between the center (0 per cent effort level) and the other end of the spoke (representing 100 per cent of the effort needed to realize maximum potential). Draw **straight lines** between the marks to create a shape that defines the actual effort profile for each action.

4 **Total** all potential contribution ratings. Add another spoke to the graph, the longest, and record the **total potential contribution** at the end of this **synthetic spoke** (see Figure 15.6). Keep in mind that the total potential contribution can surpass 100 per cent and may be more than what is required.

5 Multiply Column A by Column B ratings for each row, and record the results in the 'A × B' column. The resulting figures represent the potential contributions of actions already completed. Total these ratings (where the level of completion is weighted by its potential contribution) and record the total at the bottom of the last column. Mark this **total current contribution potential** on the synthetic spoke.

6 Discuss the picture that emerges and overall course of action based on the scores. Also discuss ways to **improve** or **combine** the actions so they make a greater contribution to resolving the problem or achieving goals, or reduce the overall level of effort still required.

Combinations

- Use *Validation* (Chapter 8), *Values, Interests, Positions* (Chapter 13) or *Levels of Support* (Chapter 14) to further explore an overall course of action that meets the criteria of contribution and feasibility.

OUTCOMES AND PROBABILITIES

Results and Risks

Purpose

To evaluate different courses of action based on the negative and the positive results expected, the value given to specific results and the probability that these results will occur. This is a group adaptation of a tool that negotiators use to determine the Best Alternative To a Negotiated Agreement (BATNA).

Step 1

Define a **situation** and make a list of the **actions** being considered. The actions should be concrete, distinct in some way and relevant to the situation.

Step 2

Create a table (see Table 15.3). List the actions in Column 1. A choice between two actions (such as 'do' or 'do not do') is the minimum you need.

Step 3

Discuss the **negative result(s)** that may be associated with each action. Using key words, record these results in Column 2.

Step 4

Give a value to each negative result, from –1 to –10; the –10 score (or 10 objects such as black pebbles) indicates the **worst** that could happen. This is **Score A**. Then, estimate how likely it is that each negative result will happen (the probability in percentage), based on current knowledge of the situation. This percentage is **Score B**. To be more precise, identify **indicators** that define the meaning of numbers and percentages on each scale. Record Score A and Score B for each action in Column 3.

Step 5

Multiply Score A by Score B (if using pebbles for Score A, reduce the number to a proportion equal to the probability percentage). This gives the **total score** for each negative result. Record the scores in Column 4.

Step 6

Discuss the **positive result(s)** that may be associated with each option. Using key words, record these results in Column 5.

Step 7

Give a value to each positive result, from 0 to 10; the +10 score (or objects such as 10 white pebbles) indicates the **best** that could happen. This is **Score C**. Estimate how likely it is that each positive result will happen (the probability in percentage), based on current knowledge of the situation. This percentage is **Score D**. To be more precise, identify **indicators** that define the meaning of numbers and percentages on each scale. Record Score C and Score D for each option in Column 6.

Step 8

Multiply Score C by Score D in each row (if using pebbles for Score C, reduce the number to a proportion equal to the probability percentage). This gives the **total score** for each positive result. Record the scores in Column 7.

Step 9

In Column 8 **total** the scores recorded in Columns 4 and 7. Review the result and decide which course of action is best. The higher the total number is, the more reason there is to take that course of action.

TABLE 15.3 *Results and Risks* assessment table

Actions	*Negative possibilities*			*Positive possibilities*			*Total score*
	Negative result	A. Value B. % prob.	Negative score A x B	Positive result	C. Value D. % prob.	Positive score C x D	
Ignore letter	Tree harmed and dies. Neighbours are enemies.	–10 40	–4.0	Harmed tree survives.	10 30	3.0	–1.0
Go to court	Fruit lost and costly battle. Neighbours are enemies.	–8 70	–5.6	Win battle.	8 50	4.0	–1.6
Sign agreement	Lose fruit.	–8 100	–8.0	Neighbours are friends.	10 90	9.0	+1.0

Summary of this example: Your family receives a letter from the neighbour. In the letter the neighbour demands the right to have 50 per cent of all the mangoes falling from the tree that your grandmother planted on the edge of your family farm about sixty years ago. You have one week to sign the agreement. If you do not agree, he threatens to cut off all the branches that are hanging on his side of the property, and possibly dig up all the roots on his side, as well. You know that if he does this, it would probably kill the tree. You must now decide how to respond to the letter. You are considering three actions: sign the letter, ignore it, or go to court in the hope that the judge will reject the neighbour's demands. Source: adapted from Means *et al.*, 2002.

Variations

If there are many possible actions, use cards to organize the actions on a continuum from the lowest total score to the highest.

Combinations

- Use *Validation* (Chapter 8), *Values, Interests, Positions* (Chapter 13) or *Levels of Support* (Chapter 14) to further explore the best alternative to a negotiated agreement.

REFERENCES

Barrs, C. (2010) *Preparedness Support: Helping Brace Beneficiaries, Local Staff and Partners for Violence*, The Cuny Center, Arlington.

Birkmann, J. (2006) 'Measuring vulnerability to promote disaster-resilient societies: Conceptual frameworks and definitions', in J. Birkmann (ed.) *Measuring Vulnerability to Natural Hazards: Towards Disaster Resilient Societies*, United Nations University Press, Tokyo, pp. 9–54.

Chandrasekhar, D. (2010) 'Setting the Stage: How Policy Institutions Frame Participation in Post-Disaster Recovery', *Journal of Disaster Research*, vol. 5, no. 2, pp. 130–137.

IIRR and LWR (2011) *Concepts and Principles of Community Managed Disaster Risk Reduction*, International Institute of Rural Reconstruction/Lutheran World Relief, Cavite, Philippines.

Lettieri, E., Masella, C. and Radaelli, G. (2009) 'Disaster management: findings from a systematic review', *Disaster Prevention and Management*, vol. 18, no. 2, pp. 117–136.

Means, K., Josayma, C. with Nielsen, E. and Viriyasakultorn, V. (2002) *Community-Based Forest Resource Conflict Management: A Training Package*, vol. 1 (Section 4.4) and vol. 2 (Activity 32), FAO, Rome.

MODULE 6

Understanding systems

MODULE 6: UNDERSTANDING SYSTEMS

Some of the tools presented so far, and the stories to illustrate them, are technically simple. Still, practitioners will know that these tools and the events or processes they support are more complex than they seem. As one colleague put it, they are 'deceptively simple'. Knowing what tools are needed, when to use them, how to adapt them, at what level of detail, in combination with what other methods and in what sequence is an art that requires practice. Engaged inquiry is a constant puzzle drawing on the judgment and skilful means of practitioners. The same applies to the analysis of the findings of each tool, and their interpretation in context. Making sense of the information collected and organized into stories, tables and diagrams, and acting on it, is not a mechanical exercise. Furthermore, success is never guaranteed.

With these lessons in mind, we turn to more advanced tools that acknowledge complexity and challenging situations from the start. The chapters in this module focus on tools and processes that involve understanding and working with systems, holistically. At first sight, holistic ventures seem to set us up for failure. Attempts at the comprehensive view, with plans to act on it in the fullness of time, can guide people and organizations into a morass of competing priorities, unprovable assumptions and inflexible responses to persistent messiness and uncertainty. Unrealistic plans and overly optimistic accounts of final outcomes often result. All the same, attempts to see the forest from the trees are essential. People and organizations are constantly struggling to understand and manage complex situations. To achieve this, they must be able to divide social and natural systems into meaningful parts, determine how the parts interact, and define methodical actions they can pursue, monitor and adjust along the way. This is no small feat.

Soft systems thinking and methods can respond to this challenge. As argued at the end of Chapters 16 and 17, they can do so by avoiding the pretension of holism and oversimplifications that ignore vast differences in local settings and cultural mindsets. In this module, three well-tested methods based on a soft systems approach to engaged inquiry are explored and narrated in detail.

The first method, *Attribution and Contribution*, attempts to answer a difficult and perennial question in the field of impact evaluation and performance measurement – accounting for the contribution of an intervention (action, project, programme) to achieving meaningful change (Mayne, 2001). The authors developed this tool in the summer of 2010 in response to pressures on civil society organizations (CSOs) working at the international level to demonstrate that their programmes are making a difference. Chapter 16 describes the tool and its use in Burkina Faso to assess the contribution of a volunteer cooperation programme to the struggle against HIV/AIDS.

Chapter 17 describes and illustrates multiple variations on *System Dynamics*, our social adaptation of the input-output matrix used in economics to depict the interaction of sectors in an economy. The tool helps identify entry points into a system based on an assessment of how elements in the system interact with each other to create specific behaviours and situations. The basic method outlined below, extensively tested by us and many partners around the world, can be extended to a wide range of topics, including systems in nature (*Ecological Dynamics*), factors in a problem situation (*Causal Dynamics*), activities in a project or programme (*Activity Dynamics*) and actors in a network (*Network Dynamics*). A synthetic version, *Social Dynamics*, explores the overall interaction of stakeholders, problems and actions in a given context.

The third method, presented in Chapter 18, is *Domain Analysis*, a powerful approach to tapping into local knowledge systems. The method helps to describe how people view a domain or topic area, and create new learning opportunities based on this understanding. The theory underlying *Domain Analysis* is Personal Construct Psychology, a well-known theory in Psychology and the Cognitive Sciences developed in the 1950s by George Kelly. Our social adaptation of the approach offers a method to explore any topic where local knowledge is at play, including things in nature (*Ecological Domain*), activities (*Activity Domain*), problems (*Problem Domain*), stakeholder profiles (*Social Domain*) and options for action (*Option Domain*).

While technically advanced, applications of *System Dynamics* and *Domain Analysis* are not as difficult as they seem. They are 'deceptively complex'. With practice, and active learning in light of errors along the way, practitioners can apply them to real-life problem solving and engaged research with great effectiveness. They can do so provided they never lose sight of the purpose of the inquiry and the real conversations the tools are meant to support. To make sure this central point is not forgotten, the last chapter in the module (Chapter 19) presents a full-length case study bringing together three meaningful applications of systems thinking: *Causal Dynamics*, *Ecological Domain* and *Social Domain*. The real-life story, set among tobacco farmers in Bangladesh, also includes an evaluative application of *The Socratic Wheel*. The research team selected, combined, adapted, sequenced and scaled these tools to facilitate authentic dialogue and address hard realities: addiction to a tobacco growing habit that is costing farmers their health and their land.

For readers that prefer to ground their learning in real stories, proceed directly to Chapter 19 and return later, as needed, to review the tools and their theoretical foundations. This example of PAR in Bangladesh reinforces a key argument developed in this book: simple and advanced action-inquiry tools can be adapted to a complex task and goals established under difficult circumstances. The story is also an instance of 'thinking outside the box' – tapping into systems of local knowledge while encouraging innovation and learning.

CHAPTER 16

Contributing to change

INTRODUCTION

Causality is often reduced to its simplest expression, i.e. linear and mechanical, leaving out considerations of complexity in society and nature or issues of human ethics and responsibility. For many adepts of hard scientific logic, causation happens without causes that are worth pleading or fighting for. Facts are established independently of values, and values are adopted and promoted without requiring scientific justification. These views on the matter of 'objective causality', widely held, are misleading in many regards. Among other flaws, they ignore a long-standing Anglo-Saxon tradition where evidence and responsibility are constantly brought together to support a complex profession and field: the practice of legal, evidence-based reasoning. In this chapter, we draw on this tradition to show how fact-finding, reasoning and the exercise of judgment can be applied to assessing meaningful change in a domain that can be attributed to a specific intervention (action, project, programme). The proposed methodology, entitled *Attribution and Contribution*, helps justify findings and recommendations that follow from a series of considerations – i.e. change observed in a domain, the scope of the intervention, the role of other intervening actors and factors, obstacles along the way, how methodical and deliberate the intervention was, what would have happened had the intervention not taken place, and the reliability of evidence provided to answer these critical questions. *Attribution and Contribution* addresses each of these in order, converging around a final judgment on the worth of specific interventions in real settings. Through this kind of reasoning the tool offers a reasonable and reasoned response to 'the attribution problem' and to broader debates raised at the end of the chapter on the concept of causation in the social sciences.

THE ATTRIBUTION PROBLEM

Attribution and Contribution

Purpose

To assess the contribution to meaningful change that can be attributed to a specific intervention (action, project, programme).

Step 1

Describe the **intervention** (action, project, programme), main **objectives** (fixed or adjusted over time), **time frame** and the implementing **partners**. Keep in mind that credit for broader interventions over long periods of time involving many actors and intervening factors is more difficult to determine. Be as specific as is necessary. Record your response under Step 1 in the diagram illustrated in Figure 16.1.

Step 2

Discuss relevant **observed changes** in the domain. Based on the available evidence or evidence collected for the purpose, indicate the magnitude of the observed changes – whether there has been major, moderate, small or no progress or whether the situation has gotten worse. Record your response on the vertical line in the centre of the diagram. Justify your response and indicate your sources of evidence. If change is unknown, describe a more specific intervention and objectives (in Step 1) or make plans to gather more evidence before proceeding to the next steps.

Step 3

Discuss four questions concerning the **scope of the intervention**. Use a descending scale of (3) to (1) to answer each question.

1. Was the intervention the **sole contributor** (3) to the observed change or did it play a role **jointly** (2) or in **parallel** (1) with other interventions (or intervening factors)?
2. Did the intervention contribute **directly** (3) to the observed change, through nearness of cause and effect, or did it act **indirectly** (2) or somewhat **remotely** (1), several steps removed from the final effects (see ice hockey example)?
3. What was the **scale** of the intervention – large (3), moderate (2) or small (1)?
4. How important were the **obstacles** blocking progress? Were they major (3), moderate (2) or minor, if any (1)?

Use a bar chart to record your responses in Step 3 of the diagram. Justify your responses and indicate your sources of evidence. For a more detailed analysis of the chain of actors and factors involved in producing observed changes, use *Timeline* (Chapter 9) and *Force Field* (Chapter 10) combined with *Stakeholder Identification* (Chapter 11).

> In ice hockey, an assist for helping a teammate score a goal is credited to one or two other players on the ice provided no opposing player touched the puck in between. While players get goals and assists, credit for winning the game goes to the whole team.

Step 4

Determine the extent to which the observed change would have occurred had the intervention not taken place, keeping in mind answers to previous questions. This is the **default scenario**, or counterfactual statement. Indicate whether there would have been major, moderate, small or no progress or whether the situation would have gotten worse. Record your response on the vertical line in the centre of the diagram. Justify your response and indicate your sources of evidence.

Step 5

Discuss and rate the **overall result** of the intervention. This is the difference between observed change and the default scenario – the distance between the two prior ratings on the vertical line in the centre of the diagram (see example in Figure 16.1). Is the overall result positive or negative? Is it significant, modest or limited? Record your response and indicate your sources of evidence.

Step 6

Discuss four questions concerning the **methodical** nature of the intervention. Use a descending scale of (3) to (1) for each question.

1 To what extent did the intervention use **effective** methods, i.e. rational steps and credible means, to achieve the observed results (assessed in Step 5)?
2 To what extent did it make an **efficient** use of available resources (human and material)?
3 Did the intervention achieve results through steps and adjustments that were **deliberate** (3) or were results partly (2) or fully (1) accidental, i.e. obtained through unintended actions?
4 How **verifiable** is the evidence used to answer all preceding questions. Is it generally sound (3), incomplete (2) or rather weak (1)?

Justify each response and use a bar chart to record your ratings in Step 6 of the diagram.

Step 7

Determine the **overall contribution** that the intervention has made, in light of answers given to previous questions, using values of 3 (high), 2 (moderate) or 1 (low). Justify your response and use a bar chart to record your rating in Step 7 of the diagram.

Step 8

Discuss the implications or **recommendations** that follow from the assessment. Should the objectives or partners involved in the intervention change (Step 1)? Should the

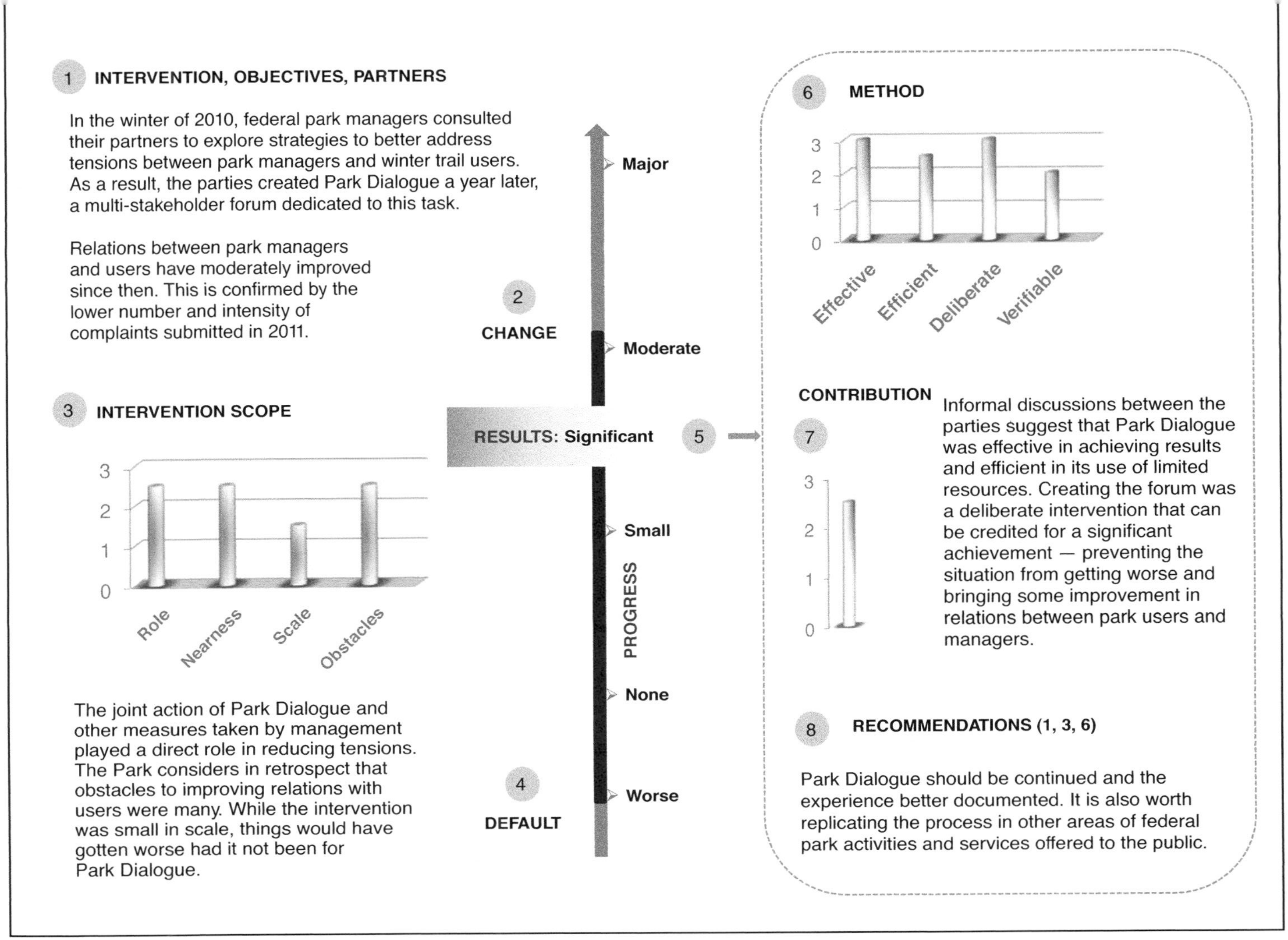
1 INTERVENTION, OBJECTIVES, PARTNERS
In the winter of 2010, federal park managers consulted their partners to explore strategies to better address tensions between park managers and winter trail users. As a result, the parties created Park Dialogue a year later, a multi-stakeholder forum dedicated to this task.
Relations between park managers and users have moderately improved since then. This is confirmed by the lower number and intensity of complaints submitted in 2011.
2 CHANGE
Major
Moderate
3 INTERVENTION SCOPE
3
2
1
0
Role
Nearness
Scale
Obstacles
RESULTS: Significant
5
Small
PROGRESS
None
Worse
4 DEFAULT
The joint action of Park Dialogue and other measures taken by management played a direct role in reducing tensions. The Park considers in retrospect that obstacles to improving relations with users were many. While the intervention was small in scale, things would have gotten worse had it not been for Park Dialogue.
6 METHOD
3
2
1
0
Effective
Efficient
Deliberate
Verifiable
CONTRIBUTION
7
3
2
1
0
Informal discussions between the parties suggest that Park Dialogue was effective in achieving results and efficient in its use of limited resources. Creating the forum was a deliberate intervention that can be credited for a significant achievement — preventing the situation from getting worse and bringing some improvement in relations between park users and managers.
8 RECOMMENDATIONS (1, 3, 6)
Park Dialogue should be continued and the experience better documented. It is also worth replicating the process in other areas of federal park activities and services offered to the public.

FIGURE 16.1 *Attribution and Contribution* – Park Dialogue.

intervention be more direct, change how it interacts with other interventions, expand or reduce its scale or find new ways to overcome existing obstacles (Step 3)? Are there ways to be more effective in achieving results or more efficient in the use of resources? Is there room for more rigorous and agile planning in response to unexpected results? What evidence is needed to verify key conclusions more reliably (Step 6)?

FAQ

- ***In what way is* Attribution and Contribution *different from results-based management (RBM)?***

Attribution and Contribution and RBM are similar in some important ways. They depend on clear objectives and sound evidence to establish links between interventions and observed outcomes. Both methods also raise questions about the efficiency and effectiveness of measures taken to achieve results. Unlike RBM, however, *Attribution and Contribution* goes beyond quantitative measurements to include any information (credible narratives, for instance) that counts as evidence in assessing outcomes. More importantly, the method is designed to support thoughtful reflection and collective learning by multiple stakeholders, not simply upward accounting for results promised. It is less about attributing change to a particular intervention (to take credit) and more about assessing a contribution to problem solving and meaningful change. Finally, *Attribution and Contribution* requires evidence to be analysed and interpreted as part of an overall argument that considers the role and nearness of an intervention in relation to observed change. As in courts of law, counterfactual thinking – assessing what would have happened had it not been for the intervention – is part of the reasoning. This default scenario is not reduced to evidence generated through controlled comparisons. In most, if not all, complex social systems it is simply not possible to compare situations as though they were identical in all ways except for the intervention (Scriven, 2008). Legal reasoning, by contrast, establishes the default scenario through arguments about reasonable expectations and credible explanations.

- ***How do you avoid complacency in discussions about results?***

You make sure that discussions reflect the views of different stakeholders, including individuals or groups that may have conflicting perspectives and information on the situation at hand. Also the evidence and reasoning used to establish links between intervention and results should be sound enough to convince third parties not involved in the exercise. Well-informed or knowledgeable parties not involved in the intervention may play a useful role in helping groups develop assessments that stand on their own.

Variations and combinations

- *Attribution and Contribution* is not a stand-alone method to evaluate results. It must be combined with methods to gather, analyse and share information on changes towards the monitoring and evaluation of project or programme results. Any number of M&E methods already in place or set up to collect and analyse information may be used. They are key to designing and substantiating an application of *Attribution and Contribution* to real-life situations involving meaningful change.

Uniterra and HIV/AIDS prevention and treatment in Burkina Faso

Uniterra, one of Canada's largest international volunteer programmes, is a joint initiative of the Centre for International Studies and Cooperation (CECI) and World University Service of Canada (WUSC). Volunteers are present in eight African, three Latin American and two Asian countries for periods ranging from a few weeks to two years, to help build the capacities of partner organizations to meet the Millennium Development Goals. In the late fall of 2011, Uniterra decided to enhance their RBM framework by incorporating results from the application of *Attribution and Contribution* into a mid-term assessment of project and sector activities undertaken since July 2009. The decision reflected a desire shared by many volunteer and international development organizations to ensure that the attribution of credit to interventions, as required by funders, not be done mechanically or without due cause. After testing the tool among their own international staff, Uniterra sponsored applications to individual projects within each country and convened broader national analyses at the sector level, with a focus on Uniterra's contribution to intermediate outcomes (i.e. medium-term changes in behaviour). A total of 108 organizations in thirteen different countries engaged in assessments using the tool, contributing to sixty-five new cooperation project proposals and fifteen new sectorial plans. What follows is a step-by-step description of reasoning emerging from the application of *Attribution and Contribution* to the health sector in Burkina Faso, with a focus on Uniterra sponsored HIV/AIDS projects. A group of seventeen participants – two representatives from each partner organization in Burkina Faso and three national government officials – took a few hours to complete the assessment, drawing on the prior data gathering and analyses done for each project. The assessment was coordinated and facilitated by Uniterra staff F. Lankoandé, Coordinator in Burkina Faso, C. Vimbamba, and Sector programme officer and regional specialist, A. Ouedraogo, with support and coaching from P. Fragnier, Team Leader Knowledge Management Unit at Uniterrra. Figure 16.2 summarises the analysis performed by one of the seven partners in Burkina Faso, used as an input into the sector-wide analysis described in the text.

Intervention, objectives and partners (Step 1)

Health conditions in Burkina Faso are cause for worry. Death rates and morbidity from disease are high. Geographic and financial access to health services is poor. While the number of persons in the country who test positive for HIV/AIDS based on blood serum specimens (seroprevalence) has gone down from 7.17 per cent in 1997 to 1.6 per cent in 2008 and 1.2 in 2010, the number of new infections has been on the increase since 2006, particularly among young men and women. Of the 120,000 adults currently living with HIV/AIDS, half of them are women. About 350,000 children have become orphans;

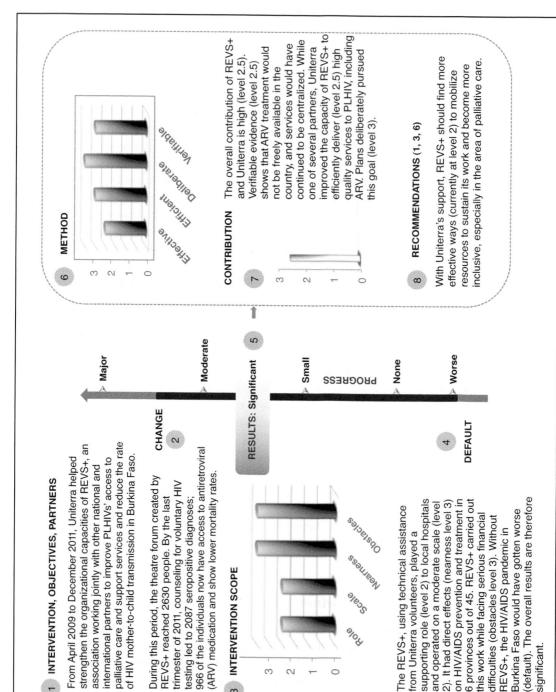

1 INTERVENTION, OBJECTIVES, PARTNERS

From April 2009 to December 2011, Uniterra helped strengthen the organizational capacities of REVS+, an association working jointly with other national and international partners to improve PLHIVs' access to palliative care and support services and reduce the rate of HIV mother-to-child transmission in Burkina Faso.

During this period, the theatre forum created by REVS+ reached 2630 people. By the last trimester of 2011, counseling for voluntary HIV testing led to 2087 seropositive diagnoses; 966 of the individuals now have access to antiretroviral (ARV) medication and show lower mortality rates.

3 INTERVENTION SCOPE

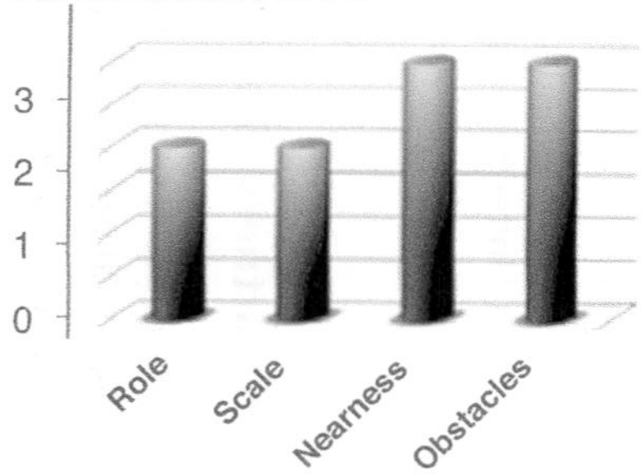

The REVS+, using technical assistance from Uniterra volunteers, played a supporting role (level 2) to local hospitals and operated on a moderate scale (level 2). It had direct effects (nearness level 3) on HIV/AIDS prevention and treatment in 6 provinces out of 45. REVS+ carried out this work while facing serious financial difficulties (obstacles level 3). Without REVS+, the HIV/AIDS pandemic in Burkina Faso would have gotten worse (default). The overall results are therefore significant.

2 CHANGE

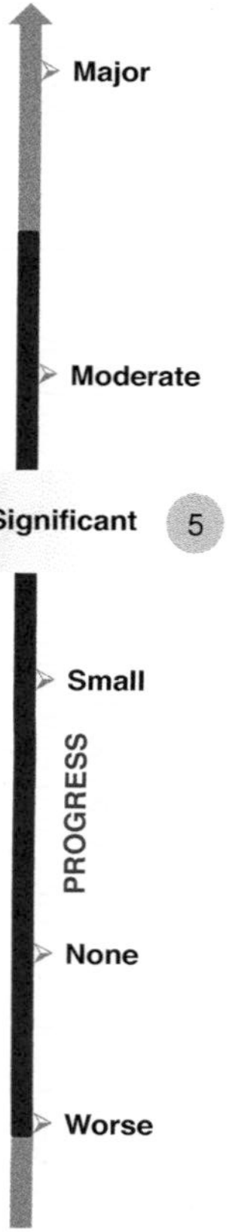

RESULTS: Significant 5

4 DEFAULT

6 METHOD

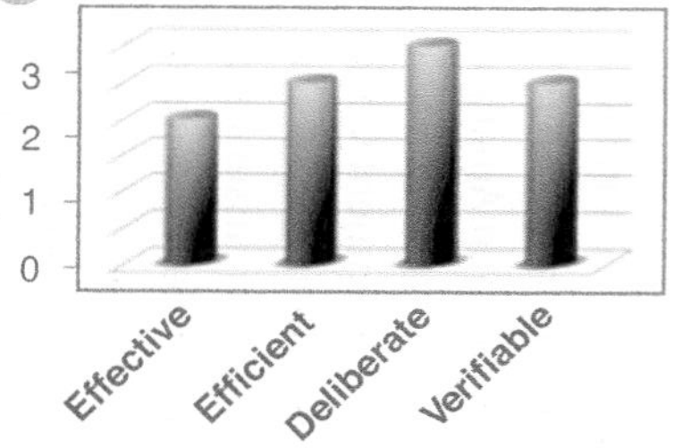

7 CONTRIBUTION

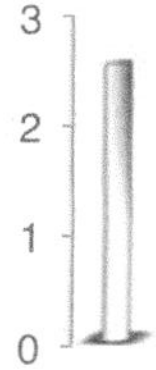

The overall contribution of REVS+ and Uniterra is high (level 2.5). Verifiable evidence (level 2.5) shows that ARV treatment would not be freely available in the country, and services would have continued to be centralized. While one of several partners, Uniterra improved the capacity of REVS+ to efficiently deliver (level 2.5) high quality services to PLHIV, including ARV. Plans deliberately pursued this goal (level 3).

8 RECOMMENDATIONS (1, 3, 6)

With Uniterra's support, REVS+ should find more effective ways (currently at level 2) to mobilize resources to sustain its work and become more inclusive, especially in the area of palliative care.

20,000 of them had HIV/AIDS in 2002. Only 45 per cent of persons living with HIV/Aids (PLHIV) have access to antiretroviral medication (ARV).

Since 2009, Uniterra has brought sixty-two Canadian volunteers (thirty-eight women, twenty-four men) to help in the struggle against HIV/AIDS and sexually transmitted diseases (STD) in Burkina Faso. These men and women have worked to build the capacities of partner organizations in areas ranging from HIV/AIDS prevention (information, education, behaviour change communication, counselling for voluntary HIV testing) to gender equity awareness and the provision of support and care services (palliative care, helping orphans and vulnerable children achieve financial autonomy, etc.). The Uniterra programme and its volunteers have also sought to strengthen organizational governance and efficiency by bringing improvements to strategic planning, the management of human resources, accounting for resources, mobilizing resources and managing knowledge (through better secretarial work, archival methods, data base management, communications, monitoring and evaluation).

During this two-year period (2009 to 2011) Uniterra partnered with seven Burkina Faso organizations and projects. They include the Association pour le développement des initiatives de prévention en santé (ADIPS), the Association Évangélique d'Aide au Développement (AEAD), the Centre d'Information, de conseil et de documentation sur le sida et la tuberculose (CIC-DOC), the Conseil Burkinabè d'appui aux associations et ONG de lutte contre le VIH/sida (BURCASO), the Programme d'appui au monde communautaire (PAMAC), Responsabilité–Espoir–Vie–Solidarité (REVS+) and Solidarité et Entraide Mutuelle au Sahel (SEMUS).

Observed change (Step 2)

Since 2009, various changes have been observed.

- **Increased outreach**
  Of the three partners working on prevention, all have increased outreach, each in their own way. AEDA offered counselling for voluntary HIV testing. REVS+ created a theatre forum involving twelve people living with HIV (PLHIV) who gave performances for a total audience of 12,192. ADIPS built a more efficient electronic management and provisioning system for pharmaceutical products used by PLHIV.
- **Enhanced support and care**
  Using a novel approach that incorporates ergotherapy and psychosocial support, three of the six partners offered support and care services to 6,217 PLHIV. Palliative care services reached seventy women and thirty men living with HIV, and another 228 received nutrition counselling (ADIPS). As for measures to promote financial independence, reports indicate that the theatre forum raised 2,000 USD. Another thirty-one PLHIVs secured micro-loans totalling 6,400 USD, 80 per cent of which were reimbursed within the expected period. Income generating activities, also supported by ADIPS, helped thirteen orphans and vulnerable children achieve greater financial autonomy. Four of these children have seen their earnings from a soap cooperative jump from 1,000 USD to 2,000 USD in 2011.

- **Improved organizational leadership and governance**
  All partners mentioned improvements in leadership and governance. For REVS+, this meant producing high-quality financial reports and delivering them on time to decision-makers; for BURCASO, a review of its by-laws helped to clarify the roles of directors and staff; for SEMUS, producing a news bulletin four times a year increased its visibility and accountability to supporters; for BURCASO, CIC-DOC and REVS+, knowing how to better mobilize financial resources and diversify sources of earnings contributed to greater organizational coherence and project sustainability; for PAMAC, rolling up timely and more reliable data from 300 associations helped to steward programmes; and for all partners, building capacities for 678 people and improving or creating seventy-three tools in the process made leadership and governance of their organizations stronger.
- **Greater gender equity**
  SEMUS and BURCASO increased substantially the number of women in key decision-making positions within their organizations. REVS+ delivered gender equality workshops to thirty elected representatives and fifty association leaders. More broadly, partner awareness of gender equity issues increased.
- **Enhanced capacity to engage in policy dialogue**
  SEMUS and REVS+ report being better prepared to participate in political dialogue, with a view to influencing policy making and the development of important HIV/AIDS services such as palliative care.

At a broader level, the seroprevalence rate in Burkina Faso has gone down from 1.6 per cent in 2007 to 1.2 per cent in 2010, according to official UNAIDS statistics. Sexual behaviour seems to be changing as well. In 2010, about 70 per cent of adults aged between fifteen and forty-nine said they used a condom the last time they had sexual intercourse. These reflect positive changes for the country as a whole.

Intervention scope (nearness, role, scale, obstacles) (Step 3)

The Uniterra programme contributed a substantial number of volunteers (sixty-two) that interacted directly with 357 women and 297 men living with HIV and AIDS alongside staff in partner organizations. This added an equivalent of twenty-six full-time staff members to the sector, distributed among seven partner organizations and projects. Overall, the total number of staff was raised by 8 per cent on average, with many of these focussed on strategic capacity-building objectives. Some obstacles were experienced along the way – e.g. delays in the assistance provided by volunteers, and interruptions in funding that hampered the implementation of project activities as planned.

It is important to keep in mind that partner organizations are ultimately responsible for using any newly acquired skills and know-how and for delivering prevention and treatment services, with support from Uniterra but other organizations as well. For example, the REVS+ theatre forum supported by volunteers also partners with the

Association Burkinabè pour le Bien-Être Familial (ABBEF), mandated by the Burkina Faso Government to implement the Programme d'Appui au Développement Sanitaire (PADS). Other partners deliver some of their programmes jointly with other national and international organizations. Thus, the role of Uniterra in achieving the outcomes of each partner can only be indirect and on a moderate scale. This was reflected in frequent ratings of 2 out of 3 in response to questions of role, nearness, scale and obstacles. The ratings indicate that Uniterra played an indirect role by jointly interacting with others to achieve the changes described in Step 2. The scale of the intervention was in most cases moderate and moderate obstacles were encountered along the way.

Default scenario and overall results (Steps 4 and 5)

Without the help of Uniterra volunteers, partners would not have had the capacities and staff to offer new services such as palliative care, the theatre forum and counselling for voluntary HIV testing. The visibility and financial viability of networks such as BURCASO would have remained low were it not for Uniterra's assistance in strategic planning, network resource mobilization and institutional reform. Financial viability would also have been compromised for three partners were it not for support to income generating activities provided by volunteers. Overall, organizations are now more competent in their own priority areas and better equipped to mobilize the financial resources they need to implement and sustain project activities. Given the default scenario and observed changes, the overall results are thus positive and significant.

Method (effective, efficient, deliberate, verifiable) (Step 6)

Step 6 of *Attribution and Contribution* asks to what extent Uniterra and its partners have been methodical in bringing about the observed results. The evidence to show this is strong and verifiable. Programme planning documents created through an RBM process show the rationale for the interventions and logical steps to be taken. They provide detailed information on M&E indicators and ongoing performance measurements using the Logical Framework and reflect careful and deliberate thinking about cause–effect relationships. Evaluation data generated through iterative reporting by volunteers, organizations and a sectorial committee also support the conclusion that the methods used were effective and deliberate. On the matter of efficiency (rated 2 out of 3), however, things could be improved in two ways: by adding more national volunteer placements to the programme and by clearly identifying the people responsible for planning, M&E and reporting activities.

Contribution and recommendations (Steps 7 and 8)

When reaching the last steps of *Attribution and Contribution*, the HIV/AIDS sector committee in Burkina Faso concluded that Uniterra made a significant joint contribution to the introduction of important new HIV/AIDS services and the development of organizational capacities in the sector. Three recommendations followed. First, some adjustments to project priorities are in order, to more directly reinforce Burkina Faso's work in the area of HIV/AIDS prevention. Second, the results of project activities such as voluntary HIV testing and the prevention of mother-to-child HIV transmission (PMTCT) should be consolidated, preferably through contributions from national volunteer placements. Third, given the current decline in funding for HIV/AIDS projects, Uniterra should continue to strengthen its contribution to capacity building in the area of resource mobilization and the development of strategic North–South partnerships.

Other applications of *Attribution and Contribution* to Uniterra programmes and sectors in Africa, Asia and Latin America were very well received, with project-related results ranging from moderate to significant and contributions by Uniterra to these results from moderate to high. In all cases participants recognized that other actors and factors intervene in the process. Overall, participants said that the discussions created space for a higher-level thinking process that will be very useful in future discussions with donors and other partners regarding strategic contributions and plans for ongoing improvements. It also challenged their assumptions regarding the availability and value of evidence on observed change, and the theory of change underlying their programme model. In Latin America, for example, where human rights based programming tends to dominate Uniterra's interventions, participants recognized that they had little concrete data on the local expressions of changes in abilities to exercise human rights. This prompted plans to gather field data differently and explore new actions other than advocacy for changes in laws.

THREADS OF THEORY: CAUSATION OR FIGHTING FOR A CAUSE

Science is a beautiful paradox. It is faith in the existence of causal interconnections – in order in things that are, or regularity in the world as we know it. But it also rebels against prison-like causation – against laws that rule out freedom of the mind, the exercise of doubt and the possibility of things being otherwise, if only through the responsible work of science. Good science is a worthy cause that postulates both the presence and absence of iron-fisted order and efficient causality. Careful inquiry based on systems thinking and involvement in the world is built on the same paradox, the same dialectical reasoning. It involves getting to know the world by changing it, and vice-versa.

Action-research is a process to both understand a situation and act on it. Root cause analysis is an essential step, followed by planning actions and the chain of causes and effects that lead to expected outcomes. In a true Einsteinian spirit, these exercises in causal reasoning must be made as simple as possible, but not simpler. Otherwise they become part of the problem. Oversimplification takes different forms. It includes converting linear design and systems thinking into enclosures of the mind. Naive thinking embraces the myth of foolproof science and ignores murky causality. It evades chaos and messiness in social and natural history. Bertrand Russell (1997) thus notes that the law of causality, 'like much that passes muster among philosophers, is a relic of a bygone age, surviving, like the monarchy, only because it is erroneously supposed to do no harm.'

The law does real harm whenever it is understood and applied mechanically – when we mistake science for magic, or magic for science. No one doubts that knowing how A causes B which causes C is important to understanding and acting on our world. But causation is an endless chain, and means many things. First of all, one thing is never entirely reducible to whatever causes it. As we argue in Chapter 17, all phenomena and contributing factors must carry some weight of their own if infinite regression (digging deeper for yet another cause) is to be avoided. Second, everything we look at is inevitably part of a bigger picture, which means that some things are bound to be left out and that whole systems are always systems with holes. Third, some degree of freedom and tolerance of loose ends must be part of 'the system' if we are to bother understanding and acting on it, as opposed to passively living our lives in chains. Even when certainty guides learning, it is no more than statistical improbability on a colossal scale (Dawkins, 1986). Given this window of freedom, many futures and system outcomes are possible. Knowing this, god-like plans to engineer reality and history constitute bad science. They deprive causality of causes worth fighting for.

Commentary

Human life is conditioned by its surrounding natural world where objective necessity seems to rule. But it also includes an inner experience, governed by the will and capacity to apply thinking to any meaningful object or phenomenon and to act freely and responsibly in our lives. Given this inner experience, impersonal relations of cause and effect, those that natural sciences abstract from the nexus of life, go only so far in making sense of reality. What humans think and the meaning they assign to life and the world they live in matter equally. This is the hermeneutic standpoint, as developed by Wilhelm Dilthey (1977) and Max Weber (1947), among others, a theory of comprehension and interpretive understanding (*Verstehen*) that values myriad human perspectives on life and its existential surroundings.

When defining the inquiry process, many theorists and practitioners of the social sciences support this hermeneutic stance, against positivism. They reject the notion that causality dictates all human affairs. A more radical attack on positivism, however, consists in rethinking causal thinking itself, embracing it fully, without restriction. To do this, causality should be recognized for what it is: not a simple and narrow path to tread, but rather an intricate playing field of moves in behaviour and language, a battleground of meaningful actions and statements about the world. The moves are essentially threefold – **cognitive, discursive and moral** – and they constantly intersect.

When fielding the difficult question of 'causality', a simple move consists in exercising reason, by examining how one thing results in another. Smoking brings about cancer, and global warming happens because of greenhouse gases, for instance. The simplicity of this **cognitive** move, however, is more apparent than real. For one thing, the link between cause and effect can never be 'simply observed'. It is always subject to reasoning, discussion and debate. If hotly disputed, a cause may easily turn into something different. It may become the grounds for legal action. When attracting attention, the action may even lead to a well-known lawsuit or *cause célèbre*, from L. *causa*, a judicial process. By definition, 'causes' are not issues of scientific inquiry alone. They also represent matters that people wish to discuss, *causer* in French, something they can do through an informal *causerie* or by going to law in order to plead their case (L. *causari*, to plead, discuss).

For science to demonstrate (or dismiss) connections between cause and effect, it too must make a 'plea' and engage in a debate or **discursive** logic meant to persuade and 'please' the mind. It must offer a justification based on evidence and adequate reasoning. This is an exercise that goes beyond Hume's 'impressions' and felt associations between them – beyond knowledge based on sense experience alone. Cancer from smoking and global warming from greenhouse gases will be acknowledged only if there is serious review and discussion of the matter at hand. Being able to debate all allegations of positive knowledge is key to the business of science. Claims and counterclaims about causes and effects are crucial in this regard. Quarrels will extend to statements about what constitutes credible connections between cause and effect, irrespective of the subject at hand. This is the playing field of causality in science, grounds of reasoning that are conducive to many moves and disputes.

The logical positivist discourse on causality, developed by leading Vienna Circle members such as James Ayer (1954), is one possible move towards hard scientific knowledge. It addresses the field of knowledge through the powers of prediction, by creating a perfect 'if-then' model of the observed phenomenon, through propositions that spell out the necessary and sufficient conditions for it to exist. Science thus looks for the 'sole cause' of an observable effect or result, the only one responsible for it. This is a hard scientific proposition, one that is hard to sell when we consider the complexity of most observable phenomena. Scientists would be ill-advised to argue that global warming is the sole cause for the decline of coral reefs. Abstracting and isolating some relationships from the web of life, natural and social, oversimplifies the facts.

Analysing 'the majority of the facts that make up the factors of a complex whole' (Dilthey, 1989, p. 433) may constitute a better plea for causal thinking. Variations on Aristotle's concepts of formal and material causes may be helpful in this regard. A formal cause is the overall form according to which a thing or event is produced or brought about (e.g. an atmosphere surrounding the earth held in place by gravity). A material cause is the means that brings the formal cause into being, hence any part, element, constituent, ingredient or factor (e.g. greenhouse gases) that goes into shaping a composite thing or event (e.g. climate change). Effects of parts on the composite whole and the composite whole on its parts can be addressed provided a distinction is made between the two, where the whole adds up to more than the sum of its parts. Part-whole and whole-part causation is an invitation to 'whole systems thinking'. It calls for the analysis of structures, laws, regularities or patterns to shed light on events of natural and social history. Functionalism in the social sciences is a response to this call. It sets out to interpret society as a structure with interrelated parts, usually with an emphasis on the functions or unintended finality that normative behaviour and cultural beliefs play in maintaining existing social institutions, those of family, religion, economy and polity (Merton, 1957).

Functionalism imposes as many constraints on scientific inquiry as does linear causal thinking. A more flexible discourse consists in toning down the 'hardness' of science, by investigating any cause that 'contributes' to an observable phenomenon and plays a part in bringing it about. While a contributing cause is neither necessary nor sufficient to produce the effect, altering it will alter the effect. The Australian philosopher Mackie (1974) thus points out that causal talk is often about contributing factors that accidentally combine to produce observable effects. For instance, a house burns down because of a short circuit that happens to occur near some flammable material, in a village that is too poor to have a fire brigade. Causal inquiry of this kind is part of day-to-day thinking in complex settings and plays an important role in explaining real events in history. Moves to deflate the claims of hard science, with a focus on things that can be shown to 'contribute' to other things, introduce a more flexible understanding of causation into evidence-based thinking.

An alternative plea for 'soft causation' consists in translating all causal propositions into true or false statements about 'possible worlds', using counterfactual thinking of the 'but for' kind. But for greenhouse gases, there would be no global warming, for instance. In this approach, known as 'modal realism', the first clause is a subjunctive statement in the past tense expressing something contrary to fact. In the writings of Lewis (1986), modal realism involves other concrete worlds that are as real as our actual world, on par with the abstract mathematical entities populating what we say about it. More importantly, counterfactual arguments about cause and effect show how the human mind must imagine all kinds of worlds that are 'possibly real' (and not just imagined), whether they be past, present or future. 'We think of a cause as something that makes a difference, and the difference it makes must be a difference from what would have happened without it. Had it been absent, its effects – some of them, at least, and usually all – would have been absent as well' (Lewis, 1973). In a similar vein, Leibniz (1985) and Luis de Molina (1988) spoke of an infinite set of logically possible worlds as a way of thinking about necessity and possibility. While 'but for' thinking may seem abstract, it is key to legal notions of causation and human responsibility. We say more on this point later.

Modal realism allows causes to actually determine their effects in some real world setting, actual or not. As in Hume's 'regularity theory', causes are invariably followed by their effects. Possibilism, however, adds a chancy dimension to this approach to science. Causation doesn't require a strict deterministic relation between smoking and cancer, for instance (Lewis, 1973). With 'chancy causation', causes simply change the probabilities of their effects; the occurrence of smoking increases the probability of cancer. Arguments for probabilism in science make a lot of sense for one of two reasons. Either our knowledge of existing determinations is always imperfect, or the causal connections under study are chancy in the first place, like the physical world posited by quantum mechanics. The implications of this perspective for evidential reasoning are many, and real. Notions of 'contributing causes' fly in the face of false science that uses the canons of necessary and sufficient causation to deny the role that tobacco plays in 'causing' cancer or greenhouse gas contributions in global warming, for instance.

Disputes about the nature of causation go to show an important point: in order to keep the field, defenders of causation must present their case through an exercise in *causari* – discussing and pleading the merits and relevance of necessary, sufficient, part-whole, contributing, counterfactual or probable causation. Proponents must show that they have cause to believe particular statements to be true, if only because no one has been able to refute them. But their plea must also contain particular assumptions or claims about the nature of causation itself. This means that every scientific hearing is also a hearing about science.

Scientists may effectively engage in discussions of causation on yet another important condition: they must have some idea of things and stakes that are worth playing and fighting for. That is, they must have a 'worthy cause' to support, some human finality or purposeful *telos*, as Aristotle calls it. This is causation understood as a **moral field** governed by a sense of purpose and direction. Principles worth fighting for may be those of objective reasoning and exact science, both of which require that a firm stand be taken against deniers of the tobacco–cancer link and human contributions to climate change, for instance. Alternatively, scientists can go in the opposite direction, towards a critical, value-laden conception of science. They can follow the footsteps of Polanyi, Kuhn, Feyerabend and post-modernist critics of positivism, by rejecting the notion that science is objective and value-free, uninfluenced by social history. With this purpose in mind, science can be shown to be always at war with something, including uncritical ways of doing science. When adopting this critical stance, no causal analysis escapes the discussion of some greater cause, subject to debate. Even the science of climate change can be scrutinized for the goal it serves. No one seriously doubts that rigorous contributions to this science are urgently needed and must be supported. Still, there are reasons to question 'objective' studies of climate variability whose agenda it is to override the multiple causes of famine and limitations on access to food in poverty-stricken Africa, one might argue. Any 'climate change and adaptation' rhetoric that silences the devastating effects of agricultural markets, technology and policy and related struggles over water and land should be questioned. What Barthes (1970) says of historical discourse and its 'reality effect' should never be forgotten: the objective world as depicted in science is never innocent. It is never anything but a meaning, revocable when the politics of knowledge demand it.

Causes that are worth fighting for, with the powers of causal reasoning and argumentation, point to the relationship between conduct and result, hence the idea of moral action and responsibility. They create grounds for ethical behaviour and legal process. This is where human agency comes into play, recognizing that people can cause things to happen, or not. Human agents are subjects responsible and answerable for what they do, such as causing intentional and foreseeable harm to others. The accountability of human agency is to be judged against rules and morals, also a matter of public discussion and responsibility. Human agency also requires demonstration through sound evidence and factual documentation. The implication here is that causation is not *either* a scientific principle *or* a cause worth defending based on moral principles. More to the point, it is both things simultaneously. Causation as understood in every court of law drives the argument home. Legal reasoning is a mix of causal, evidence-based reasoning predicting the outcomes of human action, on the one hand, and deliberation on rights and responsibilities and related claims about the common good, on the other.

Causation in English and American law goes a long way to showing the moral implications of judicial cause–effect reasoning. Key principles include the use of factual evidence, logic and clear argumentation to establish or refute causation. These concepts overlap significantly with the history of science and analytic philosophy. Factual causation, a key step in establishing liability, is often based on 'but for' reasoning, using it as a common sense test of necessity. 'But for' tobacco companies producing and selling highly addictive cigarettes, it can be argued that smoker 'x' or 'y' would not have been struck by lung cancer, for instance. While the 'but for' test is a crucial question to be asked, the complexity of real-life events also calls for other legal notions to handle situations of variable causal weight and mix. Establishing the 'proximate cause' of an injury, the closest to the harm done, is critical here, with the proviso that its actual weight can be superseded by a new 'intervening cause' – an unforeseeable event that interrupts the chain of causation and becomes the proximate cause. These notions are particularly useful in discriminating between an infinite number of 'but for' conditions that can be tied to an observed outcome. A test of 'causal sufficiency' may also help in assessing situations where several necessary conditions mix together to produce harm. Various conditions thus act as 'concurrent actual causes'; 'but for either of them', no harm would have occurred. For instance, tobacco companies are guilty as charged because they produce and sell nicotine cigarettes at the same time as they hide conclusive evidence that shows their lethal effects. Alternatively, 'independent sufficient causes' can join together to produce a particular injury, each one being sufficient to produce the same effect.

Other legal considerations include the extent to which there is deliberate human intervention to cause harm or provide help in the process. Whether the consequences of an action are 'reasonably foreseeable' also matter when trying to prove an allegation. Liability usually assumes that people are responsible for their actions if and only if they can foresee the consequences, like any reasonable person who would find himself or herself in the same circumstances. Foresight does not have to be perfect; a probabilistic, risk-based approach to liability applies in situations that warrant it. Thus, while some heavy smokers never get cancer, tobacco companies are liable for knowingly taking high risks with people's lives.

Wittgenstein (1922) once said that 'superstition is the belief in the causal nexus'. Evidence to the contrary is overwhelming. The playing field of causal inquiry is complex and astoundingly rich in its lifeworld ramifications. Letting positive science occupy the whole field and receive praise or criticism for it is unwise. Too many cognitive, discursive and moral issues are at stake – the way we experience and discuss relationships between events, the causes we fight for and the responsibility we assume (or not) in choosing efficient means to achieve moral ends. When carrying out their own business, scientists would do well to reflect on and work with the many aspects of causal thinking. To be sure, they should look for the evidence they need to develop and present arguments that are clear and convincing. But they should also open the inquiry process to public scrutiny and debate, reflect on the actual ends and people served and be critical of the moral means used to achieve the intended results. Failing this, causation may well turn into a relic of a bygone age.

REFERENCES

Ayer, J. (1954) *Philosophical Essays*, Macmillan, London.
Barthes, R. (1970) 'The discourse of history', in M. Lane (ed.) *Structuralism: A Reader*, Cape, London.
Dawkins, R. (1986) *The Blind Watchmaker*, Norton, New York.
Dilthey, W. (1977) *Descriptive Psychology and Historical Understanding*, Martinus Nijhoff, The Hague.
Dilthey, W. (1989) *Selected Works. Volume 1: Introduction to the Human Sciences*, Princeton University Press, Princeton, NJ.
Leibniz, G. W. (1985) *Theodicy: Essays on the Goodness of God, the Freedom of Man, and the Origin of Evil*, trans. E. M. Huggard, Open Court, La Salle, IL.
Lewis, D. (1973) 'Causation', *Journal of Philosophy*, vol. 70, no. 17, pp. 556–567.
Lewis, D. (1986) *On the Plurality of Worlds*, Blackwell, Oxford.
Mackie, J. L. (1974) *The Cement of the Universe: A Study of Causation*, Oxford University Press, Oxford.
Mayne, J. (2001) 'Addressing attribution through contribution analysis: Using performance measures sensibly', *Canadian Journal of Program Evaluation*, vol. 16, no. 1, pp. 1–24.
Merton, R. (1957) *Social Theory and Social Structure*, Free Press, London.
Molina, Luis de (1988) *On Divine Foreknowledge: Part IV of the Concordia*, trans. Alfred J. Freddosco, Cornell Uniersity Press, Ithaca, NY.
Russell, B. (1997) *Problems of Philosophy*, Oxford University Press, New York and Oxford.
Scriven, M. (2008) 'A summative evaluation of RCT methodology: An alternative approach to causal research', *Journal of MultiDisciplinary Evaluation*, vol. 5, no. 9, pp. 11–24.
Weber, M. (1947) *The Theory of Social and Economic Organization*, trans. A. M. Henderson and Talcott Parsons, Oxford University Press, New York.
Wittgenstein, L. (1922) *Tractatus Logico-Philosophicus*, Kegan Paul, London.

CHAPTER 17

System dynamics

INTRODUCTION

System Dynamics is our adaptation of the input–output model used in economics to depict the interaction of sectors in an economy. While a quantitative technique used by many (including Wassily Leontief, winning him a Nobel Price in Economics), the method presented in this chapter speaks to local perspectives on complex systems. It helps people explore how they define and understand differences between parts of a system (e.g. causal factors or programme activities), how parts interact with each other and how they relate to the whole. It promotes holistic thinking that is also local. *System Dynamics* also invites participants to act based on their analysis of potential entry points into a system that offers opportunities for new learning and social change. These system entry points may be where change needs to happen the most, where change is most effective and easiest to accomplish, or where new understanding challenges people to rethink existing behaviour.

In Chapter 19, we offer a detailed illustration of how one variant of the tool (*Causal Dynamics*) was combined with other PAR methods to support the transition from tobacco cultivation to alternative livelihoods in Bangladesh. Readers are encouraged to review this example in conjunction with their reading of the generic method (*System Dynamics*) presented below. Also in this chapter are instructions showing how the generic form can be adapted and applied to any topic, including systems in nature (*Ecological Dynamics*), activities (*Activity Dynamics*), problems (*Causal Dynamics*), stakeholder relations (*Network Dynamics*) and social systems involving the interaction of actors, problems and activities (*Social Dynamics*). Short stories from real-life applications in Nepal, India, Bolivia and Canada are provided to illustrate each variation.

The chapter ends with a discussion about whole systems and, in keeping with soft systems theory, proposes that we view them as 'systems with holes'.

INTERACTIONS

System Dynamics

Purpose

To identify entry points into a system based on an assessment of how elements in the system interact to create specific behaviours and situations.

Step 1

Define the **topic** area and identify the **key elements** or component parts of the system involved (see *Free List and Pile Sort*, Chapter 8). These should be **concrete**, distinct and clearly described. If the elements are vague, use the *Laddering Down* method in *Active Listening* (Chapter 8) to make them more specific and meaningful. Ask *'What do you mean by this?'* or *'Can you give an example of this?'* Another option is to use **description and storytelling** to explore the topic, and then use this information to identify the elements. Write key words or draw each element on its own card, with details on the back of the card or on a flip chart. When using a rating matrix, make a copy of each element card. For alternatives to using a matrix, see Tips below.

Step 2

Create a **table** on the floor or wall. Place one set of element cards in the top row and the other set (showing the same elements in the same order) in the first column (see Table 17.1).

TABLE 17.1 Interaction between parts (*System Dynamics*)

Elements	*A*	*B*	*C*	*D*	**Total contribution**
A	x				
B		x			
C			x		
D				x	
Total dependence					

Step 3

Decide on a **rating scale** to indicate the level of contribution that each element makes to other elements (for example, from 0 for no contribution to 10 for a maximum contribution). Develop indicators for points on the scale, if need be.

Step 4

Use the scale created in Step 3 to **rate the level of contribution** that each element currently makes to each other element. Ask 'At what level does this (name the row element) contribute to that (name the column element)?' Clarify the question and adapt it to the topic (see specific adaptations of *System Dynamics*). As in all rating exercises, the same score can be given to two or several elements.

Proceed with the rating exercise one **column** after another. Start by rating the extent to which element B contributes to the element heading the column A. This will ensure that the direction of the contribution is clear and consistent. If participants invert the question and indicate how A contributes to B, insert the score in the appropriate cell and return to the questioning by column.

Record each score on its own card and write the **reason** given for each score on the reverse side of its card or on a flip chart. Place the **score cards** in the appropriate rows and columns of the table. Leave empty all cells that **combine an element with itself** (A contributes to A), unless the element interacts with itself (as do members within a stakeholder group, for instance).

Step 5

Once the table is complete, total all scores in each row and write **Total contribution** at the top of a new column to the right. Insert the total scores in this new column, in the appropriate rows. The column shows the total contribution of each row element to all other elements. (A different term for this column is used in *Ecological Dynamics, Causal Dynamics* and *Network Dynamics*.)

Step 6

Total all scores in each column and write **Total dependence** at the beginning of a new row below. Insert the total score in this new row. This indicates the total dependence of the column element on all other elements. (A different term for this sum is used in *Ecological Dynamics, Causal Dynamics* and *Network Dynamics*.)

Step 7

Calculate the **dynamic interaction** between all elements by totalling all contribution scores (or dependency scores) and dividing the result by the maximum total score that could be obtained if all cells in the row (or the column) received the highest rating in the range. Insert the resulting percentage figure at the bottom of the last column.

Step 8

Create a **diagram** by drawing a vertical line that crosses a horizontal line of equal length. Write or draw a symbol representing the topic (identified in Step 1) above the diagram. Write at opposite ends of the vertical and horizontal lines the minimum score (usually 0) and the maximum possible score that could be obtained if all cells in a row or column received the highest rating in the range (for instance, the maximum total score that can be obtained with a list of four elements, where each element interacts with three other elements, using a scale of 0 to 10, is 30). Insert the number that represents the middle score (the sum of maximum scores in a row divided by two) where the lines cross. The **vertical line** indicates the total contribution of an element (its row total) and the **horizontal line**, its total dependence (or column total).

Step 9

Label the four corners of the diagram with the scenario obtained by combining the possible outcomes of each axis: elements that contribute and depend more (top right); those that contribute more and depend less (top left); those that contribute less and depend more (bottom right); those that contribute and depend less (bottom left). Note that the latter elements may be important even if they interact little with other elements in the system. To facilitate the analysis, find an idea or a symbol to represent each corner of the diagram.

Step 10

To **locate each element** in the diagram, mark where the element's total contribution score is located on the vertical line and the element's total dependence score is located on the horizontal line. Draw a line from each location and insert the name of the element where the two lines meet (see Figure 17.1).

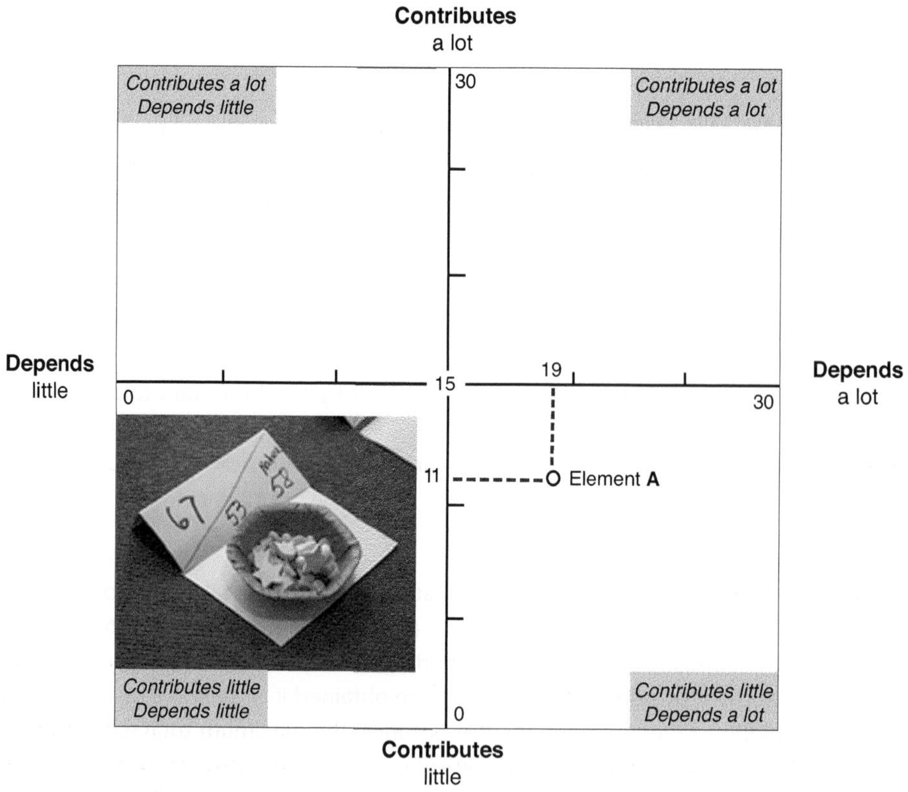

FIGURE 17.1 Locating the interacting elements in a *System Dynamics* diagram.

Step 11

Include in the diagram **other information** that may be useful for the analysis, such as the overall level of control that stakeholders have over each element in the system, the time and level of effort it would take to act on it, or the order in which people plan to act on certain elements. Use **a code** (such as capital letters, numbers, colours or circles) to identify elements with these characteristics (see examples below).

Odd scores that contradict the main tendencies of the diagram may also be important and affect the interpretation of results; one element (e.g. a project activity) that contributes little to other elements may still contribute a lot to one important element. To identify these odd scores, compare each cell score appearing in the rating table with the average row score to see if both scores are on the same lower side or upper side of the middle point of the scale (5 in a scale of 0 to 10, for instance). If a cell score is *not* on the same side as the average row score, compare the score with the average column score to see if both scores are on the same lower side or upper side of the middle point of the scale. If the cell score is *not* on the same side again, use bold font to highlight the cell score. Once these odd scores are identified, draw arrows in the diagram to indicate the relationships that **contradict the main tendencies** of the system. Use **continuous arrows** for scores above the middle point of the scale. These indicate bottom-side elements that contribute significantly to some elements located on the left side of the diagram (see example in *Ecological Dynamics*). Use **broken arrows** for scores below the middle point. These indicate upper-side elements that do *not* contribute significantly to some elements located on the right side of the diagram (see example in *Causal Dynamics*).

Interpreting the results

Step 12

Discuss the overall level of **dynamic interaction** of the elements calculated in Step 7 and review the location of the elements in the diagram, considering three possible scenarios: integration, hierarchy or dispersion.

1 There is **integration** in the system when many elements are located in the top right section of the diagram. This usually reflects a high score for dynamic interaction (above 60 per cent, as calculated in Step 7). In an integrated system increasing or decreasing the contribution of one element in the top right section may in turn affect the level of contribution of all other elements located in the same section. The result is a chain effect that influences the dynamic interaction of all elements, including the element that receives initial attention (see example in *Network Dynamics*, Figure 17.5).

2 There is **hierarchy** in the system when the diagram consists mostly of top left elements and bottom right elements. This usually reflects a middle score for dynamic interaction (between 40 per cent and 60 per cent, as calculated in Step 7). In a hierarchical system, attention to elements in the top left section will automatically have an influence on the bottom right elements.

3 There is **dispersion** or fragmentation in the system when the diagram consists mostly of elements in the bottom left section of the diagram. This usually reflects a low score for dynamic interaction (below 40 per cent, as calculated in Step 7). Elements in this section may be important even if they interact little with other elements in the system. In a dispersed system, however, the elements interact little and can only be modified through direct actions (see *Activity Dynamics*, Figure 17.4).

Step 13

Summarize the scenario or combination of scenarios that best describe the results in the diagram. Discuss the way that participants reached decisions at each step, the elements included and left out of the analysis, the kind of information or knowledge used to rate the elements, the contradictions identified and the other information added in Step 11. If need be, modify one or several elements considering the discussion, and recalculate the overall interaction of all elements (see Step 7). When completed, use this analysis to identify system entry points, rethink priorities or modify some elements so that they **interact differently** with the other elements. This is the key moment in the analysis, when participants can reflect on the meaning of their assessment and what to do to improve synergy in the system or overcome vicious circles that perpetuate problems in the system.

Tips

- Be sure to review in detail the *Scoring tips* in Chapter 8. These are critical to proper application of *System Dynamics*.
- The **elements** used in *System Dynamics* can be real or proposed (e.g. ongoing or planned activities in a project).
- A spreadsheet with **formulas** to calculate totals and create a Cartesian graph automatically is available at www.participatoryactionresearch.net.
- If some elements have a **negative** impact on other elements, use a **scale** that has negative scores (from –10 to 10, for instance; see *Ecological Dynamics*). Negative scores reflect conflict in the system.
- To focus on the rating discussion rather than the table, use a **flip chart to represent each column element**. On each flip chart place the rating cards that indicate the contributions other elements make to the flip chart element. Once the flip charts are completed, compile the scores in a table and go on directly to the diagram in Step 8. **Another option** is to make only one set of element cards and place these in a column in plain view of all participants. When discussing the elements, move the top card to one side and begin by asking to what extent do the remaining

column cards contribute to the isolated element. Continue this line of questioning down the column, always referring to the isolated element card. Once these relationships have been scored and recorded in a table, return the top card to the column and pull out the next element card. All cards remaining in the column can then be discussed as elements contributing to the isolated card. Continue until all interactions have been assessed and recorded. Once the scores are compiled in a table, go on to the diagram in Step 8 and review the results and the process. Both of these options (flip chart and single column) lend themselves to a direct **conversational style** of facilitation focussing on rating of the elements rather than the construction of a table. It also makes it easier to use objects or drawings instead of written cards, and work in a smaller space.

- To compare current levels of interaction between elements with levels people are aiming for in the future, divide each cell of the table created in Step 2 into two parts and insert a score in each part. The first score describes the **actual** contribution that an element makes to another, and the second score, the **ideal** contribution it should make. Write details on how to achieve the ideal contribution on the reverse side of each score card.

Variations

Following are instructions and brief illustrations of five thematic applications that build on the generic method. *System Dynamics* can be applied to the interaction between the components of an ecological system (*Ecological Dynamics*), factors contributing to a core problem (*Causal Dynamics*), activities that are part of a project or programme (*Activity Dynamics*) or actors involved in a particular situation (*Network Dynamics*). Another application is *Social Dynamics*, to assess the overall interaction of key stakeholders, problems and actions in a given context.

Two other applications not illustrated in this book concern the interaction between skills and the integration of values. *Skill Dynamics* asks how each skill applied to a set of activities contributes to other skills and depends on them at the same time. It supports discussions about potential complementarities between skills in a domain or set of activities and ways to integrate them further. *Value Dynamics* looks at how the values, moral principles or rules of ethical conduct that people adopt when taking a position or acting on a key problem interact with each other. The exercise focusses on the extent to which one value supports and is supported by other values people apply in a given context. The tool helps people reflect on the integration of core values that express their end goals and values to support them (acting as means). The diagram resulting from the analysis produces three possible scenarios: integration, hierarchy and fragmentation. In an integrated value system, values support each other, acting as rules of ethical conduct and end goals at the same time (top right section). In a hierarchical value system, top left rules of ethical conduct support bottom right end goals. In a fragmented value system, moral principles and rules of ethical conduct interact little and are applied to the key problem independently of each other.

Ecological Dynamics

Purpose

Ecological Dynamics helps describe how the components of an ecological system interact with each other. The tool may be used to support systems thinking concerning things in nature (such as plant species and varieties) or ecological processes (such as soil degradation or the dynamics of pollution). The understanding of the system may help people decide where to focus attention and what relationships to change.

Adaptation

Ecological Dynamics begins by defining an **ecological system** and listing the **components** of the system. The rating scale can include negative as well as positive values (e.g. –10 to +10). It focusses on the extent to which one component provides benefits to or harms other components in the system, and the extent to which each is helped by or harmed by other components. These can be seen as relations of cooperation (each component derives a benefit) or relations of exploitation or competition (one component benefits *at the expense of* another). When rating, ask 'To what extent does this component (name the row component) provide benefits to or harm that component (name the column component)?' When both situations apply, estimate the net effect. The resulting matrix produces an index for 'Helps/Harms other components' (vertical axis) and an index for 'Helped by/Harmed by other components' (horizontal axis). See *System Dynamics* for generic instructions.

TABLE 17.2 *Ecological Dynamics* of an Indian mixed cropping system

Elements	*Rice*	*Maize*	*Sorghum*	*Barbaty bean*	*Pearl millet*	*Black gram*	*Sesame*	*Pigeon pea*	*Green gram*	**Total contribution**
Rice	x	0	0	0	0	–3	0	0	–3	–6
Maize	–2	x	0	5	2	0	3	0	0	8
Sorghum	–3	0	x	5	0	–4	0	–4	–4	–10
Barbaty bean	–5	–3	0	x	0	–3	–4	–2	–3	–20
Pearl millet	–4	–5	0	5	x	–3	0	–4	–3	–14
Black gram	–3	0	0	0	0	x	0	0	0	–3
Sesame	–5	2	–3	–5	–5	0	x	–1	0	–17
Pigeon pea	–5	0	–2	4	–2	0	0	x	0	–5
Green gram	0	0	0	–3	0	0	0	0	x	–3
Total dependence	**–27**	**–6**	**–5**	**11**	**–5**	**–13**	**–1**	**–11**	**–13**	**–70**

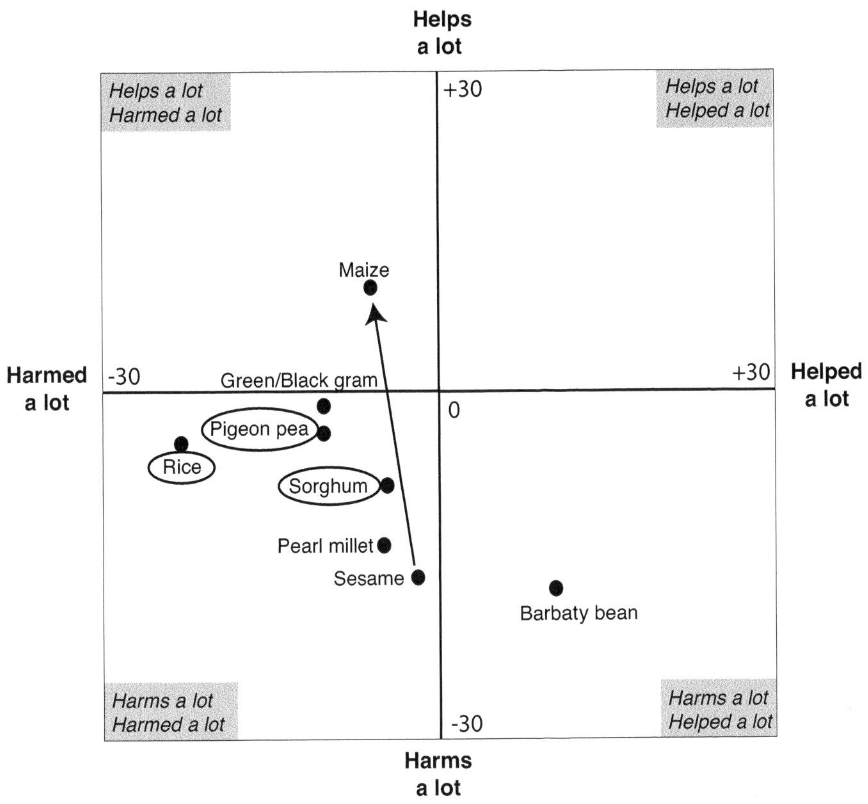

FIGURE 17.2 *Ecological Dynamics* of Indian mixed cropping.

Summary of this example: In this Indian mixed cropping system the most important crops (marked with circles) are rice, pigeon peas and sorghum. The analysis shows that some crops interact in positive ways (see Table 17.2 and Figure 17.2). For instance, maize generally affects other crops positively or does no harm. It is also positively affected by sesame cultivation (as shown by the arrow). The growth of the barbaty bean benefits significantly from climbing on the stalks of maize, sorghum, millet and pigeon pea. On the whole, however, the diagram indicates that most crops affect other crops in slightly negative ways. This is tolerated by farmers because diversity in the system allows them to manage risk. If unpredictable environmental factors such as drought or pest attack affect some crops others will survive. When this happens, competition is eliminated, allowing the remaining crops to produce better. Farmers also adjust how much of each crop they sow and the planting time to meet specific priorities (markets, home use, feed for livestock, etc.). For example, a farmer may increase the ratio of rice in their field while reducing the ratio of pearl millet if market conditions are right. Source: adapted from Lundy, 2006.

PHOTO 17.1 Millet, sorghum and pulse varieties are a treasure trove for women farmers in Medak District, India. (Source: Deccan Development Society)

Causal Dynamics

Purpose

Causal Dynamics helps assess how factors related to a key problem interact. The tool guides action when addressing a problem situation by targeting particular factors in the system (entry points).

Adaptation

Causal Dynamics focusses on relationships of **cause** and **effect** rather than relations of contribution and dependence explored in most other applications of *System Dynamics*. It begins by defining a **key problem** and listing the **factors involved**. Include the key problem in the rating matrix if it is distinct from other factors and interacts with them directly. Leave the key problem out of the rating matrix if the factors are examples of the key problem.

When rating, ask 'To what extent does this (name the row element) cause that (name the column element)?', or 'At what level does this (name the row element) produce that (name the column element) as a consequence?' The resulting matrix generates a cause index at the end of each row in the table (vertical axis in the diagram) and an effect index at the bottom of each column (horizontal axis in the diagram). Label the four corners of the diagram with the scenario obtained by combining the possible outcomes of each axis: factors that are **mostly causes** of other factors (upper left corner of the diagram), factors that are **mostly effects** of other factors (bottom right corner), factors that are both **causes and effects** (upper right corner) and factors that tend to be **independent** of each other (lower left corner). (See *System Dynamics* for generic instructions, and a detailed example in Chapter 19.)

Advanced version

The advanced version of *Causal Dynamics* incorporates two other sets of considerations: the apparent and real weight of each factor, and the overall level of integration between elements in the system. These are not needed in other applications of the generic method of *System Dynamics*.

Apparent and real weight

Some factors at the root of a key problem may have to be addressed **directly** even if they interact with other factors. To identify these, distinguish between the apparent and real weight of each factor. The **apparent weight** can be obtained by initially asking how important each factor is in relation to the key problem (as defined in Step 1). This reflects initial thinking about the weight of factors in a given context. Estimate the apparent weight using a **rating scale** of 1 to 10 and write the result in the corresponding cell in the top row of the table and the **sum** in the last cell. Factors with very low scores may be left out of the analysis.

Complete Steps 4 to 8 (assessing interactions among factors) and then revisit the weight of each factor. Estimate how important the factor would be *if all the other factors were eliminated or did not exist*. This is the **real weight** of each factor and reflects thinking informed by the rating exercise regarding *the weight of each factor in isolation from other factors under analysis*. Use the same rating scale, making sure that the real weight is **less** than or the **same** as the factor's apparent weight. Write the score next to the apparent weight in the corresponding cell in the top row of the table and the **sum** in the last cell.

Complete other steps including a diagram with the results (Steps 8 to 11). Review the apparent and real weight for each factor and adjust the **size of the dot** assigned to each factor. Use bigger dots when the **real weight of a factor is the same or close to its apparent weight**. This indicates that *the factor will remain significant even when other* *factors are eliminated.* Give special attention to these factors when interpreting the results. Factors that do not lose much of their real weight when other factors are addressed are **persistent** causes and may require more direct attention than initially thought.

Factor integration level

Step 7 in *System Dynamics* involves the calculation of the **dynamic interaction** between all elements. In the advanced version of *Causal Dynamics* this calculation may be influenced by persistent factors (factors with a real weight that is similar to its apparent weight). To take these into account, calculate the factor interaction level (FIL) by multiplying the **total cause index per cent** (the percentage figure at the bottom of the last column) by the **total real weight reduction.** the total real weight reduction is the total apparent weight (the sum of all apparent weights recorded in the last column) minus the total real weight (the total of all real weights recorded in the last column), divided by the total apparent weight. In short: FIL = total cause index per cent x (total apparent weight – total real weight) / total apparent weight. In the example provided, the total cause index per cent is 55.7 per cent, or 234/420. The real weight reduction is 45.1 per cent, or (51 – 28)/51. Thus the FIL is about 25 per cent, or 55.7 per cent x 45.1 per cent, a moderate FIL. This measure helps to guide interpretation considering the three possible scenarios described under *System Dynamics*: integration, hierarchy and dispersion.

TABLE 17.3 Factors undermining the utility of knowledge management in an international volunteer organization (*Casual Dynamics*)

Factors	*Poor KM*[a]	*Weak innovation*	*Quantitative approach*	*RBM*[a]	*Weak partnering*	*Poor HRM*[a]	*Donor dependency*	**Cause index**[b]
Weight: apparent, real	*10,2*	*7,4*	*7,4*	*6,4*	*7,6*	*8,3*	*6,5*	*51,28*
Poor KM[a]	x	0	8	8	8	2	2	28 (60)
Weak innovation	10	x	6	8	4	4	2	34 (60)
Quantitative approach	10	10	x	4	4	10	0	38 (60)
RBM[a]	8	2	2	x	4	4	0	20 (60)
Weak partnering	8	8	8	0	x	8	0	32 (60)
Poor HRM[a]	8	10	10	4	8	x	6	46 (60)
Donor dependency	6	4	6	10	4	6	x	36 (60)
Effect index[b]	**50** (60)	**34** (60)	**40** (60)	**34** (60)	**32** (60)	**34** (60)	**10** (60)	**234** (420)

a KM: knowledge management; RBM: results-based management; HRM: human resource management.
b The *cause index* and *effect index* correspond to the total factor contribution to and dependence on other factors, respectively.

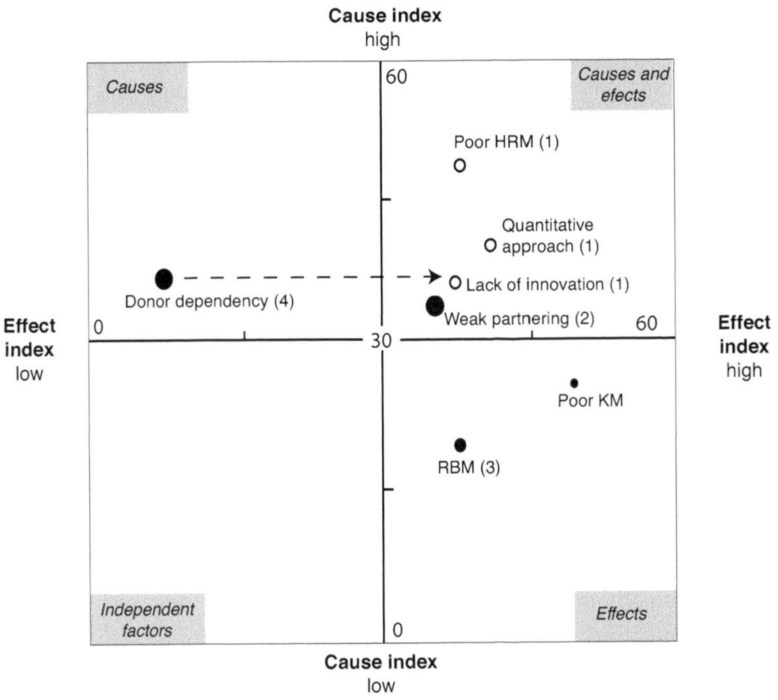

FIGURE 17.3 Knowledge management in an international volunteer organization (*Causal Dynamics*).

Legend: The **size** of each dot indicates the real weight of the factor. **Empty dots** means participants have some control over the factor; **black** indicates little or no control. **Numbers** in parentheses reflect the order in which participants plan to act on each factor. A broken **arrow** indicates a weak causal relationship (odd scores contradicting main tendencies in the diagram).

Summary of this example: This international volunteer organization feels that the way it manages knowledge is not as useful as it should be. Using the *Causal Dynamics* technique (and a rating scale of 0 to 10), participants chose to focus on the key causal factors in the top right of Figure 17.3 (see also Table 17.3) – factors that are both causes and effects of the problem (i.e. knowledge is not used). They discovered that non-strategic management of human resources (poor HRM) is a major contributing factor. Since they have some control over this (empty dot) factor, they decided to free up some human resources and apply them to innovate in the field of knowledge management (KM). They can innovate despite their donor's accounting approach to KM (see arrow in the diagram) and the organization's overemphasis on periodic accounts of measurable results (black dot) factors over which they have little control. Once these initial actions (number 1 in parentheses) are taken, the organization will then explore better ways to involve their partners in KM activities, a goal that will take time. Other objectives, such as rethinking the organization's dependence on a principal donor, are less urgent. In the long run, the organization may want to act on this factor directly or through causes not identified in this analysis.

Activity Dynamics

Purpose

Activity Dynamics helps describe how activities in a project or programme interact with each other. The tool may be used to assess and increase synergy among activities and improve the overall efficiency and effectiveness of the system. (This application comes closest to what Leontief originally intended with the input-output economic model, and lends itself to group assessments of activities in a programme, livelihoods or sectors in an economy, etc.).

Adaptation

Activity Dynamics begins by defining a **set of actions, a project or a programme** and listing the **activities involved**. It focusses on the extent to which one activity contributes to or depends on other activities. When rating, ask 'To what extent does this activity (name the row activity) contribute to that activity (name the column activity)?' The resulting matrix produces an index for 'Contributes to other activities' (vertical axis) and an index for 'Depends on other activities' (horizontal axis). See *System Dynamics* for generic instructions.

TABLE 17.4 The interaction of development programme activities, Mozambique (*Activity Dynamics*)

Activities	*National volunteering*	*International volunteers*	*Women's empowerment*	*Monitoring and evaluation*	*Institutional capacity building*	**Contribution index**
National volunteering	x	4.0	3.0	2.0	0.5	9.5 (20)
International volunteering	4.0	x	2.0	3.0	0.5	9.5 (20)
Women's empowerment	2.0	2.0	x	2.0	0.5	6.5 (20)
Monitoring and evaluation	1.5	1.5	2.0	x	0.5	5.5 (20)
Institutional capacity building	1.0	0.5	1.0	1.0	x	3.5 (20)
Dependence index	**8.5 (20)**	**8.0 (20)**	**8.0 (20)**	**8.0 (20)**	**2.0 (20)**	**34.5 (100)**

Network Dynamics

Purpose

Network Dynamics helps assess the network of information, influence or trust that exists between stakeholders involved in a particular situation or project.

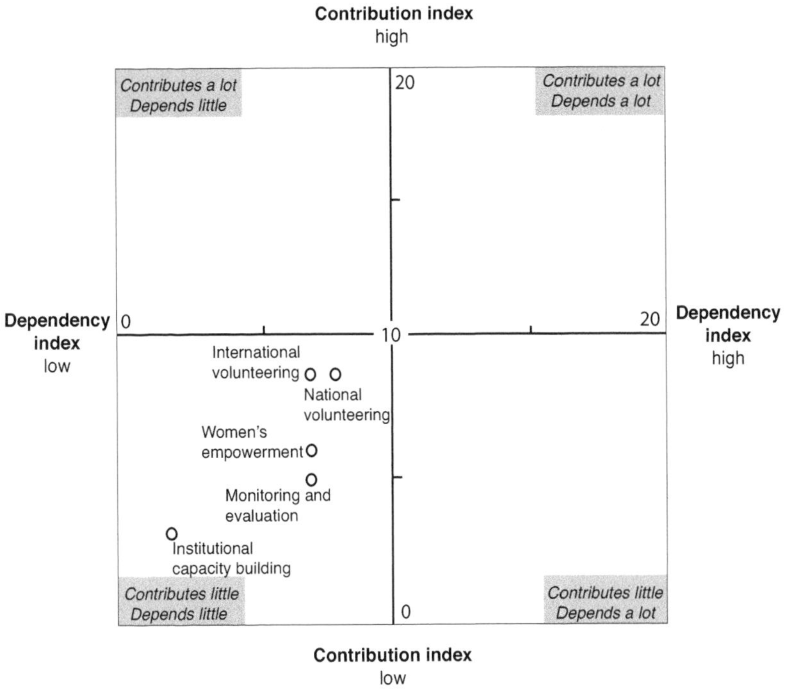

FIGURE 17.4 The interaction of development programme activities, Mozambique (*Activity Dynamics*).

Summary of this example: In Mozambique, Cuso International staff assessed the interaction of different activities in their programme as part of a strategic review held in November, 2011. The purpose was to help build a theory of change with partners by assessing the dynamic links between programme activities expected to contribute to 'bringing people together to fight poverty'. The programme mobilizes both Canadian and Mozambican volunteers, contributes to women's empowerment through a gender fund, monitors and evaluates programme activities, and builds institutional capacity through a Program Capacity Development Fund (PCDF). The result of the analysis shows that volunteering activities, both by Canadians and Mozambicans, contribute the most to other programme activities (higher in Figure 17.4). On the whole, however, the interaction between programme activities is weak; each activity makes a limited contribution to other activities. This means that activities and resources of the programme are dispersed, reflected as well in a low overall score for dynamic interaction among activities (below 35 per cent; see Table 17.4). While important in themselves, institutional capacity-building activities operate in relative isolation from other activities (lower left quadrant in Figure 17.4; see also Table 17.4). The observations supported discussion by participants, including the Country Director, Program Managers, staff and volunteers, about how to implement activities and ways to do these differently so that they could contribute more to other parts of the programme. Participants made plans to repeat the exercise after some time to see if greater synergies had been achieved. Source: Owens, 2001.

Adaptation

Network Dynamics begins by defining a situation or project and listing the stakeholders involved. It assesses an existing network using one of three criteria: the extent to which each stakeholder informs, influences or trusts other stakeholders.

1 **A network of influence** (or power) is a set of connections where people use their prestige, wealth, knowledge or position to affect other people's decisions. When rating, ask 'To what extent does this stakeholder (name the row stakeholder) influence that stakeholder (name the column stakeholder)?' The resulting matrix produces an index for 'Influences others' (vertical axis) and an index for 'Influenced by others' (horizontal axis).
2 **A network of information** is a set of connections where people pass on knowledge or views to other people. When rating, ask 'To what extent does this stakeholder (name the row stakeholder) transmit knowledge or views to that stakeholder (name the column stakeholder)?' The resulting matrix produces an index for 'Informs others' (vertical axis) and an index for 'Informed by others' (horizontal axis).
3 **A network of trust** is a set of connections where people show confidence in other parties and rely on them to provide support, to behave in appropriate ways and to do what they are expected to do. When rating, ask 'To what extent does this stakeholder (name the row stakeholder) trust that stakeholder (name the column stakeholder)?' The resulting matrix produces an index for 'Trusts others' (vertical axis) and an index for 'Trusted by others' (horizontal axis). When exploring ways to build more trust among stakeholders, discuss the indicators of trust and how to achieve them. Another option for building on the result is for participants to think of two stakeholders they trust and the reasons they trust them. The same can be done with the stakeholders that participants do not trust.

Social Dynamics

Purpose

Social Dynamics, also known as *Sinfonie* (Heussen and Jung, 2003), helps assess the ways in which key stakeholders, key problems and significant actions influence each other in a particular situation.

Adaptation

Social Dynamics begins by defining a situation and listing the key **stakeholders, problems and actions involved**. It focusses on the extent to which one element in the situation interacts with others. When rating, ask 'To what extent does this (name the row element) affect or influence that (name the column element)?' The resulting matrix produces an index for 'Influences other elements' (vertical axis) and an index for 'Depends on other elements' (horizontal axis).

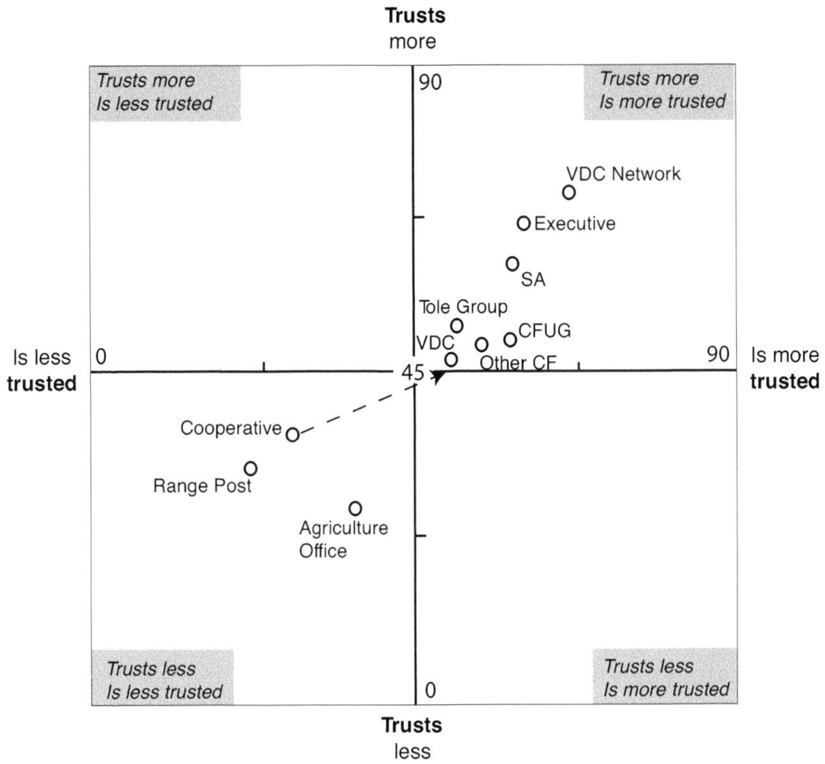

FIGURE 17.5 The network of trust among stakeholders in the Chhahare Suerini community forest, Nepal (*Network Dynamics*).

Summary of this example: Nepal has a long tradition of community forestry, a multi-stakeholder approach to forest and land use management. The process is complex, however, involving many groups and subgroups with specific and sometimes overlapping responsibilities. Coordination among the parties is key to success. In 2010 Neeraj Chapagain, Gopal Kafle and Sudil Acharya of the Livelihoods and Forestry Programme (supported by DFID, UK) facilitated an assessment among stakeholders in a community forest near Chhahare Suerini, eastern Nepal, about two hours walk from the district headquarters of Bhojpur Bazaar. Some 130 households, including many disadvantaged Dalit and Janajati (a Nepali indigenous population), benefit in some way from a mature mixed-hardwood forest type (Katus-Chilaune) common in the mid-hills. The purpose of the assessment was to determine whether or not one of the stakeholders, the Village Development Committee Network (VDCN), was in a position to play a leadership role. The network had been set up several years earlier to promote best practices and pro-poor initiatives among the Village Development Committees at the local level. Some twenty-eight people representing most of the stakeholders in the Chhahare Suerini community forest gathered for several hours to discuss the issues involved, including the network of trust on which a leadership role for the VDCN would depend.

TABLE 17.5 Ratings showing the extent to which stakeholders trust each other (*Network Dynamics*)

Stakeholders	*Exe.*	*CFUG*	*Tole Group*	*VDC*	*VDC Network*	*SA*	*RP*	*Coop*	*Other CF*	*Agr. Office*	**Trusts index**
Executive Committee (Exe.)	x	9	10	7	8	8	5	6	7	3	63
CFUG	6	x	7	3	6	8	3	4	8	4	49
Tole Group	9	10	x	3	6	6	3	2	7	5	51
VDC	6	4	3	x	8	7	2	5	5	4	44
VDC Network	9	7	5	10	x	10	4	4	9	6	64
Samuhik Abhiyan (SA)	9	7	8	8	9	x	3	2	8	4	58
Range Post (RP)	6	4	3	4	7	4	x	2	4	2	36
Cooperative (Coop)	4	6	6	7	6	2	2	x	2	4	39
Other CF	6	5	4	4	7	7	4	4	x	6	47
Agriculture Office	3	4	5	3	4	5	2	4	4	x	34
Trusted index	**58**	**56**	**51**	**49**	**61**	**57**	**28**	**33**	**54**	**38**	**485**

PHOTO 17.2 A forest user group in Western Nepal. (Source: D. J. Buckles)

The results (summarized in Table 17.5 and Figure 17.5) show that the network is strong, with many of the stakeholders recognized as both trustworthy and trusting in their relationships with others. The VDC Network is the most trusted (horizontal axis), followed by the executive committee of the Chhahare Suerini Forest Users Group (Exe.) and Samuhik Abhiyan (SA), an NGO responsible for engaging and mobilizing community people represented by the CFUG. This bodes well for the proposed leadership role of the VDC Network. They need to be sensitive, however, to the trust and expectations among stakeholders vested in the work of Samuhik Abhiyan, an organization with whom the Network has overlapping responsibilities. Fortunately, relations of trust between these two organizations are also strong, which makes it more likely the roles can be adjusted cooperatively rather than competitively. Three stakeholders, the Cooperative, the Range Post and the Agriculture Office are not fully trusted by other stakeholders. The Cooperative has a reputation of acting primarily in the interests of better-off groups within the community. They have a strong relationship with the VDC (arrow in the figure) and could be positively influenced by them. The Range Post, while responsible for providing technical advice on forestry matters, does not have a strong field presence, the kind that could help develop greater trust. To further strengthen existing relations of trust, the Executive Committee decided to involve the VDC, the Range Post and the Agricultural Office in the development of its annual management plan. It will ask the VDC Network to play a coordinating role, by virtue of its broad mandate and position of trust among all stakeholders. This should create more trust among all the stakeholders involved and improve overall coordination. Source: Chapagain *et al.*, 2010.

TABLE 17.6 Waste management in Cochabamba, Bolivia (*Social Dynamics*)

Elements	*T*	*R*	*M*	*E*	*G*	*P*	*C*	*S*	*W*	*D*	*A*	*N*	**Influences other elements**
Team (T)	x	4	4	1	1	2	0	0	0	0	3	0	15/55
Resources (R)	5	x	4	0	0	0	0	0	0	0	0	0	9/55
M&E system (M)	5	4	x	1	1	1	0	0	0	0	2	0	14/55
EMSA (E)	3	0	0	x	5	4	4	3	5	5	1	3	33/55
Municipal government (G)	2	0	0	5	x	3	5	5	5	5	1	5	36/55
Garbage pickers (P)	3	0	0	2	2	x	1	2	1	1	1	0	13/55
Citizens (C)	0	0	0	4	5	3	x	4	3	4	0	2	25/55
Socio-political context (S)	2	0	0	4	5	4	5	x	2	2	3	1	28/55
Waste collection method (W)	1	0	0	4	4	5	4	0	x	4	0	2	24/55
Dump site (D)	2	0	4	5	5	4	3	3	4	x	1	4	35/55
Agreements (A)	4	2	2	1	1	1	0	0	0	0		0	11/55
New dump site proposal (N)	0	0	1	2	4	4	2	1	2	1	1	x	18/55
Depends on other elements	27	10	14	29	33	31	24	18	22	22	13	17	261/660

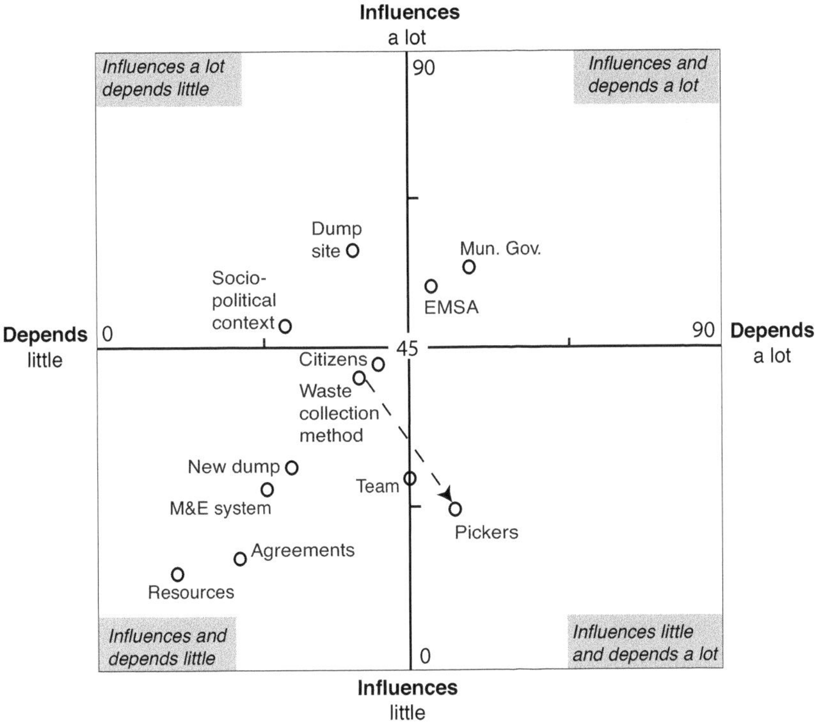

FIGURE 17.6 The interaction of stakeholders, problems and activities associated with a waste management project in Cochabamba, Bolivia (*Social Dynamics*).

Summary of this example: Waste management in any large urban centre is a complex challenge. The urban area of Cochabamba, Bolivia generates more than 400 tons of solid waste per day, passing costs but also benefits to various stakeholders including various companies in the recycling business, the municipal government, the citizens it serves and the poor (mainly women and the elderly) who collect items of value from waste sites for resale. In April 2008 the environmental NGO Sociedad de Gestión Ambiental Bolivia (SGAB) convened representatives from many of the main stakeholder groups to identify strategic entry points it could use to guide the implementation of a new project in the sector. David R. Mercado, an independent consultant based in Cochabamba, designed and facilitated the assessment using *Social Dynamics*.

The group began by listing (see *Free List and Pile Sort*, Chapter 8) stakeholders, problems or factors affecting implementation of a new project on solid waste, and actions or activities (ongoing or planned) important to the situation. Table 17.6 lists the elements in the first column and in the same order in the first row, along with estimates made by the participants regarding the level of influence of one element on every other element in the matrix. The rating used a scale of 0 to indicate no influence at all and a 5 to indicate a very strong influence. The reasoning for each rating was discussed until participants agreed, a process that generated a range of observations about the garbage pickers, laws prohibiting the collection of garbage from government waste sites, and the current waste collection system, among other things. The results, summarized in Figure 17.6, show that project management elements (Resources, M&E system, Agreements, Team), located in the lower half of the figure, have limited impact on driving elements in the system (the upper half of the figure). To make progress, the project team will need to develop its capacity to engage with players such as EMSA and the Municipal Government and bring them more directly into monitoring plans and agreements.

The analysis also shows that garbage pickers (in the lower right quadrant) exercise little influence over other parts of the system, including the current waste collection method and the socio-political context, both of which greatly affect them (see arrow in figure). The current system is problematic for them as much time is wasted and health risks taken by picking through large amounts of organic matter to reach and separate small items (such as paper, plastic and tin cans they can sell for recycling). They also lack legitimacy in the eyes of the state, which has tried to ignore their desperate situation by passing laws against picking garbage. Bringing these highly vulnerable stakeholders more directly into project planning and implementation might change that, and strengthen the position of the project team in relation to other stakeholders. Source: Mercado, 2008.

THREADS OF THEORY: WHOLE SYSTEMS AND SYSTEMS WITH HOLES

Logic is a holistic machine. It creates systems out of distinct parts, with rules on how parts interact and relate to the whole. Unlike any machine, however, human logic must cope with complexity, learn from interaction, create meaning, adapt and evolve. To achieve this, the mind must design whole systems as systems with holes, with opportunities to challenge and improve the parts and meaning in the system. As Kafka put it, logic is doubtless unshakeable. But it does not withstand humans who want to go on living and learning.

As with social philosophers, actors often find themselves in situations where they must reflect on ways to improve the dynamic integration of parts within the social whole (such as genders or classes, towards greater equality, for instance). They must advance models and measures to create synergy and whole system harmony and adaptability. Social actors cannot carry out this complex task with ready-made formula or recipes. Why? Because the contents and meanings of real-life systems and ways to harmonize them inevitably depend on how actors (and theorists for that matter) create elements and rules about their interaction in the first place. The drive to think holistically is always expressed with local colour and flavour. This means that no complete theory or unshakeable logic applies to all situations at all times. No universal rule can be imposed on all signs of logic and meaningful order. Models of the social and natural world are an integral part of an ongoing history. They feed on existing constructions of reality and guide new social experiences at the same time, by nurturing learning and taking advantage of gaps in prior understandings of life in nature and society.

Commentary

Approaches to inquiring and intervening into complex situations are many. 'Wholism,' spelled here with a 'w' to bring attention to the 'whole', is one general option. It explains a situation under study by proposing a big picture view, a wide-angle perspective where properties of the overall system determine how the component parts behave and how related events unfold. As in Aristotelian philosophy, the approach assumes that the whole is more than the sum of its parts. For instance, students of social history can make sense of situations of conflict by tying them to the laws of capitalism. They may further expand their macro view of social life by defining class conflict, regulated by forces and relations of material production, as universal principles that govern critical events and shifts in social history. Grand theory of this kind invites a capitalized writing of 'Wholism', as in Marxism (Marx and Engels, 1975), to denote the 'proper' way of understanding most situations systemically.

Contending approaches to systems thinking include Structural Functionalism (Bertalanffy, 1968; Parsons, 1951) and General Systems Theory (Kuhn, 1974), among others. Although concerned with a different set of issues, alternative medicine practitioners also advocate a 'Wholistic' strategy, an integral perspective that incorporates both the somatic and psychological aspects of health and their complex interaction in real life. They object to understanding and acting on parts of the system without reference to the whole.

Flaws in 'Wholism' are difficult to ignore. They include a tendency to reduce complex situations to manifestations of universal laws, principles that preclude competing perspectives on reality. Thinking built on properties of the 'Whole' inevitably cuts out some dimensions from the investigation, those deemed less important or less determining 'in the last instance'. For example, notwithstanding its critical insights into social history, Marxism has a hard time making sense of culture and the psyche without reducing it to considerations of power and political economy. Likewise, all psychosomatic perspectives on health claim to attend to the 'whole' person, yet some models include the spiritual and social dimensions while others don't. Let's face it. The fact that myriad formulations of 'Wholism' can coexist and make little progress in creating a single and comprehensive body of knowledge raises doubts regarding the whole enterprise.

The notion that 'Wholistic' thinking can make sense of the many wanderings of social and natural history is less convincing than the opposite view. Reflections on social history are in a much better position to shed light on the many variations of 'Wholistic' thinking. As in Hegel's conception of philosophy, a comprehensive theory requires a history of wholistic theories. All framings of knowledge are situated. The rise of biomedical science (and conceptions of the body working independently from the spirit or the mind) is a historical phenomenon specific to our era and Western world, for instance. So is the institutional and lifeworld separation of market from church, family and state. This means that systemic invitations to delve into linkages between the broken parts of Western history, as in Functionalism, make sense in the 'modern' context alone. They should not be extended to all parts of the world and the many paths of human history. Every theory that claims to explain everything (except opposing views) adopts a partial view on global history.

Organismic attempts to understand complex situations are like religions. They speak to what is 'wholesome' and 'holy' in the sense of being complete and all encompassing. All the same, much energy is expended rejecting otherness in thinking.

To remedy the flaws of 'Wholism', one can always reject every grand theory and allow real systems and frameworks to vary. Adepts of the small 'w' view on 'wholism' acknowledge plural, lower-case forms of situated theory and relinquish naive appeals to the unity of science and interdisciplinary knowledge. Each system has foundations and regularities of its own. This more modest approach to systemic reasoning admits of two interpretations: the hard and the soft. Hard systems thinking treats its object of study as simple or complicated but not complex. Key problems and intervening factors are well defined. They are mostly technical and have a limited number of optimal solutions that can be designed and applied using scientific reasoning and technology. Social and organizational measures to enhance functional efficiency in real settings are at home with this closed systems approach. They shore up a vision of social structure with interlocking parts that work like 'organs', i.e. cohesively and instrumentally, towards a proper functioning of the 'body social' striving to maintain equilibrium and achieve system goals.

Although still widely used, closed systems thinking of this sort deals poorly with the complex issues of organizational life and social change. 'Soft wholistic' thinking is better suited to the task. It acknowledges the dynamic and adaptive features and feedback loops of open systems interacting with their social and natural environments. Understanding dynamic behaviour is particularly important in systems that are nested in larger wholes characterized by mixed and overlapping topologies (local and global, for instance). Given a relaxed approach to scientific modeling, 'soft wholism' can also address non-linear transformations and incorporate the effects of seemingly random perturbations. Chaos Theory illustrates this point. It shows how starting events that seem insignificant can produce disproportionately large variations in the system, which explains why long-term weather forecasts are rarely reliable, for instance (Lorenz, 1966). In this perspective, errors in predicting observable phenomena are to be expected. More generally, complexity means that systems are conditioned but not wholly determined by their history. They have unstable components and unclear boundaries that lend themselves to fuzzy logic and partial truths. Open system boundaries and patterns also call for fractal measurements (of coast lines, for instance) that reflect the techniques and scales used by the observer and the exercise of judgment in context. These are measurements designed to quantify infinity on the dimensions of roughness, probability and perspective.

Open systems also produce emergent phenomena, i.e. novel forms of spontaneous self-organization arising out of a multiplicity of relatively simple interactions, without central control or command. Ant colony behaviour and synaptic connections in the human brain both generate aggregate effects and patterns adding up to more than the sum of parts. The dynamics of culture, language, human intelligence and social movements also show emergent properties that play a vital role in society (Logan, 2007). Emergent systems, however, are not always 'functional'. They can take their toll on world history. Speculative bubbles in stock markets are an example. Unforeseen crises in economic history suggest that self-organization may contain seeds of self-destruction, social and economic hurricanes that spell ruin for intelligent collective behaviour. The 'laissez-faire' constitution of emergent society (Hayek, 1973) is rife with contradictions, including the freedom to impose the arbitrary reign of emergency measures and self-seeking uses of the public purse (compared with Adam Smith's 'invisible hand', the metaphor of 'heavy-handed power' comes much closer to the way markets actually function). Evolution that obeys neoliberal rules is 'chaos with feedback' at best (Gleick, 1987). This is to say that trendy complexity theory should be used with caution. It is no excuse for dismissing the historic obligations of collective thinking and mindful planning for the benefit of the common good.

In short, complex systems theory models a rough and turbulent world using a spontaneous and dynamic framing of social and natural history. It pays attention to variability, instability and unpredictability in the universe. The science of complexity introduces some holes into 'holistic' thinking, the kind that can be spelled without the initial 'w' and that allows for different perspectives on social and natural history.

While refreshing, scientific insights into complexity do not eliminate basic limitations in science. Any attempt to convert 'complex situations' into 'complex systems' has inherent problems, those of scientific modelling, hard or soft. In the end, if whole systems act as systems with holes, it is not only because of the messiness of real-life events. Complexity also results from the kernel of indeterminacy planted into our experience of the world as we know it (Popper, 1993; Prigogine, 1980). The best and most critical expression of this intractable indeterminacy resides in the ethics of human freedom, a fundamental disposition to acknowledge otherness and responsibility in our relationship to being. The ethics of being call for the recognition and hosting of otherness in self – what Levinas calls the 'truth and wisdom of love', more fundamental than the 'love of wisdom and truth' (Levinas, 1994). Holes, gaps and faults pervading life and human thinking are not signs of absolute emptiness and nothingness. They do not call for a post-modern reformulation of nihilism, an epoch of moral 'Hollowness' spelled with a capital 'H', as it were. Fissures in systems as we know them are more appropriately seen as windows into meaningful conversations with otherness, uncertainty and the unknown. They constitute the source of all opportunities to create things that are entirely new on a local and global scale. Our geological epoch, known as the Holocene (*holos*, whole or entire, *kainos*, new), could use these openings.

REFERENCES

Bertalanffy, L. von (1968) *General System Theory: Foundations, Developments, Applications*, Braziller, New York.

Chapagain, N., Kafle, G. and Acharya, S. (2010) 'Trust among local stakeholders in a community forestry programme: How does reality fit with the programme's expectations?', www.forestry nepal.org/publications/article/4707, accessed 12 January, 2011.

Gleick, J. (1987) *Chaos: Making a New Science*, Viking Penguin, New York.

Hayek, F. (1973) *Law, Legislation and Liberty: A New Statement of the Liberal Principles of Justice and Political Economy*, vol. 1 (*Rules and Order*), Routledge and University of Chicago Press, London and Chicago.

Heussen, H. and Jung, D. (2003) *'SINFONIE'*, Denkmodell, Berlin.

Kuhn, A. (1974) *The Logic of Social Systems*, Jossey-Bass, San Francisco, CA.

Levinas, E. (1994) *Liberté et commandement*, Fata Morgana, Montpellier.

Logan, R. K. (2007) *The Extended Mind: The Emergence of Language, the Human Mind and Culture*, University of Toronto Press, Toronto, ON.

Lorenz, E. (1966) 'Large-scale motions of the atmosphere: Circulation', in P. Hurley (ed.) *Advances in Earth Sciences*, MIT Press, Cambridge.

Lundy, C. (2006) 'Growing seed knowledge: Shifting cultivation and agricultural biodiversity among Adivasi communities in India', M.A. Thesis in Anthropology, Carleton University, Ottawa, ON.

Marx, K. and Engels. F. (1975) *Collected Works*, International Publishers, New York and London.

Mercado, D. R. (2008) 'Segredadores y segredadoras del Departamento de Cochabamba', unpublished report, Cochabamba, Bolivia.

Owens, J. (2001) 'Measuring system dynamics in Cuso International Programming', unpublished report, Cuso, Ottawa, ON.

Parsons, T. (1951) *The Social System*, Free Press, New York.

Popper, K. (1993) *The Poverty of Historicism*, Routledge Classics, New York.

Prigogine, I. (1980) *From Being to Becoming*, Freeman, San Francisco, CA.

CHAPTER 18

Domain analysis

INTRODUCTION

The system theory underlying this chapter is our social adaptation of Personal Construct Psychology, a well-known theory in Psychology and the Cognitive Sciences developed in the 1950s by George Kelly. The key assumption is that people understand a **domain** by dividing it into parts and creating a description of the whole based on comparisons (or degrees of similarity and difference) between the parts. For example, to know the meaning of 'tasty food' requires not only a sense of what all 'tasty foods' have in common but also words and ideas to describe the opposite. In Personal Construct Psychology, domain parts are called **elements** and the contrasting characteristics are called **constructs**. The social adaptation of construct analysis presented below builds on this perspective by showing how stakeholder groups create and organize elements and their contrasting characteristics for a domain or topic area. The method uncovers ways people make sense of reality in a particular context and helps create opportunities for problem solving and learning.

Domain Analysis is a way to reconstruct or uncover local knowledge. It can be applied to any topic including things in nature (*Ecological Domain*), activities (*Activity Domain*), problems (*Problem Domain*), stakeholder profiles (*Social Domain*) and options for action (*Option Domain*). Following are detailed instructions for the generic method, and brief illustrations for each area of study. But first we offer a theoretical commentary on the challenge that construct analysis presents to our understanding of system boundaries and the classificatory tendencies of the human mind. We return to this issue at the end of the chapter, with a focus on the mixing of constructs that leads to innovation and defies the notion of closed systems of knowledge and methods for knowing.

THREADS OF THEORY: FRAMING THE PROVERBIAL BOX

A knowledge system is like a box. To step outside, we first need to know the box and its openings well enough to find our way out. Having some idea of the other boxes we may step into while on our way out of the box also helps. These are simple guiding steps for dismantling and reassembling knowledge in a world of open spaces and new horizons.

Values and knowledge systems vary greatly across time, cultures and individuals. Acknowledging this means that we must be wary of universal theories, comprehensive schemes and trendy buzzwords that show little respect for the myriad traditions of language, culture and ways of understanding the world. More than ever, inquisitive minds must tap into the great wealth of local knowledge, using measures of learning that go beyond mere observation and surface description. At the same time, knowledge traditions should not be naively glorified and fixed in time. Theories that mummify tradition, assigning a distinctive science to every people or class, spell ruin for human learning. The notion that tradition is authentic only when it remains intact forces all learning into a tight corner – what people already know, and their current habits of thinking. For tradition to flourish and endure, it must be living knowledge that thrives on problem solving and conversations across boundaries. Custom-made thinking may be a habit of mind, but so is new learning and thinking outside the box. In the end, learning is knowledge in motion. It is a verb, not a noun.

Commentary

Knowledge has long been viewed as spirit wrapped in flesh, a mind contained by the body. The resulting 'body of knowledge' is an enclosure of observations and propositions that the spirit can hold true provided they adequately frame, contain or replicate reality in the mind. Augustine, Aristotle and Thomas Aquinas held that a thing is true in the mind if it conforms to external reality. This is correspondence theory: truth is the conformity of the intellect to things that are knowable by the senses and by reason. As in Plato's cavern, the mind 'reflects', mirrors or represents what lies outside the box. The ultimate source of truth is external. To many, order in reality is determined by a higher intelligence, the divine. In this classical perspective, true knowledge is a universal frame of reference originating from Logos, as revealed by the Verb and his Creation.

To the extent that humans cannot fully comprehend the inner workings of the Spirit, some parts of reality remain forever mysterious, as in a black box. Created in the likeness of Logos, humans have nonetheless the intelligence to see certain things clearly. They can do so by applying faculties of the mind, such as the ability to identify categories. The mind can group objects based on similar properties or essential characteristics, a fundamental act in language, inference and decision-making. Introduced by Plato in his *Statesman* dialogue and further developed by Aristotle (1963) in his *Categories* treatise, the logic of categorization serves to classify objects and living beings, by assigning attributes to all elements in a given universe, using a hierarchy of higher and lower order properties. In a natural taxonomy, for instance, every living entity belongs to a discreet category where all members share the same set of properties.

In the modern era, the mind remains true to the permanence of Order in Nature. Thoughts are still developed in the likeness of things, as in Aristotle's *De Interpretatione* and Plato's *Cratylus* (Cooper and Hutchinson, 1997). Enclosures of knowledge, however, gradually detach themselves from metaphysics and the strict propositions and 'predications' of God and Church. Rational subjects are free to compete and argue for different understandings and ways of framing the world, confident that Reason and

Science will prevail. The logic of categorization is extended to all spheres of natural and cultural history, including species, nations, races and stages of evolution. Logic itself is further explored through causal reasoning, mathematics and scientific measurements (as in Newtonian physics), beyond the first principles and final causes of classical philosophy and Christian theology.

Rules of correspondence between thinking and things – laws that frame the framing process itself – continue to be debated to this day. Competing claims abound regarding the relative weight of coherent reasoning versus the senses in the human experience, and the subtle ways to connect the two. Among the contending views, Ayer's logical positivism claims that clear theoretical reasoning can be considered true and meaningful only if verified through empirical evidence and value-free experience (Ayer, 1952). Popper's critical rationalism, however, rejects the logic of empirical verification. Popper views observation as a means to test whether or not theoretical reasoning can be refuted (Popper, 1959). A scientific explanation is the right one as long as it is not proven to be wrong indirectly, by observation and experimentation. As Einstein remarks, 'no amount of experimentation can ever prove me right; a single experiment can prove me wrong'. Science thus evolves by the successive rejection of falsified theories, to be replaced by theories that have greater explanatory power and account for phenomena that were previously anomalous.

These debates are critical to our understanding of knowledge, science and the art of inquiry. Modern thinking, however, has now reached a point where mind and world can no longer accommodate the pursuit of Truth through universal rules of correspondence. The world is so complex and mind frames so numerous that attempts to unify knowledge and science are inevitably vain. Every subject, individual or collective, builds reality through a particular differentiation of parts fitted and joined together, and subject to constant alteration and transformation. Contributions to psychology, linguistics and the social sciences show that all humans are in the habit of categorizing elements, perceived or real, and making sense of relations between them. They do so through myriad systems of understanding that differ from one person or culture to another. Reasoning and rational behaviour is not the prerogative of scientists alone. The existence of a single reality or universe progressively captured through the forward march of science is no longer tenable.

Kelly's Personal Construct Psychology is one of many ways to drive the argument home (Kelly, 1963; Jankowicz, 2004). It shows how each person makes sense and copes with the world by 'construing' differences and relations between elements and testing these 'personal constructs' against experience. The insights of ethnolinguistics and structural anthropology also teach us that systems of classification and analytical categorization abound in cultural history and extend to all spheres of life, from culinary practices to systems of descent and alliance (Lévi-Strauss, 1966, 1969). Research on indigenous systems of knowledge heads in the same direction. Studies of 'sciences of the concrete' – knowledge systems attuned to both the sensible world and the cosmos – expand the horizons of knowledge beyond the confines of Western academic and corporate science. Instead of being treated as cultural oddities, observations and constructions of the 'savage mind' are valued for their effective contribution to our understanding of the world. They also keep sustainable livelihoods alive. Inspired by these principles, the Convention on Biological Diversity and various other national and international treaties acknowledge the present and future contributions of indigenous knowledge. They suggest that rationality takes many forms and is not entirely well served by the short-sighted ways of the Western world. Studies of *Stone Age Economics* (Sahlins, 1974) can testify to this. They uncover forms of rational thinking and decision-making that depart from the means-end logic of consumerism and capitalism. Principles of private property and the individual allocation of scarce means among alternative ends are not enshrined permanently in human nature.

Post-modernity reinforces these critical views, by taking science and reason out of its ivory tower and conjugating knowledge and truth in the plural. It also introduces malleability, approximation and incoherence into human reasoning. Personal Construct Psychology is a precursor of this new perspective on the framing of truth. It acknowledges that the constructs that people create and organize to make sense of the world are finite in number and have a limited range of events they can be applied to and against which they can be tested. This means that mappings of reality do not work at all times and in all situations. They cannot be derived or logically inferred from each other, as building blocks in some larger scheme that precludes other interpretations of the world. More importantly, they vary according to the people, the domain and the circumstances that give them meaning, which are limitless. Infinite variations in the construction of elements and relations between them thus point to open systems that are flexible and can adapt to changing circumstances (and failures to anticipate multiple realities). All kinds of adaptive responses can be imagined. They even include the factitious inventions of Tradition – truth strategically designed to look immemorial and immune to the passing of time. Cultural authenticity is just another grid or scheme, a 'reference to old situations, or which establish their own past by quasi-obligatory repetition' (Hobsbawm and Ranger, 1983).

Hierarchical systems of categorization mirroring attributes fixed in nature are now giving way to fuzzy, associative forms of logic endowed with freedom and adaptability. While still produced in the workspace of brain neurons, the binary differences of language can be construed, combined and transformed in ways that are practically infinite. They can be organized into ordinal and analogical signs to accommodate graded relationships on a continuum, as opposed to the digital either/or reasoning of classical logic. Hierarchical relationships are still at play in signs and constructs. Yet they can be assembled, disassembled and reorganized in different ways, depending on the circumstances of social history, prevailing interests and what matters the most to those involved.

Logic is no longer singular and permanent. Reason must now cope with plurality. It must also respond to dialectical, phenomenological and hermeneutic ways of thinking, those that call into question the Aristotelian principle of non-contradiction. This is the classical law according to which contradictory statements cannot both be true at the same time. For Leibniz and Kant, this law means that A is *not* not-A. While the interpenetration of opposites defies classical notions of logic, the contributions of Hegelian, Marxian, Freudian, Heideggerian and Ricoeurian philosophy highlight profound contradictions in the workings of consciousness, chains of signification, systems of power and the nature of being and time. Dialectical thinking and the blurring of boundaries in logic are not idle academic questions. They now pervade our lifeworld and question the existence of clear distinctions, classes and categories in social and natural history. In the global era, flows of genes, neurons, knowledge, culture and social history proceed through cracks and doors in established frames of reference. These openings are now more visible and tangible than walls built around well-insulated spaces. Webs of life and windows of learning open out in all directions. They call for new measures of reasoning, dialogue and genuine empathy. These are signs begging for a universal gathering of multiple forms of existence and perspectives on the world, conversations to be carried out caringly and carefully, with a sense of purpose and human fallibility.

SIMILARITIES AND DIFFERENCES

Domain Analysis

Purpose

To describe how people view a domain or topic area, and create new learning opportunities based on this understanding.

Step 1

Define the domain or **topic area** and identify at least **six elements** and **no more than twelve** that belong to the domain. These should be **concrete**, distinct and clearly defined. If the elements are vague, use the *Laddering Down* method in *Active Listening* (Chapter 8) to make them more specific and meaningful. Ask 'What do you mean by this?' or 'Can you give an example of this?' Another option is to use **description and storytelling** to explore the topic, and then use this information to identify the elements. Write or draw each element on its own card with a brief description on the back of the card.

Step 2

Decide on a rating scale with a range from 1 to 5 or 1 to 7 (see *Scoring tips*, Chapter 8). Create a table on the floor or wall with the term '**Characteristics**' at the top of Column 1 (see Table 18.1).

Step 3 (optional)

If necessary, discuss or provide one **key characteristic** participants want to explain in light of a problem-solving exploration of the domain. Write the key characteristic on a card, using one or two key words and give it a score of 1. Then, identify the **opposite** of the key characteristic on the same card and give it a score of 5 (or 7). Place the card showing these two opposite characteristics and the corresponding scores in the second row of the first column.

Step 4 (optional)

Rate all the elements using the key characteristic and its opposite and the rating scale (from 1 to 5, for instance). Discuss the score for each element until participants agree. Record each score on its own card and write the reason given for each score on the reverse side of its card or on a flip chart. Place each score card in the row for the key characteristic, below the corresponding element.

Step 5 (optional)

To facilitate interpretation of the table, **reorganize** all the elements in order based on the ratings given for the key characteristic.

Step 6

To elicit other characteristics from participants, choose **three** element cards from the top row at random. Identify two of them (a pair) that are the same in some important way, and different from the third. Identify what it is these two elements have in common that is *relevant to the topic.* Write the characteristic on a new card and give it a score of 1. Then, identify the opposition or contrast that makes the **third element different from the pair**. Write this opposite or contrasting characteristic on the same card and give it a score of 5 (or 7). Place the card showing these two opposite or contrasting characteristics and the corresponding scores in the third row of the first column.

Step 7

Repeat the process described in Step 6 to identify other sets of **opposite or contrasting characteristics** and add a **new row** for each set.

Step 8

Rate all the elements using each characteristic and its opposite and the rating scale created in Step 2. Discuss the score for each element until participants agree. Record

TABLE 18.1 *Domain Analysis* table

Characteristics	*Conflict A*	*Conflict B*	*Conflict C*	*Conflict D*	*Conflict E*	*Conflict F*
Rarely (1) Often (5)	1	1	2	3	5	5
Legal (1) Personal (5)	4	5	3	2	1	2
Interests (1) Values (5)	1	3	2	4	5	4

each score on its own card and write the reason given for each score on the reverse side of its card or on a flip chart. Place each score card in its row, below the corresponding element.

Interpreting the results

Step 9

To **interpret** the results, start with a **review** of the **process**, including the way that participants interacted and reached decisions at each step. Review the **substance** of the exercise, including the topic that participants selected, the elements and the characteristics identified, and the kind of information or knowledge used to rate the elements. Summarize the main points on a flip chart.

Step 10

Review the **column scores** that describe the elements. Look for obvious features such as whether the scores tend to be in the middle or closer to the poles. Also look for the elements that have **similar scores** for most characteristics, including the key characteristic. Summarize the characteristics they share and draw lines connecting elements with similar column scores to show that they are part of the same **cluster** or family of elements.

Step 11

Review the **row scores** that describe the characteristics. Look for obvious features such as scores that vary little and others a lot, or characteristics that are more meaningful compared to others. Also look for **matching characteristics**. There is a match between two or more characteristics when row scores are **similar** or show an **inverse relationship** to each other. Summarize the matches and draw lines connecting characteristics with similar (or inverse) row scores. Characteristics that match the **key characteristic** (identified in Step 3) can help explain important aspects of the topic area.

Rethinking the analysis

Step 12

Modify, delete or add to the list of elements, characteristics and scores at any time during the process.

Look for an **extra characteristic** and opposite if two elements that are very similar need to be distinguished from each other more sharply. To do this, find a meaningful difference between the two elements. Use this difference to create a new characteristic and its opposite and rate all the elements on this characteristic.

Look for an **extra element** if two characteristics that are closely matched need to be distinguished from each other more sharply. To do this, find a new element within the domain that brings together opposites (from each set of characteristics) that are *rarely* matched. Insert the new element in a new column and rate it for each characteristic and its opposite.

Step 13

Review and summarize key comments concerning the domain or topic made during the exercise. Then identify the **learning opportunity** (see *Learning opportunities*, below) and develop a strategy to act on this understanding.

Be sure to review **in detail** the *Scoring tips* (Chapter 8). These are critical to proper application of *Domain Analysis*.

Tips on elements

- **Supply** or **negotiate** some or all the elements or **elicit** them from the participants, depending on the purpose of the exercise and the facilitator's role.
- The list of elements can include an **ideal** or a **problematic element** that can be compared with other elements.

Tips on characteristics (constructs)

- **Supply** or **negotiate** any characteristic and its opposite or **elicit** them from the participants, depending on the purpose of the exercise and the facilitator's role.
- When using characteristics to describe the elements, do not interpret the descriptions as statements of facts that are either right or wrong. Statements about elements should be **accurate** only in the sense of truly reflecting people's views and informed understanding of reality.
- Characteristics should be **relevant** to the topic area, **focussed** and **clear**. They should usually consist of concrete nouns, actions or verbs ending in '–ing' rather than abstract terms, qualities or ideas.
- Characteristics and their opposites can include responses or concrete **actions** related to each element (see *Problem Domain*).
- If the characteristics are **vague** or sound like clichés, use the *Laddering Down* technique in *Active Listening* (Chapter 8) to make them more meaningful and detailed. Ask 'What do we mean by this?', 'Can we give an example of this?', 'How can we tell this?', or 'In what way is this true?'
- Don't use **negative phrases**, such as 'not legal' to describe the opposite of or contrast with a characteristic such as 'legal'. Negative phrases tend to be vague and meaningless. Opposites or contrasts phrased more precisely will describe people's views on a domain in a more meaningful way.
- If relevant, some of the characteristics may involve a **single pole** or reference point against which all the elements are rated. For example, 'cost', 'importance', 'priority' or 'feasibility' may go from low to high (see *Option Domain*).

- If participants **cannot identify** what it is that two elements have in common or what makes the third element different from the pair, ask in another way, apply the *Laddering Down* technique (see *Active Listening*, Chapter 8), choose another three elements at random or choose two cards instead of three.
- You can use other elicitation tools to identify characteristics and their opposites, without comparing elements chosen at random. A simple procedure is the **catchall question**: 'Can you think of some new, different characteristic and its opposite?' Another option is the **full context** procedure: review all elements and find two that have a characteristic in common, and then the element that is the most different from these and in what way. Use this procedure to identify one or more characteristic and its opposite. Another option is to use **description and storytelling** to explore the topic (e.g. by describing examples of success and failure), and then use this information to identify the elements as well as their characteristics organized into opposites.
- To compare two different lists and negotiate a **common list**, see *Free List and Pile Sort* (Chapter 8).
- To identify several characteristics and their opposites in **less time**, divide all participants into groups of two or three. Ask each group to choose three elements at random and to identify a relevant characteristic and its opposite. Collect these new characteristics and their opposites, discuss and clarify their meaning, and group together those that are the same (see *Social Domain*).
- Don't use a characteristic together with its opposite more than once. However, a particular characteristic can be used more than once if it is paired with a different opposite characteristic (such as 'legal' as opposed to 'personal' in one case, and then 'legal' as opposed to 'political' in the other case).
- Characteristics can be grouped together into appropriate **categories** supplied by the facilitator or created and defined by the participants (see *Free List and Pile Sort*, Chapter 8). They can also be ranked by **order of importance**. This will help with interpretation of the table at the end of the exercise.

Tips on rating

- If the characteristic and its opposite **do not apply** to an element, don't provide a score. If a characteristic does not apply to many elements, try rewording it or leave it out of the analysis.
- If the scores for a characteristic and its opposite are **nearly the same** across all elements, redefine the characteristic or leave it out of the analysis.
- The rating of elements can be done **without focussing attention on the table**. To do so, place a card representing a characteristic at some distance from another card representing its opposite or contrast. Then take each element card or an object representing the element and ask participants to locate the element somewhere on the continuum between the two characteristic cards. Convert this location into a rating, and track the scores separately in a table or directly in RepGrid. Repeat this exercise for each characteristic and its opposite.

Tips on interpreting

- When comparing elements, focus on those row characteristics and relationships that are more important or interesting. Don't assume that all relationships are meaningful. This would be **over-interpreting** the results.
- As noted in Step 5, use the ratings for the key characteristic (identified in Step 3) to **reorganize** all element cards (row 1) and score cards (row 2) from the lowest score to the highest. The reorganized table will help explain the key characteristic.
- **Group together** similar elements by moving the columns around and placing them side by side (use masking tape to stick the column cards together). Do the same with matching characteristics, by moving the rows around and placing them one above the other.
- Where you find high matches between row scores or sets of characteristics and their opposites, discuss whether one row set is an **example** or the **effect** of the other row set, or if it has the same **meaning** or the same **cause** as the other set.
- To focus on **two characteristics** and their opposites only, create a diagram by drawing a vertical line that crosses a horizontal line of equal length (see Figure 18.1). If your scale is from 1 to 5, write 1 and 5 at opposite ends of both the horizontal line and the vertical line; indicate what these minimum and maximum scores mean. Write 3 where the two lines cross. For each element, locate the score for one characteristic and its opposite on the horizontal line, and then the score for the other characteristic and its opposite on the vertical line. Connect the scores from the two lines, and write the name of the element where they meet. The closer two elements are in the diagram, the more similar they are.
- To help people participate actively in the analysis, prepare and distribute copies of the element cards among the participants. Then ask participants to identify **other elements** with row scores that are identical or very similar to theirs. Give special attention to similarities in the key characteristic and other characteristics important to the domain. **Groups formed around similar elements** can then prepare and present a brief description of what the elements have *in common*. Following this, all participants can discuss the *main differences* observed **between groups**.

Tips on mathematics

- The software RepGrid (repgrid.com) performs the calculations described below. The Focus command creates a **cluster analysis**. Elements that have the most similar ratings are placed side by side. Characteristics that are closely matched also appear side by side, with inverse relationships converted into positive relationships. A diagram with lines outside the table meeting at various points indicates the levels of similarity between elements and between characteristics.

  The PrinGrid command creates a graph with calculations based on **principal component analysis**. The graph is a two-dimensional representation of multi-dimensional relationships among elements and characteristics. Dots show the location of each element in relation to all other elements and to characteristics represented

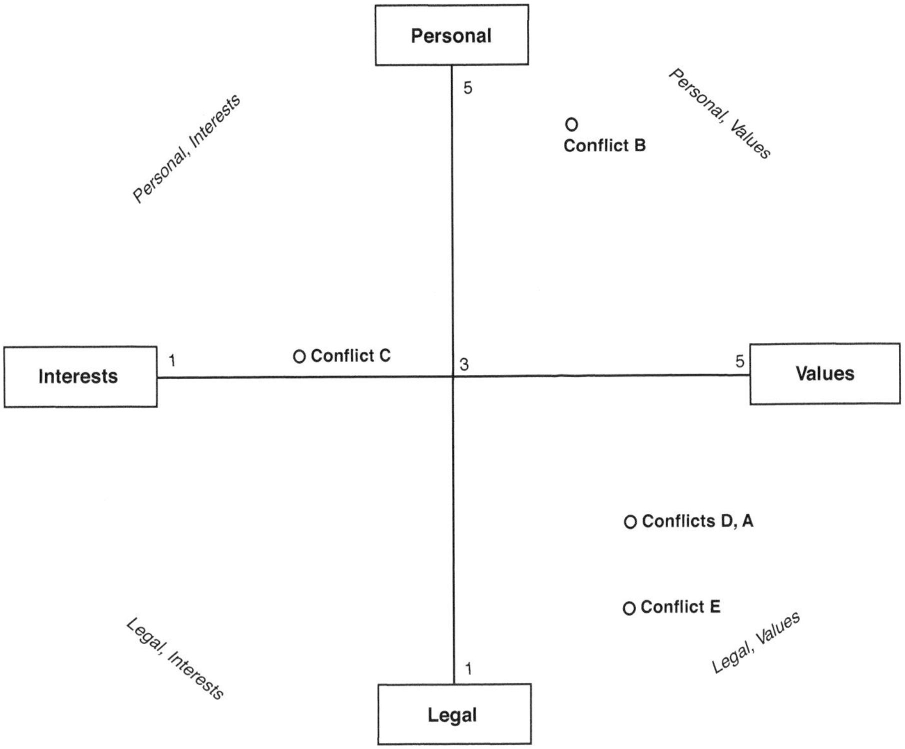

FIGURE 18.1 Comparing *Domain Analysis* elements on a Cartesian graph.

by straight lines. The shorter the characteristic line is, the less the ratings for the characteristic vary. Nearness indicates closer relationships between elements (dots), between characteristics (lines) and between elements and characteristics. The main horizontal line (principal component 1) and vertical line (principal component 2) are summary variables for these multidimensional relationships. The percentages at the end of each line indicate the extent to which each component explains these multidimensional relationships. (See examples below.)

- To manually calculate the **level of difference between two column elements,** calculate the sum of differences (SD) between same-row scores (leave out rows that have empty squares). Then calculate the total maximum difference for all scores (this is MS, the maximum score, minus 1, multiplied by C, the number of row characteristics that got ratings). The level of difference between two elements is SD divided by the total maximum difference for all scores multiplied by 100. To turn this level of difference into a percentage similarity score, subtract it from 100. In other words: [100 – (SD x 100)] / [(MS – 1) x C]. Using Table 18.1 created in Step 7 as an example, the SD between the recorded scores for elements E and F is 2 and the total maximum difference is 12, or [(5 – 1) x 3]. This results in a difference of 16.7 per cent (2/12 x 100). Looking at it another way, the two elements are similar at a level of 83.3 per cent.

- To manually calculate the **level of difference between two row characteristics,** calculate the SD between same-column scores (leave out columns that have empty squares). Then calculate the total maximum difference for all scores (this is MS, the maximum score, minus 1, multiplied by E, the number of elements that got ratings). The level of difference between two characteristics is SD divided by the total maximum difference for all scores multiplied by 100. To turn this level of difference into a percentage similarity score, subtract it from 100. In other words: [100 – (SD x 100)]/[(MS – 1) x E. Using Table 18.1 created in Step 7 as an example, the SD between the recorded scores for the last two rows is 14 and the total maximum difference is 24, or [(5 – 1) x 6]. This results in a difference of 58.3 per cent (14/24 x 100). Looking at it another way, the two elements are similar at a level of 41.7 per cent.

  If the level of similarity between two sets of row scores is very low, this indicates an **inverse relationship**. This means that if participants choose a characteristic at one end of the continuum in one row then they tend to choose the characteristic at the opposite end in the other row. When this happens, turn the inverse relationship into a positive one by reversing all the scores in one row (from 2 to 4 or from 5 to 1, in a scale from 1 to 5, for instance). Positive relationships are easier to interpret. For instance, by reversing the scores for the last row in Table 18.1 already presented, the level of similarity between the last two rows is 83.3 per cent.

Learning opportunities

Domain Analysis helps to identify **learning opportunities** based on an understanding of multidimensional relationships among elements and characteristics within the domain or topic area. Opportunities may involve structural learning, communicational learning, temporal learning or adaptive learning. Understanding the nature of the learning opportunity is key to developing an action strategy.

Structural learning

CONVERGENCE There is convergence in the system when the row scores in the table are closely matched. In this case, most characteristics can be regrouped into two categories that are opposite each other, with the elements falling somewhere along the continuum from one set of opposites to another. If convergence in the system is limiting, search for new elements that combine the characteristics in novel ways. Give special attention to novel ways of combining elements with the key characteristic identified in Step 3 (see example in *Social Domain*, Figure 18.4).

POLARIZATION There is polarization in the system when one group of elements has one set of column scores and the other group of elements is opposite in all respects. In this case, most elements can be regrouped into two categories that are opposite each other. If polarization in the system is limiting, search for new elements that combine the characteristics in novel ways. Give special attention to novel ways of combining elements with the key characteristic identified in Step 3 (see the story of *Ecological Domain* used in Bangladesh, Chapter 19).

DISPERSION There is dispersion in the system when very few elements or characteristics are closely matched. This indicates that each element is entirely different and there is no pattern in the system. If dispersion in the system is limiting, search for other elements or characteristics that may be missing and needed to introduce some meaningful pattern into the system.

VAGUENESS There is vagueness in the system when the scores for the elements do not vary much. If this is limiting, search for the likely cause. Some possibilities are: participants have very different views of the elements and negotiated the differences by assigning average scores; participants emphasize the connections and similarities between the elements, not the differences; participants have limited knowledge of the domain or topic area; or the elements chosen are too general.

Communicational learning

DISAGREEMENT There is disagreement when people give very different scores to the same elements using the same characteristics. To measure levels of agreement and disagreement between two tables or sets of scores, total the differences between same-square scores and divide this number by the total maximum difference between all squares (this is MS, the maximum score, minus 1, multiplied by E, the number of elements that got ratings). If disagreement is a limitation, identify the key area(s) of disagreement and the likely causes. Continue discussion of the causes until the scores reflect a common assessment of the situation.

To *compare many characteristics and tables* representing the views of different individuals or groups, reorder the row characteristics in each table from top to bottom, with *those at the top matching the ratings of the key characteristic* identified in Step 3. These key matching characteristics represent what each individual or group has in mind when thinking about important aspects of the topic. Then, look for key matching characteristics that participants agree or disagree with across the sample. If the tables contain many characteristics, they can be grouped into categories (see *Tips on characteristics*), reordered from top to bottom within each category, and then assessed for key match agreements and disagreements across the sample within each category. The software RepGrid will also compare tables that contain some or all the same elements and characteristics. Levels of agreement may be combined with levels of understanding (below) to produce the six possible scenarios outlined in *Disagreements and Misunderstandings* (Chapter 14).

MISUNDERSTANDING There is misunderstanding when a party with a particular profile (such as men) fails to predict how a party with a different profile (such as women) will rate certain elements. To measure levels of misunderstanding, each party must try to guess how the other party will rate the same elements using the same characteristic(s).

Then, total the differences between the original scores and the scores each group predicted for the other. Divide this number by the total maximum difference for all squares (this is MS, the maximum score minus 1, multiplied by the number of elements). If misunderstanding is a limitation, identify the key area(s) and the likely causes of misunderstanding. Compare and discuss the scores until there is a better understanding of each other's views. Levels of understanding may be combined with levels of agreement (above) to produce the six possible scenarios outlined in *Disagreements and Misunderstandings* (Chapter 14).

CONFUSION There is confusion among people when the parties use different elements or characteristics to describe the same domain or topic. If confusion is a limitation, search for common elements or shared characteristics to create some basis for mutual understanding and agreement.

Temporal learning

INSTABILITY There is instability in the analysis when the way people view a domain or topic and characterize its elements changes quickly or frequently over time, without any clear justification. If instability is limiting, identify the factors that may explain this. Look for elements or characteristics that are more meaningful, or take more time to discuss the ratings or to gather the information needed to complete the exercise.

RESISTANCE TO CHANGE There is resistance to change when people become aware of specific learning opportunities described above yet prefer to leave the views expressed in their analysis unchanged. If resistance to change is limiting, identify the factors that may explain this or take more time to discuss the topic, the elements and their characteristics. Note that elements and characteristics (which reflect *how* people think) are generally more difficult to change compared with element ratings (which reflect *what* people think about the elements and characteristics).

Adaptive learning

FAILURE TO PREDICT There is a failure to predict when experience and real events do not confirm the characteristics and the ratings applied to the elements in the analysis. To assess the predictive value of the analysis, select key characteristics and their opposites, and then identify **indicators** that define the meaning of each number on your rating scale. Collect reliable information on these indicators related to each element to see if the characteristics are relevant and the ratings are confirmed. If the failure to predict is limiting, change the ratings or look for characteristics that have better predictive value.

Ecological Domain

Purpose

Ecological Domain examines how people view existing elements in nature using terms and characteristics that participants choose and negotiate. The tool may be used to classify things in nature (such as rice varieties or soils) or ecological processes (such as effects of climate change). The understanding of the domain generated in this way may help people innovate, solve problems or test views against experience and other sources of knowledge. (See Figures 18.2 and 18.3 and the example in Chapter 19.)

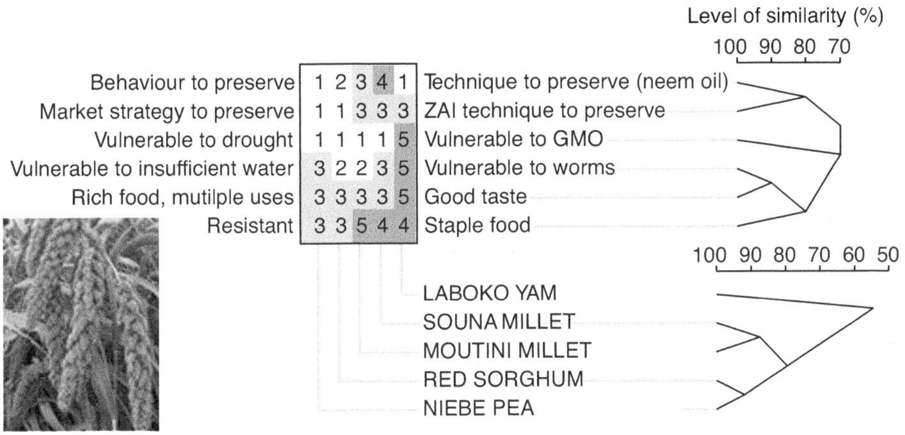

FIGURE 18.2 Biodiversity and seed preservation in West Africa (*Ecological Domain*, Cluster Analysis).

Activity Domain

Purpose

Activity Domain examines how people view existing activities or actions using terms and characteristics that participants choose and negotiate. The tool may be used to identify different types of actions or activities and explore associated levels of difficulty, forms of knowledge, benefits and the values or skills involved (see Figure 18.4). An understanding of the activity domain may help people innovate, solve problems or test views against experience and other sources of knowledge.

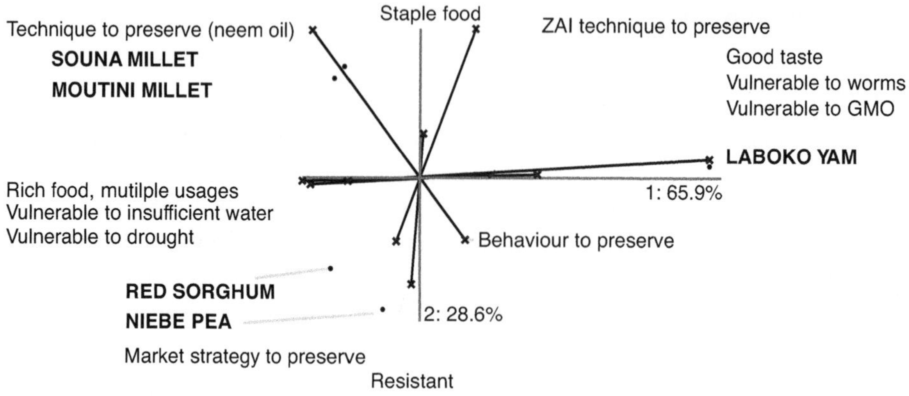

FIGURE 18.3 Biodiversity and seed preservation in West Africa (*Ecological Domain*, Principal Component Analysis).

Summary of this example: In March 2009 COPAGEN held in Dakar, Senegal a West African colloquium (facilitated by J. M. Chevalier) on strategies to preserve and promote peasant varieties of agricultural crops, partly in response to the risks posed by the spread of genetically modified organisms (GMOs) in Africa. Participants tested *Ecological Domain* to see how the technique could help develop a strategic and methodical approach to promoting local knowledge on peasant seeds (different from the conventional use of questionnaires and interviews). To start the analysis, the participants identified five **strategic** and **vulnerable** agricultural crops grown in their respective countries (see Figures 18.2 and 18.3). They also identified a series of characteristics and their opposites that reflected three basic questions: in what way are the crops *strategic*, what makes them *vulnerable* and what kind of *action* is being taken to preserve them. The results represented in the two graphs reveal that niebe peas and red sorghum are strategic because they produce rich and tasty food and have multiple uses. The source of vulnerability for these crops is their extreme sensitivity to drought conditions. Actions to preserve these crops involve marketing measures and customary rules of farmer behaviour. While millet crops (souna, moutini) are also rich, tasty and vulnerable to drought, they can be preserved through technical measures (using neem oil and the Zai planting pit method). The remaining variety, laboko yam, is even tastier but is vulnerable to worms and GMO contamination. These patterns, represented in the Principal Component graph, account for about 94.5 per cent of the variance within the system (see percentages on the horizontal and vertical axes). Considering these findings, participants decided to focus their attention on actions such as conventional plant breeding to preserve and reduce the vulnerability of crops to drought.

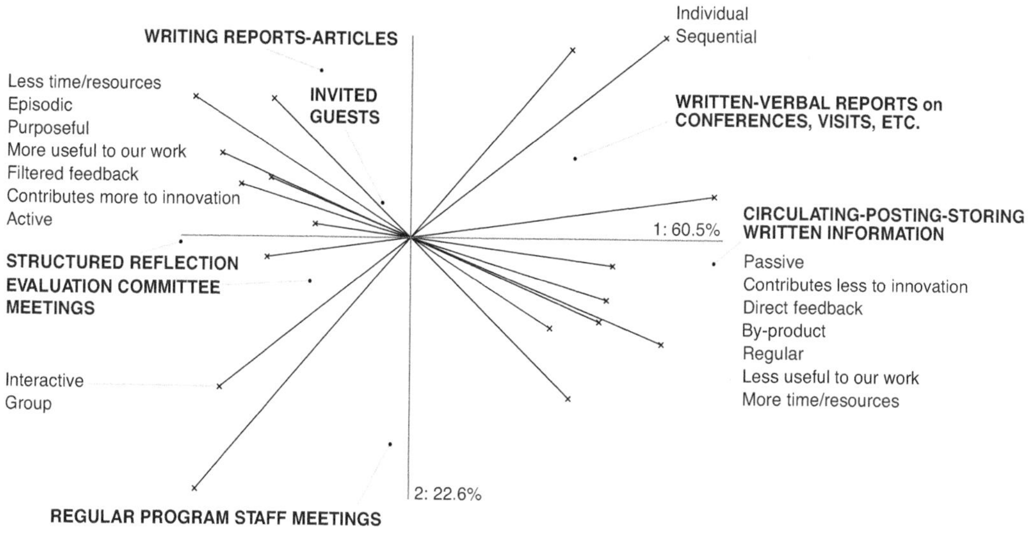

FIGURE 18.4 Assessing a knowledge management system (*Activity Dynamics*, Principal Component Analysis).

Summary of this example: In this Canadian organization most knowledge sharing (KS) activities fall into two categories (see Figure 18.4). On the one hand, KS that participants consider **more useful** to their work (on the left hand side) includes 'structured reflection' (rated the most useful), 'writing report articles' and 'invited guests' (both rated second), and 'evaluation committee meetings' (rated third). These activities tend to be planned ('purposeful') and are done episodically. They involve an active sharing of information and careful feedback on existing projects. Except for 'writing report articles', these more useful KS activities also involve real-time teamwork. By contrast, more time and resources are actually dedicated to the **less useful** KS activities (on the right hand side) that are regular by-products of other work. These activities include 'circulating, posting and storing written information' (rated fifth, the least useful) as well as 'written/verbal reports' (on conferences, visits, etc.) and 'regular programme staff meetings' (rated fourth). Except for 'regular programme staff meetings', these activities involve a passive sharing of knowledge. They are done individually, sequentially (not in real-time), and they contribute less to innovation. These patterns, represented in the Principal Component graph, account for about 83 per cent of the variance within the observed system (see percentages on the horizontal and vertical axes). Based on this analysis, participants plan to allocate more time and resources to the most useful KS activities, and find ways to do the less useful ones such as regular programme staff meetings differently so that they can be more useful to KS.

PHOTO 18.1 Participants discuss the patterns shown by white, grey and black cards, while the ratings are entered into the RepGrid software.
(Source: D. J. Buckles)

Problem Domain

Purpose

Problem Domain examines how people view existing problems using terms and characteristics that participants choose and negotiate (see Figure 18.5). The tool may be used to identify different types of problems, levels of difficulty and responses adopted in the past. The understanding of the problem domain may help people innovate, find appropriate solutions or test views against experience and other sources of knowledge.

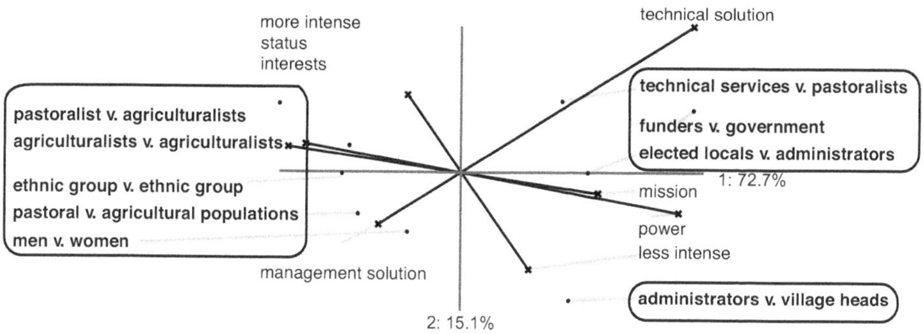

FIGURE 18.5 Looking at recurrent conflicts over natural resources (*Problem Domain*, Principal Component Analysis).

Summary of this example: In a worskhop designed and facilitated by J. M. Chevalier, about twenty-five representatives of French-speaking African countries working on issues of natural resource management (NRM) identified the most frequent types of NRM conflicts occurring in their respective countries. Examples are conflicts between pastoralists and agriculturalists, elected locals and administrators, men and women, etc. They also identified contrasting characteristics to describe these conflicts (see Figure 18.5). Each kind of conflict was rated against each characteristic and its opposite, using a scale of 1 to 9. The analysis showed that conflicts amongst agriculturalists and between agriculturalists and pastoralists are the most intense. Clashes between ethnic groups are also intense, although less so. All of these conflicts usually involve conflicts of status and economic interests and are currently addressed through land management solutions. By contrast, tensions between funders and governments and between technical services and pastoralists are much less intense. They involve conflicts in power, mandate and 'mission', and they are currently addressed through technical and administrative solutions (e.g. formal procedures and agreements). These patterns represented in the Principal Component graph account for about 88 per cent of the variance within the observed system (see percentages on the horizontal and vertical axes). Discussion focussed on ways to introduce technical and administrative solutions into the more intense conflicts, as complements to current strategies. While no decisions were made, participants agreed that innovation in the response to conflicts was needed and that the analysis pointed to unconventional approaches and ways of looking at the problem that were worth exploring further.

Option Domain

Purpose

Option Domain examines how people view different proposed actions (options) using terms and criteria that participants choose and negotiate. The tool may be used to identify different kinds of options, evaluate them on specific criteria, establish priorities and support decision-making. Understanding an option domain may help people innovate, solve problems or test views against experience and other sources of knowledge.

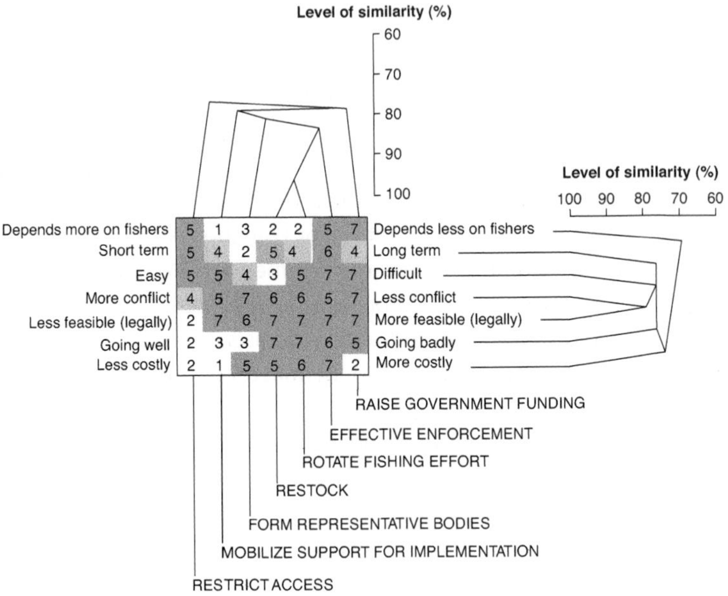

FIGURE 18.6 Assessing coastal fishery management options (*Option Domain*, Cluster Analysis).

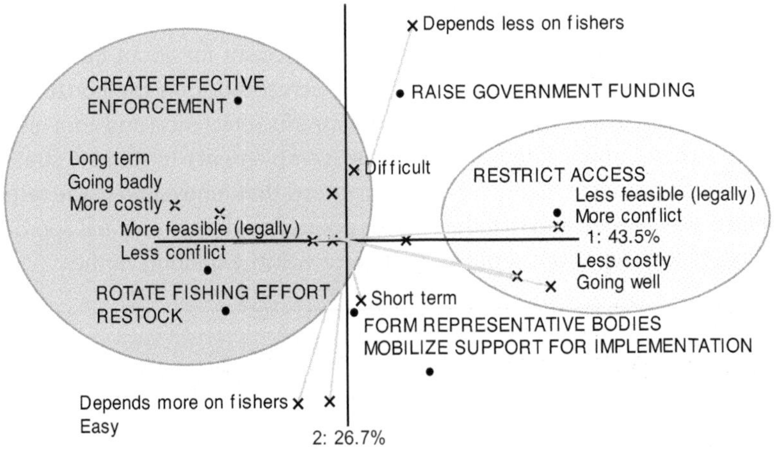

FIGURE 18.7 Assessing coastal fishery management options (*Option Domain*, Principal Component Analysis).

Summary of this example: About 2,000 artisanal fishers exploit a range of aquatic resources in the Common Fishery Zone of Ancud in central coastal Chile. The Fund for Fisheries Research invited some fifty-seven fishers, officials and scientists to a two-day meeting to discuss better fishery management strategies in the zone. With facilitation by J. M. Chevalier and Carlos Tapia of CESSO in Chile, participants identified seven possible actions together with seven criteria that could be used to evaluate the proposed actions. A scale of 1 to 7 was applied to each criterion (see Figures 18.6 and 18.7). Participants noted that restricting access to the fishery may not be costly but will take time and is less feasible legally. Also it is likely to generate some conflict, at least at the beginning. Current enforcement measures, while more feasible legally, are not going well and represent a costly, longer-term approach that depends a great deal on other actors. Raising funds from the government also creates dependence and will continue to be difficult. On the whole, the most favourable ratings lined up behind two options: mobilizing support for better implementation of current management practices and bringing excluded fishers into representative bodies. All of these observations and related patterns, represented in the Principal Component graph, account for about 70 per cent of the variance within the observed system (see percentages on the horizontal and vertical axes). In addition to identifying the two best options, the analysis also generated new thinking about ways to improve enforcement, raise funds and gain better control over the rotation of fishing effort.

PHOTO 18.2 Artisanal fishers rely on a wide range of aquatic resources in communities such as Caleta Quintay, south of Valparaiso, Chile. (Source: D. J. Buckles)

Social Domain

Purpose

Social Domain examines how people view themselves and others using terms and characteristics that participants choose and negotiate. The tool may be used to identify different groups or categories of stakeholders based on the types and levels of interests they have in a project or programme (see Table 18.2 and Figure 18.8); the forms and levels of organization or power they can apply to a situation; the degrees and ways in which they are trusted or viewed as legitimate by others; the actions or positions they take in a conflict; or the information, skills, values or leadership styles they might apply in a situation. Understanding the social domain may help people innovate, solve problems or test views against experience and other sources of knowledge.

Variations

Social Domain can be facilitated **without the use of a table**, thereby focussing attention on the discussion and the active engagement of participants in describing meaningful similarities and differences between them. There are five steps to this variation on *Social Domain.*

TABLE 18.2 Tobacco farmer profiles, Bherama, Kushtia, Bangladesh (*Social Domain*)

Characteristics	*Aminul*	*Hakim*	*Razzak*	*Azizul*	*Nazmul*	*Alim*	*Abu*	*Huq*	*Salam*
1 Little or no tobacco 6 Large tobacco fields	1	2	2	2	2	2	3	3	6
1 Little or no farmland 6 Big farm	6	4	1	2	6	4	2	3	6
1 Few food crops 6 Many food crops	5	3	4	4	5	2	2	4	3
1 Rare tobacco trade 6 Frequent tobacco trade	1	1	5	4	2	1	1	6	6
1 Young 6 Old	3	6	4	2	4	6	5	4	2

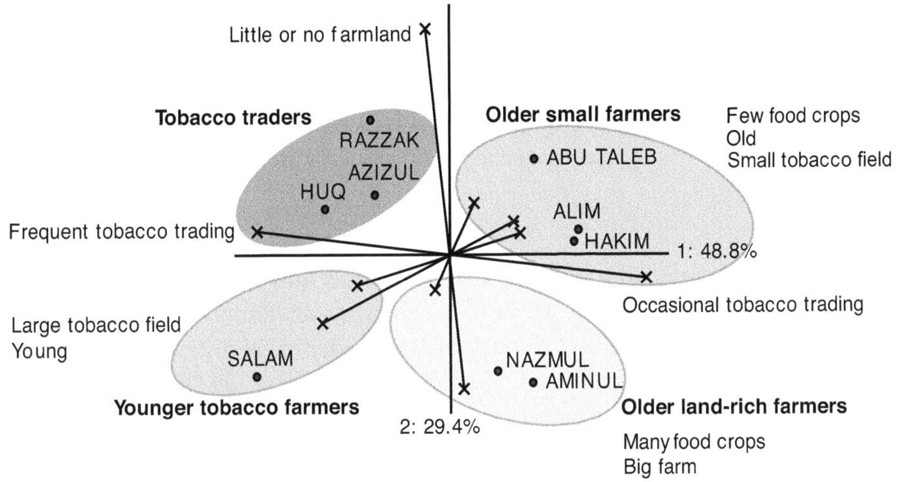

FIGURE 18.8 Tobacco farmer profiles, Bherama, Kushtia (*Social Domain*, Principal Component Analysis).

Summary of this example: Farmers grow tobacco on some 80,000 acres of agricultural land in Bangladesh, often under direct contract with the British American Tobacco Company. While tobacco is a cash crop for farmers, tobacco farming causes a wide range of environmental, social and health problems in farming communities. The Bangladesh non-governmental organization UBINIG is working with tobacco farmers who have expressed a desire to move away from tobacco into other kinds of farming. As it cannot work with all households at the same time, the initiative needed to form subgroups that could conduct experiments and assess alternatives to tobacco. In a process designed and facilitated by D. J. Buckles, UBINIG used *Social Domain* to identify different farmer profiles they would need to work with in each major region. The exercise revealed that farmers in a well-established tobacco growing area were made up of households with one of four profiles: (1) younger tobacco farmers; (2) older farmers with small areas of tobacco and food crops; (3) tobacco traders with limited tobacco production of their own; and (4) older, land-rich farmers who no longer engaged in tobacco farming directly. It also suggested that being involved in the tobacco trade is particularly important to land-poor farmers (such as Razzak, Azizul and Huq in Table 18.2 and Figure 18.8), giving them a distinct profile that should be taken into account when evaluating alternatives to tobacco production. These patterns, represented in the Principal Component graph, account for about 78 per cent of the variance within the observed system (see percentages on the horizontal and vertical axes). A plan was developed to engage each of the household types in monitoring and evaluation of the impact of alternatives to tobacco on livelihoods. Different profiles were identified in regions with a shorter history of tobacco farming, or where ethnic minorities were an important part of the farming population. (For more details on this story, see Chapter 19.)

Step 1

Divide all participants into random **groups of three**. Ask each group of three to identify two people in the group (a pair) that are the same in some way relevant to the domain or topic, and different from the third. Find a characteristic that is shared by the pair, and then the characteristic that makes the third person different.

Step 2

Make a list of the distinctions between **characteristics and their opposites** obtained from all the groups. Discuss and clarify the meaning of each distinction. Group together the distinctions that are the same. Reduce the list to four to six distinctions that matter the most in the domain or topic area. To help interpret the results of the analysis, rank the pairs of characteristics in order of importance (see *Tips on characteristics*).

Step 3

Each participant **rates** himself or herself on each characteristic and its opposite, from 1 to 5. Ensure that participants have a common understanding of what the numbers on the scale mean for each characteristic and its opposite, or develop indicators. Each actor can record their ratings on a card showing the same characteristics, in the same order, and with the same format (see Figure 18.9).

Step 4

Ask each participant to find others that have cards with many row scores that are **identical or similar** (only one point apart in a majority of rows) to theirs. Give special attention to similarities in the rows that describe the most important characteristics. Encourage all participants to compare their cards with others until groups or 'families' with similar profiles are formed.

Actor's card: John S.						
Characteristics	**1**	**2**	**3**	**4**	**5**	**Characteristics**
Good listener				x		Good speaker
Organized			x			Creative
Efficient		x				Committed
Rallying person				x		Visionary
Experienced						Adventurous

FIGURE 18.9 Actor's card.

Step 5

Groups formed around similar cards can then prepare and present to the whole group a brief description of *the characteristics group members have in common.* When a group presents their profile, other participants (individuals or groups) can **move closer** if they feel they are similar in significant ways or **distance** themselves if the differences are more important than the similarities. At the end of the exercise, participants should discuss the main differences observed between groups and plan strategies that draw on different but complementary profiles.

THREADS OF THEORY: THE TWAIN SHALL NEVER PART

All forms of knowledge, including well-developed theories and methods, are like living organisms. They come to life by virtue of the distinctive features they possess and display. But their existence also hinges on their ability to adapt and mix characteristics and ideas scavenged from elsewhere. When life thrives on learning, the twain can never fully part. This means that apostles of either pure models or absolute muddles err on the side of simplicity. They ignore the fact that bodies of knowledge can be different from each other at the same time as they are profoundly mixed-up, just like humans.

In the global era, connectivity achieved through co-mingling and fraying of edges has reached a point where every culture is merely another hybrid, a special combination of behavioural and symbolic DNA enduring and moving among myriad ways of life. Original varieties have been lost, if they ever really existed. The same principle applies to knowledge systems, packaged methods and coherent theories, each aspiring to the status of 'a species of thinking', one whose 'right to exist is coextensive with its power of resisting extinction by its rivals' (Huxley, 1893, p. 229). By nature, every species of coherent thinking is profoundly mixed-up with others. Human learning thrives on borrowing, adapting and juggling objects, facts, words, ideas and beliefs, co-opting them into serving variable ends and new systems of meaning. This is to say that cross-fertilization rules over all knowledge, culture and even living organisms. Every way of life and understanding is a model and a muddle at the same time, a twofold exercise in Greek order and Babylonian confusion.

Commentary

Every human being is thrown into the world together with other humans and ways of living, manifestations of being in time and in space. The same applies to language and acts of speech. They too are deeply engaged in webs of life and history. Theories intended to shed light on the world are no exception. They never emerge or dwell in a vacuum of everlasting truth. A theory exists by virtue of what it borrows or rejects from other bodies of knowledge and the manner in which it responds to and anticipates other intentions and viewpoints. As with Bakhtin's understanding of the self, every frame of mind develops its own sense of identity by virtue of being truth-for-other-theories, statements attuned to their possible interpretations and incorporation into other frames (Bakhtin, 1981). Each viewpoint is also a theory-of-other-truths that appropriates meaning from different perspectives, using outside learning essential to its development. In other words, like selfhood, a theory never exists alone, without the medium of time, language and social life. While it contains itself, each theory carries otherness and context within itself, and is contained in otherness and context at the same time.

It follows from this that no theory can ever be finalized. Threshold conversations between selves and viewpoints are bound to change. Impermanence is the rule. For a theory to contribute to knowledge and learning, it must accept to exceed its own boundaries, by acknowledging difference and dialogue. The argument echoes Bakhtin's call for a polyphony of theory – a heteroglossia of living knowledge and learning at the boundaries, on the borders of conventional knowledge and language. As in the Indian tradition of Jainism, heteroglossia means that it is in the nature of theory to express a particular perception of reality claimed to be true 'in some ways' only. No single point of view can stand as the complete truth.

Truth can never be boxed into a comprehensive body of knowledge and definitive propositions about self and reality. If it is to be 'contained', it is in selves, minds and voices engaging with each other and honouring the disagreements and inconsistencies that pull them apart and together at the same time. At stake here is the need for a porous display and interaction of plural meanings and methods. To use the subject matter of physics, truth on the origins of the universe lies neither in general relativity theory nor in quantum mechanics. Nor will it simply emerge from a dialectical synthesis that overcomes the opposition of thesis and antithesis, as might be proposed in a universal theory of gravity or some other 'theory of everything'. Grand syntheses are flawed as soon as they pretend to bring an end to all conversations of science and the human imagination.

Universal knowledge lies in Einstein's tireless commitment to careful conversations across perspectives, with a constant involvement of reasoning, experience and openness to dialogue. Theorizing of this kind is essentially oecumenical. It draws attention and interest by putting up with contradiction, and bringing different viewpoints and people into a conversation. If anything, truth is an invitation to connect, with an open mind as to what each good debate has in store for history and the people involved.

REFERENCES

Aristotle (1963) *Categories and De Interpretatione*, trans. John Lloyd Ackrill, Clarendon, Oxford.

Ayer, A. J. (1952) *Language, Truth and Logic*, Dover, New York.

Bakhtin, M. M. (1981) *The Dialogic Imagination: Four Essays*, M. Holquist (ed.), trans. Caryl Emerson and Michael Holquist, University of Texas Press, Austin and London.

Cooper, J. M. and Hutchinson, D. S. (eds) (1997) *Plato: Complete Works*, Hackett, Indianapolis and Cambridge.

Hobsbawm, E. and Ranger, T. O. (eds) (1983) *The Invention of Tradition*, Plato, Cambridge.

Huxley, T. H. (1893) 'The coming of age of the origin of species', in *Collected Essays: Darwinia*, vol. 2, Macmillan, London, pp. 227–243.

Jankowicz, D. (2004) *The Easy Guide to Repertory Grids*, Wiley, Chichester.

Kelly, G. (1963) *A Theory of Personality. The Psychology of Personal Constructs*, Norton, New York.

Lévi-Strauss, C. (1966) *The Savage Mind*, University of Chicago Press, Chicago.

Lévi-Strauss, C. (1969) *Elementary Structures of Kinship*, trans. James Harle Bell, John Richard von Sturmer and Rodney Needham, Beacon, Boston, MD.

Popper, K. R. (1959) *The Logic of Scientific Discovery*, Basic Books, New York.

Sahlins, M. (1974) *Stone Age Economics*, Aldine-Atherton, Chicago.

CHAPTER 19

Breaking the dependency on tobacco production

Practitioners of the art of engaged inquiry do not look for problems that match the tools they know best. They choose, mix, adapt or create methods that fit the situation. This means they must develop their own understanding of action-research at the same time as they engage with people and content in real settings. Designing the right PAR process can never be a mechanical exercise. Each situation calls for skilful means to inquire into a situation and act on it. Judgment and complex reasoning are needed to apply simple methods in some situations. Equal skill goes into selecting, adapting and applying more advanced tools to systems thinking and problem solving, with full participation of the parties involved. In either case, purpose comes first.

In this chapter, we offer a story to illustrate how PAR methods, including *Causal Dynamics* and *Domain Analysis* (i.e. *Ecological Domain* and *Social Domain*), were combined in a complex setting to fit a purpose – breaking the dependency of farmers in some parts of Bangladesh on tobacco production as a livelihood. Tobacco farmers are, in their own way, as dependent on tobacco as smokers of the final product. Debt to the tobacco companies, and the seductive appeal of facilities they offer, bind tobacco farmers to an industrial mono-crop that depletes soils, denudes forested hillsides and compromises the health of field workers and the women and children curing the leaves. Many tobacco farmers, especially older ones who have seen the impacts on their families and on their lands, are desperate to shift into other livelihoods, but don't. Breaking the dependency is not easy, and many farmers that try end up going back to the companies asking for more. The British American Tobacco Company (BATC), the largest in the country, is particularly effective at drawing farmers into tobacco farming. For decades they have been setting up operations in prime agricultural areas in Bangladesh such as river valleys and flood plains close to abundant sources of firewood for curing kilns. As these resources are depleted the company shifts to new areas, leaving damaged landscapes, neglected agricultural markets and indebted people in their wake. From both a farmer and national perspective, tobacco production in Bangladesh is a disaster.

The problems of tobacco production are not widely known outside of specialist circles. The World Health Organization-sponsored Framework Convention on Tobacco Control does, however, call for the reduction of the supply of tobacco products by calling on governments to support a transition out of tobacco production. Some 168 states are parties to the convention, including Bangladesh. Special anti-tobacco legislation in Bangladesh also establishes the principle of support to tobacco farmers wanting to shift out of tobacco production, in recognition of the many detrimental effects it has on the environment and public health. How to do so remains a key challenge. Little detailed research has been undertaken on the constraints farmers face or practical ways to make the transition to alternative systems.

A participatory action research initiative funded by IDRC and launched in 2006 by UBINIG, a Bangladeshi policy and action research organization, and D. J. Buckles at Carleton University sought to address this gap by engaging with tobacco farmers interested in shifting out of tobacco production. The initiative, currently being turned into a book by D. J. Buckles, F. Akhter and R. Tito, proposed to combine research with action and participation to change key factors keeping farmers addicted to producing tobacco. Work was undertaken and is ongoing in three districts of Bangladesh, including Kushtia, Cox's Bazaar and Bandarban. Informal discussions with tobacco farmers in each of these areas determined that many tobacco farmers acutely feel the negative impacts of tobacco production and want to stop. This felt need prompted an exploration of the constraints tobacco farmers face and strategic entry points, from the perspective of both men and women, older and younger farmers as well as small- and medium-sized farms. The analysis and interpretation by participants led in turn to a critical realization: farmers hold the key to successful transition strategies. The discussions that followed, about what farmers know and think about crops and crop choices, prompted thinking outside of the box. New crop choices and transition strategies emerged that had not been considered previously. Using these insights, farmers designed and tested innovative field experiments and evaluated the results over several agricultural seasons. The story reported below describes this cycle of participatory inquiry into strategic constraints, innovative experimentation and evaluation. It also includes brief accounts of the methods used (explained in greater detail in previous chapters). D. J. Buckles designed and facilitated this action–inquiry process in close collaboration with Farida Akhter and Rafiquel Haque Tito of UBINIG. The process was part of a broader study of transition strategies for tobacco farmers involving more than 500 families trying to break their dependency on tobacco.

WHY GROW TOBACCO?

Why do farmers continue to grow tobacco, despite the many concerns they have about its impacts on their health, environment and land? This question launched the first full cycle of diagnostics, planning, implementation and evaluation in 2006. Tobacco farmers in each of the three regions of the project sat together to state their reasons for growing tobacco, develop a common understanding of the situation and decide what to do about it. During the first diagnostic step the facilitators supported the discussion by eliciting the reasons behind decisions to grow tobacco and facilitating an assessment of the interaction of these reasons using the *Causal Dynamics* tool (Chapter 17). The final discussion converged around potential entry points for action, and decisions by the group to plan and implement a strategic intervention.

Participants in one of the assessments included seven men and three women living in Daulatpur village in Kushtia district. All had grown tobacco for many years and decided that they had to find a way out without completely undermining their livelihoods in the short term. After tea and introductions, they identified six reasons why people continue to grow tobacco. To paraphrase the views expressed:

- Tobacco production **pays well**. The price for the highest grade of cured tobacco set by the BATC is higher than for any other crop we know. We hope we will get the top price, but often we don't – the price drops a lot for leaf judged by the BATC as of lesser quality.
- The BATC issues a **card** to farmers they buy from, and will only buy from farmers with a card. This creates an obligation to the BATC, cemented by access to credit for fertilizers, pesticides and tobacco seed. We can also use the card to buy cured tobacco from farmers that don't have one, setting ourselves up as tobacco traders as well as producers.
- Tobacco farmers usually receive a **single payment** for their entire crop. This is attractive because we can use the lump sum to repay debt, buy land, improve our houses or pay for other large expenditures such as marriages and social obligations. We can also use the cash to buy tobacco from other farmers and thereby join the tobacco trade. Lump sums of money are not available for other crops.
- There are currently **few cash crops** for us to consider or compare with tobacco. Markets for traditional crops have withered away over the years and no new crop has emerged to challenge tobacco.
- Most farmers in the area grow only tobacco. We feel **peer pressure** to also farm this way because it is what all farmers do here.
- Tobacco farming makes use of **family labour**, especially women and children at home. By tending the fires to cure the tobacco leaves, we contribute directly to generating household cash income.

Men and women in the group discussed each of these factors, and others set aside by them as less important. They did so with a focus on the relative weight of each factor, and interactions between the factors at play. The key question posed for each factor is simple: to what extent does it contribute to other factors in the list? In other words, what is the causal weight of one factor on another? To answer the question each time it is asked, the group used a scale from 1 indicating a very minor weight to 5 indicating a major cause. The group justified and negotiated ratings for each factor's causal interaction with other factors until a consensus emerged. Table 19.1 shows the ratings given in one exercise, numbers reflecting the complex rationale for continuing to grow tobacco. The last column records the total active score of the row factor, i.e. its overall weight on all other column factors. This is the cause index. The third row from the bottom records the total passive score of the column factor, i.e. the overall weight that all other row factors exercise on it. This is the effect index. The two indices tell us to what extent each factor is a cause and an effect of other factors.

For readers, a brief discussion of causal attribution is in order. Any analysis that unravels the root cause of each factor at play in a system is logic operating at its best. Logic and causal reasoning has countless implications for science and pragmatic interventions in real life. It can, however, create what might be called a farmer's nightmare – 'root digging ad infinitum'. If we know that problem X (unemployment) is the root cause of problem Y (poverty) and that Y acts in turn as the root cause of problem Z (indebtedness), chances are we will target X in order to do away with both Y and Z. But why stop the causal chain at point X? Should we not go back to the root cause of X (why is there unemployment in the first place?), and so on, ad infinitum, cognizant that there will never be a problem A at the end of the line?

Causal Dynamics proposes a common sense solution to this puzzle, expressed in the last two rows of the table. It assumes that each factor has a weight of its own that will persist stubbornly even in the absence of contributing cause(s). We call this the 'real weight' of any given factor. For instance, indebtedness may not disappear entirely even if the unemployment problem is fully resolved. It will continue to exercise 'real weight' on people's livelihoods. This notion differs from the 'apparent weight' of a factor – the weight it seems to have at first sight, before factor interaction and real weights are assessed.

Back to our story. The second row from the bottom of Table 19.1 records the conclusions of discussions with farmers about the 'apparent weight' of each factor (as a first estimate of its overall weight in the system), using a scale of 1 to 7. For example, people felt that the single lump sum payment and the lack of an alternative cash crop carried the greatest weight in keeping farmers engaged in tobacco farming; each received the highest score in the scale (7). After giving scores to indicate the interaction of all factors (i.e. after completing the rating matrix), participants reviewed their earlier assessment of apparent weight, and revised it to determine the 'real weight' of each factor. This involved thinking about each factor in isolation from all other factors, as if these were resolved or did not exist. Ratings for real weights are recorded in the last row and represented in Figure 19.1 by the relative size of each factor marker. They point to **persistent reasons** for continuing to grow tobacco, factors (e.g. the lack of alternate cash crops) that people may choose to address regardless of what else may change in the system along the way.

Debate among participants and the negotiation of ratings took place largely as a direct conversation with the facilitators and among themselves. The assistant facilitators working on the side compiled the numbers in a table once agreement was reached. A tree metaphor and image with roots supported the discussion and helped people keep track of which relationship they were talking about – is it A causing B, or B causing A? While the basic question became repetitive, the discussion remained lively due in large part to the good humour of the Bangladeshi co-facilitators and the high relevance of the topic for participating farmers. The facilitating team applied a light touch to turn the reasoning by participants into a final score, verified pointedly and adjusted when needed along the way. The focus was on understanding farmer perspectives on the direction of the causal relationship and where, roughly, it fit in the scale of interactions. A tea break also helped, bringing the first part of the discussion (reasons, weight and ratings) to completion within three hours.

Interpretation of the results and discussions about what they meant to farmers and to UBINIG as a supporting organization followed on another tea break and brief tour of

Table 19.1 The interaction of factors behind farmer decisions to continue to grow tobacco (*Causal Dynamics*)

Factors	*Pays well*	*BATC obligations*	*Lump-sum payment*	*Scarcity of cash crops*	*Uses family labour*	*Most grow tobacco*	**Cause index Total score**
Pays well	x	2	4	3	3	4	16/25
BATC obligations	3	x	4	4	3	3	17/25
Lump-sum payment	4	2	x	4	3	4	17/25
Scarcity of cash crops	4	2	3	x	1	5	15/25
Uses family labour	3	0	0	2	x	3	8/25
Most grow tobacco	4	2	3	5	3	x	17/25
Effect index Total score	**18/25**	**8/25**	**14/25**	**18/25**	**13/25**	**19/25**	**90/150 (62%)**
Apparent weight	6	6	7	7	4	5	
Real weight	3	4	4	6	1	3	

the gardens at UBINIG's rural facility. Meanwhile, the facilitation team turned the results from the table into a large Cartesian graph showing the exact location of each factor based on the intersection of the cause index and the effect index (Figure 19.1). The graph was an unfamiliar image to the farmer participants. They nonetheless understood what it meant when they saw that most of the reasons for growing tobacco were both causes and effects of each other (upper right quadrant of the figure), roots and their own ramifications at the same time. This pointed to a vicious circle of reasons for growing tobacco. Participants summed up this interpretation up as a seductive trap reinforcing the decision to continue to grow tobacco.

The reasoning is as follows:

1 The **obligation to the BATC**, symbolized by the BATC card (upper left quadrant), is a direct cause of all other factors in the system. Participants agreed with the summary statement represented by the medium-sized marker on the graph that ownership of a BATC card would remain a persistent and compelling reason for farmers to continue to grow tobacco even if the other factors did not exist (i.e. the real weight would not change). After all, the BATC card gives farmers an assured market and access to credit, a rare benefit in the world of farming.

2 The **lump-sum payment** for an entire season's output gives the impression that the product pays well, even though prices are unpredictable and costs spread out over a much longer period. This factor acts as a moderately persistent cause, linked to the perennial hope that their leaf will be judged of high quality and receive a high price.

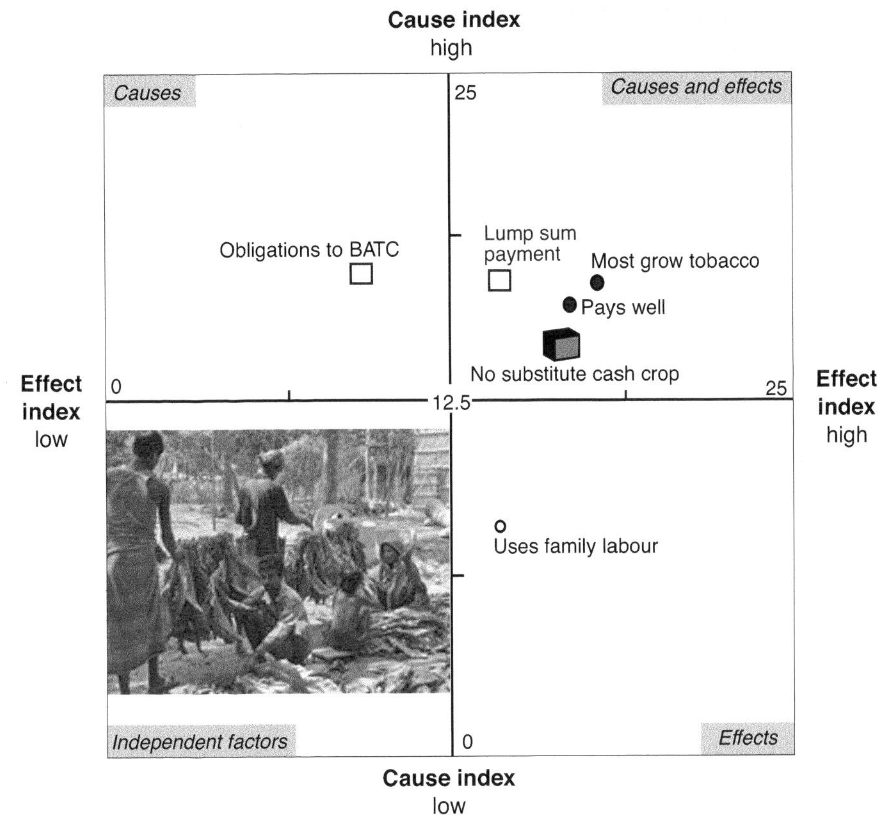

FIGURE 19.1 The interaction of factors behind farmer decisions to continue to grow tobacco (*Causal Dynamics*).

3 Together with the appeal of a lump-sum payment, the **scarcity of cash crops** accounts for the fact that **most grow tobacco**. In turn, this dominant land use has undermined experimentation with new crops and the development of a range of crop choices. Over time, the diverse technologies of farming (native seed, knowledge, integration with livestock, etc.) and markets for food and other economic crops withered away. Productive uses of **family labour** also declined (e.g. livestock management and marketing of foodstuffs used to employ women and children), making family labour primarily an effect of the other factors (lower right quadrant). Farmers also noted many other effects downstream from the set of immediate reasons for continuing to grow tobacco (not appearing on the graph), including poor health from processing the tobacco leaf and deforestation of the hillsides.

The scarcity of substitute cash crops is the most strongly persistent reason (shown by the larger square in the graph) farmers continue to grow tobacco. The gap would persist even if all other reasons were not at play. It is also the only factor that participants felt they could address themselves. This, as we shall see, became the focus of their actions.

All of these factors combine to keep farmers prisoner to an entrenched monocropping system with no process in place to find substitute crops or support farmer experimentation and innovation.

Later that day, one of the farmers, a practitioner of the rural art of song improvisation, composed a spontaneous musical lament about the pain and suffering of tobacco cultivation. He also added a few lines about tree roots becoming spoiled fruits on branches, a humorous reference to the work of the day and powerful imagery to capture the notion of a vicious circle where causes turn into their own effects.

Since 'scarcity of cash crops' is a persistent factor that partly accounts for other intervening factors, the group decided to focus its attention on doing something about it. The course of action that emerged from the assessment was to start experimenting on a small scale with other agricultural crops with cash potential. If successful, farmers might be able to create a positive chain effect on the other factors as well. Talk within the group focussed on crops such as peanuts, jute, mustard seed, lentils and pulses that were traditionally grown in the region and remain important in other areas. These crops could generate a smaller but steady stream of cash income and ultimately pay more than the single payment obtained through tobacco farming. Fewer farmers would grow tobacco, encouraging others to make the shift as well. Meanwhile the real weight and appeal of a lump-sum payment and obligations to the BATC would remain. Farmers have no control over these practices of the BATC. Nothing could be done to act on these factors directly. Developing new cash crops, however, was within their sphere of influence and became the focus for later explorations of farmer ecological knowledge and innovative ideas for field experiments in the coming season.

PHOTO 19.1 Aminul Begum composes a song about freedom from tobacco before a group of farmers discussing the results of their research. (Source: D. J. Buckles)

FOOD FOR LOCAL THOUGHT

Tobacco farmers in Daulatpur and in various other communities doing a similar analysis converged in their decisions to experiment on a small scale with crops they could sell. It was a necessary step within their control and key to breaking out of the addiction to tobacco production. The strategy made sense to the research team as well, and was more feasible than trying to compete directly with the financial services provided by BATC or to simply campaign for a total ban against tobacco production. An alternative was needed to guide any political or policy initiative to create or reinforce incentives to grow other crops. Efforts to put in place disincentives to restrict tobacco production would hurt farmers if there were no viable cash crops available to them.

Conducting field experiments is no small matter for farmers, even on a small scale. Land and other resources dedicated to an experiment expose farmers to risk. Furthermore, potential crops are many but few will work economically for farmers. To help plan experiments that farmers would actually implement and that responded to the concerns they had about growing tobacco, a process was needed to develop new crop options for farmers to consider. Radical innovation was needed. The research team responded by inviting tobacco farmers from various parts of Bangladesh to sit together and share ideas about crops of interest and ways to shift out of tobacco production. The underlying strategy was to tap into traditions of knowledge *and* continuous learning – what farmers actually know about crops and people's capacity to 'think outside the box'.

During the first day of the meeting participants used *Causal Dynamics* again, but this time to assess the impacts of tobacco production on the farmer's resource base and understand how these impacts (listed below) interact. The exercise gave the group an opportunity to reflect on what needed to improve first in order to create the possibility of change in the cropping system. The main conclusions from the assessment, not presented here for lack of space, were that the **degradation of soil** by years of tobacco cultivation and the **lack of locally available seed for other crops** were prominent causes of other technical constraints faced by tobacco farmers. These other technical constraints included:

- the low productivity of other crops grown on tobacco soils;
- persistent weed infestations;
- the loss of fishponds in the community that provide sources of irrigation and food;
- the loss of deep-rooted trees useful to the management of surface water;
- the decline of livestock in the farming system.

A few participants used this assessment to directly identify and experiment on their own with varieties of crops well adapted to tobacco-degraded soils. (Since everyone had contributed directly to the analysis and results were shared immediately, farmer participants had the option to act on their own based on the learning they had achieved on the first day.)

The research team used this systemic assessment of the impacts of tobacco production on the resource base as an input into a deeper assessment of crop characteristics of interest to farmers. *Ecological Domain* is the method we chose to build on farmer knowledge of a wide range of crops and explore novel options farmers could consider through field experiments. Our reasoning was that innovation would be key to going beyond what was immediately available to farmers from within their own knowledge system. The key assumption of *Ecological Domain* is that people understand a natural resource domain by dividing it into distinct elements and 'constructing' similarities and differences between them. Application of the method produces clusters of similar elements (in this case, crops) that differ from each other along characteristics organized into contrasting pairs (e.g. 'farmers can market the product' versus 'the product must be sold through a broker'). In keeping with its clinical origins in the work of George Kelly, the method supports breakthrough thinking about novel ways to resolve tensions within a domain, using the language and knowledge of the people involved.

To ground the discussion in specific ecosystems and agricultural histories, farmers from each of the three regions did their own comparisons of crops separately and then shared their results. The assessments followed the same steps in the three groups, starting with making a list of crops participants thought would be useful to farmers wanting to shift out of tobacco production. For example, five farmers from Daulatpur (two men and three women) sat together and listed about thirty-five crops grown in their area, from which they selected thirteen, including tobacco, various grains, pulses,

PHOTO 19.2 Women farmers in Cox's Bazaar establish similarities and differences between crops, and rate each crop on a grey scale. (Source: Abdul Zabbar)

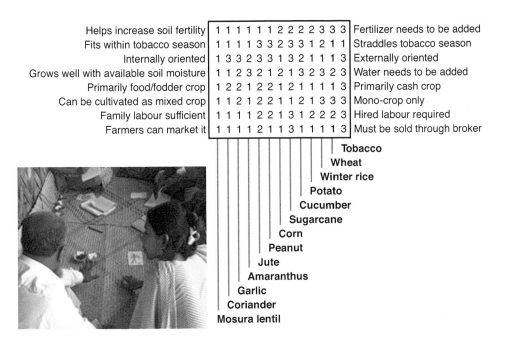

	Mosura lentil	Coriander	Garlic	Amaranthus	Jute	Peanut	Corn	Sugarcane	Cucumber	Potato	Winter rice	Wheat	Tobacco	
Helps increase soil fertility	1	1	1	1	1	1	2	2	2	2	3	3	3	Fertilizer needs to be added
Fits within tobacco season	1	1	1	1	3	3	2	3	3	1	2	1	1	Straddles tobacco season
Internally oriented	1	3	3	2	3	3	1	3	2	1	1	1	3	Externally oriented
Grows well with available soil moisture	1	1	2	3	2	1	2	1	3	2	3	2	3	Water needs to be added
Primarily food/fodder crop	1	2	2	1	2	2	1	2	1	1	1	1	3	Primarily cash crop
Can be cultivated as mixed crop	1	1	2	1	2	2	1	1	2	1	3	3	3	Mono-crop only
Family labour sufficient	1	1	1	1	2	2	1	3	1	2	2	2	3	Hired labour required
Farmers can market it	1	1	1	1	2	1	1	3	1	1	1	1	3	Must be sold through broker

FIGURE 19.2 Alternative crops rated against eight contrasting sets of characteristics, Daulatpur, Kushtia (*Ecological Domain*).

vegetables and other plants with industrial uses. Participants collected samples of seed for each crop from UBINIG's seed collection and placed them in small bowls laid out on the floor for systematic comparisons. To establish similarities and differences between the sampled crops, they selected three bowls at random and identified a feature shared by two crops different from the third crop. For instance, participants from Daulatpur said that lentils and amaranthus, two of the crops selected at random, help increase soil fertility while the third crop (maize) requires fertilizers to be added. This process (known as triadic elicitation) generated a contrast using terms and concepts meaningful to the farmers. All in all, participants in Daulatpur generated eight sets of contrasts to describe crops in terms of differences and similarities they felt were important to understanding their cropping systems. The facilitating team proposed a simple rating scale of 1 to 3, represented by white, grey and black cards, to score each crop in the list on a continuum between the two poles of each contrast. Rows of cards on the floor were used to record the scores and facilitate group discussion of patterns.

The Daulatpur exercise revolved around a dependent variable – whether a crop 'helps increase soil fertility' or 'fertilizer needs to be added'. This central question, revealed by the earlier analysis of technical constraints, helped guide the discussion about different clusters of crops. To help visualize the variable, the facilitators organized the seed samples in order from one end of the continuum ('helps increase soil fertility') to the other ('fertilizer needs to be added'). Organizing the pots of seed along this main variable made it easier to analyse other ratings recorded in the table (Figure 19.2). Participants then rated each crop on the seven other elicited contrasts, and added the values to the table using the three grades of cards. This active organization of the information and visual presentation of the findings helped to facilitate progressive and collaborative interpretation of the results as the exercise proceeded. For example, participants observed that crops that increase soil fertility also tend to grow well in available soil moisture and can be cultivated as mixed crops. Crops requiring the addition of fertilizers tend to have the opposite characteristics. Figure 19.2 showing the associations using specialized software confirms and quantifies this clustering performed directly by participants.

The research team used the software RepGrid to enter and analyse the data that emerged from farmer-led discussions. The team did not attempt to use the software jointly with the farmers because they were unfamiliar with the technology. Also electricity was often interrupted. By comparing row and column cards (differentiated on a grey

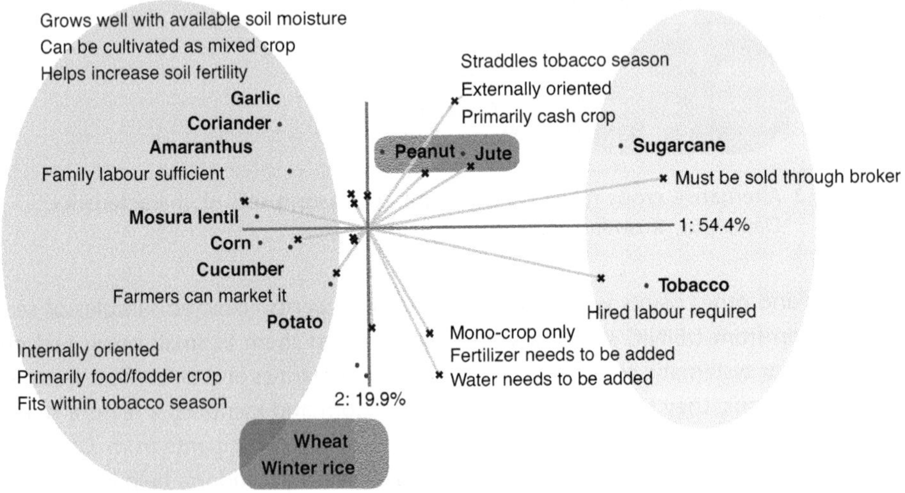

FIGURE 19.3 Principal component analysis of crops and crop characteristics, Daulatpur, Kushtia (*Ecological Domain*).

The statistical technique used to create this figure is called principal component analysis. It simplifies a data set by reducing the multi-dimensional relationships among observed variables to a cross-shaped, two-dimensional representation. Shorter distances between crops (dots) and crop characteristics (crosses) indicate closer relationships. In the figure, the scores assigned to crops and crop characteristics (the observed variables) are mapped in relation to two fictive variables. The horizontal line (first component) represents a fictive variable that in this case accounts for 54.4 per cent of the total variance in the data (pattern of relationships among dots and crosses). The vertical line (second component) represents a fictive variable that accounts for another 19.9 per cent. Together, the two principal components account for 74.3 per cent of the total variance.

scale), participants were able nonetheless to identify the main patterns shown in Figure 19.2. For example, farmers could see that crops that require added fertilizer tend to be mono-crops that also need extra water. They also noted that cash crops tend to be external to the food and fodder system, and crops that require hired labour typically are sold through a broker. The research team later shared their statistical analysis with participating farmers, which helped inform subsequent actions.

Figure 19.3 shows a principal component analysis of the same table data. It confirms and quantifies the main patterns observed by participants in the session based on row and column comparisons. Importantly, crops and crop features combine to form two major groups. One group is composed of crops integral to the current local food and fodder system. They can be taken to market by farmers themselves and can be managed using family labour. They tend to be planted and harvested during the same season as tobacco, lend themselves to mixed cropping, grow well with available soil moisture and increase soil fertility. Examples of these crops are *mosura dal* (a pulse), garlic, coriander, amaranthus and cucumber. The other major group is composed of crops grown in response to external market demand. These crops must be sold to brokers, mill owners or company buyers before they get to market. They tend to be grown as a mono-crop and require inputs such as water, fertilizers and hired labour. Tobacco and sugarcane are examples of crops with these features.

Participants explained that by combining these two sets of crops farmers can grow food and fodder for their households and also secure some cash income. They felt that this dual strategy was necessary but also problematic. The two kinds of crops are grown in the same season and therefore compete directly with each other for land and other resources. This forces farmers to choose between them or split their land into two separate blocks. They also explained that current local food and fodder crops are at a disadvantage compared to the externally oriented crops such as tobacco and sugarcane. That is, they receive little policy support, and markets for them have declined locally or do not exist. Under these circumstances, the current set of local food and fodder crops, while important to them, cannot be viable substitutes for tobacco.

> In Figure 19.3, crops and crop characteristics combine to form two major groups: crops integral to the current local food and fodder system (left side), and crops grown in response to external market demand (right side). Two smaller sets of crops combine characteristics in other ways, opening opportunities for middle-of-the-road strategies that farmers and the research team can further explore.

Figure 19.3 also shows that some crops stand apart from all others in that they combine features quite differently, an observation that created an important learning opportunity for the farmer participants and the research team. Crops such as wheat, rice and to some extent potato are grown in a way similar to externally oriented crops (mono-crops, external inputs needed). Unlike the external crops, however, they contribute strongly to the current local food and fodder system and can be marketed by farmers themselves. These crops usually occupy the land at the same time as tobacco. A second group of crops (jute and peanut for instance) combine features in odd ways as well. They are like local food and fodder crops in many respects but also have well-established external markets. Furthermore, they do not compete directly with tobacco but rather straddle the tobacco season, either before or after.

These unusual combinations of features generated a lot of excitement in the group, especially with respect to jute and peanut. These would be new crops in Daulatpur, and good candidates to compete with tobacco. More importantly, the clustering of crops and crop features based on local knowledge stimulated thinking about how to **unblock** the dual strategy in the current cropping system. Rather than trying to find the perfect crop to substitute for tobacco during the same season, participants started to think about crops that could support a transition out of tobacco into different cropping patterns. In practical terms, the innovation strategy would begin in the season before tobacco is grown. This would allow for gradual and steady improvements in soil quality and a better stream of financial benefits throughout the year.

The **distinction between substitute crops and transition strategies** had not occurred earlier to farmers or the research team, and provided a new lens to reflect on ways to shift out of tobacco production. It moved thinking by the group beyond current local knowledge and conceptual categories into a new space of innovative thinking and experimentation. This group insight parallels the psychological process of breakthrough thinking central to Kelly's Personal Construct Psychology.

One of the women farmers in the group, Sheuli Begum, gave shape to this new thinking with an example. She explained that recently, while going to the local market looking for new cash crops, she saw a spice that she and other rural women regularly buy. It contained seeds of three different plants not currently grown in her region. She sprouted and planted all three types, and then chose one (*Methi*) that she believed could be easily grown in her current mixed cropping system. It needed to be planted before the tobacco season, and would help create some cash income at a time when she would be tending to other crops that would mature later on. Inspired by this idea, participants decided to also search local markets for products that combine crops and crop features in novel and fruitful ways – crops that have a demand in markets they can access themselves (either locally or regionally), that can be grown in mixed cropping systems, or that straddle the tobacco season.

EXPERIMENTING OUTSIDE THE BOX

Participatory action-research into the social and technical constraints faced by farmers seeking to shift out of tobacco, and the development of a new conceptual model for thinking about innovation in cropping systems, helped to create independent research capacities among tobacco farmers. Participants immediately started to design a number of new cropping systems. For example, farmers from Cox's Bazaar thought that potato, French bean and felon would combine well in their cropping system, and help with the transition out of tobacco production. Potato, maize and lentil combinations seemed promising to farmers in Kushtia, and potato, tomato, felon and coriander combinations in Bandarban. To support this process, and scale up the learning that had occurred, the final days of the weeklong regional meeting focussed on developing a tool for planning farmer-led field experiments. This involved creating and using a local adaptation of *The Socratic Wheel* that could help identify specific crop combinations to support a transition out of tobacco farming, in particular agro-ecosystems.

The Socratic Wheel (Chapter 7) drew on elements from the analysis of the previous days to create criteria for assessing the balance of benefits from particular crop combinations. The criteria selected by participants were: labour requirement, cash requirement, nutrient contribution, early harvest potential, storage attribute, pest resistance, input requirement, health benefits, fodder/fuel contribution and market access. For each criterion an example crop or other symbol was identified to express the maximum positive value on the criteria, including:

- potato for market access as it was very easy to sell directly;
- leaves of the pumpkin for early harvest potential because it produces some yield very soon after planting;
- the Ginga gourd for storage because it stores extremely well;
- rice for fodder and fuel because it supplies both;
- a green coconut for health because the water and soft pulp are used to nurse people back to health after suffering from stomach problems.

Participants reproduced these criteria and symbols on the ground using bamboo sticks for each spoke in the wheel and a sample or picture of the plant symbolizing the maximum positive value (Photo 19.3). Farmers then proposed a crop combination and assessed how well it balanced the various criteria at play. For example, the group judged that the potato, French bean and felon combination for Cox's Bazaar was a good decision because the mixed crop system met all criteria reasonably well. It recognized the initial proposal in Bandarban to combine potato, tomato and felon as potentially problematic and corrected it by adding coriander to the mix, allowing for a better balance in terms of harvest time.

Participants discussed the various crop combinations emerging from the analysis at length and presented them to other farmers for feedback. In the weeks following the initial meeting, the farmers in each region converged in their thinking about the best decisions, and requested support from the research team for access to seed of the selected crops and crop combinations. The research team then acquired seed of the candidate crops and made a fixed amount of seed available to farmers committed to establishing field experiments. We did not tie access to seed for the experiments to any kind of contractual arrangement other than a commitment to consider the combinations that seemed most promising and to use the seed for experiments with some combination of crops during the upcoming season. While many opted to test the recommended combinations in their entirety, others adopted slightly different combinations in light of their own judgments and preferences. Over a period of two years, some 351 farmers

PHOTO 19.3 Farmers assessing specific crop combinations against a range of criteria. (Source: D. J. Buckles)

established field experiments, generating a wealth of new experience and stimulating a concerted effort to innovate and evaluate outcomes.

Before launching the farmer-led experiments, the research team also developed a simple application of *Social Domain* analysis to form groups of farmers with similar characteristics so they could support each other during their experiments. Working in separate groups of men and women, and, in the case of Bandarban, separate groups of ethnic and Bengali communities, the research team engaged groups from the same or neighbouring villages in each area to elicit household features and identify major subpopulations within each setting. The household typology that would result from this analysis could greatly help organize farmer-experimenters into meaningful groups and provide a reference point for the evaluation of alternative cropping systems by each subpopulation (see *Social Domain* in Chapter 18).

Between twelve and twenty people participated in ten different exercises held in parts of the village with shade and mats for outdoor seating. They listed the different kinds of **livelihoods** they and immediate family members engaged in, and the kinds of **resources** at their disposal. The triad method used with crops helped elicit from the group meaningful differences in these two factors among households. The research team arranged cards with family names and opposing characteristics in a table on the ground and farmers scored each household on the characteristics. In some cases this involved a three-point grey scale and in other cases a numerical scale represented with piles of seeds or stones. Clusters of similar families emerged. Participants immediately discussed and verified these as accurate and relevant to the process of experimentation and evaluation. For example, in the Kushtia area the analysis converged around four household types: young tobacco farmers, older very small-scale tobacco farmers, tobacco traders and older land-rich farmers (see Figure 18.8). Age tended to separate the farmers focussed on tobacco production from those that adopt a mixed strategy. The amount of land is also a factor determining the extent to which farmers engage in tobacco production. In Bandarban and Cox's Bazaar wage workers and forest workers emerged as additional household types likely to be affected negatively by a wholesale shift out of tobacco production (they rely on the sale of wood to kilns and labour in the tobacco fields). They represented important groups to consider when assessing the economic performance and impact of transition strategies out of tobacco production.

The results of the analysis informed the creation of two different groups in each village: farmer experimenters and village evaluators. The experimenter group ultimately included any tobacco farmer, regardless of household profile, interested in testing specific transition strategies. The research team decided not to treat the socio-economic distinctions mechanically during group formation but rather to use them to inform ongoing discussions with farmers about the crop choices they were making. For example, young farmers needed additional encouragement to experiment because they tend to dedicate all of their land to tobacco production. The concept of village evaluators emerging from the analysis also informed latter efforts to engage different segments of the population in an evaluative process.

TASTING THE RESULTS

The outputs of the two diagnostic processes – the formulation of specific crop combinations for experimentation, and the formation of groups of farmers to implement and evaluate field experiments – helped the research team plan new activities. In the months following the launch of the field experiments we used the findings of our collaborative research to design various researcher-led evaluative studies, including a survey of the economic performance of particular crop combinations, an assessment of demand for firewood produced by forest workers, and an inventory of plant species and varieties that used to be cultivated but were no longer available. These provided detailed information on matters of direct concern to farmers and other stakeholders such as forest workers and wage labourers.

The survey incorporated measures of economic performance from a farmers' perspective. As detailed in Chapter 12, farmers used *Interests* to assess the gains and losses associated with working capital, yield, product quality, food independence and impact on the well-being (happiness) of the household. These grounded, sociopsychological criteria and indicators were included in the questionnaire along with detailed measures of land and labour use, inputs purchased, actual yield, sales, etc. Sixty farmers were interviewed using a purposive sampling procedure based in part on meaningful socio-economic differences discovered in the household profile exercise reported above.

The results consistently showed that the costs and benefits of the alternative crop combinations provided higher financial returns on both land and labour compared to tobacco farming (UBINIG, 2007, 2008). The farmer-generated criteria, analysed separately for the 2006–2007 season only, indicated that about 20 per cent of the tobacco farmers surveyed experienced severe difficulties repaying their loans and 30 per cent did not have enough food to meet their needs for three months or more. Only a few farmers testing alternative combinations experienced food shortages and none had problems repaying loans. On one criterion, yield expectations, the alternative combinations did not do as well as tobacco production. Farmers produced enough food to meet their subsistence needs, but surplus yield fell below expectations for almost half of the farmers testing alternative combinations. Only a third of tobacco farmers experienced a similar level of disappointment in the yield of tobacco leaf. Farmers explained that they did not achieve expected yields for alternative crop combinations because the soils had been degraded after many years of tobacco cultivation. This finding underlined the need to focus the transition strategy on steps to improve soil quality incrementally.

While interesting in many ways, the farmer-generated criteria and indicators were dropped for the 2008 economic performance survey. The research team decided that standard measures of financial returns to land and labour were good enough for discussion with policymakers, and that the survey purpose did not merit the greater level of effort needed to analyse and interpret the additional farmer criteria and indicators. We opted instead to develop a tool farmers could adapt and use independently to assess the economic performance of particular crop combinations. A simple version of *The Socratic Wheel* was introduced to farmers, with criteria they developed but not detailed indicators. Less attention was given to collating individual farmer responses and more to explanations in a group context of why one farmer did better on a certain criterion compared to another farmer growing the same crop combination. Women in farming households led this process, sometimes forming separate groups to develop their own collective position on what criteria to include and rating the performance of particular crop combinations. These adjustments allowed for a grounded and gender-sensitive discussion of how household and field circumstances affect economic performance from one situation to another, and what goes into making 'the best decisions' for each situation. Adjustments also enabled the research team to engage with non-farming sub-populations in communities where the sale of wood and labour were important livelihood considerations.

FROM FIELD TO POLICY DEBATES

The action-research process launched with tobacco farmers is ongoing in its search for ways to break the addiction to tobacco production. The initial work focussed on engaging farmers, developing a detailed understanding of the system of economic and technical constraints they face, and stimulating innovation and experimentation with viable alternatives building on their own ecological knowledge. The complete cycle of diagnosis, innovation, intervention and grounded evaluation reported here contributed to the development of a number of promising transition strategies. Importantly, key principles such as the distinction between transition crops and substitute crops emerged from the analysis with farmers, and opened up a wide set of possibilities. It shifted thinking from the search for a perfect alternative to a strategy for shifting out of tobacco production in a series of steps. Innovation in the selection of crop combinations for the transition was considerable, going beyond what farmers have traditionally grown in the study areas. Assessment criteria important to farmers were also identified, along with the major categories of households that would be affected by any widespread shift out of tobacco production. At the end of the cycle we could confidently conclude that there was much more optimism among tobacco farmers about the possibility of a transition than was initially the case. For every farmer that had already joined in the research there were many more that had expressed interest, in the same villages as well as in neighbouring villages. This was an encouraging situation. Even the BATC took notice, opting to increase tobacco prices in the areas where the experiments were most advanced.

Key questions remained unanswered, however, following two years of engaged research. The technical and economic feasibility of promising crop combinations and transition strategies had to be validated broadly before governments could promote widespread adoption and provide support through significant investments. The policy implications of the findings also required the attention of government officials. The need to scale up findings from field to policy debates prompted and guided a new cycle of participatory action research. While still ongoing, this new cycle has involved repeated farmer-led experiments, support to community-based seed production, the development of marketing cooperatives, and education and communication strategies to engage the general public, scientists and government officials in an informed discussion about the public policy implications of shifting out of tobacco production. These efforts go beyond the farm and village level, to engage multiple stakeholders in assessing the problem, designing interventions and evaluating outcomes. (See www.participatoryactionresearch.net for links to this ongoing story).

REFERENCES

UBINIG (2007) 'Economic performance of tobacco and alternative Rabi crops', *UBINIG Technical Report*, Bangladesh.

UBINIG (2008) 'Evaluation of Rabi crops (combination) cultivation against tobacco production', *UBINIG Technical Report*, Bangladesh.

Conclusion

Rethinking higher education and the discovery process

This book is about the process of doing action research with people, investigating and solving problems in real settings. On a broader level, it is a response to the pressure on higher education to deliver meaningful learning and research. Efforts to rethink the university experience in the global era are all the more relevant as more and more students enrol in post-secondary institutions around the world, especially women and youth in the global South. Over the last four decades enrolment has soared by 471 per cent, going from 35 million students in 1970 to 165 million in 2009, according to UNESCO. Regions other than North America and Europe now represent about half of all enrolment in tertiary education establishments, compared to 25 per cent in 1970. In the same period, the ratio of female to male students has risen from 0.75 to 1.08.

Access to higher education nonetheless remains a problem for some populations and regions, particularly in countries of South and West Asia and Sub-Saharan Africa. The gross enrolment ratio for higher education is still below 20 per cent in about a third of the countries (158) for which UNESCO statistics are available. Poorer segments of the population are still massively excluded. Also, while women are the principal beneficiaries of improved access overall, gains do not always translate into enhanced career opportunities, especially in the field of research.

The quality and relevance of higher learning is another cause for concern. As the demand for higher education increases, universities are forced to compete globally and tailor their offerings to students anxious about their employment prospects in fields of their choice. As a result, institutions now pay more attention to the ways in which they can support student learning and career development more efficiently and effectively (through the use of ICT and distance learning, for instance). The process of 'assisting discovery', as Van Dore aptly calls it, is no longer taken for granted. The academic community does not assume that teaching and learning are things that can be delivered routinely, without skilful handling and innovation. The assumption that a professor's job is simply to demonstrate and 'profess' scholarly wisdom, a view dating back to the Middle Ages, no longer holds.

Exploring new pedagogical strategies in support of higher learning is a relatively recent trend. The endeavour takes much of its inspiration from a long history of experimentation with non-traditional approaches in basic education. Audio-visual aids, didactic manuals, interactive and group learning, hands-on experience and differentiated instruction have now proven their worth in university teaching. What is still missing, however, is more probing into strategies adapted to the core mission of university life. Unlike basic schooling, universities and colleges are dedicated to creating knowledge and mobilizing it in the complex setting of professional work and life in society. While enlightening in many ways, ground-breaking methods to enhance primary and secondary education are not sufficient to achieve this mission.

Traditional instruction methods, focussed on teachers transmitting existing bodies of knowledge and received ways to do research, remain a major obstacle. Before we address this issue, however, it is important that we give due credit to 'traditional education' for its critical contribution to the hopes of Modernity, including freedom of thought and speech, the ideals of reason and the standards of literacy, science, advanced technology and workplace rationality. Humanism is part of this long-standing legacy (Gauthier and Tardif, 2004; Peters, 1966). With it comes the notion that humans are inherently perfectible in a world of infinite horizons. Humans can forever 'grow' provided they explore new frontiers of knowledge and never yield to dogmatism and obscurantism. However routinized higher education may be, it is still a contribution to constant learning and self-determination, dedicated to the discovery of otherness on a global scale and the hosting of other possible worlds in mind and self. Higher learning institutions carry forward teachings of the Enlightenment, the Age of Reason, the French Revolution and Modern Science, legacies never to be taken for granted let alone forgotten (as many widely publicized expressions of denialism keep reminding us).

To remain true to this legacy education must nonetheless go beyond 'instructing' students in a closed and orderly environment using a linear and piecemeal approach to discoveries of the world. As many have already remarked (ever since Rousseau's *Emile*), traditional instruction methods follow rules of learning that are fatally mechanical. In their current university version, they involve a gigantic array of silos where discrete bodies of knowledge and steps to learning gradually are organized into rows of courses, programmes, disciplines, academic levels and degrees. Learning proceeds from simpler studies to more advanced curriculum. Courses in general theory and 'small-m' methods are taught in the same spirit, i.e. separately, as distinct cogs in the assembly line of learning. Knowledge is in turn differentiated from its actual use and application in the work context, outside the confines of university life. Students are expected to first master knowledge and only later gain professional experience. To prepare themselves, they take one course after another, compile notes and grades, perform countless literature reviews, pass exams and debate **abstract theory**, all in the hope of eventually receiving the licence to practice in the profession of their choice.

The research profession has similar standards of 'linear discovery'. Building on the principles of mainstream science, research moves one careful step at a time, from stating a question to reviewing the relevant literature, developing a conceptual model or theory, formulating a working hypothesis, gathering and analysing sound data, and revisiting the hypothesis and theory in light of the findings. If ethical considerations come into play, they become another logical step in the inquiry process (and another topic for course-based teaching). In this little-by-little approach to academic life, all hopes of meaningful discovery are tied to Einstein's famously stated definition of insanity – 'doing the same thing, over and over again, but expecting different results'. To the extent that it remains linear, fragmented and removed from the world, the whole experience can never be more than the sum of its parts.

A direct consequence of traditional instruction methods is that students spend an inordinate number of years completing their university degrees, if they ever do. OECD statistics indicate that 30 per cent of enrolled students never obtain a university degree. Part of the explanation for this institutional failure is the fact that students prepare endlessly for a full learning experience that constantly recedes into the distant future. The living knowledge, useful and meaningful, that learners wish to encounter at school is like Godot: everybody claims to be a close acquaintance yet no one can recognize the character because forever expelled from the present scene. Unfortunately, waiting for Godot doesn't stop after students graduate and find employment. Complaints that graduates are not ready to handle the many challenges that society now faces are heard so often they have become a cliché.

Academic institutions must rethink the nature of thinking and learning and the logic of the inquiry process. This is particularly pressing in the social sciences, a field that places too much emphasis on students applying general theoretical reasoning to social issues, at considerable cost to teamwork and collaborative problem solving. Little attention is given to developing the skills required to facilitate careful reasoning and dialogue across social divides. University learning in the engineering, health and hard sciences has a different problem: students typically learn to apply technical knowledge to problems stripped of their social aspects. Graduates in both fields end up applying narrow frameworks to situations otherwise messy and begging for creative and flexible thinking.

The many critiques of traditional teaching methods, widely known in the field of education, are devastating. So what sustains the edifice? The answer to this puzzle points in several directions, all of which take us back to the foundations of Western thinking. The first answer has to do with analytic or classificatory thinking, a cornerstone of both ancient philosophy and modern culture. The practice consists in gaining knowledge of the world by dividing it into its component parts and mastering each in turn. Academic disciplines as we know them exist by virtue of this well-established 'pigeon-holing' perspective on reality. The tradition started more than a thousand years ago, with the seven arts of the trivium and the quadrivium, a framework first developed in late Antiquity by Martianus Minneus Felix Capella (fifth century) and then promoted throughout the Middle Ages via the work of Alcuin of York (c. 735–804) and his followers. In medieval universities, learning began with the 'three ways' of the trivium, or the liberal arts of grammar, rhetoric and dialectics. This led in turn to studies of the quadrivium, comprising music, geometry, arithmetic and astronomy (precursors of the natural sciences). Together the seven arts were preparatory work for the even more serious study of philosophy and theology. These distinctions became an integral part of the classical education movement in the West, which lasted well into the twentieth century.

The fact that classificatory reasoning and teaching continues to be at home in modern thinking has other roots as well. The growth of biology as a pivotal discipline in science is one of them. Modern biological classification, originating in the work of Carolus Linnaeus (1707–778), extended Aristotle's law of non-contradiction to our scientific observation and classification of entities in nature. Linnaeus showed the way to modern biology by arranging species and genuses in a hierarchical series of nested classes. Throughout modernity, this Linnaean framing of 'classes organized hierarchically' provided an authoritative language for describing and rank-ordering human beings, races and types of society along evolutionary lines. In the twentieth century, conceptions of society as living macro-organisms evolving from simple to complex forms provided further impetus to the multiplication and growth of separate disciplines, each tasked with applying science to a distinct component part of life in society. Economics and management sciences took responsibility for discovering the laws of business, markets and industry. Political science focussed on State authority and governance. The matters of Church and spirituality became the subject matter of religious studies. Anthropology investigated 'primitive' forms of social organization. Psychology studied the individual mind, and social psychology looked at self within society. The same logic helped organize the natural sciences into different fields of knowledge and research. Specialization in science was thought to mirror functional divisions in social and natural history.

The linear arrangements of class and rank in nature, society and history are key to understanding the politics of 'higher learning' and teachings of the 'civilized world'. They also support three other pillars of modernity: class-based distinctions between mental activity and manual labour, the mechanical assembly line of modern industry and the ever-growing rule of bureaucracy. Academic life has greatly contributed to the revolution of modern science, bureaucracy and industry. While doing so, the higher learning enterprise has also borrowed and adapted the linear workflow and procedures of bureaucracy and industry. As students well know, university life functions as a bureaucracy, with its own routinized, step-by-step implementation of the regulations, rules and procedures of organized teaching, accountable learning and disciplined research. Some principles of the progressive assembly line have also made inroads into systems of higher education via a sequential organization of learners, class tools and bodies of knowledge divided into parts. As in industry, each act of (intellectual) labour is minimized to the extent possible, through an incremental process in which parts are added one step at a time, towards creating the finished product – a degree obtained through a graduated series of lessons. The final graduation helps in turn reproduce the basic division and rank order of physical labour and mental work in industry and economic activity. The division between mind and matter is also part of physical labour, which can be skilled or not, according to the line of work. Likewise, mental work is divided into different career paths. Some apply knowledge gained to vocational work (by exercising a profession). Others choose to carry out research that is either applied or fundamental.

Traditional education breaks down the learning process into disciplines and programmatic steps to produce 'intellectuals', i.e. knowledgeable professionals and experts licensed to distance themselves, rise above and exercise control over physical labour and the 'social body' as a whole. Much of this methodical framing of classroom teaching and classes in society harks back to Greek notions of pure knowledge (*epistêmê*) rising above knowledgeable craft work (*technê*) and empiric practice based on experience of the senses alone (*empeiria*). These concepts have been discussed at length in previous chapters. Academic activity owes an even more important debt to Western divisions between mind and body, spirit and flesh.

The judgment is harsh, but the stakes are high. The era in which we are now thrown is fraught with messy problems on all scales, threats and challenges that cannot be met in a piecemeal manner, through a short-sighted application of disciplines disconnected from each other and from practical experience. Life in our times is not conducive to hard scientific explanations and easy solutions designed by experts alone. What is needed instead are multiple skills and dynamic strategies to inquire into real-life situations with multiple stakeholders and myriad knowledge systems. This calls for new methods to assist the experience of discovery. Instead of proceeding from simple course material to advanced studies, higher education must commit to placing students in complex situations from the start, and help them progressively develop the capacity to deal with difficult obstacles, persistent confusion and the proverbial unknown. By leaving the comfort of well-controlled lab-like environments, learners may develop the art of discovery in a messy world. They may also learn to apply greater creativity and flexibility in designing research, as opposed to relying on the packaging of standard inquiry tools (such as survey, interview and focus group methods endlessly used in the social sciences).

Many conditions required to rethink and develop a dynamic approach to higher learning are already in place. Perspectives on what learning is all about have evolved to the point that the idea of experiential education and problem-based learning, now used in many medical schools, is no longer limited to experiments in basic education. Notions of 'capacity building', 'professional skill sets' and 'differentiated learning' are widely discussed and translated into educational objectives and practice centred on student competencies. This means that deference towards high-profile institutions that show little regard for student needs is becoming a thing of the past. So is deference towards professors 'that can and do (research), and therefore can't teach'. Universities now compete globally to attract students and must develop novel ways to enhance the learning experience, through the promotion of interactive classroom activities and group learning dynamics, among other strategies. Another important trend is the proliferation of interdisciplinary programmes and new fields of studies and career opportunities that crossover or go beyond the liberal arts and professions. Education focussed on well-delineated bodies of stable knowledge and learning trajectories no longer fits with reality. Instead of being fixed, classifications of fields of knowledge are now pragmatic and constantly evolving. Last but not least, the global ICT revolution is radically transforming our ways of learning, sharing and advancing knowledge. No university worth attending can afford to ignore the effervescence of a knowledge society in the twenty-first century.

More than ever, professionals are expected to work at developing new knowledge-based technology and skills. This means that students must become expert learners. It also implies that teachers and researchers must keep rediscovering the 'art of assisting discovery'. All must skilfully engage in constant learning activity. While these transformations are already under way, the shift presents enormous challenges for the way universities actually organize the experience of learning, teaching and research. Instead of carving up and sequencing the component parts of learning, academic activity must strengthen connections between fields and disciplines, between theory, method and practice, and also between teaching and research. None of this will happen if professors continue to teach and do research in relative isolation from each other and from life in society, adopting what is essentially a territorial and ivory-tower mindset in their work. As should be expected, resistance to change is fierce. Individualism, key to understanding modern culture, remains a major obstacle to rethinking university education.

An argument often levelled against skill-based, student-centred education is that university learning is not a business and that knowledge is not up for sale. Students are not clients, and faculty are not entrepreneurs. General culture and the pursuit of knowledge for its own sake is an invaluable legacy of modern history and should never be traded for greater efficiency and profits in corporate business. Student distance and academic autonomy vis-à-vis market forces and state intervention should therefore be preserved. As for experts in competency theory and skill-based education, they should not be allowed to dictate how other academics facilitate student learning.

The idea that each discipline and university life as whole should maintain some independence in defining its mission – making judgments about the transmission of worthwhile knowledge and ways to transform our understanding of the world (Peters, 1966, p. 17; Barrow, 2011, p. 13) – is a critical point with which we are in total agreement. But we agree for radically different reasons. The relative autonomy we have in mind is not of the ethereal kind, i.e. independence from all considerations of material existence and life in society. In our view, the claim that higher learning has been and should remain essentially 'unpractical' is pure historical fiction. If society can institute the learning or teaching of music, painting or philosophy, it is because of those who actually practice and hopefully make a decent living from the art of music, painting or philosophical investigation. As with other walks in life, these are professions that deploy tangible 'skills in means'. The notion that fundamental research, pure science and high culture (spelled with a capital C) have no bearing on technology, politics and economics is equally deceptive. Any course in art history, cultural studies or the history of science worth attending will drive this argument home.

The independence of academic activity does not lie in isolation from everyday life and material concerns. Rather it lies in its capacity to question 'being' and let it be more than what it is or appears to be. If anything, education is an invitation to explore all of our possible futures, by acting on our conditions of existence and hopefully transforming them for the better. This means that learning is 'higher' on condition that it brings us all closer to 'another world', one that belongs to the whole of humanity rather than the few committed to reproducing their own 'cultural capital' (Bourdieu, 1984; Bourdieu and Passeron, 1977). To achieve this, students, teachers and researchers must acknowledge and build on the contributions of both knowledge-centred and skill-based approaches to learning. But they must also address a third aspect of learning and the critical question it raises: knowledge and skills to what end – for what kind of human existence and life on earth?

In this book, we offer inquiry tools and methods that underscore the role of evidence-based thinking and rigour in research. The illustrative material we provide shows how these methods can support engaged inquiry and effective learning for all parties concerned, including student learning in real settings – the kind of learning that university programmes can reinforce through modular seminars of variable duration, compulsory or optional, planned or not, depending on the inquiry or task at hand. In this collaborative approach to discovering the world, we value science. That is, we do not short-change the requirements of knowledge in favour of consensus at any cost, or real-life experience above all; as Heine once said, experience is a good school, but the fees are high. But we also spell out and illustrate the skills that we think are essential to carrying out action inquiry in real settings; scientific knowledge makes for good instruction, but it doesn't beat capable learning. All in all, our goal has been to integrate collaborative fact-finding and skill building in a dynamic approach to living knowledge. In our view, the combination is powerful and much needed. Still, it is not enough. Another key ingredient is missing: the ability to create meaning and hope.

At the end of his Foreword to Freire's *Pedagogy of the Oppressed* (1970, p. 34), Shaull reminds us that 'There is no such thing as a *neutral* educational process. Education either functions as an instrument that is used to facilitate the integration of the younger generation into the logic of the present system and bring about conformity to it, *or* it becomes "the practice of freedom," the means by which men and women deal critically and creatively with reality and discover how to participate in the transformation of their world. The development of an educational methodology that facilitates this process will inevitably lead to tension and conflict within our society. But it could also contribute to the formation of a new man [i.e., Humanity] and mark the beginning of a new era in Western history.' Our work is committed to this task. What this book proposes, as many others do, is 'another possible world' in the field of science and education, one that values authentic dialogue and democracy in the pursuit of sound reasoning and knowledge for the common good.

In many ways, our plea for reason and the art of dialogue is a reinstatement of the Socratic ethics of dialectics and argumentation in the public sphere. Over the centuries, universities have traded this full integration of mind, *technê* and moral life in society for the privileges of power. Church-led universities of the Middle Ages disconnected reasoned dialogue (part of the trivium) from the public sphere, preferring instead to debate questions of life in the great beyond. Modernity further disconnected dialectics from society: first by stripping scientific discipline of all sense of 'moral discipline' (a concern limited to child education), and then feigning disinterest in the language, the values and the struggles of lay existence. As a result, higher education in the modern era celebrates another world once again 'not of this world'.

As a new century unfolds, another 'flight from this world' looms large on the university horizon: the virtual world of wireless disconnection from our senses, life in society and well-being in all corners of the global community. While redefining social life and humanity's relationship to *technê*, ICT resembles any learning or skill: it can serve many purposes – supporting distance learning, leaking government documents, reshaping the entertainment industry, launching nuclear missiles or enhancing global surveillance, to name just a few. Given these many potential applications, some more worthy than others, higher learning must lead. It must harness this new revolution to explore meaningful futures that are challenging but nonetheless within our reach – futures where existence evolves 'mindfully', i.e. carefully and caringly, for the benefit of all sentient beings on earth.

Now is the time to rethink higher education, beyond its traditionally narrow framing. A broader and bolder vision consists in reintroducing knowledge making and dialogue in the public sphere, using the methods and technology at our disposal. Teaching, learning and research must adjust accordingly, along lines described in this book and inspired by the many lessons of PAR, Community-Based Research, Problem-Based Learning, Community Service Education and Deliberative Democracy. These innovative approaches to scholarly activity converge on means to rediscover and transform the *world before us*, engaging minds and people in collaborative inquiry and action in meaningful settings.

The university experience must re-examine its commitment to history and society. The myriad social movements supporting alternative forms of globalization will not settle for anything less. Nor will the current revolution in ICT and its many political applications simply give the 'ivory towers' a passing grade on relevance, social inclusion and scientific accountability. Higher learning has no choice: it must boldly relaunch the discovery process to bring about another world on a human scale.

REFERENCES

Barrow, R. (2011) 'Was Peters nearly right about education', in *Reading R. S. Peters Today: Analysis, Ethics, and the Aims of Education*, Wiley-Blackwell, Oxford, pp. 6–23.

Bourdieu, P. (1984) *Distinction: a Social Critique of the Judgment of Taste*, trans. Richard Nice, Routledge, London.

Bourdieu, P. and Passeron, J.-C. (1977) *Reproduction in Education, Society and Culture*, trans. Richard Nice, Sage, London.

Freire, P. (1970) *Pedagogy of the Oppressed*, Foreword by Richard Saull, trans. M. Bergman Ramos, Continuum, New York and London.

Gauthier, C. and Tardif, M. (eds) (2004) *La pédagogie. Théories et pratiques de l'Antiquité à nos jours*, Gaëtan Morin, Montréal.

Peters, R. S. (1966) *Ethics and Education*, Allen and Unwin, London.

Index